# CNA/CNE STUDY GUIDE

# CERTIFICATION SERIES

BOONE, Barry: *Java Certification Exam Guide for Programmers and Developers*, 0-07-913657-5

MUELLER, John Paul; GATLIN, Anthony (MCSE): *The Complete Microsoft Certification Success Guide, Second Edition*, 0-07-913201-4

MUELLER, John Paul; WILLIAMS, Robert A.: *CNA/CNE Study Guide: IntranetWare Edition*, 0-07-913619-2

NET GURU TECHNOLOGIES, Inc.: *WEBmaster Engineer Certification Exam Guide*, 0-07-913287-1

NEW TECHNOLOGY SOLUTIONS: *Visual Basic 5 Exam Guide: Everything You Need to Pass Microsoft's Visual Basic 5 Certification*, 0-07-913671-0

PARKS, Sarah T.; KALMAN, Bob: *The A+ Certification Success Guide for Computer Technicians*, 0-07-048596-8 (paperback); 0-07-048595-X (hardcover)

THOMAS, Scott L.; PEASLEY, Amy E.: *Lotus Notes Certification Exam Guide: Application Development and System Administration*, 0-07-913674-2

# CNA/CNE Study Guide
## IntranetWare Edition

John Mueller
Robert A. Williams

**McGraw-Hill**
New York • San Francisco • Washington, D.C. • Auckland • Bogotá
Caracas • Lisbon • London • Madrid • Mexico City • Milan
Montreal • New Delhi • San Juan • Singapore
Sydney • Tokyo • Toronto

**Library of Congress Cataloging-in-Publication Data**

Mueller, John, date.
    CNA/CNE study guide / John Mueller, Robert Williams.—
IntranetWare ed.
      p.   cm.
    Includes index.
    ISBN 0-07-913619-2
    1. Novell, Inc.—Examinations—Study guides.  2. Computer
networks—Management—Examinations—Study guides.  3. Electronic
data processing personnel—Certification.  I. Williams, Robert A.
(Robert Allen)  II. Title.
TK5105.5.M8  1997
005.3'76—dc21                                                   97-26275
                                                                                       CIP

# McGraw-Hill
*A Division of The McGraw·Hill Companies*

Copyright © 1998 by The McGraw-Hill Companies, Inc. Printed in the United States of America. Except as permitted under the United States Copyright Act of 1976, no part of this publication may be reproduced or distributed in any form or by any means, or stored in a data base or retrieval system, without the prior written permission of the publisher.

1 2 3 4 5 6 7 8 9 0   DOC/DOC   9 0 2 1 0 9 8 7

P/N 044454-4
PART OF
ISBN 0-07-913619-2

*The sponsoring editor for this book was Judy Brief and the production supervisor was Clare Stanley. It was set in Century Schoolbook by North Market Street Graphics.*

Printed and bound by R. R. Donnelley & Sons Company.

McGraw-Hill books are available at special quantity discounts to use as premiums and sales promotions, or for use in corporate training programs. For more information, please write to the Director of Special Sales, McGraw-Hill, 11 West 19th Street, New York, NY 10011. Or contact your local bookstore.

---

Information contained in this work has been obtained by The McGraw-Hill Companies, Inc. ("McGraw-Hill") from sources believed to be reliable. However, neither McGraw-Hill nor its authors guarantees the accuracy or completeness of any information published herein and neither McGraw-Hill nor its authors shall be responsible for any errors, omissions, or damages arising out of use of this information. This work is published with the understanding that McGraw-Hill and its authors are supplying information but are not attempting to render engineering or other professional services. If such services are required, the assistance of an appropriate professional should be sought.

---

 This book is printed on recycled, acid-free paper containing a minimum of 50% recycled de-inked fiber.

This book is dedicated to our families. Like the families of network administrators who spend weekends searching frantically for broken cables, our families had to spend many weekends without us as we put this book together. We would like to thank our wives, Rebecca and Cyndie, for their endless support, tireless resolve to keep our homes together, and loving care when things didn't go well.

# CONTENTS

| | | |
|---|---|---|
| **Preface** | | xv |
| **Chapter 1** | Getting Started | 1 |
| | Introduction | 2 |
| | What is a CNA? | 3 |
| |     The NetWare 3.x Route | 6 |
| |     The NetWare 4.x Route | 7 |
| |     The GroupWise Route | 8 |
| |     The SoftSolutions Route | 9 |
| |     The InForms Route | 10 |
| | What Is a CNE? | 12 |
| |     The NetWare 3.x Route | 16 |
| |     The NetWare 4.x Route | 17 |
| |     The GroupWise Route | 19 |
| | What Is an MCNE? | 19 |
| | What Is an NCIP? | 22 |
| | What Is a CNI? | 25 |
| | Creating a Certification Checklist | 31 |
| | Conclusion | 46 |
| **Chapter 2** | Understanding the Certification Process | 51 |
| | Introduction | 52 |
| |     Why Do You Need Certification? | 53 |
| |     Professional Recognition | 56 |
| |     Internet/Internetworking/Network Skills | 57 |
| |     Industry Trend | 58 |
| |     Novell Support | 59 |
| |     Other Reasons | 61 |
| | What Is the Certification Path? | 62 |
| |     CNA | 62 |
| |     CNE | 64 |
| |     MCNE | 67 |
| |     NCIP | 68 |
| |     CNI | 68 |
| | How Long Does Certification Take? | 74 |
| |     Training | 74 |
| |     Testing | 74 |
| |     Paperwork | 75 |
| |     Continuing Education | 75 |
| | Conclusion | 76 |

| | | |
|---|---|---|
| **Chapter 3** | Learning the Trade | 77 |
| | Introduction | 78 |
| | Is Training Really Required? | 78 |
| | Deciding What Level of Training You Need | 79 |
| | Obtaining the Required Financing | 84 |
| |    Company-Sponsored Support | 87 |
| |    Student Loans | 91 |
| |    Scholarships | 92 |
| |    Veterans' Benefits | 93 |
| |    Personal Savings | 94 |
| |    Other Prrograms | 95 |
| | Who Do You Talk to About Training? | 96 |
| |    Hands-on Training | 96 |
| |    Instructor-Led Training | 98 |
| |    Self-Study Training | 100 |
| |    Other Types of Training | 101 |
| | Getting the Most from Your Training | 103 |
| | Conclusion | 107 |
| **Chapter 4** | Taking the Tests | 109 |
| | Introduction | 110 |
| | Gathering the Information You Need | 111 |
| |    The Importance of the Novell Courses | 111 |
| |    Taking Good Notes | 112 |
| | What Are the Requirements? | 114 |
| | The Test Taker's Study Guide | 117 |
| |    Setting Aside Adequate Study Time | 119 |
| |    Creating the Right Study Environment | 121 |
| |    Goal-Setting Strategies | 124 |
| |    Developing Good Study Habits | 126 |
| |    Getting the Job Done Right | 128 |
| | Registering for the Exam | 130 |
| | Things to Watch for While Taking the Exams | 131 |
| |    Standard Testing Technique | 134 |
| |    Adaptive Testing Technique | 135 |
| | What Do You Do If You Fail? | 136 |
| |    Understanding the Mechanics of Failure | 136 |
| |    Understanding the Emotions of Failure | 137 |
| | Conclusion | 138 |

# Contents

| | | |
|---|---|---|
| **Chapter 5** | **Getting the Paperwork Finished** | **139** |
| | Introduction | 140 |
| | Getting the Paperwork Started | 140 |
| | How Long Is Too Long? | 141 |
| | Maintaining a Log of the Paperwork | 142 |
| |     Using the Paperwork Log | 142 |
| |     Using the Phone Log | 146 |
| | Filling Out the Paperwork | 148 |
| |     Standard Paperwork Requirements | 148 |
| |     CNI Paperwork Requirements | 149 |
| | Verifying that Novell Receives and Processes the Paperwork | 150 |
| | Victory—Getting Your Certificate | 151 |
| | Conclusion | 152 |
| **Chapter 6** | **Using Your Certification to Your Advantage** | **153** |
| | Introduction | 154 |
| | Advancing Within Your Present Company | 155 |
| |     Creating a Company-Based Strategy | 155 |
| |     New Status Recognition | 157 |
| |     Advancement Through Promotion | 158 |
| |     Advancement by Creating a New Position | 162 |
| |     Recognition Through Title Change | 168 |
| |     Getting Paid for What You Do | 171 |
| | Moving to a Different Company | 173 |
| |     Getting Your Résumé Together | 173 |
| |     Emphasizing Your Qualifications During an Interview | 180 |
| |     Talking About a Rate of Pay | 181 |
| | Conclusion | 182 |
| **Chapter 7** | **Planning for Continuing Education Requirements** | **185** |
| | Introduction | 186 |
| | Looking for More Information | 187 |
| |     Filtering Your Input | 187 |
| |     Sources of Information | 188 |
| |     Organizing Your Information | 190 |
| |     Magazines | 192 |
| |     Trade Papers | 195 |
| |     Books | 196 |
| |     Online Services | 198 |
| |     Electronic Media | 207 |
| | CNE Continuing Education Requirements | 207 |
| | MCNE Continuing Education Requirements | 208 |
| | NCIP Continuing Education Requirements | 209 |
| | CNI Continuing Education Requirements | 209 |
| | Conclusion | 210 |

# Contents

| Chapter 8 | The Consulting Approach | 213 |
|---|---|---|
| | Introduction | 214 |
| | Using the Novell Logo | 215 |
| |    Advertisements | 215 |
| |    Brochures, Business Cards, and Price Lists | 217 |
| |    Advertising on the Internet | 219 |
| | Carrying Your ID Card | 220 |
| | Determining What Services to Offer | 221 |
| | Making Clients Aware of What Certification Means | 225 |
| | Determining What to Change | 227 |
| | Professionalism | 229 |
| | Conclusion | 233 |

| Chapter 9 | DOS Micro Hardware | 235 |
|---|---|---|
| | Introduction | 236 |
| | Case Study | 237 |
| |    Workstation Inventory | 238 |
| |    Workstation Setup | 241 |
| |    Workstation Optimization | 243 |
| | Study Questions | 249 |
| | Fun Test | 258 |
| | Brain Teaser | 264 |
| | Disk Time | 264 |

| Chapter 10 | NetWare 3.x Administration | 267 |
|---|---|---|
| | Introduction | 268 |
| | Case Study | 269 |
| |    Setting Up the Directory Structure | 269 |
| |    Creating the Users and Groups | 271 |
| |    Setting Up the Network Environment | 278 |
| |    Printing | 281 |
| |    The Final Test | 283 |
| | Study Questions | 285 |
| | Fun Test | 292 |
| | Brain Teaser | 297 |
| | Disk Time | 300 |

| Chapter 11 | NetWare 3.x Advanced Administration | 301 |
|---|---|---|
| | Introduction | 302 |
| | Case Study | 303 |
| |    File Server Startup Procedures | 304 |
| |    File Server Memory Management | 306 |

# Contents

xi

|  |  |  |
|---|---|---|
| Performance Tuning | | 311 |
| Maintenance Procedures | | 313 |
| Study Questions | | 315 |
| Fun Test | | 323 |
| Brain Teaser | | 328 |
| Disk Time | | 329 |

**Chapter 12** NetWare 3.x Installation and Configuration Workshop  331

| Introduction | 332 |
|---|---|
| Case Study | 333 |
|    File Server Software Installation | 333 |
|    Workstation Software Installation | 340 |
| Study Questions | 343 |
| Fun Test | 354 |
| Brain Teaser | 360 |
| Disk Time | 362 |

**Chapter 13** NetWare 3.x to 4.x Update  363

| Introduction | 364 |
|---|---|
| Case Study | 365 |
|    Introduction to ET | 366 |
|    Defining Terms and Concepts | 374 |
|    Practice Session | 380 |
|    Answers to Terms and Concepts | 382 |
|    A Look at the DynaText Viewer | 386 |
| Study Questions | 389 |
| Fun Test | 398 |
| Brain Teaser | 405 |
| Disk Time | 405 |

**Chapter 14** NetWare 4.x Administration  407

| Introduction | 408 |
|---|---|
| Case Study | 409 |
|    Setting Up the Directory Structure | 410 |
|    Creating Organizational Units, Users, and Groups | 411 |
|    User and Group Definitions | 414 |
|    Testing the Setup | 422 |
|    Setting Up the Windows 95 Client | 424 |
| Study Questions | 430 |
| Fun Test | 439 |
| Brain Teaser | 445 |
| Disk Time | 447 |

## Contents

| | | | |
|---|---|---|---|
| **Chapter 15** | NetWare 4.x Advanced Administration | | 449 |
| | Introduction | | 450 |
| | Case Study | | 451 |
| | | Print Queue Setup | 453 |
| | | Print Server Setup | 455 |
| | | Printer Setup | 455 |
| | | Printing Software Installation | 459 |
| | | DSREPAIR | 462 |
| | | VREPAIR | 463 |
| | | Adding Long Filename Support | 464 |
| | Study Questions | | 466 |
| | Fun Test | | 474 |
| | Brain Teaser | | 480 |
| | Disk Time | | 480 |
| **Chapter 16** | NetWare 4.x Installation and Configuration Workshop | | 485 |
| | Introduction | | 486 |
| | Case Study | | 487 |
| | | Install the Workstation ODI/VLM Software | 496 |
| | Study Questions | | 498 |
| | Fun Test | | 507 |
| | Brain Teaser | | 513 |
| | Disk Time | | 514 |
| **Chapter 17** | GroupWise System Administration | | 517 |
| | Introduction | | 518 |
| | Case Study | | 520 |
| | | GroupWise Installation on a Windows Workstation | 520 |
| | | Creating a Post Office and Setting Up Users | 524 |
| | | The Final Test | 535 |
| | Study Questions | | 537 |
| | Fun Test | | 547 |
| | Brain Teaser | | 553 |
| | Disk Time | | 556 |
| **Chapter 18** | GroupWise 4.x Asynchronous Gateway and Remote Client Support | | 557 |
| | Introduction | | 558 |
| | Case Study | | 560 |
| | | Installing the GroupWise Message Server | 561 |
| | | Configuring the GroupWise Message Server | 563 |

# Contents

xiii

| | |
|---|---|
| Creating Links Between Domains | 565 |
| Checking Your Installation | 570 |
| Study Questions | 575 |
| Fun Test | 587 |
| Brain Teaser | 594 |
| Disk Time | 596 |

**Chapter 19** GroupWise 4.x Advanced System Administration  597

| | |
|---|---|
| Introduction | 598 |
| Case Study | 600 |
|    Adding a New User | 601 |
|    Changing a User Setup | 602 |
|    Adding New Post Offices | 609 |
|    Adding New Domains | 614 |
|    Merging Domains | 619 |
|    Performing Database Maintenance | 623 |
| Study Questions | 627 |
| Fun Test | 638 |
| Brain Teaser | 644 |
| Disk Time | 647 |

**Chapter 20** NetWare Service and Support  649

| | |
|---|---|
| Introduction | 650 |
| Case Study | 651 |
|    CompuServe | 652 |
|    Virus Protection | 658 |
|    NetWare Support Encyclopedia | 662 |
| Study Questions | 665 |
| Fun Test | 677 |
| Brain Teaser | 684 |
| Disk Time | 687 |

**Chapter 21** Networking Technologies  689

| | |
|---|---|
| Introduction | 690 |
| Case Study | 691 |
| Study Questions | 698 |
| Fun Test | 707 |
| Brain Teaser | 714 |
| Disk Time | 714 |

## Contents

**Chapter 22**  SoftSolutions 4.x Administration — 717

    Introduction — 718
    Case Study — 720
        SoftSolutions Installation — 720
        Document Desktop Installation — 726
        Correcting Database Errors — 729
        Index Compaction — 733
    Study Questions — 734
    Fun Test — 745
    Brain Teaser — 752
    Disk Time — 754

**Chapter 23**  InForms 4.x Administration and Form Design — 755

    Introduction — 756
    Case Study — 757
        Installation — 758
        First Time Configuration — 763
        Designing a Form — 766
        Testing a Form — 773
        Assigning Security — 775
    Study Questions — 783
    Fun Test — 794
    Brain Teaser — 800
    Disk Time — 803

**Appendix A**  List of Acronyms — 805

**Appendix B**  Fun Test Question Answers — 817

**Appendix C**  Brain Teaser Answers — 825

**Appendix D**  Important Phone Numbers — 835

**Appendix E**  Sources of Additional Information — 837

**Appendix F**  Course Descriptions — 841

**Glossary** — 871

**Index** — 891

# PREFACE

## Why You Need Certification

Many people don't understand what a Novell certification is or why they need it. This includes employers as well as clients. Even if you understand why the certification is important, presenting these facts to an employer or client may prove difficult. The *Novell CNA/CNE Study Guide* provides you with a full description of each of the certifications and why they are important. This not only increases your own knowledge, but helps you explain it to potential clients and employers as well. Knowing this information could mean the difference between getting a job or losing it to someone less qualified. It also helps you get the level of compensation you deserve for having a certification.

## What This Book Will Do for You

The overall purpose of the *Novell CNA/CNE Study Guide* is simple. It helps CNA or CNE candidates prepare for the Novell certification examination, then use that certification to further their career goals. The major reason that many people fail the Novell examinations is a lack of preparation, not necessarily a lack of knowledge. Setting reasonable goals and learning good study techniques are a major part of any examination preparation. This book helps you do both. Of course, getting a certification is only part of the task. A failure to follow through once you get your certification will prevent you from getting the kind of job that you deserve. This book will help you see some of the potential job enhancements that a CNA or CNE certification can provide.

If the *Novell CNA/CNE Study Guide* stopped here, you would probably feel it was well worth the investment. However, it also covers four essential areas to help you fully prepare for your certification exams and your new career goals once you pass. We'll begin by telling you about the various Novell certification requirements and help you come up with a plan to get the certification you need. Many network administrators need to get their certification, but are unaware of the requirements or are unsure of who to contact.

The second area where the *Novell CNA/CNE Study Guide* will help you out is in *defining certification strategy*. Of course, everyone knows that the ultimate goal of this process is receiving the certification. Our book goes much further—it provides you with the milestones you need to reach before you can pass the required examinations. Disorganization hurts many people who seek certification. Providing you with a set of goals helps you get ready for the examination more than just about any other form of preparation.

The third area where you can depend on the *Novell CNA/CNE Study Guide* to help is in *job performance*. Of course, improving job performance is one step toward many goals. For example, you may want a job with more responsibility, better pay, or greater advancement potential. This part of the book helps you gain those goals by showing you how to present your certification to potential employers or clients. Learning how to present your certification is as important as getting it in the first place. In total, the first three areas of the book help you in 10 specific ways.

1. *Learning the differences between the various certifications offered by Novell: CNA, CNE, ECNE, MCNE, and CNI.* Many users are unsure what level or type of certification they need. Especially unclear are the differences between CNE, MCNE, and ECNE. This book helps you understand the differences and plan for the level of certification that meets your needs.

2. *Enhancing your career by getting a Novell Certification today.* Many people face a Novell certification as an extra responsibility they neither want nor need. The *Novell CNA/CNE Study Guide* helps you over this hurdle by showing the benefits of such a certification. In many cases a positive attitude could mean the difference between becoming certified, or not.

3. *Planning for the certification process.* It's unfortunate, but many people start CNA or CNE training with no idea of what to expect or how to prepare for it. There are instances where someone has never even used a computer before, but now has to learn to run a network. The *Novell CNA/CNE Study Guide* will help you prepare for certification by helping you understand the certification requirements. It also helps you create a checklist tailored to your needs. Writing down what you need to do is at least half the battle in planning for certification.

# Preface

4. *Understanding what support you can expect from Novell.* Part of the benefit of becoming certified is the support that Novell provides. While the documentation provided with the certification package outlines some of the benefits, a mere list is not enough. The *Novell CNA/CNE Study Guide* helps you understand what you can do with these additional support items.

5. *Planning for continuing education requirements.* Many people approach a Novell certification as they would a high school education. Once it's over, they peacefully go back to their old routine, never acknowledging the need to continue their education. Fortunately, the Novell recertification requirements will quickly make you aware of the need for continuing education. This book will help you prepare for it before you lose your certification due to lack of planning.

6. *Finding all your certification questions answered in one place.* One of the big problems in getting a Novell certification is that prospects spend many hours searching for answers to their questions. This problem isn't new or unique; college and university students face the same problem. Many authors have addressed the issues of getting from point *A* to point *B* in these institutions. For example, just look at all the books that tell you how to get a GED or take an SAT test—both requirements for getting into a college or university. Currently, there's no guide for people who want to become a CNE; this book answers that need.

7. *Getting your certification quickly and easily.* The *Novell CNA/CNE Study Guide* provides tips and hints that reduce the chance of failure when taking a test. This could shave days or even weeks from the certification process. Add to this the time saved researching the certification itself, and you could end up saving a month or more in the certification cycle.

8. *Learning what courses are available.* Many people miss opportunities to learn something they really want to know about NetWare simply because they don't know what courses are available. The *Novell CNA/CNE Study Guide* provides a list of classes provided by Novell. All you need to do is decide which courses you want to take (as long as they meet certification requirements), sign up, and take the courses.

9. *Getting answers to your questions quickly and easily.* The *Novell CNA/CNE Study Guide* provides a list of important phone numbers that you can call whenever you need help with a problem. Instead of writing these numbers on scraps of paper that get lost whenever you

really need them, using this guide can quickly provide you with the help you need. In addition, instead of playing telephone tag with the one person you thought could help—only to find out that they can't—this book helps you find the right person the first time.

10. *Finding sources of additional information.* There is no one book solution to every problem. Rather than strand you without the resources you need, this book provides a list of places you can go for additional help. This resource is very important to both the novice and the expert reader.

Finally, the bulk of this book looks at the test itself. It starts with a hands-on exercise designed to show you what you need to know. It then tests this ability through the use of sample questions. Each question includes an explanation of why the answer is important. This is one of the most common questions that people ask: *"Why is this answer more correct?"* Every Novell question features at least four possible answers. The first type of answer (not necessarily the first answer) is always incorrect. The second type is meant to fool people who don't really know what the question is asking. The third type of answer is always correct, but it doesn't represent the Novell way of doing things. The fourth type of answer always contains the Novell answer to the question. This section answers the "Why more correct?" question by showing you how to look at things from a Novell perspective. The section ends with some fun exercises designed to help you learn the material to an even greater extent. It also includes some exercises based on the disk that is included with this book.

By now you are probably asking what more the *Novell CNA/CNE Study Guide* could offer. There are many features that differentiate this book from others on the market. The most important features are the test questions and exercises. The most important items of interest to you are the questions you will need to answer. Digging information out of a text filled with facts is not necessarily the best way to get that information. This book provides you with questions, the appropriate answers, and the reason that each answer is correct. Using this study method helps you learn the test faster than any other method available.

This book also features three visual and two tactile methods of learning the information. First, it starts with a hands-on approach to learning the information through an exercise called a *case study*. You use both tactile and visual capabilities to work through a series of problems to get to a desired end result. Then, the book shows you what kind of questions you can expect from Novell. This provides another form of visual input.

# Preface

Finally, you go through some fun exercises that include a *Jeopardy!*™-type game. The game will provide the answers; you'll have to provide a corresponding question. This provides yet another form of tactile and visual input. These three different types of input will fully prepare you to take the examination. (Make sure you read about the new brain teasers feature in the "Brain Teasers—A New Feature to Help You Study" section of this introduction.)

The glossary and appendixes in this book provide a useful set of tools as well. Acronyms confuse many people; App. A provides definitions for the acronyms used in the networking industry. Novell has a reputation for making this problem worse. Yet many of these acronyms and obscure words will appear in the examination and within the text of this book. In addition, this section of the book provides useful information about where you can receive additional information in the form of courses and people (contacts).

## How This Book Is Organized

This book provides all the information you need to get your certification and to use your certification once you get it. Setting goals, learning to study, and then actually studying the right material are the tasks you need to accomplish to reach this goal. The modular format of this book helps you find the information you need quickly and easily. The following paragraphs describe the contents of each chapter.

**CHAPTER 1—GETTING STARTED.** Everyone needs to learn about the basics before they can start a new task. Getting a Novell certification isn't any different. This chapter explains what types of certifications Novell offers, what differentiates them from other certifications, and the criteria for getting the certifications. The most important feature of this chapter is that it tells you all about the duties and responsibilities associated with the various certifications. This allows you to focus on the certification you actually require to get your job done, rather than trying to figure out what you need based on course outlines.

Once you figure out which certification to get, the chapter helps you design a checklist for your particular certification course. Since each person starts at a different knowledge threshold, each company's requirements are different, and Novell offers elective courses in some areas, your checklist will contain unique requirements.

**CHAPTER 2—UNDERSTANDING THE CERTIFICATION PROCESS.** Once you gain a full appreciation of what the certification accomplishes, you can concentrate on how certification helps you on the job. This chapter answers questions like *Why is certification important?* Once you understand this concept, you can take a detailed look at the certification requirements. This will help you complete the certification checklist you started in Chap. 1. This chapter also helps you schedule the time required to complete the certification. Some participants in the certification process never become certified because they don't schedule the time required to complete the process. The guidelines in this chapter help reduce the probability of such an occurrence.

**CHAPTER 3—LEARNING THE TRADE.** After you get all the planning done, it's time to get the required training. Currently, some candidates choose to avoid training classes altogether. At an average cost of $600 it's not too difficult to figure out why they would want to do so. Unfortunately, these people usually end up dropping out of the process or taking the classes anyway. Rather than waste time and effort trying to take the tests without the proper training, it's to your benefit to take the courses. This chapter helps explain the need for training and what goals you should set as part of the training process. It also helps you see places where you could take a test immediately instead of going through a class first. Finally, the book takes a look at what you can do to get the maximum benefit from your training experience.

**CHAPTER 4—TAKING THE TESTS.** Taking tests is the least favorite part of any training experience. Professional examinations are more difficult than just about any other examinations you can take. Novell's examinations aren't any different. Even if you go through all the training courses, study hard, and take the proper approach to testing, there's a good chance you'll fail at least one examination. This chapter helps you cover the first three areas by telling you how to study and what to study. It also stresses the importance of taking the Novell viewpoint when answering questions. Most important of all, this chapter helps you over the ultimate hurdle—*dealing with failure*. The better prepared the person taking the test, the more devastating the failure becomes. Helping you get back on your feet is a very important feature of this book.

This most important way in which this chapter helps you get your certification is to help you develop good study habits. There are four major areas of concern. The first section helps you *set aside time to study*. If you

# Preface

are too busy taking care of other things that you cannot concentrate on what you want to study, then your retention rate will fall to near zero, and there is no reason you should even make the effort. Study requires your full attention! Nothing else will work.

The next area is *creating a good study environment*. Every time you change the conditions for one of your senses, you also change your chances of getting a good exam grade. We'll look at things like getting the correct materials together and making sure that you have enough light. Even a comfortable seat can change your outlook on life. We look at all the things you can do to improve your study environment. In other words, this section looks at the physical requirements for study.

The third section looks at *setting goals for a study session*. You need to know what you plan to accomplish during any given session. This isn't the same as your overall goal, or even the goal of passing an exam. It's a small goal that you can accomplish in one study session. Positive feedback in the form of goal accomplishment goes a long way toward making every study session an event that will help you pass your exam. A failure to set goals may lead you to random study that does not accomplish the goal of passing the test.

Finally, we look at *study techniques*. Not every reader can use the same technique. Each person is unique and requires a unique study environment. The rote memorization that works for one person may result in pure boredom for someone else. This section looks at several viable ways to study. At least one of the methods will meet the needs of every reader. You may even find that using a combination of study methods is the right method for you.

**CHAPTER 5—GETTING THE PAPERWORK FINISHED.** *The job's never finished until the paperwork's done.* This is a truism for Novell certification as well. Even if you finish all the required tests and training, you can still fumble around for several weeks just getting all the paperwork finished. The problem is that Novell lacks a written procedure for finishing this paperwork. This chapter deals with this problem by providing you with step-by-step instructions on filling out the paperwork and getting all the required documentation together. It also provides you with a list of people you need to talk with and where you need to send the paperwork. Finally, it tells you what kind of paperwork you should get back from Novell and how long it usually takes to receive it.

**CHAPTER 6—USING YOUR CERTIFICATION TO YOUR ADVANTAGE.** Gaining access to a skill is only the first step in using it as a career enhancing tool. This chapter helps you understand what you need to do to use certification to your benefit. This particular chapter focuses on the individual working for someone else. We cover a number of topics from advancing in your current company to getting a new (and hopefully better) job based on that training.

**CHAPTER 7—PLANNING FOR CONTINUING EDUCATION REQUIREMENTS.** All Novell certifications require some maintenance. Lack of maintenance is the number one reason that people lose their certification. Every time Novell releases a new NetWare product, the certificate holder must take another test proving proficiency with that product. Even though the time allotted to perform this task is usually more than sufficient, many people fail to make the grade because of a lack of planning. This chapter emphasizes two forms of continuing education. The first is *professional level training*. It answers questions like, *What types of new equipment is industry creating?* The second is *Novell-specific training*. It helps you prepare for and pass that recertification examination. This chapter also helps you see the importance of both types of continuing education.

**CHAPTER 8—THE CONSULTING APPROACH.** Many consultants make a living from installing and maintaining Novell networks. This chapter specifically targets the networking expert. It provides the consultant with ideas on how to improve business through the proper use of Novell-supplied aids. It also examines some ways that consultants can use the certification to gain and keep new clients. Finally, this chapter examines some thorny issues like what to charge the client for network services and how to maintain a professional relationship with the client.

**CHAPTERS 9 TO 23.** Chapters 9 to 19 follow the same format, but look at different courses. This is the heart of the book, the section that every reader will want to review in detail. Of course, you won't need every chapter. There's one chapter for every major test that you'll need to take. Simply look at the chapters you need to get your certification.

Every chapter begins with an introduction. The introduction tells you about the purpose of the chapter and what you should know when you finish it. In essence, this tells you how to set your goals for a particular test. Make sure you use it as your source for goal setting. It will also tell you who should use this chapter. Remember, you only need to read the chapters that pertain to your particular certification. Don't waste time looking at nonessential material.

The first major section of the chapter is a *case study*. You will perform some hands-on tasks that will help you learn what you need to know to pass the examination. This section of the chapter assumes that you are sitting at a workstation on your network. It helps you through a set of exercises designed to teach you about the important features of your network. It's the tactile part of the exercise that makes this section so valuable. Even though you'll get a lot more from this section if you perform it on your own network, the inclusion of screen shots will help you get something out of it even if you don't have a network handy. This means that you can still read this section on a plane or any other convenient place. Unfortunately, the screen shots are a poor substitute for performing the exercise yourself.

The second area will contain *actual Novell questions* for that course. It will also include the correct answer and an explanation of why that answer is correct. The way you should use this section is to ask yourself the question, look at the answer to see if you were correct, then read the reason why this answer is more correct than any of the other questions presented. Using a three-step process of this nature will reinforce the information you need to pass the examination. Make sure you take the time to fully understand why a particular answer is correct before you go on to the next question.

The next section is a *fun test*. This is an exercise where you'll look at some sample test questions and answer them. The answers will appear in an appendix at the back of the book. This will help you test what you learned in the previous section. Taking this test will also give you some idea of how well you will do on the actual exam. Of course, there's no way that our fun test can provide the ultimate in accuracy, considering the number of variables in every Novell exam.

# Disk Time—Using the Disk That Comes with This Book

Spending time with the online study tools provided on the disk that comes with this book offers a different way to study the material required to pass your certification exam. Think of it as the visual corollary to the text-based material presented in the book. Unlike the book, you must use the Disk Time materials at your computer. However, the advantage is that the Disk Time study aids offer an interactive environment that you can't get from a book.

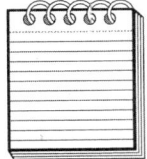

**NOTE** *Windows must be installed on your system in order for you to take full advantage of the disk that accompanies this book. Even though the disk is designed to work with Windows 3.x, it was tested under Windows 95 as well.*

There are three Disk Time presentations for this chapter. Each presentation is different. The *Big Red Test* provides you with a sample exam. The exam looks just like the one that you'll see at the Drake Testing Center. Of course, there are differences. Like the exams in this book, you can only take Big Red Test a limited number of times before you begin to memorize the answers. Fortunately, you can get a larger test base for Big Red Test than the one provided on our disk. Simply follow the ordering instructions you get with the product.

The *Windows Help* file provides the same questions and answers you find in the third section of this chapter, plus a few more. You can use this method of study to enhance your ability to learn in one specific area. The Windows search engine allows you to look up the questions and explanations you need to build a knowledge base in one particular area. The search engine also allows you to use the questions and answers for reference. In other words, you can use the questions and answers as a source of information even after you take the exam.

The final Disk Time aid is the *Jeopardy!*-type game called *Red Zone*. The questions and answers in this section come from a random sampling of questions from the entire database presented in this book. You'll select a question and a point value. Answer the question within the time allotted and you get the points. Failure to answer the question results in a loss of points. The game presents a few twists and turns. For example, you won't always get the same amount of time each time you answer a question. You can also select from one of three experience levels. The higher the experience level, the more challenging the game. The game will tell you if you got your certificate when you finish. Just like real life, the prize in this game is your certificate and all that it brings.

## What's New in This Edition

There are quite a few new materials in this edition of the book. The first thing you'll notice is that we cover all the new requirements for becoming a CNE or a CNA. All the tables, figures, and questions contain updated

# Preface

information that reflects Novell's changing certification requirements. Most of these tables are also enhanced with additional information from the previous edition. For example, all the elective courses covered in Chap. 1 now include course and test numbers in addition to the course names provided in the previous edition.

We've also improved all the disk materials. Not only are they completely updated to reflect the changing certification requirements, but you'll find additional questions in this edition as well. Look on the disk if you didn't find enough questions in the book. We're sure you'll be surprised at just how many more questions you'll get to look at. Of course, questions aren't the only resource that the disk provides. The Red Zone (our *Jeopardy!*-style game) has been enhanced to include all the new certification routes and topics that Novell tests for. As always, the online help utility provides you with the complete list of questions provided in the book, along with a few bonus questions for each chapter.

## Brain Teasers—A New Feature to Help You Study

Almost everyone likes puzzles. A lot of people look forward to the daily crossword puzzle in the paper or a word-search puzzle book at the store. Just think about all of the words and bits of information you've picked up over the years by working with puzzles. In essence, they provide a fun way to learn new information or at least reinforce what you already know.

That's why this edition of the book contains a new brain-teaser feature. It's designed to make learning new information, or at least reinforcing what you already know, just a bit more fun. Every chapter, beginning with Chap. 9, will include this new feature to help you learn what you need to know for your certification exam.

The brain-teaser section of the book isn't designed for stand-alone use. You won't learn everything you need to know to pass the exam by looking at this section of the chapters to the exclusion of everything else. That's sort of the same as bypassing the vegetables on your plate and going right for dessert. No one ever built a strong body by eating sweets alone—likewise, you'll want to spend a lot of time reading the questions and using the other study aids in this book to prepare for your exam before you go on to the fun stuff.

# CHAPTER 1
# Getting Started

## Introduction

Everyone needs to research and practice a task before they can actually perform it. Getting a Novell certification isn't any different from any other task you've performed. You'll need to research your certification before you can understand what you need to do to get it. Once you understand the requirements, you'll need to practice some set of skills before you can actually perform them.

The overall goal of this chapter is to explain what types of certifications Novell offers, what differentiates them from other certifications, and the criteria for getting them. We also discuss all the duties and responsibilities associated with the various certifications. We even include a procedure for creating your own certification checklist, a must for anyone serious about obtaining this useful and beneficial credential.

Since this is a CNA- and CNE-oriented book, this chapter focuses on the requirements for those two certifications. It provides you with many of the specific things you need to know about becoming a CNA or CNE. This chapter also tells you what a CNA or CNE is and what you need to do to become one. Many people compare certification efforts like becoming a CNA or CNE with a journey. Knowing where you are now and where you want to go is one of the most important parts of any journey. Look at this book as your road map and this chapter as the *You Are Here* pointer on that map. Of course, this is only the beginning of your journey. Any certification effort will require you to learn the theory behind networking in general and NetWare in particular. Chapters 9 through 23 help you achieve this goal.

This chapter also outlines the various routes you can follow for a specific course of study for the CNA and CNE certifications. We'll cover the process one step at a time, so don't worry about getting lost in a mire of information overload. To use this chapter, first find the major section for either CNA or CNE (depending on the level of certification you require). Now find the particular course of study you need to follow. There's one subsection each for the NetWare 3.x and 4.x courses of study. We also cover the Novell GroupWise course of study, along with a couple of special options for CNA candidates. All you need to do is find the course you intend to take and follow the goal path to completion. Using this method takes all the guesswork out of certification.

Novell patterned its certification process after the credit system used by colleges. Each exam passed earns a predetermined number of credit points. There are two types of credits: required and elective. The *required* credits cover the base or core exams while the *elective* credits allow

# Getting Started

you to pick exams that are in your field of expertise or that interest you. Each certification requires a certain number of both required and elective credits.

Novell offers five classes of technical certification: *CNA* (Certified Novell Administrator), *CNE* (Certified Novell Engineer), *MCNE* (Master Certified Novell Engineer), *NCIP* (Novell Certified Internet Professional), and *CNI* (Certified Novell Instructor). The ECNE program was phased out; Novell stopped allowing people to pursue this certification after June 1996. The replacement program is the MCNE. The NCIP is also a new certification for people interested in the Internet; it concentrates on managing a Web site versus a LAN. Make sure you take the time required to at least look at all five certifications. You may find that you have the experience and knowledge required to participate in one of the higher-level programs like MCNE or CNI.

**NOTE** *Novell used to use the term* NetWare *as part of all its certifications. For example, CNE used to stand for* Certified NetWare Engineer. *In the ensuing years, the NetWare moniker didn't seem relevant anymore because Novell offered more than just NetWare certification. For those of you who are used to the older term, just remember that CNE now stands for* Certified Novell Engineer—*it's a reasonable change considering the new scope of Novell's offerings.*

## What Is a CNA?

The *Certified Novell Administrator* (CNA) is Novell's entry-level certification. It's for the person who needs to administer the network on a day-to-day basis. The duties of this person include adding users, assigning security to the users, writing login scripts, backing up the system, installing applications onto the network, and managing the printing environment. Individual companies may assign this person other network administration tasks as well. The CNA is usually a full-time employee of the company and often is required to perform other duties besides managing the network.

The CNA certification provides current or prospective employers the assurance that you have a good understanding of the Novell operating system (or a non–operating system alternative). It also certifies that you have knowledge of the different administration tools and the various aspects of managing a network. It doesn't certify that you are a hardware guru or are capable of performing some of the advanced tasks that a CNE could.

Once you become a CNA, you can use the knowledge and information that you acquire on the job to become a *Certified Novell Engineer* (CNE). Of course, you'll still need to learn all of the advanced networking technology that you didn't learn as part of your CNA certification. Unfortunately, the CNA test doesn't count toward the CNE certification. The CNA certification requires that you know the basic and advanced concepts of the Novell operating system, along with more than a basic understanding of microcomputers.

Before you rush out to your nearest (NAEC) Novell Authorized Education Center or (NEAP) Novell Education Academic Partner, you need to decide whether you should even pursue the CNA certification route. Some people go the CNA route only to find that they really don't have the credentials required to get the job they want. Figure 1-1 shows a decision tree you can use to help you decide between CNA and CNE certification. Obviously, it can't take every contingency into account, but it will help you define the kinds of questions you should ask before you start the certification process.

One of the first decisions that you must make once you've decided to pursue a CNA certification is which Novell product you want (or need) to work with. Novell offers two operating system and three non–operating system certification routes for potential CNAs: 3.x NetWare or 4.x NetWare; and SoftSolutions, InForms, or GroupWise.

*NetWare 3.x* is the oldest-technology operating system now offered by Novell. The reason so many people like it is that it looks and feels like the very popular NetWare 2.x operating system of days gone by. Some people also view it as easier to implement than NetWare 4.x in a small network setup since NetWare 3.x doesn't rely on (NDS) NetWare Directory Services. The second choice is the *NetWare 4.x* operating system. This is Novell's latest version of the operating system for a LAN setup, though you'll see a lot of new installations use IntranetWare in its place. (Although there isn't an IntranetWare certification available right now, Novell is in the process of setting one up.)

*GroupWise* is the oldest non–operating system (groupware) route for CNAs. This product is similar to other groupware offerings, like Lotus Notes. You can also choose the InForms and SoftSolutions routes, both of which are groupware choices. *InForms* is a forms creation and data-handling product. It depends on structured query language (SQL) to interact with any databases on your server. *SoftSolutions* is a document management system. Essentially, it maintains a database of all of the documents on your server, which allows people to find what they need a lot

# Getting Started

**Figure 1-1**
CNA Decision Tree.

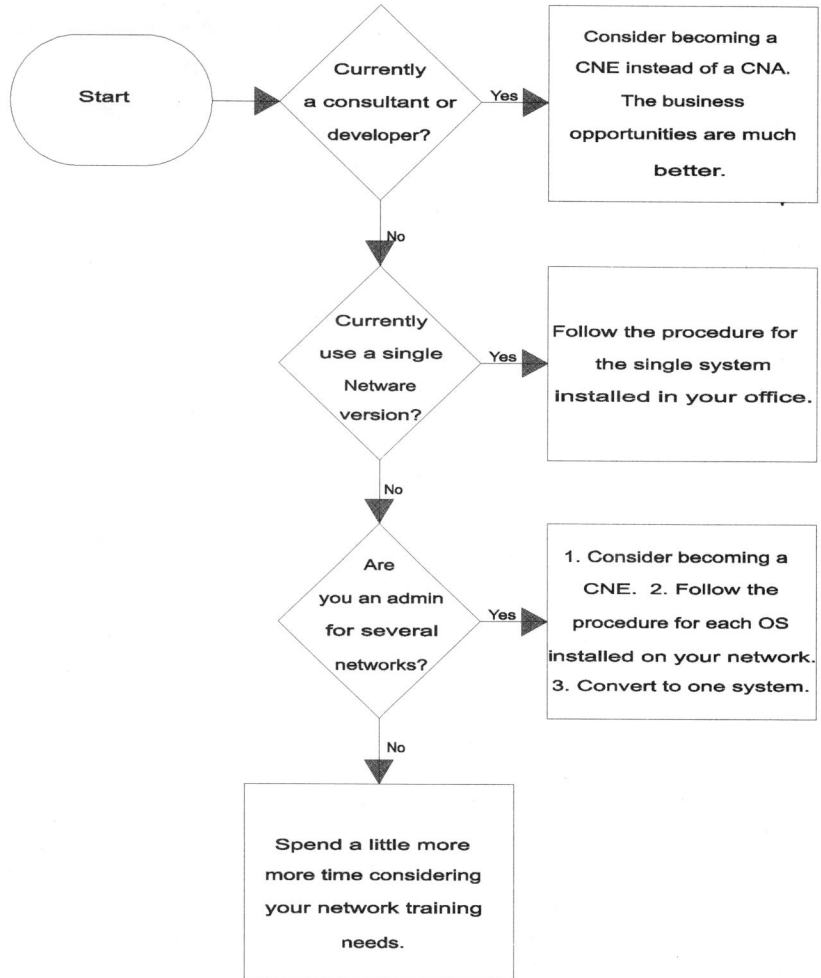

faster than searching for the information by hand. Fortunately, GroupWise, InForms, and SoftSolutions are all designed to work with each other. This allows you to build on one groupware certification to provide a broader range of services to a potential employer.

The decision of which certification route to choose is going to depend on which type of system you have in your office or which system you have the most experience with. It could also depend on the particular type of business that you intend to work in. For example, GroupWise certification would lend itself more to large businesses than small ones. The same can be said of both the InForms and SoftSolutions routes. If you're targeting smaller companies, then it's more likely that you'll run into older technology like NetWare 3.x.

The criteria for getting the CNA certification involves passing one competency exam. The exam covers the system administration for any of the following products: NetWare 3.x, NetWare 4.x, SoftSolutions, InForms, or GroupWise. There is no exam, and no questions on the exams, about DOS or microcomputer concepts. However, you must have a very good understanding of how to operate a computer before you'll pass any of the CNA examinations. A passing understanding of the interior workings of the computer is a plus as well, though certainly not required.

## The NetWare 3.x Route

The 3.x route includes three steps. First, you need to decide whether you want to take the Novell certification course. If you do, then ask about course number 508 (3.x Administration) at your local NAEC or NEAP. Once you complete the course, study Chaps. 9 and 11 in this book. This will prepare you for the one exam required for this certification. (Make sure you spend time working on an existing or test network, if you have one available, as well.) Finally, call the Sylvan Prometric testing center and ask for exam number 50-390.

That's all there is to it. If you pass your exam, you're a CNA. If not, spend some additional time learning NetWare by using the hands-on training exercises provided in this book. You should receive your paperwork in a few weeks.

So, what is Novell interested in as far as your CNA qualifications with NetWare 3.x? The following list tells about the various tasks you'll need to be able to perform. Remember that simply performing the tasks doesn't guarantee you'll pass the exam, but performing them competently does help.

- *Customize the desktop.*   One size no longer fits. As PC operating systems become more complex, so does the job of the CNA. The user is going to rely on you to help gain the right kind of access to the network and to make that access as easy as possible.

- *Optimize the desktop.*   In today's information age, you need to provide the quickest possible access to the data that the user requires to perform a task. This usually means some type of optimization, like

# Getting Started

changing system settings. However, it could also mean performing tasks like installing the latest drivers.

- *Automate access to the network.* You'll need to demonstrate your ability to write scripts, map drives, and perform other network-related tasks to help the user gain access quickly, yet maintain the required level of security.
- *Run system backups.* Getting a backup of the data on the server is an important task. Everyone responsible for any form of maintenance on the file server needs to know how to perform this task, even if it's not part of their regular duties.
- *Maintain printer services.* Users will need your help in accessing a printer, choosing the right print job, and capturing a printer port. You'll also need to know what to do when the unexpected—like a printer failure—happens.

## The NetWare 4.x Route

The 4.x route includes three steps. First, you need to decide whether you want to take the Novell certification course. If you do, then ask about course number 520 (4.x Administration) at your local NAEC or NEAP. Once you complete the course, study Chaps. 9 and 15 in this book. This will prepare you for the one exam required for this certification. (Make sure you spend time working on an existing or test network, if you have one available, as well; spend extra time working with NDS, since that's the NetWare 4.x management strategy.) Finally, call the Sylvan Prometric testing center and ask for exam number 50-394.

That's all there is to it. If you pass your exam, you're a CNA. If not, spend some additional time learning NetWare by using the hands-on training exercises provided in this book. You should receive your paperwork in a few weeks.

Novell will want you to know specific kinds of information before allowing you to become a CNA. The following task list tells you what kinds of tasks you'll need to know how to do. Even if you can perform these tasks, you're still not guaranteed of passing the exam, but you'll be a lot closer.

- *Share software resources using NetWare Directory Services (NDS).* NDS is the central network management strategy for NetWare 4.x. It uses object technology to make sharing resources of all kinds easier.

In addition, you can manage every resource from one location. Needless to say, learning to use this feature is essential to certification.

- *Implement a company security strategy.* Security has always been a major issue, but it's becoming more so as companies start working on the Internet. Even if you're part of a small company, security is a major concern. Just think about the damage one hacker could cause to your data and you'll see that learning about security isn't just an option.
- *Monitor network performance.* Getting more work done with fewer resources is what performance is all about. You'll need to know how to wring every ounce of power from the file servers and workstations you work with. This normally means tuning various system parameters to the optimum levels for your particular setup. However, it could also mean doing extra work, like installing new drivers as needed.
- *Handle routine software maintenance.* A lot of the work you'll need to do involves some type of software maintenance. For example, every time a vendor comes out with a new version of its word processor, you'll probably be the first one to know about it. A CNA spends a lot of time working with users in getting their workstations fully operational, and that means installing software updates from time to time.

## The GroupWise Route

Even though the GroupWise route itself includes three steps, you may want to add a fourth intermediate step to the process. First, you need to decide whether you want to take the Novell certification course. If you do, then ask about course number 325 (GroupWise 4.x Administration) or course number 350 (GroupWise 5.x Administration) at your local NAEC or NEAP. Here's the intermediate step—spend some time working with a network administrator who actually uses GroupWise to learn some of the ins and outs of this product, since it's unlikely that you'll get to test every aspect of the product while you perform your normal job. Once you complete the course and optional hands-on training, study Chaps. 9 and 17 in this book. This will prepare you for the one exam required for this certification. Finally, call the Sylvan Prometric testing center and ask for exam number 50-395.

That's all there is to it. If you pass your exam, you're a CNA. If not, spend some additional time learning GroupWise by using the hands-on

# Getting Started

training exercises provided in this book. You should receive your paperwork in a few weeks.

Novell will expect you to be able to perform certain tasks before taking the test. The following list outlines the tasks for you. Spend some time with another administrator to learn the Novell way of performing these tasks. You'll find it easier to pass the exams if you do.

- *Create post offices.* This is one of the first tasks you'll need to do as part of setting up GroupWise. Unfortunately, that's about the only time you'll do it unless your company is growing relatively fast. The need for new post offices is fairly infrequent, but you need to set them up right the first time when you do create a new one.
- *Create users.* You'll find that you perform this task fairly often, especially if your company is growing fast or has a high turnover rate. Make sure you know how to perform all of the user-related tasks, like adding and removing them from groups.
- *Create links between domains.* Domains are a big part of your GroupWise setup if you are part of a larger company. A domain could be as large as the entire company, or as small as a specific workgroup within that company. Normally, you'll find that domains are divided along subsidiary lines and that you'll use groups to make smaller divisions.
- *Install and administer GroupWise clients.* Getting GroupWise to work is only part of the task. Once you have GroupWise set up, you'll want people to use it. That requires a client. Normally, you'll need a separate client for each kind of PC operating system, like Windows 95, that your network supports.
- *Perform basic troubleshooting.* Even the best setup will eventually get into trouble. When it does, you can bet that someone will call for help. Some of the more typical problems you'll run into are lost mail and the inability to call outside of the building. Of course, once problems reach the hardware level, you'll probably hand them off to a CNE or another higher-level network administrator.

## The SoftSolutions Route

Even though the SoftSolutions route itself includes three steps, you may want to add a fourth intermediate step to the process. First, you need to decide whether you want to take the Novell certification course. If you do, then ask about course number 345 (SoftSolutions 4.x Administration) at your local NAEC or NEAP. You may want to take the intermediate step of spending some time with an experienced administrator once you complete your course, since this is about the only way that you'll be able to put the information you've learned into practice. Once you complete the course and optional hands-on training, study Chaps. 9 and 22 in this book. This will prepare you for the one exam required for this certification. Finally, call the Sylvan Prometric testing center and ask for exam number 50-397.

That's all there is to it. If you pass your exam, you're a CNA. If not, spend some additional time learning SoftSolutions by using the hands-on training exercises provided in this book. You should receive your paperwork in a few weeks.

You can improve your chances of passing the exam the first time around by making sure you know how to perform specific tasks. Even though knowing how to perform the tasks in the following list doesn't guarantee you'll pass, they're the things that Novell is looking for during the testing process.

- *Add users.* If you plan to create a document management system, then it pays to know who is using those documents. That's what this part of the testing criteria is all about, knowing who can access which documents.

- *Set up basic applications.* SoftSolutions is a document manager, not an actual application that can read the documents. As a result, you'll need to set up applications to handle the document requests made by the users of your system.

- *Operate full text indexers.* Before anyone can find what they need on your system, you'll need to create an index of what it contains. That's where the full text indexer comes into play.

- *Design screens, reports, and workstation IDs.* Having a full text database of the documents at your company isn't much use unless you can generate reports to show how they're being used.

## The InForms Route

Even though the InForms route itself includes three steps, you may want to add an intermediate step to the process. First, you need to decide whether you want to take the Novell certification course. If you do, then ask about course number 335 (InForms 4.x Administration and Form Design) at your local NAEC or NEAP. You'll probably want to take the

# Getting Started

intermediate step of spending some time with an experienced administrator once you complete your course, since this is about the only way that you'll be able to put the information you've learned into practice. Once you complete the course and optional hands-on training, study Chaps. 9 and 23 in this book. This will prepare you for the one exam required for this certification. Finally, call the Sylvan Prometric testing center and ask for exam number 50-396.

That's all there is to it. If you pass your exam, you're a CNA. If not, spend some additional time learning InForms by using the hands-on training exercises provided in this book. You should receive your paperwork in a few weeks.

You'll probably want to spend some additional time training before you take your exam. This means making sure you know how to perform certain tasks before you step into the testing room. Knowing how to perform the following list of tasks is one way you can improve your chances of passing, but is by no means the only way.

- *Create forms, queries, and reports.* Databases are used to contain a wealth of information in an organized, yet sometimes difficult to access, manner. Part of your job as a CNA will be to create the forms used to view information, the queries used to gather specific kinds of information, and the reports used to summarize or combine various types of information.

- *Create dynamic forms.* Most databases allow you to create static forms with ease. But what if the content of the record you're viewing changes after the user downloads it? Normally, this isn't much of a problem unless you're working with time-critical information. Then you'll want to use dynamic forms that automatically provide updated information on screen as the database contents change.

- *Link forms to a database.* Creating the forms required to view the contents of a database is only the first step. You need to create a connection to that database before you'll actually see anything. Unfortunately, databases use a wide variety of connection schemes and as a CNA you'll probably end up dealing with many of them.

- *Create simple macros.* Automation is one of the ways that humans avoid repetitive tasks. After all, the computer doesn't care how many times it performs a task. As a CNA it's important for you to know how to create macros, not just to save yourself time, but to save the time of other people in your organization as well.

## What Is a CNE?

This is Novell's certification for people who are more than system administrators. Many of the people that obtain the CNE certification are consultants, system integrators, or employees of a company that needs a person with more skill and knowledge than a CNA to help maintain the overall network.

CNE responsibilities include managing the network in day-to-day activities, repairing and upgrading the hardware at both the workstations and the file server, troubleshooting problems on the network, and fine-tuning the network for maximum performance. In general, the overall job of the CNE is to make sure that the network stays up and running. GroupWise CNEs perform more specific tasks than many CNEs do, but they still spend a lot of time working with the network itself.

To obtain the CNE certification, you should have a good general understanding of microcomputers and how they work. You should also have an intermediate knowledge of DOS and Windows. Other areas that you should be very familiar with are the NetWare operating system, network hardware, network cabling, and network diagnostic and troubleshooting tools. Even the GroupWise certification route requires you to know Windows, DOS, and NetWare.

**NOTE** *While you could probably qualify for GroupWise certification by knowing NetWare 3.x, all the Novell documentation states that you must know NetWare 4.x to meet the requirements. The only exception to this rule is if you are currently a NetWare 3.x CNE in good standing who wants to also obtain the GroupWise certification. Check with your CNE administrator to make sure you understand the GroupWise requirements.*

A CNE must provide a level of service well beyond the CNA level. In fact, a good number of people who would probably make great CNAs try to become CNEs. The results are usually disastrous because they are ill-equipped to handle the extra demands placed on them by the CNE certification. On the other hand, there are some people who stop with the CNE certification when they really need to go on to the MCNE level. Figure 1-2 shows a decision tree for the various CNE certification routes. While this decision tree won't cover every potential situation, it does give you some things to think about, like whether you're choosing the correct certification route.

CNEs can pursue three different certification routes: NetWare 3.x, NetWare 4.x, or GroupWise. Unlike CNAs, CNEs cannot pursue the non-

# Getting Started

**Figure 1-2**
CNE Decision Tree.

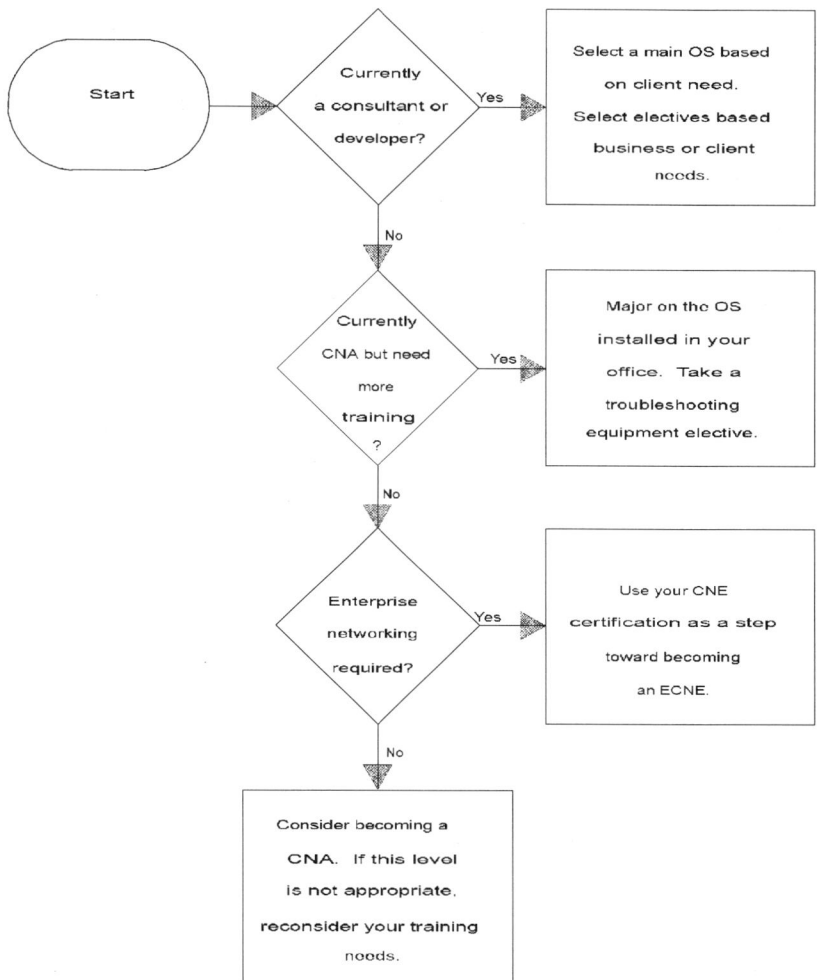

operating system specific SoftSolutions and InForms groupware routes. However, the CNE can pursue these products at an elective level and to a greater depth than the CNA will. (There is a fourth CNE certification level called *Classic CNE,* which is for people who have moved from older NetWare operating system products to newer products through continuing education requirements. You can't pursue this route as a new CNE.)

To become certified as a CNE, you must pass a minimum of 7 or 8 competency exams to obtain a total of 19 credits, and submit an application to Novell. The exams are broken into three categories: core, target, and elective. The *core exams* consist of NetWare Service and Support and Networking Technologies. These required exams will give you a total of 8 credits. The next category is the *target exam;* this area contains four different exams. The actual contents of the exams depend on the certification route that you choose. Figure 1-3 shows the target exam requirements for each route. In all cases the target exams are worth 9 credits. The CNE *elective exams* are worth 2 credits. The electives you can choose depend on the certification route that you intend to pursue. Table 1-1 shows the electives available to the NetWare 3.x or the NetWare 4.x CNE candidate. Table 1-2 shows the electives available to the GroupWise CNE candidate.

**NOTE** *Even though Novell no longer explicitly tests your knowledge of the old DOS Micro Hardware exam, you'll still have to demonstrate a proficiency in this area. For that reason, we've maintained the DOS Micro Hardware exam materials in Chap. 9. Make sure you spend some time in that chapter before taking any exam.*

Novell doesn't place an actual limitation on the time you take to get your certification, but there are practical time limits. From the time you take the first exam, you have about one year to complete all other require-

**Figure 1-3**
Target Exam Requirements for Three CNE Certification Routes.

### NetWare 3.x CNE

| NetWare 3.x Administration<br>Course 508<br>Test 50-130<br>3 Credits | NetWare 3.x Installation & Configuration<br>Course 802<br>Test 50-132<br>2 Credits |
|---|---|
| NetWare 3.x Advanced Administration<br>Course 518<br>Test 50-131<br>2 Credits | NetWare 3.x to NetWare 4.x Update<br>Course 526<br>Test 50-162<br>2 Credits |

### NetWare 4.x CNE

| NetWare 4.x Administration<br>Course 520<br>Test 50-152<br>3 Credits | NetWare 4.x Installation & Configuration<br>Course 804<br>Test 50-163<br>2 Credits |
|---|---|
| NetWare 4.x Advanced Administration<br>Course 525<br>Test 50-161<br>2 Credits | NetWare 4.x Design & Implementation<br>Course 532<br>Test 50-601<br>2 Credits |

### GroupWare CNE

| GroupWise 4.x Administration<br>Course 325<br>Test 50-154<br>3 Credits | GroupWise Async. Gateway & Remote Client<br>Course 326<br>Test 50-155<br>1 Credit |
|---|---|
| GroupWise 4.x Advanced Administration<br>Course 328<br>Test 50-604<br>2 Credits | NetWare 4.x Administration<br>Course 520<br>Test 50-152<br>3 Credits |

# Getting Started

**TABLE 1-1**

*NetWare Elective Courses*

| Course name | Course number | Exam number | Credits |
|---|---|---|---|
| **Network Management** | | | |
| Fundamentals of Network Management | 210 | 50-606 | 2 |
| Printing with NetWare | 535 | 50-137 | 2 |
| NetWare Navigator | 550 | 50-138 | 2 |
| LANAlyzer for Windows | 1125 | 50-105 | 1 |
| **Infrastructure and Advanced Access** | | | |
| Fundamentals of Network Management | 210 | 50-606 | 2 |
| LAN WorkPlace for DOS 4.1 | 601 | 50-104 | 2 |
| NetWare TCP/IP Transport | 605 | 50-145 | 2 |
| NetWare NFS | 610 | 50-87 | 2 |
| NetWare NFS Gateway | 625 | 50-119 | 1 |
| NetWare IP | 630 | 50-603 | 1 |
| NetWare NFS Services: Management and Printing—NetWare 4 Edition / NetWare NFS Services: File Sharing—NetWare 4 Edition (You must take both courses for this exam.) | 640 and 645 | 50-160 | 2 |
| NetWare Connect | 718 | 50-607 | 2 |
| NetWare for SAA | 720 | 50-605 | 3 |
| NetWare Global MHS | 750 | 50-108 | 2 |

ments. If Novell changes the requirements or adds additional requirements while you are in the process of certifying, you must follow the new certification requirements. That's why you want to get through the examination process as quickly as possible—to avoid potential certification delays due to changes in the ever-changing computer industry.

Once you become a CNE, you are required to maintain your certification by taking additional courses and/or exams. This usually happens if Novell releases a new or updated product or feels that CNEs should know about significant technology changes concerning networking. If continuing certification requirements are imposed, Novell will notify you by mail. After being notified of the continuing requirements, you normally have six

**TABLE 1-2**

GroupWise Elective Courses

| Course name | Course number | Exam number | Credits |
|---|---|---|---|
| Fundamentals of Network Management | 210 | 50-606 | 2 |
| Soft Solutions 4.x Administration | 345 | 50-158 | 3 |
| Soft Solutions 4.x Advanced Administration | 348 | 50-159 | 2 |
| InForms 4.x Administration and Form Design | 335 | 50-156 | 3 |
| NetWare TCP/IP Transport | 605 | 50-145 | 2 |

months to pass the proficiency exams (though Novell has been known to extend the time limit because of the large number of CNEs taking the courses and exams). If you let your CNE certification expire by not following up on the continuing certification requirements, you will have to start the certification process from the beginning to become a CNE again. (Make sure you contact a CNE administrator first; there are extenuating circumstances that could help you reduce recertification time.)

**NOTE** *Since every CNE is required to take the two core examinations, Networking Technologies and NetWare Service and Support, we won't talk about them in the individual sections that follow. You'll want to study Chap. 20 for the NetWare Service and Support requirement. Chapter 21 talks about the Networking Technologies exam.*

## The NetWare 3.x Route

The NetWare 3.x route consists of four required operating system exams and at least one elective exam. You need to take the 3.x Administration and 3.x Advanced Administration exams as a starting point. Chapters 10 and 11 will help you study for these two tests. Once you get past the operating system, you'll need to take the NetWare 3.x Installation and Configuration and NetWare 3.x to NetWare 4.x Update exams. Chapters 12 and 13 will help you prepare for these two exams. Figure 1-4 provides you with a training-at-a-glance chart. This chart provides a quick method of seeing which tests you need to take. Make sure you look at Table 1-5 at the end of the chapter—it contains the test numbers you'll need when scheduling your exams.

Once you complete your operating system requirements, you need to select at least one elective exam. Novell requires that you gain a total of 2

# Getting Started

**Figure 1-4**
CNE Netware 3.x
Training at a Glance.

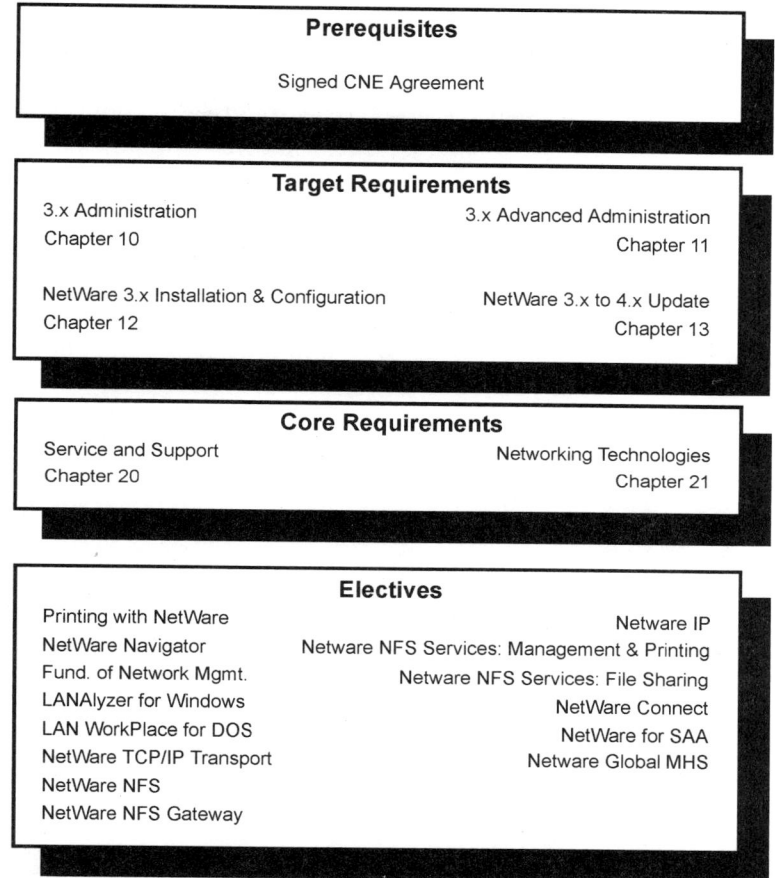

credits in this area to complete your certification. Of course, they won't penalize you if you go beyond this limit. Table 1-2 shows the tests you can take. Since there are so many different electives you can take, we chose not to cover them in the book. You'll need to contact your local NAEC for course materials and testing information.

## The NetWare 4.x Route

The NetWare 4.x route consists of four required operating system exams and at least one elective exam. You need to take the 4.x Administration and 4.x Advanced Administration exams as a starting point. Chapters 14 and 15 will help you study for these two tests. Once you complete these requirements, you must pass the NetWare 4.x Installation and Configuration and the NetWare 4.x Design and Implementation exams. Chapter 16 will help you study for these two tests. Figure 1-5 provides you with a training-at-a-glance chart. This chart provides a quick method of seeing which tests you need to take. Make sure you look at Table 1-5 at the end of the chapter—it contains the test numbers you'll need when scheduling your exams.

Once you complete your operating system requirements, you need to select at least one elective exam. Novell requires that you gain a total of 2 credits in this area to complete your certification. Of course, they won't penalize you if you go beyond this limit. Table 1-2 shows the tests you can take and the corresponding chapters you need to study. Since there are so

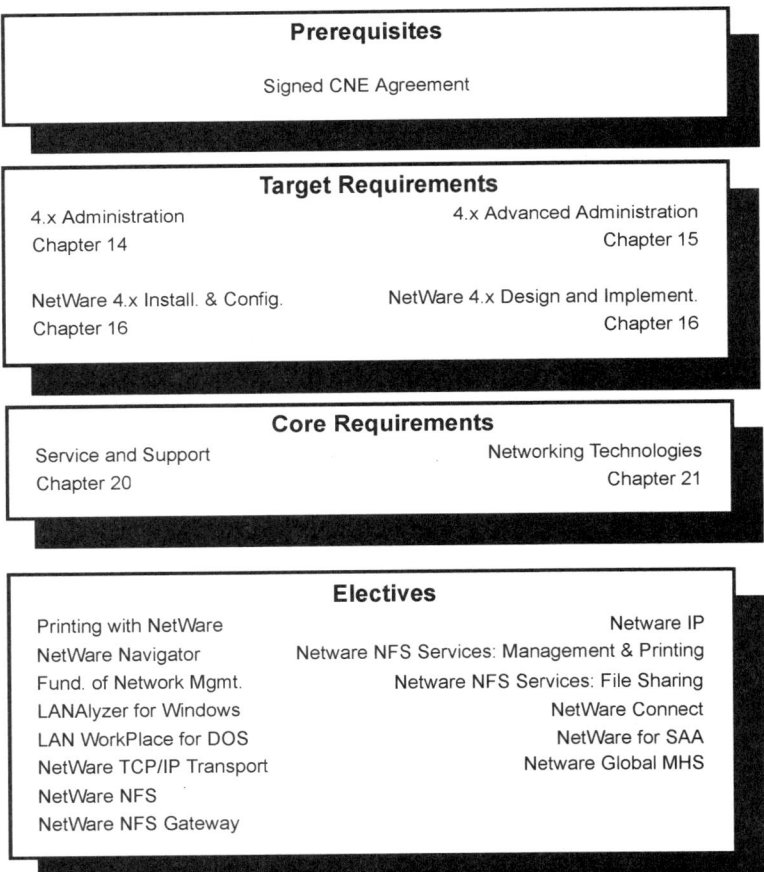

**Figure 1-5**
CNE Network 4.x Training at a Glance.

# Getting Started

many different electives you can take, we chose not to cover them in the book. You'll need to contact your local NAEC for course materials and testing information.

## The GroupWise Route

The GroupWise route consists of four required operating system exams and at least one elective exam. You need to take the GroupWise 4.x Administration and GroupWise 4.x Advanced Administration exams as a starting point. Chapters 17 and 19 will help you study for these two tests. Once you complete these requirements, you must pass the NetWare 4.x Administration and the GroupWise 4.x Asynchronous Gateway and Remote Client Support exams. Chapters 14 and 18 will help you study for these two tests. Figure 1-6 provides you with a training-at-a-glance chart. This chart provides a quick method of seeing which tests you need to take. Make sure you look at Table 1-5 at the end of the chapter—it contains the test numbers you'll need when scheduling your exams.

**NOTE**  *You can substitute the GroupWise 4.x Asynchronous Gateway and GroupWise Remote exam for the GroupWise 4.x Asynchronous Gateway and Remote Client Support exam. However, because the two courses are so similar, we only cover the GroupWise 4.x Asynchronous Gateway and Remote Client Support exam in this book.*

Once you complete your operating system requirements, you need to select at least one elective exam. Novell requires that you gain a total of 2 credits in this area to complete your certification. Of course, they won't penalize you if you go beyond this limit. Table 1-2 shows the tests you can take and the corresponding chapters you need to study. Since there are so many different electives you can take, we chose not to cover them in the book. You'll need to contact your local NAEC for course materials and testing information.

## What Is an MCNE?

Novell's *Master CNE* (MCNE) certification replaced the older Enterprise CNE (ECNE) program. It's been around for a while now, so most people are

**Figure 1-6**
CNE GroupWare Training at a Glance.

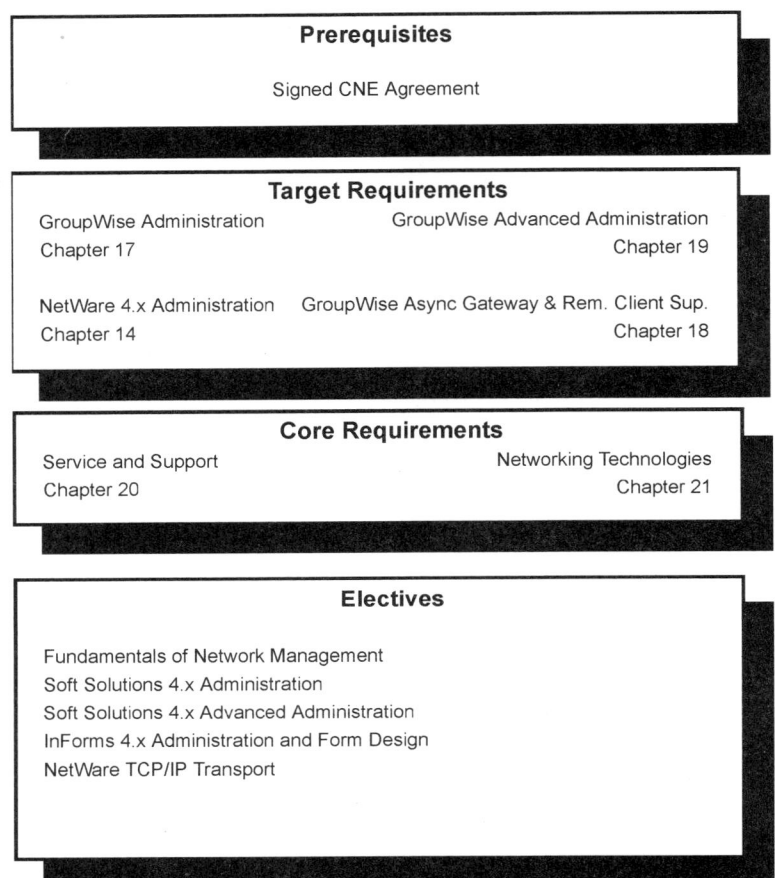

used to the change. The MCNE program is for people who need to specialize in a particular area of network management besides providing the more general services that a CNE provides. Normally, an MCNE would be in some type of managerial position, though this isn't always true. Most of the people who obtain the MCNE certifica-tion are consultants or system integrators. Large companies may also require a person with more skills and knowledge than a CNE to help maintain the overall network. There are five areas of MCNE specialization: Management, Connectivity, Messaging, Internet/Intranet Solutions, and Client/Network Solutions. There are three subspecialties in the Client/Network Solutions area: IntranetWare and AS/400 Integration, IntranetWare and Windows NT Integration, and IntranetWare and UNIX Integration.

# Getting Started

MCNE responsibilities include managing the network in day-to-day activities, repairing and upgrading the hardware at both the workstations and the file server, troubleshooting problems on the network, and fine-tuning the network for maximum performance. In general, part of the overall job of the MCNE is to make sure that the network stays up and running. Besides these physical network management requirements, MCNEs will usually oversee the work of other network specialists, provide input to management on network-related requirements, and maintain control over their specialty area of the network.

To obtain the MCNE certification, you must be a CNE in good standing. You should have an advanced knowledge of DOS, Windows, and computer hardware. Other areas that you should be very familiar with are the NetWare operating system (especially NDS), network hardware, network cabling, and network diagnostic and troubleshooting tools.

To become certified as a MCNE you must pass a minimum of 5 competency exams to obtain a total of 10 credits, and submit an application to Novell. The exams are broken into three categories: core, target, and elective. The *core exams* for everyone consist of NetWare 4.x Design and Implementation and Fundamentals of Internetworking. There are also special core requirements for the Internet/Intranet Solutions (NetWare TCP/IP Transport) and Client/Network Solutions (varies by subspecialty) specialties. These required exams will give you a total of 4 or 6 credits, depending on your specialty.

The next category is the *target exam*. The following list shows the target exams associated with each specialty.

- *Management.* Network Management Using NetWare ManageWise
- *Connectivity.* Internetworking with NetWare Multi-Protocol Router
- *Messaging.* No target required
- *Internet/Intranet Solutions.* Web Server Management and DNS/FTP Server Installation and Configuration
- *Client/Network Solutions (IntranetWare and AS/400 Integration subspecialty).* IntranetWare and AS/400 Integration
- *Client/Network Solutions (IntranetWare and Windows NT Integration subspecialty).* IntranetWare and Windows NT Integration
- *Client/Network Solutions (IntranetWare and UNIX Integration subspecialty).* SCO Open Server Release 5 ACE for Master CNE or SCO UnixWare 2.1 ACE for Master CNE

The MCNE *elective exams* are worth 0, 2, 4, or 6 credits, depending on your specialty (some specialties don't require you to take any electives). The electives you can choose depend on the certification route that you intend to pursue. Table 1-3 shows a complete list of elective courses for each of the specialties, along with the number of elective credits you require.

Novell doesn't place an actual limitation on the time you take to get your certification, but there are practical time limits. From the time you take the first exam, you have about one year to complete all other requirements. If Novell changes the requirements or adds additional requirements while you are in the process of certifying, you must follow the new certification requirements. That's why you want to get through the examination process as quickly as possible—to avoid potential certification delays due to changes in the ever-changing computer industry.

Once you become an MCNE, you are required to maintain your certification by taking additional courses and/or exams. This usually happens if Novell releases a new or updated product or feels that MCNEs should know about significant technology changes concerning networking. If continuing certification requirements are imposed, Novell will notify you by mail. After being notified of the continuing requirements, you have six months to pass the proficiency exams. If you let your MCNE certification expire by not following up on the continuing certification requirements, you'll have to start the certification process from the beginning to become an MCNE again.

## What Is an NCIP?

The Internet is the place to be in today's computing environment. Just about every vendor you can think of has a Web site. In fact, most major and many smaller companies have a Web site. The need for people trained in maintaining Web sites increases every day, which is why Novell has created the new *NCIP* (Novell Certified Internet Professional) program.

Right now, there aren't enough people in this program to really come up with a definitive picture of a typical NCIP. However, there are some criteria for this program that'll help you see whether or not you're a good NCIP candidate. Obviously, you have to have spent some time working on the Internet before you can even think of applying for this program. You'll also need to have some knowledge of how to design Web pages using hypertext markup language (HTML). It doesn't hurt to have a knowledge of database viewers, Java, ODBC, and a variety of search engines, either.

# Getting Started

**TABLE 1-3**

MCNE Elective Courses

| Course name | Course number | Exam number | Credits |
|---|---|---|---|
| **Management (4 credits required)** | | | |
| Fundamentals of Network Management | 210 | 50-606 | 2 |
| Printing with NetWare | 535 | 50-137 | 2 |
| Printing in an Integrated NetWare Environment | 537 | 50-622 | 2 |
| NetWare Navigator | 560 | 50-138 | 2 |
| LANAlyzer for Windows | 1125 | 50-105 | 1 |
| **Connectivity (4 credits required)** | | | |
| Fundamentals of Network Management | 210 | 50-606 | 2 |
| Printing in an Integrated NetWare Environment | 537 | 50-622 | 2 |
| LAN WorkPlace for DOS 4.1 | 601 | 50-104 | 2 |
| NetWare TCP/IP Transport | 605 | 50-145 | 2 |
| NetWare NFS | 610 | 50-87 | 2 |
| NetWare NFS Gateway | 625 | 50-119 | 1 |
| NetWare IP | 630 | 50-603 | 1 |
| NetWare NFS Services: Management and Printing—NetWare 4 Edition / NetWare NFS Services: File Sharing—NetWare 4 Edition (You must take both courses for this exam.) | 640 and 645 | 50-160 | 2 |
| NetWare Connect | 718 | 50-607 | 2 |
| NetWare for SAA | 720 | 50-605 | 3 |
| NetWare Global MHS | 750 | 50-108 | 2 |
| **Messaging (6 credits required)** | | | |
| Fundamentals of Network Management | 210 | 50-606 | 2 |
| Soft Solutions 4.x Administration | 345 | 50-158 | 3 |
| Soft Solutions 4.x Advanced Administration | 348 | 50-159 | 2 |

**TABLE 1-3**
(Continued)

| Course name | Course number | Exam number | Credits |
|---|---|---|---|
| InForms 4.x Administration and Form Design | 335 | 50-156 | 3 |
| GroupWise 5 Workflow | 362 | 50-621 | 1 |
| NetWare TCP/IP Transport | 605 | 50-145 | 2 |
| **Internet/Intranet Solutions (2 credits required)** | | | |
| Fundamentals of Network Management | 210 | 50-606 | 2 |
| Advanced Web Authoring | 655 | 50-705 | 2 |
| Internetworking with NetWare Multi-Protocol Router | 740 | 50-142 | 2 |
| **Client/Network Solutions—IntranetWare and AS/400 Integration (0 credits required)** | | | |
| **Client/Network Solutions—IntranetWare and Windows NT Integration (2 credits required)** | | | |
| Fundamentals of Network Management | 210 | 50-606 | 2 |
| Printing in an Integrated NetWare Environment | 537 | 50-622 | 2 |
| NetWare Connect | 718 | 50-807 | 2 |
| **Client/Network Solutions—IntranetWare and UNIX Integration (0 credits required)** | | | |

As with any other Novell certification, you can take a variety of courses to prepare for the NCIP certification exams. Table 1-4 provides a complete list of the courses and tests for this program.

To get your NCIP certification, you must pass the Web Authoring and Publishing, NetWare TCP/IP Transport, Advanced Web Authoring, and Web Server Management exams. Each of these exams is worth 2 credits. You also have a choice between the IntranetWare: NetWare 4.x Administration (5 credits) or IntranetWare: NetWare 3.x to NetWare 4.x Update (4 credits) exams.

# Getting Started

**TABLE 1-4**

*Novell Certified Internet Professional (NCIP) Course Listing*

| Course name | Course number | Exam number | Length |
|---|---|---|---|
| Web Authoring and Publishing | 654 | 50-700 | 2 days |
| IntranetWare: NetWare 4.11 Administration | 520 | 50-613 | 5 days |
| IntranetWare: NetWare 3.x to NetWare 4.x Update | 526 | 50-615 | 4 days |
| NetWare TCP/IP Transport | 605 | 50-145 | 2 days |
| Advanced Web Authoring | 655 | 50-705 | 2 days |
| Web Server Management | 656 | 50-710 | 2 days |

Novell doesn't place an actual limitation on the time you take to get your certification, but there are practical time limits, especially when you consider how volatile Internet technology is. From the time you take the first exam, you have about six months to complete all other requirements. (This may seem like a short time, but consider the fact that some browser vendors out there release a new product in far less time.) If Novell changes the requirements or adds additional requirements while you are in the process of certifying, you must follow the new certification requirements. That's why you want to get through the examination process as quickly as possible—to avoid potential certification delays due to changes in the ever-changing computer industry.

Once you become an NCIP, you are required to maintain your certification by taking additional courses and/or exams. This usually happens if Novell releases a new or updated product or feels that NCIPs should know about significant technology changes concerning networking. If continuing certification requirements are imposed, Novell will notify you by mail. After being notified of the continuing requirements, you have six months to pass the proficiency exams. If you let your NCIP certification expire by not following up on the continuing certification requirements, you will have to start the certification process from the beginning to become a NCIP again.

## What Is a CNI?

This certification is for the individual who wants to teach certified NetWare courses. These courses are taught at Novell Authorized Education

Centers (NAECs) or by a Novell Education Academic Partner (NEAP). The classes must use the Novell courseware. There are two basic types of CNIs: NAEC/NEAP-employed CNIs and contract CNIs. The *NAEC/NEAP-employed CNIs* are employed full or part time by the NAEC or NEAP and teach exclusively for that education center. Often, these CNIs are required to perform other tasks besides teaching. Such duties include installing systems, acting as technical support for other employees or customers, maintaining the computer network at the NAEC or NEAP, repairing and maintaining the equipment in the classroom, and teaching other non-Novell courses, such as applications.

The *contract CNI* is normally not connected with any NAEC or NEAP on an employee basis. They are usually self-employed or are an employee of a consulting firm that hires out the services of the CNI. Contract CNIs are hired by NAECs and NEAPs on a class-by-class need. While many NAECs and NEAPs employ full- or part-time CNIs to teach the scheduled classes, there are times when more classes are added to the schedule and the NAEC or NEAP does not employ enough CNIs to cover the added courses. NAECs and NEAPs also hire contract CNIs at times, to cover classes when the employed instructor becomes ill or to cover classes when instructors are on vacation. Other NAECs and NEAPs do not employ any CNIs; they hire only contract CNIs. This eliminates the overhead cost of an employee and allows the NAEC or NEAP to teach classes only when profitable.

The responsibilities of the CNI vary greatly in scope. The basic responsibility is to present the Novell courseware in a professional and understandable format. The CNI must make sure that the classroom is properly set up and that all the hardware and software needed to conduct the class is in functioning order. Besides these responsibilities, the CNI must remain current on certifications and must keep up with changing technologies that impact the course subject. Other responsibilities may include any other jobs or tasks that the company feels that the CNI should perform.

Every CNI candidate has to have some basic qualifications before attempting to pursue a certification. The following list provides a quick overview of the minimum qualifications you should have. Obviously, exceeding these minimums is a big plus and will help you get your certification much faster.

- *Computer knowledge.* An instructor needs better-than-average knowledge about the interior of the computer. After all, you can't expect to teach an MCNE about hardware if your computer knowledge isn't up to par. You'll also need the same level of knowledge when

# Getting Started

it comes to operating systems. Keeping yourself up to date with the latest operating system developments is an absolute necessity. This includes operational considerations as well as maintenance items, like device driver updates.

- *Hands-on experience (networking and interoperability candidates only).* Nothing shows up more in the classroom than hands-on experience. You'll do a much better job as an instructor if you spend at least a year plying your trade before you try to teach someone else to do it.

- *Presentation skills.* If you're afraid to talk in public, forget about becoming an instructor. You're trying to teach other professionals about a new aspect of their trade. They aren't going to be a very easy audience to talk with, so you're going to need better-than-average presentation skills to get the job done. Novell requires you to have at least one year of classroom experience teaching adults before you even apply as a CNI. You can also take a presentation skills course offered by Novell, though this isn't a requirement.

- *Communication skills.* Obviously, you have to know how to talk about technical information in a way that other people can understand.

- *Classroom management skills.* Fortunately, adult students are far less likely to run amuck than younger students are, but you still have to maintain control over the classroom.

- *Attitude.* If you aren't excited about the material you have to teach, the student won't be either. Novell looks for people who have a positive attitude and can present material with some level of enthusiasm.

- *Motivation.* Spending entire days in a classroom can become boring if you don't have some type of motivation. Novell looks for people who want to advance both professionally and personally when choosing instructors.

The first thing you need to decide before starting down the CNI route is the area in which you want to specialize. There are two main areas: networking and interoperability. (There used to be two additional areas—applications and development—but Novell has ended these programs.) The *networking area* is the one most familiar to people who qualified under the older certification program. It includes all of Novell's network operating system products, like NetWare, and groupware products, like GroupWise. The *interoperability area* concentrates on connections to other types of machines, like mainframes and the Macintosh.

You can actually simplify the CNI certification process to four steps, as follows:

1. Fill out an application and get it approved.
2. Attend the required courses, then submit the course certificates to Novell.
3. Successfully complete all the required exams.
4. Complete an Instructor Performance Evaluation (IPE) successfully.

Obviously, this is an oversimplification of a much lengthier process, but it helps to get an overview before you take the plunge. Now let's look at how you complete each of the steps in detail.

The application process begins when you find a NAEC or a NEAP to act as a sponsor. All of your training has to take place at a NAEC or a NEAP since you have to actually attend the courses you plan to teach (unlike the other certification options offered by Novell, where course attendance is an optional part of the training). Then you have to submit the following pieces of information to the regional CNI program contact:

- A completed and signed CNI application form
- A signed CNI agreement
- A résumé
- Three references, including one from a NAEC or a NEAP manager
- Target course selection (the course you want to teach)

The first two items on your paperwork list, a completed and signed CNI application form and a signed CNI agreement, come directly from Novell. All you need to do is call Novell Education at one of the numbers provided in App. A and they'll mail them out to you. Make sure your résumé reflects the experience required to teach the course you want to start with. Novell wants people who already have real-world experience, so if your résumé doesn't show this experience they'll probably turn down your application. The three references must include either a NAEC or a NEAP manager. Make sure that the other two references come from professionals that you worked with in the past. It helps if these references are directly related to the courses you want to teach. You must also tell the Novell regional CNI program contact which course you want to teach. This means that you have to decide on a general area (applications, networking, interoperability, or development) and on a specific course within that area before you start the paperwork process. You must choose an Instructor Performance Evaluation (IPE)

# Getting Started

eligible course when selecting the interoperability and networking areas to become certified as a CNI. The four specialty areas for the CNI certification program allow a lot of flexibility as far as course choices go. These courses include:

- Networking (IPE-eligible)
    - GroupWise 4.x Administration
    - GroupWise 4.x Advanced Administration
    - NetWare 3.x Administration
    - NetWare 3.x Advanced Administration
    - NetWare 4.x Administration
    - NetWare 4.x Advanced Administration
    - Printing with NetWare
    - NetWare TCP/IP Transport
    - NetWare Service and Support
- Networking (additional courses—may not be used for IPE)
    - Introduction to Networking
    - Networking Technologies
    - GroupWise Asynchronous Gateways and Remote Client Support
    - NetWare 3.11 to 3.1x Update Seminar
    - NetWare 3.1x to 4.x Update
    - NetWare 4.x Directory Services Design and Implementation
    - NetWare Navigator
    - Understanding and Applying Internet Concepts
    - Web Authoring and Publishing
    - Advanced Web Authoring
    - Web Server Management
    - NetWare 3.x Installation and Configuration Workshop
    - NetWare 4.x Installation and Configuration Workshop
- Interoperability (IPE-eligible)
    - NetWare NFS
    - NetWare Connect
    - NetWare for SAA: Installation and Troubleshooting
    - NetWare Internetworking Products

- Interoperability (additional courses—may not be used for IPE)

  Fundamentals of Network Management

  Fundamentals of Internetworking

  LAN WorkPlace for DOS Administration

  NetWare Flex/IP

  NetWare NFS Gateway

  NetWare/IP

  NetWare NFS Services: Management and Printing (NetWare 4 Edition)

  NetWare NFS Services: File Sharing (NetWare 4 Edition)

  NetWare for LAT

  NetWare Management Using ManageWise

  NetWare for Global MHS

A CNI candidate can begin the certification process as soon as Novell accepts the application. The best way to start the process is to fulfill any prerequisite courses. The following lists provide you with the prerequisites for each general area.

- Networking

  NetWare 3.x or NetWare 4.x Administration

  NetWare 3.x or NetWare 4.x Installation and Configuration

- Interoperability

  NetWare Service and Support

  NetWare 3.x or NetWare 4.x Administration

The CNI candidate must also attend a certified class for the target course and any prerequisites for that course. This course must be led by a CNI and the courses must be conducted at a NAEC or a NEAP using Novell's suggested format and course materials. The candidate must then mail or FAX a copy of the certificate received to Novell CNI administration. Once the course is complete, the CNI candidate must take the test for that course (and any prerequisite courses) and pass it. The only exception to this rule is if there is no test for the target course.

One of the more difficult parts of the CNI certification process is the IPE. Most candidates will want to gain some experience teaching, or at least attend a teaching course, before attempting the IPE. (In fact, Novell requires that you have at least one year of technical experience and

# Getting Started

another year of experience teaching adults.) You must pass the IPE before you can become certified.

Following this process helps you become qualified to teach one course in a particular specialty area. You need to follow the same route for each additional course that you want to teach. Of course, Novell doesn't expect you to pass the prerequisites each time. If you have already fulfilled the prerequisites, then all you need to do is concentrate on the new course, the corresponding exam, and the required IPE.

The CNI certification is an ongoing process. CNIs must continue to stay current with each new course that is added to the category that they are certified for. CNIs must also pay a yearly registration fee that covers, among other things, updates on courseware.

## Creating a Certification Checklist

Now that you have a basic idea of what each certification entails, you can create a checklist. This checklist will help you get organized and help safeguard against missing or forgetting any of the requirements. It's easy to get lost in paperwork and testing concerns as you progress toward your certification goal. The use of the checklist, along with understanding why you want or need the certification (covered in depth in Chap. 2), will help you maintain the proper focus to succeed.

The checklist that you create should have information about the certification that you'll pursue, the courses and the related exams. This includes dates of training courses, course numbers, dates of the exams, and exam numbers. Other pieces of information included in the checklist are the telephone numbers of your contacts at Novell, the Novell Authorized Education Center (NAEC) or Novell Education Academic Partner (NEAP) facility where you attend classes, the Sylvan Prometric registration office, and the Sylvan Prometric testing office. You may also want to include addresses of the preceding contacts, an area for reference material, and an area for any notes.

There are two very important contacts mentioned in the previous paragraph. First, the *NAEC* is a training center that provides Novell-certified training. NEAPs are educational centers like universities and colleges that include Novell-developed courses as part of their curriculum. The difference between someone who teaches Novell and a NAEC or a NEAP is much like the difference between a nonaccredited and an accredited college or university. You may learn something from either source of information, but people tend to view your credentials with less enthusiasm if you don't use a NAEC or a NEAP. In fact, some people will disregard your Novell training altogether if you don't receive your training from a NAEC or a NEAP. The reason is obvious: you receive training from a known good source if you use a NAEC or a NEAP. The level of training from any other source is dubious at best.

The second contact is the *Sylvan Prometric testing center*. This is a company that provides testing for a wide range of certifications; everyone from CPAs to Registered Nurses goes to Sylvan Prometric to take exams. The person sitting next to you during an exam may not even know very much about computers; he or she may fly planes for a living. Sylvan Prometric testing centers appear in a wide variety of locations. You can find them in dedicated test centers or borrowing space at a training facility like a college or university. In fact, you may even find one at your local NAEC or NEAP.

The Sylvan Prometric testing center always uses someone who is certified by them to administer the examinations you take. They make certain that you do not have an opportunity to cheat on the examination. They also make sure that you have any required testing materials and that your test environment is as quiet and comfortable as possible. You are required to follow any instructions the administrators may provide and you can talk only to them during the examination.

One thing that these test center administrators do not do is handle your examination. Sylvan Prometric downloads the examinations from the test center on a daily basis and sends them to the appropriate places. The computer automatically grades the examinations after you take them. As you can see, your examination is untouched by any human hands but your own. If you fail, there's little chance that you will convince anyone that there was any problem except a lack of study on your part. If you do notice a flaw in your examination, make sure you point it out to the test center administrators immediately. They can provide feedback to Novell and may help you if you narrowly missed passing your examination. Reporting the problem will also reduce the risk of someone else stumbling over the same problem. As a result, you will also want to report the problem to your contact at Novell.

Now that you understand what you want to do and whom you need to contact, it's time to start a checklist. The following sample checklists will give you an idea of what you may want to include in your checklist. If you decide to use the checklists in this book, use a highlighter to mark which courses and exams you are going to use in obtaining your required credits. Be sure to add any information that will help you reach your goals.

# Getting Started 33

The checklist for the CNA certification usually is not as detailed as the ones for the CNE, ECNE, and MCNE certifications. The example in Fig. 1-7 lists the basic information.

Note that the first two items indicate when you understand the responsibilities of a CNA and when you complete the goals worksheet. This is the preplanning section, knowing what you are doing and why you are doing it. The second area defines the exam description, exam date, and exam pass date. This is what you need to do to fulfill the certification requirements for a CNA. As you pass the exams, fill in the dates. In the last section of the checklist, we provide a space for information such as the phone numbers of the testing center and Novell. The form includes other areas for dates of exams and the location of the test center. When

**Figure 1-7**
Sample CNA Certification Checklist.

### CNA Certification Checklist

**Item description** — **Date**

Understand the responsibilities of a CNA _____

Complete goals worksheet _____

| Exam description | Exam number | Exam pass date |
|---|---|---|
| NetWare 3.x Administration | 50-390 | _____ |
| NetWare 4.x Administration | 50-394 | _____ |
| GroupWise 4.x Administration | 50-395 | _____ |
| SoftSolutions 4.x Administration | 50-397 | _____ |
| InForms 4.x Administration and Forms Design | 50-396 | _____ |

**Other information**

Phone number: _____

Date of exams: _____

Location of test center: _____

Date paperwork sent to Novell: _____

Reference materials (books, software, etc.): _____

Misc.: _____

_____

filling in the test center location, make sure you include the street address, cross streets, and any special directions about how to get to the test center. The next line documents when you sent your paperwork to Novell. Also provided is space for any references that may help you study or prepare for the exams and a space for any other comments or ideas that you may find important. Filling out each area of the checklist ensures that you complete each step necessary to become certified.

The CNE and MCNE checklists are a little more involved than the one for the CNA. Both certification checklists include a list of required and elective credits that you must keep track of. Note that this form contains additional information designed to keep you on the right path. For example, in addition to the preplanning section, we include all of the required and elective requirements. This allows you to see all of the possible selections in one place. The sample checklist in Fig. 1-8 shows the requirements for the CNE certification.

You can easily divide the CNE certification checklist into four areas. The first area contains the same preplanning blocks that the CNA certification form does. Once you complete the planning process, you need to complete the target certification requirements in the next section. We've included both the target course names and course number for ease of reference. You'll also see an exam number for each of the courses. The third section contains all of the elective course names, course numbers, and exam numbers. The fourth section helps you keep all of your essential information in one place. A note area allows you to keep track of any notes or comments that you may want to make about the subject. At the end of the checklist is a section for the phone numbers, addresses, contact names, and reference material. We even supplied some space for any additional information that may assist you in your quest.

The MCNE checklist in Fig. 1-9 basically follows the CNE checklist with just a few changes at the beginning of the list. This certification checklist includes an area you'll want to fill out after completing the CNE certification. All the other modifications deal with differences between the various programs. We discussed those differences at the beginning of this chapter, so there is no need to go into them again here.

The NCIP checklist in Fig. 1-10 combines features of the CNA and CNE checklists. Most of the other modifications deal with differences between the various programs. We discussed those differences at the beginning of this chapter, so there is no need to go into them again here.

The CNI checklist shown in Fig. 1-11 is modeled after the CNE checklist. However, it contains blanks that help you plan for many of the prerequisites that this program requires. The checklist also includes extra

# Getting Started

## CNE Certification Checklist

| Item description | | | Date | | |
|---|---|---|---|---|---|
| Understand the responsibility of a CNE | | | _____ | | |
| Complete goals worksheet | | | _____ | | |

| Core requirements | Course number | Course date | Exam number | Exam pass date | Credits |
|---|---|---|---|---|---|
| NetWare Service and Support | 801 | _____ | 50-602 | _____ | 5 |
| NetWorking Technologies | 200 | _____ | 50-147 | _____ | 3 |

| Target requirements | Course number | Course date | Exam number | Exam pass date | Credits |
|---|---|---|---|---|---|
| **NetWare 3.x Track** | | | | | |
| Administration | 508 | _____ | 50-130 | _____ | 3 |
| Advanced Administration | 518 | _____ | 50-131 | _____ | 2 |
| Installation and Configuration | 802 | _____ | 50-132 | _____ | 2 |
| NetWare 3.x to NetWare 4.x Update | 526 | _____ | 50-162 | _____ | 2 |
| **NetWare 4.x Track** | | | | | |
| Administration | 520 | _____ | 50-152 | _____ | 3 |
| Advanced Administration | 525 | _____ | 50-161 | _____ | 2 |
| Installation and Configuration | 804 | _____ | 50-163 | _____ | 2 |
| Design and Implementation | 532 | _____ | 50-601 | _____ | 2 |
| **GroupWise Track** | | | | | |
| NetWare 4.x Administration | 520 | _____ | 50-152 | _____ | 3 |
| GroupWise 4.x Administration | 325 | _____ | 50-154 | _____ | 3 |
| GroupWise 4.x Asynchronous Gateway and Remote Client Support | 326 | _____ | 50-155 | _____ | 1 |
| GroupWise 4.x Advanced Administration | 328 | _____ | 50-604 | _____ | 2 |

**Figure 1-8**
Sample CNE Certification Checklist.

| Elective requirements | Course number | Course date | Exam number | Exam pass date | Credits |
|---|---|---|---|---|---|
| **NetWare Track** | | | | | |
| Fundamentals of Network Management | 210 | _____ | 50-606 | _____ | 2 |
| Printing with NetWare | 535 | _____ | 50-137 | _____ | 2 |
| NetWare Navigator | 550 | _____ | 50-138 | _____ | 2 |
| LANAlyzer for Windows | 1125 | _____ | 50-105 | _____ | 1 |
| LAN WorkPlace for DOS 4.1 | 601 | _____ | 50-104 | _____ | 2 |
| NetWare TCP/IP Transport | 605 | _____ | 50-145 | _____ | 2 |
| NetWare NFS | 610 | _____ | 50-87 | _____ | 2 |
| NetWare NFS Gateway | 625 | _____ | 50-119 | _____ | 1 |
| NetWare IP | 630 | _____ | 50-603 | _____ | 1 |
| NetWare NFS Services: Management and Printing and NetWare NFS Services: File Sharing (You must take both of these courses to gain the knowledge required to pass the exam.) | 640 and 645 | _____ | 50-160 | _____ | 2 |
| NetWare Connect | 718 | _____ | 50-607 | _____ | 2 |
| NetWare for SAA | 720 | _____ | 50-605 | _____ | 3 |
| NetWare Global MHS | 750 | _____ | 50-108 | _____ | 2 |
| **GroupWise Track** | | | | | |
| Fundamentals of Network Management | 210 | _____ | 50-606 | _____ | 2 |
| SoftSolutions 4.x Administration | 345 | _____ | 50-158 | _____ | 3 |
| SoftSolutions 4.x Advanced Administration | 348 | _____ | 50-159 | _____ | 2 |
| InForms 4.x Administration and Form Design | 335 | _____ | 50-156 | _____ | 3 |
| NetWare TCP/IP Transport | 605 | _____ | 50-145 | _____ | 2 |

**Figure 1-8**
(*Continued*).

# Getting Started

**NAEC/Course Information**

NAEC name: _____

Phone number: _____

Contact name: _____

Location: _____

Course start times: _____

Comments: _____
_____
_____

**Testing Information**

Phone number: _____

Date of exams: _____
_____
_____

Location of test center: _____

**Novell Information**

Date called Novell to order CNE application: _____

Date paper work and picture sent to Novell: _____

Reference materials (books, software, etc.): _____
_____
_____

Other: _____
_____
_____
_____

**Figure 1-8**
(*Continued*).

## MCNE Certification Checklist

| Item description | Date |
|---|---|
| Understand the responsibility of a MCNE | _____ |
| Complete goals worksheet | _____ |
| Complete required CNE certification (NetWare 3.x or NetWare 4.x for the Network Management or Infrastructure and Advanced Access routes. GroupWise for the Groupware Integration route.) | _____ |

| Core requirements | Course number | Course date | Exam number | Exam pass date | Credits |
|---|---|---|---|---|---|
| NetWare 4.x Design and Implementation | 532 | _____ | 50-601 | _____ | 2 |
| Fundamentals of Internetworking | 216 | _____ | 50-611 | _____ | 2 |
| **Additional core requirements for Intranet/Internet Solutions** | | | | | |
| NetWare TCP/IP Transport | 605 | _____ | 50-145 | _____ | 2 |
| **Additional core requirements for Client/Network Solutions—IntranetWare and AS/400 Integration** | | | | | |
| NetWare for SAA | 720 | _____ | 50-605 | _____ | 3 |
| **Additional core requirements for Client/Network Solutions—IntranetWare and Windows NT Integration** | | | | | |
| NetWare TCP/IP Transport | 605 | _____ | 50-145 | _____ | 2 |
| **Additional core requirements for Client/Network Solutions—IntranetWare and UNIX Integration (choose one)** | | | | | |
| NetWare TCP/IP Transport | 605 | _____ | 50-145 | _____ | 2 |
| SCO TCP/IP | N/A | _____ | 90-004 | _____ | 2 |
| SCO Open Server Network Administration | N/A | _____ | 90-054 | _____ | 2 |

**Figure 1-9**
Sample MCNE Certification Checklist.

# Getting Started

| Target requirements | Course number | Course date | Exam number | Exam pass date | Credits |
|---|---|---|---|---|---|
| **Management** | | | | | |
| Network Management Using NetWare ManageWise | 730 | _____ | 50-164 | _____ | 2 |
| **Connectivity** | | | | | |
| Internetworking with NetWare Multi-Protocol Router | 740 | _____ | 50-142 | _____ | 2 |
| **Messaging** | | | | | |
| There are no target requirements for this track. Select 6 elective credits worth of courses instead. | | | | | |
| **Internet/Intranet Solutions** | | | | | |
| Web Server Management | 656 | _____ | 50-710 | _____ | 1 |
| DNS and FTP Server Installation and Configuration | 658 | _____ | 50-625 | _____ | 1 |
| **Client/Network Solutions—IntranetWare and AS/400 Integration** | | | | | |
| IBM 1100 IntranetWare and AS/400 Integration | NA | _____ | 00-051 | _____ | 3 |
| **Client/Network Solutions—IntranetWare and Windows NT Integration** | | | | | |
| IntranetWare and Windows NT Integration | 555 | _____ | 50-624 | _____ | 2 |
| **Client/Network Solutions—IntranetWare and UNIX Integration (choose one)** | | | | | |
| SCO Open Server Release 5 ACE for Master CNE | NA | _____ | 95-153 | _____ | 4 |
| SCO UnixWare 2.1 ACE for Master CNE | NA | _____ | 95-154 | _____ | 4 |

| Elective requirements | Course number | Course date | Exam number | Exam pass date | Credits |
|---|---|---|---|---|---|
| **Management (4 credits required)** | | | | | |
| Fundamentals of Network Management | 210 | _____ | 50-606 | _____ | 2 |
| Printing with NetWare | 535 | _____ | 50-137 | _____ | 2 |

**Figure 1-9**
(Continued).

| Elective requirements | Course number | Course date | Exam number | Exam pass date | Credits |
|---|---|---|---|---|---|
| Printing in an Integrated NetWare Environment | 537 | | 50-622 | | 2 |
| NetWare Navigator | 550 | | 50-138 | | 2 |
| LANAlyzer for Windows | 1125 | | 50-105 | | 1 |
| **Connectivity** | | | | | |
| Fundamentals of Network Management | 210 | | 50-606 | | 2 |
| Printing in an Integrated NetWare Environment | 537 | | 50-622 | | 2 |
| LAN WorkPlace for DOS 4.1 | 601 | | 50-104 | | 2 |
| NetWare TCP/IP Transport | 605 | | 50-145 | | 2 |
| NetWare NFS | 610 | | 50-87 | | 2 |
| NetWare NFS Gateway | 625 | | 50-119 | | 1 |
| NetWare IP | 630 | | 50-803 | | 1 |
| NetWare NFS Services: Management and Printing and NetWare NFS Services: File Sharing (You must take both of these courses to gain the knowledge required to pass the exam.) | 640 and 645 | | 50-160 | | 2 |
| NetWare Connect | 718 | | 50-607 | | 2 |
| NetWare for SAA | 720 | | 50-605 | | 3 |
| NetWare Global MHS | 750 | | 50-108 | | 2 |
| **Messaging** | | | | | |
| Fundamentals of Network Management | 210 | | 50-606 | | 2 |
| SoftSolutions 4.x Administration | 345 | | 50-158 | | 3 |
| SoftSolutions 4.x Advanced Administration | 348 | | 50-159 | | 2 |
| InForms 4.x Administration and Form Design | 335 | | 50-156 | | 3 |
| GroupWise 5 Workflow | 362 | | 50-621 | | 1 |
| NetWare TCP/IP Transport | 605 | | 50-145 | | 2 |

**Figure 1-9**
(*Continued*).

# Getting Started

| Elective requirements | Course number | Course date | Exam number | Exam pass date | Credits |
|---|---|---|---|---|---|
| **Internet/Intranet Solutions** | | | | | |
| Fundamentals of Network Management | 210 | _____ | 50-606 | _____ | 2 |
| Advanced Web Authoring | 655 | _____ | 50-705 | _____ | 2 |
| Internetworking with NetWare Multi-Protocol Router | 740 | _____ | 50-142 | _____ | 2 |
| **Client/Network Solutions—IntranetWare and Windows NT Integration** | | | | | |
| Fundamentals of Network Management | 210 | _____ | 50-606 | _____ | 2 |
| Printing in an Integrated NetWare Environment | 537 | _____ | 50-622 | _____ | 2 |
| NetWare Connect | 718 | _____ | 50-807 | _____ | 2 |

**NAEC/Course Information**
NAEC name: _____
Phone number: _____
Contact name: _____
Location: _____
Course start times: _____
Comments: _____

**Testing information**
Phone number: _____
Date of exams: _____
Location of test center: _____

**Novell information**
Date called Novell to order MCNE application: _____
Date paperwork and picture sent to Novell: _____
Reference materials (books, software, etc.): _____

Other: _____

**Figure 1-9**
(*Continued*).

## NCIP Certification Checklist

**Item description**             **Date**

Understand the responsibility of a NCIP    _____

Complete goals worksheet    _____

| Prerequisite requirements | Course number | Course date | | | |
|---|---|---|---|---|---|
| Understanding and Applying Internet Concepts (or equivalent experience) | 652 | _____ | | | |

| Standard course requirements | Course number | Course date | Exam number | Exam pass date | Credits |
|---|---|---|---|---|---|
| Web Authoring and Publishing | 654 | _____ | 50-700 | _____ | 2 |
| IntranetWare: NetWare 4.x Administration or IntranetWare: NetWare 3.x to NetWare 4.x Update | 520 or 526 | _____ | 50-613 or 50-615 | _____ | 5 or 4 |
| NetWare TCP/IP Transport | 605 | _____ | 50-145 | _____ | 2 |
| Advanced Web Authoring | 655 | _____ | 50-705 | _____ | 2 |
| Web Server Management | 656 | _____ | 50-710 | _____ | 2 |

**NAEC/Course Information**

NAEC name: _____

Phone number: _____

Contact name: _____

Location: _____

Course start times:: _____

Comments: _____

_____

_____

**Figure 1-10**
Sample NCIP Certification Checklist.

# Getting Started 43

**Testing information**

Phone number: _____

Date of exams: _____

Location of test center: _____

**Novell information**

Date called Novell to order NCIP application: _____

Date paperwork and picture sent to Novell: _____

Reference materials (books, software, etc.): _____

_____

_____

Other: _____

_____

_____

**Figure 1.10**
(Continued).

blanks for the other requirements of this certification program, like the IPE. A CNI candidate will have to spend a lot more time than any of the other certification program candidates will in planning for the certification process. As a result, the certification checklist provided here is a lot more complex than those provided for the other programs. The important thing for a CNI to remember is that, eventually, all the candidates for other programs will rely on you to provide them with the best possible level of training.

Now that you have a good idea of what to expect, it might be kind of handy to have a list of all the courses you can take. Table 1-5 provides you with the reference list of all the courses and exams that Novell offers. The list includes course names and numbers, exam numbers, and credit values. We provided space at the end of the list to allow you room for course and exam additions.

## CNI Certification Checklist

| Item description | Date |
|---|---|
| Understand the responsibility of a CNI | _____ |
| Complete goals worksheet | _____ |
| Complete CNI application form | _____ |
| Complete CNI agreement | _____ |
| Complete resume | _____ |
| Get three references | _____ |
|  | _____ |
|  | _____ |

| Prerequisite requirements | Course number | Course date | Exam number | Exam pass date |
|---|---|---|---|---|
| **Networking specialty** | | | | |
| NetWare 3.x Administration or NetWare 4.x Administration | 508 or 520 | _____ | 50-230 or 50-252 | _____ |
| NetWare 3.x Installation and Configuration or NetWare 4.x Installation and Configuration | 802 or 804 | _____ | 50-232 or 50-263 | _____ |
| **Interoperability specialty** | | | | |
| NetWare Service and Support | 801 | _____ | 50-218, 50-253, or 50-802 | _____ |
| NetWare 3.x Administration or NetWare 4.x Administration | 508 or 520 | _____ | 50-230 or 50-252 | _____ |

| Other prerequisite courses | Course number | Course date | Exam number | Exam pass date |
|---|---|---|---|---|
| Any NetWare 4.x Course: NetWare 4.x Design and Implementation | 532 | _____ | 50-801 | _____ |
| Any Internet Course: NetWare TCP/IP Transport | 605 | _____ | 50-245 | _____ |

**Figure 1-11**
Sample CNI Certification Checklist.

# Getting Started

| Target course requirement (select 1) | Course number | Course date | Exam number | Exam pass date | IPE date |
|---|---|---|---|---|---|
| **Networking specialty (IPE-eligible courses only)** | | | | | |
| GroupWise 4.x Administration | 325 | _____ | 50-254 | _____ | _____ |
| GroupWise 4.x Advanced Administration | 328 | _____ | 50-804 | _____ | _____ |
| NetWare 3.x Administration | 508 | _____ | 50-230 | _____ | _____ |
| NetWare 3.x Advanced Administration | 518 | _____ | 50-231 | _____ | _____ |
| NetWare 4.x Administration | 520 | _____ | 50-252 | _____ | _____ |
| NetWare 4.x Advanced Administration | 525 | _____ | 50-261 | _____ | _____ |
| Printing with NetWare | 535 | _____ | 50-237 | _____ | _____ |
| NetWare TCP/IP Transport | 605 | _____ | 50-245 | _____ | _____ |
| NetWare Service and Support | 801 | _____ | 50-218, 50-253, or 50-802 | _____ | _____ |
| **Interoperability specialty (IPE-eligible courses only)** | | | | | |
| NetWare NFS | 610 | _____ | 50-33 | _____ | _____ |
| Enterprise Access with NetWare Connect | 718 | _____ | 50-807 | _____ | _____ |
| NetWare for SAA: Installation and Troubleshooting | 720 | _____ | 50-805 | _____ | _____ |
| Internetworking with NetWare Multi-Protocol Router | 740 | _____ | 50-242 | _____ | _____ |

**NAEC/Course Information**

NAEC name: _____

Phone number: _____

Contact name: _____

Location: _____

Course start times: _____

Comments: _____

**Figure 1-11**
(*Continued*).

**Regional CNI program contact information**

Contact name: _____

Phone number: _____

Location: _____

Comments: _____

_____

**Testing information**

Phone number: _____

Date of exams: _____

Location of test center: _____

**Novell information**

Date called Novell to order MCNE application: _____

Date paperwork and picture sent to Novell: _____

Reference materials (books, software, etc.): _____

_____

_____

Other: _____

_____

**Figure 1-11**
(*Continued*).

## Conclusion

So, what are you waiting for? It's time to figure out which level of certification you need. Once you figure that out, consider the courses you want to take. Make sure you use the certification checklists to help you achieve your goal. It's important to maintain a certain level of organization when completing your certification, and the certification checklist is one way to stay organized. Obviously, our checklists are just examples. Make sure you customize your checklist to meet your individual needs.

# Getting Started

**TABLE 1-5**
Course/Exam List

| Course title | Course number | Course length | CNE/MCNE exam number | CNI exam number | Credits |
|---|---|---|---|---|---|
| Product Information | None | | 50-100 | | 1 |
| Networking Technologies | 200 | 3 days | 50-80 or 50-147 | 50-81 or 50-247 | 3 |
| Fundamentals of Internetwork and Management Design | 205 | 2 days | 50-106 | 50-206 | 2 |
| Fundamentals of Network Management | 210 | 2 days | 50-606 | 50-806 | 2 |
| Fundamentals of Internetworking | 216 | 2 days | 50-611 | 50-811 | 2 |
| GroupWise 4.x Administration (CNA exam number 50-395) | 325 | 3 days | 50-154 | 50-254 | 3 |
| GroupWise 4.x Asynchronous Gateway and Remote Client Support | 326 | 2 days | 50-155 | 50-255 | 1 |
| GroupWise 4.x Asynchronous Gateways and GroupWise Remote | 327 | 2 days | 50-612 | 50-812 | 1 |
| GroupWise 4.x Advanced Administration | 328 | 2 days | 50-604 | 50-804 | 2 |
| InForms 4.x Administration and Form Design (CNA exam number 50-396) | 335 | 3 days | 50-156 | 50-256 | 3 |
| SoftSolutions 4.x Administration (CNA exam number 50-397) | 345 | 3 days | 50-158 | 50-258 | 3 |
| SoftSolutions 4.x Advanced Administration | 348 | 3 days | 50-159 | 50-259 | 2 |

**TABLE 1-5** (Continued)

| Course title | Course number | Course length | CNE/MCNE exam number | CNI exam number | Credits |
|---|---|---|---|---|---|
| GroupWise 5.x Administration (no CNA exam available yet) | 350 | 3 days | TBD | TBD | 3 |
| NetWare 3.x Administration (CNA exam number 50-390) | 508 | 4 days | 50-130 | 50-230 | 3 |
| NetWare 3.x Advanced Administration | 518 | 2 days | 50-131 | 50-231 | 2 |
| NetWare 4.x Administration (CNA exam number 50-394) | 520 | 4 days | 50-152 | 50-252 | 3 |
| NetWare 4.x Advanced Administration | 525 | 3 days | 50-161 | 50-261 | 2 |
| NetWare 3.x to 4.x Update | 526 | 3 days | 50-162 | 50-262 | 2 |
| NetWare 4.x Directory Services Design | 530 | 2 days | 50-125 | 50-225 | 2 |
| NetWare 4.x Design and Implementation | 532 | 3 days | 50-601 | 50-801 | 2 |
| Printing with NetWare | 535 | 3 days | 50-137 | 50-237 | 2 |
| NetWare Navigator | 550 | 2 days | 50-138 | 50-238 | 2 |
| LAN WorkPlace for DOS 4.x Administration | 601 | 2 days | 50-104 | 50-204 | 2 |
| NetWare TCP/IP Transport | 605 | 2 days | 50-145 | 50-245 | 2 |
| NetWare NFS (NetWare 3.x Edition) | 610 | 2 days | 50-87 | 50-33 | 2 |
| NetWare NFS Gateway | 625 | 1 day | 50-119 | 50-219 | 1 |

# Getting Started

**TABLE 1-5**
(Continued)

| Course title | Course number | Course length | CNE/MCNE exam number | CNI exam number | Credits |
|---|---|---|---|---|---|
| NetWare IP | 630 | 1 day | 50-603 | 50-803 | 1 |
| NetWare NFS Services:Management and Printing (NetWare 4 Edition) | 640 | 2 days | 50-160 | 50-260 | 2 |
| NetWare NFS Services: File Sharing (NetWare 4 Edition) | 645 | 2 days | 50-160 | 50-260 | 2 |
| Understanding and Applying Internet Concepts | 652 | 1 day | NA | NA | None |
| Web Authoring and Publishing | 654 | 2 days | 50-700 | 50-750 | 2 |
| Advanced Web Authoring | 655 | 2 days | 50-705 | 50-755 | 2 |
| Web Server Management | 656 | 2 days | 50-710 | 50-760 | 2 |
| NetWare Connect | 718 | 2 days | 50-607 | 50-807 | 2 |
| NetWare for SAA Installation and Troubleshooting | 720 | 3 days | 50-605 | 50-805 | 3 |
| NetWare for LAT | 725 | 2 days | 50-140 | 50-240 | 2 |
| Network Management Using ManageWise | 730 | 2 days | 50-164 | 50-264 | 2 |
| NetWare Management System for Windows | 730C | 2 days | 50-205 | 50-205 | 2 |
| NetWare Internetworking Products | 740 | 3 days | 50-142 | 50-242 | 2 |
| NetWare Global MHS | 750 | 2 days | 50-108 | 50-208 | 2 |
| NetWare Service and Support | 801 | 5 days | 50-118, 50-153, or 50-602 | 50-218, 50-253, or 50-802 | 5 |

**TABLE 1-5**
(Continued)

| Course title | Course number | Course length | CNE/MCNE exam number | CNI exam number | Credits |
|---|---|---|---|---|---|
| NetWare 2.2/3.x Installation and Configuration Workshop | 802 | 2 days | 50-132 | 50-232 | 2 |
| NetWare 4.x Installation and Configuration Workshop | 804 | 2 days | 50-163 | 50-263 | 2 |
| LANAlyzer for Windows | 1125 | 1 day | 50-105 | NA | 1 |

# CHAPTER 2
# Understanding the Certification Process

# Introduction

The first chapter provided you with a better understanding of what each certification will help you accomplish. However, this is the company view of the certification. It only answers part of the question, *What can the certification do for my current company?* This is great for your employer, but it doesn't help you understand how to accomplish this feat or why you should even attempt it. Everyone wants more from an educational experience than to simply fulfill a company requirement. (Even a consultant is theoretically working for a company and should have some reason for getting a certification other than to satisfy some specific company need.)

Fortunately, a Novell certification can help you in a more personal way by paving the way to a new job with higher pay and more interesting work. It's not unusual for consultants to double or even triple their rates after adding networking services. For example, typical network consultants in California can get anywhere from $90 to $125 an hour for their services.*

An employee can usually get an increase on the basis of a new networking-based job title, as well. It's unlikely that you'll see an immediate large increase in pay, but many companies will allow smaller, incremental pay increases over time. A typical network administrator in California earns anywhere from $35,000 to $70,000 a year.†

The bottom line is that you get to do something more fulfilling than the work you used to perform and gain the benefits that increased computer knowledge provides, and still get paid more to do it. Instead of helping the boss juggle paperwork all day, you can run your own department in a larger company with the right certification. In many cases, a certification provides the basis for starting your own networking business. A consultant could go from a small computer servicing business to running a full-fledged network with all the opportunities and work variety it provides.

---

* This rate is based on a survey of 100 California network consultants. The actual rate you can charge depends on factors like the standard rate charged by other consultants in the area, your personal level of expertise, the type of client that your business services, and the number and type of services that your business offers.

† This rate of pay is based on a survey of 70 California network administrators. Your rate of pay will vary by locale, level of expertise you can offer the company, local laws regarding pay rates, your company's pay policy, and the size and complexity of the network you administer.

# Understanding the Certification Process

One day might find you installing new applications. On another day you might train users to use the network. A third day could find you installing new network hardware and testing it out.

This chapter helps you concentrate on how the certification helps you. It answers questions like *Why is certification important?* and *How do I obtain my personal goals as well as the company's goals?* Once you understand these concepts, you can take a detailed look at the certification requirements. This chapter will help you complete the certification checklist you started in Chap. 1.

We'll also look at some of the mechanics of certification. For example, you'll learn how to schedule the time required to complete the certification. Believe it or not, the major reason that many people fail to become certified is a lack of time. Certification requires a personal investment just like any other educational experience. You must schedule time to take the classes, study for the exams, and take the exams. What's more important, you must schedule time for continuing education.

A typical failure scenario begins when someone starts to attend classes, but cuts a few because they don't quite have the time required to attend. Then they try to take the exams without studying. Finally, because they are totally unprepared to take the exams, they become frustrated after the first few questions and rush through the rest. This is a sure way to fail. Even people who are certified can lose that certification if they don't attend to continuing education requirements. More than anything else, certification means that you are willing to devote the time required to maintain a specific level of education and competency. The guidelines in this chapter help reduce the probability of failure.

## Why Do You Need Certification?

There are many people who look at certification as simply another "sheepskin" to hang on the wall. Fortunately, certification is a lot more than completing a few hours of classroom study and passing one or more exams. It's a commitment by you to maintain a precise level of training in order to perform a set of very specific tasks. You'll have to get some hands-on experience in addition to the classroom study to really appreciate how certification can help. Unlike many other forms of education, you'll also get the personal satisfaction of knowing that you have the skills to perform that job to the standards set by the industry.

It usually helps to take a look at your reasons for doing something before you actually do it. There are a lot of reasons why people decide to get certified, some of which have nothing to do with higher pay or a more interesting job. In fact, you can easily break these reasons into five categories, as follows:

1. Professional recognition
2. Internet/internetworking/network skills
3. Industry trend
4. Novell support
5. Other

Discovering exactly what certification will do for you is a big part of completing the requirements successfully. Things like higher pay or a more interesting job are lights at the end of the certification tunnel—they're the goals that you're trying to reach. You need to keep these goals in mind as you choose classes and prepare for exams. Having a goal in view also helps when you take the exams and set the time aside to maintain your proficiency. Figure 2-1 provides some ideas for how to create your own goals worksheet. You can use this worksheet to help you throughout the certification process.

**NOTE** *Make sure you sign off the* completed goals worksheet *section of the certification checklist you created in Chap. 1 once you complete Fig. 2-1.*

As you can see, the form is very straightforward. It contains blanks for your name, the certification you intend to pursue, and the date you plan to obtain it. Make sure you keep both the *certification* and *anticipated date of completion* fields up to date as you progress. Explanations of the *goals*-area fields appear in the following sections. You should couple this form with the proper certification checklist from Chap. 1.

The following paragraphs examine the five goal categories in detail, which should make it easier for you to brainstorm your own goals for getting certified. We'll talk about some typical goals that people have in each category—feel free to use these goals, or come up with some of your own. Listing the reasons you are doing something at the beginning of a project often helps you complete it. These reasons help you to focus on the goals you set at the start of the certification process and emphasize the personal need to complete it.

# Understanding the Certification Process

**Novell Certification Goals Worksheet**

Name: _____

Certification: _____

Anticipated date of completion: _____

**Goals**

Professional recognition: _____

_____
_____
_____

Internet/internetworking/network skills: _____

_____
_____
_____

Industry trend: _____

_____
_____
_____

Novell support: _____

_____
_____
_____

Other: _____

_____
_____
_____

**Figure 2-1**
Novell Certification Goals Worksheet.

## Professional Recognition

There are many people stuck in dead-end jobs who would prefer to do something else. Many administrative assistants or other semiskilled personnel would prefer a job with a little excitement, rather than performing the same old work every day. A Novell certification can help you reach that goal. Even if you do have a fairly interesting job, a Novell certification can provide the variety that makes work interesting. Instead of spending all day every day shuffling papers, you could spend part of that time working with the network.

Another group of people who really need Novell certification to gain professional recognition is consultants. How many times have clients asked why they should use you rather than Mark or Christine down the street? Have you had to lower your per-hour charge just to get the job? Wouldn't it be nice to have a reason that you could show in no uncertain terms to the client? These are all reasons why a consultant would want professional recognition, not only to increase self-satisfaction and gain a reputation among peers, but to gain the respect of clients as well. A certification, like the NCIP certification, can also help a consultant gain access to specialty business. For example, if you can show that you know how to work with the Internet based on your certification, you might find it easier to get cutting-edge technology jobs.

Professional recognition is more than just an interesting job. Consider, for a second, the kind of people you would like to associate with and the types of discussions you'd like to have. Some people want to talk about technology, what's happening today in the world of computers. You aren't going to have that kind of discussion as an administrative assistant. From a very personal perspective, getting a certification can raise your self-esteem and make your life more interesting even when you aren't at the job site.

There are some subtle forms of professional recognition, as well. It's frustrating when you're not in control of a given situation, such as an equipment failure. Being certified can give you a certain level of control over the work environment. Instead of being the one waiting for a technician to arrive, you can be that technician. Now you're the one in control.

As you can see, professional recognition goes a long way toward making every day an adventure rather than an exercise in boredom. A Novell certification is a good way of getting the professional recognition you need to gain this goal. Of course, these are only two ways that professional recognition can help. Now's the time for you to think about how professional recognition will help you. Make sure you write it down on your goals worksheet.

## Internet/Internetworking/Network Skills

This is one area that you may or may not feel concerns you. Perhaps you have had some hands-on experience with a network, and you keep up with the latest news in the trade journals. Certainly the Internet is the latest craze to grace the trade press headlines, and more than a few people are trying to get the skills required to make the Internet a profitable venture. Lest you think that all the old technology is going out the door, people still need to make mainframes and minicomputers work with LANs. In fact, the need for internetworking is greater than before. No matter what you think your level of experience is, certification training is always the best method for gaining the skills required to pass the exam and get your certification.

Let's look at certification training for a moment. While on-the-job training (OJT) is a viable way of gaining some information, it does not give you the full effect of certification training. In addition, you're relying on the experience of one person—you. When you go through network classes, the instructor provides you with information based on the input of hundreds, or even thousands, of other people. There's no way to gain this type of information in the vacuum of OJT. Even if you could gain the book knowledge, certification training provides you with at least one other valuable asset: you get to test this input in a laboratory environment. Your company won't let you test the knowledge you gain from OJT on the company LAN, but you can test it at a training center.* This ensures that you really know how specific networking conditions normally look and how to fully install all the features of the Novell NetWare operating system.

Skills include both knowledge from books and practical experience from hands-on training. You'll likely spend as much time using your new skills as you will learning about them from the manuals. The instructor at a training center can help you understand the contents of the manuals. How often have you read the manuals only to feel like you didn't know any more when you finished than when you started? In many cases you understand what the manuals say, but fail to implement the procedures correctly. In other cases you may think you understand what the manuals are saying, but lack the knowledge needed to fully understand the implications of what you've learned. Learning from an instructor through certification

---

* Some courses provide more hands-on training than others. See the course descriptions in App. F for further details.

training really helps you to know NetWare, rather than simply taking your best guess about what you think will happen. (The same principle holds true for other certification routes—an instructor can help you better understand what's going on in the documentation.)

You'll find that you get very little hands-on help from the instructor when it comes to hands-on training in the courses you take (unless you're experiencing some kind of difficulty). The reason is simple: the hands-on portion of each course is there to help you actually learn a skill and to get the practical experience you'll need to work on a real network. A laboratory environment like the one at a training center helps you gain this practical experience without damaging a real network.

Since every trainee begins with a different level of knowledge, it is important that you gauge what you know with what you expect to learn. This is one of the goals that'll help you keep on track. Once you determine what you expect to gain from the certification process regarding network skills, then you need to write it down. Keep this goal in mind as you take each of your courses. Also use it as a guide for helping you study. Concentrate on your weak areas before taking the exam.

## Industry Trend

A weak, but viable, reason to become certified is that it's an industry trend. Novell plans to train 115,000* more CNEs in the near future to supplement the existing 65,000 CNEs; this is the result of industry's need for fully qualified individuals to manage networks. The number of new CNAs that industry will need is even greater. Some analysts predict there will be four or five times as many CNAs as CNEs. Of course, the number of CNIs will increase proportionately to handle the influx of new certification candidates. Even though the MCNE program has gotten established, it hasn't been around long enough to get a good estimate of the number of participants. However, you can be certain that many network managers will become MCNEs instead of CNEs. The industry's internetworking needs are just too great to ignore the benefits that the MCNE program provides. Needless to say, it's impossible to gauge the need for NCIPs at this point, but the need will be there. The Internet is a boomtown at the moment. There are too many variables to take into consider-

---

* All numbers in this section are approximate.

# Understanding the Certification Process

ation. Fortunately for the NCIP candidate, this is actually good news. The sky's the limit for your certification.

So, what started this industry trend? Many companies do not want to trust the valuable information on their network to someone who doesn't possess the proper training and you can bet they'll take even greater precautions when it comes to distributing information over the Internet. References are nice, but a certificate is just as good in many cases. Having a CNA, CNE, MCNE, NCIP, or CNI certificate will open many employment opportunities for you. Of course, having both experience and a certification is almost a sure winner at the negotiation table. As you can see, having the proper credentials always works to your benefit.

This is probably a good time for you to write down some of the ways that you can use your certification once you get it. Make sure you look at the various trade papers* that will show how industry trends will help you in gaining the type of employment you want. You could write these trends down, or even take clippings from the trade papers to use for future reference.

Clippings from trade magazines and newspapers are especially important for consultants. They provide an extra level of credibility when bidding on a large networking job. Remember that the client is more apt to listen to what industry has to say than to simply take your word that certification is a good and necessary requirement of finding someone to install a network.

## Novell Support

Novell provides an added layer of support for people who become certified to use their products. After all, it only makes good business sense for them to do so. There are several mechanisms that Novell uses to accomplish this.

- Special assistance on the Novell product support line.
- A special place on the Internet where you can discuss new advances in networking technology or get a little help with an especially thorny problem. (There's also a forum on CompuServe that provides this special meeting capability, though it's existence isn't ensured now that the Internet is at the forefront of Novell's support strategy.) You can

---

\* See App. E, "Sources of Additional Information," for ideas on what trade papers you should read to find out what's going on in the networking industry.

also use this forum to download new versions of drivers and programs.

- Use of the Novell logo for your price sheets, advertising pamphlets, business cards, and résumé. Only a certified person may use this logo.
- One year's free subscription to the *Network Support Encyclopedia Professional* (NSEPro) *Edition,* a software library crammed with information about Novell products. It also contains articles and papers describing how to overcome specific networking problems.
- Monthly issues of *NetWare Application Notes,* a magazine that contains information about current product support problems and how to get around them. It also contains news about technological advances and new products. This is also the first place where most certification holders will hear about new product details. (The trade press normally provides the first look at a new product, but seldom do they provide the information you'll need to implement that new product until its release.)

The CNI gets a few additional support items. Most of these benefits reflect the CNI's need for additional information. Since CNIs spend the day in a classroom teaching other potential candidates, it's important that they receive the latest information possible as quickly as Novell can get it to them. Other candidates often find that the instructor has information that supersedes what is in the manuals. These additional benefits are the source of that information in many cases. The following list describes the items that a CNI gets above and beyond the other certification levels.

- *Ongoing development and distribution of instructor materials.* Even CNIs spend time going through the latest materials relating to their specialty. This allows Novell to provide other certification candidates with the best possible information.
- *Instructor kit updates.* This is the physical component of the new material that an instructor requires to remain up to date. It contains the materials that CNIs will use to teach classes about advances in Novell products, changes in the certification program, or updates to educational programs.
- *CNI update training.* There are times when an update to a manual or some additional materials will not get the job done. The instructor needs to spend time with Novell representatives learning about new technology or updates to existing products. It is very important that Novell provide this updated information in the form of hands-on or classroom training to CNIs.

# Understanding the Certification Process

- *Informational mailings (including* Novell Educational Bulletin*).* CNIs require constant input to remain current about their own trade as well as on the information they need to teach others. Novell uses informational bulletins to help CNIs remain current on the requirements for maintaining their certification. The mailings also help CNIs improve their training approach and provides them with new teaching methods. The *Novell Educational Bulletin* also provides information about new courses and test announcements.

- *CNI support on NetWire.* This is support above and beyond what the other certification levels receive.

As you can see, Novell's commitment to the certificate holder is just as great as the commitment you must have to become certified. The ability to receive special support from a company also works to both an employer's and a client's benefit. If these people know that you can provide them with better-than-average support because of your relationship with Novell, it could work to your advantage in getting the job. You need to keep this support in mind as part of the method you will use to sell your skills to a potential employer or client.

## Other Reasons

By now your head is buzzing with other ideas about how certification can help you. Make sure you write them down while they are fresh in your memory. These ideas can prove to make the difference between failing and passing as time progresses. In addition, personalizing your goals list may provide the edge you need to gain an advantage over the competition.

What if you decide to bid on a job that another certified person has already bid on? Telling your client how your approach to networking differs from the competition's can make the difference between getting the job or giving it to your competitor. You need to base part of this reasoning on how you approach your certification.

How about a job opportunity where more than one certified person has applied? Telling a potential employer how you see your certification may make them take notice. Make sure you let people know that you took the time and effort to get the most out of your valuable certification training. Give them a reason to view you as someone who is willing to put a little more effort into doing the job right.

# What Is the Certification Path?

Now that you have a better idea of why you would want to become certified, we need to take a detailed look at how you can do so. Getting from point $A$ to point $B$ is usually a matter of following a map or procedure. The certification process is no different. It helps to have a map to guide you through the process. The following subsections provide you with a detailed look at the certification path for each level of certification.

## CNA

The Certified NetWare Administrator (CNA) is the lowest-level certification you can obtain. Essentially, this certification teaches you to administer a LAN or work with a specific Novell product. There are five certificates available: 3.x NetWare, 4.x NetWare, SoftSolutions, InForms, and GroupWise. The path for this program appears in Fig. 2-2.

As you can see from Fig. 2-2, the certification process for CNA is fairly simple. Take the time to go to all of the courses you require, not just those that are recommended. If you don't feel that you know enough about DOS, you'll want to go to the DOS for NetWare Users and Microcomputer Concepts for NetWare Users courses as well. InForms users can go to the InForms 4.x Introduction for New Users (331a) course. Many people feel that going to these courses is unnecessary. However, even if you have previous NetWare experience you'll want to know the Novell way of maintaining the network. This is the most correct way to perform a task based on the experiences of literally thousands of other administrators.

The next step is to study for the exam. Concentrate on the manual you got in class, and avoid cluttering your mind with information from too many sources. Take the time required to study your class notes and the student manuals thoroughly. This represents the best possible method for passing the exams. Make sure you spend the time required to study weak areas. You may even want to have someone else quiz you on various aspects of the material contained in the CNA manuals.

Once you feel that you know enough about NetWare, schedule your exams. If you are a morning person, schedule the exams in the morning; likewise if you are an afternoon person. Always schedule the exams when you are most alert. Remember that you'll only have your brain to work with when it comes to taking the exam. There are no books allowed in the examination room. You may want to consider the day of the week as well.

# Understanding the Certification Process

**Figure 2-2**
CNA Certification at a Glance.

### CNA Certification Path

1. If you don't work with DOS on a daily basis, you may want to start your study with the DOS for NetWare Users course. You will also want to take the Microcomputer Concepts for NetWare Users course. Novell will not test you on this information, but you will need it for your certification-specific classes.

2. Take the appropriate course. This consists of NetWare 3.x System Administration for the NetWare 3.x Administrator certification, NetWare 4.x Administration for the NetWare 4.x Administrator certification, InForms 4.x Administration and Form Design for the InForms certification, SoftSolutions 4 Administration for the SoftSolutions certification, or GroupWise 4.x Administration for the GroupWise certification.

3. Study the student manuals provided during the class. Make sure you study any weak areas in your knowledge skills. Check any notes you may have for information that does not appear in the manuals.

4. Schedule your exam by calling 1-800-RED-EXAM. Take the appropriate test: 50-390 Certified NetWare 3.x Administrator, 50-394 Certified NetWare 4.x Administrator, 50-396 Certified InForms Administrator, 50-397 Certified SoftSolutions Administrator, or 50-395 Certified GroupWise Administrator.

5. Submit your paperwork to Novell (you'll have to sign a certification agreement at the test center). You can call 1-800-NETWARE to find out about the status of your paperwork. (Ask for the CNA administrator when you call.)

6. Subscribe to one or more trade journals that allow you to keep up on industry events and advances in network technology. Examples of trade journals for this level of certification include *PC Magazine* and *PC Week*. Both periodicals include network-specific sections on a regular basis. If you have a specialty area, you may want to pursue a magazine that leans toward that bias. For example, if you mainly work with database management systems, you may want to get a periodical like *Data Based Advisor* for the database-specific networking tips.

7. Watch your mailbox for your certification papers and any other Novell-sponsored information.

Some people schedule their exams on a Monday, when they feel most rushed. Don't fall into this trap. Schedule your exams for a day when you really have time to take them.

Immediately after you complete your tests, make sure you submit your paperwork to Novell. You'll probably need to call Novell from time to time to check on the progress of your paperwork. Novell also issues a picture identification card to you. Therefore, you'll need to provide a photograph. You can usually obtain a suitable picture from any passport photo store. Getting a picture of this type ensures that it'll fulfill Novell's needs—there's only so much space for the picture on the identification card.

While you wait for your certification papers to arrive, you may want to go to your local bookstore and browse the shelves for books and periodicals that pertain to networking. Make sure you get material you can understand. It doesn't matter how well the book or periodical explains networking technology if you can't grasp what it means. B. Dalton's Software Etc. and Walden Books both provide well-stocked periodical stands you can check. If you don't have one of these stores in your area, look for a technical bookstore. *PC Magazine* and *PC Week* both contain a wide variety of materials that a network administrator needs to know. For example, they both contain product reviews along with networking articles. Periodicals include any Novell-supplied materials as well. You may want to maintain a subscription to *NetWare Connection* so you keep abreast of the latest innovations in NetWare.

## CNE

The Certified NetWare Engineer (CNE) certification is one of the most common certifications that people get. This is the level of certification that a consultant would want to get in most cases. The revamped MCNE program makes this option very attractive if most of your clients use large networks or have special internetworking requirements. CNE is also the level of certification that an administrator of a large network would want to get.

Since this certification allows you to work with the operating system at a low level, it requires a lot more preparation and training than the CNA course. Of course, many of the points that we present in that section are equally applicable here. We assume that you know these particular skills and therefore don't discuss them again in this section. Figure 2-3 provides an overview of the CNE certification process.

# Understanding the Certification Process

**CNE Certification Path**

1. Take the appropriate courses. Chapter 1 provides a complete listing of the courses you can take. Make sure you take all the required courses and exams. You will want to spend a little time considering which elective courses to take. For example, you may want to take the LANAlyzer for Windows course if you maintain a large network and need to perform troubleshooting on a regular basis.

2. Study the student manuals provided during the class. Make sure you study any weak areas in your knowledge skills. Check any notes you may have for information that does not appear in the manuals. Studying one student manual at a time may help reduce your confusion level when taking the associated exam.

3. Schedule your exams by calling 1-800-RED-EXAM. Table 1-3 provides a complete list of the exams required for the CNE certification. We also talk about these requirements in Chap. 1. Take the appropriate exams for both the required and optional courses you attended. Make sure you leave enough time between exams to allow for study. Don't rush the exams. However, you must make sure that you do take all the exams within about a year since Novell could change the certification requirements if you take longer.

4. Submit your paperwork to Novell. You can call 1-800-NETWARE to find out about the status of your paperwork. (Ask for the CNE administrator when you call.)

5. You probably already subscribe to one or more trade journals, like *PC Magazine* or *PC Week*. Make sure you also subscribe to one or more network-specific trade journals that allow you to keep up on industry events and advances in network technology. Examples of trade journals for this level of certification include *LAN Times*. This magazine provides a much more intense view of networking than more generic magazines like *PC Magazine* do. If you have a specialty area, you may want to pursue a magazine that leans toward that bias. For example, if you mainly work with database management systems, you may want to get a periodical like *Data Based Advisor* for the database-specific networking tips.

6. Watch your mailbox for your certification papers and any other Novell-sponsored information.

7. Check with various printers about prices for adding your new certification sticker to your résumé, price lists, or advertisements. When your certification papers arrive, make sure you add the Novell logo to show that you've completed the required certification.

**Figure 2-3**
CNE Certification at a Glance.

As you can see from Fig. 2-3, the process for becoming a CNE is very straightforward. You go through about the same steps as a CNA does, but at a much more intense level. Of course, there are more courses and tests to take as well. While the CNA only takes one exam, the CNE must take 19 credits worth of exams. You may want to read through the explanation in the CNA section if you have any questions about the basic process for becoming a CNE.

Of course, there are other differences between the CNE and CNA certification as well. For example, you get to choose between several elective courses. This is one area where the CNE can really hone his or her skills for the environment they intend to pursue. As stated in Fig. 2-3, you could decide to pursue LANAlyzer for Windows as one of your electives. This is one of those areas where you must think about what you want to do with your certification before you actually begin the process. Make sure you fill out your goals worksheet (Fig. 2-1). This is one of those items that you could place in the *other* category.

CNEs who run their own business will also want to check the price for placing their logo on price lists and advertisements. Even if you do have to spend a little more money, the recognition you receive by placing this logo on your forms will really increase business. No one will know that you went through all the training required to receive this valuable certification unless you advertise it. Make sure you get all the value you can out of the certification process.

CNEs who are going to work for a company may want to place the CNE logo on their résumé. A logo of this type can really help differentiate your résumé from all the others on the stack. In fact, it can make the difference between a potential employer actually reading your entire résumé or tossing it after looking at the first few lines. The logo will definitely attract the attention of anyone who looks at your résumé; use it to your best benefit.

One final place that the CNE differs from the CNA is in the literature that they read. We assume that you already read magazines like *PC Magazine* and *PC Week*. These are the magazines that anyone who really wants to know about the computer industry will read even before they become a CNE. The magazines you will need to consider subscribing to include those like *LAN Times* and *Network World*. These magazines really cover networking in detail. They provide you with that added advantage in knowledge that you will need when talking with a client. Keeping yourself up to date on all the latest industry trends really makes a difference. For example, you may know of some new technology that works better and costs less than the old technology recommended by a competitor.

# Understanding the Certification Process

## MCNE

The MCNE is a continuation of the CNE program. It emphasizes various forms of connectivity. This is the certification for people who need to work with large networks or WANs. It is also the route that many managerial level candidates will take since it provides a lot more information in the way of network management (versus administration). As shown in Fig. 2-4, you start as a CNE before you go to this program. You can find out about all the requirements for this program by reading Chap. 1.

Figure 2-4 shows you how to become an MCNE. Notice that you must start as a CNE and work your way through the MCNE program. The bulk of the difference between this program and the CNE program is the additional credits you must obtain prior to certification. Most of these credits

**Figure 2-4**
MCNE Certification at a Glance.

### MCNE Certification Path

1. Perform all the steps required to become a CNE (see Fig. 2-3). Once you complete this step and feel comfortable with your skills as a CNE, you can go on to complete the requirements for MCNE.
2. Complete the MCNE core and target requirements for your selected area of expertise. Chapter 1 goes through the various specialties in detail.
3. Complete all required elective courses and exams. Make certain that you do not choose any courses used to complete your CNE certification. It is also important to select electives from your specialty. Chapter 1 defines the elective courses that you can take to complete the requirements for MCNE.
4. Make sure you file the required paperwork after you take each exam. You can call 1-800-NETWARE to find out about the status of your paperwork. (Ask for the MCNE administrator when you call.)
5. Watch your mailbox for your certification papers and any other Novell-sponsored information.
6. Check with various printers about prices for adding your new certification sticker to your résumé, price lists, or advertisements. When your certification papers arrive, make sure you add the Novell logo to show that you've completed the required certification.

are for courses that a CNE wouldn't take. They all deal with connectivity and other higher-level issues that a MCNE will deal with. Remember that a MCNE usually supervises the network in some way in addition to providing a much broader range of experience.

## NCIP

This is the latest certification from Novell. If you have an interest in working with the Internet, then you'll want to pursue the NCIP route. The biggest thing you need to do before you start this certification route is to spend some time getting familiar with the Internet. You not only have to know how to surf the net, but you have to have some experience with Internet servers as well. Considering that Microsoft makes Personal Web Server available with both the OSR2 version of Windows 95 and with Windows NT Workstation, you should be able to get the experience you need without too many problems.

Figure 2-5 shows the certification path for the NCIP program. Chapter 1 covers all of the requirements for this certification. Make sure you pay special attention to Table 1-4 in that chapter.

## CNI

The CNI certification is far different from any of the other certifications that we have discussed in this chapter so far. To become a CNI, you must go through extra preparation and intense training. Unlike the other certifications, you must attend the Novell classes to become a CNI. In addition, these classes must be taught by someone certified by Novell to do so. Figure 2-6 provides you with an overview of the requirements for this certification.

Novell has greatly streamlined the CNI certification process since its inception (especially so during the last two years), yet has made it more flexible as well. Figure 2-6 shows the basic certification route. It's very important to note the various decisions you'll make along the way. We discussed the various types of CNI certification in Chap. 1, so we'll only cover the route itself in this chapter.

This certification starts differently than the other certifications. You must first get approval to even start the process of becoming a CNI. This certification also requires you to obtain an NAEC or NEAP sponsor. There are also some paperwork requirements that the other certification levels

# Understanding the Certification Process

> **NCIP Certification Path**
>
> 1. Spend some time working with the Internet. Make sure you spend time as both a user and an administrator of an Internet server. (You can use the personal Web server products that Microsoft provides to set up a mini-Internet with two machines.)
> 2. Take the appropriate courses. Chapter 1 provides a complete listing of the courses you can take. Make sure you take all the required courses and exams. The only course-related decision you have to make is whether to take the IntranetWare: NetWare 4.11 Administration or IntranetWare: NetWare 3.x to 4.x Update course.
> 3. Study the student manuals provided during the class. Make sure you study any weak areas in your knowledge skills. Check any notes you may have for information that does not appear in the manuals. Studying one student manual at a time may help reduce your confusion level when taking the associated exam.
> 4. Schedule your exams by calling 1-800-RED-EXAM. Table 1-4 provides a complete list of the exams required for the NCIP certification. We also talk about these requirements in Chap. 1. Take the appropriate exams for both the required and optional courses you attended. Make sure you leave enough time between exams to allow for study. Don't rush the exams. However, you must make sure that you do take all the exams within about a year since Novell could change the certification requirements if you take longer.
> 5. Submit your paperwork to Novell. You can call 1-800-NETWARE to find out about the status of your paperwork. (Ask for the NCIP administrator when you call.)
> 6. You probably already subscribe to one or more trade journals, like *PC Magazine* or *PC Week*. Make sure you also subscribe to one or more network-specific trade journals that allow you to keep up on industry events and advances in network technology. Examples of trade journals for this level of certification include *LAN Times*. (Remember that you'll be spending plenty of time working with a Web server and not just surfing the Net or creating Web sites.) This magazine provides a much more intense view of networking than more generic magazines like *PC Magazine* do. You'll also want to subscribe to one or more Internet-specific trade journals—weekly trade journals are probably the best bet here since the monthly magazines will have a hard time keeping up with the hectic pace of Internet innovation.
> 7. Watch your mailbox for your certification papers and any other Novell-sponsored information.
> 8. Check with various printers about prices for adding your new certification sticker to your résumé, price lists, or advertisements. When your certification papers arrive, make sure you add the Novell logo to show that you've completed the required certification.

**Figure 2-5**
NCIP Certification Path.

**CNI Certification Path**

1. Submit an application to become a CNI, a signed CNI agreement, and a résumé to the Novell regional CNI program contact. Once you complete this task, you must convince a Novell Authorized Education Center (NAEC) or Novell Educational Alliance Program (NEAP) representative to sponsor you during the certification process. You must include an NAEC or NEAP reference with your application (along with two other professional-level references). Contract CNIs do not have to actually maintain a relationship with the NAEC or NEAP, but Novell counts this lack of contact against you during the certification process.

2. Determine which target course you want to teach. (As part of this process you will select a specialty area.) You must provide this information to the regional CNI contact before your application will be approved by Novell. Chapter 1 contains a complete list of available courses and divides them into specialty areas.

3. Take any prerequisite courses. Study for the required exams and pass them. You should complete the prerequisite requirements before you proceed to your target course. (Even though Novell does not require you to pass the exams in any specific order, passing your prerequisite exams first will enable you to pass the target exam a lot easier.)

4. Attend the class for your target course at any NAEC, NEAP, or Novell training site. The training site must use CNIs for instructors and Novell course materials. (This may not be a requirement for some Applications specialty courses; check Chap. 1 for details.)

5. Study the student manuals provided during the class. Make sure you study any weak areas in your knowledge skills. Check any notes you may have for information that does not appear in the manuals. Studying one student manual at a time may help reduce your confusion level when taking the associated exam.

6. Schedule your target course exam by calling 1-800-RED-EXAM. Take the appropriate target course exam. Make sure you leave enough time between exams to allow for study. Don't rush the exams. However, you must make sure that you do take all the exams within the 12-month time frame allotted by Novell.

7. Obtain the required training for oral presentations.

8. Attend and pass your IPE. Make certain that you attend the IPE for your specialty and target course. This is especially important for some Development specialty target courses. Chapter 1 provides specific IPE numbers where required. Make sure you talk with your sponsor before you actually schedule the IPE time.

**Figure 2-6**
CNI Certification Path.

# Understanding the Certification Process

9. Submit your paperwork to Novell. Make sure you include the class certifications from each class you took. You can call 1-800-NETWARE to find out about the status of your paperwork. (Ask for the CNI administrator when you call.)
10. You probably already subscribe to one or more trade journals, like *PC Magazine* or *PC Week*. Make sure you also subscribe to one or more network-specific trade journals that allow you to keep up on industry events and advances in network technology. Examples of trade journals for this level of certification include *LAN Times*. This magazine provides a much more intense view of networking than more generic magazines like *PC Magazine* do. If you have a specialty area, you may want to pursue a magazine that leans toward that bias. For example, if you mainly work with database management systems, you may want to get a periodical like *Data Based Advisor* for the database-specific networking tips.
11. Watch your mailbox for your certification papers and any other Novell-sponsored information.
12. Check with various printers about prices for adding your new certification sticker to your résumé, price lists, or advertisements. When your certification papers arrive, make sure you add the Novell logo to show that you've completed the required certification.
13. Follow steps 2 through 9 for any other target courses that you want to certify for. You may skip any steps that you have already satisfied during a previous certification effort. Make certain that you do fulfill all the requirements for each certification.

**Figure 2-6**
*(Continued)*.

do not require. Unlike the other certifications, you cannot immediately start this certification process by taking classes. You must do a little preparation in advance.

There's one requirement that really differentiates a CNI candidate from all others. It's the IPE that you see in Step 8. Passing the IPE is critical to your certification. However, the IPE is never really over. You get tested every time you step in front of the classroom. Your students will test your ability to teach on a daily basis. Their input after the course equates to the test results from the IPE. In fact, the IPE is so critical that Novell requires you to get some professional training before you attempt to pass it (see Chap. 1 for details). Figure 2-7 provides you with an overview of what will happen during your IPE. As you can see, it reflects a typical day in the classroom. However, this classroom is only a lab. Once you become certified, that lab will become a daily experience.

### CNI Instructor Performance Evaluation (IPE) at a Glance

*Day 1 activities*

1. *CNI orientation.* This is where you will learn about what Novell expects from you during the IPE. The head of the group evaluating your performance will talk about grading criteria and other IPE-specific topics.
2. *Assignments given.* The evaluation group will give you a teaching assignment. You will not know what this assignment is before you take the IPE. The whole purpose of this exercise is to see your performance during the entire teaching cycle.
3. *Lunch.* It isn't too difficult to figure out what you do now.
4. *Candidate preparation.* You will spend the entire afternoon of the first day preparing for your assignment. It is very important that you fully outline everything you intend to present during the "test" class the next day.

*Day 2 activities*

1. *Presentations.* This is where the real IPE begins. The evaluation group will judge you on all the criteria that you were told about the previous day. The criteria include the following items:

   *Presentation characteristics*
   - Confident when presenting the course materials
   - Modulates voice properly
   - Wears appropriate attire
   - Maintains eye contact with student
   - Enthusiastic about subject
   - Avoids filler words and other distractions
   - Presents materials at an appropriate pace
   - Provides for student autonomy and security
   - Encourages class participation

   *Presentation mechanics*
   - Introduces section and identifies objectives
   - Provides an verbal outline of the course topics

**Figure 2-7**
CNI Instructor Performance Evaluation (IPE) at a Glance.

# Understanding the Certification Process

- Talks about the relevance of each topic
- References appropriate manual page for current topic
- Defines new terms and acronyms
- Shows proper preparation for actual topic discussion
- Talks about the topics in a logical order
- References the topics to subjects the student already knows about
- Uses analogies to describe and illustrate the topic
- Uses visual aids to help describe the topic
- Uses questions to help the student remember the topic
- Promotes class discussion
- Summarizes the topic
- Avoids introducing new material during the summary

2. *Lunch.* This is the same as the day before.
3. *More presentations.* The IPE evaluation group will use the remainder of the day to test any candidates they did not test in the morning.

**Figure 2-7**
(*Continued*).

CNIs who run their own business will also want to check the price for placing their logo on price lists and advertisements. Even if you do have to spend a little more money, the recognition you receive by placing this logo on your forms will really increase business. In fact, no NAEC or NEAP will hire you without proof of this certification. While you could continue to use your certification as a consultant installing LANs, this isn't the reason you went through all that training. Be sure you make it very clear that you have all the required credentials. As you can see, the value of this certification is in actually acquiring it. You can't teach certified Novell courses without it.

CNIs who are going to work for a company (usually an NAEC or NEAP) may want to place the CNI logo on their résumé. A logo of this type can really help differentiate your résumé from all the others on the stack. In fact, a potential employer will likely toss your résumé if the certification is not immediately apparent. An NAEC or NEAP won't want to waste the time interviewing someone who isn't qualified.

# How Long Does Certification Take?

Some people look at the time required to gain certification as the number of hours spent in class and the time required to take exams. Nothing could be further from the truth. The certification process is ongoing and requires a commitment if you want to maintain it. There are paperwork and continuing education requirements that you must consider in addition to the more obvious requirements. The following subsections will provide you with the information you need to take all these factors into account.

## Training

The time you spend in training depends on the certification you plan to achieve. In most cases the courses are two to five days long. Chapter 1 contains a table that tells you the exact length of each class. To obtain the total time required to complete the training requirements for certification, simply add the lengths of each class you intend to take.

The important consideration for this time requirement isn't really the length of each class, but coordinating the class time. It helps to talk with your local NAEC or NEAP representative to get a listing of course availability and dates. Simply mark out the days for each course on a calendar to plan for the time you need to spend in training.

There's another way to look at the training time investment. It's very unlikely that time will allow you to schedule more than one class per week. As a result, you can simply count the number of classes you need to take, and count it as the number of weeks you need to set aside for training. Of course, you'll still have some time each week to get work done at your job or business.

## Testing

As a practical rule, no one can tell you exactly how long testing will take. The problem is that while the exam times are a constant, study time is not. Taking an exam before you study for it is likely to produce very frustrating results. You need to plan sufficient study time or you will fail the exam.

A general rule of thumb that you can follow is to plan at least two hours of study per day for the same number of days it took you to com-

# Understanding the Certification Process

plete a course. For example, if you have a four-day course, then you should plan eight hours of study time. Of course, you will not want to try to get all your studying done in one day. Plan for a maximum of three hours per day. Any more study time during one day will reduce the effectiveness of your study time.

Make sure you include at least one hour plus travel time to take the exam itself. For example, if it takes about 20 minutes to travel from your office to the testing center, plan on at least 1 hour and 40 minutes for the exam. Remember that you need to get to the testing center at least 15 minutes early. As a result, you may want to add this additional time to your estimate as well.

## Paperwork

Novell doesn't place any restrictions on how long you can take to submit your paperwork (which usually amounts to nothing more than signing a certification agreement and getting any requirements for your photo identification out of the way). It really depends on the availability of resources to get the required documentation together and the time required in communication with Novell. A good rule of thumb is to plan at least two hours for completing the paperwork. This includes an hour at the photographer to take your picture, about 15 minutes reading and signing your certification agreement, about half an hour in communication time with the testing center or NAEC, and 15 minutes talking with a Novell representative. CNI candidates have more paperwork, so they should plan on spending more time to complete it. You'll also need to spend more time getting your logo put on business forms and price lists.

## Continuing Education

How much time is too much or too little for continuing your education? It really varies by individual requirements, past experience, and the type of certification you have. Make sure you spend time learning about technology and techniques that will actually help you in your work as well as in maintaining your certification. The certification path guides in Figs. 2-1 to 2-6 make suggestions on the kind of magazines and trade journals you should consider subscribing to. A few hours with the Novell manuals and using the various server utilities is probably a good idea as well, since you'll find that you only use a subset of the utilities that Novell provides on the job.

A good rule of thumb is at least one hour of training time per day for CNEs without any special requirements, like database management tasks. An MCNE will probably need about an hour and a half per day at a minimum because of the specialty tasks that an MCNE performs. A CNA can probably get by with about half that investment, while a CNI probably requires quite a bit more. Most CNIs will require a minimum of two hours of training each day, plus one full day of training per week (if you teach all week, then you'll probably want to set Saturday aside for this task). It's hard to tell precisely how much time an NCIP should spend learning new technology since the Internet changes on a daily basis, but an hour per day is a good starting point. Make sure you spend time looking for new technology on the Web since it's unlikely that you'll see new developments in a trade journal before they're old news.

You should plan on increasing your training time every time Novell introduces a new product. Make sure you spend enough time both reading and practicing that you feel comfortable with your level of skills. Trying to learn at least one new item per day is probably a good idea. Make sure you spend a little time trying out new ideas with the network itself. Perhaps a different directory arrangement or a new menuing system will help improve overall system efficiency. Investing in yourself is good for both you and the company. Besides, you'll never maintain your certification if you don't take the time required to train.

## Conclusion

By now you should have a clear idea of what certification you want to get, why you want to get it, what courses are required to get it, and the procedure for getting it. You should also have an appreciation for things like continuing education requirements and the need to keep up to date on current technology. It's very important that you view certification as an ongoing process because that's what it is. No one who gets their certification today can truly say that they no longer need to learn anything new tomorrow.

# CHAPTER 3
# Learning the Trade

## Introduction

In days gone by, people who worked a trade usually started out by working as apprentices for someone else. After some period of time, when the apprentices had learned enough about their trade, they became journeymen in their selected profession. In some respects, getting a certification is a sort of apprenticeship. It takes time to learn the trade you've selected. Whether that trade is network- or Internet-related doesn't make a lot of difference; the process for learning your trade is just the same. Of course, we no longer use the term *apprenticeship* for this training period. In many cases, people simply refer to it as *on-the-job training* (OJT).

Just like modern apprenticeships, you'll gain experience in a variety of ways. While the most common way of learning new techniques for some people is OJT, you can also gain much needed experience by reading trade magazines, attending seminars or lectures, or by hands-on trial and error. Other ways to get the experience you need for advancement may be through formal education. This formal education could come in different ways, such as attending Novell courses, taking vendor training from companies like Compaq or 3Com, or obtaining a degree from a college or university. Often, an organization will want you to have a certification like the Novell CNE before they'll let you maintain the network. If you want to advance into a higher position or into management, the company may require you to have a college degree.

In Chap. 2, we cover the requirements needed to become certified by Novell as a networking expert. In this chapter we'll explore different ways to learn the trade. We'll look at two questions. First, we'll ask if you actually need a specific type of formal training to get your certification. Second, we'll look at the best way to get training if a formal education isn't really required to learn a particular task. It's very important to get the proper level of training so you can advance as easy as possible. Finally, we'll cover how to get the most from what you learn.

## Is Training Really Required?

Is some form of training required to pass the Novell certification exams? *Yes.* However, the level and amount of training required depends on your level of experience. If you want to improve your position—and we assume that you do, or you would not have picked up this book or even considered getting a Novell certification—you'll need more training.

# Learning the Trade

Even an expert may not know everything required to get a certification from Novell. It may be true that you're an expert in a particular area, but there's no one who knows everything there is to know about networking (or even computers in general). The persons who believes that they're experts in everything are only fooling themselves. They're cheating themselves out of really learning, growing, and becoming all that they can be in this business. Remember this important rule: You have a *specialized* knowledge of computers based on the requirements of your job—Novell is going to test your *general* knowledge, perhaps in areas where you don't have any OJT or experiential knowledge.

Of course, knowing that you require training doesn't necessarily tell you what type or even how much. You'll need to spend time looking at the kind of experience you have and the OJT you've gotten in the past. If you can't honestly evaluate your current level of experience, looking at your job description may provide helpful clues into the kinds of things that you're supposed to know for your current job. You could use this information to evaluate the knowledge you have now versus the knowledge required to pass a Novell exam. The point is that you need to determine that you need training. If you walk into a classroom with the idea that you already know everything about your trade, then it's also pretty likely that you won't get much out of the training. Be certain about your need for training before that first day of class—attitude is everything.

Here's another helpful tip. Novell always publishes the requirements for its exams. All you need to do is get a copy of the test description and read what information Novell will test. If you know all of those things, then you might be able to get by with just a bit of a refresher course in the manuals. If not, you may want to invest in some formal training. No matter how well you think you know the information, though, always take time to get some training before you walk into the testing center.

## Deciding What Level of Training You Need

Let's assume for a minute that you intend to get formal training from an NAEC, or at least use the student manuals that Novell provides as a means for studying. The level of training you'll need depends on how comfortable you feel with the subject matter. You may only need a few hours of review with a student manual, or you may need to spend a few years developing the skills required to reach your goal.

There are a lot of different criteria to take into account when deciding how much training to get. For example, you might be a CNA and want to become a CNE. All you may need are a few courses at your local NAEC to get the job done. On the other hand, if you haven't had much hands-on experience with NetWare (or Novell's new IntranetWare) or don't know much about networking, you'll have a hard time becoming certified. (The same thing can be said for Novell's groupware products.) This isn't to say that it's impossible. There are many people who have become certified by only studying the student manuals they borrowed from someone else. Unfortunately, once they get out into the work place it becomes apparent that they aren't qualified to service or administrate a network (the same thing holds true for other types of certifications, like GroupWise). These are the people that give the certification a bad name. Luckily, these people get weeded out of the marketplace in a short time—clients and employers hear of their bad reputations and refuse to have anything to do with them. It doesn't take long for their reputations to get passed around.

Before you can determine what level of training you need, it's important to consider your current skill level compared to the skills you need to pass the Novell exams. Since the skills Novell is looking for are readily available, all you really need to do is perform an honest evaluation of your current skills. The chart in Fig. 3-1 will help you determine your skill level (candidates pursuing something other than NetWare or IntranetWare can use this chart as an example of what to look for in the way of skills). This chart, along with your goals worksheet from Chap. 2, will help to pinpoint your level of expertise.

The key to making these worksheets and charts work, though, is being truthful with yourself. We all want to believe that we have more expertise or knowledge than we really have. Remember that only you will see this chart. No one else needs to know how you rank yourself. When ranking yourself on the skills chart, choose the lower level of the skill ranking if you have any doubts about your skill. This will help you to strengthen any weak areas that you may have or will reinforce the subject matter at hand.

The chart can be separated into four areas. The first area lists the *skills* that an expert in Novell networks must know and will perform in the field. This is only a general sampling of the different skills. Most of these skills are easily broken into subcategories. If you rank yourself very high on the chart for a particular skill, try breaking it into subcategories to see if you have an area of weakness within that particular skill. Remember, the key is to be honest with yourself. We've included extra space at the bottom of the skills list so that you can add any additional skills you think

# Learning the Trade

| Skills | Skill Level Ranking Chart | | | | | | | | | |
|---|---|---|---|---|---|---|---|---|---|---|
| | Level | | | | | | | | | |
| | High | | | | | | | | | Low |
| | 10 | 9 | 8 | 7 | 6 | 5 | 4 | 3 | 2 | 1 |
| DOS (Not as important as it used to be, since most people now use Windows.) | | | | | | | | | | |
| Microcomputer hardware (Includes a wide variety of standard hardware like serial ports, as well as specialized network hardware like NICs, bridges, and routers.) | | | | | | | | | | |
| NetWare concepts | | | | | | | | | | |
| NetWare features (Should know both NetWare 3.x and 4.x feature set.) | | | | | | | | | | |
| NetWare 3.x system administration | | | | | | | | | | |
| NetWare 4.x system administration | | | | | | | | | | |
| NetWare 3.x installation | | | | | | | | | | |
| NetWare 4.x installation | | | | | | | | | | |
| Workstation installation/setup (Make sure you know Windows 3.x, Windows NT, and Windows 95 client installation and problem areas.) | | | | | | | | | | |
| Fine-tuning NetWare 3.x | | | | | | | | | | |
| Fine-tuning NetWare 4.x | | | | | | | | | | |
| System back-up | | | | | | | | | | |
| Printing | | | | | | | | | | |
| Security (Make sure you know the differences between various NetWare versions, plus bindery emulation versus NDS management for NetWare 4.x.) | | | | | | | | | | |
| Troubleshooting network problems (Includes using console utilities like DSRepair.) | | | | | | | | | | |
| User/group accounts | | | | | | | | | | |
| Console utilities | | | | | | | | | | |

**Figure 3-1**
Skill Level Ranking Chart.

## Skill Level Ranking Chart

| Skills | Level | | | | | | | | | |
|---|---|---|---|---|---|---|---|---|---|---|
| | High | | | | | | | | | Low |
| | 10 | 9 | 8 | 7 | 6 | 5 | 4 | 3 | 2 | 1 |
| Command line utilities | | | | | | | | | | |
| Using NWAdmin to manage NetWare Directory Services (NDS) | | | | | | | | | | |
| NetWare Upgrading (Make sure you know how to upgrade NetWare 3.x to 4.x.) | | | | | | | | | | |
| Installing patches and fixes (Includes knowing where to find the patches and fixes.) | | | | | | | | | | |
| Topologies (Includes things like cable distances and connection schemes. Make sure you understand the various network standards.) | | | | | | | | | | |
| Network technologies | | | | | | | | | | |
| Other skills (List all skills relevant to your area of specialty.) | | | | | | | | | | |
| | | | | | | | | | | |
| | | | | | | | | | | |
| | | | | | | | | | | |
| | | | | | | | | | | |

**Prepared**              **Areas needing improvement**

_____              _____

_____              _____

_____              _____

_____              _____

_____              _____

**Figure 3-1**
(*Continued*).

# Learning the Trade

are necessary. If you're a manager who's helping your employees get certified, you'll want to include any unique or special requirements for your company. You may also want to include supplementary skills that you feel a candidate will need for certification.

The second section within the chart is the *ranking* area. This is the section where you'll rank yourself on a scale of 1 to 10. The rankings are listed from high to low, with 10 being a high ranking and a 1 being a low ranking. Remember to be honest when ranking yourself—this is for your eyes only and will be a study index. If you overrank yourself, you may miss out on studying an area that you are weak in. Just check the box that most closely represents your current skill level. If you feel that you are between levels, place your checkmark on the low side of the scale.

At the bottom of the skills chart is the third section, *areas needing improvement*. Use this area to write down the specific areas that you need to improve in. Make sure you include both general topics from the skills section and specific subtopics from within the general skills. Be specific when filling out this area, because it'll form the basis for study. If you feel that you need more room to document your improvement areas, continue them on another piece of paper. It's important to create a complete list of potential weak areas. Doing so will not only help you pass your exam, but will help you become a better networking professional as well.

The fourth and final section can be found to the left of areas needing improvement. Any goals-oriented approach to training includes *milestones* so that you know where you're at. Consider each entry in this area a milestone. When you've studied long enough to raise your skills to the level required to pass the exam, add a date. Using the skill level ranking chart, this will help you get a feeling of accomplishment as you study.

Now it's time to come up with a plan of attack. Compare the contents of the certification goals worksheet in Chap. 2 with the skill level ranking chart in Fig. 3-1. Make sure you've listed all of the skills required to accomplish each goal you want to attain. For example, if your goal is to become a CNE and you have been working as a network administrator, then you know the administration side of NetWare (IntranetWare) but have never installed or configured a NetWare (IntranetWare) file server. Instead of spending time in the system administration course, your time is better spent attending the service and support course. This course is where you will learn how to configure and install NetWare, the shell, and to troubleshoot the network. Taking this route is more productive in helping you reach the goals you set than taking every course or studying every aspect of NetWare. You may find that no courses are necessary, just some light study in the Novell manuals. (You may want to find someone with a copy of the student manuals and study them as well. This improves your chances of passing the exams.)

When you feel that you have completed studying and preparing yourself for the exams, reevaluate yourself again using the skill level ranking chart in Fig. 3-1. This time, use a different color pen when ranking yourself so you can compare your skill level now to the first time you completed the chart. You may still find some weak areas. If you do, then concentrate on those areas as you study for the exam. Repeat this process until you feel that you know the topics cold.

## Obtaining the Required Financing

Financing your training is an important step in the certification process. Everyone can get financial support, but finding the correct source takes time and effort. Before you begin the actual process of funding your education, take time to figure out how much financing you need. The following points summarize the things you need to take into consideration.

- Training costs
- Testing costs
- Travel expenses
- Lost work time
- Miscellaneous expenses

The first step is to add up all the costs of classes and testing. Make sure you add a little extra for failed tests in your estimate. Even though you probably won't fail an examination if you prepare properly, it's best to plan for a failure just in case. You need this money in addition to your normal paycheck and a little bit of additional money for emergencies and miscellaneous expenses. Failure to plan ahead will certainly cost you your certification.

Also take time to consider hidden costs. For example, you need to factor in additional travel expenses if the test and training centers are farther away than your usual place of work. In some cases, you may need to take time off work to attend class. Some companies will not allow you to miss work to attend class; others will ask you to make up the time by working extra hours later. If your company won't pay you during this time, you need to factor in the amount you would need to pay your bills. As an alternative, you could always take vacation time. Try to think about all the

# Learning the Trade

possible sources of trouble and the alternatives you can exercise. As you can see, there's a lot to consider in the financial arena before you even begin the process of getting the financing.

There are a number of ways to get the money you need for certification training. The sources you use really depend on a number of factors, including who will benefit from your training and what length of time you will need to pay for the training costs. Of course, the most important factor is the technique you plan to use to get the aid. Do you go to your company or simply rely on your own resources? The technique you use greatly affects your chances of success. Figure 3-2 provides you with some ideas on techniques you can use to get this financial aid. As you can see, there are at least three different techniques that you can use.

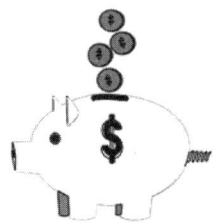

Some people save the money they need for education, then begin to go to school. While this method does mean a delay in getting your training, it does reduce the after-training expenses you'll encounter. This is ideal for consultants.

A common source of money for training is company sponsorship. You convince your company that it is in their best interest to supply the money required for training. This usually involves some type of payback period.

One option that many people don't consider is combining support from a number of sources. For example, you could get your company to support half the cost, a loan to support a quarter of the cost, and savings to support the rest.

**Figure 3-2**
Getting Financial Aid.

Some people save for the training before they actually begin; that way there are no costs to burden them after they graduate. Consultants or people who plan to start their own business often use this technique. Trying to pay for your education and get a business going at the same time usually doesn't work very well. However, most people take a *learn now, pay later* approach to the whole process.

*Company sponsorship* is the method that most people use to get certification training. Convincing your company to sponsor you is relatively easy if they just installed a LAN or the network administrator recently left the company. The need for someone to manage the LAN is usually pretty obvious by the time all the hardware and software gets installed. Of course, convincing them that you're the right person for the job might prove a little more difficult. This is a situation where you need to provide proof that you not only can do the job, but do it better than anyone else in the company. There are other forms of sponsorship as well. For example, you might get a state or federal government agency that promotes work programs to sponsor your training. Other forms of sponsorship cover everything from veterans' programs to scholarships and grants.

What happens, though, if a certification candidate can't get all the support from one source? For example, a candidate who won't be employed as a full-time network administrator may only get 50 percent support from a company, or a candidate might be part of a small business that can't afford the total cost of training. In these cases, you might need to spend time putting together a package deal. One or more sources help you get the training you need and reap the benefits of that training. To use this technique you spend time getting part of the support from one source, then use that source as a means to get other people to join in. For example, what if you are part of a small company? The company may recognize the need to obtain the services of a trained network administrator, but may not have the financial resources to pay for the training. If you could put part of your own money into the support fund (or get a scholarship or other form of financial support), the company might provide the other part.

As you can see, there are a lot of sources you can tap for financial support during your training. Experience or the current political environment often determine which sources you try to tap. For example, many military people can use their GI benefits to get the training. (Of course, this assumes you spent time in the military.) There are also student loans and scholarships that you can use. Quite a few states in the United States are now supporting training programs in an effort to get more people working. You might be able to use state resources to finance part of your training costs if you've been laid off for a long time. Some of these sources

# Learning the Trade

won't be available to you simply because you don't qualify for one reason or another. Make sure you don't waste time trying to tap a financial source that you can't possibly use.

Figure 3-3 shows just some of the sources that you can use to acquire the capital required for certification training and testing. These six sources represent the ones that people most commonly use. The following subsections describe all these options in detail. Use your imagination and detective skills to track down other sources of potential financial support you can use. Some jobs offer more potential sources of financial support than others do. Remember, only a lack of research and motivation can prevent you from finding the financial support you need.

## Company-Sponsored Support

Getting financial support from a company is the most common method that people use. You usually need to provide proof that the company needs

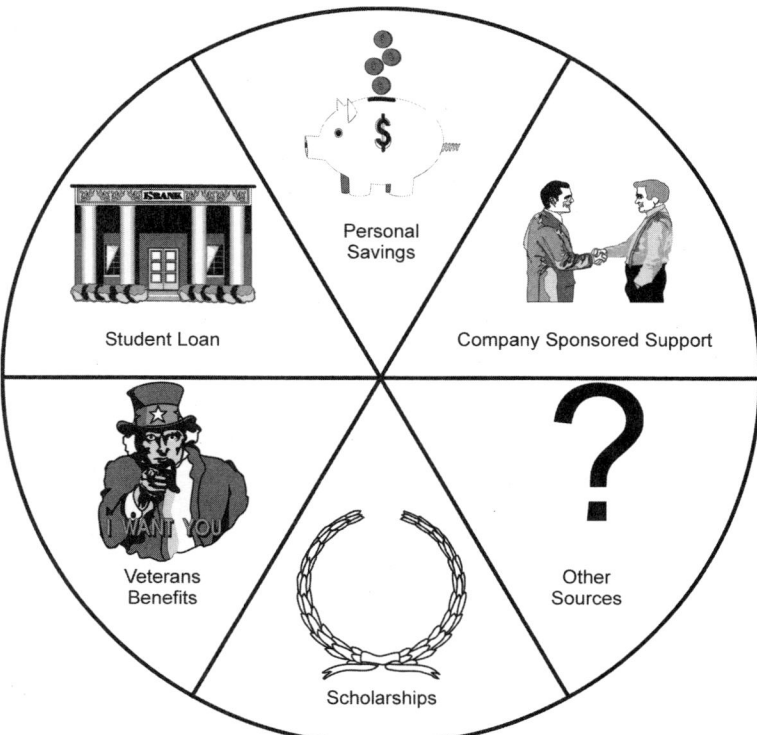

**Figure 3-3**
Sources of Financial Support.

the services that your training will provide and that you are the best person for the job. In most cases, you must show a willingness to repay the company by promising to work for them for a specified period of time after you complete the training. There are also instances where you'll have to repay the company any moneys they expended if you fail to get certified or need to change positions before the required payback time has expired. These are all considerations you need to take into account if you plan to go this route to getting financial support.

At this point, you may think that getting company support is an all or nothing proposition. There are a lot of different possibilities when you attempt to get support from your company. You could offer to pay for half of your training (or to get financial assistance from another source) and ask the company to pay the other half. This shows that you're willing to invest in your own future and makes it a lot more likely that the company will help provide financial assistance. Some companies also offer interest-free education loans. Essentially, you take an advance against your salary to pay for the training. Every week (or whatever your pay period is) the company takes a small portion of the loan out of your paycheck. The interest-free nature of this loan makes it especially appealing to people on a lower income scale.

Some people think that getting company support is only for full-time employees. There are many situations in which a company might consider providing educational benefits to a part-time employee as well. For example, you might qualify for the educational loan benefit described in the previous paragraph. Other scenarios include going full-time for a specific payback period or, in rare cases, showing that you'll provide a very great benefit to the company with the training you get. Never limit your horizons to what you think you can get. Remember, all the company can do is say no if it doesn't like your proposal.

Getting a proposal together is one of the most important parts of this method of getting financial support. You need to prove two things. First, you need to provide proof that the company needs the services of a network administrator for its LAN. Second, you need to prove that you are the only person, or the most qualified person, to fill that role.

There are quite a few tools in this book that help you get started on this proposal. The Novell certification goals worksheet in Chap. 2 (Fig. 2-1) helps you determine what you plan to achieve from this training. A goals worksheet can also show management that you are serious about obtaining the training. It can also provide you with reasons that the company needs a network administrator. The skill level ranking chart in Fig. 3-1 not only can show personal weak and strong areas, but can provide a basis for showing why you are the best candidate for the job. Much of the material in Chap. 6 can also help you get the information needed to create a convincing proposal.

Figure 3-4 provides a sample outline you can use to get started on your proposal. Of course, you'll need to modify it to meet any company-specific requirements or to meet your own personal needs. Make sure you don't go to management empty-handed. Even if you don't write a formal proposal, you can at least get all the answers to questions they are likely to ask together. Make sure you are prepared to provide them with the best possible reasons to help you achieve your goals and provide you with the financial support you need.

As you can see, there are a number of things that you need to put in the proposal. The introduction allows you to quickly summarize the reasons that you put the proposal together. Make sure you include any relevant company rules or guidelines. You also need to define any nonstandard terms you use within this section. Likewise, the conclusion summarizes the contents of the proposal. It won't contain a repeat of the information

**Figure 3-4**
Sample Company Financial Aid Proposal Outline.

Introduction
    A description of the proposal
    A synopsis of any relevant company rules, regulations, or benefits
    Definitions of terms and acronyms

How will this training benefit the company?
    Demonstrated need for a network administrator
    Cost/benefits analysis
    Resident LAN expert available at all times

What am I willing to provide the company in exchange for the training?

Why am I the best person for the job?
    Existing skills
    Existing training
    Training goals
    Personality traits
    Other considerations

Conclusion

the proposal contains; it will simply summarize the high points of your proposal. A manager should get a good idea of what you are trying to say by simply reading the introduction and conclusion of the proposal. Then, if they want more details, they can read the contents of the proposal.

There are three main areas in the body of this outline; your outline may include more. The first thing you need to do is concentrate on the needs of the company. Show management that you are thinking of the company first, yourself second. The first part of the section tells them about the need to have a network administrator available. Of course, one of the first questions that comes to mind is *Why not use an outside consultant to perform this work?* You need to demonstrate the need to keep a staff administrator. One way to do this appears in the second part of this section. Showing management that it is actually cheaper to maintain a staff network administrator is one way to prove your point. There are also intangible benefits that you can cite. For example, one intangible benefit is the security in knowing that no one outside the company has access to vital data. This information appears in the third part of this section.

The second area of the proposal tells management what you are willing to exchange for the financial support. Of course, what you offer is up to you. The standard items include a promise to stay with the company for a specific amount of time and other concessions. Make sure you let management know that you are willing to negotiate. If you offer something they don't want and make it obvious that you are not willing to negotiate, then your proposal will fail even if management is interested in getting a trained network administrator on staff. Don't kill your chances of becoming certified by being inflexible or unimaginative.

The third area of the proposal must concentrate on you. Tell management why you are the best person for the job. This is the place where you can brag about your capabilities a little bit (don't brag too much, though). Initially, you can concentrate on tangible evidence, like your current job skills and training. Then let management know about your training goals. Showing them the tangible parts of your plan makes it obvious that you want to succeed in your certification goals. Finally, you can tell them about the intangible benefits you can offer the company. For example, are you good at working with people? Make sure you offer management some evidence of this intangible skill. Does your work record demonstrate that you're a hard worker? Make sure you let management know about this, too.

As you can see, writing a financial support proposal requires an investment in time and effort. The results are well worth the effort, though. Getting your certification can open new doors of opportunity that you might not get otherwise. In addition, some of the work you need to do for the proposal is a direct result of the work you would need to do for certification anyway. Many of the pieces of information that you need to convince management to provide you with financial support already appear in other areas of this book. You can also use them for other certification goals.

## Student Loans

There are many sources you can tap for student loans, even though most people look no further than their local bank. Of course, the number and type of sources vary by region of the country and with your personal situation. So, the first objective is to find out where you can get a student loan. The following paragraphs provide some pointers you can use in this area.

- In most cases your local college or university can supply you with this information. Just look in the student catalogs or other brochures provided by them. The writers of these books pack them with great ideas for finding financial aid. (Obviously, the college or university wants to make it as easy as possible for someone to attend; you're simply using this source of information for another purpose.)
- You should also check with friends. You might be surprised at the bits of information you find out this way.
- Life insurance companies and other financial planning institutions also make good places to check for this type of information.

Once you determine where you can get a student loan, you need to find out the criteria for getting the loan. For example, any student loan will require that you provide evidence of income. A government loan may require that you fall below a specific income level, while a bank loan may require that you exceed a specific income level. The one loan that may require the least financial information is a student loan provided by an insurance company or fraternal organization. In most cases, you secure this type of loan with your insurance policy or other tangible asset.

You need to take other things into consideration with a student loan as well. For example, what type of payback period does the institution offer, and how high is the interest? By shopping around, you can usually optimize these features to your benefit. Especially important is the interest rate. Even waiting a few days can change the amount of interest you pay on the loan. A check on the stability of the bank or other lending institution is important too, since most loans contain a clause that forces you to pay back the entire loan in one lump sum should the lending institution request it. Consider any stipulations that the lender may have about the loan. For example, some lenders may require that you provide proof of schooling in the form of a graduation certificate. You need to find out everything you can about the institution, what types of loans they offer, and what you can expect from them in the way of payment plans.

Of course, you also need to consider what you can afford. Unfortunately, some people find that they get into more debt than they can repay (as witnessed by the number of government student loans that remain unpaid). Make sure you aren't taking out too large a loan for your education. If you don't plan ahead, you may find yourself living on peanut butter and jelly sandwiches for a long time before you get the loan repaid. Even worse, you may end up filing for bankruptcy. A little planning goes a long way toward ensuring that you achieve your goals without worrying about money all the time.

Now comes the important part of the process. Once you decide on a particular lender, get all the paperwork filled out. They usually require a lot of financial information. For example, a potential lender will want to know where you work and live, in addition to what you make. The best idea is to get a copy of the loan paper and fill it out at home, if possible. That way, you will have all the required information at your fingertips. After you get the form filled out, take it back to the lender. Take any required documentation with you, as well. For example, some lenders require that you bring in a pay stub or other proof of income. They may also require that you bring in a birth certificate and other forms of identification. Make sure you ask the lender about these requirements when you get the loan forms.

## Scholarships

The number and variety of scholarships available to you are probably limited when compared with other forms of education. Unlike your local college or university, it is doubtful that your local NAEC will have any type of scholarship plan available. Most of these scholarships are tied to a specific institution of learning. A scholarship gets created when someone endows the university or college with the money required to fund it.

# Learning the Trade

Don't let the paucity of scholarships deter you from exploring this avenue of financial aid. Fortunately, there are a few other places to get a scholarship that could help in this situation. For example, many life insurance companies and fraternal organizations provide scholarships. Some of these scholarships are aimed at technical schooling rather than more traditional subjects. Your local church or other organization may have scholarships available, as well. In many cases, there are very few stipulations placed on these scholarships by the people setting up the fund. A check with the leaders of these organizations may reveal a scholarship that very few people know about.

Unfortunately, most of these scholarships are fairly small. Most of them will pay for one or, perhaps, two of the courses you require for certification. If you do go this route, plan on supplementing your scholarship funds with money from personal savings or other sources. In many cases, a scholarship offers just the right amount of additional funding to get company support for your educational needs. This is especially true of smaller companies that want the services of a network administrator but lack the funds for training. As you can see, even if the scholarship is small, it can make the difference between getting and not getting your education.

Once you do get a scholarship, make sure you understand all the qualifications. For example, many scholarships require that you pass the course before you receive payment from the scholarship fund. You need to supply proof that you passed the course in the form of a graduation or other type of certificate. If this is true, you'll have to pay for your certification course from a savings account, then reimburse the account once you receive the scholarship money. (Most NAECs require you to pay for your classes in advance.) Some scholarships have other types of requirements, or the person who started them may have restricted their use to specific types of education. Make sure you understand all these requirements before you use the money you expect to receive from the scholarship. In some cases, failure to observe a specific requirement could result in a loss of scholarship moneys.

## Veterans' Benefits

It's amazing how few veterans actually use their GI benefits to further their education, especially when you consider the time they spent in the service to get these benefits. In many cases, the perception is that the veterans' educational benefits are only for college, not for technical or vocational training. However, there are many forms of technical and vocational training that qualify for these educational benefits, as well.

There are a few things that you'll need to prepare for if you use veterans' benefits. First, there is the usual amount of ever-changing government paperwork to fill out if you go this route. Make sure you talk to your local VA representative well in advance to get all the required paperwork. Spend some time learning how to fill it out correctly. Also, make sure you check that the certification training qualifies for VA benefits, since the requirements for these programs change on an almost continual basis.

Once you determine that you qualify, that the training qualifies, and that you have all the paperwork filled out correctly, make sure your local NAEC will accept government payment. Some NAECs require payment in advance of the course. If not, then you'll need to work out some type of arrangement with the NAEC since the government pays only after you successfully complete the course. Unfortunately, they also pay the educational institution directly, making it more difficult to work something out. You may need to spend some time working with the NAEC on this issue.

## Personal Savings

All the previous methods of getting financial aid had one thing in common—someone else paid the bills for your training. Of course, this is the best way to pay for your training, but it doesn't always work out that way. If you do plan to pay for all or part of your training using your own financial resources, make sure you have enough to complete your training before you even start. This is a good rule of thumb, since it is all too common for someone to start certification training only to drop out later due to a lack of funds. In fact, the best plan is to make sure you have all your bills covered, plus a little for emergencies, plus the total amount required for certification classes and testing. Remember, paying for the classes isn't the end of your financial responsibility. You also need to set aside the money required for testing and for continuing education.

There are other sources of personal income that you can tap besides your savings account. For example, some people have paid-up life insurance policies that they can borrow against. In many cases, the money contained in these policies can pay for the entire schooling process. The interest on such a loan is usually pretty small; almost always below the

# Learning the Trade

rate that you'll get from a bank or other financial institution. In essence, an insurance loan is one where you borrow from yourself.

You can also take money out of an IRA or other long-term savings account if you're willing to pay the penalties and don't want to wait until you have the money saved in your regular savings account. Of course, you need to spend some time with your bank working out the details of this solution. The penalties and other legal considerations vary by bank and savings plan.

One final solution to get the last bit of support you need is to pay for part of your classes using a credit card. Many people will pay for all their classes using a credit card, then pay off the credit card company through their monthly bill. Of course, to pay for the entire cost of certification classes and testing using a credit card, you need a fairly high line of credit. The big disadvantage to this method is the high interest rate you'll pay for your training. On the other hand, you may need to get the training today rather than tomorrow to take advantage of an opportunity.

## Other Programs

There are other payment programs that you can try to use. For example, some states and the federal government have job training plans for minorities (in addition to student loans or other forms of assistance that you must repay). If you qualify for one of these plans, then the money you receive may pay for all or part of your schooling costs. As with the veterans' benefits mentioned earlier, there is usually a lot of paperwork involved with this approach. Make sure you know all the requirements before you start signing up for classes. In most cases, you'll need to combine the money you get from these programs with some type of other financial aid package. For example, your company may help pay for part of the cost if you can get government support for the other part. In fact, the personnel office of your company is a good place to begin your search for appropriate aid programs.

You might be able to get grants from corporations or other organizations in exchange for some type of consideration. For example, a consultant might get a grant from a company in exchange for free maintenance service for a specific amount of time. Of course, it takes time and effort to ferret out these sources of financial aid. You might want to consider this as a final option if all the other plans in this section of the book fail to produce results.

# Who Do You Talk to About Training?

You realize the need for training of some sort. (Proper training will help you gain the expertise needed to complete your certification goal.) So where do you go, and who do you talk to about obtaining the proper training? That's the question we'll answer in this section of the chapter.

Training comes in many forms and from several sources. For example, you may learn more in an hour of hands-on training than you could ever learn in the classroom (though classroom training or an equivalent is still very important to get the global view of networking). In essence, the type of training you choose will depend on your personal work and study habits.

As previously mentioned, there are several kinds of training to choose from. The two most common types of training are *on-the-job training* (OJT) and *structured classroom time* with an instructor. OJT relies on your ability to learn on your own, while classroom time relies on your ability to work with other people. Other types of training include third-party lectures, videotapes, audiotapes, self-study manuals, instructor-led classes, and—of course—the trial-and-error method.

## Hands-on Training

*Hands-on training* is just a broader term for OJT. Whenever you think about hands-on training, remember that it involves some type of physical participation by you with the software that you plan to get certified on. OJT is the easiest way to get hands-on training, but it's a little limiting since you don't get to explore the full range of software features. You can also get directed hands-on training using third-party aids, as in the case studies you'll find later in this book.

Hands-on training could also be the most time-consuming method of learning new skills. While this type of training will supply you with the most real-world way of performing a task, the amount of time you must invest before you have enough information to become certified may take years. However, no matter how much knowledge you obtain from other sources, nothing will replace the knowledge acquired from on-the-job experience. There's something special about going through all of the procedures for installing, configuring, maintaining, and troubleshooting software and hardware yourself that makes the learning experience more complete.

The best place to acquire on-the-job training is on a live system at an existing company. All you need to do is find a job that's related to your education requirements. Of course, actually getting hired by a company that can offer OJT before you have a certification in hand is a lot harder than it might seem. Unfortunately, most companies will require you to have the same skills that you are trying to learn before they'll hire you. If this is the case, you may have to work out an arrangement with the prospective employer to work as an entry-level person or to work at a reduced rate. Other times you may be able to work out an arrangement to help out and assist on projects free of charge in return for the hands-on experience. While this is not putting any money into your pocket, you'll be getting the necessary training that you are looking for. Consider it as a payment toward your education.

When you start to look for places of employment, either on a training basis or as a permanent placement, remember that you're not locked into a long-term permanent job. If at some point in time you find that you aren't learning what you need to learn or that you are not happy where you are, you can always find another job that will give you what you are looking for. Just because you are trying to get some education or are currently certified, you don't have to stay at a place you aren't happy with. If you aren't happy or comfortable with your situation, you won't be as apt to learn what you need to know as quickly as if you really enjoyed the job.

So where and how do you start to look for this job? The first place to start should be to check your personal resources. These are people who may be in a position to help you. They may include family members, friends, neighbors, or people you work with. Oftentimes these people won't be able to directly help you, but they may know of someone who may know someone who will be able to help you. You'll then have a warm lead and a name that you can use as a possible reference and as an icebreaker. The more people you let know what you are doing and what you are looking for, the better your chances are of getting that warm lead. The more personal contact with a prospective employer, the higher the chances are of obtaining a position.

Another area to turn to for a prospective employer for on-the-job training would be the help wanted section of the newspaper. This source of leads will point you to employers that have a need for some type of assistance. You'll find that this is usually a tougher way to land a position than finding a warm and personal lead. Normally, there will be many people applying for the same position, and some of the applicants will often be better qualified or overqualified. This will make it very difficult for you to get very far. You may need to find some type of angle to make your services more attractive. This may include working at a lower pay rate or signing on with the company for a long time.

Other sources to look at for on-the-job training would be job services, job counselors, employment agencies, and headhunter services. These are all good places to contact for opportunities. You'll more than likely find that they'll want or need someone with some type of experience. You are, again, caught in the loop of not being able to find a job without experience and not being able to get experience without a job.

The final way to find the OJT you need would be to knock on doors. Look in the phone book for computer and Novell dealers in your area and then just visit them. The in-person approach will normally yield the best results. You are presenting yourself to possible employers so that they can see what you are like. They can talk face to face with you and get to know you. A face-to-face meeting also allows you to present your goals and needs in a way that a phone call won't allow. Remember that you must provide a reason for them to help you. You must create an incentive for the company to hire you.

## Instructor-Led Training

The fastest way to get the training needed and bring yourself up to speed is to enroll in a professional education program (this is also the most expensive route). The courses will present you with a lot of information in a relatively short amount of time (two or three days for most classes). The instructor will normally present you with a series of lectures, along with oral or written question and answer periods, lab exercises, and hands-on experience.

Instructor-led courses are available from a variety of different sources. These sources include Novell, Novell Authorized Education Centers (NAECs), Novell Education Academic Partners (NEAPs), colleges, universities, vendors, and different third-party educational facilities. Each of these different educational facilities provides a vast myriad of services. The services offered by these institutes range from the very general to the very specific. The lengths of classes also range from just a few hours to four or more years. The cost of the different educational services will range from nothing to thousands of dollars.

# Learning the Trade

Since the educational facilities will vary in class size, materials offered, length, cost, and types of services, you'll need to talk with them to see if they meet your needs. To locate the different institutes in your area check the phone book, talk to your local chamber of commerce, and check with the local computer dealers. In many cases, the local computer dealers will be able to tell you where the best place in town is to get training. Since they are in the trade and see many of the qualified people working in the industry, they will know which institute has the best reputation in a particular area.

The best place to obtain the required information for the Novell certifications would be from a Novell education center. Novell provides excellent training for its certifications as well as for its line of products. While Novell does offer some training directly, most of the training comes from the NAECs or NEAPs. Novell authorizes the centers to teach its courses at a strict quality level. Novell inspects the centers for proper hardware and software, as well as for the general overall condition of the facility. Each center must use Certified NetWare Instructors (CNIs) to teach its courses. The instructors have passed a series of competency exams and have attended special courses designed to make sure that they meet the Novell standards for teaching the course.

The NAECs and NEAPs are located worldwide, with the largest concentration being in the United States. Some of the NAECs are quite large, with upwards of 10 classrooms in one location. NEAPs are usually smaller. There are also a few NAEC companies that have education centers in different parts of the country. The centers are all basically the same, since Novell must authorize each one and each center must meet the Novell guidelines.

What distinguishes the different centers from each other is the quality of the instructors. While each instructor is Novell certified, many of the instructors teach only what is in the Novell course manuals. While this is the base information required for the Novell certifications, it may not always lend itself to real-world experiences. The extras that the better instructors include usually come from years in the field practicing what they teach. We have all had instructors or professors who really know the book material that they are teaching, but ask them a question about something that doesn't appear in the manual and they don't have a clue. When selecting the education center that you want to attend, be sure to ask for references from former students. Talk to these people and get a feel about how the instructor handled the class, subject matter, and questions about related topics not included in the course material. You'll find that most of the instructors will get good reviews.

Other items that separate the NAECs and NEAPs will be the courses that they offer. Many of the classes require the latest in computer technology and some of the smaller NAECs and NEAPs cannot cost-justify the expense of the equipment. These centers are then left teaching only the basic core classes. This is okay for the basic certifications, but if you want to become a CNE or MCNE then you will have to find an NAEC center that teaches the advanced classes. The amount and frequency of courses are also an issue. If the class that you want to attend is offered only quarterly, you may have to wait a few months before attending the class. Some of the larger NAECs and NEAPs offer most of the core classes on a monthly rotation and the advanced classes on a four- to six-week rotation.

Whether you attend a large or small NAEC you will be receiving quality training from some of the most credible institutes around. Novell has long been recognized by the industry for its proactive approach to training its dealers, users, and technicians. You can always count on the course materials written for Novell's software to be current with what's on the market.* To get a list of Novell Authorized Education Centers in you area you can call Novell directly at 1-800-NETWARE (1-800-638-9273) or the Novell FaxBack service at 1-800-233-3382 or 1-801-429-5363. Both of these numbers will get you in touch with either the Novell education group or the FaxBack service. You'll then have the opportunity to order a list of NAECs and NEAPs centers. The list will be sent to your fax machine free of charge. You can also look at Novell's Web site at http://education.novell.com/. This Web site contains a complete list of courses, current certification requirements, and NAECs and NEAPs. You can even leave an e-mail for the NAEC or NEAP of your choice and have them call you back within information regarding certification programs.

## Self-Study Training

Novell offers self-study programs, as do other sources. The self-study programs are good for self-starters who have both the time and the attitude to study on their own. By using the self-study programs offered by Novell and the NAECs and NEAPs you can save yourself a few dollars. The courses are designed to supply you with the course manuals offered by Novell and usually include some form of lab training. Most of the NAECs

---

* With advancements in the industry being made almost daily, the course materials are maintained to be as current as possible.

and NEAPs will send you all the course manuals so that you can study them at a time that is convenient for you. After you have had some time to study the manuals, usually a month or so, you will then attend some type of lab session. This lab session is usually one week long and has a CNI present. The instructor may lead you in different exercises or lectures, depending on how the NAEC structures the class. If you have any questions or problems during the exercises, the instructor is more than willing to help you in any way possible.

The self-study programs are an excellent way to get some form of training, hands-on experience, and knowledge needed to obtain the Novell certification. The biggest advantage of the self-study program is that it'll save you money by not having to attend the more expensive instructor-led courses. You'll also get to study at your own pace, a decided advantage for many people who can't afford to sit through eight hours of class each day.

If you decide to participate in the self-study program, you'll need to spend the time required to really learn the material. Giving yourself too many breaks or fooling yourself into thinking that you know more than you really do won't make self-study work. The biggest disadvantage to the self-study program is the amount of individual work it takes to prepare yourself. You won't have the luxury of a structured class and an instructor who will lead you by the hand through each chapter of the manuals. You'll have to devote at least two hours a day to studying the Novell manuals and researching any questions that you have about the subject matter. Before you attend the lab session of the program you need to know the book material completely. The lab session will provide you with the resources to bring together all loose ends and any questions that you may have about the operating system, installation, software, hardware, concepts, or any other area dealing with networks.

To find out more about the self-study certification programs, contact your local NAEC or computer dealer, or call Novell. The programs will vary from education center to education center, so be sure to thoroughly investigate what each has to offer.

## Other Types of Training

There are times when the standard approaches to training, like OJT or instructor-led training, won't fit into your schedule or don't meet some personal need (you may not study well on your own). For this reason, alternative forms of education are very popular. The alternative forms of education may include books, audiotapes, videotapes, and computer-based training (CBT) programs. These are all excellent sources of information that will help to augment your training process.

From the experienced computer technician down to the beginner, a bookcase with a wide variety of computer books will be a necessity. This library will prove to be a great asset in your quest for advancement in the computer industry. With a well-rounded library, you'll be able to reference the topics and subjects that you may not know very well. You'll find that your library will grow immensely in a short time. Many of the books that you get will have just a few pages on the subject that concerns you right now, but will provide a source of reference on other material in the future.

There are many books written about the Novell NetWare operating system on the shelves of bookstores. You'll also find some about Intranet-Ware and Novell's groupware products. Many of these books are very general in nature, and include the same material as books supplied by Novell. They're usually someone's interpretation of the subject. In some cases, they're more concisely written than the Novell books. Most of these books go into great detail on how to install the operating system and how to manage the system once NetWare's been installed. If you attended the Novell courses you will find that many of these books repeat the information that the instructor presented in class. On the other hand, these Novell-specific books are very helpful in teaching you about the system if you haven't had any formal training on NetWare or any OJT. If you're new to the world of NetWare, you'll find that these books help supplement your knowledge.

There's another good reason to buy some of these general Novell books for your library. The Novell classes focus on the current operating systems. This is acceptable for learning about the latest systems that are being sold, but you'll find that many businesses still have old versions of the operating systems. The old versions serve these business with everything that they need. There's no reason for them to spend the money on a new system. In their mind, a new version of the operating system will not provide them with anything that they need. As a Novell expert, you'll need to know about the early versions of NetWare and how they work. You should know the different commands and the different terminology that was a part of old versions of NetWare. There are many differences in the versions of NetWare. Version 2.0a is different from NetWare v2.2 and NetWare v4.0. This is one reason why books written about the different operating systems will be an asset to your library. It's sometimes difficult, if not impossible, to get books from Novell on past operating systems.

# Learning the Trade

Don't ignore the general networking books. Many of these books have a lot of practical information about how to administer your network.* While these books may not provide Novell-specific information, they will help you gain a better understanding of networks in general. Even if you don't use this information immediately, you'll find it essential later.

Finding books related to your Novell certification isn't that difficult, just look in the same sources as you would for other books. Most bookstores carry at least a few. The large bookstore chains normally carry a good line of Novell books written by many different authors. Don't forget your local computer store—they normally carry several networking books as well. You'll find that in many of the larger cities there will be a technical bookstore that specializes in computer books. Most of these stores will carry most of the books written about the NetWare operating system. Technical bookstores will normally carry IntranetWare and Novell groupware books as well—you'll have a more difficult time finding these books in a regular bookstore. You can normally find a list of the bookstores in your area by looking in the yellow pages of your phone book.

Another good source on finding computer books is to talk to the Novell instructors from your area. They normally stay current on a variety of computer-related topics. They also visit the more technical bookstores on an ongoing basis to stay current with technology. You'll also find that most technical bookstores will supply you with a list of titles that they have access to, and will ship books worldwide.

Besides books, another great source of training material is the use of audio- and videotapes. Both Novell and third-party companies make tapes that are basically the Novell courses. These tapes will supply you with a great deal of information about NetWare, IntranetWare, and groupware products like GroupWise, but are usually fairly expensive. While the cost puts them out of reach for most individuals, they're good for companies that need to train a few people in their organization. This allows them to buy one tape and then let all of their employees use it. This is more cost effective than sending all of their employees to a certification class. A note here for companies that may plan to do this: Send one person to the certification course, or have at least one person on hand who knows NetWare when using a audio- or videotaped presentation. You'll find that

---

* See John Mueller and Robert Williams, *Hands-On Guide to Network Management* (McGraw-Hill, ISBN 0-8306-4440-7), for more information about network administration in general.

the tapes present a lot of material to you, but they won't be able to answer the questions that arise from watching them.

Novell offers a vast array of tapes on different NetWare, IntranetWare, and Novell groupware topics. The tapes include both basic and advanced topics. The tapes are professionally done, and Novell continues to update them as new products are released. You can order the tapes from Novell or from your Novell dealers. To get a list of tapes offered by Novell, call the Novell FaxBack service or your Novell dealer.

Novell also offers a computer-based training (CBT) program that will help you to train for both the certifications, as well as just to get a better understanding of NetWare and IntranetWare. The CBTs are a computer program that first offers information that you read and then exercises that require input from the reader (sort of a miniexam that you can use to test your knowledge). These are good programs that will help you understand how NetWare and IntranetWare work but will usually stimulate many other questions not addressed by the program. The programs are also quite expensive for the individual, but are very attractive to companies that need to train more than one person. To get a list of available CBTs and their part numbers, refer to your Novell FaxBack information sheet or contact your Novell authorized dealer.

## Getting the Most from Your Training

As you've seen, there are many different approaches to training for becoming a certified Novell expert and for general knowledge of the computer industry. It's normal to feel a bit overwhelmed because of the vast amount of information that you'll receive in preparation for your certification exams. The best advice available to help you obtain your certification is to *stay focused*. By using the goals worksheet presented in Chap. 2 and the information presented in this chapter, you'll be able to formulate what your goals are and how to obtain them. Keep your goals worksheet with you all the time and look at it often. This will keep you focused.

To get the most from your training you will also want to take the training one step at a time. It's very easy to get caught up in the frenzy of trying to learn as much as you can as fast as you can. Take one topic at a time and work with it until you feel that you know the subject matter. Don't try to learn all the other related subtopics that are part of the main topic.

# Learning the Trade

You'll find that every topic or subject will have many other related subtopics, and each one of them has many other topics and subtopics as well. Soon you'll find that the subject that you had originally started to study is now replaced by a new topic and you haven't learned anything more about the original item of study. Take one item at a time and stick with it until finished.

Another good way to get the most from your training is to take many notes. If you're in a class, you'll want to take brief notes. Don't take notes on everything the instructor says. If you do this, you'll find that you miss many things that the instructor says. You may not even catch enough of the discussion to ask questions. Try to write just the key words that are being used, then after the class is over or at a break period you can fill in some of the other information. Usually, just the key words will start a thought process that will replay the lecture in your mind. Now, at this point you can write down as much information as you would like. You'll have the time and be able to concentrate on how to convert the information from a thought to a written idea.

When reading the books and manuals with the information you are looking for, use a highlighter and sticky notes for references. Many people highlight sections of the text that they know. What you should be highlighting are the parts that you don't know or the parts that you'll need additional help on. Once you highlight the text, use a sticky note to mark the page for future use.

You'll find that one of the best ways to study the course manuals is to break the process down into three parts. First, quickly read the material in a summary fashion. Don't spend much time reading the material; you only want to get familiar with the content of the book. For example, you may want to scan the headings and the first sentence of each paragraph. This will help you understand the author's intent in writing the book. Second, get a note pad, your sticky notes, and your highlighter. Then reread the manuals making notes and highlighting the important information, as well as the information that's new to you or that you don't understand. The third step is to to study your notes and marked pages and then research any areas that you do not understand.

Using this process will take a little more time than other techniques that you could use to study, but you'll find that you'll retain a lot more information. There's something special about converting the information from a thought in your mind to letters on a piece of paper. The final step in this process will be different for each of you. Many times you'll want to reread the manual and your notes again. If you feel that you know the materials, consider taking the exams. You'll have to make that decision when you get to that point, and it may change with each manual you read.

The secret to making this work and passing the exams will be to find the style, type of training, and studying technique that best stimulate your mind. This may take some time and you may have to change your approach to it. Be aware of what techniques work for you and which techniques produce the best results.

When doing your studying you'll find that short bursts of studying will produce better results than long periods of intense concentration. Remember the long, all-night cram sessions preparing for high school and college exams? All that did was put your mind in a state of exhaustion—more likely than not, you didn't retain any of the information you studied. You'll be able to concentrate longer and remember better if you have a rested mind. You'll find, too, that your exam scores will be higher if you take the test when you are rested and alert.

When doing your studying, hit it hard for 10 to 15 minutes then take a short break. Your actual study time will vary from day to day. It also varies from person to person. The best rule of thumb is to study until your mind starts to wander. The moment your mind starts to wander, you aren't getting any real work done; it's time to take a break. Get up and walk around, get a drink of water or a breath of fresh air. You'll find that your concentration will be much higher and your retention will also be better. If you just study for hours on end, your concentration is usually high at the start and near the end. Most of the information in between becomes diluted. The short burst prevents your mind from getting overwhelmed and tired.

Other study techniques include the use of flash cards or posters, and recording your notes on a cassette tape. All these methods are proven ways to study and improve your knowledge base. When using the flash cards, use $3 \times 5$ cards with a question on one side and a complete answer on the other. You can use these while stuck in traffic, watching TV, or just about any time. You can also give them to friends and have them ask you the questions.

The posters are similar to the flash cards. Get a package of poster paper and a large dark marker. Write just a few key words on the posters, then hang them around your house and office. The key words that you put on the posters should start a thought process that gets you thinking about some subject. The flash cards and the posters will not only help you in studying for the exams by using them over and over, but the process of making them also enforces the concepts in your mind.

# Learning the Trade

The use of cassette tapes is another way to get the most from your training. By recording your notes onto a cassette, you can play the tapes over and over at any time. They're especially useful while you are driving; just plug them into your tape player. You'll find that by listening to your notes in your own voice, your mind will retain more. You'll also be able to reuse the tapes for different classes and different manuals. Use the tape recorder to also record notes in class. It then becomes possible to replay the course lectures at your convenience and at your own pace. Often times, you'll find that you missed something the instructor was talking about. This is especially true if the material is new to you—as you're thinking about what is being presented, the instructor moves onto another subject and you miss some part of what is now being said.

All the mentioned training techniques will help you to reach your goal of certification if you apply them. By staying focused on your goals, selecting a training program that's acceptable, and then applying the proper study technique and refining them to your style, you find yourself prepared for the exams.

## Conclusion

At this point, you should know what certification you want to get, why you're getting it, and how to get it. By now, you should also know what your weak areas are so that you can do a better job of studying during the courses and right before your exam. You should also have a pretty good idea of how you are going to finance your certification efforts. It's important to figure out all of the details before you actually begin the certification process. The more problems you take care of now, the fewer distractions you'll have while studying.

# CHAPTER 4
# Taking the Tests

# Introduction

Taking tests is the least favorite part of any training experience—they seem to evoke the worst feelings from all of us. While general exams are difficult, professional examinations are more difficult than just about any other exam you can take. With most general exams, you have a wide range of study aids available. If nothing else, you have a group of fellow students to talk with. Professional exams usually don't offer these aids; in most cases, only a small group of people interested in something more than just a general knowledge of the world around them takes these types of exams. Novell's exams aren't any different. Not only is there a lack of third-party study aids, but each exam is unique. Therefore, you can't even rely on the input from fellow students to help very much.

The emotional pressures of a professional exam are greater than a general exam's, as well. Of course, the reason that emotions run the gambit from agony to ecstasy is easy to understand: the stakes are high—a career is up for grabs. Every professional exam you take has the potential of helping your career if you pass it, or reducing your potential if you don't.

Learning to take an exam is just like any other skill—you gain the knowledge to perform the task, practice until you become proficient, and then demonstrate your ability. To become a proficient test taker you learn how to study, how to think when taking the exam, and how to prepare yourself emotionally. This chapter takes a look at all these elements and more. It helps you prepare for the Novell exams not only at the knowledge level, but at the emotional level as well.

There's another event you have to prepare for, too. Even if you go through all the training courses, study hard, and take the proper approach to testing, there's a good chance you'll fail at least one examination. After all, if there really wasn't a chance of failure, would anyone really want to become certified? The potential for failure helps differentiate between those who really want the professional recognition that comes with certification and those who don't. Dealing with that failure is an important element of passing the exam the next time. Looking for places where you made mistakes in the first attempt will help you prepare for the second attempt.

This chapter helps you cover the three areas of testing by telling you how to study and what to study. It also stresses the importance of taking the Novell viewpoint when answering questions. Most important of all, this chapter helps you over the ultimate hurdle, dealing with failure. The better prepared you are to take the test, the more devastating a failure becomes. Helping you get back on your feet again is an important feature of this chapter.

# Gathering the Information You Need

The student guides you receive while taking the Novell courses listed in Table 1-1 are your most important asset in taking an exam, especially if you take good notes during class. There are two operative phases here. First, you must take the Novell courses to obtain the Novell view of networking (or of any other certification-related task). Second, you must take good notes in class. Unless you perform both of these steps, there's a good chance that you'll fail at least once on each exam. The reason for this failure is simple: while you may have a great understanding of networks in general, you need to know the Novell way of doing things to pass the exam.

## The Importance of the Novell Courses

Your instructor is specially trained to help you understand networking from a Novell perspective. A Novell certification is a credential that tells the world you know what you're talking about when it comes to Novell networks and the Novell way of doing things.

It may seem that prescribing one way of doing things when there are many other equally correct ways of doing them is unnecessarily restrictive and oppressive. However, Novell can't test everyone's methods of doing a task, yet must ensure that the methods used by the people Novell certifies are correct. Any other course would make people ask, "Why should I trust anyone you certify to maintain my network?" As you can see, what may seem restrictive at first is simply a way of making sure that everyone can perform networking tasks in a way that works every time. It also ensures that someone certified by Novell fully tests those techniques in a real-world environment. When people hire you based on your certification, what they are really hiring is someone who knows the Novell way of performing a task—an extension of Novell, if you will.

So how does this relate to test taking? Since Novell must test your ability to maintain a network, and we've seen there's logical reason for everyone performing those tasks in the same way, it follows that Novell will test that one way of doing things. If you walk into the examination room without a knowledge of Novell's way of performing the task, then there's no way for you to answer the questions correctly. (The passing requirements are high enough to void just about any possibility of someone guessing their way through the exam.) This is the first point you must remember, then. When you take a certification exam, you are being tested on your knowledge of Novell's way of performing a task, not your networking knowledge in general. This is a very important concept to grasp. Failure to grasp it could cost you the exam.

By now you're saying, "But Jane over there never went through the courses and she passed the exams without any problem." There's a simple answer to this question as well. You can perform some tasks only one way. When you come across questions that ask about that one way, you'll find that you can answer them even if you haven't gone through the Novell courses. This is how some people get by without taking the Novell courses. They learn enough about the Novell methods to pass the exam based on their own knowledge. Of course, these are usually people who have several years' worth of networking experience and a few degrees as well. Unfortunately, unless you're very skilled in networking, the cost of approaching the exams from this angle can prove costly. Failure to prepare yourself costs you both time and the money paid for failed exams.

## Taking Good Notes

Another piece of information you need to collect before you can study for an exam is a set of good notes. What makes the difference between a good note and a bad one? Actually there aren't any bad notes (with the exception of wrong information). There are good notes that help you study, and ones that won't. While both convey information, one doesn't provide the correct type of input.

Notes are somewhat difficult to quantify until you actually need to use them. You may think something the instructor said is of the greatest importance during class, only to find that you never use the information afterward. Watching what information you use and what information you don't is one way to improve your note-taking skills. Everyone differs in their ability to retain information. Some people need to write down on paper just about everything they hear or they won't remember it later, while others will fail to hear an important fact if they are too busy taking notes.

# Taking the Tests

Part of the problem is your level of concentration. How well do you concentrate? Can you work on complex problems for hours without getting mentally tired? Do you remember what you read in trade journals long after the information is no longer useful? You may find that taking a minimum of notes and really concentrating on what the instructor has to say is your best method of retaining information. In fact, some people don't take any notes at all during class. They save that activity until after class, as a technique for going back over the information the instructor presented.

If you find that you can't remember anything without writing it down first, you may want to consider two other methods of taking notes. Some people use the outline approach. They write quick notes about what the instructor said as an outline on a separate sheet of paper. This allows the note taker to concentrate on what the instructor has to say. After class they fill in the outline. This helps reinforce what the instructor said during class.

Another group can actually concentrate on two things at once. They can write complete notes and still pay attention to what the instructor is saying. These are the same people that you find talking on the telephone while working away on a computer. This is a talent that some people possess, and it can be used to good effect in class. Make sure you use every resource to ensure that you get a good set of notes for later study.

A final group of people needs to resort to high technology to make sure they get all the facts. Simply take a tape recorder with you to class, record what the instructor has to say, and transcribe it later. This tends to reinforce the lessons you learn in class and still allows you to get complete notes. (Make sure you ask the instructor's permission before you start recording the session; some people may object to the use of recording equipment in class.)

As you can see, there are a variety of ways to take notes. This is the first thing that you must learn to do. Get the information down on paper so you can use it later to study. If you find that you can't remember what the instructor said at the end of the day, then you may be using the wrong note-taking technique. You should rely on your notes as an aid to memory, not as a replacement for your memory. Force your brain to do a little of the work required to remember what the instructor said during the day. Work with a variety of methods until you find the one that works best for you.

The second part of this note-taking procedure is to take notes that you will actually use. This differentiates a good note from one that you took and don't need. Taking good notes always helps you in the long run; the other kind of note is a waste of time. Unfortunately, this is something that you learn from experience. A valuable note for one person may not provide any information for someone else. Here are some rules of thumb that you can follow to maximize the possibility that the notes you take are as useful as possible:

- *Take complete notes.* Never write down just a few words without filling the note out later. This is especially important if you use the outline approach to note taking. Some people take good notes during class, but fail to fill them out immediately afterward. When they try to use the notes to study for an exam or part of their work later, they find the notes are incomplete or indecipherable.

- *Take specific notes.* Don't talk about generalities in your notes. Always make them as specific as possible. If the instructor provides an example in class, adding this example to the note can help you get the most out of the note later. Making the note specific also helps trigger the memory process later. We tend to remember specific, not general, occurrences.

- *Don't take notes out of context.* Always provide enough surrounding information so you can get the full flavor of the note. Never jot down a quick idea that you could misinterpret later. Always provide yourself with all the details. Have you ever heard of the guy who took notes about preparing a chicken for dinner? One of the notes said *Cut off head.* So he cut off his own head instead of the chicken's head. Don't let this happen to you—take complete notes that give you the whole story.

As you can see, note taking is an important part of the learning process. Always increase your chances of passing an exam by taking good notes in class. Take the time to check the usefulness of your notes after you write them. If you find that you don't use the contents of a note later, then don't waste the time required to take that type of note again. In addition, if you find that you can almost but not quite remember something the instructor said, it's a sure sign that you needed to take a note. Make sure you remember to record this type of information during courses you take in the future.

## What Are the Requirements?

The precise requirements for the CNA and CNE certifications vary by the course of study you plan to follow. We've already covered the specific

# Taking the Tests

issues in Chap. 1. There are, however, general educational and practical requirements for any certification that you want to pursue. You can break these general requirements into four areas: (1) gaining the required knowledge, (2) practicing what you learn, (3) taking your exam, and (4) filling out any required paperwork. It's really that simple.

This chapter helps you look at two of those steps: *gaining the required knowledge* and *practicing what you learn*. That's what study is all about—getting the knowledge you need to know to do something, then putting that knowledge into practice before you're called upon to do it in real life.

There are two levels of knowledge required to get your certification: practical and Novell. The *practical knowledge* is what you need to get your work done every day. For example, formatting a floppy or installing a new network card are examples of practical knowledge. This is where hands-on training comes into play. Practical knowledge will get you around many of the trickier exam questions, but it won't prepare you to do things the Novell way.

The *Novell knowledge* is what you need to see things from the Novell perspective. Some people may not see this as very valuable, but it is. There are many situations where you can perform a task in more than one way. One way isn't theoretically better than any other, but Novell wants you to do things its way to enforce a consistent way of handling problems. In some cases, Novell's way of doing things is also slightly better than any other way of performing the task. You may not even notice the difference immediately; it takes time and experience to learn what Novell is trying to show you up front.

Of course, Novell is providing you with this training for a very specific reason. Training of this sort reduces the number of technical support calls Novell receives. It also makes it a lot easier for Novell to help you during a crisis. The technical support person can better anticipate the problems that you may encounter if he or she knows what procedure you'll use to fix an error. (This is a gross oversimplification of the two levels, but it's a good way to look at them for right now.)

You can gain the knowledge required to pass your certification exams in any number of ways (see Fig. 4-1):

- *Attend classes.* Some people take the Novell-sponsored classes provided by their local NAEC. This provides you with the head knowledge of the Novell way of doing things, but falls short in the practical experience area.

- *Read the manuals.* A lot of people read the Novell manuals, then try the things they learn on their local network. This method cer-

**Figure 4-1**

Three Ways to Learn about Novell.

Class study provides the best level of Novell specific knowledge. You need to enhance it with practical experience to pass your exams.

Practical experience will help you accomplish your everyday tasks, but it won't help you gain a Novell perspective on networking.

Self-study using the Novell manuals will provide you with a little of the Novell perspective; practicing what you learn will help you gain the practical experience you need.

tainly provides a lot more practical experience, but it usually falls short in teaching the precise Novell way of learning things. Of course, you'll get at least some of the Novell view going this route since Novell writes the manuals. One potential drawback is that your boss may not look at your practice sessions on a live network favorably.

- *OJT.* Experienced networking people spend so much time on a network that they learn the things they need to know over time. This method certainly helps you excel in practical knowledge, but almost guarantees that you won't know the Novell way of attacking a problem. Gaining only practical knowledge may get you into a situation where you'll feel that Novell marked a question on your exam wrong, even though you provided the correct answer. Remember that you must provide the *Novell* view on every test answer.

There's no *best* way to achieve your goals. You may want to take classes in areas where you don't feel comfortable. On the other hand, reading the manuals may provide sufficient information in areas where you have a lot of practical information. This book will help you study for your exams. Someone with a lot of practical experience will be able to pass the Novell exams simply on the merit of what they learn here. However, if you do find that you can't pass the exams in this book, then you may want to invest in some courses and other forms of education.

As you can see, the basic requirements for passing the Novell certification exams are quite simple. You need to possess a combination of Novell and practical knowledge in the area tested by your exam to pass it. Even though it looks simple, gaining the knowledge required may prove daunting in some situations. The following section provides you with a better understanding of the complexities of the situation.

## The Test Taker's Study Guide

You're sitting at a table or desk, your student manuals on one side and a stack of notes on the other. What do you do now? What's the best way to study for your certification exam? These questions plague almost anyone who takes an exam. If you leave your study area and go to the exam with this feeling, you may actually psyche yourself into failing it.

No matter how you cut it, passing an exam means that you'll need to perform some type of study before you take it. Whether you use the formal approach of classes or something a little less conventional, like tapes and self-study guides, you need to prepare yourself to take the exam before you enter the test area. This section helps you develop the good study habits that you need to get the most out of your study time.

A good study regimen doesn't mean spending a long time in study, it means studying efficiently. There are four major areas of concern, as shown in Fig. 4-2: *quality, environment, goals,* and *techniques.* Each area will help you improve your study habits to obtain the best overall efficiency without reducing the effect of your study. If anything, these techniques will help you study faster and better.

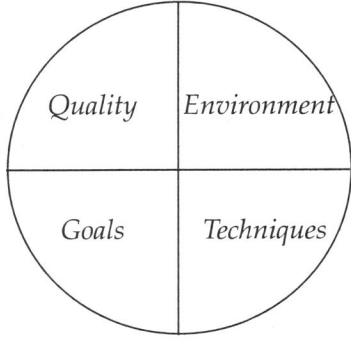

**Figure 4-2**
The Four Cornerposts of Any Study Regimen.

The first part of this section helps you set time aside to study. Let's face it, everyone has a very busy schedule and it's not always easy to get somewhere quiet to study. In fact, home and job probably consume more time and energy than you really want to admit. However, here's another fact to consider: if you're so busy taking care of other things that you can't concentrate on what you want to study, then your retention rate will fall to near zero, and there's no reason to even make the effort. This may seem a bit harsh until you really think about it. Why waste your time? Part of studying smart is to set aside a special time and place to study. Don't let anyone or anything interfere with it. You'll find that you can study for a lot less time and actually get more out of it. This will help you free more of your time for those home and work duties in the long run.

The next area we look at is creating a good study environment. Some people try to study in the living room with both the TV and the radio blaring. Of course, this type of setup is hardly conducive to a good study environment. There are innocuous things that affect the study environment as well. You may not notice how much direct light tires you out, but your retention rate will certainly reflect this factor. The right kind of comfort is essential to a good study environment. This part of the section looks at the total study environment. We'll look at things like getting the correct materials together and making sure that you have enough of the right kind of light. This section also looks at the physical requirements for study. For example, the type of chair you choose can greatly affect comfort, which affects how much you get out of a study session.

The third part looks at setting goals for a study session. You need to know what you plan to accomplish during any given session. Few people realize just how much the mind can wander during a study session. Do you find yourself thinking about the work you need to get done tomorrow while reading that test question? Setting goals keeps your mind focused. A failure to set goals may lead to random study that does not accomplish the goal of passing the test. Consider how well you would do on the job if you didn't set and meet goals. You may not always meet those goals within the time frame you set, but you meet them to maintain your productivity. Studying is no different from any other human activity in this regard.

Finally, we look at study techniques. The technique that works best for you is a very personal thing. Not every test taker can use the same technique. The same individuality that lends interest to life in general makes it difficult, if not impossible, to create a sure-fire study technique that will work for everyone. As a result, we won't even try to propose one standard way to study for your certification test. This part of the section looks at a variety of study techniques that you can choose from to create your own strategy. At least one of the methods will meet the needs of every reader. Hopefully, you'll use a variety of study methods to make your study time interesting.

## Setting Aside Adequate Study Time

Time is a quantity that seems in shorter supply than ever today. Its use is closely guarded by all of us in our everyday dealings. In fact, many of us are even more careful with our time than we are with our money. Time is a quantity that you can never have enough of. This time shortage invariably extends into your studies as well.

Unfortunately, some people will try to cram everything in this book into just one or two days' worth of study. They'll further cheat themselves by using only one of the teaching aids that we provide. While this may work for some of the simpler exams, it probably won't do much good for the majority of them. The average human being really needs a lot more in the way of study to pass the certification exams. You'll want to set aside at least a full week of study for each exam. Most people will require two weeks of study to really understand what the exam requires.

Fortunately, there's an answer to this problem of time and how it impacts your certification. There are two things you need to do to ensure that you get the maximum benefit from your study time: control the starting time and control the length of study. *Controlling the starting time* is important because that influences how you approach your study time. *Controlling the length of study* ensures that you maximize the effect of your study time. The following rules of thumb should help you in both regards.

- *Always study when you feel well rested, never study when you feel tired.* Not only are you apt to get facts that you study confused when you feel tired, but you'll remember them for a shorter length of time. Studying with a clear mind helps you maintain the facts you learn for a longer period of time. Studying when you feel well rested also improves your attitude.

- *Try to study at the same time each day.* This helps you develop a study habit rather than forcing yourself to go through the inconvenience of study. It also improves your ability to study. You will find that your body actually anticipates the demands of studying and prepares for it. Make your study time a treat instead of a dreaded job each day.

- *Choose a time of day when you are relaxed and there are few interruptions.* Trying to study right before or right after meals probably isn't a good idea in most cases. (Most people are a little too relaxed right after a meal.) You'll want to pick a time when your surroundings are quiet and you can spend some time hitting the books. This means that you won't want to study during your lunch hour at work. Use your lunch hour as a time to rest in preparation for your study time that night. Trying to take care of the kids while you're trying to study probably won't work well either.

- *Use an alarm or other timing device to keep yourself on track.* This will help reduce the chance that you'll spend more time watching the clock than you do studying. Decide how long you need to study for a particular session, set the timer, and then forget about clocks until you hear the alarm. Of course, using this technique will also keep you from studying too long and losing the good effect of your study time.

- *Never study for more than two hours.* Most researchers indicate that one hour of study is about what most people can tolerate. Have you ever gone to a seminar where they try to cram as much as possible into the two or three hours allotted? With all the excitement, it would seem that everyone should be ready to go for at least that long. What happens is that after about an hour, people start leaving for places unknown or begin to fidget in their seats—they simply can't absorb more than one or two hours' worth of lecture. Likewise, as a person spends more time in study, the attention slowly drifts to other topics and finally away from the area of study. If you really want to study for more than two hours, make sure you take plenty of breaks. One way to extend your study time is to study for an hour, take a 15-minute break to relieve the stress, then study for another hour.

■ *Try varying your study technique.* You might try having someone quiz you one night and do some memorization another night. Another way to vary your schedule is to spend the first half hour studying and the second half hour having someone quiz you. Make sure you use more than one of the methods of study presented for each test in this book to help obtain this goal. Varying your study technique can reduce the boredom that naturally occurs as study progresses.

As you can see, planning for your study time is fairly important. It really helps if you can study without fear of interruption or of going to sleep. It also helps if you can maintain the most positive attitude possible—you want to study without becoming bored.

One technique that helps to prevent dozing or boredom is to read or study with a big bowl of popcorn. As you study, munch on the popcorn—the action of moving your hand from the bowl to your mouth will stimulate your other muscles just enough to keep you alert. (Make sure you don't douse your popcorn with too much butter—you don't want to complete your certification weighing in at 400 pounds.) Of course, the game-type study programs provided with this book accomplish the same purpose by combining action with study.

Variety is essential to meeting your nightly study goals. After all, this is your future livelihood. Why should you work at something that bores you? Give yourself every advantage, and pick the times when you are best able to study. Make sure you study long enough, but not too long.

## Creating the Right Study Environment

Creating a productive study environment can prove daunting in the average home. No one wants to maintain a quiet environment after spending the day locked in a classroom or office. In addition, few homes contain a dedicated study area. More likely than not, you'll find your study area located in the kitchen or a bedroom. Other possible areas you may want to use for study include the library, a park bench, the beach, or your own backyard. Problems aside, you need to find a place that satisfies at least the majority of the hints provided in this section, even if it means studying outside your home. With a little work you can probably satisfy most of them. Figure 4-3 shows some typical study area needs.

Notice that the requirements for a good study area are fairly simple. You can group them into three areas, as shown in the picture: (1) optimum study environment, (2) personal study needs, and (3) a lack of distrac-

**Figure 4-3**
Creating a Good
Study Environment.

Make sure you observe all precautions for using your computer. This includes sitting at least 30 inches from the screen and using a wrist pad to prevent carpal tunnel syndrome. Keep your display and other parts clean too.

Go ahead and get relaxed, but not too relaxed. Remember, the whole idea is to study for your certification exam. Maintaining the correct posture and body position can help you focus on the job ahead.

Avoid study area distractions. A lack of light or the right kind of light can reduce your ability to see. Try to use indirect light. TV and radio can interfere with studies as well. Never try to study while doing chores.

tions. Actually, obtaining these goals is a whole different matter. Let's look at the requirements in a little more detail.

You have the greatest control over the *study environment*. It doesn't get tired or have a bad day. In addition, it usually stays in place once you set it up. As a result, this is the area you should concentrate on first. Make sure you take some time to get the study environment up to par since the other areas are subject to change. For example, a few dollars spent for a better computer chair today can continue to net results for many tomorrows. Normally, you'll spend a lot of time in front of your computer studying for the certification exams, so it really pays to invest in this area. Don't overlook things like an antiglare screen if you need it. Many newer displays provide an antiglare surface, but you may require more.

One of the most important, yet often overlooked, requirements is the screen distance. If you can't see the screen at 30 inches without squinting, then there's something wrong. Take the time to check for glare conditions or dirt. You may want to change the size of the font to make it easier to see from a distance. Getting glasses specifically designed for computer work can help a great deal, as well.

A comfortable office chair that's adjusted to fit your body is also a must. Take the time to adjust it to meet your needs. Your calf and thigh should form a 90° angle and your thighs should be parallel to the floor when you adjust the chair properly. Check out your arms. Do you have to reach up to touch the keyboard? Your upper arms should rest against your body and your upper arm should form a 90° angle with your lower arm. Make sure you provide plenty of support for your wrists. A wrist rest is a very inexpensive way to make certain you don't end up with carpal tunnel syndrome or other repetitive stress injuries.

You can usually control the second area pretty well. A look at your *personal study needs* is always a good idea. Maintaining a positive mental attitude will help you get the most from your study. Trying to study while tired does not accomplish much. If you feel bad, take the night off. Get relaxed, but not too relaxed. If you're too tense, then you'll tire easily. You need to relax to go the distance during your study time. Of course, getting too relaxed will allow your mind to wander. A wandering mind doesn't remember much, not even what you were thinking about instead of your studies.

*Distractions,* the third area of concern, are the hardest part of the equation to get under control. Don't try to study while performing chores around the house. One of two things always results. Either you'll perform the chore with your usual flair and forget everything you studied, or you'll end up frustrated because you cannot perform both tasks at the same time. Don't fall into the trap of having someone quiz you while you perform chores either. This is still a form of study; give it the respect it deserves.

Avoid too much noise as well. A television or radio is a good companion when you work around the house, but they produce devastating results when you study. Do you ever find yourself singing a song on the radio instead of paying close attention to your studies? This is the natural result of noise in the study area. Of course, the same thing holds true for people who insist on talking to you while you study. Take the time to look away from your work, listen to what they say, take care of anything they need, politely ask them to leave you alone, and get back to work. Any other course will surely frustrate both of you.

Subliminal distractions are the worst of the group. Ever have a dripping faucet ruin a good night's sleep? The same thing happens when you get distractions that are just beyond the range of your senses during your study time. The amazing part of this is the variety of forms that subliminal distraction can take. For example, you might need to remove the clock from your study area because it makes too much noise. Even a source of light can provide a subliminal distraction. Try using indirect light instead of a lamp while you study. You'll probably feel more relaxed because you don't have light glaring in your eyes. Using indirect lighting also means that you can use the proper light level. Some people get rid of the glare by getting rid of the light. (The 500-W halogen lamps that you get in most department stores provide the best possible level of indirect light and they don't cost very much—usually less than $30.) Taking time to figure out those subliminal distractions may not rapidly improve your test scores, but they will make your study time a lot more comfortable.

Setting up the right study environment is just as important as any other factor in the study environment. Make sure you don't ignore it. A good study environment can help you optimize your study time and can reduce the fatigue most people associate with study.

## Goal-Setting Strategies

Setting goals for each study session is extremely important. You need to decide where you are now and where you want to get to by the end of the study session. Using this technique will help you keep your mind focused on what you want to do. Maintaining your focus is one of the most important parts of any study regimen. If you don't keep your mind on what you are doing, it'll drift to other, more "interesting," topics, and you may as well not spend any time studying at all. Any effort spent from the time you stop thinking about the exam, and start thinking about that next vacation in Tahiti, is totally wasted.

Of course, it's equally devastating to rush through a study session simply to meet your goals. Think of your goals as the target that you want to obtain. Get as close as possible to that target, but don't shoot yourself in the foot in the process. Rushing is one of the worst things you can do if you

# Taking the Tests

want to retain what you learn. Make sure you take the time to fully study each topic.

Getting somewhere between these two extremes is the best way of setting goals for your learning time. Make sure you set a reasonable goal. After all, who are you trying to impress? Only you will know what takes place during your study sessions, so make your goals difficult but not impossible to reach. The following tips will help you set reasonable, yet worthwhile, goals.

- *Check your actual progress from session to session.* Use this as a gauge for setting your goal for each session. Set a goal a little higher than what you achieve during an average study session. This will challenge you, but will keep the goal within the realm of the achievable.

- *Use the tests in this book to measure your retention.* Make the first goal of each new session to test the amount of information you retained from the previous session. The score you obtain will tell you whether you are rushing or not. The combination of materials provided in your courses, plus this book, plus the Novell manuals and any third-party books, should allow you to retain a minimum of 80 percent of what you learn. (You should be able to retain a minimum of 70 percent of what you learn if you don't go to the Novell courses.) If you don't retain this level of information, then consider slowing down a little and spending a little more time on each topic. If you still can't achieve a high enough retention level and you haven't taken any courses, then consider taking classes at your local NAEC or NEAP.

- *Maintain a point system based on the goals you achieve each session.* This makes the study session more of a game and ensures that your interest level remains high. Compete against yourself. That is what you really do anyway, so make a game of it. You could use the following scoring system. Assign each goal a point level: hard (3), medium (2), or easy (1). Add up the goal points for each goal that you accomplish during a session. Now, multiply this number by the test score you obtain during the following session to obtain your final score. For example, you study 2 hard, 1 medium, and 1 easy goal(s) during an evening. You obtain a score of 80 percent on the test during the following session. Your score for the evening is: $(2 * 3) + (1 * 2) + (1 * 1) * 0.8 = 7.2$. See how easy it is to use this system? Now you have an easy way to track your progress from day to day. Make sure you reward yourself for above-average performance. This is one sure way to ensure continued success.

- *Set goals based on your ability, not on someone else's desires.* It's too easy to destroy a study session if you are trying to live up to a boss' expectations or what a coworker achieved. On the other hand, it's equally devastating to hold back your progress because you think you need to spend a specific amount of time on each topic. Each person is an individual and requires their own special goal-setting strategy. Use the other tips in this section to stay on track.
- *Use a weekly test to check your overall retention level.* If you plan to spend a few weeks studying for each exam, then keep an overall look at your progress. Don't fall into the trap of thinking that you're doing fine only to find that you don't remember the things you studied during the early part of your study sessions.
- *Set your goals based on your current workload.* If you have an easy week, then set higher goals. A stress-filled week probably calls for a lower goal level. Don't add to a burden by thinking that you need to maintain the same level of achievement every day.

As you can see, what looked like a difficult task at first may prove to be easier than you think. Setting goals is easy. Checking to see that those goals are reasonable takes a little more time, but is definitely worth the effort. Make sure you optimize your study time by optimizing your study goals.

## Developing Good Study Habits

Developing good study habits is also important if you want to pass an exam—using the appropriate study technique is an important part of developing good habits. You always want to maximize the impact of each study session by varying your technique over the time allotted. Study techniques are a personal part of the picture. Each person has different needs in this area.

Developing good study habits means a lot more than just getting into the right frame of mind or using good study practices. Using the right study technique can mean the difference between a boring study session and one that fully meets your objectives. If you enjoy spending a lot of time with other people, a good study technique could include taking the time to converse with your peers about the topics that will appear on the test. You may even want to exchange telephone numbers and addresses with your classmates and set up a study session at one of their houses. Make it a study party and you could be miles ahead in your study goals.

Talking with friends is just one more technique you can add to your bag of study techniques. Of course, you'll surely fail if this is the only technique you use. You need to combine this technique with some individual study time or other study methods.

There are many ways to improve your study time. Some methods work for some people, others for others. Everyone is different. You need to develop a set of study habits that works for you. The best rule of thumb is to always analyze both your successes and failures to determine what works and what doesn't. The following hints will help you develop a study strategy that maximizes the effectiveness of your study time.

- Ask someone to quiz you. Make sure they concentrate on one test at a time, but that they vary the questions from one session to the next. Ask them to ask the same question in several different ways. This will help you develop a pattern of thinking centered around question *content* rather than around the questions themselves.
- Discuss the test and other study materials with your peers. You can ask them about problem areas they have and express your own problem areas. Having a group help you with your problem areas not only increases your chances of getting a great answer, it forces you to consider areas that you may not think about normally.
- Make a game out of the test. That is the purpose behind the games in this book. It puts the test in a different light, making it more of a challenge than something you have to do. Try creating your own set of flash cards. You may even want to create your own Trivial Pursuit game cards. Try modifying existing games to meet your needs, or use other traditional game methods. For example, you might want to combine correct answers with the ability to move on the game board. (Make sure you spend some time looking at the "Brain Teaser" sections in the later chapters of this book for other ideas.)
- Spend some time in concentrated book study. Look over the Novell manuals in depth. Try to find at least one new fact during each study session. Perform the same process with your third-party books and the student manuals. The search will help you focus your thoughts on the test and reduce the chances that they'll wander.
- Some people find that memorization is an easy way to learn. Try to memorize as many of the facts in this book and in the Novell manuals as possible. Recite them to yourself as you perform other network or application-related tasks. (Always avoid mixing study and chores.)

- Consider the hands-on activities in this book, your student manuals, and the Novell manuals as the basis for your own exercises. Create your own case studies based on your weaknesses and the guidelines presented in this book. Make sure you set a starting point and an ending point. Figuring out how to get from point $A$ to point $B$ is a good way to study. You can even use this in a group setting. Challenge one of your peers to a race. Each of you can set the starting and ending points for the other person. The first person to accomplish their goal wins.
- Use association to study. Take the time to associate the items you need to know for the exam with things that you do every day. Some people even create acrostic sayings to learn various elements of the exams. For example, this works especially well when learning the security portions of an operating system, like the different types of access or the attributes you can assign to a file. Of course, it works equally well when memorizing the various menu functions of an application. You can also use mnemonics for association. To learn the names of the seven OSI model layers in order, try taking the first letter from each word of the saying "All People Seem To Need Data Processing." The initial letters in this saying are the same as in the ordered OSI layers—Application, Presentation, Session, Transport, Network, Data-link, and Physical.
- Take notes as you read the Novell manuals and study the questions in this book. Then, refer back to the notes and see if you can remember what you read. See how accurately the notes reflect what the manuals actually say. This can help you find and define problem areas. An alternative to this method is to create an outline of the topics you study, then fill in the blanks later. This forces you to remember what you read and then reinforces it by having you write the information down.

Of course, this is not the list to end all lists. Do yourself a favor, develop a set of study strategies that work for you. Then, take the extra time to use a variety of techniques to keep your study time from getting boring. The time you spend in this additional effort will pay for itself quickly when it comes time to get down to work.

## Getting the Job Done Right

Learning to study is essential if you want to pass your certification exams. Any other course of action is deadly. This section looks at four major areas

# Taking the Tests

in optimizing your study time. More important, this section shows you how to retain what you learn. You'll never pass the exams if you don't know how to study and retain information. The following hints will help you develop a study strategy that maximizes the effects of your study time.

- Always study your weak areas first, then study the areas you feel more confident about. If you have someone quiz you, make sure they quiz you about the weak areas first and the strong areas second. To help determine where your weak areas lie, make sure you look at your notes. If you spent the time to take notes about a particular topic, then you are probably weak in that area.

- Have someone quiz you on what you have learned. (The instructor will provide you with sample test questions; form your quiz questions using the same format.) Make a game out of studying. Reward yourself with something special if you get a specific number of points toward your goal. You can use the questions you miss as the basis for the next day's study.

- Create a good study environment. Make sure you have a clean desk or table to work at. Reduce any distractions by turning off the radio, closing windows, and asking others in the study area to remain quiet. Adding a good indirect light source and sitting in a comfortable chair can help, as well. Make sure you wear comfortable clothing while you study.

- Study the appropriate student guide for the test you want to take. Some people tend to race ahead or look at previously studied areas when they become bored with the current test material. Doing this can actually confuse you rather than help you study. For example, you may find that you start confusing the security rules for NetWare 3.x with those used in NetWare 4.x. Each exam tests only one specific course. Make sure you study for that course. If you find yourself becoming bored with the current material, take a short break—get up and move around instead of racing ahead or looking at previously studied material.

- Fill out your notes if you use the outline method of taking notes. Even if you don't, you may want to spend part of your study time expanding the notes you took in class. This forces you to remember what the instructor said and what went on during class. It also increases the usefulness of your notes when you need to use them later.

- Spend time discussing the topics you studied in class with your classmates. This allows you to compare notes and ideas about the topics.

You may find that someone else has a different viewpoint about what actually took place during class. (The same thing happens when you ask two people about what happened at an accident site—both will have seen something different.) Talking with your classmates helps you enhance your notes by incorporating their viewpoints as well. It may also help you fill gaps in your notes. Even the most conscientious person misses things during a discussion.

- If you're a very self-motivated person who tends to rush things, never register for the exam until you feel ready to pass it. Even though there's a limited time in which to take all the exams, you won't want to repeat one because you weren't prepared to take it. Make sure you are ready to take the test before you call to register.

- If you tend to procrastinate, you may want to register for your exam immediately after the class is completed. Try setting the date for two weeks from the time your class finishes. This will give you a goal to achieve and enhance your study efforts. Don't let your certificate pass you by—register now for the exam.

As you can see, there are a lot of ways to improve your chances of passing an exam. These include creating and maintaining a positive study environment, reemphasizing important points through quizzes and discussions with your peers, and taking the exam only when you're ready. Following any or all of these suggestions may just make the difference between passing the exam and failing it. You may want to take some time to add your own ideas to this list. For example, some people may find that studying outside is more beneficial than studying in the house. Each person is different. The study methods used by one person may not help another. Make sure you optimize your study methods to meet your needs.

## Registering for the Exam

Registering for the exam is one of the easiest parts of the process. All you need to do is have a credit card ready and call the Drake testing center. You can register for any test by calling 1-800-RED-EXAM. The person on the other end of the line will ask you a few questions. That's all there is to registering.

Of course, there are a few pieces of information you need to know before you can call. You'll need to know the number of the examination you want to take and the location of your nearest test center. (You can check Table 1-5 for a list of exam numbers.) If you don't know the location of the nearest test center, the person registering you can provide a list of locations in your area. They can usually provide you with directions to the test center as well. You may want to drive to the test center from work sometime before the exam so you know how long it takes to get there. This also allows you to test the directions you get from the test center and make any required changes. Make sure you add or subtract some time to compensate for differences in traffic flow at the time you plan to travel to the test center. If you make the trip from work during your test run in light traffic, but then try to make it in the same time in heavy traffic, you may end up arriving late.

Make sure you have several exam dates in mind before you call the test center. Otherwise, you may find that the test center has filled the date you originally wanted and you might have to rush to find another one. Once you do get a test date, write it down in several places. Talk to your boss about taking the needed time off well in advance of the test. Make sure you don't schedule other appointments on your test day. Set this day aside for testing and nothing else, if possible. (Of course, most people will have to go back to work after the exam.)

## Things to Watch for While Taking the Exams

There are quite a few things people do during the examination. Many of them are big time wasters. Some people wander between the drinking fountain and their desk. Others seem more interested in staring at the dots on the wall instead of answering questions. Make sure you use all the time allotted to take the test—don't waste any of it doing other activities. Try to maintain your concentration during the entire exam—don't allow interruptions to rob you of the chance to pass. Of course, time isn't the only thing you need to watch during the exam. The following hints should help you take the test faster and improve your chances of passing.

- *Look at the time indicator on your screen from time to time, but don't waste time staring at it.* Make sure you pace yourself, allotting enough time for each question you need to answer. You may want to take a quick glance at the time indicator after each question and ignore it the rest of the time.*

---

*Novell uses adaptive exams for the most part now, so there isn't any time indicator to worry about. The exam ends once you've answered enough questions to confirm either that you know enough to pass the exam or that you lack the required knowledge.

- *Read the entire question.* Don't skip over small words like *and* or *not* when reading the question. Small words make a real difference—skipping them could cost you the question. People often miss questions not because they didn't know the answer, but because they failed to read the question fully. Make sure you understand the question before you read the answers.
- *Read all the answers provided.* Sometimes there is more than one correct answer on the screen. You need to pick the *most correct* answer that you find.
- *Remember to put on your Novell hat before you enter the testing area.* Novell uses the student manuals as the basis for all the answers in the exam. Even if there is more than one correct way to perform a task, only the Novell way is the correct answer on the exam. In some cases, you may see more than one correct Novell answer to a question. Always pick the most complete answer.
- *Go with your first instincts.* Some people get so psyched out before an exam that they actually overthink the answers to questions. Going with the first answer that comes to mind is correct more often than not, especially if you took the time and effort to study. Don't kill your chances to pass the exam by overthinking the answers.
- *Maintain your level of concentration.* Even though the exam center administrator tries to provide the very best testing environment possible, there are always distractions to reduce your concentration level. Concentrate on the test—ignore any outside influences that tend to reduce your level of concentration. You can't perform well on a test that you aren't concentrating on.
- *Make sure you take care of your comfort needs before the exam.* For example, even if you don't normally need to eat breakfast, you may want to do so on the day of the exam to boost your energy levels. You'll also want to wear comfortable clothing. Wear your glasses or contacts so you can see the screen without squinting.

As you can see, how well you do during the exam is really a matter of how well you prepare before you go into the test center. For example, your body's energy level always affects your concentration level. It's also affected by all the environmental factors under your control, like the ability to see the screen and wearing comfortable clothing.

Realizing the effects of environmental factors on your mind during an exam is very important. For example, some people go so far as to make out a schedule for the day of the exam. This can help you get from place

# Taking the Tests

to place without rushing. Make sure you allow plenty of time to get from place to place. Taking an exam while you feel relaxed is a lot easier than taking one after you have rushed all day. Figure 4-4 shows a typical schedule. Of course, you will need to tailor your schedule for your test needs.

Note that our schedule contains little housekeeping notes like calling work and placing the test results in a folder where you can find them later. These may seem like things you shouldn't have to write down, but writing them down does provide a certain peace of mind while you're taking the exam. You don't need to worry whether you took care of a specific item since you have all of the things you need to take care of on paper.

There's one especially important note in this group. Putting on your red glasses isn't an option, it's a requirement for passing the exam. You must provide the Novell way of doing things during the exam, not just an answer that works. The other part of this line is important, as well. Studying on the day of the exam is a sure-fire way to ensure that you'll fail. If you don't know the material when you get to the test center, any studying you could do won't help.

**Figure 4-4**
A Typical Test Day Schedule.

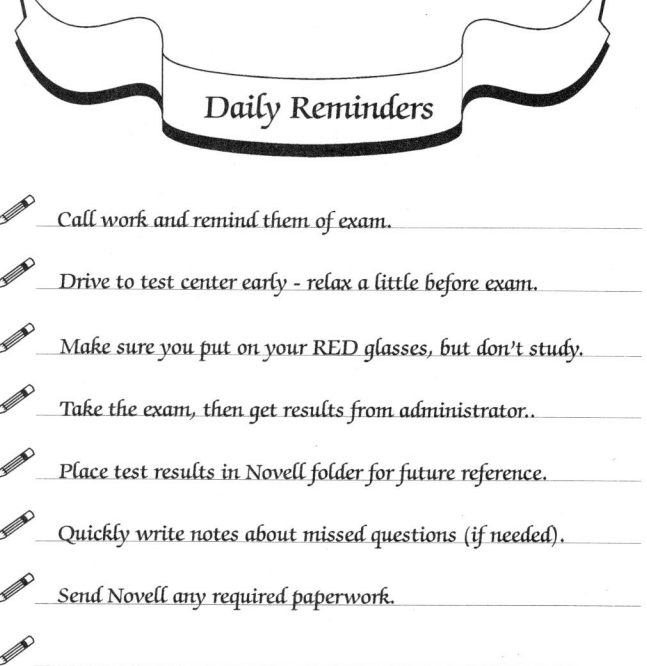

Daily Reminders

- Call work and remind them of exam.
- Drive to test center early - relax a little before exam.
- Make sure you put on your RED glasses, but don't study.
- Take the exam, then get results from administrator..
- Place test results in Novell folder for future reference.
- Quickly write notes about missed questions (if needed).
- Send Novell any required paperwork.

Once you do get into the test area, you'll take one of two types of exams. The first type is the *standard testing technique*. This is the method that Novell originally used when its certification program started, and some tests still use this method. The second type of exam is called the *adaptive testing technique*. This is a new, knowledge-based method of testing. We describe both test methods in detail in the following subsections.

## Standard Testing Technique

The standard testing technique uses the same methodology as your instructor used for most of your classes in school. You'll receive an exam with anywhere from 60 to 100 questions. Novell creates a unique exam for each person by drawing a specific number of questions at random from the testing base. For example, you might get 10 questions about printing from a test base of 100 questions. Another 10 questions might ask you about security.

Think of this testing method as the Chinese menu approach. You get so many questions from column *A*, so many from column *B*, and so forth. You'll never know which questions will appear on the exam—Novell creates a unique test for each candidate by selecting the questions at random. About the only thing you might be able to count on is getting so many test questions in a specific area.

It's very important to study everything completely when you take a standard exam. You need an even amount of knowledge about all the testing areas to complete the exam successfully. However, there are a few things you can do to improve your chances of passing the exam.

- *Talk to other people about their testing experience and the types of questions they saw.* Even though your chances of getting precisely the same questions as any one individual are very small, you can build an overview of all the test questions if you ask enough people. It's important to remember that Novell constantly updates its test base and that you'll get a random set of questions.

- *Make absolutely certain that your strong areas really are strong.* It is possible to have a weak area and still pass the exam. For example, you might find that you don't know printing very well, yet pass the exam by knowing security perfectly. Of course, having more than one weak area is still deadly—you need to answer enough questions correctly to pass the exam.

- *If you do fail an exam, make sure you write notes about your weak area as soon as possible.* Drake won't allow you to record any answers or take any other notes. However, you can take the time to commit these facts to memory and write them down after you leave the test center. It's very important to improve on your weakest areas for the next exam if you want to pass.

## Adaptive Testing Technique

The adaptive testing technique is a different approach to testing. There's no way to predict how many questions you'll get before you start the exam because everyone receives a different number. In addition, there's no way to predict how many questions you'll get in any one area unless you are really honest about your skills.

An adaptive test actually changes to meet your specific testing needs. For example, if you are very weak in printing, then you'll get a lot of printing-related questions. Likewise, if you are very good when it comes to security, you will see very few security questions. The adaptive test bases the next question on the results of the previous question. If you get a question wrong, you can be certain that you'll see more of those questions during the exam. The adaptive exam won't continue to pound away at one area of knowledge. It'll give you enough questions to determine whether you know the information. Once it determines that you are weak in an area, the adaptive exam will move on to another area.

It may seem like Novell is making the exam process more difficult than it needs to be. You may be surprised to learn that there are some situations where an adaptive exam is actually easier to pass because you get fewer questions. Fatigue is a major problem with the standard testing technique. A candidate who answers 100 questions is likely to miss some of them because he or she is tired. This is one of the problems that led to the adaptive testing technique. Even if adaptive tests are harder to pass in some respects, there are ways that you can improve your chances of passing.

- *You can count on an adaptive exam concentrating on your weak areas.* It pays to study your weak areas a lot more than your strong areas. Since an adaptive exam won't give you any extra boost for really knowing a topic area, demonstrating a general knowledge of all your strong topics is sufficient.

- *If you start seeing a lot of questions about a specific topic, then you know you aren't doing well in that area.* This means that you really need to slow down and take your time answering the next question in that area. Make sure you don't kill off your chances of passing the exam by rushing through the areas you don't know.
- *Novell requires you to provide some answer for every question.* Since you can't bypass a question you really don't know the answer to, take the time to rule out the obviously wrong answers, then select that answer you think is correct. Novell still uses a policy of one absolutely wrong answer, one answer that's either a trick answer or has some minor flaw, an answer that is correct, but less correct than some other answer, and finally the most correct answer. Always choose the most correct answer from those presented.

# What Do You Do If You Fail?

Even if you do fully prepare for an exam, there's still a chance that you'll fail it. There's no means for you to take every variable into account to guarantee that you'll pass the exam. You may not realize that you have a weak area that the test asks you about. A cold or flu may strike on the day of the exam. An accident may delay part of your schedule, forcing you to rush to the exam. Any or all of these reasons may prevent you from performing your best on the exam.

How you recover from a failure partially determines how you will react during the next attempt. It may even determine whether you make another attempt to pass the exam. Many people try the exams once, fail, then give up on their certification because the failure was so demoralizing. Remember, certification requires a lot of input from you in the form of dedication and hard work. If certification were an easy task, then the benefits of certification would be a lot less valuable. Don't give up after one attempt to pass an exam.

## Understanding the Mechanics of Failure

Of course, nothing's more demoralizing than failing the same test twice. There are several things you should do after failing an exam to make sure it won't happen again. For example, you can plan to study the areas that gave you the most trouble in the first exam. The following tips will help you pass the exam the second time around. Unlike the other tips in this chapter, these tips usually work for everyone. Make sure you try them all.

- *Write down the areas where you did well and the areas where you did not.* This will tell you where you need to concentrate your study before you take the next exam. (The test center administrator will provide you with a blank sheet of paper and a pencil you can use for this purpose.)
- *Maintain a positive attitude.* If you convince yourself that you're going to fail, you surely will. Literally thousands of other people have gotten their certification; there's no reason that you can't get it with the proper training and study. You need to keep this fact in mind while you study for the retake.
- *Don't overcompensate by studying too much.* Many people make the mistake of punishing themselves for failing by spending hour after hour in front of their desks studying for the next exam. This is probably the worst mistake you can make. While it's important to study for the next exam and try to find the weak areas that caused you to fail the first time, studying too much can confuse you and cause you to fail again. Make sure you don't study more than two hours per day. (You may want to review the study tips in the previous section of this chapter.)
- *Try to remember specific questions that you may have had trouble with.* In fact, you should try to write these down while they're fresh in your memory. Even though it's unlikely that you'll see these questions on the next test, they may help you find weak areas in your study strategy. In some cases you may even see the same question worded in a different way. This is where reading the question and understanding what it says really helps.
- *Always study for a general exam, not the specific exam you took the first time.* Trying to study for a specific exam is pointless since each exam contains different questions. Novell writes a new exam from questions in a database for each person who takes an exam. That's why it's so unlikely that you'll see the same question again.

## Understanding the Emotions of Failure

Besides the mechanical methods for getting to the next exam, you must deal with the emotional issues as well. Failing an exam always lowers your self-esteem and causes you to doubt your abilities. You need to find outlets for dealing with this problem. Some people perform some physical activity like bowling or tennis after a failure. The activity helps them release the frustration they feel over failing the exam. Other people work on crafts. A creative endeavor allows them to take their mind off the failure and put it to useful work. Whatever method you use to release the tension of failure, make sure you do it as soon as possible afterward. Don't give yourself time to think about the failure too long.

You also need to convince yourself that you can pass the exam. Many people who start the certification process never complete it because they don't think they can pass the exam. Remember, anyone with reasonable computer skills can pass the exams with the proper training and the right amount of study. A positive attitude is one of your best weapons in passing the exam the next time around. Make sure you maintain a positive atmosphere as you study and when you take the exam. Keep telling yourself that you can pass the exam.

## Conclusion

This chapter provides you with information about the three major areas of taking a test: getting ready for the exam, taking the exam, and recovering from failure. The way that you approach these three areas can greatly affect the final outcome of your certification efforts. After all, the main purpose of going through the course and all the effort to study is to pass the exams. Of course, the only reason you would want to take the exams is to get your certification.

We also looked at what you need to do to register for your exam. This is a fairly easy procedure, but you need to do some advance planning before you call to register. Make sure you give yourself every advantage possible by taking the exam when you are best prepared to pass it.

CHAPTER 5

# Getting the Paperwork Finished

## Introduction

*The job's never finished until the paperwork's done.* This is a truism for Novell certification, as well. Even if you finish all the required tests and training, you can still fumble around for several weeks just getting all the paperwork finished. Failure to take care of the paperwork properly won't cost you your certification, but it'll cost you time—and, as we all know, time is money.

Normally, Novell downloads your test scores from the testing center automatically. You'll also need to complete a certification agreement for every certification that Novell supports; CNIs have additional paperwork, as covered in Chap. 1. However, everything doesn't always go as planned. Test results can get lost and hardware failures can trash the test center files. If any of the test results do get lost, you must provide Novell with all the documentation required to prove that you passed the required exams and took the required courses. (Having a copy of your certification agreement isn't a bad idea, either, since a certification agreement can get lost in the mail.) Needless to say, every time a piece of paperwork like an exam result or certification agreement gets lost, you'll have to resubmit it and, perhaps, some additional paperwork as well.

Of course, the paperwork doesn't end when you submit a few forms to Novell, using the most reliable means possible. That's where the work begins. Even though Novell has made the paperwork process as close to automatic as you can get, the system still fails occasionally. Considering the investment you've made in your certification, it doesn't take much additional effort to call to make sure that Novell has everything it needs to issue your certificate. You also need to call Novell to make sure that nothing gets lost or overlooked. The bottom line is that you need to maintain a line of communication between yourself and Novell to make sure that the certification gets issued promptly.

This chapter deals with this problem by providing you with step-by-step instructions on filling out the paperwork and getting all the required documentation together. It also explains which departments you need to talk with and where you need to send the paperwork. Finally, it tells you what kind of paperwork you should get back from Novell and how long it usually takes to receive it.

## Getting the Paperwork Started

It's very important that you begin the paperwork process by getting organized. Make sure you can find the items you need when you talk with Novell by putting them in one easy-to-find place. Putting all your paperwork in one or two folders is a good idea as well. You may even want to create one folder for each course you attend. This way you can keep the notes, certificate, and test results for that course in one place. Whatever techniques you use, make sure you keep good records of all the certification items that Novell requires. You want to make it as easy as possible to find this information when you need it during a conversation with a Novell representative.

You'll also want to make a list of the paperwork required for your certification. The figures in Chap. 1 help you to do this. Make sure you keep this information in your folders, as well. If there was a mistake in what you thought you required for certification, then you'll want some basis to discuss the mistake with Novell. This may help improve the level and quality of information that Novell provides to other candidates in the future. It may also grant you some leeway on getting the required exams taken or other certification requirements finished.

## How Long Is Too Long?

The problem you face now is figuring out when to panic if you don't receive word from Novell regarding your certification. It's always a good idea to take a proactive approach to your certification. Novell downloads the data from the test center about once a week. They compare the information they receive to their current database. If someone passes a test, they add it to their existing record. If Novell can't find your name on its lists, then it adds you to the database as a new applicant. People who complete all their requirements are issued a certificate. A computer performs all these database functions automatically, making the process nearly foolproof. There's little chance that your examination scores will get lost.

Based on this information, you'll want to call Novell 10 to 14 working days after you take your exam to make sure they received the results (ask your NAEC or NEAP for additional guidance in this area if you need it). Calling Novell ensures you'll receive your certificate on time and that both of your records are in synchronization. It also reduces the last minute rush you'll experience if you wait until you complete all the requirements to call Novell. You can take care of each mishap as it happens.

Once you complete all your requirements, take time to call Novell again. Make sure you wait the requisite 10 to 14 working days after you complete your last requirement. Make sure they received everything. This is the time to ask the Novell representative how long it'll take to receive your certification. Asking this question will help you know when you've waited too long for your certificate to arrive. Always allow a few days after the deadline before you call Novell again. This compensates for slow postal deliveries, especially during the holiday season.

## Maintaining a Log of the Paperwork

Keeping records is an important part of the certification process. It helps you keep track of where you need to go and what you need to do. Of course, records fulfill an even more important need. Maintaining these paperwork logs may seem like a lot of fuss for nothing—until something gets lost. Chances are good you won't have any problems, but if you do, the time spent creating these logs will help to resolve any problems or misunderstandings. Make sure you cover all the contingencies by keeping a record of what you do, when you do it, and how you do it. That way you won't have to rely on your memory later when it comes time to figure out what happened. You also want to make sure you maintain good contact with the Novell administration department for your level of certification without making a nuisance of yourself. Maintaining these logs will help you maintain constant contact without calling too often. Remember that you are the one interested in certification. The Novell representative is only there to help you achieve your goal.

### Using the Paperwork Log

The time may arrive when you need to provide Novell with proof that you passed your certification exams. Since proof of requirement completion is your responsibility, it really helps to keep a complete log of every certification requirement you complete. Knowing when the testing center sent proof of this completion to Novell is a good idea as well (normally all you need is the date of your exam, since the testing center keeps a complete set of logs). You'll also want to make notes on what method you used to send the certification material. For example, did you fax the material or send it by overnight mail. (If you completed the requirement and simply relied on Novell to download the information from the test center, make sure you record this information as well on the appropriate Chap. 1 form. The forms in this chapter are for emergency use only.) Figure 5-1 provides an emergency log you could use for the CNA certification. Figures 5-2 to 5-5 provide the same logs for the CNE, MCNE, NCIP, and CNI certifications, respec-

# Getting the Paperwork Finished

**Figure 5-1**
CNA Paperwork Log.

**CNA Paperwork Log**

Name: _____

Date started: _____ Date completed: _____

| Requirement | Course number | Date sent | Method of mailing | Register number | Date received |
|---|---|---|---|---|---|
| Submit test results | _____ | _____ | _____ | _____ | _____ |

tively. Use these logs to record any paper correspondence with Novell. For example, if Novell loses your paperwork, you would want to use these forms to record the time, date, and method you used to send them paper copies.

As you can see, each of the forms addresses the needs of one of the certifications. Using this type of form allows you to make sure not only that

**Figure 5-2**
CNE Paperwork Log.

**CNE Paperwork Log**

Name: _____

Date started: _____ Date completed: _____

| Requirement | Course number | Date sent | Method of mailing | Register number | Date received |
|---|---|---|---|---|---|
| Target 1 | _____ | _____ | _____ | _____ | _____ |
| Target 2 | _____ | _____ | _____ | _____ | _____ |
| Target 3 | _____ | _____ | _____ | _____ | _____ |
| Target 4 | _____ | _____ | _____ | _____ | _____ |
| Networking technologies (core) | _____ | _____ | _____ | _____ | _____ |
| Service and support (core) | _____ | _____ | _____ | _____ | _____ |
| Elective credit 1 | _____ | _____ | _____ | _____ | _____ |
| Elective credit 2 | _____ | _____ | _____ | _____ | _____ |
| Elective credit 3 | _____ | _____ | _____ | _____ | _____ |
| Elective credit 4 | _____ | _____ | _____ | _____ | _____ |
| Elective credit 5 | _____ | _____ | _____ | _____ | _____ |

**Figure 5-3**
MCNE Paperwork Log.

| | | MCNE Paperwork Log | | | |
|---|---|---|---|---|---|
| Name: | | | | | |
| Date started: | | | Date completed: | | |
| Requirement | Course number | Date sent | Method of mailing | Register number | Date received |
| Core 1 | ____ | ____ | ____ | ____ | ____ |
| Core 2 | ____ | ____ | ____ | ____ | ____ |
| Core 3 | ____ | ____ | ____ | ____ | ____ |
| Target 1 | ____ | ____ | ____ | ____ | ____ |
| Target 2 | ____ | ____ | ____ | ____ | ____ |
| Elective credit 1 | ____ | ____ | ____ | ____ | ____ |
| Elective credit 2 | ____ | ____ | ____ | ____ | ____ |
| Elective credit 3 | ____ | ____ | ____ | ____ | ____ |
| Elective credit 4 | ____ | ____ | ____ | ____ | ____ |
| Elective credit 5 | ____ | ____ | ____ | ____ | ____ |

you sent everything that Novell needed, but that you can keep track of when and how you sent it, as well. The first few fields of the form contain personal information like your name, the date you started the certification process, and the date you finished it. The table contains a list of the requirements for certification. Some of the information needed to fill in the blanks will come from the worksheets that you completed in the previous chapters. Note that the course information is blank. This allows you to tailor the form to your specific needs. The course numbers you place in these blanks reflect your operating system specialty. The other fields in this form contain the date you sent proof of passing the requirement to Novell, the method used to mail the package, the registered mail number (you never want to send this information by regular mail), and the date Novell received it. You may even want to include the name of the person who verified that Novell did receive the package. (This information also appears in the telephone log described in the next paragraph.)

One good alternative to using the mail service is faxing your information to Novell. You may want to consider this alternative whenever possible. It

# Getting the Paperwork Finished

**Figure 5-4**
NCIP Paperwork Log.

### NCIP Paperwork Log

Name: _____

Date started: _____ Date completed: _____

| Requirement | Course number | Date sent | Method of mailing | Register number | Date received |
|---|---|---|---|---|---|
| Web Authoring and Publishing | 654 | _____ | _____ | _____ | _____ |
| IntranetWare: NetWare 4.x Administration or IntranetWare: NetWare 3.x to 4.x Update | 520 or 526 | _____ | _____ | _____ | _____ |
| NetWare TCP/IP Transport | 605 | _____ | _____ | _____ | _____ |
| Advanced Web Authoring | 655 | _____ | _____ | _____ | _____ |
| Web Server Management | 656 | _____ | _____ | _____ | _____ |
| IPE eligible test 4 | _____ | _____ | _____ | _____ | _____ |
| IPE eligible test 5 | _____ | _____ | _____ | _____ | _____ |
| Additional course 1 | _____ | _____ | _____ | _____ | _____ |
| Additional course 2 | _____ | _____ | _____ | _____ | _____ |
| Additional course 3 | _____ | _____ | _____ | _____ | _____ |
| Additional course 4 | _____ | _____ | _____ | _____ | _____ |
| Additional course 5 | _____ | _____ | _____ | _____ | _____ |

is much faster than using the mail and you can call Novell immediately after you send it to make sure they received it. Make sure you call and verify that you have the correct fax number and alert them that you plan to send the information immediately. Once you send the information to Novell, verify that someone at the other end of the fax line received the material in good condition. If they didn't receive the information in good condition, resend it right away.

**Figure 5-5**
CNI Paperwork Log.

```
                          CNI Paperwork Log
Name: _____

Date started: _____ Date completed: _____
```

| Requirement | Course number | Date sent | Method of mailing | Register number | Date received |
|---|---|---|---|---|---|
| Required category testing 1 | _____ | _____ | _____ | _____ | _____ |
| Required category testing 2 | _____ | _____ | _____ | _____ | _____ |
| Required category testing 3 | _____ | _____ | _____ | _____ | _____ |
| Required category testing 4 | _____ | _____ | _____ | _____ | _____ |
| Other course-specific prerequisite test 1 | _____ | _____ | _____ | _____ | _____ |
| Other course-specific prerequisite test 2 | _____ | _____ | _____ | _____ | _____ |
| IPE-eligible test 1 | _____ | _____ | _____ | _____ | _____ |
| IPE-eligible test 2 | _____ | _____ | _____ | _____ | _____ |
| IPE-eligible test 3 | _____ | _____ | _____ | _____ | _____ |

## Using the Phone Log

There is at least one other log you should consider maintaining—a record of your telephone conversations with people at Novell. Make sure you record when you call, whom you talked to, pertinent facts about the conversation, and a few notes about what transpired. Figure 5-6 provides a sample telephone log.

This log file contains enough space for two entries per page. You may want to make a few copies of this sheet to keep on hand for easy reference. Maintaining the log on your computer will allow you to scan the records quickly during a telephone conversation. It also helps you ensure that no information gets overlooked while you talk with the Novell representative. This also makes it a lot faster and easier to maintain your logs and to make sure you haven't forgotten to take care of anything you talked about on the phone or by mail. Some database managers, like AskSam or

# Getting the Paperwork Finished    147

**Figure 5-6**
Certification Telephone Log.

---

**Certification Telephone Log**

Date: _____ Time: _____ Contact person: _____

Phone number: _____ Ext.: _____

Topic: _____

Notes: _____
_____
_____

Problem: _____
_____

Resolution: _____
_____
_____


Date: _____ Time: _____ Contact person: _____

Phone number: _____ Ext.: _____

Topic: _____

Notes: _____
_____
_____

Problem: _____
_____

Resolution: _____
_____
_____

---

Folio Views, will allow you to enter this type of free-form information quickly. When you need to search for a particular topic, these database managers will look for phrases or whatever else you can remember about the conversation.

   Note that the telephone log contains space for the date, time, and contact person's name. These items are pretty self-explanatory. You'll want to include the person's telephone number and extension in the *Phone number* and *Ext.* fields of the form.

The *notes* field allows you to maintain a record of what each party said during the conversation. Reserve this section for conversation of a general nature. Be specific when taking notes. The more information that you can include, the better your chances of resolving any difficulties. Make sure that you record times, dates, phone numbers, and any names mentioned. If there were any commitments made by either party, be sure to make a note of that, as well. After you finish your conversation, summarize the conversation from your notes before hanging up. This will help to prevent any miscommunications.

If you called about a problem, make sure you record it in the *problem* field of the form. Use descriptive terms for this field. Don't write something like "Lost package in the mail." Provide yourself with exact details by writing "Lost copy of the Advanced System Manager exam results in the mail." At least this tells you what test the postal service lost for you. In addition to this information, you may want to record the registration number and other important facts. If the field does not provide enough room to record all the pertinent information, at least make a note about where you can find the information.

Record the resolution that you and the Novell representative talked about in the *resolution* field. Again, document as much of the conversation as possible immediately after the conversation. If you wait very long before documenting your conversation, you may forget something. You can use the contents of the resolution field to help make a *to do list* later. Creating a to do list ensures that you won't forget to follow through on your certification requirements. It also helps you remember when you need to call Novell to recheck the results of a problem resolution.

## Filling Out the Paperwork

There are two sets of paperwork requirements. The *standard set* applies to anyone who wants to obtain any of the certificates. The *CNI set* applies only to people who want to become CNIs. The following subsections explain these requirements in detail.

### Standard Paperwork Requirements

The paperwork required for certification by Novell is very minimal. Besides the test scores, the paperwork consists of a release form and a picture ID request. (Remember that you are responsible for maintaining a copy of your test scores.) As you complete and pass each test, Sylvan Prometric sends a copy of your test scores to Novell. The people in the CNA, CNE, MCNE, or NCIP administration will then enter that information into a database. If you are just starting the certification process, Novell adds your name and records to the database. As you take each test, Novell will add that information to your name. Once you complete all the exams, Novell will automatically register your certification. This applies to the CNA, CNE, MCNE, and NCIP certifications.

The paperwork for the picture ID instructs you about the specifications concerning the photograph. The picture ID is proof of your certification and is used by clients and employers as justification for your services. In most cases, you can get this picture taken at any studio that specializes in passport or VISA photographs. While color pictures are nice, Novell doesn't require that you provide one. Black and white photographs work fine for your identification card. Make sure that you provide Novell with the best picture you get. The photo studio normally takes four pictures unless you request more. You may also want to dress in your normal work clothes and wear anything you normally wear on the job (like glasses). This provides the client with a better idea of what you look like when you present your certification card. It also makes it more difficult for someone else to use your certification card.

## CNI Paperwork Requirements

The paperwork required for the CNI is just about the same as for the other certifications. The only real differences are in the initial application and in having to send Novell a copy of your course certificates. Remember that to become a CNI you must attend each of the classes that Novell certifies you to teach. You'll also need to take care of any required category testing and other course-specific prerequisites.

Once you complete the courses and exams, call the CNI administration department and tell them that you have completed all your courses. They will then want you to send them a copy of the course certification for each class. This can be faxed or mailed. You should also include a cover page detailing your name, address, phone number, and why you are sending the certificate copies. Make sure you take the extra step of sending your certificates by fax or by registered mail. Never send the original certificate—always send a copy. After you complete this step you are ready to go through an *IPE* (Instructor Performance Evaluation).

You must call Novell to register for the IPE. If you have not completed an IPE-eligible exam, you won't be able to attend the IPE. You'll want to make sure that all test scores and passing dates are on your paperwork log form. After registering for the IPE, Novell will send you a confirmation letter with the IPE dates, times, location, lodging information, and directions. Keep this information in your paperwork folder until the date of the IPE.

On the first day you attend the IPE, make sure that you have the confirmation letter in case you have any problems or mix-ups. After completing the IPE, you'll want to retain this letter with your other paperwork for future reference. Upon completion of the your IPE, Novell will send you a letter stating whether you passed the IPE. You'll want to retain this letter with your other documents, as well.

If you were successful in completing the IPE, you'll be eligible to teach the appropriate classes. At the end of each year Novell sends you a recertification invoice. Novell applies the fee toward updating your manuals and provides you with the education bulletins and *Application Notes*. Again, you'll want to retain a copy of this invoice with your records.

## Verifying that Novell Receives and Processes the Paperwork

Even though Novell will automatically register your certification, it is your responsibility to follow up. You can never take too many precautions when it comes to your certification. After all, you've just spent many hours and dollars to get this far. The last thing you want now is to have some lost or misplaced paperwork hold up your certification or, worse yet, cause you to have to retake a test. After completing your last test, give Novell 10 to 14 working days to process the paperwork. After that time, call Novell administration for your test level to check the status of your certification. Chances are very good that Novell will have already processed your certification, and it may be on its way to you. If Novell has not processed the paperwork yet, then you'll be able to inform them of your standings and they can start the process moving.

Make sure you're armed with all the information you need to talk intelligently with the Novell representative before you call. This includes your logs and the actual documentation. The more information that you can give the Novell representative, the faster and more accurately Novell can take care of your paperwork.

When you call into Novell certification administration, make sure you have a list of important telephone numbers, as well. For example, if you work for a company, make sure you have a fax number that Novell can use to send you any required information, if necessary.

## Victory—Getting Your Certificate

The day of victory is the day your certificate finally arrives in the mail. Your certificate will arrive in your *welcome aboard* kit from Novell. There's nothing like the feeling you get when you finally see the certificate you worked so long to get. However, before you rush right out to your next client and tell them about your new certification, spend a little time looking at your credentials. Make sure Novell filled in your name and other important information on your certificate correctly. You may want to write down some of the vital information, like your CNA, CNE, MCNE, NCIP, or CNI number, as well. You can provide this number to your clients or potential employers for verification purposes.

The welcome aboard kit contains many other items besides your certification certificate. These include your NSEPro (covered in Chap. 7) and some other paperwork. This paperwork includes a release form granting Novell permission to publish your name in the appropriate section of *Netwire*. Another form instructs you to send a passport-style photo of yourself to Novell. The photograph is placed on your ID badge, and it is sent back to you. Once you receive your ID badge, display it to your customers or employers as proof of certification. Chapter 6 tells you how to use your new badge when you want to work for someone else. Chapter 8 covers the use and purpose of the badge when you use it as a consultant.

You'll also want to take time to get your certification logo put on any brochures or sales literature. If you aren't a consultant or in the retail business, you may want to put your logo somewhere on your résumé. This may attract the attention of a future employer. You may also want to make some photo copies of the certificate and include it at the end of your résumé. It's important to let everyone know that you finally got your certification. After all, you shared your dreams of certification with them. They supported you throughout the courses, the long hours of studying, and the testing process. This includes not only telling your friends, family, and coworkers, but also framing your certificate and displaying it. Many companies and resellers will use your certification to add credibility to their organizations. This is an important part of making your certification work for you.

## Conclusion

You've learned a lot about the most dreaded part of any process in this chapter, the paperwork. Novell really does its best to make sure you don't have a lot to do, and most of the time these automated procedures work surprisingly well. The real purpose of this chapter is to help you through those times when the certification machinery doesn't work as well as it should. Keeping logs and making multiple copies of everything you do during the certification process may seem like a waste of time, but you'll find that these bits of information are invaluable when something goes wrong.

# CHAPTER 6
# Using Your Certification to Your Advantage

# Introduction

Have you ever seen someone who had all the advantages lose out to someone else because they didn't know how to use what they had? It happens all the time in the movies. We find ourselves cheering for the underdog as he or she overcomes the resources of some villain to win in the end. Of course, the movies don't truly reflect real life. In real life, the consequences of not using an advantage you may earn aren't nearly as entertaining—in fact, they're downright devastating. Imagine losing a job you really wanted to someone less qualified than you are simply because you didn't market your skills properly. Gaining access to a skill is only the first step in using it as a career-enhancing tool. You must learn to use the skill to your advantage in the marketplace.

As you can see, the trick to gaining the full benefit of your certification is in marketing those skills to a potential employer. This chapter helps you understand what you need to do to use the certification you acquire to your benefit. This particular chapter focuses on the individual working for someone else. We cover a number of topics from advancing in your current company to getting a new—and, hopefully, better—job based on that training. (See Chap. 8 for information on how consultants can use their Novell certification to good advantage in the marketplace.)

We cover two main methods of enhancing your career in this chapter. Either method will help you gain the full benefit of obtaining your certification, but they use entirely different approaches. The first section following covers the possibility of advancing within your own company. This is the route that will appeal to people who are happy with their current company. Many people are very happy with their jobs. If you fall into this category, there's absolutely no reason to move to a new company.

We do spend some time, however, talking about getting paid for what you can do for the company. This is a big problem for some people. They get a brand-new title and added responsibility, but very little recognition from the boss in the form of pay. Of course, it's always nice to be recognized for your contribution to a company, and a change in title can help you find a better job later, but it does little for you now. You have to make sure that the time you spend getting your certification is going to pay some dividend today. This subsection of the chapter shows you how to get this concession from management before you start the certification process.

There's a group of people, however, who only take a job for the short term until they can get something better. (In fact, some employers hire people knowing that they don't intend to stay.) Moving from one company to another can help you gain the recognition you need, in addition to improved company benefits. If you want to make a change from your current company, then it pays to follow the two-step plan outlined in the second section following. The first step is *preparing your résumé;* the second step is *making the best possible impression during an interview.*

## Advancing Within Your Current Company

There are a lot of ways to advance within your current company. For example, your boss may get promoted or leave for another company. If you demonstrate the abilities required to take over your boss' position, then your company may choose to promote you rather than hire someone from outside the company. Unfortunately, there isn't much chance that you'll get an opportunity like this in some companies.

Another method of advancing is to create your own position. Your company may want to get rid of an old method of doing something and replace it with a newer, more efficient method. If you provide your company with enough reasons to make the change, you may find yourself in charge of the group responsible for implementing the change. After the change is finished, you may find yourself in an entirely new position as head of the group. Some companies will simply change your job title to match the work that you're doing. In some cases this includes additional pay or other benefits.

These are just two ideas for advancing within your current company; a lot of other potential methods exist. Whatever method you choose to follow, you need to create an *advancement plan.* Don't wait for opportunity to knock, because it seldom does. Create your own opportunities within the workplace.

### Creating a Company-Based Strategy

The fact that your company chose to pay for your certification shows that there is an advancement opportunity waiting for you when you return. Even if your company already has a network and support staff in place, your training is part of some overall company goal. In some cases, the company will let you know about its vision of your future job before you begin training. This is simply a beginning, not the ultimate goal you should be trying to achieve. You need to combine company-based goals with a plan of attack of your own.

Your first goal in getting a promotion or new position is to find out all the reasons why you're getting trained (not just the ones that a manager is willing to part with immediately). Use this information as the basis for your advancement plan. You may find that you have to do a lot of detective work before you can work out an advancement plan. Management often treats new network installations or the departure of a manager as a closely guarded secret. Finding out your company's plans will help you prepare for the future by allowing you to see the overall picture. The following tips will help you form some advancement goals and strategies.

- If your company already has a network, try to find out if anyone from that section is leaving the company. You may find that you will eventually fill their position if you demonstrate the proper skill level. Make sure you concentrate on ways of enhancing these skills. If your company doesn't have a network in place, you can be sure they will. The company wouldn't train you for a position that won't exist. Try to become part of the planning process for the new network. Not only will the information you gain help you prepare for the new position, it'll show the company you have the dedication required for the position.

- There are situations where a CNE and a CNA may work together on a larger network. The CNA may provide training services in order to free the CNE to take care of the more technical network needs. If your company already has a training program in place, try to find out if it is expanding that training or if someone plans to leave the department. Make sure your training will sufficiently prepare you to take over the departing person's position. This includes training on all the applications they currently support. If your company doesn't currently have a program in place, you may become the founding member of such a group. It always pays to find out what the company plans before you get too far into the certification process. Your attitude has a lot to do with the way the company views your skills. This includes your attitude before, during, and after training.

- Check to see if your company is increasing the size of the network or installing a new network. If it is installing a new network, you may find that you were chosen to maintain it. An expanding network may show that you are at least in line for a title change.

- Find out if your company is creating a new workgroup. Some companies create splinter organizations when they want to introduce a new

# Using Your Certification to Your Advantage

product or when the current group becomes too large. If there are no plans to expand the current network, then your company may want to create such a splinter group. You may become the network administrator for the new workgroup.

- See if your company recently won a large contract. A company may create a small workgroup to deal with a specific contract. If so, your new position may only last the term of the contract. Figuring out ways to make this new position permanent is a very important consideration. You need to consider the longevity of any advancement or title change you get.

## New Status Recognition

Some employers won't recognize your new status unless you bring it to their attention. Even if a company pays for your training and recognizes that fact that you have new skills, they won't pay much attention to your new status as a certified professional. In some cases, this lack of attention is a mere oversight; in others it's actually part of a plan to get the services you can provide for little or no recognition. After all, why should a company pay for your new skills if you don't realize what you can provide? Having a certificate to hang on the wall, then, is really just part one of a longer process to gain the recognition you deserve.

There are also situations where you may find that your certification is more of a handicap than an asset. For example, you may find yourself doing twice the work for the same pay as before. A company may be so nearsighted as to expect you to maintain the network and still keep up with your old job as well. Take whatever steps you need to prevent this situation from happening. In most cases, your employer won't want to lose the investment in time and money that the company made to get you certified. You can use this as leverage when you try to correct these problem situations. The following list discusses some of the problems you may experience.

- In some cases, a company will help you get your certification and promise you the sun, the moon, and the stars until you achieve your goal. As soon as you get back to work, you find that instead of a promotion you got more work instead. Your company may feel perfectly justified in forcing you to perform all your previous tasks in addition to the new network administration tasks. Don't let this happen. If your company promises you anything to get your new certification, make sure you get the promises in writing. Verbal promises last only as long as you can hear the words.

- Some companies will ask you to sign a contract promising to work for them for a specific amount of time after you receive your certification. They may also ask you to sign a document promising to pay back the cost of certification (which could include company-paid time off to attend classes) if you fail to obtain it. Make sure you get some concessions from the company in exchange for these guarantees. Never give your company something for nothing. In many states, it's illegal to hold you to such a contract or to make you pay the employer back for education. Make sure you check local laws before you sign such a contract.

- You may find that the level of management cooperation drops drastically once you complete a network installation. Without the proper tools and support, you'll never maintain the network in peak operating condition. Make sure you talk to the company about these problems in advance. Don't make your new certification a source of problems.

## Advancement Through Promotion

Many people start at a particular company and stay there for their entire working careers. They wait for the person ahead of them to either get a promotion or leave the company. As new positions open, these people try to fill them before someone else does. This is a perfectly good way to advance your career. There are several different ways that you can enhance your chances of getting that new position based on your new certification and the longevity of your relationship with the company.

- You can demonstrate an extensive knowledge of the company's ways of doing things. This translates into a network administrator who is familiar with company policies. It means that you can do the job faster and more efficiently than someone hired from outside the company. You can also demonstrate how this knowledge will enhance specific network-related tasks, like security. One of the most common problems cited with networks right now is that the administrator is more interested in keeping the network running than keeping the data it manages secure.

- Longevity also translates into knowledge of the people working at the company. You probably have a better idea of who is working at the

# Using Your Certification to Your Advantage

company, how long they have worked there, what their job responsibilities are, and what you can do to help them. All of this knowledge means that you'll spend less time getting the network set up and maintaining it. It also means that you'll probably make fewer mistakes.

- The fact that you have held several positions in the same company means that you can better identify with problem areas within the company. This is especially important as companies move to the Internet or implement intranets. You have a greater understanding of why certain policies are in place and what each person needs to do their work since you have done their job in the past. Knowledge of how the company operates also translates into more informative Web sites with fewer security problems. Application specialists can also use their knowledge to set up training plans that will actually work, rather than build up resentment over broken schedules and interrupted meetings.

- The Novell certification you receive opens new doors of responsibility. Your past job performance will help you get an advancement based on positive proof that you can handle the added responsibility. Everyone in the company knows that you are capable of doing the job. They don't have to rely on secondhand information provided by someone you worked for in the past. Make sure you foster the idea that you're a known quantity when you present an advancement plan to management.

As you can see, the means of getting the promotion once a door of opportunity opens is there. Of course, simply because the door opens does not mean that management will put you in the new position. You must earn the new position. As a result, there are other things you need to do, as well. For one thing, you can't advance if you don't know where all the windows of opportunity exist. Figure 6-1 shows a typical company organization chart.

If you are Mary on the chart, the first thing you may think is that your next promotion opportunity is limited to Harvey's job. But, in reality, there are many other windows of opportunity just waiting for you. For example, as you help administer the network you'll find out about the tasks performed by Amy Hart or William Poe. You may even set your sights higher by trying for the position held by Sedrick Barlow. Of course, your ultimate goal might include the vice president's job. The important thing to remember is *the organization of your company*—look for opportunities to advance yourself. You may even want to take this

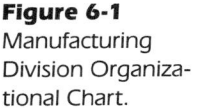

**Figure 6-1**
Manufacturing Division Organizational Chart.

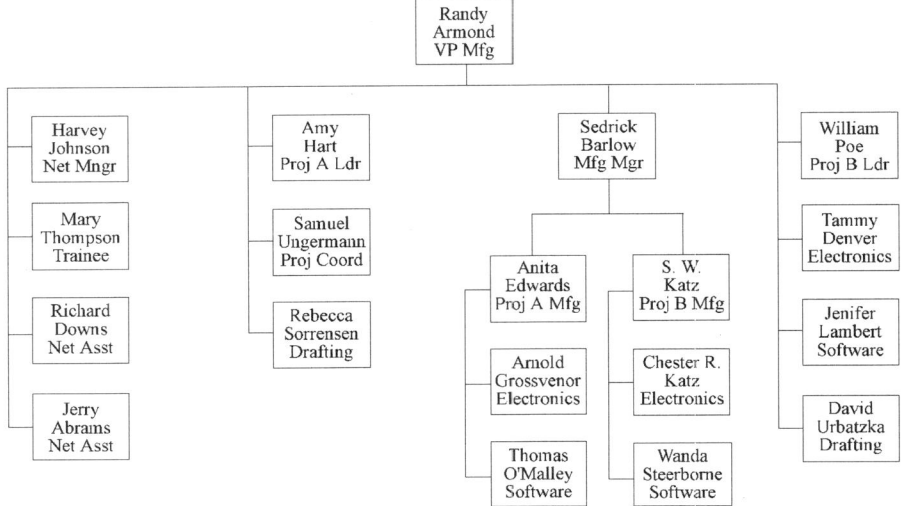

time to get a copy of your company's organizational chart (or make one of your own).

So how does this relate back to your certification? Remember that there are many ways to use your certification as a key to future promotions. Don't limit your thinking to a single area or to one possible means of using it. You can use the information you obtain from administering the network to prove your worth in other areas of the company, as well. Companies look for people who are willing to take charge, who show real involvement in their careers. They won't promote someone who simply does their work.

Now it's time to combine everything you learned from the preceding paragraphs into a plan of attack. Learning the various pieces of information we discussed should provide you with all you need to know to fill out the advancement form in Fig. 6-2. Note that this form is specially designed for those who want to use the advancement route to improve their position at the company.

The form begins with a little self-examination. It asks you to provide your current position and salary. This gives you a starting point; it shows where you are now. You need a starting point to see how much progress you've made toward your goal. It also provides a reality check as you set your future goals. Trying to reach president of the company in one step isn't very reasonable. Reaching for a management position from a technician's job is a little more obtainable.

The next two sections of the form provide spaces for two goals. These are positions you want to target as places for potential advancement.

# Using Your Certification to Your Advantage

**Figure 6-2**
Advancement through Promotion Worksheet.

---

**Advancement through Promotion Worksheet**

Date: _____ Current job title: _____

Current pay rate: _____ Target pay rate: _____


1st advancement goal: _____

Date of anticipated advance: _____

How will your networking experience help you attain your goal? _____
_____
_____

Experience needed to attain goal: _____
_____

Education needed to attain goal: _____
_____


2nd advancement goal: _____

Date of anticipated advance: _____

How will your networking experience help you attain your goal? _____
_____
_____

Experience needed to attain goal: _____
_____

Education needed to attain goal: _____
_____

---

Make sure you pick realistic goals or you'll find disappointment rather than advancement. Picking two goals is an essential part of the planning process; doing so encourages you to look for possible avenues of promotion in more than one area of the company. Make sure you pick goals that you really want to obtain—there aren't any good reasons to advance to a job that doesn't provide satisfaction in ways other than a pay raise. You'll also want to pick diverse goals—try to expand your horizons if possible.

Once you pick two goals, you need to define them. What is it about these positions that make them worthwhile, and what do you need to get them? There are four questions you need to answer in each goal-related section:

1. *Define the goal.* Make sure you include the title, potential pay, and any responsibility you would like to take on as part of the advancement.
2. *Relate your networking experience to the position you want to attain.* This serves as a reality check. It asks you to determine how you can use the experience you gain now to help in later promotions.
3. *Decide what other experience you need to gain to get to the next position.* This is an important consideration because it helps you see opportunities to gain the needed experience. For example, when the boss asks for volunteers for a project, it's really an opportunity to grab some experience.
4. *Determine what educational requirements the new position will require.* Management is interested in both knowledge and experience. Don't let someone fresh from college take your position from you. Make sure you prepare for both areas.

We have one final piece of advice for those who want to advance in their current company. You need to grab opportunities, because they seldom knock very loud. Look for opportunities to gain experience and show management that you are ready for a promotion. Always think about the possibilities; don't stoop to reactive attempts at advancement. The proactive approach always yields some result; the reactive approach always yields stagnation. Of course, you need to think about the consequences of your plan before you present it. A proactive approach can have negative as well as positive results. Make sure you find the opportunities that yield positive result.

## Advancement by Creating a New Position

Some people still possess the frontier spirit. They go where no one else will go and do the things that no one ever thought about doing. Inventors and scientists commonly fall into this category. This same set of skills can work to your benefit in the corporate environment, as well. Many people have made fortunes by inventing their own position and then showing management that the company can't survive without it. This is where the network administrator is today, especially if you plan to work with the Internet. You have an opportunity to break new ground, to create your own position. The network administrator is truly at the forefront of technology.

Of course, the network administrator doesn't always start with many benefits and may receive even less recognition. Sometimes a network administrator starts as a grunt laborer under someone who doesn't appear to understand what the company needs and has no desire to learn. Many CNEs end up working as computer repair personnel instead of spending much time with the network. CNAs are in an even worse position, because they have less training than a CNE does. They'll often end up trying to train other people and still maintain their old position. (Fortunately for NCIPs and MCNEs, your positions are relatively well defined and you shouldn't run into any problems from a job description perspective.)

Instead of forcing yourself to endure untold hardship under someone who cares little about what you do, turn the situation around. Look at this situation as an opportunity to create a new position. If you can show management that you can produce better results without your current boss standing over your head, you may find that you can create your own position. Management is almost always interested in hearing about ways to improve work flow, but picking a time when they're looking for ways to streamline the current setup usually produces the best results. Of course, the payment for failure to convince management of the benefits of the new position is dismissal in many cases. (Your old boss will never trust you again, at the very least.)

As you can see, this method of advancement involves taking risks, but the risks are worth it to someone prepared to take advantage of the results. Creating your own position means that you control how your job takes shape. It also means that your chances of being promoted to upper management are much better. If you prove that you're an idea person, someone capable of thinking on your own, management may sit up and take notice.

So how do you start planning for a new position? Everything requires planning. You must take time to create a proposal that demonstrates that the company needs the new position you want to create. More than that, you must demonstrate that you are the best candidate for the position. Just because you prove the company needs a new position doesn't mean that you'll get it. You must prove that you're the only person for the job, through both qualifications and in repayment to the company. Figure 6-3 shows a sample of what you can do to start the planning process.

There are several interesting features on this form. The first section states a starting and ending date to accomplish your goal. Make sure you enter both dates to give yourself a target to reach. It's easy to procrastinate when developing a plan of this sort; motivation in the form of a deadline really helps some people keep a project moving. Don't be afraid to change the ending date, if necessary; you'll want to prepare the best presentation possible. The important thing to remember is that *you need to*

**Figure 6-3**
A Sample Plan for Creating Your Own Position.

---

**New Position Worksheet**

Current date: _____ Planned presentation date: _____

New position title: _____

Reason the new position is important: _____
_____
_____
_____
_____

Cost of creating the position: _____

Potential cost benefit: _____ Payback time: _____

Intangible benefits: _____
_____
_____

Reasons you should take the new position: _____
_____
_____
_____

❑ Cost analysis ❑ Full presentation
❑ Time analysis ❑ Handouts
❑ Benefits analysis ❑ Graphs and charts
❑ Requirements for the position ❑ Presentation scheduled

---

*maintain a sense of balance.* Get the proposal finished as quickly and as well as possible.

Don't think that your presentation will come together flawlessly, though, no matter how much time you spend on it. You can always count on one thing, no matter how well you prepare for your presentation—someone in management will ask the one question that you didn't think about. The bottom line is that you have to prepare for the unexpected and remain flexible throughout the presentation. Make the best possible preparations, but don't put your presentation on hold in an attempt to figure out every potential answer in advance. That's why two dates are absolutely essential—give yourself a deadline that you can actually meet, and then give the presentation even if you don't feel you're quite ready.

The next section covers the position itself. It's very important to define a potential title name, explain why the position is important, conceptualize any potential costs and problems associated with creating the posi-

# Using Your Certification to Your Advantage

tion, and provide management with a projected payback period for their investment. Make sure you list both tangible and intangible benefits. In most cases, you'll want to create a position that provides a payback in both areas to the company. This doesn't mean that management never considers a new position that provides only intangible benefits. However, you'll likely find your job on the chopping block at the first sign of economic troubles if you take this approach. It's always better to show the company management that you can make some money for them.

The third section states why you're the person to fill this position. Write these reasons down and back them up with good arguments. Make sure you demonstrate beyond a shadow of a doubt that you're the person to fill the position. Of course, it helps that you are the person defining the new position. You can modify the job definition as required to make yourself the only person who can fill the position. This process of give and take provides another reality check. Once you do get to the point where you completely define the job and your reason for filling it, make sure the job still makes sense. Otherwise, you may find that management won't even talk to you about it. Don't try to create a position whose sole advantage is a promotion for you.

The final area is a checklist of items you need to complete before you make your presentation. Each of these items will help you present your ideas in a way that management can quickly understand. The idea here is to present the information completely in the shortest amount of time possible. Management will give you more time if they have questions once your presentation is over, but you need to get them interested before you'll get a second meeting to fully explain your proposed position. Here are the details for each of the check boxes in Fig. 6-3:

- *Cost analysis.* You'll want to create a full cost analysis showing exactly what it will cost the company to create the new position that you propose. At the very least, it'll cost the company a pay raise. (Hopefully, you aren't going through all this work for the sheer gratification of doing the work.) Make sure you look for hidden costs as well. Consider items like additional staff and equipment. Make sure you show how the company can amortize this investment over a period of time. Any friends you have in accounting can probably help you in this area.

- *Time analysis.* At a minimum, you need to create a milestone chart with goals that you expect to meet by specific dates. Some of the more advanced project management programs could help you in this regard. You might find a computer with one of these programs in the engineering or manufacturing area of your company. Ask the supervisor if you can use the program. (You may need to come in after working hours to perform this work.) Of course, you could even use a standard drawing program to create the charts you need, but the project management software will help you look for potential scheduling conflicts. The project management software will also make it easy to incorporate changes to your plan.

- *Benefits analysis.* This is one of the most important parts of your presentation. Management tends to focus on the negative elements of any form of change: the cost of making it and the cost of maintaining the change afterward. You need to focus their attention on the positive elements of what they'll obtain from the change. Make sure you look at the company's interests when you write the list of benefits, not at the elements that are attractive to you. For example, while you may find the increased responsibility interesting, management won't. However, they'll find increased revenues or other company-related benefits interesting. One common way for network personnel to make their case is to show that the new position will make the company more efficient. A more efficient operation usually spells lower operating costs and higher income.

- *Requirements for the position.* This entry accomplishes two purposes. First, it defines the position and shows management that you took the time to think this idea through. It also helps you define your position later. One of the reasons that some new position ideas fail is that they're ill-defined at the very start. Some people actually make their jobs more difficult by not defining what they mean at the start of a project. This leaves the door for interpretation open. Second, you can use the requirements as part of your arguments later. For example, you can use the requirements to show management that you're the only person who can perform the job adequately. Make all the pieces of your presentation fit together into a well-coordinated plan.

- *Full presentation.* Include slides, graphs, charts, handouts, and anything else you can think of to make the presentation interesting for management. Remember that you're trying to sell an idea that many of them will want to resist. This isn't a situation where you're starting with an open-minded audience—you have to open their minds to the potential benefits of the new position.

- *Handouts.* A good handout really helps keep people interested if you use it correctly. There are several rules you need to observe during the presentation. For example, have someone help you with this element

# Using Your Certification to Your Advantage

of your presentation. Don't make the mistake of providing management with all your handouts at once. Give them out as management needs to look at them. Otherwise, you may find that you'll lose your audience to the handouts that were supposed to keep them interested in your presentation. The people you gave the handouts to will skim through them trying to find the bottom line and won't get the full picture that you're presenting to them. You should also refer to your handouts frequently during the presentation. Otherwise, management will wonder why you took the time to prepare them.

- *Graphs and charts.* This is an extremely important part of your presentation. Studies show that people can absorb information in graphic form much better and faster than they can in printed form. The printed material is abstract; the graphic form is a lot more concrete. Rather than burden management with a lot of tabular data, present it in graphic form and offer to allow them to see the tables later. Make sure you make the actual data available, but keep your presentation interesting by using graphics.

- *Presentation scheduled.* Make sure you get a specific date from management. A common problem that people face is that management will use the excuse that they want to see your presentation "sometime soon." They keep putting the presentation off until (hopefully) you forget about showing it to them. To get their approval you may need to tell them about some aspects of your idea. Make sure you don't tell them everything; keep some surprises for the meeting itself. Get management as excited as you are about this new position. Schedule a conference room for the meeting. Avoid presenting your idea in someone's office. Reduce the chances of political posturing by holding the meeting in a neutral setting. This helps alleviate the problem of trying to answer questions from someone who only asks them to increase his or her political stature in the company. In addition, holding the meeting in a conference room reduces the risk of interruptions such as phone calls and other people walking in. Get everything ready for the meeting well in advance. Don't wait until the last minute.

As you can see, creating a successful presentation is a challenge in many ways. You need to do a lot of preparation before you'll be able to present your idea to management. Take the time to research your company thoroughly. Make sure you can tell management everything they'll need to know about your idea. Show them you did your homework—that you're interested enough in the company to devote the time required to find out about it. You may want to spend some time viewing presentations made by other people in your company, as well. Notice the ideas and presentation methods that seem to attract the attention of key management personnel. These are the methods that usually guarantee some measure of success when you make your presentation. Make sure you write these ideas down to use in your presentation, as well.

Of course, there are several ways you can use your certification to attain these goals. For one thing, as network administrator you will meet many of the people you need to influence. This personal contact can make the difference between getting the new position approved and looking for a new job. Make sure you take the personalities of the individual members of management into account as you prepare your presentation.

You can also use your position to obtain information about the company and its operations. As network administrator you'll gain access to many areas of the company that many other people may not see. You'll see the broad view of all the jobs that people in the company perform. Your position will expose you to all the products that the company makes and give you inside information about how those products could be improved. The possibilities for gaining knowledge are almost unlimited.

Finally, your position as network administrator will give you a unique view of both management and the employees. You can use this view to provide unique insights as you present your idea to management. Present some of the employee needs from a management viewpoint during your presentation.

## Recognition Through Title Change

Everything that we've told you about so far assumes that you want to advance in some way—perhaps even move into a management position in the company. What if you're happy working at your current position and don't really want the added responsibility that a promotion brings? This isn't necessarily a bad idea. Someone has to fill these positions and if you're happy working where you are, a management post may not provide the type of work environment that you want.

Of course, you should still get some form of recognition for your achievement. After all, you did go through all the effort required to get your certification and you want management to recognize that achievement. One of the best ways to get recognition is to provide management with a reason to change your title. You'll work for the same boss at the same pay doing about the same work, but the title change will show that you have made some type of change in your qualifications. So what good is a title change?

# Using Your Certification to Your Advantage

It'll make a big difference if you ever leave your current company. The title change shows a potential employer that you made some type of effort to get a promotion, even if it didn't result in a pay raise. Of course, a title change could lead to some additional pay as well. You may not receive it right away; it may come during your annual review instead.

So what do you do to get this title change? First, you could simply schedule a meeting with your boss and ask for the change. You might be surprised to find that your boss will help you get the title change with no additional effort on your part. (You may have to shuffle some paperwork, but this is really a very minor consideration.) A title change on your part reflects favorably on your boss. It shows that he or she is doing the job by helping each employee under his or her control provide a greater contribution to the company as a whole. You may even want to remind your boss of this fact. It never hurts to show bosses that you have their welfare in mind, too.

If this first approach doesn't work, put your request in writing. Make sure you state some reasons why the title change is so important. This will give your boss an incentive to tell you why he or she won't consider a title change. It'll also provide your boss with something to pass up to his or her superior. The reason that your boss didn't provide the title change could involve a lack of authority to do so. The following list provides some ideas on arguments you can use to get a title change.

- Since your job tasks have changed since you got your Novell certification, why not a title change to go along with the increased responsibility? Changes in job tasks should show up in your job title as well. An MCNE will want to pursue this route because their certification usually involves some type of change to a managerial level job. You could even argue that the job title change will help show that the company got value for the money it invested in your training.

- A new job title will help distinguish between the tasks you perform and those performed by other employees with the same title. This is especially important for government contractors since the government usually looks to see that they have enough personnel to do the job in a given category before granting the contract. MCNEs will want to point out that government representatives usually want to deal with someone in a management position. Of course, this also reflects well on other companies, especially when it comes time to impress visiting dignitaries.

- The new job title is a lot less expensive than a raise. (Of course, you can always argue later that your new title entitles you to a pay raise.)

CNAs will want to look at this option since their certification usually entails an additional responsibility rather than an entirely new job.

- The new job title could potentially add to the company's prestige by showing they have an up-to-date networking system specialist, an especially important consideration now that the Internet is such a big part of the company environment. You would need to add some arguments that would show whom this would affect. It may help to show how this new job title could help the company gain new contracts. An NCIP will probably want to get their title changed to Webmaster (the standard title for someone who manages a Web site).

- Providing you with a new job title could enhance the way management views your boss' position. It would show that he or she has a wider area of responsibility than before. This particular argument appeals to the boss' vanity, but it pays to use whatever will work.

Of course, these are just a few of the arguments you could use to convince your boss to grant you a new job title. The important factor is that you deserve the new title. If your current title is administrative assistant, it hardly reflects your new position as a network administrator, training specialist, or Webmaster. Even if you perform this job on a part-time basis, your job title should reflect your change in status.

There are several ways that a job title change can help you in the future, even if it doesn't appear to help you today. First, if you do decide to go to another company, the title change will appear to be a promotion. There is no way that your future employer will know that you didn't receive any additional benefits for the change in title unless you tell them. Second, it could help you get better raises in your current company. If you demonstrate an increased level of knowledge, then many companies are willing to pay for that increased knowledge. The only problem is that upper management will never know that your status has changed unless you get it down on paper somewhere. The change in title is one of the most efficient and most noticeable methods of doing so.

There are a few certification-specific title change issues to consider, as well. What happens if you are already a CNE and work as a network administrator? In some companies, that is all you'll ever need. However, a large company may need more than one network administrator. You may end up as one of many CNEs on staff. So, where do you go from there? The MCNE program allows people who work in larger companies to advance to higher positions. Rather than act as one of several network administrators in a large company, getting some additional education and the MCNE certification will allow you to become a supervisor. Just look at other areas of

# Using Your Certification to Your Advantage

your company. It takes more than just political power and astute powers of observation to create or advance to a supervisory position. You have to prove you are the right person for the job. Other managers in your company probably got their positions because they have a college degree and have proved their ability to get the job done. You need to do the same thing. Having the right certification (in other words, physical evidence of your knowledge) and job experience are the keys to getting to the managerial level in many large companies. Once you get this additional level of training and recognition, it is absolutely essential that you get the title change to go with it. Otherwise, you'll end up with an MCNE certification that doesn't really help you reach a goal that advances your career.

The same holds true for a CNA. What happens when you no longer want to work as an administrative assistant? If you took the first step of getting a title change when you got your CNA certification, then it'll be a lot easier to show management that they need to support you in your attempt to get a CNE certification. (This is especially important for growing companies where a CNA may meet their needs to begin with, but the company grows to the point where they really need a CNE to manage the network.) Once you get your CNE certification, it's very important to get another title change, one that shows you have obtained a higher level of knowledge. (You'll probably need to talk about a new position at this point, since it is unlikely you'll perform any administrative tasks after getting your CNE certification.)

Getting a title change may not seem very exciting. In fact, it may seem as if you have accomplished nothing at all. Of course, nothing's further from the truth. A title change may not dramatically affect your career today, but it could help a great deal in the future. Even if you don't want to get into management in your current company, it's very important that you gain the recognition you deserve for getting your Novell certification.

## Getting Paid for What You Do

The matter of how much of an increase in pay you can expect from a promotion or new position is always a touchy subject. There are no hard and fast rules, and the policy in your company and the effects of the local economy make things even harder. Someone who gets a 15 percent raise in pay in Wisconsin may get only a 3 percent increase in Texas. There are some general things you can do to get an idea of what kind of increase you should expect. The following tips provide guidelines, but you'll need to tailor them to your specific situation.

- *Check around the company for clues.* Some people will tell you what type of raise they got when going to a new position. However, some companies will fire someone for even talking about their salary, so this may not be an option. Don't expect to go to the personnel department and ask about salary ranges in the company; they won't provide you with the information.

- *Talk to someone at your local Chamber of Commerce.* They track all kinds of business statistics, including pay-raise rates. You may even find that they can provide you with an approximate range of pay for your type of position. If you can't get this information at the Chamber of Commerce in your town, then go to the nearest large city and try to find the information there.

- *Just about every large community has a local business magazine.* You won't see it on your newsstand, but you may see it in the lobby or other public areas. Take time to look through the magazine. Many of them provide current trends in business for your area.

- *Read the business section of your local newspaper.* This will give you some economic information for your area. It may also contain news about your company or other information you can use.

- *Listen to the radio.* I was surprised when a local radio station revealed that the average pay raise in my area was running at 3 percent. Few radio stations will provide you with everything you need to know, but many will provide you with some clues.

- *Talk to people in your local users' group.* If you don't belong to a users' group, then join one. The people in your users' group work in the same area as you do. Just find someone who performs the same work as you do and talk to them. What could be easier? Make sure you ask them how long they've worked in that area of expertise and take this into consideration when you look for a promotion.

There are a few absolutes that you should expect when it comes to pay. You'll always receive a salary instead of an hourly rate when working as a network administrator. The reason you get a salary is simple: No company in its right mind will pay you for the extra hours required when working these types of jobs. The same thing holds true for Webmasters or network managers; both positions require a lot of extracurricular activity. A CNA who works as a training specialist may be able to get an hourly rate in some circumstances, but don't count on it.

You absolutely will not get the same amount of pay as a consultant doing the same work. There are a few reasons for this. First, your company pro-

# Using Your Certification to Your Advantage

vides benefits like health insurance that a consultant doesn't receive. Second, the consultant pays business taxes and other expenses out of the money he or she earns that you don't need to consider. Don't forget that your employer pays half your social security tax, a benefit that the consultant doesn't get. However, you can use the local consultants' fee as a point of reference for your pay. In most cases, an employee will earn 25 to 33 percent of the fee charged by a consultant in the same area. Call at least three consultants in your area, average their hourly rates, multiply by 25 percent, and then multiply by 40 hours to get your new weekly pay (or 160 hours to get your monthly pay). The differential between this weekly pay rate and your current pay rate probably reflects the pay raise you should expect. Remember that this is only an estimate, not a hard and fast reality.

## Moving to a Different Company

Some people work at a company to gain experience and a specific level of education, then move to another company. The reason for this strategy is quite simple—you can advance a lot faster using this technique than you can by staying at your current company. Of course, you give up quite a bit to use this strategy. For example, many companies won't provide you with any kind of retirement unless you stay there for a specific number of years (anywhere from 10 to 20 years). There are other benefits that companies offer, as well. For example, in some companies you share in the stock program after you work there for five years. If you move from company to company in pursuit of a better position, you may never meet this requirement.

Once you weigh the consequences of moving around and decide that you want to improve your position more than you want to gain these other benefits, you need to consider how to present yourself to a potential employer. This includes both a written and a verbal presentation. Of course, the written presentation is commonly called a *résumé,* while the verbal presentation is called an *interview.* The following subsections show you how to leverage your Novell certification as part of both processes.

### Getting Your Résumé Together

Any good book on business writing or communication will show you how to write a stock résumé and cover letter. That isn't the purpose of this section. What you need to know is how to modify these stock presentations to emphasize your qualifications. The following tips point out several ideas you need to present in these written forms of communication.

- If you're currently a network administrator, place your experience first on the résumé. Make sure you provide detailed information on your network-related jobs. Provide one or two sentence summaries of other jobs.
- If you recently passed your CNA, CNE, MCNE, or NCIP certification tests, place your education first. Emphasize the fact that you passed your certification test. Don't be afraid to use bold type for this credential to make it stand out from any others you may have. Add a date of certification to show that you are current.
- MCNE certification holders will want to emphasize their CNE-level experience as well as their education. It's vital to show a potential employer that you did not move from one certification to the next without getting the proper experience at the CNE level first.
- Place a reference to your certification in the first sentence of the cover letter. Many managers don't read past this point before both letter and résumé end up in the circular file.
- Always add your logo to both the cover letter and the résumé. This will make them stick out from other stock input. Use a half-inch square logo.

Now that you have some ideas on what to include in your letter and how to present it to an employer, it's time to look at an example. Figure 6-4 provides you with an example cover letter.

As you can see, this letter uses the Novell certification label in the lower left corner. This helps to differentiate the letter from others that the employer may look at. Note that there's a lot of white space—the letter doesn't look cramped or difficult to read. Make your letter as inviting to read as possible. The letter also contains the names and addresses of both parties; this is for your benefit as well of that of your future employer. The first paragraph tells your future employer how you meet the qualifications set by the advertisement. It also tells them where you saw the advertisement. The second paragraph tells the employer why they should consider you before someone else. This is an important part of the cover letter. You have to gain the interest of the person reading the letter or they'll never read your résumé.

We also mentioned the things you should do to modify a stock résumé to emphasize your certification. Let's look at an example or two of a modified

**Figure 6-4**
Example Cover Letter.

John Mueller
2020 Twin Palms Street
River City, CA 92104-3703
(619)881-7732 Business
(619)881-7733 FAX

25 February, 1997

Mary Jones
Engineering Manager
The Industrial Place
3288 The Place Street
Somewhere, CA 92112

Dear Ms. Jones

I recently saw your advertisement for a CNE in the California Job Times. According to the ad, you need someone with a minimum of two years experience and proof of certification. As you can see from the attached resume, I can meet both qualifications. I worked two years at Jobber Industrial and three years at Technical Stuff, Inc. I can provide my certification papers to you on request. (There is a copy of the certification attached to the back of the resume.)

The important consideration for you is that both of my former employers produced about the same products as your company does. In addition, according to your annual report, the corporate structure of all three companies is similar. These similarities mean that you will spend less time training me to fill the position at your company. Hopefully, these qualifications will allow you to consider my application in preference to others who applied.

Sincerely,

*John Paul Mueller*

John Paul Mueller

stock résumé. Figure 6-5 provides you with an example of an experience-based résumé. Figure 6-6 provides you with an example of an education-based résumé. Note that each résumé provides a different view of the information. This flexibility helps you tailor your résumé to the employer's needs.

**Figure 6-5**
Example Experience-Based Résumé.

**John Mueller**
**2020 Twin Palms Street**
**River City, Ca. 92104**
**Home Phone: (619) 775-2123**

**EXPERIENCE:**
**Network Administrator, Technical Stuff, Inc.**
**(July 1990 - August 1993)**
In charge of two assistants at Technical Stuff, Inc. The combination Ethernet and token ring LAN supports 150 users and 4 file servers. There are eight print servers attached to the network as well. Most of the print servers had two printers attached, one HP Laserjet III and a high speed dot matrix. All maintenance scheduling went through my office. In addition, I supervised the installation of a new DBMS (database management system) on one of the file servers.

**Assistant Network Administrator, Jobber Industrial**
**(January 1988 - July 1990)**
Assist the LAN Administrator in maintaining the company LAN (local area network). The LAN supports 40 users and 3 file servers. There are four print servers attached to the network as well. Part of my LAN responsibilities include installing and maintaining Windows. I also performed much of the hardware maintenance.

**Sonar Technician, US Navy (July 1976 - September 1987)**
Maintained computer controlled sonar and fire control equipment. This equipment ranged from tube-based technology, to solid state discrete circuitry, to modern CMOS circuitry. Learned to operate and maintain every type of data storage device available today. Most equipment was hybrid digital and analog circuitry.

Designed and was paid for a design change to audio recording equipment. Change decreased recording reproduction time by a factor of four, reducing the per recording cost to the government for a training tape.

**Figure 6-5**
(*Continued*).

Operated sonar equipment which included acoustic signal analysis equipment. Supervised work center personnel. Wrote six-part training course using tapes and training books.

**EDUCATION:**

Technical Diploma in Electrical Trade, Milwaukee Technical High School, June 1976

Various Military Electronic Equipment Maintenance Courses:
- Basic Electronics and Electricity
- Sonar Specific Advanced Electronics
- Acoustic Analysis Schooling
- Fire Control System Maintenance/Operation Schooling
- Computer Controlled Sonar Maintenance/Operation Schooling
- Other Peripheral Equipment Maintenance Schooling

Bachelors in Computer Science, National University, June 1986

Artificial Intelligence Programming Course, Cubic Corporation, October 1986

Certified Netware Engineer Courses, VITEK Corporation, April 1991

**COMPUTER LANGUAGES:**
- Pascal - IBM PC knowledge only
- BASIC - IBM PC and Perkin-Elmer mainframe experience (Includes various Windows 3.1 dialects like Access BASIC and Visual BASIC)
- Assembler - IBM PC (DOS, OS/2, and Windows NT environments), Macintosh, and various military computers
- dBase III (Clipper, Force, and FoxPro) - IBM PC
- Prolog - Learning stages, IBM PC knowledge only
- Machine Code (Hex) - IBM PC, Macintosh, and various military computers
- C - IBM PC (DOS, OS/2, and Windows NT environments)

**Figure 6-6**
Example Education-Based Résumé.

**Robert Williams**
**9845 Harbor Road Suite 22**
**Some Region, CA 92112**
**(619)234-7890**

**CERTIFICATIONS:**

1991    LanAlyzer Basic and Advanced for Ethernet
Network Technologies
Novell 3.11 Advanced System Manager

1990    Novell Certified Instructor (CNI) Category I & II:
Novell Certified to teach 286 System Manager
Update & Advance features
386 OS/Features and Review
386 System Supervisor
Service & Support
Novell Enhanced Support Training
Introduction to Data Communications

1989    Novell Certified Engineer (CNE)

**EDUCATION:**

1989    Novell Authorized Education.
System Manager
Update & Advanced Features
Service & Support
Diagnostics & Trouble Shooting
Introduction to Data Communications
Novell Enhanced Support Training
Novell 386 Training

1987    Mt. San Antonio College, Walnut, Ca.
Construction Estimating
Elements of Construction
4.0 G.P.A.

1977    Citrus College, Azusa, Ca.
Industrial Engineering Technology
3.8 G.P.A.

**Figure 6-6**
(*Continued*).

> **EXPERIENCE:**
> **Very Impressive Systems, Hard Rock, Ca. (1989 - Present)**
> Novell Authorized Distributor, Novell Authorized Education Center, Distribution center for major brands of computer equipment.
>
> Novell Certified Instructor: Duties include: Education of Resellers and end users in the use of the Novell Operating System. The classes include 286 system mgr., Update & Advanced Features, 386 OS/Features and Review, 386 System Supervisor, Service & Support, Introduction to Data Communications, Novell Enhanced Support Training, Basic and Intermediate DOS, Hardware Basics.
>
> Other Duties include: Operate and maintain the Education Facility in San Diego, Ca.
>
> **Great West Computers, Hard Rock, Ca. (1989 - 1989)**
> Novell Authorized Reseller, Novell Authorized Education Center, Network Installations, Technical Support.
>
> SERVICE AND SUPPORT TECHNICIAN: Duties include: Technical Support for customers, Education of customers on the use of the Novell Operating System, Network sales.
>
>

The first résumé uses a lot of white space and bold lettering to draw the reader's attention to particular areas of the document. This helps the manager read the highlights of your résumé quickly, then concentrate on any important areas. The résumé is slightly over one page long, but all the information relates to the position offered by the company. The author mentions network experience twice in the experience section and once in the education section. There's a special computer languages section that draws the manager's attention to the special qualifications of this candidate. Note that this special qualification is mentioned in the experience and education areas as well. The résumé writer does a good job of relating the special qualification back to networking in the first paragraph of the résumé. (Knowing computer languages is a good asset for network administrators who need to administer large database management systems.) The writer also spells out each acronym the first time it appears in the document. This is an important part of writing the résumé.

The second résumé looks somewhat the same as the first one. It uses the same amount of white space and the same bold lettering. However, this résumé places education first. Note that the certifications appear in an entire category by themselves. This tells the reader that the certifications are something of great value that you have to offer. The rest of the educational skills appear second to these all-important job skills. Note that the job information in this case is very short and concise. The emphasis here is on education supported by experience, not the other way around.

As you can see, modifying a stock letter and résumé is essential if you want to use your certification to your advantage when getting a new job. It is the content of that résumé that makes the difference. You get two pages—one for the résumé and another for the cover letter—to convince someone to hire you. It's your job to use those pages to good effect.

## Emphasizing Your Qualifications During an Interview

Everyone knows the basics of going in for an interview. You're supposed to get dressed up and present a clean appearance. Of course, breath mints and a good attitude are important too. All these things are just a part of any interview. However, there are several things you can do to enhance your interview by leveraging your Novell certification. The following list provides you with some ideas on how to do this.

- Many Novell certificate holders receive lapel pins. Make sure you wear this pin on your lapel during the interview. It serves to reinforce your qualifications every time your potential employer looks at you and sees it.
- Take your badge along with you. Your employer may ask you to present proof of your certification.
- Prepare a listing of the hardware you worked on in the past. You can use this information during the interview.
- Create a list of questions you want to ask the employer. Every employer asks if you have questions during a successful interview. Make sure your questions are based on your knowledge of the company and what it does. This is your opportunity to impress the employer with your knowledge of their company.
- The interview is a two-way street. They are not only interviewing you—you're interviewing the company, as well. You need to make sure that this is the company that you want to invest your time and effort

# Using Your Certification to Your Advantage

into. Just because you conducted some preliminary research on the company doesn't mean it is a good company to work for. The only time you find out this information is during your conversation with your prospective boss. The company must also pass your interview.

- During the interview, make sure that you maintain eye contact with the person giving the interview, speak clearly, and portray confidence in yourself. If asked a question that you do not know the answer to, do not make one up. It's better to say that you don't know the answer than to lie to them; it shows honesty. You can usually avoid looking like a dunce when this happens by showing interest in the topic. Use the occasion to feed your potential boss' ego. Phrases like, "I didn't know that!" go a long way toward making the interview a success. Make sure you show an interest in what the boss knows and what the company needs rather than irritation at not knowing the answer to a question.

## Talking About a Rate of Pay

How much should you be paid for your qualifications? That's a tough question for a lot of reasons. Your past work greatly affects how people view your certification. Someone who has managerial experience in addition to their certification should expect to receive a better job than someone who only has the certification. Likewise, someone with a computer-related degree will receive more than someone who does not possess this credential. The following tips should help you determine what type of pay increase you should expect.

- Always use a point of reference based on fact to compute your new rate of pay. You need to know that a change of company is worth the effort. One point of reference that you can use is any proposed pay increase your current company offers. You can also talk to people at a local users' group to find out what other companies pay for similar work. Finally, you can check statistical information contained in business magazines or other sources.

- Try to get a pay increase equal to at least twice the current average pay raise rate in your area if your new job title is about the same or only one level higher than your old one. For example, suppose the newspaper in your area states that the average pay raise in your area is 5 percent and you currently make $30,000 a year. Simply multiply the rate by 2, then add that percentage to your current pay. In this case you should expect a pay increase of at least $3000 a year, or a salary of $33,000.

- Make sure your new company recognizes any supplemental capabilities you can provide. For example, if you have a degree in computer science, then there is a good chance you can perform some programming tasks in addition to your network responsibilities. A network administrator who also has training experience can provide a lot more than simple user assistance. Your new company will try to make use of these capabilities, so you should get paid for them.

- Be sure you consider any benefits your new company offers that your old company doesn't. For example, your new company may offer a dental plan when your old company didn't. This is a benefit you can use even as a short-term employee. On the other hand, a stock option benefit may not be worth much if you don't plan to stay with the company. You also need to ensure that the new benefit is tangible. Use the value of these new benefits to you as part of the basis for the level of pay increase that you're willing to accept.

Of course, these tips merely help you home in on a rate of pay. Here are some absolutes you need to consider. First, you always have to get more for a transfer to a new job than a promotion at your current company. There are a few simple reasons for this, but most of them have to do with a loss of benefits. Companies don't provide very many benefits to short-term employees. If your current company offers you a promotion, double the amount of pay increase (not the pay itself) and add it to your current salary. This is what you need to receive from your new company to make the move worthwhile.

The second absolute is that no one ever got a pay increase for doing the same job at a new company. If you're a network training specialist with the current title of administrative assistant, then you should look for some type of network-related title in the new company that emphasizes your training skills. Your old title doesn't match your new job and you won't get the pay raise you deserve using that old title. The same holds true for other types of network specialties. If you previously had a title of maintenance technician, look for a new title of network administrator or assistant network administrator.

## Conclusion

There are two ways to improve your position using your new certification. You can stay at your current company and get a pay raise or other tangible benefit, or you can move to a new company. Whatever course of action you pursue, the most important thing you need to do once you have your certification is to get some recognition. Your certification is important to you and it should be important enough to the people you work for that they'll give you some additional recognition.

If you can't get the recognition you deserve, it may be time to go out on your own. Chapter 8 provides invaluable information for starting your own business as a consultant. You may want to read this chapter even if you don't plan to make such a big move right now.

The next chapter looks at continuing education requirements. Everyone needs to keep their tools sharp and ready for use. The same holds true of the intellectual skills that you learned for the certification exams. Following the advice in Chap. 7 can play a big role in helping you maintain that edge.

CHAPTER 7

# Planning for Continuing Education Requirements

## Introduction

You've finally made it! The certification level that you worked so hard for is finally yours! Take some time to feel good about yourself and your accomplishment. After all, you've worked hard for it and you deserve it. Once you've had time to reflect, it's time to think about and plan for what it'll take to maintain your precious certification. The bottom line is that Novell can revoke your certification if you don't meet the continuing education requirements. However, even if you meet the continuing education requirements, there are other real-world requirements you'll need to meet, as well. In other words, you'll need to think about two levels of education.

The continuing education requirements that Novell will ask you to meet aren't difficult. Don't worry about getting a letter every other month with additional education requirements designed to squeeze more money out of you. Novell only asks you to recertify if there's a major change in networking technology. In other words, you only have to get additional training when there's a new product to work with—which is quite reasonable, if you're a networking professional. You're Novell's best representative and sales person since you're the one on the front line with the customer. If your knowledge of the product isn't current, or is inaccurate, Novell's credibility, as well as yours, may be in question. The last thing you want is to have customers think that your skills aren't what they expected. If customers aren't comfortable with Novell's reputation or yours, they'll most likely take their business elsewhere. What this means to you is a loss of sales, resulting in lost income to you and to Novell.

Planning for continuing education doesn't stop at what Novell requires of you. This only skims the surface of what you need to know in the real world to conduct business. For example, if you're a consultant, Novell won't test your ability to train someone how to use Microsoft Word or how well you present yourself to a client. Even if you work in a company setting, you'll need to keep abreast of current industry trends, like moving to the Internet and the use of new hardware. Novell won't ever ask how much you know about network computers, but your company or client will most certainly do so. In every respect, your Novell certification is like the main course, but a meal usually has an appetizer and dessert included as well.

In this chapter we discuss what you'll need to do to maintain your Novell certification in the real world. Since the education process doesn't

# Planning for Continuing Education Requirements

stop with the Novell training, we'll also cover topics that help you to remain current in the networking market. These additional topics will include where to find this valuable information about networking. The ideas in this chapter are certainly only a beginning—as you gain experience and accumulate time in the networking business, you'll find additional sources of information that meet your particular needs.

## Looking for More Information

The real expert in this business, be it the system administrator, consultant, analyst, Webmaster, or instructor, always has a desire for more information. It's like an obsession. The more information and knowledge that you have, the more you want. This is probably the only industry where the more you learn about a topic, the more you find that you need to learn. It's also the only industry where technology changes and advances so fast that the trade journals have a hard time keeping up.

The key to staying current is finding the information that relates to your situation. We're living in the information age, and there's more than enough to go around. In fact, there may actually be too much to go around—the problem that faces most of us is *information overload*. The faster you read the information, the faster it seems to arrive. Every vendor wants you to know about his or her great new product. Every magazine says that it's the key resource you need to improve your business. The way to control information overload is to know where your interests lie. For example, if you're a consultant, then you need to look at what your clients are doing. (Consultants have the worst time fighting information overload because they're normally working with multiple clients with diverse interests.)

### Filtering Your Input

One key to remembering more of the information you gather is to focus on the topics that interest you. For example, suppose you're a systems administrator of a small firm with 10 to 12 users and you're using Novell NetWare 3.1 with no access or connections to a mainframe computer. Unless you're personally interested in mainframe computers and may someday need this information, spend your time gathering information about products and techniques related to smaller local area networks (LANs). Think of this process as filtering—you're eliminating everything you don't need so that you can spend more time learning what you do need.

This doesn't mean that all the other information sent your way isn't important or worthwhile, because it is. For example, you might want to take the time to at least skim articles on Internet strategies for small companies even if your company doesn't have plans to build its own Internet site. Make a mental note of this other information for future reference. If you need this information someday, you'll know where to start looking for it. Figure 7-1 helps you get a handle on what information you need to read. It contains a survey of the things that you need to read about to maintain your client's or company's LAN in peak condition.

The survey provides you with some ideas of what you need to read to maintain your network. Simply fill out the form and then look for those areas in the magazines and trade papers that you read. There's another way that you can use this survey. Some people get so much mail and so many magazines to read that even a focused approach to reading won't help them get through everything they need to look at. They usually resort to using a *clipping service,* a company that sends you clippings from magazines and trade papers in your areas of interest. A more cost-effective method of doing the same thing is to have an administrative assistant or other subordinate use the survey as the means for going through the magazines and trade papers for you. They simply clip out the articles that you're interested in. This alleviates the need to go through all the magazines and trade papers manually. It also helps you maintain your concentration level by removing sources of other nonessential information.

## Sources of Information

The basic information needed to maintain your certification will come from Novell. This may include instructor-led courses, videotapes, manuals, bulletins, or seminars. This information is very Novell-specific and relates only to Novell, the NetWare products, and your certification. Since most people have an interest in the complete scope of networking, using Novell as your only source of information won't get you very far. In the real world, people use a variety of solutions; you must make sure you're ready to handle them. For this reason, other sources of information

# Planning for Continuing Education Requirements

**Figure 7-1**
Reading Interest Survey.

---

**Reading Interest Survey**

Name: _____ Date: _____

Position: _____

**Hardware needs**
- ❏ PC
- ❏ Macintosh
- ❏ Workstation
- ❏ Mainframe
- ❏ Minicomputer
- ❏ Internet-specific

**Software needs**
Word processing: _____ Database: _____
Spreadsheet: _____ Accounting: _____
Maintenance: _____ Server: _____
Internet browser: _____ Internet server addon: _____
Other communications: _____ Other: _____

**Peripheral devices**
- ❏ Tape drive
- ❏ Sound board
- ❏ Modem
- ❏ Printers: _____
- ❏ Other: _____
- ❏ CD-ROM drive
- ❏ Mouse
- ❏ Multimedia

**Network-specific**
Network type: _____ Bridges/routers: _____
Operating system version: _____ Print servers: _____
Other: _____

---

include magazines, trade papers, books, online services, and electronic media. Figure 7-2 shows these typical sources of information and provides a little guidance on how to allocate your time.

These other sources of information will help you not only to maintain your Novell certification but will help you to advance to the next level of certification or to a better job position. Don't fall into the trap many people do of thinking that now that you have your certification you can stop studying. Nothing can be further from the truth. Now that you have your certification, you must work just as hard to maintain it.

**Figure 7-2**
Sources of Continuing Education Information.

Follow the 30/70 rule when updating your knowledge base.
30% Novell and 70% Other

## Organizing Your Information

*Organization* is a major key to retaining a vast amount of knowledge without juggling it in your head all the time. Trying to keep all your knowledge balls in the air at the same time is just plain silly. Put the balls down so you can get some real work done. The important idea here is to group the information into easily digested chunks, then find a way to access those chunks quickly. Of course, the exact method of organization you use varies by the type of information you want to store. The most flexible media are trade magazines and books. Notes and brochures from seminars are also fairly easy to store. You'll find it a lot more difficult to store information from satellite conferences and special training sessions. Information collected at user group meetings may prove to be the most difficult source of all to organize.

One way that'll help you to organize textual information, like books and magazines, in an easy to retrieve form is to photocopy the tables of contents. Put the photocopied tables of contents in a notebook. Divide the notebook into sections such as *magazines, trade papers, books, electronic sources,* and others. You can also divide it by magazine or trade paper title or by general category of information, like *network hardware.* Ordering your magazine and trade paper articles in this manner will allow you to quickly locate what you need. Of course, part of this maintenance is removing old information from the folder as well. For example, you wouldn't want to keep articles that told you about the latest version of the PC—the 8088. Keeping your information up to date is part of the work required to reduce information overload.

Another way to reference information is to use a program such as *AskSam,* DynaText storage for data that may or may not fall within a predictable pattern. In fact, it's the perfect database for storing notes and other hard to organize information. *Folio Views* is the same program Novell uses for its online help and the NetWare Buyer's Guide (we discuss the NetWare Buyer's Guide later in this chapter). Newer versions of NetWare use a different online help viewer called *DynaText;* it offers a much better interface than Folio Views. Any of these programs allow you to quickly and easily create an infobase with all the previously mentioned information. You can also add a paraphrased summary of the articles, books, or other information to help narrow your search of a particular topic. In fact, you could scan entire articles into the database using a scanner. While this requires a little more time creating and maintaining the infobases, you'll be able to find the information that you're looking for faster.

Of course, other methods of recalling this information may include creating a database using one of the popular database programs or by converting the data into some other electronic format that you can retrieve at a later time. Whatever method you use to keep track of the information you find, the key is to *record and document* your findings. Don't trust the information you need to make a living to memory.

Ziff Publishing provides a unique method for accessing its articles and reviews. You can order *Computer Library Plus* for a nominal fee. Every month you receive a new CD-ROM disk containing the latest articles and reviews about any topic you can think of. The CD contains the complete text (excluding graphics and advertisements) of over 170 publications. It also includes 13,000 company profiles and a complete computer glossary. The search engine included as part of the library system allows you to conduct key word searches throughout the entire database. You can order Computer Library Plus by calling 1-800-827-7889. The cost is about $1000 per subscription.

Microsoft provides the same type of library through the *Microsoft Developer Network*. It contains the latest issues of *Microsoft Systems Journal* and many of the Cobb Group newsletters. You can order the Microsoft Developer Network by calling 1-800-227-4679. There are currently four levels of support, and each one offers different features. Make sure you get the level of support you actually need for your business. Of course, Microsoft charges more for each level, so make your purchasing decision wisely.

## Magazines

Magazines are an excellent source of information. By subscribing to a few good magazines you'll be able to remain current on most areas of networking. Many publishers produce their magazines on a biweekly or monthly basis. Since you have a couple of weeks to read the magazine, you'll be able to study when you have the time. You're also better able to absorb and retain what you read if you're not under pressure or rushed.

Finding the magazine doesn't present a problem either. There are many excellent magazines on the shelves at your favorite bookstore. You'll also find that there are as many magazines that never make it to the bookstores or the magazine racks. It's not that these magazines are of any less quality, they may just target a different market. They're usually mailed directly to your home or business. You can usually find business reply mail cards for these magazines in the card stacks that you get in the mail, as part of software packages, or within other magazines. For example, most of the Cobb Group newsletters are sold as part of the software package you purchase. They also perform direct mail based on the registration cards you send back to the vendor.

Deciding which ones you'll buy is a very difficult decision and one you shouldn't rush. Spend the time to research each magazine before you subscribe, looking for the ones that center on the topics that concern you. You can't buy and read every one of them. Even if you had the money to do so, it would require many hours or days to read them all. Narrow your search to the few good magazines that address your areas of interest. By reading the magazines written with a focus on your area of interest you won't have to wade through a group of articles that don't interest you.

Many magazines on the newsstands contain too many advertisements, and, in some cases, the ads get top priority over the articles. This becomes very annoying when articles are too short and the editor leaves out important information because the ads need more room. Sometimes you can't get around this kind of magazine. Even though they have a lot of ads, they may still contain some good information that you can't get elsewhere. However, you'll want to concentrate on magazines that have a good editorial-to-ad ratio. So, how do you find a good magazine? Spend a few months looking through the magazine and you'll begin to notice whether it contains mostly ads or articles. A good rule of thumb regarding the editorial-to-ad ratio is 40/60. You'll see 40 percent editorial and 60 percent ads in a good magazine.

You'll also begin to see patterns in the type of articles written for the different magazines. Some magazines are into home computing, some the latest gadgets, others focus on networking, and still others cover every other aspect of computers or electronics. A magazine normally has an editorial style, as well. For example, the editorial staff may favor large corporations over small businesses. They might have a certain attitude in some areas as well. A magazine may have a pessimistic or optimistic view of events in the computer industry; make sure you look for a balance. Once you find a group of magazines that provides a balanced view combined with an approach that matches your company size, make them your required reading list. Make sure that you read them first each month; they're your windows into the industry.

Look through the tables of contents for the magazines you read on a regular basis. Read the articles that pertain to your business needs first, and then spend some time skimming the other ones to get an overview of what they are trying to convey. If you find something interesting, read it. After you have read the required magazines, read the others if you have time or want to. If you try to read everything, you're just wasting your time.

Those of you who spend most of your time on a network will want to pay particular attention to two magazines: *LAN TIMES* and *NetWare Application Notes*. McGraw-Hill publishes *LAN TIMES* biweekly. It's a Novell-based magazine that covers everything taking place within the PC computer networking industry. Even though it's a Novell-based magazine, *LAN TIMES* is also one of the most objective magazines available. It provides fairly even coverage of both good and bad events in the computer industry. The magazine includes articles on the latest technologies, internetworking, applications, and network management, to name a few. There's also an article in every issue that covers a *hands-on* topic. This article covers some networking-specific topic, usually one directly relating in some way to Novell, in detail, giving you the theory, use, and procedures. Current coverage includes a heavy emphasis on the Internet, coverage that should help the NCIPs out there, as well.

The second must-read magazine publication for networking professionals is *NetWare Application Notes*. This is a Novell-published magazine that provides in-depth coverage of the topic at hand. There are usually three to five articles in each publication, with absolutely no ads. The articles cover such topics as installation, integration, testing, theory, and management, to name a few. When you become a CNE, Novell will send you one complementary copy of the *Application Notes* (also referred to as "*APP Notes*"). If you want to continue to receive the magazine after that—and we recommend that you do—you can find the ordering information in the front cover of the magazine.

There are many other magazines that also deal with PC networks. You need to research each of them to find the ones appropriate for you and your needs. Some of the magazines are free to consultants, administrators, and businesses. When you find the magazines that you like, call or write to the circulation manager and ask about a complementary subscription. Often, you'll find that complementary subscriptions are available for the asking. Sometimes they're on a trial offer of one to three issues for free; sometimes even longer. If you can't get them for free, then spend the money for them; you need some access to the technology. In most cases, the magazine subscriptions are tax deductible as a business or education expense.

Always remember to document the contents of a magazine once you finish reading it, and then store the publication in a safe place. You'll only remember a small fraction of the information contained within the articles, but by using the search techniques we discussed earlier you'll be able to access the information when you need it in the future. (Check out the preceding "Organizing Your Information" subsection if you need tips on how to build your own information retrieval system.)

Some magazines are good for anyone to read, while others concentrate on the novice or expert reader. As you move from novice, to intermediate, and finally to expert status, you may need to change some of your magazines as well. If you find that a particular publication is no longer teaching or informing you, then it may be time to drop the subscription. If you keep reading the same material over and over again, then you're just wasting your time.

## Trade Papers

The weekly trade papers that you receive are packed with the latest information about the computer industry. Subscriptions to one or two of the more popular ones will keep you up to date on what the hardware and software vendors are doing. They always have articles about new gadgets, state of the art technology, and trends. Also included are columns about what certain industry people are doing and what company they are working for this week.

As with magazines, choose one or more trade papers that meet your needs and make them your top reading priority. There are just too many on the market to read every one of them.

Trade papers are even more opinionated than magazines are. Some of the trade papers you'll find are very pro-IBM or -UNIX, while others only concern themselves with what Novell is doing, or what Microsoft is doing wrong. It's important to remember the "news" orientation of a trade paper when it comes to controversial articles. Remember that these articles express the opinion of the author. They don't necessarily represent the right or wrong view of the industry, simply one person's view. Of course, these people maintain their position because they either are controversial or are correct more often than not. The best course of action is to choose a trade paper that objectively covers the areas that interest you most.

*Timeliness* is the important consideration with trade papers. You'll find that reading trade papers to get the current industry gossip and magazines to get hard facts will keep you informed about what's going on in the industry.

Unlike magazines, trade papers will normally have a lot of articles that have nothing to do with your business. Just skip past them. Trade papers also contain a ton of ads when compared to magazines. Since many trade papers rely on advertising for income to the exclusion of everything else, you'll just have to ignore the ads like everyone else.

Even though trade papers contain very time-sensitive information, you'll still want to hold on to them for a while. Make sure you keep track of the articles that interest you, using some form of document retrieval database. The easiest way to do this is to find the articles of interest, make photocopies of them, and then place the articles into a binder. Record the entries in a table of contents for future reference. After you save the articles that interest you, discard the original trade paper or recycle it. If you try to save every back issue of the paper, you'll soon find that you need a large storage garage to keep them all.

A few of the trade papers that you may want to invest in are *Network World, Computer Technology Review, Computer Reseller News, PC Week,* and *LAN Times.* Since you only have a week to read a trade paper, one or two of them is about all you'll be able to handle. Appendix E contains a list of the most popular trade paper vendors and tells you how to contact them.

## Books

Books are another excellent source of information for continuing education. You'll want to invest in books for long-term information (at least, *long term* in the computer sense). It takes between four and eight months to produce a book from the time the author begins writing until you see it on the bookshelf. This means that you can't rely on books for time-sensitive material like the current state of the computer industry. The best use of books is for long-term theory or usage information. Books are also a good way to train yourself on new technology once the smoke has cleared in the trade papers. Make sure you can get at least a year's worth of use out of every book you buy (unless the topic is the Internet, which changes about every six months).

Most of the books written about a software product begin with the same information that's supplied by the vendor manuals. A good author will add all of the undocumented information about the product that he or she can find. The information you find in third-party books is usually better organized and more concise than the vendor manuals as well, though this isn't always the case. In many cases, you'll also find real-world examples in the third-party books. A third-party book may be easier to understand than the vendor manual, as well. For these reasons, and more, you'll want to invest in at least a few third-party books if you maintain a lot of applications.

You'll need to spend some time looking at the book before you buy. An author normally addresses a specific audience, which determines the kind of information you'll see in the book. Even though the label on the back of the book says *intermediate,* you'll want to page through it to make sure you'll get something for your money. Even if you know all of the information in the book, one that's well organized can always serve as a quick reference while you're on the road. You can also use it to review what you already know on an occasional basis.

One book that the network administrator will want to check out is *The Hands-On Guide to Networking* by John Mueller and Robert Williams (Windcrest/McGraw-Hill, ISBN 0-8306-4439-3). This book provides you

# Planning for Continuing Education Requirements

with a lot of tips and techniques for getting your network running smoothly and keeping it that way.

For the dedicated NetWare professional, one book that should be mandatory for your library is the *NetWare Buyer's Guide*. This book is published by Novell and usually updated twice a year. You can get it free of charge by calling Novell. *NetWare Buyer's Guide* is published in both paper and electronic versions. The electronic version has the same appearance and interface as the Novell help utility with NetWare. Novell divides the contents of *NetWare Buyer's Guide* into four sections:

1. *Novell Corporate and Strategic Overview.* This section details Novell's company background and market leadership and the Novell integrated computing architecture. The roll that Novell plays in computer networking is defined. How Novell works with other computer vendors is also discussed. This ensures that all the products that Novell produces will work with any third-party products that you use. Also included in this section is the theory of operations for the Novell operating systems.

2. *Novell Product Overview.* Section 2 outlines all the products Novell sells and supports in an overview fashion. Described in this section is the history of the Novell products and the reasons for using them. Since this section is a Novell product overview, there's no discussion of the inner workings of the products. All CNAs, CNEs, MCNEs, NCIPs, CNIs, administrators, consultants, and anyone who's working with the Novell operating system should read this section. You'll learn about all the different products that Novell has to offer. Knowing what products are available will give you ideas about making your system work better.

3. *Novell Products.* This section lists the Novell products by type. You'll find the following subheadings: "Operating System," "Network Services," "Communication Services," "Internetwork," "Network Connectivity," "Network Management," and, finally, "Distributed Application Development Tools." Under each subheading is a listing of every Novell product that relates to the topic. You'll get both an overview and some technical information in this section. This section also explains product features. Included in the product descriptions are implementation details—the hardware, software, and any other materials required to install the product. The final area of this section covers specifications and ordering information, along with part numbers. This is an excellent section for learning how each product works and what the hardware and software requirements are.

**4.** *Novell Support and Education.* This section deals with the customer support programs offered by Novell for both resellers and end users. The information in this section is an overview of the Novell services that includes technical support, NetWire information, and the reseller authorization program. Also included is an overview of the Novell education and training programs.

The *NetWare Buyer's Guide* is an important addition to your reference library and will help you learn about the Novell products. Whether you work with the book or the electronic version, be sure to contact Novell on a regular basis for upgrades to keep your *NetWare Buyer's Guide* current.

## Online Services

Novell offers a wide range of services to all NetWare users and support technicians. Besides the standard publications of magazines and books, Novell offers electronic online services, as well. With these services you can use your computer to stay in touch with Novell.

The Internet has become all the rage in recent months, and Novell has followed the trend by offering a variety of Internet related services. You can always reach their Web site at http://www.novell.com. It contains links you can use to reach a variety of other Novell related sites. For example, if you want to find out about educational opportunities, then check out http://education.novell.com/. Another interesting place to look at is the course catalog at http://db.netpub.com/nov_edu/x/qsearch.pl. If you need patches, check http://support.novell.com/search/patlst.htm.

As you can see, there are a lot of interesting places to look at to get information from Novell on the Internet. As of this writing, Novell hasn't created a newsgroup on the Internet. That means you'll have to visit a more generic network newsgroup if you want to keep up to date with networking on the Internet. It also means you won't get much in the way of direct human contact when you need help for a specific Novell product.

You can also visit Novell's CompuServe forums, a vast array of places you can use to get answers for every conceivable question. Unlike the Internet, you can actually exchange ideas with other people who are specifically interested in Novell products when visiting CompuServe. The forums on CompuServe also offer download services that provide you with free updates for your Novell products. (Of course, you'll only see this service when the update is free of charge.) Figure 7-3 provides an overview of Novell's CompuServe forums.

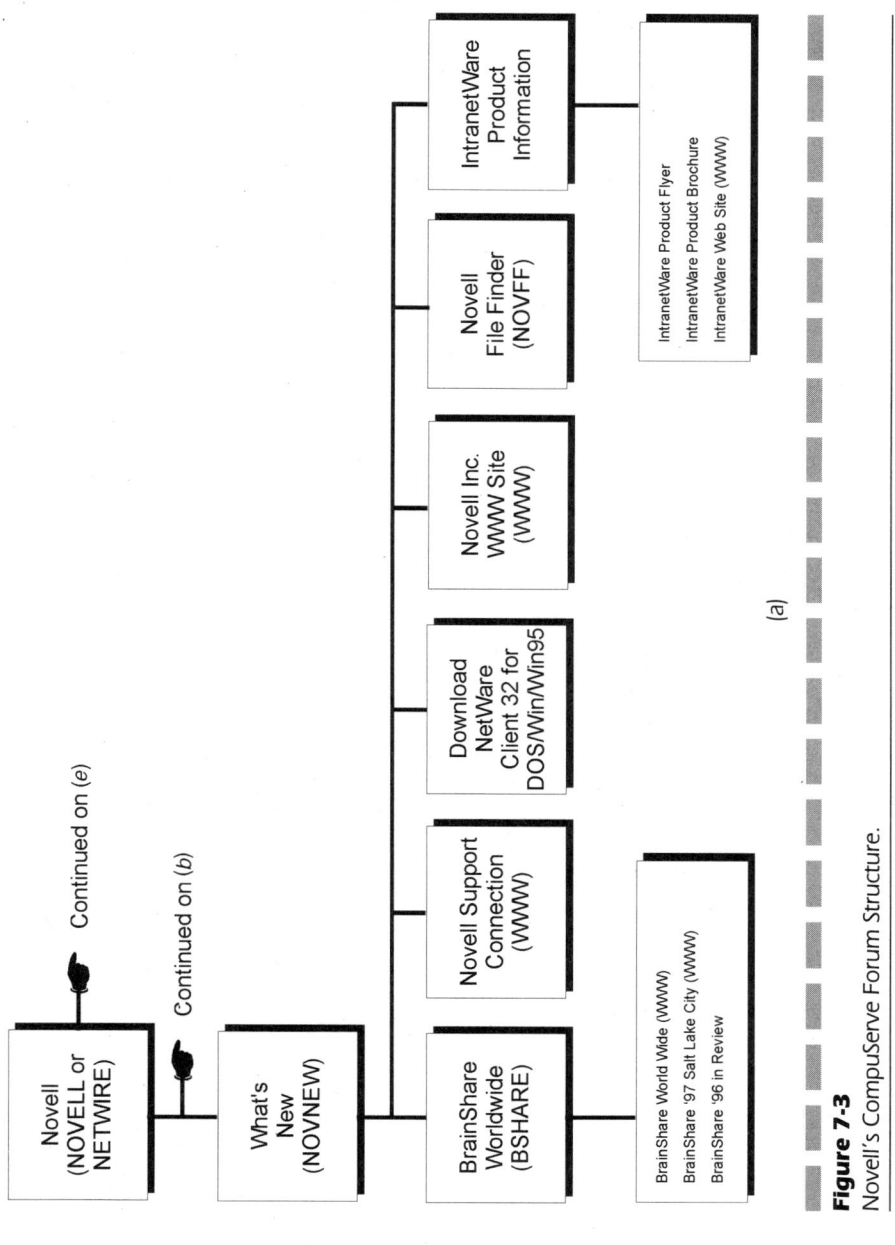

**Figure 7-3**
Novell's CompuServe Forum Structure.

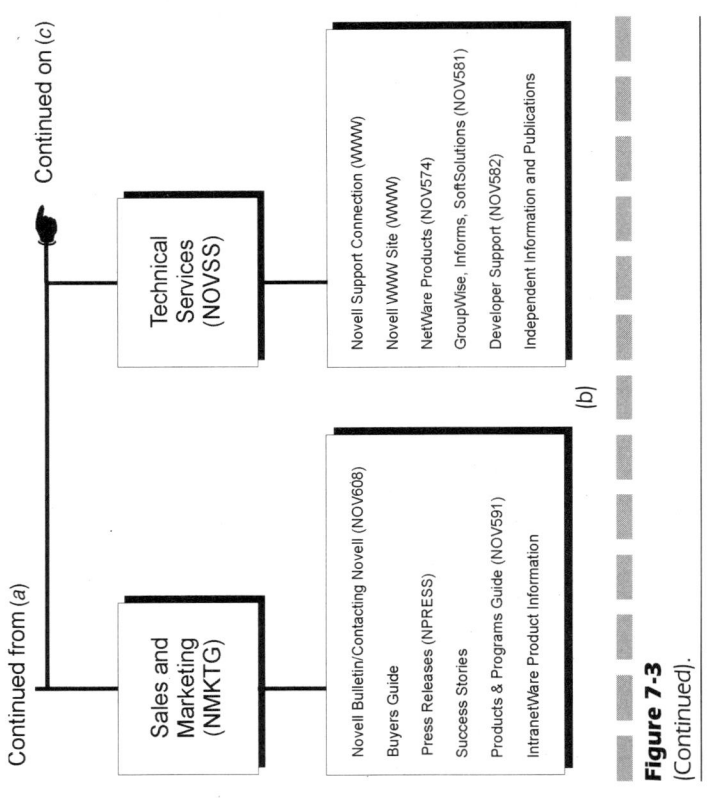

**Figure 7-3**
(Continued).

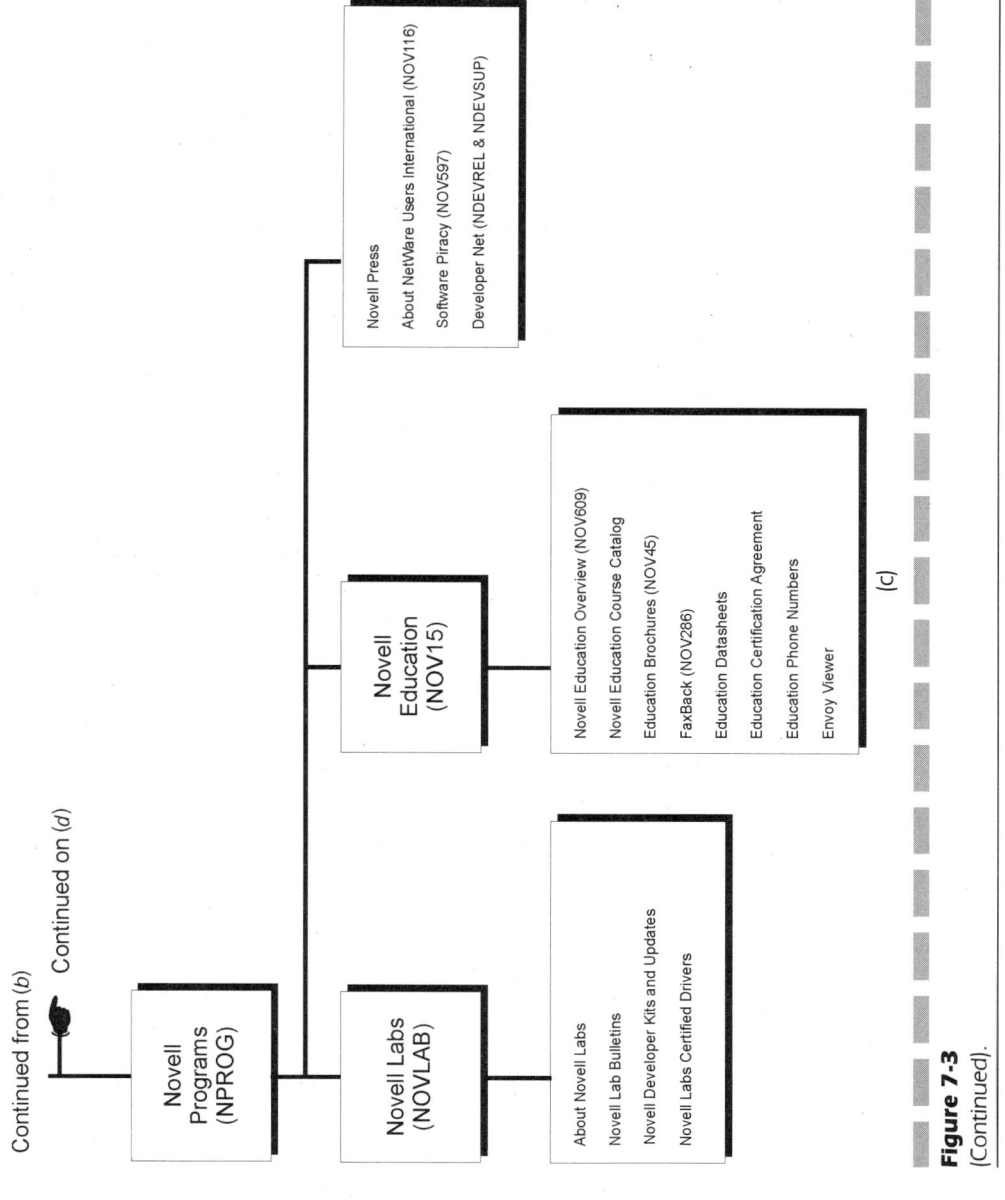

**Figure 7-3** (Continued).

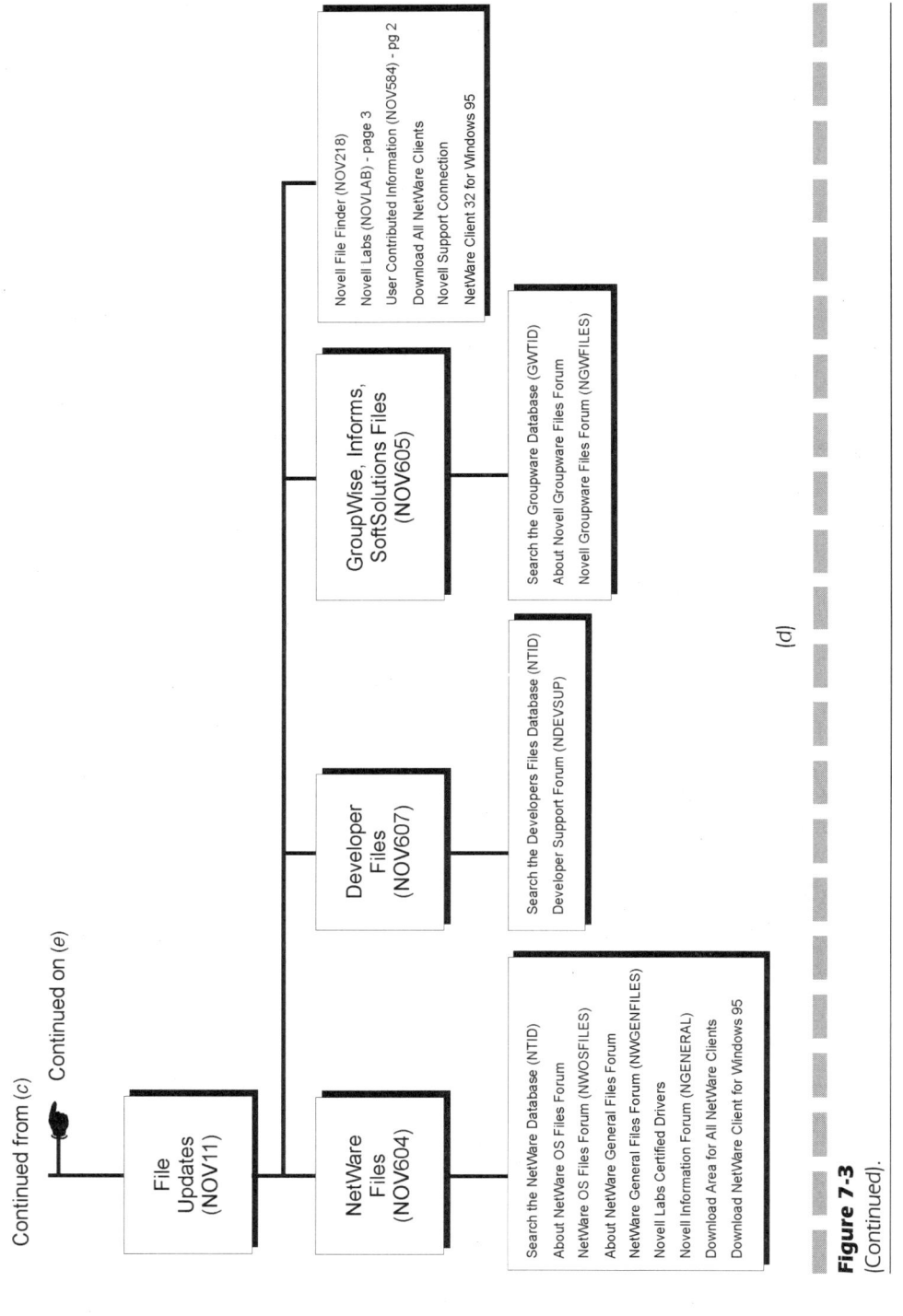

**Figure 7-3**
(Continued).

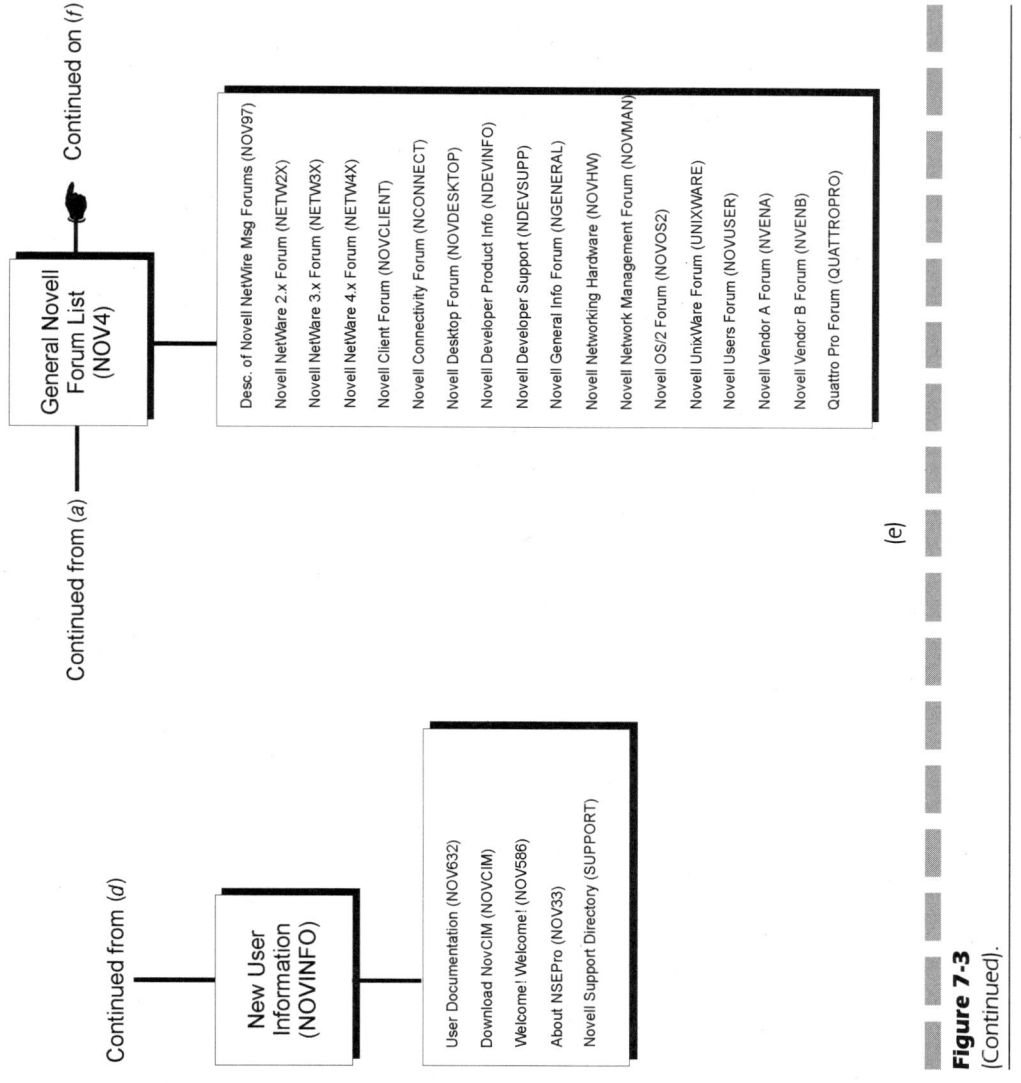

**Figure 7-3** (Continued).

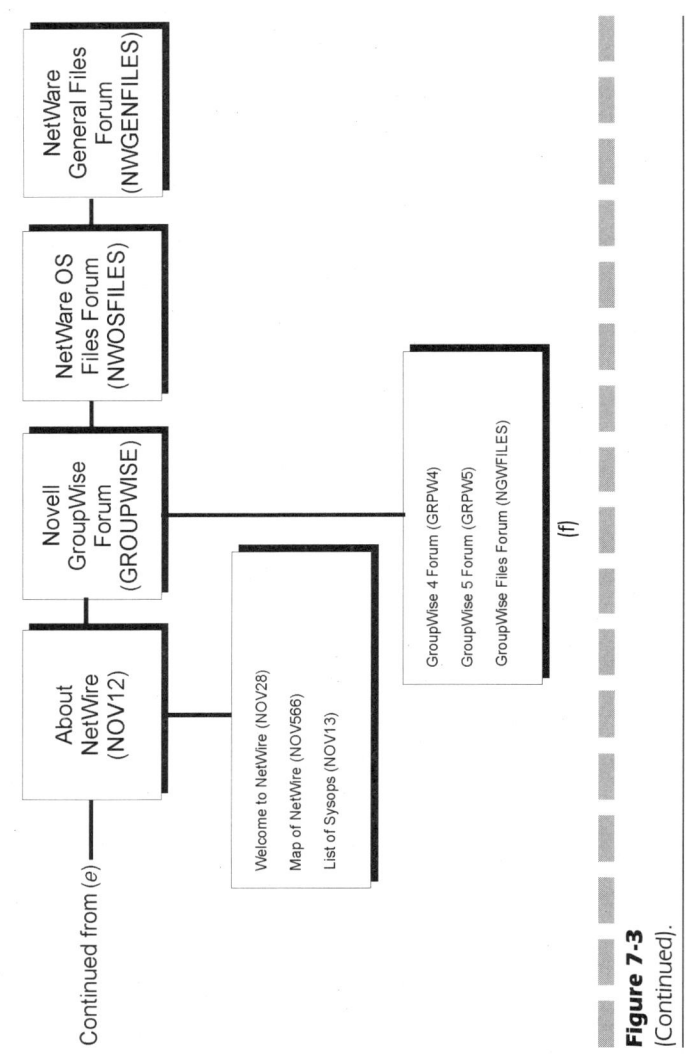

**Figure 7-3** (Continued).

As you can see, Fig. 7-3 is huge. If you feel a little overwhelmed by the number of services that Novell offers, you're not alone. You could spend days just trying to find the right forum for your particular needs. For that matter, unless you use a product like *WinCIM* to maneuver through the labyrinth of CompuServe menus, you may not even reach your destination. (Novell does offer a special version of WinCIM that includes all of its forums as standard entries; the problem is that other vendors, like Microsoft, offer this same service, and you can't combine the various specialty versions of WinCIM into a single program.) Using Fig. 7-3 should make your job a lot easier and allow you to use more cost-conscious tools, like *TapCIS* or *OzCIS* for Windows, to find your way on CompuServe. (You can download shareware versions of either product from their CompuServe forums—GO TAPCIS for TapCIS or GO OZCIS for OzCIS for Windows.)

One of the first things you should notice about the forum map in Fig. 7-3 is that a lot of the support you'll receive comes from the Internet. In the past, Novell provided all of its support on CompuServe. Now some of those same menu selections take you to a Web page on the Internet, also known as the *World Wide Web* (WWW). Whenever you see (*WWW*) next to an entry in Fig. 7-3, you know that the forum is on the Internet and Novell is only using CompuServe to provide a link. You must use WinCIM as your communications program to access an Internet site from CompuServe.

Figure 7-3 is arranged in a *hierarchical* format. This means that the upper-level menus appear first. The actual forums appear at the bottom of the hierarchical tree. Notice the *go words* in parenthesis beside each menu or forum name. A go word provides a short cut on CompuServe. If you know the go word, you can go directly to the menu or forum that you want to see. Not every menu entry has a go word, but there are enough provided in Fig. 7-3 to greatly decrease your search time. Every forum does have a go word, making it easy to get to any forum you want to visit.

The online Novell services fall into two classes of services: *dial-in voice services* and *computer access services*. We just covered the computer access services. The *dial-in voice service* is Novell's technical information service, update information service, education information and enrollment, and direct product ordering service. This service is available 7 days a week, 24 hours a day. If you have technical questions about any Novell product and would like to talk to a Novell technician, you can call the Novell technical support department. As a CNE, Novell entitles you to two free incident calls the first year of your certification. If you need more technical support after two calls or following your first year of certification, you may purchase additional support at a reduced rate.

Other services that you may take advantage of include the ability to order many Novell products, including, among other things, updates to your current products. You may also obtain information about the NAEC education centers and listings of the latest courses.

Now that you have a good overview of the online services offered by Novell, it's time to take a detailed look at them. The following paragraphs provide you with a detailed synopsis of each Novell online offering. It's always important to know where you need to go to find the information required to get the job done. This material helps you find that resource.

**NETWIRE.** For the latest up-to-date information about Novell or the NetWare products, Novell offers the services found on NetWire. This is a type of bulletin board service. NetWire, referred to as the *Novell forum* or *NetWire forum,* is available through CompuServe. Once you have access to CompuServe, NetWire is free.

*Sysops* (short for system operators) perform maintenance and control of the NetWire forum. In the case of NetWire, the sysops are Novell employees and volunteer Novell experts. These people monitor the files being uploaded and downloaded on the system. They're also available to answer any questions about where to find information or how to use the forums and to answer any technical questions concerning Novell and its products.

One of the services offered by NetWire is the ability to post questions about NetWare onto the forum. Then anyone having access to the forum can read and answer the questions. The answers to the questions that you post on the forum may come from the other users or from the sysops. These users might be end users, system administrators, CNEs, CNIs, or anyone else with an interest in Novell. With thousands of people using NetWire every day, there's a very good chance that someone has had a problem similar to yours. They can answer with a solution.

Other services offered by the NetWire are product updates and conferences. The *product updates* includes the latest patches, fixes, drivers, and enhancements available for the Novell product line. These updates are downloadable from the service and are free to users of NetWire. The other service, *conferences,* allows a group of NetWire users to have an online discussion about some topic. Some of these discussions are preplanned and are conducted by a Novell sysop or engineer; others are spur of the moment conferences with a group of users. Topics range from a problem someone has been having to the theory and implementation of some technology.

Anyone who holds a Novell certification will want to visit NetWire or the Internet equivalents. You'll find that cost of joining CompuServe is more than justified when compared to the cost of using Novell's technical support for every question you might have. It's also an asset for obtaining

# Planning for Continuing Education Requirements 207

the most current drivers and patches. For more information about CompuServe and NetWire, please refer to Appendix E.

**FAXBACK.** The Novell FaxBack service, as mentioned in Chap. 3, is another electronic service offered by Novell. This service is part of the Novell education department and allows you to receive a listing of the authorized education centers and class information by fax. Besides the NAEC or NEAP and course information, you can get general information about the CNA, CNE, MCNE, NCIP, and CNI certifications. You'll also find information about every other educational service that Novell provides. The FaxBack service is a good way to find information about the certifications and education without contacting the respective certification division every time you have a question.

## Electronic Media

Novell offers a product called the *Network Support Encyclopedia Professional* (NSEPro). This is an electronic information base containing technical data about Novell networking. It contains Novell's technical notes, hardware and software test information, product documentation and product information, product specifications, NetWire information, Novell press releases, and the *NetWare Buyer's Guide*.

You'll also find downloadable information on NSEPro. The downloadable information is the same information that is available on NetWire. Some of the things that you can download include NetWare patches, product fixes, device drivers, product enhancements, troubleshooting charts, *NetWare Application Notes* (*AppNotes*), and additional manuals.

NSEPro is only available on CD-ROM. Novell updates it once a month for as long as your subscription lasts. Even though the subscription may seem expensive, you'll find that NSEPro is a good investment if you spend a lot of time working as a networking professional. Once you become a CNE, you'll receive one free issue of NSEPro.

## CNE Continuing Education Requirements

You must update your certification from time to time as a CNE. These continuing education requirements are to help you maintain a certain level of expertise with Novell products. You'll also find out about new products that can help resolve problems in the workplace or help optimize network throughput. The continuing education requirements also help Novell maintain a specific level of customer support. Remember that your certification essentially guarantees the customer a specific level of support using Novell techniques.

You'll normally need to meet a continuing education requirement when Novell introduces a new product, and then only if they feel that all the CNEs should be aware of the updates. In most cases, you'll need to meet a continuing education requirement every one or two years, depending on what your specialty is and how fast the technology changes. If there's a continuing education requirement, Novell will notify you by mail of the necessary requirements. After Novell notifies you of the update, you usually have 90 days to fulfill the requirements. In many cases, all you'll need to do is pass a competency exam. If you don't know the new material, Novell and NAECs will offer classes on the subject. Even though you have 90 days to meet the certification requirements, don't wait too long. Try to certify as soon as possible, but make sure you give yourself plenty of time to prepare for the exam. Remember that the more pressure you are under, the higher the odds of failing.

## MCNE Continuing Education Requirements

An MCNE's education requirements are about the most intense of any certification, except for the CNI's. In fact, MCNEs require a broader range of information than many CNIs, since an MCNE works with more than just Novell products. In addition to this broad base of general knowledge, the MCNE needs to stay abreast of Novell-specific product information. Remember that an MCNE's specialty area requires a fuller understanding of the inner workings of the product.

MCNEs are required to meet all of the continuing education requirements for CNEs, since you must be a CNE before you can become a MCNE. Novell may require MCNEs to meet special continuing education requirements, as well. For example, a new set of drivers or patches may affect the way you interface NetWare with other operating systems. Even though a CNE may not need to meet a continuing education requirement, the MCNE most likely will. Since MCNE is a more specialized certification, Novell wants to make sure you have all the facts needed to maintain a specific level of service to the customer.

## NCIP Continuing Education Requirements

NCIPs will likely have more continuing education requirements than anyone else, simply because the Internet is a moving target right now. These continuing education requirements are to help you to maintain a certain level of expertise with Novell products and to stay apprised of new Internet standards and technologies. You'll also find out about new products that could help maintain a Web site with less work or help to optimize network throughput. The continuing education requirements also help Novell maintain a specific level of customer support. Remember that your certification essentially guarantees the customer a specific level of support using Novell techniques.

Aside from a higher frequency of continuing education requirements, NCIPs will find that they follow essentially the same course as CNEs do. You'll need to update your certification whenever Novell introduces a new product or technology that changes the way you do your job. In most cases, you'll get the same 90 days as a CNE for meeting the continuing education requirement.

## CNI Continuing Education Requirements

The Novell CNI is a little different from the CNE and MCNE when it comes to recertification. Since CNIs teach everyone else, a product has to change a lot less before Novell requires the CNIs to meet a continuing education requirement. However, since CNIs are responsible for fewer classes for any given certification than someone like an MCNE, they'll usually need to be recertified less often for a particular certification. The bottom line is that CNIs will need to recertify any time Novell releases a new product, changes testing procedure, or modifies the classes because of support line trends.

**NOTE** *It's unlikely that a CNI will be certified to teach just one class. If you're serious about becoming a CNI, then expect to spend a lot of time keeping up to date on current technology. The more classes you can teach, the more valuable you are to the NAEC. The down side of this is that you'll also spend a lot of time maintaining all of those certifications.*

Recertification usually begins by attending the course. These classes are taught either by a Novell-employed instructor or by a certified instructor at a NAEC. After completing the course and receiving the certificate, the instructor must pass the CNI version of the competency exam. After passing the exam, the CNI must fax a copy of the course certificate to the CNI administration department. When the CNI candidate satisfies these requirements, Novell permits the CNI to teach the course.

Novell can require CNIs to perform additional tasks to maintain their certification. For example, a CNI may be required to attend an IPE to remain certified. In the IPE the instructor will be videotaped while conducting lectures on the material that will be part of the course. The instructor must pass a critique based on presentation skills and technical accuracy. Most of the time, instructors will only have to attend the IPE if they wish to teach the MCNE or specialty classes.

Another possible requirement for a CNI would be to attend a seminar-style class. At this seminar a Novell-employed instructor presents information that Novell considers to be essential for CNIs to know. The CNI may or may not have to take an exam on this material.

## Conclusion

If you're not convinced of the need for continuing your education once you are certified, just think about the alternatives. There are a lot of professions that don't require constant schooling. You could work as a janitor for some large corporation and never pick up a book again. However, we doubt that you'd be reading this book if you fell into that category.

As a professional, education isn't an option—it's a necessity. Every time someone else learns something that you don't, you've given them an opportunity. Whether that opportunity is advancement or a new customer is immaterial—the point is that without constant updates you've lost your competitive edge. Keeping up to date on current technology is money in the bank.

Make sure you don't go into information overload, though. We've told you about some techniques that you can use to filter the information. Make sure you take the time to learn what you need to learn, but do not get so overwhelmed by technology that you can't function. Being a professional also means knowing what you want to specialize in.

CHAPTER 8

# The Consulting Approach

# Introduction

Many consultants make a living from installing and maintaining Novell local area networks (LANs). Installing and maintaining LANs became a very lucrative business when large corporations decided to downsize their database applications from mainframes and minicomputers to PCs. In addition, many small businesses are starting to see the benefit of networking their computers to enhance productivity. Add to this the increasing number of middle-size businesses and you have a climate ripe for the entrepreneur. As the business market gets more competitive, the consultant should see an increase in business.

The recent Internet craze has only increased the networking frenzy. A consultant can now specialize in Internets, intranets, or the old standby networks. Even the variety of networks has increased, though, as companies have begun to mix and match networking models and machine capabilities. If you're a consultant who's serious about working with networks, be prepared to work with a variety of equipment and networking models. In fact, if you're a CNE today, you may want to broaden your horizons by getting Novell's NCIP certification as well. It's no longer *if* the Internet will a play a role in your business, it's a matter of *when*.

Of course, not every consultant will see an increased customer base immediately after being certified. The difference between a successful consultant and those who simply maintain their current installed base is *recognition*. Unless you get recognition for your achievements as a businessperson, there's less of a chance that you'll increase your client base. Learning to leverage your certification when talking with potential clients is almost as important as getting the certification itself.

There are other benefits to getting certified than simply working more hours per day as your client base increases in size. For example, with an increase in capability, you can charge higher per-hour fees. You may find that you can afford to hire a helper. This allows you to concentrate on the "fun" jobs and give someone else the headaches. You'll also have more opportunities for interesting work, rather than working grunt-labor consulting jobs. As you can see, the benefits of a Novell certification are many. However, to get the benefits you must first gain recognition.

This chapter specifically targets the networking expert. It provides the consultant with ideas on how to improve business through the proper use of Novell-supplied aids. It also examines some ways that the consultant can use the certification to gain and keep new clients. Finally, this chapter examines some thorny issues like what to charge the client for network services and how to maintain a professional relationship with the client.

# Using the Novell Logo

Once you get your certification, you need to tell someone about it. Clients usually aren't very thrilled about wasting time hearing about your latest achievement, so you need to tell them in an almost subliminal manner. One of the ways you can do this is to add the Novell logo to all your business correspondence, price lists, business cards, and other areas of your business. If you're an NCIP, you may want to emphasize the Internet aspect of your business in addition to the Novell logo. The following subsections discuss some ways that you can use the Novell logo to tell your clients about your capabilities.

## Advertisements

There are two elements to advertising: *design* and *distribution*. The first topic is subject to much debate. The number and variety of advertising brochures that you get in the mail demonstrate this problem. The second topic's a little easier for the consultant to master. As a consultant, there are only a handful of truly effective ways to distribute your advertisements.

Lets tackle the first problem—how to *design* your brochure. Your best source of information on how to solve this problem is the junk mail you receive. What kinds of mail attract your attention? Give the same junk mail to a few people willing to help you out. Ask them to show you the junk mail that attracts their attention. Now, throw the rest of it away (unless you really need it). Going through all the mail that attracts your attention will give you ideas of what works and what doesn't. You may want to perform the same kind of analysis on magazine advertisements and store brochures if you intend to pursue those routes. Always look at what the successful competition is doing, then add a few ideas of your own to come up with a truly winning combination.

Once you do get a few ideas together, you need to create an advertisement. Creating an advertising brochure is not a scientific process—it lies on the artistic edge of maintaining a business. Of course, part of the problem is that an effective advertising brochure usually attracts our attention because we can understand what the author is trying to say. As a result, a brochure that works fine in one area of the country may fail in another because the cultural connection isn't as strong. When someone calls your business, you may want to take the time to ask them why they called. Keep track of what types of advertising work and what types don't.

Make sure you weight the scores to account for the types of client that you like to work with. If your advertisements always attract the wrong kind of client, it's a sure sign that you need to create a different type of advertisement.

There are several common elements that you need to put in an advertisement. First, you need to identify yourself. Unless people know whom they're dealing with, you won't get any sales. Second, you need to consider adding a list of services. You can do this in a number of ways. For example, stores usually use *graphics* to tell people what services they offer. (What else do you call a picture of a computer with a price listed below it?) Some businesses use a simple list that looks much like a *price list*. Still other businesses use *descriptive paragraphs* or other methods to tell people what services they offer. The choice is up to you. You may want to include price as part of your brochure, but this usually isn't the best idea for consultants. Giving the client a price list after you make your sales pitch is usually a better idea. Of course, every form of advertising you create should contain your Novell certification. Have you ever noticed how other vendors use this technique to attract potential clients? You need to avail yourself of this potential sales tool as well. Make sure you look at these other sales brochures for ideas on how to present your certification. Two methods that you should always consider are including the actual logo as part of your advertisement and adding some text that says, *Fully Novell Certified to work on your network.*

The second problem that you need to deal with is *distribution*. Some businesses resort to mass mailings and all kinds of other methods to attract new clients. While this may work fine for your local food store, it usually doesn't work all that well for a networking professional. Studies show that the rate of response from mass mailings is approximately 7 to 10 percent. That's 2 to 3 people per 100 mailings. If you close 2 percent of your sales, you need to mass mail to 1,000 companies to get 2 new clients. So how do you get new clients? An advertising brochure is still a good method of gaining new clients, but the method of distribution can make all the difference in the world.

*Word of mouth* is a very good way for a consultant to gain new clients. Other professionals, like doctors and lawyers, have relied on this method for years. Have you ever noticed the other method that they use? *Referrals* are a common method of gaining new clients in both of those fields. A generalist will refer you to a specialist for particular kinds of work. The same holds true for professionals certified by Novell. You need to rely on both word of mouth and referrals for new clients. However, the job doesn't end there. The computer business is a lot more complex than other businesses. Every day there are new developments in industry that other people may not know about. Certainly, they won't know everything you do about your business. The reason for advertising becomes very clear when you look at it from this perspective.

You may find that your local newspaper or computer magazine are good places to advertise. This means of gaining new clients is secondary to word of mouth and referrals. Experience shows that about 50 percent of people respond to either word of mouth or referrals. Only 1 percent of the people you reach with a magazine advertisement will respond. Of those who do respond, only about 1.5% will actually become clients.* This means that you have to reach a minimum of 10,000 people with a newspaper or magazine advertisement to get a potential client. The numbers for telephone book advertisements are even smaller, since the audience is less likely to need computer services. As you can see, the one or two clients you gain using advertising need to pay off with large work loads and lots of referrals to make the effort worthwhile.

## Brochures, Business Cards, and Price Lists

There are three classes of document that do not fall into the advertisement category, but can act as subtle reminders of the services you offer: *brochures, business cards,* and *price lists*. All three of these items end up in the hands of your current clients. If you can get clients to look at these items from time to time, the subtle reminders you leave will help them to remember what services you offer. They'll also serve as the reminders that your clients need if they are to tell others about the services you offer. Remember, referrals are one of the best means at your disposal for gaining new clients.

*Business cards* offer very little room for advertising, much less subtle reminders. By the time you add a name, address, telephone number, and fax number, there's little room left for anything else. However, you can usually add a logo or two, plus a slug line. You normally add your business logo on the same line as the name of your business or directly below it. The logo identifies your business to people. They may actually look for the logo instead of your name when they look for your business card. Adding your Novell certification logo to the bottom right or left corner of your

---

*Results obtained from a survey of 50 computer consultants who relied on all three methods of gaining new clients.

business card adds a subtle reminder about one of the types of service that you offer. This little graphic says a lot about you and your business. The slug line usually includes one- or two-word reminders of the services you offer or, perhaps, the guiding ideas of your business. Make sure you add a reference to your Novell certification here, as well. It doesn't have to contain many words. Simply saying *Novell Certified* usually gets your point across to the client.

*Price lists* are a very important part of your business. Some clients may actually believe that you go out of your way to overcharge them if you don't provide such a document. In addition, some clients view the lack of a price list as an indication that you're willing to negotiate on your prices. If you aren't willing to make this concession, a price list is the best means of telling clients. Providing them with a document that spells out what you charge and how you apply those charges is very important to maintaining good client relations. However, printing those brochures may provide the client with a little peace of mind, but it doesn't do much for your pocketbook. You need to make the price list pay some dividend in increased sales or other tangible benefits. This is where adding your Novell certification logo comes into play. Adding something as small and unobtrusive as a logo can provide a big payback. As clients peruse your price list, they also get a complete reminder of why you charge more than Joe or Sally down the street. Your certification logo reminds them that they're paying for a higher quality of service than they might otherwise obtain. It also reminds them to tell their friends about the quality service they receive from you. Even a price list can serve as an advertisement. Make sure you get the full benefit from the investment you need to make in this document.

The final document is the *brochure*. This is a relatively undefined piece of information that you provide to the client. It includes everything from advertising brochures (covered in the previous subsection) to documents designed to help clients use your services more efficiently. For example, how often have clients asked you what your certification really represents? It makes good sense to create a brochure that tells clients about your certification and why it is important. If your business uses more than one level of certification, you can use the brochure to help clients understand what services they can expect from each of your employees. Make sure you create valuable tools of this type to reduce the time you spend answering client questions. Of course, adding the logo to brochures of this type only serves to show clients your level of dedication and professionalism. Make sure you add the certification logo whenever possible.

## Advertising on the Internet

Advertising your business on the Internet may be one way of gaining an edge over your competition. Creating a Web site is a lot different than other types of advertising. For one thing, you can make the environment interactive and more informative than any other type of advertisement. Someone visiting your site can get an overview from the first page of the Web site, and then drill down as needed to get amplifying information. You don't have to worry about getting everything on one page. In addition, you can add a few special effects to really dramatize the services you offer.

The best part about advertising on the Internet is that you can offer special features that you can't when using other techniques. For example, you can let the visitor download a price list. You could also offer updates for any custom software you create. Current clients could also check their appointments with you. In fact, you could even make it easy for clients to check on the current maintenance status of their networks without disturbing you. (Some of these features would require passwords and other forms of protection.) A Web site really can offer a wealth of features, limited only by your imagination.

In addition to providing features that will certainly help potential clients, you can update Web sites a lot easier than advertisements. Consider the fact that it takes a minimum of three months to run an advertisement in a magazine. Such a long delay doesn't allow you to offer the kind of instantaneous updates that are possible with a Web site. You could update your Web site on a daily basis if necessary.

Don't get the idea that a Web site on the Internet is going to be a perfect advertising solution. In fact, it's really the riskiest of all of the solutions in this section. There are quite a few pitfalls that you need to take into consideration. For example, unlike a magazine, you can't be sure who will visit your Web site. You could get literally thousands of hits and not a single customer for your efforts. You can't provide the same kind of focus using the Internet that you can using other forms of advertisement. Fortunately, you can ease this problem a little by working with the Webmasters of other Web sites to get pointers to your site in the right places.

Another potential problem with maintaining a Web site is cost. You can choose whether you want to run a print advertisement during a certain month depending on a lot of factors. A Web site has to be available all the time or people will get tired of trying to visit it. That means you'll always be out the advertising dollars for a Web site every month—even if you really don't need to advertise. Don't forget that you'll also have to pay for equipment and a connection. Maintenance costs for a Web site could get rather high unless you take the time to do things right the first time around.

## Carrying Your ID Card

The first thing that comes to many people's minds about a badge is identification. It's true that your Novell badge will identify you to your clients. It provides them with a picture, a name, and a certification number they can use for reference. This provides clients with a sense of security; they know who you are and what you represent. Of course, this really doesn't tell you much more than you already knew.

If you spend any time at all going from site to site, you soon realize that clients judge you by your appearance and not your professionalism on the first visit. Your manner in dealing with client questions also makes a big impact. A charming idiot will obtain more clients than a surly genius. (Keeping them is another matter—the surly genius who gets the job done usually wins on this count.)

The most obvious answer to the question of physical appearance versus reality may appear to lie in good communication skills. You may want to tell the client who you are and what you represent. Unfortunately, blurting out all your qualifications may make it appear that you're more a boastful oaf than a professional and thoughtful consultant. So, how do you tell the client about all your qualifications without making your sales pitch seem rude? Brochures, price lists, and advertisements all help with the sales pitch. However, there's another method that many consultants fail to consider. We all know the importance of dressing for the job and making sure we present a clean appearance, but this only skims the surface. Use subliminal methods to tell people about you and your business. For example, wearing your Novell badge can go a long way toward starting a client-initiated conversation about your qualifications. (They may simply ask why you're wearing the badge.) If you can get clients to ask about your qualifications, they're less apt to think that you're boasting about your qualifications and more likely to think that you provide complete and reasonable answers to their questions.

Your badge says a lot more about you than just what you can do. Wearing your badge helps people see that your qualifications mean a lot to you. It also shows your professionalism, that you have the knowledge required to keep a network running or to get it installed. People tend to maintain the first impression that they get from you. It's very difficult for a consultant to overcome a negative first impression. Make sure you make the right first impression by helping people see the professional side of your business.

## Determining What Services to Offer

Determining what services you want to offer is a matter of taking inventory of what skills you have to offer and what skills pay the best. You also need to consider what the clients in your area need the most and what they view as the most valuable. This is one of the reasons that you decided to pursue your Novell certification. The first part is fairly easy—simply create a list of your skills, then rank them from 1 to 10. Figure 3-1 provided you with an opportunity to survey your networking skills. Figure 8-1 provides the same opportunity with your skills as a whole. Note that each section provides additional space for you to add specialized skills.

Note that there are four sections to this survey. The first section asks you about your *hardware experience*. The second and third sections ask about your *software* and *training experience,* respectively. These are the three major areas of participation for a consultant. Of course, there are other areas as well. For example, the fourth section contains a listing for the lucrative area of *technical writing*. How do these four areas relate to your Novell certification? As you gain knowledge and experience with networks, your hardware experience will grow. In addition, companies will call on your networking experience when they try to get their software to work. Passing this knowledge onto other people is always a marketable skill. And how many times have you walked into a situation where the client had little or no documentation for a network? The need for technical writers becomes obvious when you look at this need. As you can see, you can enhance each of these skills when you get your Novell certification. Marketing these advanced skills is the sign of good business management.

You can answer the second part of the new services equation in two ways. First, you can simply survey your clients or ask them what they need in the way of service. You may want to ask leading questions that produce more than a yes or no answer. Make sure you look at their businesses for opportunities. You might find that the clients hadn't considered this service item in the past. Don't be surprised if clients turn down some of the ideas you have. They may not see a need to pursue them and any arguments on your part may serve to alienate them. Figure 8-2 provides a simple survey that you can ask clients to fill out or can simply use as a reference document when you ask the questions in person.

### Overall Skills Survey

*Hardware*

| Skills | Level | | | | | | | | | |
|---|---|---|---|---|---|---|---|---|---|---|
| | High | | | | | | | | | Low |
| | 10 | 9 | 8 | 7 | 6 | 5 | 4 | 3 | 2 | 1 |
| Cable installation | | | | | | | | | | |
| Computer system building | | | | | | | | | | |
| Computer system installation | | | | | | | | | | |
| Computer system repair and maintenance | | | | | | | | | | |
| Routers, bridges, hubs, etc. | | | | | | | | | | |
| Mini and mainframe connections | | | | | | | | | | |
| Scientific and specialty installations | | | | | | | | | | |
| Others: | | | | | | | | | | |
| | | | | | | | | | | |
| | | | | | | | | | | |
| | | | | | | | | | | |
| | | | | | | | | | | |

**Figure 8-1**
Network Consultant Skills Survey.

The sample survey shows you how to phrase an open-ended question. Note that we don't ask the clients if they plan to expand the number of products they produce, but what new products they already have in mind. This open-ended question assumes that the clients' businesses are in good shape and that they plan to grow. You really wouldn't want to assume anything else. You also want to explore the outer reaches of networking with your questions. For example, we ask the clients about their mainframe databases. Many clients don't even think of downsizing their current applications until you ask them about it. Make clients see your visions as their own ideas. Asking questions like the ones shown in Fig.

## Overall Skills Survey

*Software*

| Skills | Level | | | | | | | | | |
|---|---|---|---|---|---|---|---|---|---|---|
| | High | | | | | | | | | Low |
| | 10 | 9 | 8 | 7 | 6 | 5 | 4 | 3 | 2 | 1 |
| Programming | | | | | | | | | | |
| Installation and upgrades | | | | | | | | | | |
| Configuration management (the software configuration for each machine) | | | | | | | | | | |
| License management | | | | | | | | | | |
| Fault resolution (making the hardware and software work together) | | | | | | | | | | |
| Others: | | | | | | | | | | |
| | | | | | | | | | | |
| | | | | | | | | | | |
| | | | | | | | | | | |
| | | | | | | | | | | |
| | | | | | | | | | | |

**Figure 8-1**
*(Continued).*

8-2 will make it appear that the client had the idea, not you. (Putting clients in the driver's seat is the easiest way to ensure that they will accept any proposals you make as a result of the survey.)

The second way you can answer the question of what services the clients need is to look in your local newspaper and to read the case studies in the magazines or trade papers. These all serve as sources of ideas that you can add to your survey. You may even want to simply offer a service and see how many clients respond. Often clients will say they aren't interested in a service if you ask them first, but will respond favorably if the service is already in place.

Notice that Question 9 of Fig. 8-2 starts with a yes or no question and then adds an open-ended second part. Sometimes you need to ask a yes or

| Overall Skills Survey | | | | | | | | | | |
|---|---|---|---|---|---|---|---|---|---|---|

*Networking*  See Fig. 3-1 in Chap. 3.

*Training*

| | Level | | | | | | | | | |
|---|---|---|---|---|---|---|---|---|---|---|
| | High | | | | | | | | | Low |
| **Skills** | 10 | 9 | 8 | 7 | 6 | 5 | 4 | 3 | 2 | 1 |
| Database | | | | | | | | | | |
| Spreadsheet | | | | | | | | | | |
| Word processing | | | | | | | | | | |
| Graphics software | | | | | | | | | | |
| Custom software | | | | | | | | | | |
| Network maintenance and administration | | | | | | | | | | |
| Hardware maintenance and repair | | | | | | | | | | |
| Technical support technician | | | | | | | | | | |
| Peripheral device support (print server support) | | | | | | | | | | |
| Others: | | | | | | | | | | |
| | | | | | | | | | | |
| | | | | | | | | | | |
| | | | | | | | | | | |

**Figure 8-1**
(*Continued*).

no question to avoid wasting the customer's time. Make sure you don't stop at just yes or no, though. Always add a second part that makes customers think about what you actually want them to do.

Figure 8-2 also shows two common Internet-related questions. Remember that the Internet is likely going to be your future. Even if you can't help a client with the Internet very much today, you can always keep this form on file as a source of potential clients later. It's important to keep all of your options open when you design a questionnaire.

# The Consulting Approach

**Overall Skills Survey**

*Other*

| Skills | Level High 10 | 9 | 8 | 7 | 6 | 5 | 4 | 3 | 2 | Low 1 |
|---|---|---|---|---|---|---|---|---|---|---|
| Technical writing (network documentation and user manuals) | | | | | | | | | | |
| Others: | | | | | | | | | | |
| | | | | | | | | | | |
| | | | | | | | | | | |
| | | | | | | | | | | |
| | | | | | | | | | | |

**Figure 8-1**
*(Continued).*

## Making Clients Aware of What Certification Means

Your clients may not even know what your certification means. After all, until you read this book you may not have known what certification involved or what you would get out of it. Your clients are probably less informed than you are about Novell certification, yet this is one area that they really do need to know about. It always pays to keep your clients informed. A little information goes a long way when it comes to helping the client see the need for a particular course of action.

As a Novell-certified professional you can usually charge a little more than your noncertified competition for the same service. The reason is simple—you've demonstrated that you possess a set of fully developed skills, while the competition hasn't. (*Demonstration* in this case means a full examination by a competent authority.) Clients won't see the value of this demonstration until you tell them about it. Until they do understand the significance of certification, their reaction to the higher rates you

**Figure 8.2**
Sample Customer Survey.

---

**Sample Customer Survey**

1. In what ways do you see your need for customized software support growing in the future? How far into the future?

2. What types of new products are you planning to build in the future? How will this affect your network?

3. When do you plan to downsize your current mainframe database to a PC LAN?

4. How can we improve the reliability of your network? What types of hardware and software purchases are you willing to support to make these changes?

5. Are there tasks that you would like the network to perform but that you can't get it to do?

6. Have you considered any contingency plans if the network fails? If so, have you actually tested them?

7. Which methods do you find most effective for protecting your software investment?

8. Are there any other ways you could see my business helping to make yours grow?

9. Do you intend to get on the Internet sometime in the future? If so, why?

10. What kind of expectations do you have for your Web site, and is there a way that I can help you achieve those expectations?

---

charge will range from accusations of overcharging to threats of retaining someone else's services. However, many of these objections go away once you make them aware of the advantages of certification.

The approach you take to this education process depends on the techniques you use to run your business. A hard-sell consultant may want to schedule a meeting with the client to talk about this new certification and to make a proposal based on what it represents. A soft-sell consultant may choose to simply print a brochure that fully explains what certification means and provide it to the client during a scheduled visit. Other consultants may use a combination of both approaches or may even simply mention it during the course of a regular meeting. Your methods of managing your business determine which techniques feel the most comfortable to you. However, the question of informing the client is clear. If you don't tell your clients why your certification is

# The Consulting Approach

important, then they will never know. An uninformed client is your very worst enemy.

There are specific advantages to each technique we describe for keeping your clients informed. For example, brochures can double as advertising. If a client passes your brochure on to a friend, you may find yourself with a new client. On the other hand, the direct special meeting approach may yield a new networking job. The instant cash after you get your certification can improve your self-esteem. A mention during a regular meeting may improve the intimacy between you and your clients. They may feel that you're letting them in on something special. This often translates into greater customer loyalty and support.

You need to consider the temperament of your clients as well when approaching them with news of your certification. Some clients like to talk with a consultant who lets them think about whatever the consultant has to say. They like to take the time required to fully think about what the new certification does mean to their business. For example, many educational and professional organizations, like those for lawyers and doctors, fall into this category. Other clients may appreciate the hard sell. They take it as a sign that you are an aggressive businessperson when you present your certification quickly and then add a proposal on how they could use the certification within their businesses. Many retail customers fall into this category. Using the mention-during-a-meeting approach with a small-business client really works wonders. Small businesses need to maintain a feeling of intimacy, rather than the cold business approach used by corporations. Whatever method you use, make sure you take your temperament and that of your clients into account before you pursue it.

## Determining What to Charge

Figuring out what to charge is always difficult. Charging too much will yield a dead business when your clients go to your nearest competitor for their networking needs. Charging too little may give you more business but not much profit. You need to find the middle ground between charging too much and too little. Unfortunately, this is like one of those psychology tests that we all hate. There are no right answers—just right answers for *you*. No matter how little you charge, someone who really wants a lower price can probably find it. The same holds true for higher prices. Of course, the people who determine this middle ground are your competitors. Your competitors are the ones who'll steal your clients and put you out of business if possible. (Of course, you'll do the same to your competitors, given the chance.) The bottom line is that if a client sees an opportunity to get the same level of support that you provide from someone else for less money, you can be sure they'll use it.

So how do you determine what the middle ground is? You can start by doing a little research. Simply call the competition to see what they charge. There is no reason for them to withhold the information from you if you call as someone looking for information rather than as a competitor. Another place to look is your local computer magazine or newspaper. Vendors often publish their rates for specific types of installations.

Sometimes the previous methods don't produce any results. When this happens, you can resort to a number of alternative methods to get the information you need. For example, if you have a large enough client base with fairly new LANs, you can always ask them what they paid for the service. Of course, this only helps if you didn't install the LAN yourself. Federal, state, and local governments keep statistics of what businesses charge for certain services. You could find what you need to know from these sources, as well.

There are other resources you should consider using. For example, CompuServe and other online services host a wide variety of consultant-based forums. You can usually find out the current rate for a given service by polling this group of people. One word of caution here: many of the consultants who frequent these online services are at the upper end of the pay scale. You may not get a true reading on what the actual average rate of pay is for a specific service.

As you can see, the only limits on the sources of information you use are the resources you want to tap. Deciding what you want to charge doesn't stop here. You also need to resolve such issues as what to charge for parts. Some consultants don't charge anything at all. They make up for any parts sales by charging a higher hourly rate. Other consultants tack 10 to 15 percent onto the price of the parts they sell and charge a lower hourly rate. Both approaches are equally useful. You need to decide which approach your clients will appreciate more.

There's also the issue of when to apply different rates. Some consultants offer more than one service. You need to decide if you want to charge the same rate for software installation as you do for network maintenance. If you do decide to charge one inclusive rate, you may find that some customers balk when you present a bill for training that costs as much as their network installation.

If you decide to use different pay scales for different services, you need to decide when one pay scale ends and the other begins. This is one area where consultants can run into trouble. Some clients will try to cheat the consultant by saying that the service performed was subject to a lower rate than the service the consultant actually performed. For example, what happens if clients constantly interrupt you with questions during a network installation? Do you charge the network installation rate or the lower training rate? The clients may choose the training rate. They may not feel that you deserve the full networking rate since you spent that time training them. The best course of action is to tell clients what rate you are charging for the work you are performing. Make sure you inform them when the rate has changed because the task you're performing has changed.

As you can see, rate setting isn't the easiest part of consulting. You need to expend the energy required to provide clients with written rates and the methods you use for charging them. You also need to make them aware of when that rate changes and why. If possible, always make sure you write down the rules for rate changes and get the customer's signature. (Many consultants refuse to work without a signed contract. It's very easy to see why.)

## Professionalism

*Respect—it's not given, it's earned.* That's a saying many of us hear from more than one source as we advance along our career paths. Yet, how many of us really know what the saying means? Professionalism in the way you perform your job is what earns the respect of your clients. Professionalism means that you are proud of your abilities and of the work you do. It also means that you set certain standards for yourself and stand by the work you do. Some people call this type of behavior old-fashioned or out-of-date, but most clients appreciate a professional when they see one.

Where do you stand on this issue? How do you know when you achieve professional status? Some people set up a stiff set of rules and call it professionalism. Nothing could be further from true professionalism than a set of stiff rules. Even crooks and thieves set up rules for themselves. They always use the rules as a means to skirt their real responsibilities and neglect to fulfill their promises. Professionalism is more a mind-set and less a stiff set of rules than many people think. A professional needs to bend with the changing circumstances of everyday living. Figure 8-3 provides a checklist that you can use to measure your professional standing.

**Figure 8.3**
Professional Network Consultant's Business Guide.

### A Guide to Professionalism

- Consider using high-quality parts whenever possible. High quality does not necessarily mean high cost. Look for product reviews in trade magazines and newspapers. It also helps to look for opinions from other network professionals via CompuServe or other online media.

- Try to reduce costs whenever it will not affect the quality or usefulness of a product the client needs. If a product breaks the first time you use it or the part does not perform the task the client requires, then buying it at a discount does not solve any problems. In fact, it actually creates more problems. However, buying a high-priced product simply to get the name value discredits your ability to help the client make prudent buying decisions.

- Always consider the cost of losing a client versus the cost of losing money on one job. Losing a client always costs you more money than you'll lose from one job. If the client assumes that you mistreated him or her, find out what it will take to restore confidence. Often this means that you'll lose the profit from one job to save the client's trust.

- Never break the law to meet the demands of an unyielding client. For example, some clients will insist that you install pirated software on their networks even though they know such an act is illegal. It is always better to lose a client than to knowingly break the law. Otherwise, clients will expect you to break the law as often as they see fit. In addition, you will share in the client's guilt if you get caught performing an illegal act.

- Try to honor your warranty whenever possible. Many clients will try to convince you to honor unreasonable interpretations of the warranty you offer as part of your services. It often helps to honor an unreasonable request to maintain the client. Of course, this can backfire if the client starts expecting you to perform this service every time there is a dispute. The most reasonable course of action is to make sure the client understands that you are honoring an unreasonable request in the hope of maintaining a good relationship.

- Use the clearest wording possible in any written documentation that you provide the client. This includes contracts and warranties. Make sure you go through the contract or warranty with clients

**Figure 8.3**
(*Continued*).

> and explain anything they don't understand. Using this technique helps reduce confusion later. It may also prevent you from losing valued clients by reducing the chances of misunderstandings.
>
> - Always perform the work to the best of your ability. Even if the clients do not possess the level of technical competence that you do, they do know what tasks the network should perform when you finish. Make sure that both hardware and software are up to par. Alert the users to potential problems with equipment that you did not install. Help clients understand why there are specific limitations to the installations you create for them.
>
> - Never be afraid to admit that you can't perform a specific task. The clients can respect you if you simply say that you can't perform a specific task that they need help with. Trying to perform a task when you lack the skills will make customers less likely to hire you again in the future.

As you can see, there are many situations where you might need to take time to think about the consequences of your actions before you actually do them. For example, when does a client deserve warranty service rather than paying for a new piece of hardware? There are gray areas that make this a hard question to answer. Yet, if you don't answer the question you may find yourself in a no-win situation. Imagine that a client calls you in for warranty service on a drive that broke during use. If it appears that the client broke the part, you might feel they should pay for it. On the other hand, what if the part is so poorly made that there isn't any way to use it without breaking it? If this is an expensive part and the vendor has a reputation for not honoring the warranty, you may have to replace it yourself. (This happens more often than you might think with inexpensive parts.) Choosing to perform the warranty service means that you'll lose money on the job. On the other hand, if you don't provide warranty service, you'll lose a valuable client.

Perhaps the most difficult part of being a professional is figuring out when actions on your part could prevent a situation from happening at all. For example, in our previous example you might choose to use a higher-quality part during installation. The higher-quality part will last longer and you won't need to figure out whether to honor your warranty. Because you used a higher-quality part, both you and the client are happy with the results. Setting a standard for yourself means you could lose a few jobs because you can't compete on cost, but it may prevent you from losing money later when the inexpensive parts break down. Every job has potential risks and paybacks. The professional weighs the cost of each action during a job and chooses the course that produces the best long-term results.

Professionalism is important for another reason. When people see you as a technician certified by Novell to maintain their network, they expect a higher standard of service. After all, you convinced the client to pay you a higher hourly rate based on the assumption that they would receive better service. You're supposed to represent the best that the client can get in regard to quality workmanship. Your certification proves that you care more about how people perceive your services than someone who doesn't choose to get certification. When you're on the job you represent not only yourself, but every other certified individual who follows you.

As you can see, *professionalism* is not a mere word. It represents a way of doing business and a particular mind-set. There are many "experts" performing network installations today, but few professionals. You need to work to maintain a professional mind-set if you expect people to regard you as something more than a hammer mechanic. Maintaining such a high standard is hard work, but it pays many dividends.

So what will professionalism buy you? It may buy you some peace of mind. Peace of mind may not seem like very much until you face hostile clients a few times. Professionals get a happy greeting from the client every time they go in to do work. The reason is simple—the client knows that the professional will do the very best he or she can to get the network up and running. More important than a great customer relationship, professionalism will buy you customer loyalty. Customer loyalty translates into regular paychecks with a lot less effort than finding a new client. Every time you have to find a new client, you need to set up a new contract, get to know the installation, and perform a lot of nonpaid work. This really reduces the benefit you see from working for the client. It isn't until you work for the client for a time that the relationship begins to pay off. (This does not mean that one-time jobs are not profitable, it simply means that long-term relationships are even more profitable.)

Even if professionalism is old-fashioned, people still respect it and look for it whenever possible. They want to know someone who takes the time to get the job done right the first time. Any other course of action is a waste of their time, of your time, and of materials, and will reduce the impact of your certification. Remember, you worked hard to become certified by Novell to do the work you do. Keep up the good work—maintain your professionalism.

## Conclusion

OK, are you all charged up and ready to get that price list together? A consultant needs to consider a lot more than just getting the network up and running. Not only do you have to learn to present your skills in a way that people understand, you have to learn to follow through on those skills to keep the customer happy. Getting certified is only the first part of a much longer process for the consultant. Building a happy client base can take years.

# CHAPTER 9

# DOS Micro Hardware

# Introduction

This chapter looks at the requirements for the DOS Micro Hardware exam. There are several discrete sections in this chapter. Each section helps you study for the exam in a different way. You can improve your chances of passing the exam by using two or more of the study methods provided in this chapter. In fact, it'll probably help if you study all the sections once and your favorite sections at least twice. Remember to review the study guidelines in Chap. 4 as required to ensure that you maintain the best possible study atmosphere.

The first section of this chapter is a *case study*. You'll perform some hands-on tasks that'll help you learn what you need to know to pass the examination. The case study will also come in handy for daily tasks, since we look at how to do such things as perform a workstation inventory. Even though you'll get a lot more from this section if you perform it on your own machine or a spare machine that you've borrowed, the inclusion of screen shots will help you gain something from the section even if you don't have a machine to work on.

The second area contains actual Novell *questions* for this course. It also includes the correct answers and an explanation of why those answers are correct. Try to answer each question yourself, look at the correct answer, and then determine where you went wrong if you did not answer correctly. We'll concentrate on DOS issues in this particular chapter, but be prepared for the occasional question on other issues, like Macintosh hardware configuration.

The next section is a *fun test*. This is an exercise where you'll look at some sample test questions and answer them. The answers appear in App. B at the back of the book. This will help you test what you learned in the previous section.

The final text section of the chapter is the *brain teaser*. You'll get to have a little fun working on some DOS Micro Hardware–related puzzles. In this case you'll spend some time looking at acronyms in a word-search puzzle. Remember that Novell will test your knowledge of acronyms, so learning as many of them as possible is very important. You may even want to take the opportunity to look these acronyms up in the glossary once you've completed the puzzle itself.

Finally, we'll spend some time using the *Jeopardy!*-type game. This section helps you look at the test from the opposite viewpoint. The game provides you with an answer—you need to come up with the corresponding question. The game awards points for correct answers, and takes points away for incorrect answers. You'll receive a score at the end of the game proclaiming that you either did or did not get your certificate.

# DOS Micro Hardware

By the time you finish this chapter you should have all the knowledge you need to perform basic DOS-related tasks. Even though Novell no longer tests this knowledge in a separate exam, you'll find DOS- and hardware-related questions in other certification exams. Use all the learning methods that we provide in this chapter to improve your chances of passing the exam. It's a good idea to save the fun test section until you are almost certain that you possess all the required knowledge. Remember, you can probably go through the test only two or three times at most before you'll start to remember the answers without really knowing the material. You'll likely want to save the brain teaser section as a treat for after you've completed the fun test successfully.

Everyone who wants their certification needs to learn the material in this chapter—there are no exceptions. This chapter provides the basics that you'll use to learn other computing concepts in this book. Without a firm foundation of knowledge, there's no way that you'll fully understand the material in the other chapters. Make sure you pass this exam before you go on.

## Case Study

There are two sections to this exam. First, you need to know about the hardware that forms the basis for your workstations and servers. Second, you need to know about the operating system used by the Intel architecture machines. There is little doubt as to why you need to know about the hardware. Any network contains a great deal of hardware, much of it network-specific.

It's all too easy to tell yourself that there is little that a network setup requires from the DOS prompt. The setup looks simple. All you have to do is load a couple of device drivers and/or TSRs and you're ready to go. However, if this is where your setup stops, your client will never obtain all the functionality possible from a workstation. The workstation may not even work properly. There are a number of things you must do to improve the workstation environment after you finish the initial network installation.

This case study helps you build a knowledge base of both the hardware and software required to make your LAN work. It assumes that you're using an Intel 80x86 architecture machine and that you have access to a few hand tools, like screwdrivers and pliers. Here are the situations that we'll work with:

- You need to document the contents of every workstation on the network in preparation for an inventory.

- The company decided to hire a few more employees and you need to get their machines ready by installing a network adapter and the appropriate software.

- A user needs updated hardware to get the job done. You need to add the hardware, then reconfigure the machine for best performance.

## Workstation Inventory

In this section, you perform a visual check on the contents of a workstation attached to your LAN. You could rely on a program like CheckIt or MSD to perform the check for you, but you need to perform the visual check for inventory purposes. In addition, these inventory aids wouldn't provide the valuable serial and model numbers needed for future reference.

**WARNING:** Remove power from your computer before opening the case. Failure to do so can result in severe electrical shock.

1. Unplug the power cords for the computer, monitor, modem, and any other external peripherals from their outlets.

2. Look at the back and sides of your computer for screws used to hold the case cover in place. Loosen and remove these screws. Make sure you don't loosen and remove any ancillary screws, like the ones used to hold the power supply in place.

3. Open the case of your computer and identify the following parts: CPU, disk drives, video adapter, hard disk controller, serial and parallel ports, and floppy and hard disk drives. Use the form in Fig. 9-1 to record the number and type of these components.

**NOTE** *Even though Fig. 9-1 includes places for I/O port, IRQ, and DMA settings, most modern hardware uses software setups or plug-and-play instead. If your hardware uses a software setup, use the diagnostic or setup program provided by the vendor to determine the current settings. Using plug-and-play means that the operating system may take over the job of configuring the hardware (in the case of Windows 95). You still need to know what these settings mean and how to reconfigure the hardware should the operating system run into difficulty. Make sure you record the ideal hardware settings for plug-and-play–configured machines.*

# DOS Micro Hardware

**Figure 9-1**
Workstation Data Sheet.

**Workstation Data Sheet**

ID number: _____

Date purchased: _____

Place of purchase: _____

CPU type: _____   Brand: _____   Speed: _____ MHz

Bus Type:   ISA ❏   EISA ❏   Microchannel ❏   PCI ❏

Serial number: _____

Warranty info: _____


RAM type: _____   Brand: _____   Speed: _____   On/above: _____

Above brand: _____   Settings: _____


Video type: _____   Brand: _____

Serial number: _____

Controller brand: _____   Settings: _____


Floppy disk:   A brand: _____

Size:   360 ❏   1.2 ❏   720 ❏   1.44 ❏   Other: _____

Serial number: _____


Floppy disk:   B brand: _____

Size:   360 ❏   1.2 ❏   720 ❏   1.44 ❏   Other: _____

Serial number: _____


Disk controller: _____   Brand: _____

Settings: _____   Channel: 0   ID: _____   Other: _____

Hard disk 1: _____   Brand: _____

Purchase date: _____   From whom: _____

Size: _____   Heads: _____   Cyls: _____   SPT: _____

Serial number: _____

**Figure 9.1**
(*Continued*).

Hard disk 2: \_\_\_\_\_   Brand: \_\_\_\_\_

Purchase date: \_\_\_\_\_   From whom: \_\_\_\_\_

Size: \_\_\_\_\_   Heads: \_\_\_\_\_   Cyls: \_\_\_\_\_   SPT: \_\_\_\_\_

Serial number: \_\_\_\_\_

NIC type: \_\_\_\_\_   Brand: \_\_\_\_\_

Date purchased: \_\_\_\_\_   From whom: \_\_\_\_\_

IRQ: \_\_\_\_\_   I/O: \_\_\_\_\_   Base mem: \_\_\_\_\_

DMA: \_\_\_\_\_   Slot: \_\_\_\_\_   Cable type: \_\_\_\_\_

Node addr: \_\_\_\_\_   Boot prom: \_\_\_\_\_

Serial number: \_\_\_\_\_

Tape drive type: \_\_\_\_\_   Brand: \_\_\_\_\_

Date purchased: \_\_\_\_\_   From whom: \_\_\_\_\_

IRQ: \_\_\_\_\_   I/O: \_\_\_\_\_   Base mem: \_\_\_\_\_

DMA: \_\_\_\_\_   Slot: \_\_\_\_\_   Cable type: \_\_\_\_\_

Serial number: \_\_\_\_\_

CD-ROM type: \_\_\_\_\_   Brand: \_\_\_\_\_

Date purchased: \_\_\_\_\_   From whom: \_\_\_\_\_

IRQ: \_\_\_\_\_   I/O: \_\_\_\_\_   Base mem: \_\_\_\_\_

DMA: \_\_\_\_\_   Slot: \_\_\_\_\_   Cable type: \_\_\_\_\_

Serial number: \_\_\_\_\_

Other equipment type: \_\_\_\_\_   Brand: \_\_\_\_\_

Date purchased: \_\_\_\_\_   From whom: \_\_\_\_\_

IRQ: \_\_\_\_\_   I/O: \_\_\_\_\_   Base mem: \_\_\_\_\_

DMA: \_\_\_\_\_   Slot: \_\_\_\_\_   Cable type: \_\_\_\_\_

Serial number: \_\_\_\_\_

Other information:_____

_____

4. While you have the case open, perform any required maintenance. For example, you could use compressed air to blow any dust out of the interior. You could also perform a visual inspection of the components. Look for things like loose and frayed cables or other physical damage.

5. Put the case cover and screws back into place. There's no need to tighten the screws until they break. All you need to do is make them snug.

6. Plug the computer and associated peripheral devices into their associated outlets.

7. Turn the machine on and perform any required diagnostic checks.* Always check the machine's operation after you open the case—even if you did nothing more than a visual inspection. This extra step could save you time later.

## Workstation Setup

In this section of the case study, you prepare a new workstation for use by someone on the network. This means that you need to check the machine for the required hardware, add a NIC, and then install the appropriate software. It also means that you need to check the machine itself and the initial network connection. Normally, you would include creating the required accounts and other network-specific tasks in the workstation setup. We cover these situations in other chapters.

**WARNING:** Remove power from your computer before opening the case. Failure to do so can result in severe electrical shock.

1. Unplug the power cords for the computer, monitor, modem, and any other external peripherals from their outlets.

2. Look at the back and sides of your computer for screws used to hold the case cover in place. Loosen and remove these screws. Make sure you don't loosen and remove any ancillary screws like the ones used to hold the power supply in place.

3. Open the computer case and determine if the user will require any additional hardware. Take this opportunity to configure and install the NIC. Make sure that you configure the card for an unused IRQ,

---

*You can use a variety of diagnostic aids to check your machine. The most common aids include products like CheckIt from Touchstone Software.

**NOTE**  *Step 3 assumes that you'll need to perform some level of manual configuration for your hardware. Most of the new hardware available on the market today uses either software or plug-and-play configuration. This mean that you install the hardware, then configure it later using a utility supplied by the vendor (or allow the operating system to perform the configuration if it supports this feature).*

   I/O address, network address, and DMA as required. Follow the vendor instructions that you received with the card. Many vendors don't use hardwired setups any more; they use software setups instead. Wait until Step 9 to perform any software setups.

4. Put the case cover and screws back into place. There is no need to tighten the screws until they break. All you need to do is make them snug.

5. Plug the computer and associated peripheral devices into their associated outlets.

6. Put your DOS setup disk in drive A and turn the machine on. Get into the BIOS setup by pressing Ctrl-Alt-Escape or other key combination; your machine usually displays a message that tells how to get into the BIOS setup. Perform any required BIOS setup. This includes defining things like your equipment setup and inputting the system time and date. Once you complete the setup, press F5 or whatever key your BIOS uses to save the setup. This information normally appears at the bottom of the display.

7. Once the machine reboots, it should read the setup disk in drive A. Simply follow the vendor instructions to partition and format drive C (if required). After you finish this step, you can install DOS (or another operating system, like Windows 95). Most of the setup is automated with newer versions of DOS. All you need to do is answer a few questions and swap a few disks.

8. Now you have the machine set up and ready to go. Reboot the machine again and perform any required diagnostic checks. Always check the machine's operation after you open the case—even if you did nothing more than a visual inspection. This extra step could save you time later.

9. It's time to check how the workstation interacts with the network. Make sure you connect a network connector onto the back of the NIC. In some cases, the NIC displays some sort of status light to

# DOS Micro Hardware

**NOTE** *Step 9 assumes that you're using DOS or an older version of Windows on your network. Newer operating systems, like Windows 95 and Windows NT 4, perform the network setup as part of the installation process. Even if you add a NIC later, operating systems like Windows 95 will automatically detect the NIC and lead you through the network installation process. Make certain that you understand the requirements for your operating system before you attempt to install network support.*

show that you are using an active connection. This is the time to perform any NIC software setups. Just follow the vendor instructions to get the IRQ, network address, I/O address, and DMA setup. Install any required network drivers on drive C, add any required commands to AUTOEXEC.BAT and CONFIG.SYS, and reboot the machine.

10. Log onto the network using your password. Observe how the workstation reacts. If you don't see any problems, turn the workstation off. This doesn't complete the setup; it merely prepares the workstation for use. Refer to the case studies in the other chapters of this book for complete setup examples.

## Workstation Optimization

This case study provides you with some of the basics required to optimize a workstation after you add a new piece of hardware or software.* A network administrator performs this task a lot as users get promoted, change job profiles, or simply update their equipment. While you could rely on vendor-supplied optimizers like the MEMMAKER utility supplied with DOS versions 5.0 and above, there are times when you need to provide a little hand editing to get the most from your machine. In addition, knowing how to edit the machine's configuration by hand helps a lot when it comes time to troubleshoot your configuration.

In this case study a user gets promoted and needs additional workstation capability to get the job done. You already added the required hardware and software to the workstation. All you need to do now is optimize the system configuration. The case study assumes that you're using DOS 6.x (we'll

---

*Get *Memory Management and Multitasking Beyond 640K* by Lenny Bailes and John Mueller (Windcrest/McGraw-Hill, ISBN 0-8306-3476-2) for complete details on how to improve workstation performance. This includes setups for Windows, DESQview, and OS/2.

# Chapter Nine

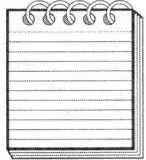

**NOTE** *Advanced operating systems like Windows 95 and Windows NT 4 require special tuning techniques that lie outside the scope of this book. Make sure you take the time to learn about the various tuning options at your disposal if you work with one of these operating systems. Every operating system offers tradeoffs that you need to know about to get the very best performance from the machine. You'll also want to look at hardware-specific performance inhibitors, like lack of memory.*

use DOS 6.2) with EMM386 as your memory manager, and that your DOS directory contains all the utilities normally provided with the operating system. There's little chance you can perform the case study unaltered since each PC contains different hardware and uses different software. However, you can easily modify the case study to meet your specific needs and software. Simply follow the commands as listed, but modify any changes to AUTOEXEC.BAT and CONFIG.SYS to reflect your setup.

1. At the DOS prompt, type *MEM /C* and press Enter. You should see a display similar to the one in Fig. 9-2. Of course, your display will reflect the software and hardware loaded on your machine.

2. This display provides you with a lot of information. Depending on your setup, you may need to use the MORE command to display all of it. Simply type *MEM /C | MORE* and press Enter to see the information one screen at a time. You could also use the /P parameter for the MEM command. What you are looking for in this display is opportunities to increase the amount of conventional memory.

3. Note that there are quite a few TSRs and device drivers loaded into conventional memory. If we load those programs high, then applications that need the conventional memory will have it. The way to optimize workstation memory use is to change or add entries in

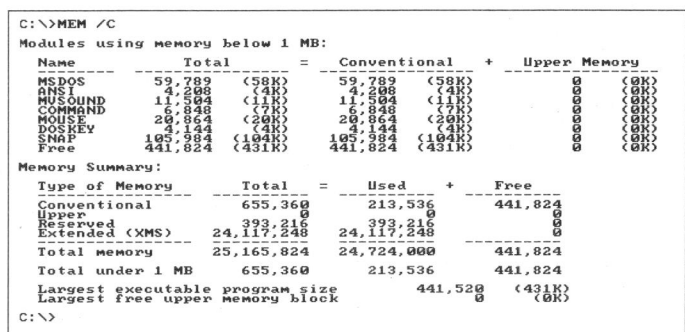

**Figure 9-2**
Sample MEM Display.

# DOS Micro Hardware

```
FILES=60
BUFFERS=10
DEVICE=C:\DOS\ANSI.SYS
SHELL=C:\DOS\COMMAND.COM C:\DOS\ /E:2048 /p
DEVICE=D:\PROAUDIO\MVSOUND.SYS D:3 Q:7 S:1,220,1,5 M:0 J:1
LASTDRIVE=E
BREAK=ON
STACKS=9,256
FCBS=1,0
```

**Figure 9-3**
Default CONFIG.SYS File.

```
ECHO ←[1;37;44m
C:\DOS\MODE CON: LINES=43
PATH C:\DOS;D:\WIN;D:\PKZIP;D:\PCTOOLS;D:\UTILS\MOUSE;D:\PROAUDIO;D:\TAPCIS\SCAN;
SET PCTOOLS=D:\PCTOOLS\DATA
C:\DOS\SMARTDRV.EXE 6144 6144 /V
D:\UTILS\MOUSE\MOUSE.COM 2
C:\DOS\DOSKEY.COM
SET BLASTER=A220 D1 I5 T3
D:\PROAUDIO\PAS SET VOLUME TO 40
```

**Figure 9-4**
Default AUTOEXEC.BAT File.

CONFIG.SYS and AUTOEXEC.BAT. Figure 9-3 shows the current CONFIG.SYS. Figure 9-4 shows the current AUTOEXEC.BAT.

4. As you can see, these files contain very simple entries. The first step in optimizing workstation memory use is creating the proper environment. Adding three simple lines to CONFIG.SYS can greatly improve the memory picture:

   ```
   DEVICE=C:\DOS\HIMEM.SYS
   DEVICE=C:\DOS\EMM386.EXE NoEMS NoVCPI
   DOS = UMB, HIGH
   ```

   Add these lines to your CONFIG.SYS if you haven't done so. Figure 9-5 shows the results of adding these lines to our example system. As you can see, we now have 471 K, an increase of 40 K over the previous configuration. Notice the two command line switches added to the EMM386 line. The NoEMS entry removes expanded memory support

**Figure 9-5**
Sample MEM Display after Modifying CONFIG.SYS.

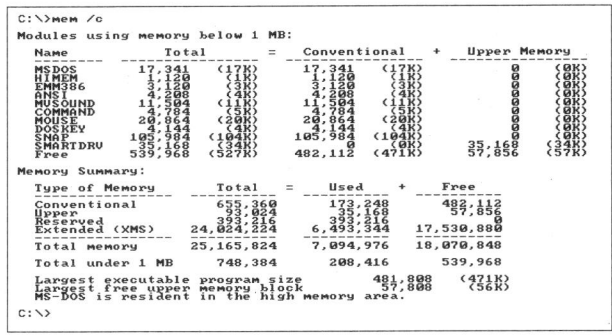

from the machine, while the NoVCPI entry removes support for an alternate XMS manager.

5. There's a lot more we can do to improve the memory picture. Type *MSD* and press Enter at the DOS prompt. MSD will take a few seconds to examine your system. Type *M* to select the Memory option. You should see a display similar to the one in Fig. 9-6.

6. As with the previous displays, there's a lot of information offered here. Look at the memory diagram (graphic representation of your memory setup). The entry of interest for our example system is the free area between D1FFh and DFFFh. You can add this memory to your UMB by adding the following switches to the EMM386 line of CONFIG.SYS: I=D1FF-DFFF.

7. There's more than meets the eye here, though. Note that there's an area above DFFFh that MSD can't guarantee is free for use. This is where hand tuning comes into play. You can research this area by looking through the various vendor manuals provided with the

**Figure 9-6**
Sample MEM Display with Memory Option Selected.

workstation and peripheral components. In this case, you find that the area is free, so you change the CONFIG.SYS EMM386 entry to I=D1FF-EFFF. Press Escape, and then F3 to exit MSD. Make any required changes to CONFIG.SYS, and then reboot by pressing Ctrl-Alt-Del.

8. Type *MEM /C* and press Enter. You won't see any increase in conventional memory at this point (unless there is more space for an application to automatically load itself into upper memory). However, you should see an increase in the UMB entry. Figure 9-7 shows the results for our test machine. The amount of UMB memory changed from 56 to 120 K. Now it's time to use that memory to improve the overall picture again.

9. The first step in this process is to determine how that upper memory is arranged. Type *MEM /F* to display the free memory arrangement. Figure 9-8 shows the results for our test machine. Notice that all the

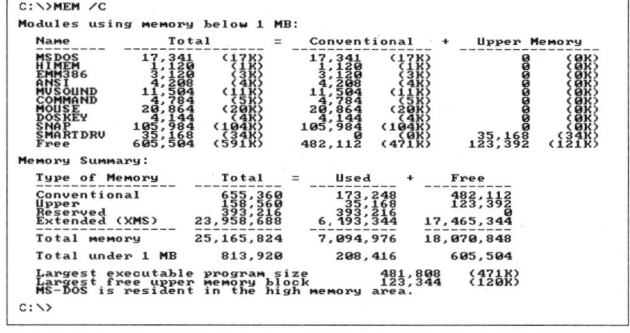

**Figure 9-7**
Sample MEM Display Showing Increase in UMB.

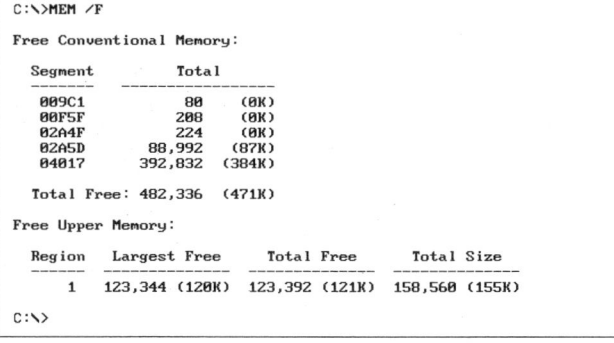

**Figure 9-8**
Sample MEM Display Showing Free Memory Arrangement.

free UMB memory appears in one big region. Depending on your hardware configuration, you may see two or more memory regions.

10. Refer to Figs. 3-3 and 3-4 for this step. Change the DEVICE= entry to DEVICEHIGH= for both the ANSI.SYS and MVSOUND.SYS lines in CONFIG.SYS. This change loads the drivers into UMB memory instead of taking valuable conventional memory. Add a LOADHIGH entry in front of the MOUSE and DOSKEY lines in AUTOEXEC.BAT. As with the CONFIG.SYS changes, this change places the TSRs into UMB memory. Once you make the required changes, reboot your machine.

11. Type *MEM /C* at the DOS prompt. Your display should look similar to the one in Fig. 9-9. Notice that our conventional memory increased to 538 K. This is quite a change from the 431 K that we originally had. The figure also shows that we still have some UMB memory left that could hold other TSRs and device drivers.

Of course, this case study presents only the coarsest of system adjustments. There are a number of other things you can do to hand-tune your workstation. For example, you could change the order in which the TSRs and device drivers load. This occasionally nets you an additional increase in available memory. There are a lot of other things you can do to improve system performance as well. For example, a disk cache can greatly improve system performance, but it uses up some of your precious memory. The Novell exams will test your ability to use the optimization utilities. You may as well enhance your overall system performance while you learn to use them.

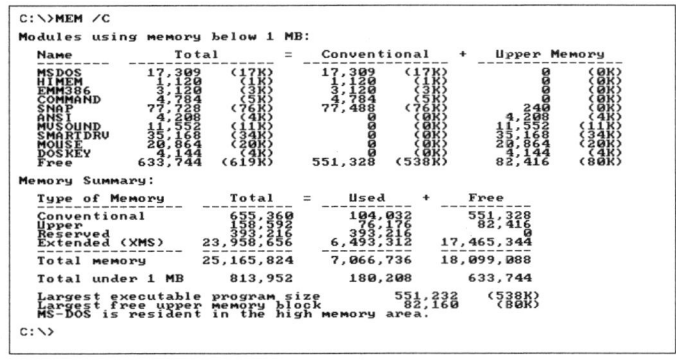

**Figure 9-9**
Sample MEM Display after Modifying CONFIG.SYS and AUTOEXEC.BAT.

# Study Questions

1. The letters CPU stand for:
   a. Critical processing unit
   b. Central processing unit
   c. Current process union
   d. None of the above

   *b.* The central processing unit (CPU) is the unit responsible for performing calculations, monitoring input and output, and assuming other responsibilities as needed.

2. The MEM command allows you to:
   a. Check the computer's memory for faults.
   b. Determine the amount of conventional, extended, and expanded memory available.
   c. Configure the computer's memory.
   d. Analyze the way that TSRs and device drivers use memory.

   *b and d.* MEM tells you how much and what type of memory you have available. It also provides a number of switches you can use to analyze memory usage on your machine.

3. The serial port outputs information _____.
   a. As a continuous stream
   b. 8 bits at a time
   c. 16 bits at a time
   d. 1 bit at a time

   *a and d.* The serial port uses special flow control signals or signal lines to output data as a continuous stream. It outputs this data one bit at a time (hence the name *serial*).

4. The /F parameter of the FORMAT command allows you to:
   a. Specify that you want the disk format verified.
   b. Format a 5.25-in disk with a write-protect tab attached.
   c. Override the default capacity of the formatted disk.
   d. Reduce the number of files that the root directory will accept.

c. You can use the /F parameter to specify the amount of space that the disk will contain. Of course, this is limited by the sizes that the disk can provide. For example, /F:1440 will format a 1.44-MB 3.5-in disk.

5. CONFIG.SYS contains:
   a. Entries for any device drivers you need
   b. An entry for the number of file handles you want
   c. The number of operating system stacks and their size
   d. All of the above

   *d.* CONFIG.SYS contains all the entries you see above. Make sure you know all the available entries and their parameters before you take the exam.

6. You can find the MC68000 processor on a(n):
   a. IBM PC
   b. Sun Workstation
   c. Apple Macintosh
   d. All of the above

   *c.* The Apple Macintosh uses the MC680x0 series of processors. This includes the 512K, 512Ke, Plus, Mac Classic, and SE models.

7. You can press _____ at the opening DOS menu to start DOS without any device drivers or TSRs.
   a. F1
   b. F3
   c. F5
   d. F7

   *c.* Pressing F5 bypasses both CONFIG.SYS and AUTOEXEC.BAT. This provides a clean environment that you can use for workstation testing and other purposes.

8. You can find the following expansion bus configurations on an Intel architecture machine:
   a. EISA 32-bit
   b. MCA 32-bit
   c. ISA 32-bit
   d. ISA 8/16-bit

# DOS Micro Hardware

*a, b, and d.* The reason that industry created the EISA and MCA buses is that the ISA bus can support only 8-bit and 16-bit (AT class machines only) cards. (Of course, this is only one of several reasons for the change.)

9. The major NIC card types include:
   a. Token Passing, EtherLink, and Proteon
   b. Token Ring, Ethernet, and Arcnet
   c. Token Ring, Ethernet, and Bus
   d. Bus, Star, and Ring

   *b.* This represents the three major NIC types available for the PC today.

10. The display adapter:
    a. Presents visual information created by the computer
    b. Connects the monitor to the computer
    c. Interprets digital computer information and generates video output
    d. Inputs video information to the computer

    *c.* The display adapter converts digital representations of data and outputs it to the monitor in a form that you can understand.

11. The computer normally uses SRAM for:
    a. Disk cache on the hard disk controller
    b. Storage on the display adapter
    c. To store the computer's configuration data
    d. As a short-term cache to speed CPU memory fetches

    *d.* Static RAM is far too expensive to use in place of the standard dynamic RAM used for system memory or hard disk storage. Some video adapters use a specialized form of memory called VRAM, but most use DRAM as well. The system configuration data normally gets stored in CMOS RAM, a special low-energy battery-backed RAM.

12. Most PCs support the following display standard(s):
    a. SVGA
    b. EGA
    c. MDA
    d. RGA

*a, b, and c.* Most PCs will support super video graphics array, enhanced graphics adapter, and monochrome display adapters.

13. The baud rate and bits per second rate of a serial port are always the same.
    a. True
    b. False

    *b.* The baud rate is almost never the same as the bit rate in modem to modem communications.

14. The DOS TREE command allows you to:
    a. Display the directory structure of the specified drive.
    b. Grow a tree in an outdated PC.
    c. Create an unlimited number of subdirectories.
    d. Connect subdirectories on network drives to the local drive.

    *a.* The TREE command displays the directory structure for the selected drive.

15. You can use a maximum of _____ root directory entries on a hard disk.
    a. 128
    b. 256
    c. 512
    d. 1024

    *c.* DOS allows a maximum of 512 root directory entries. You'll want to use subdirectories to keep the files organized long before you reach this limit.

16. The COUNTRY.SYS device driver provides support for:
    a. Foreign languages under DOS
    b. Use of DOS outside the United States
    c. Code page support under DOS
    d. Useful DOS commands in rural areas

    *a and c.* DOS can provide support for a variety of foreign languages. The information for each language appears within a code page. Selecting a code page will change the default language supported by DOS.

# DOS Micro Hardware

17. The maximum length of the PATH environment variable is:
    a. 256 characters
    b. 128 characters
    c. 127 characters
    d. 64 characters

    *c.* The maximum path length supported by DOS is 127 characters.

18. A 3.5-in 1.44-MB floppy disk contains:
    a. 80 tracks and 18 sectors per track
    b. 80 tracks and 9 sectors per track
    c. 40 tracks and 18 sectors per track
    d. 80 tracks and 15 sectors per track

    *a.* The 1.44-MB floppy disk contains 80 tracks, 18 sectors per track, and 512 bytes per sector for a total of 1,474,560 bytes of usable disk space.

19. A standard VGA display adapter can present a maximum of:
    a. 640 × 320 resolution and 16 colors
    b. 640 × 320 resolution and 256 colors
    c. 640 × 480 resolution and 16 colors
    d. 640 × 480 resolution and 256 colors

    *d.* A standard VGA can display 640 by 480 pixels and 256 colors. Advanced adapters can display more pixels and colors.

20. You will find the following types of RAM in most computer systems:
    a. CMOS
    b. SRAM
    c. VRAM
    d. DRAM
    e. ROM

    *a, b, c, and d.* The computer uses a variety of RAM to speed performance and enhance system usability.

21. You can create a path longer than 127 characters using the _____ command(s).
    a. JOIN and SUBST
    b. JOIN and APPEND

**Chapter Nine**

   c. MORE and APPEND

   d. SUBST and APPEND

   *d.* You can use the SUBST and APPEND commands to shorten the length of specific path parameters, enabling you to create a path longer than 127 characters.

22. Differences between the 8088 and 80286 include the ability to:

   a. Run in real mode.

   b. Use 16 MB of RAM.

   c. Run in protected mode.

   d. Use a 24-bit address.

   *b, c, and d.* The 80286 offered many advantages over its predecessor, the 8088.

23. A hard disk requires _____ while a floppy disk doesn't.

   a. Formatting

   b. Certification

   c. Partitioning

   d. Verification

   *c.* You must partition a hard disk before you can DOS format it (some hard disks also require a low-level format). A floppy doesn't require this intermediate step.

24. DOS is a _____ operating system.

   a. Protected mode

   b. Real mode

   c. Virtual 86 mode

   d. None of the above

   *b.* DOS runs on the entire Intel line of processors because it runs in real mode.

25. You always have to provide DOS with an AUTOEXEC.BAT file.

   a. True

   b. False

   *b.* You can easily boot DOS without either an AUTOEXEC.BAT or CONFIG.SYS file.

26. The MenuItem command allows you to:

   a. Define a menu item within AUTOEXEC.BAT.

# DOS Micro Hardware

    **b.** Create an alternative boot method.
    **c.** Define a menu item within CONFIG.SYS.
    **d.** All of the above.

    *c.* The MenuItem command is one of the commands you can use to create a startup menu for DOS. The menu allows you to select from one of several configurations.

**27.** DOS allows you to load as many device drivers as your system requires to operate.
    **a.** True
    **b.** False

    *a.* You can load as many device drivers as you require to operate your system as long as you don't exceed available conventional and upper memory.

**28.** The Apple Macintosh uses a _____ bus.
    **a.** ISA
    **b.** EISA
    **c.** MCA
    **d.** NuBus

    *d.* The Macintosh uses a bus that isn't compatible with the bus systems found in PCs.

**29.** The MODE command allows you to:
    **a.** Adjust the speed and other settings of your COM ports.
    **b.** Change the number of lines of text displayed on your monitor.
    **c.** Adjust the speed and other settings of your LPT ports.
    **d.** Toggle your computer between real and protected mode.

    *a and b.* The MODE command allows you to adjust your COM ports, change the number of text lines displayed on your monitor, and redirect your LPT ports (among other things).

**30.** A standard VGA display adapter outputs digital signals to the monitor.
    **a.** True
    **b.** False

    *b.* The VGA was one of the first widely distributed display adapters to use analog output. Older display adapters used digital signals.

**31.** The SYS.COM program allows you to:
   a. Reboot the system without pressing Ctrl-Alt-Del.
   b. Transfer the system files to another drive.
   c. Adjust the system operating parameters.
   d. Create a different operating system setup.

   *b.* You can use the SYS.COM program to transfer the two hidden operating system files to a floppy or hard disk drive.

**32.** DOS allows you to multitask applications.
   a. True
   b. False

   *b.* DOS allows you task switch applications. It can't perform true multitasking.

**33.** The TYPE command allows you to:
   a. Define the font used to display information on screen.
   b. Display the contents of a file.
   c. Send messages over a teletype.
   d. Create new types of files.

   *b.* You use the TYPE command to display the contents of a file.

**34.** Parallel ports provide _____ data line(s).
   a. 1
   b. 7
   c. 8
   d. 16

   *c.* A parallel port provides 8 data lines numbered 0 through 7. This allows the port to transfer 1 byte at a time to an attached device.

**35.** The term ROM means:
   a. Read-occasionally memory
   b. Random oxide memory
   c. Real orbital memory
   d. Randomly oriented money
   e. Read-only memory

   *e.* The computer uses read-only memory to store the computer's BIOS. Many add-on cards also provide some form of BIOS held in ROM.

# DOS Micro Hardware

36. DOS versions _____ and older support only 32-MB hard disk partitions.
    a. 4.01
    b. 4.0
    c. 3.4
    d. 3.3

    *d.* DOS versions 3.3 and older support only 32-MB hard disk partitions. You'll want to replace this old version of DOS with a newer version on networked machines.

37. One TB equals:
    a. 1 terabyte
    b. 1024 MB
    c. 1024 GB
    d. 1024 K

    *a and c.* A terabyte is equal to approximately a million, million bytes.

38. A standard serial port uses nine signals which include:
    a. TxD, RxD, GND, Strobe, RTS, CD, RI, DTR, DCE
    b. TxD, RxD, RTS, CTS, DSR, SG, CD, DTR, RI
    c. TxD, RxD, RTS, CTS, DCE, SG, CD, DTR, RI
    d. TxD, RxD, RTS, CTS, DTE, SG, CD, DCE, RI

    *b.* The standard serial port connections include transmitted data, received data, request to send, clear to send, data set ready, signal ground, carrier detect, data terminal ready, and ring indicator.

39. The ST506 interface:
    a. Transfers data at 5 MB/s and uses MFM encoding
    b. Transfers data at 15 MB/s and uses MFM encoding
    c. Transfers data at 7.5 MB/s and uses RLL encoding
    d. Transfers data at 10 MB/s and uses RLL encoding

    *a and c.* There are actually two different ST506 encoding methods. RLL supports a higher transfer rate and capacity.

40. Many hard disk controllers provide a BIOS.
    a. True
    b. False

*a.* The only way your computer knows how to interact with the hard disk controller is by accessing the hard disk controller BIOS or through a device driver.

# Fun Test

1. You can use a maximum of _____ root directory entries on a hard disk.
   a. 128
   b. 256
   c. 512
   d. 1024

2. The serial port outputs information:
   a. As a continuous stream
   b. 8 bits at a time
   c. 16 bits at a time
   d. 1 bit at a time

3. The display adapter:
   a. Presents visual information created by the computer
   b. Connects the monitor to the computer
   c. Interprets digital computer information and generates video output
   d. Inputs video information to the computer

4. The DOS TREE commands allows you to:
   a. Display the directory structure of the specified drive.
   b. Grow a tree in an outdated PC.
   c. Create an unlimited number of subdirectories.
   d. Connect subdirectories on network drives to the local drive.

5. The letters CPU stand for:
   a. Critical processing unit
   b. Central processing unit
   c. Current process union
   d. None of the above

**DOS Micro Hardware**                                                                                      259

6. Many hard disk controllers provide a BIOS.
   a. True
   b. False

7. The maximum length of the PATH environment variable is:
   a. 256 characters
   b. 128 characters
   c. 127 characters
   d. 64 characters

8. Differences between the 8088 and 80286 include the ability to:
   a. Run in real mode.
   b. Use 16 MB of RAM.
   c. Run in protected mode.
   d. Use a 24-bit address.

9. Most PCs support the following display standard(s):
   a. SVGA
   b. EGA
   c. MDA
   d. RGA

10. The MEM command allows you to:
    a. Check the computer's memory for faults.
    b. Determine the amount of conventional, extended, and expanded memory available.
    c. Configure the computer's memory.
    d. Analyze the way that TSRs and device drivers use memory.

11. The MenuItem command allows you to:
    a. Define a menu item within AUTOEXEC.BAT.
    b. Create an alternative boot method.
    c. Define a menu item within CONFIG.SYS.
    d. All of the above.

12. DOS versions _____ and older support only 32-MB hard disk partitions.
    a. 4.01
    b. 4.0

c. 3.4

d. 3.3

13. The SYS.COM program allows you to:
    a. Reboot the system without pressing Ctrl-Alt-Del.
    b. Transfer the system files to another drive.
    c. Adjust the system operating parameters.
    d. Create a different operating system setup.

14. The major NIC card types include:
    a. Token Passing, EtherLink, and Proteon
    b. Token Ring, Ethernet, and Arcnet
    c. Token Ring, Ethernet, and Bus
    d. Bus, Star, and Ring

15. The Apple Macintosh uses a(n) _____ bus.
    a. ISA
    b. EISA
    c. MCA
    d. NuBus

16. You can find the following expansion bus configurations on an Intel architecture machine:
    a. EISA 32-bit
    b. MCA 32-bit
    c. ISA 32-bit
    d. ISA 8/16-bit

17. DOS allows you to multitask applications.
    a. True
    b. False

18. A standard VGA display adapter can present a maximum of:
    a. 640 × 320 resolution and 16 colors
    b. 640 × 320 resolution and 256 colors
    c. 640 × 480 resolution and 16 colors
    d. 640 × 480 resolution and 256 colors

19. The /F parameter of the FORMAT command allows you to:
    a. Specify that you want the disk format verified.
    b. Format a 5.25-in disk with a write-protect tab attached.

# DOS Micro Hardware

      c. Override the default capacity of the formatted disk.

      d. Reduce the number of files that the root directory will accept.

20. The TYPE command allows you to:
    a. Define the font used to display information on screen.
    b. Display the contents of a file.
    c. Send messages over a teletype.
    d. Create new types of files.

21. You can press _____ at the opening DOS menu to start DOS without any device drivers or TSRs.
    a. F1
    b. F3
    c. F5
    d. F7

22. A standard VGA display adapter outputs digital signals to the monitor.
    a. True
    b. False

23. The COUNTRY.SYS device driver provides support for:
    a. Foreign languages under DOS
    b. Use of DOS outside the United States
    c. Code page support under DOS
    d. Useful DOS commands in rural areas

24. DOS is a _____ operating system.
    a. Protected mode
    b. Real mode
    c. Virtual 86 mode
    d. None of the above

25. One TB equals:
    a. 1 terabyte
    b. 1024 MB
    c. 1024 GB
    d. 1024 K

26. CONFIG.SYS contains:
    a. Entries for any device drivers you need
    b. An entry for the number of file handles you want
    c. The number of operating system stacks and their size
    d. All of the above

27. The baud rate and bits per second rate of a serial port are always the same.
    a. True
    b. False

28. A standard serial port uses nine signals which include:
    a. TxD, RxD, GND, Strobe, RTS, CD, RI, DTR, DCE
    b. TxD, RxD, RTS, CTS, DSR, SG, CD, DTR, RI
    c. TxD, RxD, RTS, CTS, DCE, SG, CD, DTR, RI
    d. TxD, RxD, RTS, CTS, DTE, SG, CD, DCE, RI

29. You can create a path longer than 127 characters using the command(s).
    a. JOIN and SUBST
    b. JOIN and APPEND
    c. MORE and APPEND
    d. SUBST and APPEND

30. You can find the MC68000 processor on a(n):
    a. IBM PC
    b. Sun Workstation
    c. Apple Macintosh
    d. All of the above

31. DOS allows you to load as many device drivers as your system requires to operate.
    a. True
    b. False

32. The ST506 interface:
    a. Transfers data at 5 MB/s and uses MFM encoding
    b. Transfers data at 15 MB/s and uses MFM encoding
    c. Transfers data at 7.5 MB/s and uses RLL encoding
    d. Transfers data at 10 MB/s and uses RLL encoding

# DOS Micro Hardware

33. You always have to provide DOS with an AUTOEXEC.BAT file.
    a. True
    b. False

34. The computer normally uses SRAM for:
    a. Disk cache on the hard disk controller
    b. Storage on the display adapter
    c. To store the computer's configuration data
    d. As a short-term cache to speed CPU memory fetches

35. A hard disk requires _____ while a floppy disk does not.
    a. Formatting
    b. Certification
    c. Partitioning
    d. Verification

36. A 3.5-in 1.44-MB floppy disk contains:
    a. 80 tracks and 18 sectors per track
    b. 80 tracks and 9 sectors per track
    c. 40 tracks and 18 sectors per track
    d. 80 tracks and 15 sectors per track

37. You will find the following types of RAM in most computer systems:
    a. CMOS
    b. SRAM
    c. VRAM
    d. DRAM
    e. ROM

38. The MODE command allows you to:
    a. Adjust the speed and other settings of your COM ports.
    b. Change the number of lines of text displayed on your monitor.
    c. Adjust the speed and other settings of your LPT ports.
    d. Toggle your computer between real and protected mode.

39. Parallel ports provide _____ data lines.
    a. 1
    b. 7
    c. 8
    d. 16

40. The term ROM means:
   a. Read-occasionally memory
   b. Random oxide memory
   c. Real orbital memory
   d. Randomly oriented money
   e. Read-only memory

## Brain Teaser

Now it's time to spend a little time flexing your brain in a new way. There isn't any reason why learning can't be fun. The brain teaser for this chapter is a word search puzzle. Figure 9-10 shows a grid of letters and an accompanying acronym list. All you need to do is find the acronym in the letter grid. Make sure you look forward, backward, diagonally, and vertically since the acronyms could be hidden in any of those positions. You'll find the solution for this brain teaser in App. C, "Brain Teaser Answers."

Once you complete the puzzle, you may want to take a second look through the word list. Look for any acronyms you can't identify in App. A, "List of Acronyms," and the glossary. Make sure you look at the meaning (when supplied) for each acronym as well. You may want to design your own word search puzzle of acronyms. Looking for acronyms using this kind of puzzle really embeds them in your mind.

## Disk Time

Don't forget to spend some time working with the CD-ROM that accompanies this book. It provides valuable, fun-to-use teaching aids that'll help you prepare for your exam. See "Disk Time" in the preface of this book for details about what the disk contains. Make sure you pay special attention to the parts of the Windows help file and Red Zone game that pertain to this chapter. Also, check out the acronym areas provided in both disk features—they'll help you get up to speed on what's going on in the industry faster.

# DOS Micro Hardware

| | | | | | | | | | | | | | | | |
|---|---|---|---|---|---|---|---|---|---|---|---|---|---|---|---|
| Y | I | S | N | A | B | D | N | D | Q | W | V | L | N | 2 | / | E | R |
| D | R | C | E | W | R | Q | X | F | D | D | I | T | T | Q | S | N | H |
| P | I | S | W | R | C | P | D | S | S | C | X | O | N | G | R | M | P |
| W | R | I | T | D | B | Z | A | / | B | C | M | E | E | Q | S | T | F |
| G | 2 | E | A | S | W | C | Q | N | J | I | K | P | L | B | M | R | R |
| I | E | E | E | / | C | Z | S | N | E | T | B | I | O | S | N | M | A |
| I | B | O | R | 2 | S | C | D | N | E | T | X | Z | R | W | F | H | I |
| N | C | J | C | V | S | H | E | W | S | S | C | C | L | D | H | M | D |
| R | D | T | Q | Z | X | Y | U | P | O | M | M | D | N | R | Q | Q | X |
| P | I | S | O | G | L | X | S | A | U | O | A | P | / | E | R | Q | X |
| Z | C | A | I | A | N | M | I | C | S | M | A | / | C | D | Q | D | B |
| L | V | S | R | N | T | F | S | T | Y | L | N | M | A | W | C | B | Z |
| J | M | S | O | D | M | F | T | R | L | G | G | K | A | A | S | T | Y |
| S | S | M | S | A | U | B | N | E | R | N | W | T | A | Y | Z | K | L |
| H | X | 2 | / | / | X | Q | W | E | A | D | C | C | P | E | R | X | Q |
| V | B | E | 2 | H | J | W | Q | E | Z | X | R | A | P | I | D | O | J |
| T | V | Y | R | P | N | W | C | D | R | Z | R | L | C | S | B | K | X |
| R | R | T | M | P | B | N | M | A | I | C | E | L | N | A | M | A | D |

**Figure 9-10**
Acronym Word Search Brain Teaser.

*Acronym List*

1. ADCCP
2. ANSI
3. APPC
4. ARPANET
5. BSC
6. CCITT
7. CMOS
8. CSMA/CD
9. DDCMP
10. DQDB
11. EBCDIC
12. EISA
13. FDDI
14. GOSIP
15. HDLC
16. IEEE
17. ISDN
18. LLAP
19. MSAU
20. MUX
21. NAEC
22. NETBIOS
23. NTFS
24. ODI
25. OS/2
26. PARC
27. RAID
28. RTMP
29. SCSI
30. SMTP

CHAPTER 10

# NetWare 3.x Administration

# Introduction

This chapter looks at the requirements for the 3.x Administration exam using several different study methods: case study, sample questions, fun test, and brain teaser. Each section of the chapter helps you study for the exam in a different way. You can improve your chances of passing the exam by using two or more study methods. It'll help if you study all the sections once and your favorite sections at least twice. Remember to review the study guidelines in Chap. 4 as required to ensure that you maintain the best possible study atmosphere.

The first section of this chapter is a *case study*. You'll perform some hands-on tasks that will help you learn what you need to know to pass the examination. In this case, we set up a simple network. You'll learn how to configure the hard drive, add users, and set up security. Even though you'll get a lot more from this section if you perform it on your own network, the inclusion of screen shots will help you gain something even if you don't have a network.

The second area contains sample questions for this course. We concentrate on setup and security questions for the latest version of NetWare 3.x in this section. It also includes the correct answers and an explanation of why those answers are correct. Try to answer each question yourself, look at the correct answer, and then determine where you went wrong if you didn't answer correctly.

The next section is a *fun test*. This is an exercise where you'll look at some sample test questions and answer them. The answers appear in App. B at the back of the book. This will help you test what you learned in the previous section.

The final text section of the chapter is the *brain teaser*. You'll get to have a little fun working on a NetWare 3.x–related puzzle. In this case, you'll get to pit your installation skills against a crossword puzzle. You'll need to know all about installing a NetWare 3.x network to complete this crossword since some of the clues are a little on the obscure side.

Finally, we'll spend some time using the *Jeopardy!*-type game. This section helps you look at the test from the opposite viewpoint. The game provides you with an answer—you need to come up with the corresponding question. The game awards points for correct answers, and takes points away for incorrect answers. You'll receive a score at the end of the game proclaiming that you either did or did not get your certificate.

You have three goals in this chapter. First, you need to know how to install and configure NetWare. This includes things like creating an effective directory setup. Getting the directory setup wrong will definitely affect your ability to protect the company's data. The second goal is to learn how to add users. This includes everything from the simple act of adding their names to the bindery to giving them specific rights through group assignments. Make sure you really understand everything that the users require. Your final goal is to learn all about NetWare 3.x security. Learning the Novell way to implement security is the only way to pass the certification exam.

Use all the learning methods that we provide in this chapter to improve your chances of passing the exam. It's a good idea to save the fun test and brain teaser sections until you're almost certain that you possess all the required knowledge. Remember, you can probably go through the test only two or three times at most before you'll start to remember the answers without really knowing the material. Obviously, the brain teaser is only good once—after that you'll have all the answers filled in.

## Case Study

In this case study, you'll prepare a network for use by a small company. After talking to the owner of the company you find the following information:

- There are four users. All of them are experts in their respective fields, but have very little network experience.
- There are four different applications, consisting of a word processor, a database, a spreadsheet, and an accounting package.
- One of the users will use all the applications. The other three users will use the spreadsheet, word processor, and database applications.
- Security is at a moderate level.
- All the users will print to a common laser-jet printer.

Once you obtain information about the company, you can start to configure the network. In the following sections you'll go through the steps necessary to make this network functional. Note the logical organization of the procedure. This is the most efficient method of configuring a network.

### Setting Up the Directory Structure

The first step is to create the directory structure you'll use. For this exercise you'll create a directory off the root of volume SYS called APPS. This will hold subdirectories for all the applications that the users of the network will need. You'll then create a DATA directory off the root to store the users' data. The DATA directory contains subdirectories that each application uses to store data. Each network user will also have a personal directory. NetWare will automatically create the directories for you later in the exercise.

Log into the network as supervisor to perform the tasks ahead.

1. At the F:> prompt, type *LOGIN SUPERVISOR,* then press Enter.

2. Create the directory structure for the network applications. At the F:> prompt, type *CD \\,* then press Enter.

3. You're now at the root of volume SYS. Type *MD APPS,* then press Enter.

4. You've created the master directory for all of your networked applications. Move into the APPS directory and create the individual directories for each application. At the F:\\> prompt, type *CD APPS* and press Enter.

5. Your prompt should now indicate F:\\APPS>. Create a directory for the spreadsheet application. Type *MD SS* and then press Enter.

6. Create directories for the word processing, database, and ACCOUNTING applications. Repeat Step 5, replacing *SS* with *WP, DB,* and *ACCT.*

7. Return to the root of volume SYS to create the data directory. Type *CD \\,* then press Enter.

8. Now make a DATA directory that the applications can use to store their data. To make the DATA directory from the root of SYS, type *MD DATA,* then press Enter.

9. You now have the master directory where your networked applications will store data. Move into the DATA directory and create individual data directories for each of the applications. At the F:\\> prompt, type *CD DATA* and press Enter.

10. Your prompt should now indicate F:\\DATA>. Create a data directory for the spreadsheet. Type *MD SS* and then press Enter.

11. Create directories for the word processing, database, and ACCOUNTING applications. Repeat Step 11, replacing *SS* with *WP, DB,* and *ACCT.*

12. Return to the root of volume SYS by typing *CD \\,* then press Enter. Figure 10-1 displays the directory structure that you've just created. Use the Novell LISTDIR utility to view your directory structure. At

**Figure 10-1**
Display of the LISTDIR Command Output.

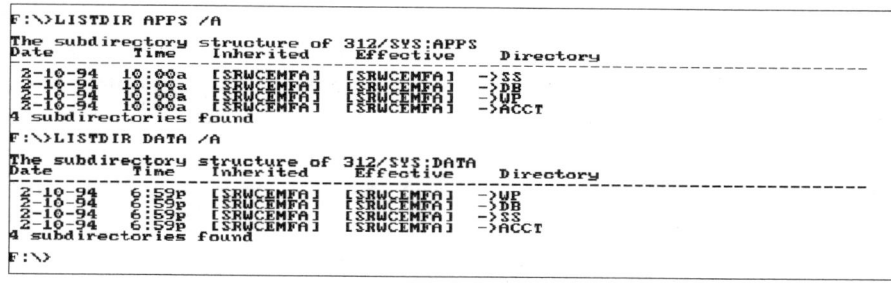

your F:\> prompt, type *LISTDIR APPS /a* to produce a listing of the applications directory, and then type *LISTDIR DATA /a* to produce a listing of the data directory.

## Creating the Users and Groups

Once you have created the directory structure, the next step is to create the user and group accounts. The NetWare utility to create the users and groups is SYSCON (system configuration).

1. To use the SYSCON utility, from the F:\> prompt type *SYSCON* then press Enter.

2. Move the menu highlight bar to *Supervisor Options* and press Enter. The Supervisor Options menu will appear just to the right of the previous menu.

3. The first option to modify is *Default Account Balance/Restrictions*. With the highlight bar on Default Account Balance/Restrictions, press Enter. A new option window will appear in the center of the screen.

4. The first option to change is *Limit Concurrent Connections*. Change this value from No to Yes. Move the highlight bar to Limit Concurrent Connections. With the highlight bar on Limit Concurrent Connections, type *Y*. This changes the option from No to Yes. Press Enter. This moves the highlight bar to the *Maximum Connections* option and will place a 1 in the highlight field. Accept this value by pressing Enter.

5. Move the highlight bar to *Create Home Directory for User*. The default setting for this option is YES. Press Enter to accept this value.

6. The next option is *Require Password*. With the highlight bar on the Require Password option, type *Y*, and then press Enter. This will change the value from No to Yes and automatically assign values to the rest of the options on the menu. For this exercise, you'll accept the default values that appear in the final options. Figure 10-2 displays all the changes made in this menu. Compare what's on your screen with Fig. 10-2. This completes our changes to the Default Account Balance/Restrictions menu.

7. Press the Escape key to return to the Supervisor Options menu.

8. Move the highlight bar to the *Default Time Restrictions* option and press Enter.

9. Your users will have access to the network from 6:00 A.M. to 7:00 P.M. Monday through Friday. The quickest way to restrict your user's access is to first remove all the asterisks from the window. With the cursor in the upper left corner of the screen, press F5. This is the *mark* or *toggle* key. Press F5 now to start the marking feature. Now press End, then Page Down to mark the entire window. After marking the entire window, press Delete to delete all the asterisks. Figure 10-3 shows the window after removing the asterisks.

10. You'll now replace the asterisks in the appropriate locations. This allows users to access the network. Move the cursor to the position

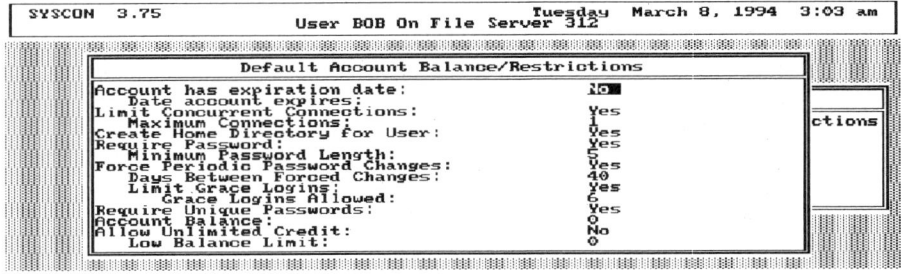

**Figure 10-2**
Default Account Balance/Restrictions Dialog Box.

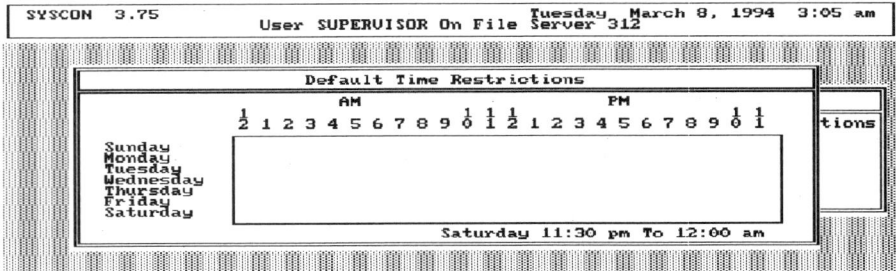

**Figure 10-3**
Default Time Restrictions Dialog Box (Part 1).

of Monday 6:00 A.M. Note the cursor status indicator at the lower right corner of the screen. This indicates that your cursor is at Monday 6:00 A.M. to 6:30 A.M. Press F5 to start blocking. Move the cursor to the right and down until the status indicator in the lower right shows Monday 6:00 A.M. To Friday 7:00 P.M. After highlighting this area, press Enter to insert the asterisks. Figure 10-4 shows what your screen will look like after completing these steps.

11. This completes setting up the default account restrictions for the network users. Press Escape twice to return to the Available Topics menu of SYSCON.

12. From the Available Topics Menu of SYSCON, move the highlight bar to *User Information* and press Enter. Now you're ready to create the users' accounts.

13. A list of current user accounts will appear on the screen. To create a new user for the network, press the Insert key. A dialog box will appear in the center of the screen.

14. Type the user name *PAUL,* then press Enter.

15. A dialog box will appear across the top of the screen showing the path that NetWare will use to create the user's home directory. Use the Left Arrow to move the cursor to the left until it is under the letter P. Type the word *USERS* followed by a \ (backslash) and press Enter. A dialog box asking you to verify the creation of the new directory will appear in the center of the screen. Move the highlight bar to the *Yes* option, and then press Enter. Figure 10-5 displays the proper syntax of the path and the verification dialog box. Note that the path shows the file server name followed by the volume, the USERS directory, and, finally, the name of the user's home directory.

16. Repeat Steps 12 through 15 to create the other three users: John, Rebecca, and Cyndie.

**Figure 10-4**
Default Time Restrictions Dialog Box (Part 2).

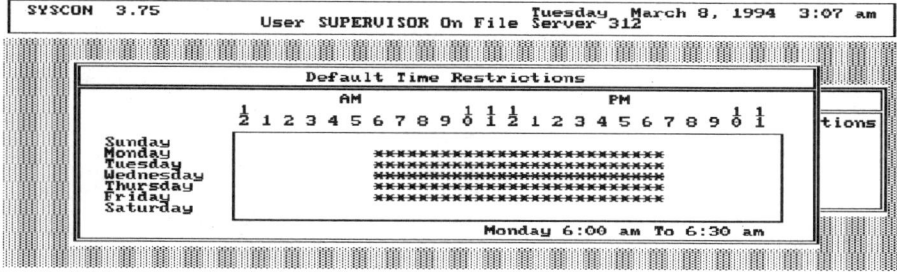

# Chapter Ten

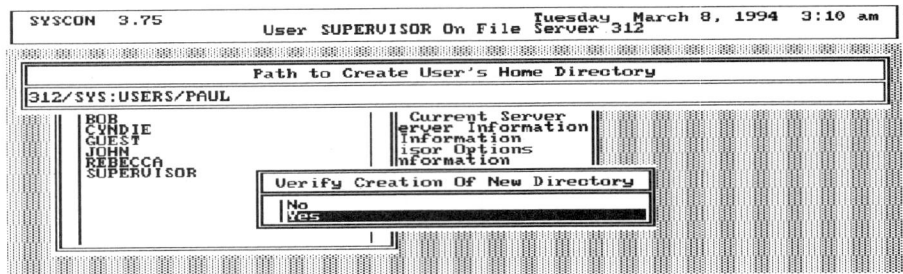

**Figure 10-5**
Path to Create User's Home Directory Dialog Box.

17. To define the account for user PAUL, move the highlight bar to *PAUL,* and then press Enter. The User Information menu will appear to the right of the screen after selecting a user.
18. With the highlight bar on *Account Restrictions,* press Enter.
19. Verify that the information in this window is the same that you set up in the Default Account Balance/Restrictions menu. Figure 10-6 shows the complete menu.
20. After verifying that the options in the Account Restrictions window are correct, press Escape to return to the User Information menu.
21. Move the highlight bar to the *Change Password* menu option and press Enter.
22. At the bottom of the screen, a dialog box will appear asking you to type a password for the user. Type *NOVELL* and press Enter, then retype *NOVELL* and press Enter again.
23. Move the highlight bar to the *Trustee Directory Assignments* option and press Enter. A window will appear on the right side of the screen listing the directories that the user has rights to and what those rights are.
24. Assign all rights except Supervisory to user Paul for the DATA directory. Press Insert to add Paul as a trustee for a directory. A dialog box will appear across the top of the screen asking for the directory path.

**Figure 10-6**
Account Restrictions for User PAUL Dialog Box.

# NetWare 3.x Administration

**Figure 10-7**
Directory in Which Trustee Should Be Added Dialog Box.

Type the path *SYS:DATA*, then press Enter. Match your screen with the one in Fig. 10-7. This will assign Paul to the path SYS:DATA and automatically assign him the Read and File Scan rights.

25. Now assign more rights to Paul for this directory. With the highlight bar on SYS:DATA, press Enter. This will display a list of Paul's rights. Since Paul needs more rights, press the insert key to view a list of Rights Not Granted. Figure 10-8 displays the *Trustee Rights Granted* and the *Trustee Rights Not Granted* windows. Move the highlight bar to the Create right and press F5 to mark the selection. Move the highlight bar to the Erase right and press F5, then highlight Write and press F5 again. You've just marked the three additional rights you want Paul to have. Press Enter to move the rights from the Trustee Rights Not Granted window to the Trustee Rights Granted window. Press Escape to return to the Trustee Directory Assignments window.

26. Next, assign Paul to the APPS directory. Press Insert, type *SYS:APPS* in the dialog box that appears across the top of the screen, and press Enter. Since the default NetWare trustee directory assignments are Read and File Scan, you'll need to make no other modifications. Figure 10-9 shows the two directory assignments for user Paul, and the rights he has in each directory plus the two assignments the system automatically created.

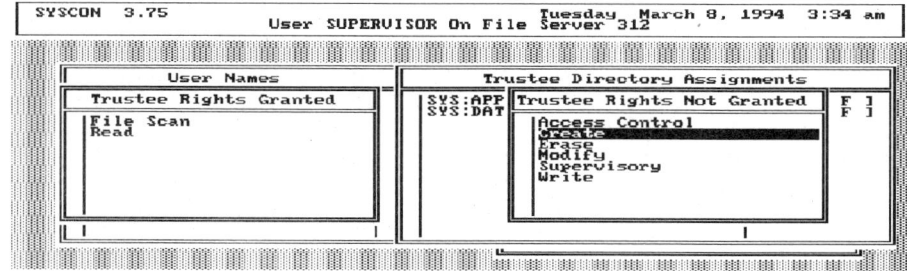

**Figure 10-8**
Trustee Rights Granted and Trustee Rights Not Granted Dialog Box.

**Figure 10-9**
Trustee Directory Assignments Dialog Box (Part 1).

27. Press Escape twice to return to the Users Names window.

28. Define accounts for the other three users. The setup for each user is nearly the same as for Paul. The only difference is in the assignment of trustee rights. The three remaining users all need Read and File Scan rights to the spreadsheet, database, and word processing applications. They also need Read, Write, Create, Erase, and File Scan rights to the spreadsheet, database, and word processing data directories. Since all three users have the same rights for the APPS and DATA directories, you'll create and assign rights by groups instead of by users. Repeat Steps 17 through 22 for the other users. Substitute the names Rebecca, Cyndie, and John in place of Paul. Press Escape twice to return to the Users Names window.

29. You are now ready to create the groups. Press Escape until you are at the Available Topics menu.

30. Move the highlight bar to the *Group Information* option and press Enter.

31. A window will appear listing groups. To create a new group, press the Insert key. Type the word *SALES* in the New Group Name dialog box and press Enter. You'll then return to the Group Name window, with SALES in the list.

32. With the highlight bar on the group name SALES, press Enter.

33. Move the highlight bar to the *Member List* option and press Enter. A window will appear listing the members of this group.

34. To add users to the group SALES, press Insert. A window will appear to the left, listing the users that are not a member of the group.

35. Mark the users Rebecca, Cyndie, and John by pressing F5, then press Enter. The names of the three users will move to the *Group Members* window.

36. Press Escape once to return to the Group Information window.

# NetWare 3.x Administration

37. Move the highlight bar to the *Trustee Directory Assignments* option and press Enter. A blank window will appear indicating there are no Trustee Directory assignments for this group.
38. Press Insert to open the *Directory In Which Trustee Should Be Added* dialog box.
39. The first directory to assign the SALES group is the spreadsheet application. In the dialog box titled Directory In Which Trustee Should Be Added, type *SYS:APPS\SS,* then press Enter. This will assign the Read and File Scan rights to the group SALES for the SYS:APPS\SS directory.
40. Repeat Steps 39 and 40, replacing the *SS* directory with *DB* and *WP.*
41. Next, assign the group SALES to the spreadsheet data directory. Press Insert to open the Directory In Which Trustee Should Be Added dialog box. Type the path *SYS:DATA\SS,* then press Enter. This will add the path SYS:DATA\SS to the Trustee Directory Assignments with only Read and File Scan rights.
42. You must assign more rights to the group SALES for this directory. With the highlight bar on SYS:DATA\SS, press Enter; this will open a window that shows the rights granted to the group SALES.
43. Press Insert to view a list of the Trustee Rights Not Granted.
44. Press F5 to mark the Write, Create, and Erase rights, and then press Enter. This grants the rights to the group. The rights will then move to the Trustee Rights Granted window. Press Escape once to return to the Trustee Directory Assignments window.
45. To assign the group SALES to the word processing and database data directories, repeat Steps 43 and 44, replacing *SS* with *WP.* Figure 10-10 displays the Trustee Directory Assignments for the group SALES after you add the group to the application and data directories.

**Figure 10-10**
Trustee Directory Assignments Dialog Box (Part 2).

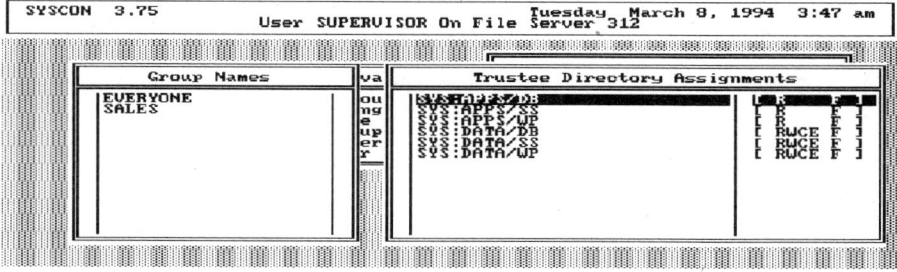

# Chapter Ten

46. This completes the steps necessary to create users and groups, define the account restrictions, and assign the trustee assignments. Press Escape three times to return to the Available Topics menu.

## Setting Up the Network Environment

For this portion of the exercise you'll create a system login script that sets up the network environment for all the users. Your system login script will set up drive mappings, display a message to the users, and execute user applications.

1. To create a system login script, use the SYSCON utility. At the DOS prompt, type *SYSCON* and press Enter.

2. From the Available Topics menu of SYSCON, highlight *Supervisor Options* and press Enter.

3. Use the Down Arrow key to highlight the *System Login Script* option and press Enter. A blank window will appear on your screen. This is the system script editor.

4. The first section of the login script file contains basic system setup. Press the Cap Lock key, then type the following lines into the system login script:

   ```
   REM THIS IS THE BASIC SYSTEM SETUP
   MAP ERRORS OFF
   MAP DISPLAY OFF
   MAP INS S1:=SYS:PUBLIC
   COMSPEC=C:\COMMAND.COM
   ```

   Figure 10-11 displays these five lines of text after you type them into the script.

5. The next group of commands set up search mapping to the applications directories and drive mappings to the data directories. Figure

**Figure 10-11**
Sample System Login Script (Part 1).

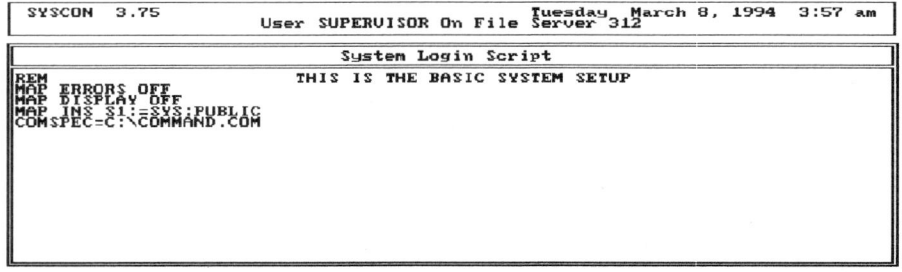

**Figure 10-12**
Sample System Login Script (Part 2).

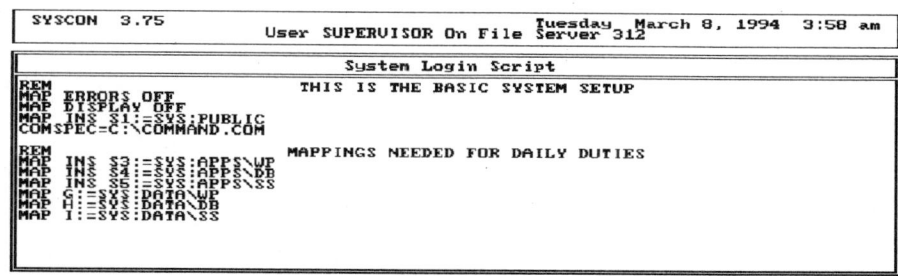

10-12 shows both the first group of commands and the following set of commands. Press Enter to put a space between information groups, then type the following lines into the login script:

```
REM MAPPINGS NEEDED FOR DAILY DUTIES
MAP INS S3:=SYS:APPS\WP
MAP INS S4:=SYS:APPS\DB
MAP INS S5:=SYS:APPS\SS
MAP G:=SYS:DATA\WP
MAP H:=SYS:DATA\DB
MAP I:=SYS:DATA\SS
```

6. Now customize the mappings for user Paul. Press Enter to put a blank line between the last group of commands. Indent the commands between the BEGIN and END statements to make this portion easy to read. Type the following lines into the script:

```
REM CUSTOM MAPPINGS FOR PAUL
IF LOGIN_NAME = "PAUL" THEN BEGIN
     MAP INS S6:=SYS:APPS\ACCT
     MAP J:=SYS:DATA\ACCT
END
```

7. The next section places the users into their home directories. Press Enter to put a blank line between the group of commands. Figure 10-13 shows both the commands from Step 6 and the following commands. Note that the first set of commands from Step 4 has scrolled

**Figure 10-13**
Sample System Login Script (Part 3).

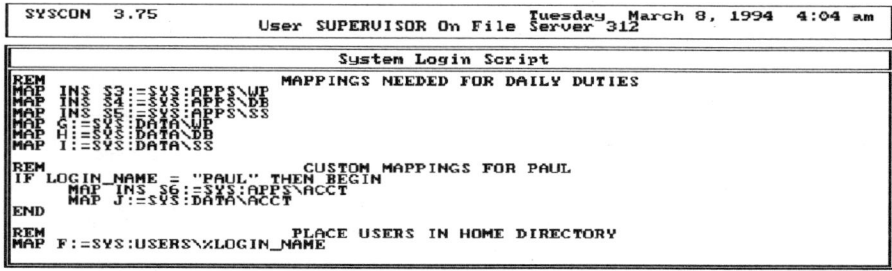

off the screen and out of the figure. Type the following lines into the script:

```
REM PLACE USERS IN HOME DIRECTORY
MAP F:=SYS:USERS\%LOGIN_NAME
```

8. Press Enter to insert a blank line between command groups. Type the following lines to execute the DOS command CLS, and to display a personal greeting to the user in the middle of the screen. On the line that starts with the word WRITE, place 27 spaces before the word GOOD. This moves the text to the center of the screen.

```
REM PERSONAL GREETINGS
#COMMAND /C CLS
REM ENTER INFO FOR WRITE ON 1 LINE, IT WILL LINE WARP TO NEXT
LINE
WRITE "\n\n\n\n\n\n\n Good %GREETING_TIME %LOGIN_NAME
\n\n\n\n\n\n\n"
PAUSE
```

9. The next group of lines you add to the script define how the users will print. Figure 10-14 shows both the commands from Step 8 and the following commands. Press Enter to insert a blank line between command groups, and then type the following lines into the script:

```
REM PRINTING SETUP
#CAPTURE Q=LASER TI=5 NT NFF NB
```

10. Next, clear the screen and display the drive mappings to the users. Press Enter to insert a blank line between the command sets, and then type the following lines into the script:

```
REM SHOW USER THE MAPPINGS
#COMMAND /C CLS
MAP DISPLAY ON
MAP
PAUSE
```

11. The final area of the login script will end the login process and start windows for the users. Figure 10-15 shows the commands from

**Figure 10-14**
Sample System Login Script (Part 4).

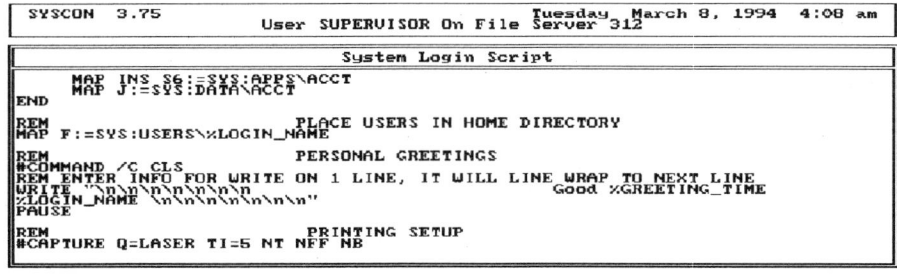

# NetWare 3.x Administration

**Figure 10-15**
Sample System Login Script (Part 5).

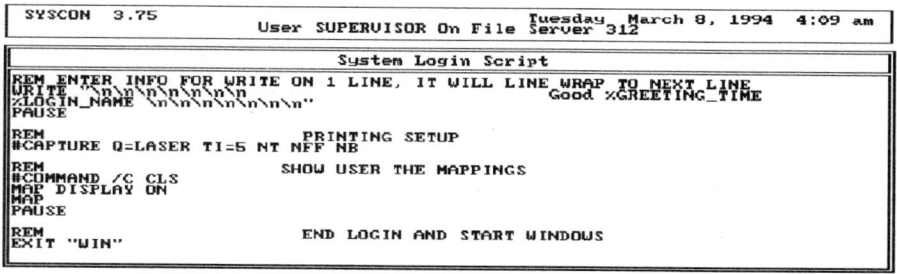

Steps 10 and 11. Press Enter to insert a blank line between command sets, and then type the following lines:

```
REM END LOGIN AND START WINDOWS
EXIT "WIN"
```

12. Before exiting and saving the system login script, double-check every line and word for correct spelling and syntax.

13. To save the information in the System Login Script, press Escape, then answer *Yes* to the Save Changes window that appears. You return to the Supervisor Options menu.

14. Press Escape two more times to exit SYSCON. Press Enter on the *Yes* option in the Exit SYSCON window.

## Printing

The final area to set up is the print servers and print queues. In this exercise you create one print server and one print queue. The steps outlined describe the shortest, easiest, and most efficient way to set up printing on your network.

1. At the DOS prompt, type *PCONSOLE* and press Enter to start the print console utility.

2. First, create a print queue. Highlight the *Print Queue* information option and press Enter. A blank window titled Print Queues will appear on the left side of the screen.

3. Press Insert, type *LASER* in the dialog box, and press Enter.

4. After you define the print queue name, press Escape to return to the Available Options menu.

5. Next, define the print server information. Move the highlight bar to the *Print Server Information* option and press Enter. This opens the Print Server window.

6. Press Insert. Type *LASER-PS* in the dialog box and then press Enter. This will return you to the Print Server window.

7. With the highlight bar on LASER-PS, press Enter. This opens the Print Server Information menu.

8. Move the highlight bar to the *Print Server Configuration* option and press Enter. This will open the Print Server Configuration Menu.

9. Move your highlight bar to the *Printer Configuration* option and press Enter. A Configured Printers window will appear on the left side of the screen.

10. Next, define the configuration for the printer. With the highlight bar on *Printer 0,* press Enter. This opens the Printer 0 Configuration menu.

11. With the highlight bar on *Printer Name,* press Enter. Backspace over the name Printer 0, type *LASER-JET,* and then press Enter. The highlight bar will automatically move to the Type option.

12. With the highlight bar on the *Type* option, press Enter to open the Printer Types menu. Move the highlight bar from the *Defined Elsewhere* option to the *Parallel, LPT1* option, then press Enter. NetWare automatically fills in the rest of the options on the top half of the menu.

13. Accept the default options that NetWare defines for the Parallel, LPT1 printer. Compare your screen to Fig. 10-16. To save the information, press Escape. A confirmation dialog box will appear; place the highlight bar on *Yes* and press Enter. This will return you to the Configured Printer window. It will also show the name LASER-JET as a Configured Printer.

14. Press Escape again to return to the Print Server Configuration Menu.

**Figure 10-16**
Printer 0 Configuration Dialog Box.

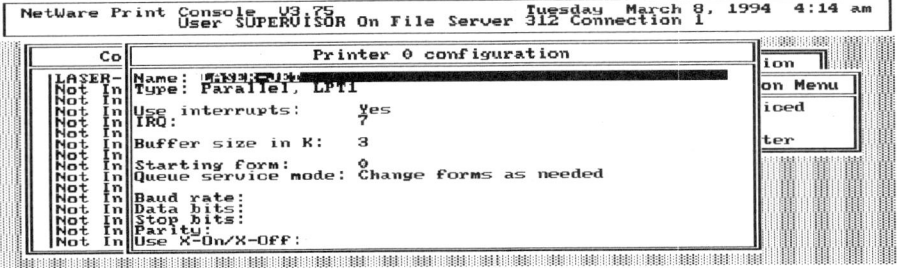

# NetWare 3.x Administration

15. You now link the printer to the print queue. Move the highlight bar down to the *Queues Serviced By Printer* option, and then press Enter. A Defined Printer window will open on the left side of the screen.
16. Your LASER-JET printer appears in this window. With the highlight bar on your printer, press Enter. A new window will appear in the center of the screen.
17. Press Insert to open a window of available print queues. Move the highlight bar to the print queue *LASER* and press Enter. This will open a dialog box to set the priority. Press Enter to accept the default value of 1. NetWare adds your print queue, the priority, and the file server to the window.
18. This completes the definition portion of the printing setup. Press Escape 6 times and answer *Yes* to the Exit PCONSOLE prompt. This returns you to the DOS prompt.
19. Now, prepare the file server and printer. Go to the file server and attach the printer to the LPT1 port. Make sure that the printer has power, and that you turn it on, set it online, and place paper in the paper bin.
20. With the printer set up, you're now ready to load the print server software on the file server. At the file server prompt, type *LOAD PSERVER LASER-PS* and press Enter. The print server software will load into memory and the print server monitor will show printer 0 as *LASER-JET* and *Waiting for job*. Figure 10-17 shows the print server monitor at the file server.

## The Final Test

The final step is to make sure that everything you set up works properly. Before you allow any of the users to power up their workstations and

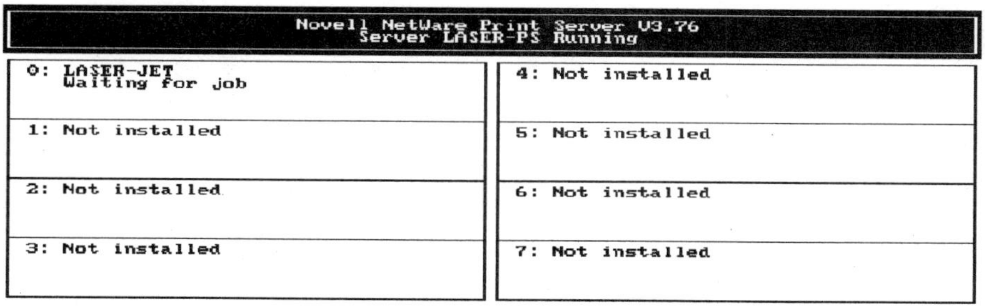

**Figure 10-17**
Print Server Monitor Screen.

**Figure 10-18**
Workstation Setup Checklist.

| Activity | Paul | Rebecca | Cyndie | John |
|---|---|---|---|---|
|  |  |  |  |  |
| Password required? |  |  |  |  |
| Asked for new password? |  |  |  |  |
| Errors during login? |  |  |  |  |
| Display Greeting? |  |  |  |  |
| Did Screen Pause? |  |  |  |  |
| Display Mapping? |  |  |  |  |
| Did Screen Pause? |  |  |  |  |
| Did Windows start? |  |  |  |  |
| Exit Windows—do you have access to the network? |  |  |  |  |
| Change to each of the APPS directories, type RIGHTS—are they correct? |  |  |  |  |
| Change to each of the DATA directories, type RIGHTS—are they correct? |  |  |  |  |
| Will each of the APPS start? |  |  |  |  |
| Can you save data from the APPS? |  |  |  |  |
| Can you print from all the APPS? |  |  |  |  |
| Can you return to Windows? |  |  |  |  |
| Can you logout properly? |  |  |  |  |
| Other: |  |  |  |  |
| Other: |  |  |  |  |
| Other: |  |  |  |  |
| Other: |  |  |  |  |

attempt to log into the network, test each of the users' accounts. Make sure that the login script works properly, that the security is as you intended, and that users can print.

1. Using the chart in Fig. 10-18 as a checklist, mark the box under the user name and next to each task that you verify as working properly.
2. Log into the network as user Paul. Check each item on the checklist.

# NetWare 3.x Administration

3. Make any necessary changes or modifications on items that didn't work properly.
4. Repeat Steps 1 to 4 for users Rebecca, Cyndie, and John.

## Study Questions

1. Basic Network services include:
    a. Printing
    b. Security
    c. File Storage
    d. None of the above

    *a, b, and c.*   NetWare provides *a, b,* and *c.* Many exam questions will ask you to select all the correct answers.

2. NetWare supports UNIX workstations as clients.
    a. True
    b. False

    *a.*   The NetWare operating system supports not only UNIX, but also Macintosh computers as workstations.

3. To connect a DOS machine to NetWare, you need:
    a. A hard drive
    b. A user
    c. Special hardware and software
    d. A telephone

    *c.*   The workstation must have a physical connection to the file server and software that establishes a logical connection.

4. Important information about your network connection is stored in:
    a. The net$log.dat file
    b. The DOS requester
    c. The IPX.COM file
    d. None of the above

    *b.*   As you log into and out of the network, NetWare stores the connection information in the NetWare DOS requester.

5. The acronym VLM stands for:
   a. Very Low Memory
   b. Virtual Loadable Module
   c. Vital Link Module
   d. Virtual Link Module

   *b.* With the release of NetWare 3.x and above, Novell replaces the previous workstation shells with a group of files known as Virtual Loadable Modules (VLMs). The modular structure of these files allows you to use only the services you require.

6. NetWare uses the _____ communication protocol.
   a. ODI
   b. Netx
   c. English
   d. IPX

   *d.* The Internetwork Packet eXchange (IPX) protocol is Novell's proprietary communication system, allowing workstations to communicate with file servers.

7. NetWare 3.x requires an MLID driver at the workstation.
   a. True
   b. False

   *a.* NetWare 3.x conforms to the Open Data-Link (ODI) specifications. The Multiple Link Interface Driver (MLID) is software program that translates the physical link of the network to the logical communication protocol of the computer.

8. During the installation of the client software, NetWare creates a:
   a. STARTNET.BAT file
   b. Bindery file
   c. Password file
   d. All of the above

   *a.* The workstation installation program creates the STARTNET.BAT file to automate the process of loading the workstation files and connecting to the network.

9. Upon executing the _____ file, NetWare prompts you for your user name and password.

a. STARTNET.BAT
   b. LOGIN.EXE
   c. AUTOEXEC.BAT
   d. SERVER.EXE

   *b.* The LOGIN.EXE program will register you with the operating system by asking you to enter your user name and password. The program will then query the bindery files and authenticate your login request.

10. NetWare provides _____, _____, and _____ for network access, usage, and management.
    a. DOS text, Command line, graphical utilities
    b. Macintosh, DOS, UNIX
    c. you, me, everyone
    d. supervisor, guest, everyone

    *a.* The three types of interfaces Novell offers users to interact with NetWare are DOS text utilities (menus), Command line utilities (text entered at the prompt), and graphical utilities (Windows-based programs).

11. To prevent receiving all messages, execute the following command:
    a. DISALLOW
    b. CASTOFF
    c. CASTOFF /ALL
    d. CASTON /ALL

    *c.* The CASTOFF command is a command line utility that will prevent the workstation from receiving messages sent by other users. The /ALL option prevents the workstation from receiving messages that the system or the supervisor might send.

12. The NetWare file system provides the following benefits:
    a. Shared file storage
    b. Private file storage
    c. Data security
    d. Both A and C
    e. All of the above

*e.* One of NetWare's main functions provides for file management. This includes the ability to share files, to provide for private file storage, and to protect both shared and private files.

13. A single NetWare volume may span more than one hard drive.
    a. True
    b. False

    *a.* NetWare 3.x and above allow for up to 32 hard drives to become segments of a single volume.

14. The first NetWare volume can be any name you want up to 15 characters long.
    a. True
    b. False

    *b.* The first volume on each NetWare file server must have the name *SYS:*. NetWare will allow only the following characters as part of the volume name: the letters A to Z, the numerals 0 to 9, ~, !, #, $, %, ^, &, (), -, _, and {}.

15. Directory names can contain up to _____ characters.
    a. 8
    b. 11
    c. 31
    d. 255

    *b.* NetWare follows the same file and directory naming conventions as DOS. Both allow files and directories to have up to 8 characters in the first part of the name and 3 characters in the extension.

16. The full directory path includes the:
    a. User name, directory, and file
    b. Server, volume, and directory
    c. Directory name and file name
    d. Server name, directory name, and file name

    *b.* The full NetWare path to a directory includes the file server name, volume name, and the directory name(s). If you have only one file server, you can shorten the full path by omitting the file server name.

17. The system-created directories include Public, System, Doc, and Mail.

a. True

b. False

*a.* When NetWare first installs on the file server, NetWare automatically creates the following directories: LOGIN, PUBLIC, SYSTEM, MAIL, ETC, DELETED.SAV, and DOC. These directories contain files for use by the operating system or NetWare-specific files for the users.

18. The NetWare suggested directories include:

   a. Users

   b. DOS

   c. Shared

   d. Both *a* and *b*

   e. All of the above

   *e.* By creating directories for the network users, shared data, and DOS, network administrators efficiently manage the network file system, applications, and data.

19. Drive pointers are used by:

   a. DOS

   b. NetWare

   c. The freeway systems

   d. Driving instructors

   e. Both *a* and *b*

   *e.* Both NetWare and DOS can use a single letter followed by a colon to point to a directory or area where you can store files.

20. NetWare 3.x requires a last drive statement of E in the CONFIG.SYS file.

   a. True

   b. False

   *a.* CONFIG.SYS contains a LASTDRIVE=Z statement when you use the NetWare VLMs. You must specify the first network drive letter in the NET.CFG file.

21. To access a NetWare drive, you must:

   a. Have an Ethernet card.

   b. Map a drive letter.

   c. Enter a Password.

   d. None of the above.

b. By mapping a drive letter to NetWare, you make the services available for use. The drive mapping makes a logical link between your computer and the network resource.

22. You can change to another NetWare volume with the CD command.
    a. True
    b. False

    *a.* Since the NetWare drive pointers are pointing to logical areas rather than physical devices, changing the pointer to another volume is just like changing to another directory.

23. The correct syntax for the MAP command is:
    a. MAP G:=FS1/SYS:DATA/SS
    b. MAP G:+SYS:DATA\SS
    c. MAP G:=SYS;DATA\SS
    d. NET MAP G:=SYS;DATA\SS

    *a.* When creating a drive mapping, specify a drive letter followed by a colon and equal sign. Following the equal sign, enter the path starting with the file server name, then the volume, and finally the directory path.

24. Changing directories on a network drive changes the mapping.
    a. True
    b. False

    *a.* The NetWare drive pointers are dynamic links to a directory. If you CD from one directory to another, the drive letter will then point to the new directory.

25. There are _____ network search drives available.
    a. 5
    b. 16
    c. 26
    d. No limit

    *b.* NetWare reserves 16 letters of the alphabet for search mappings. The system will automatically assign the letters, starting with the letter Z.

26. The NetWare 3.x bindery consists of:
    a. NDS
    b. NET$BVAL.SYS and NET$BIND.SYS

# NetWare 3.x Administration

  **c.** NET$OBJ.SYS, NET$PROP.SYS, and NET$VAL.SYS
  **d.** All of the above

 *c.* The NetWare bindery files, NET$OBJ.SYS, NET$PROP.SYS, and NET$VAL.SYS, contain information about the systems objects, their properties, and the values assigned to them.

**27.** The NetWare bindery files are in the _____ directory.
  **a.** Public
  **b.** Security
  **c.** System
  **d.** ETC

 *c.* Since the bindery files are part of the operating system, NetWare stores the three bindery files in the system directory.

**28.** The function of NCP packet signature is to:
  **a.** Protect against forging packets.
  **b.** Check the connection of the workstation.
  **c.** Stop NetWare Core Printing.
  **d.** None of the above.

 *a.* Implemented as another level of security, packet signature assigns a key to the workstation as a way of authenticating the source of the data.

**29.** Directory and file rights include:
  **a.** Supervisory
  **b.** Delete
  **c.** Scan File
  **d.** Access Change

 *a.* The Supervisory right includes all seven other rights: Read, Write, Create, Erase, File Scan, Modify, and Access Control.

**30.** To execute a file, you must have the _____ and _____ rights.
  **a.** File Scan, Execute
  **b.** Read, Execute
  **c.** Read, File Scan
  **d.** None of the above

 *c.* The Read and File Scan rights allow you to locate the file and then read or execute its contents.

**31.** Users can receive rights in the following ways:
   a. User account
   b. Group membership
   c. Security equivalence
   d. All of the above

   *d.* Any user of the network may inherit access rights at an individual level, by association with a group, or by becoming equivalent to another user.

**32.** The IRM can block all rights to a user.
   a. True
   b. False

   *b.* The IRM will block all rights except supervisory. Once granted the Supervisory right, the user or group carries that right to the bottom of that directory structure.

**33.** Your effective rights to a directory or file can never be more than the IRM will allow.
   a. True
   b. False

   *b.* If a user or group has an explicit trustee assignment to a file or directory, the explicit assignment supersedes the IRM.

**34.** To install the workstation client software, you run the _____ program from the _____ diskette.
   a. STARTNET, WSGEN
   b. SETUP, WSGEN
   c. WSGEN, WSGEN
   d. INSTALL, WSDOS_1

   *d.* The WSDOS_1 diskette contains the files necessary for a workstation to log onto a file server. The install program copies the files from the diskette to the workstation.

# Fun Test

**1.** The full path to a directory includes the:
   a. Directory name and file name
   b. Server name, directory name, and file name

c. Server, volume, and directory
d. User name, directory, and file

2. The program that prompts you for a user name and password is:
   a. AUTOEXEC.BAT
   b. STARTNET.BAT
   c. SERVER.EXE
   d. LOGIN.EXE

3. Which of the following are benefits provided by the NetWare file system?
   a. Data security
   b. Private file storage
   c. Shared file storage
   d. Both *a* and *c*
   e. All of the above

4. NetWare provides a maximum of _____ search drives.
   a. 5
   b. 16
   c. 26
   d. No limit

5. With NetWare, a volume may span more than one hard drive.
   a. True
   b. False

6. The first NetWare volume must be SYS.
   a. True
   b. False

7. To install the workstation client software, run the _____ program from the _____ diskette.
   a. WSGEN, WSGEN
   b. STARTNET, WSGEN
   c. SETUP, WSGEN
   d. INSTALL, WSDOS_1

8. When installing the workstation software, NetWare creates a:
   a. Bindery file
   b. Password file

c. STARTNET.BAT file
d. All the above

9. Users can receive rights in the following ways:
   a. Security equivalence
   b. User account
   c. Group membership
   d. All of the above

10. The Public, System, Doc, and Mail directories are automatically set up by the system.
    a. True
    b. False

11. The CD command is one way to access another NetWare volume.
    a. True
    b. False

12. Changing directories on a network drive changes the mapping.
    a. True
    b. False

13. Directory names on NetWare can be _____ characters long.
    a. 31
    b. 11
    c. 255
    d. 8

14. A UNIX work station can be a NetWare client.
    a. True
    b. False

15. Basic Network services include:
    a. Printing
    b. Security
    c. File storage
    d. None of the above

16. To execute a file, you must have the _____ and _____ rights.
    a. READ, EXECUTE
    b. FILE SCAN, EXECUTE

c. READ, FILE SCAN
d. None of the above

17. The correct syntax for the MAP command is:
    a. MAP G:=SYS;DATA\SS
    b. NET MAP G:=SYS;DATA\SS
    c. MAP G:+SYS:DATA\SS
    d. MAP G:=SYS:DATA/SS

18. The NetWare stores the bindery files in the _____ directory.
    a. Public
    b. ETC
    c. Security
    d. System

19. To connect a DOS workstation to a NetWare file server, you need:
    a. A telephone
    b. Special hardware and software
    c. A user
    d. A hard drive

20. NetWare 3.x requires a last drive statement of E in the CONFIG.SYS file.
    a. True
    b. False

21. An MLID driver is a requirement for a workstation using NetWare 3.x VLMs.
    a. True
    b. False

22. Your effective rights to a directory or file can never be more than the IRM will allow.
    a. True
    b. False

23. The NetWare 3.x bindery consists of:
    a. NET$OBJ.SYS, NET$PROP.SYS, and NET$VAL.SYS
    b. NET$BVAL.SYS and NET$BIND.SYS
    c. NDS
    d. All of the above

24. The IRM can block all rights to a user.
    a. True
    b. False

25. NetWare suggests that you create which of the following directories?
    a. Users
    b. DOS
    c. Shared
    d. Both *a* and *b*
    e. All of the above

26. _____ is the communication protocol of the NetWare operating system.
    a. English
    b. Netx
    c. IPX
    d. ODI

27. The acronym VLM stands for:
    a. Virtual Loadable Module
    b. Vital Link Module
    c. Virtual Link Module
    d. Very Low Memory

28. To access and manage the network, NetWare provides _____, _____, and _____.
    a. Supervisor, guest, everyone
    b. DOS, Command line, graphical utilities
    c. Macintosh, DOS, UNIX
    d. You, me, everyone

29. Information about the workstation connection to the network is in:
    a. The IPX.COM file
    b. The DOS requester
    c. The net$log.dat file
    d. None of the above

30. To prevent receiving all messages, execute the following command:
    a. Castoff /All
    b. Caston /All
    c. Castoff
    d. Disallow

**31.** Directory and file rights include:
   a. Scan File
   b. Access Change
   c. Supervisory
   d. Delete

**32.** To access a NetWare drive, you must:
   a. Enter a Password.
   b. Have an Ethernet card.
   c. Map a drive letter.
   d. None of the above.

**33.** The reason for NCP packet signature is to:
   a. Stop NetWare Core Printing.
   b. Protect against forging packets.
   c. Check the connection of the workstation.
   d. None of the above.

**34.** Drive pointers are used by:
   a. DOS
   b. NetWare
   c. The freeway systems
   d. Driving instructors
   e. Both *a* and *b*

## Brain Teaser

Are you ready to perform your first NetWare installation? The installation crossword in Fig. 10-19 may not test your ability to actually perform the installation, but it's a fun way to test your installation knowledge. Just work it like you would any other crossword. The clues appear in two columns, for *Across* and *Down*. If you find that you have a hard time completing the crossword, you may want to take another look at the case study in this chapter. Like most crosswords, you'll find a lot of acronyms in this one. Make sure you check out App. A and the glossary if you're having trouble figuring out one of the acronyms in the crossword puzzle. We also have used some fairly obscure common knowledge clues, just to make the puzzle more interesting. You'll find the solution for this Brain Teaser in App. C, "Brain Teaser Answers."

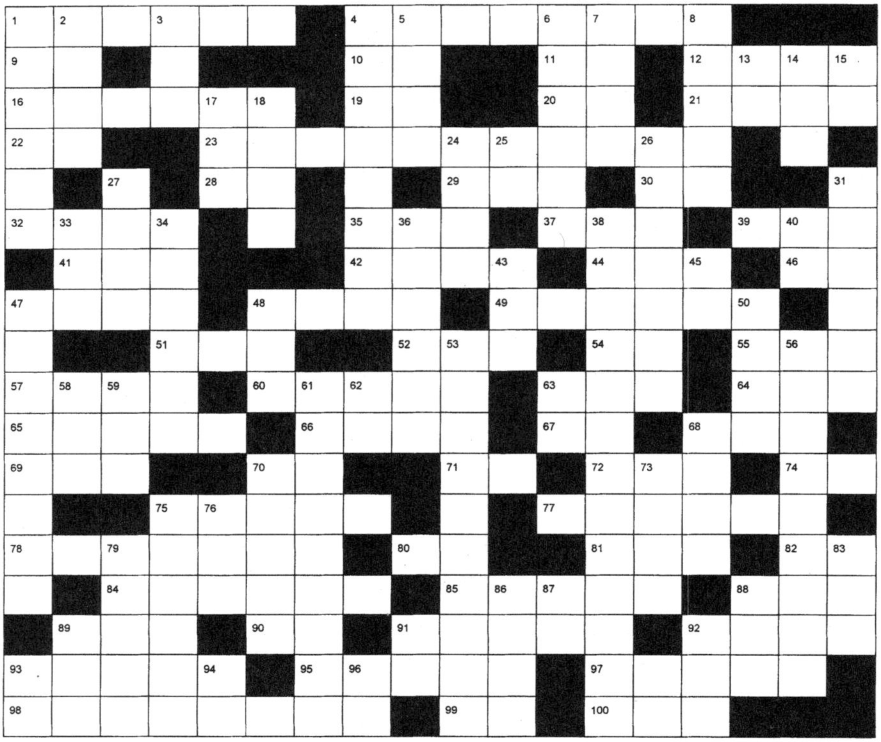

**Figure 10-19**
Installation Crossword Puzzle.

*Across*
1. Maximum letters in a directory name
4. Printer configuration utility
9. Compass point (abbreviation)
10. File attribute (abbreviation)
11. End of line (abbreviation)
12. Multiple drive technology
16. Mountain in Israel
19. Ego
20. After do
21. An Apple communication method (abbreviation)
22. Sumerian god of heaven
23. Limit Concurrent _____
28. Storage media for music and data
29. Drive redirection command
30. Electrical engineer (abbreviation)
32. Certification prerequisite
35. International group responsible for making rules (abbreviation)
37. Making knotted lace of cotton or linen
39. A child's question
41. Communication hardware (abbreviation)
44. Nonfunctional driver condition (abbreviation)
46. International standard (abbreviation)
47. Computer memory type (abbreviation)
48. Road information media
49. Saturday funnies
51. Body of water
52. Data dropout
54. Data communication based on light (abbreviation)
55. At least once (abbreviation)
57. The *C* in NCP
60. Personal NetWare installation requirement
63. Number of print queues required for each print server

# NetWare 3.x Administration

64. Paneled truck
65. Network clients
67. Serial port signal
68. Affirmative
69. Edge of a canyon
70. Not stop
71. Beast of burden
72. IBM standard protocol (abbreviation)
74. Modem control signal
75. Doesn't hide
77. Put away
78. _____ File Transfer Protocol
80. Egyptian sun god
81. High speed walking
82. Doctor's assistant (abbreviation)
84. Several songs sung together
85. Giant
88. Electronics standards group
89. Barrel (abbreviation)
90. Modem control signal
91. Colored lightly or faintly
92. An ocean occurrence
93. Religious devotion
95. African story teller
97. A formal speech
98. A method of grouping areas of a script together
99. Not yes
100. The color glasses needed to pass the exam

*Down*

1. Exit key in Novell utilities
2. Not fat
3. Workstation shell file type
4. NetWare service
5. Secret _____
6. Login command source
7. Cookie
8. NetWare trustee right
13. Vendor product notification
14. Internet communication supplier
15. Text work in progress (abbreviation)
17. Hard drive fix-it (abbreviation)
18. A veinlike deposit
24. Computer configuration memory
25. Thank you (British slang)
26. Novell's CompuServe forum
27. Application storage directory
31. Utility for users and groups
33. An application's presentation of data
34. _____ List, group configuration in SYSCON
36. A _____ NetWare volume may span more than one hard drive
38. Holds the network reins
40. Hello
43. Internet communication methodology
45. Computer chips (abbreviation)
47. Major access concern during installation
48. First NetWare volume name
50. End of editing message, _____ Changes
53. File _____ Table (FAT) disk format
56. Drive setting CONFIG.SYS command
58. Networking model
59. Script file comment command
61. Learning result
62. Computer communication
63. Either
68. Response of the bored
70. Final objectives
73. Part of speech for things
75. Suave
76. Concealed in the past
83. Scottish no
86. He walked _____ the house
87. Symbol for the element technetium
88. Food consumption
89. Storage container
91. Comes after LA
92. A large piece of gum
93. The value 3.14159
94. An abbreviation for yes/no
96. Modem control signal

## Disk Time

Don't forget to spend some time working with the CD-ROM that accompanies this book. It provides valuable, fun-to-use teaching aids that'll help you prepare for your exam. See "Disk Time" in the preface of this book for details about what the disk contains. Make sure you pay special attention to the parts of the Windows help file and the Red Zone game that pertain to this chapter. Also, check out the acronym areas provided in both disk features—they'll help you get up to speed on what's going on in the industry faster.

CHAPTER 11

# NetWare 3.x Advanced Administration

# Introduction

This chapter looks at the 3.x Advanced Administration exam. This exam is a lot more in-depth than the 3.x Administration exam we looked at in the previous chapter. You'll want to study security in depth, as well as most of the console commands. Obviously, you could get questions on anything you tested for in the previous exam as well, though Novell probably won't spend a lot of time on this area unless it looks like you don't know the material. (The adaptive exams look for weak areas and then see if you know the material well enough to pass.) Remember, at the time you complete this exam, Novell is saying that you're ready for full network duty.

There are several discrete sections in this chapter. Each section helps you study for the exam in a different way. You can improve your chances of passing the exam by using two or more of the study methods provided in this chapter. It'll probably help if you study all the sections once and your favorite sections at least twice. Remember to review the study guidelines in Chap. 2 as required to ensure that you maintain the best possible study atmosphere.

The first section of this chapter is a *case study*. In this case, we concentrate on the file server itself. You'll learn how to set the file server up, tune it for optimum performance, and then perform any required maintenance checks. All of these hands-on tasks are designed to help you prepare for the kind of exam that Novell gives. Even though you'll get a lot more from this section if you perform it on your own network, the inclusion of screen shots will help you gain something from the section even if you don't have a network.

The second area contains *questions* for this course. This chapter provides an overall view of NetWare 3.x. We really won't concentrate on the server, though it probably wouldn't hurt to spend extra time working with a server if you have one. This section also includes the correct answers and an explanation of why those answers are correct. Try to answer each question yourself, look at the correct answer, and then determine where you went wrong if you did not answer correctly.

The next section is a *fun test*. This is an exercise where you'll look at some sample test questions and answer them. The answers appear in App. B at the back of the book. This will help you test what you learned in the previous section.

The final text section of the chapter is the *brain teaser*. You'll get to have a little fun working on a NetWare 3.x–related puzzle. This chapter provides two cryptograms that should give you some ideas of ways to study for the exam. Obviously, it helps to have a good overall knowledge of NetWare 3.x in this case, since the cryptograms will be easier to solve if you can spot specific patterns in the way they're encrypted. By the way, the cryptograms use different encryption methods, so you'll have to solve each puzzle separately.

Finally, we will spend some time using the *Jeopardy!*-type game. This section helps you look at the test from the opposite viewpoint. The game provides you with an answer—you need to come up with the corresponding question. The game awards points for correct answers, and takes points away for incorrect answers. You'll receive a score at the end of the game proclaiming that you either did or did not get your certificate.

Use all the learning methods that we provide in this chapter to improve your chances of passing the exam. It's a good idea to save the fun test section until your are almost certain that you possess all the required knowledge. Remember, you can probably go through the test only two or three times at most before you'll start to remember the answers without really knowing the material. Obviously, the brain teaser is only good once—after that you'll have all the phrases decrypted.

Everyone who wants a NetWare 3.x certification needs to learn the material in this chapter—there are no exceptions. Make sure you pass this exam before you go on to the other chapters.

## Case Study

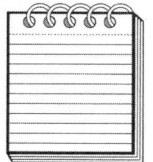

**NOTE**  *This case study assumes that you completed the case study in Chap. 10. If you didn't complete that case study, make sure you have a network available that already has the proper setup. You'll probably need to modify this case study a bit to make it work if you're not using the setup from Chap. 10.*

In this case study, you'll focus on the procedures for managing the file server and network. Anyone who manages a network will benefit from this chapter because that is where you'll spend most of your time. You won't install networks every day and, hopefully, troubleshooting will be minimal, but there are always management tasks to perform. The areas of study include:

- File server startup procedures
- File server memory management
- Performance tuning
- Maintenance procedures

The case study walks you through the necessary steps to take a proactive approach to network management. Each step looks at a different area of the network that can cause your users to lose productivity and you to lose sleep.

## File Server Startup Procedures

The first step in managing any type of network is to have the file server operating system automatically start when the computer powers up. In this section, you'll create the configuration files for the file server. The configuration files allow the file server and the network to restart automatically at any time of the day or night.

1. Boot the file server computer to DOS.
2. Once the computer boots DOS, create an AUTOEXEC.BAT file that will launch the NetWare operating system. At the C:\> prompt, type *COPY CON AUTOEXEC.BAT* and press Enter. The cursor will drop to the next line. On this line type the word *SERVER,* and then press the F6 key. This will place a ^Z after the word SERVER. Press Enter to save the file.
3. Restart your computer by pressing the Control, Alt, and Delete keys at the same time. The computer will reboot and load SERVER.EXE into memory.
4. Once the program loads into memory, NetWare will prompt you for the name of the file server. Type *312* and press Enter.
5. A prompt appears asking for the internal IPX network number. Type in the number *A312* then press Enter. This displays a prompt of the file server name followed by a colon.
6. Now you are ready to load the hard disk controller NLM. At the file server prompt, type *LOAD ISADISK\** and press Enter. NetWare will prompt you to select an I/O port address and an interrupt address. Press Enter twice to accept the defaults of 1F0 for the I/O port address and E for the interrupt number value. If the settings for your controller are different, replace with the appropriate values.
7. Now that NetWare can communicate with the hard disk controller, you must mount the volume. At the file server prompt, type *MOUNT ALL* and then press Enter.

---

\* If you are using a hard disk controller other than a standard ISA type controller, load the NLM that came with your controller. For example, if you have an ADAPTEC 1542 SCSI adapter, type *LOAD AHA1542*.

# NetWare 3.x Advanced Administration

8. The next step is loading the LAN driver for the NIC. At the file server prompt, type *LOAD NE2000* and press Enter. NetWare will prompt you to enter the I/O port value and the interrupt value. The default values are 300 for the port and 3 for the interrupt. Press Enter to accept each of these values.

9. After loading the LAN driver, bind the IPX protocol to the LAN card. At the prompt, type *BIND IPX TO NE2000* and press Enter. At the prompt, type *E100* and press Enter.

10. Save this information to NetWare's configuration files. At the file server prompt, type *LOAD INSTALL* and press Enter. After the install menu appears on the screen, move the highlight bar to *System Options,* and then press Enter. Move the highlight bar to create AUTOEXEC.NCF, then press Enter. NetWare automatically inserts all appropriate information typed at the prompt into this file.

11. Add two more lines to the bottom of the file, to load support for the remote console utility. Move the cursor to the end of the last line and press Enter. Type *LOAD REMOTE < NOVELL* and press Enter. Now, type *LOAD RSPX* and press Enter. This loads the remote NLM and assigns the password of *NOVELL.* Figure 11-1 shows what your AUTOEXEC.NCF file will look like. Press Escape and answer *yes* to save the file.

12. Create the STARTUP.NCF file by moving the highlight bar to *CREATE STARTUP.NCF,* then press Enter. NetWare displays a prompt showing the file save location. Verify that the path shows C:\STARTUP.NCF, then press Enter. An edit window appears showing the contents of the file. Do not make any changes. Press Escape and answer yes to save the file. Figure 11-2 shows the completed STARTUP.NCF file.

13. Press Escape two times and answer *Yes* to Exit Install.

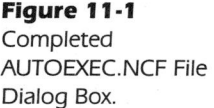

**Figure 11-1**
Completed AUTOEXEC.NCF File Dialog Box.

**Figure 11-2**
Completed
STARTUP.NCF File
Dialog Box.

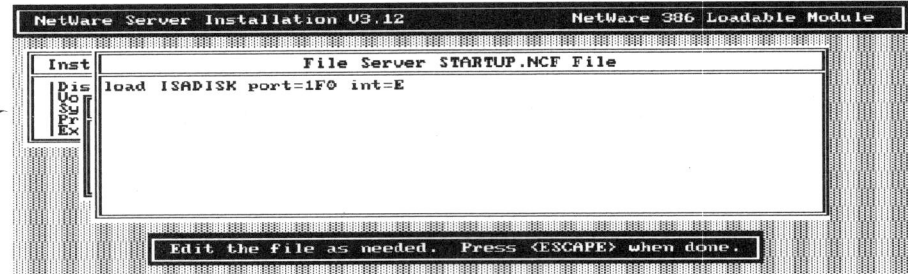

14. To verify the configuration files are setup properly, type the word *DOWN* at the file server prompt and press Enter. Type *EXIT* and press Enter. This returns you to the DOS prompt. Now reboot your computer. NetWare will automatically load into memory.

This completes the steps necessary to automatically start the NetWare operating system. After the file server reboots and loads the NetWare operating system into memory, you can verify the configuration using the NetWare commands MODULES and CONFIG. To view a list of NLMs loaded into the file server memory, type *MODULES* at the file server prompt. To verify the file server name, internal IPX number, configuration of the LAN driver, LAN protocol, and the network address, type *CONFIG* at the file server prompt. Figure 11-3 shows the output from the CONFIG command, and Fig. 11-4 shows the output from the MODULES command.

## File Server Memory Management

To effectively maintain your file server, you must first know your server's statistics. If you don't know the statistics about your file server when it's operating properly, you won't have a baseline of information to trouble-

**Figure 11-3**
Display of the CONFIG Command Output.

# NetWare 3.x Advanced Administration

**Figure 11-4**
Display of the MODULES Command Output.

```
312:MODULES
RSPX.NLM
    NetWare 386 Remote Console SPX Driver
    Version 3.12    March 29, 1993
    Copyright 1993 Novell, Inc. All rights reserved.
REMOTE.NLM
    NetWare 386 Remote Console
    Version 3.12    May 13, 1993
    Copyright 1993 Novell, Inc. All rights reserved.
NE2100.LAN
    Novell NE2100
    Version 3.22    June 1, 1993
    Copyright 1993 Novell, Inc. All rights reserved.
ETHERTSM.NLM
    Novell Ethernet Topology Support Module
    Version 2.14    May 17, 1993
    Copyright 1993 Novell, Inc. All rights reserved.
MSM.NLM
    Novell Generic Media Support Module
    Version 2.14    March 11, 1993
    Copyright 1993 Novell, Inc. All rights reserved.
ISADISK.DSK
    NetWare ISA Device Driver
    Version 3.12    April 28, 1993
    Copyright 1993 Novell, Inc. All rights reserved.
```

shoot future problems. This section will help you to identify and document important statistics about your file server.

1. At the file server prompt, type *LOAD MONITOR* and press Enter. This loads the utility that displays the statistics for the file server. Figure 11-5 displays the main screen for the monitor utility.

2. Use the chart in Fig. 11-6 to record statistics about your file server. The following steps help you perform this task. The first piece of information to enter is the date.

3. Look at the monitor statistics screen. The first line in the top window shows *Information For Server 312*. Record the file server name on your chart.

4. The next line shows how long the file server has been up. Record the information from the line titled *File Server Up Time*.

5. The next value to record is the processor utilization value. On the line titled *Utilization,* note the approximate value and write it on the chart.

6. Record the number of buffers from the line *Original Cache Buffers*.

7. Under the Original Cache Buffers line is the information for *Total Cache Buffers*. Enter this information on the chart.

**Figure 11-5**
Monitor Utility Screen.

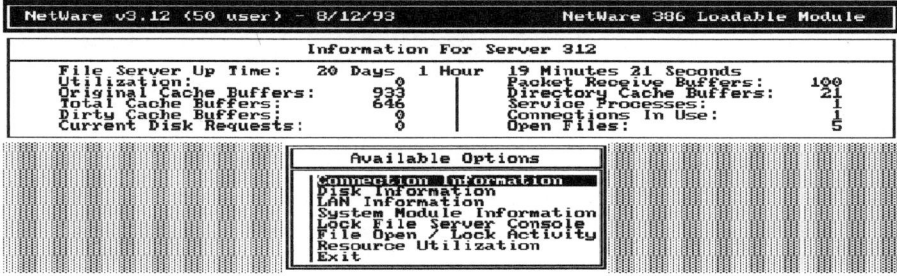

**Figure 11-6**
File Server Statistics Tracking Chart.

| File Server Statistics Tracking Chart |||||
|---|---|---|---|---|
| Date | | | | |
| File server name | | | | |
| File server up time | | | | |
| Utilization | | | | |
| Original cache buffers | | | | |
| Total cache buffers | | | | |
| Dirty cache buffers | | | | |
| Packet receive buffers | | | | |
| Directory cache buffers | | | | |
| Service processes | | | | |
| Drive type | | | | |
|    Card number | | | | |
|    Controller number | | | | |
|    Drive number | | | | |
|    Redirection blocks | | | | |
|    Redirected blocks | | | | |
| Drive type | | | | |
|    Card number | | | | |
|    Controller number | | | | |
|    Drive number | | | | |
|    Redirection blocks | | | | |
|    Redirected blocks | | | | |
| Permanent memory pool, bytes | | | | |
|    Percentage | | | | |
|    Bytes in use | | | | |
| Alloc memory pool, bytes | | | | |
|    Percentage | | | | |
|    Bytes in use | | | | |
| Cache buffers, bytes | | | | |
|    Percentage | | | | |
| Cache movable memory, bytes | | | | |
|    Percentage | | | | |
| Cache nonmovable memory, bytes | | | | |
|    Percentage | | | | |
| Total server work memory, bytes | | | | |

# NetWare 3.x Advanced Administration

8. The next line to record is *Dirty Cache Buffers*. Record this value on the chart.

9. *Packet Receive Buffers* is the next item to record. This information is at the top of the next column.

10. Record the information from the next line, *Directory Cache Buffers*.

11. The last item to record on this screen is *Service Processes*. Enter the information on the chart.

12. From the Available Options menu on the lower portion of the screen, move the highlight bar to the *Disk Information* option and press Enter. This will open a new window, titled *System Disk Drives*.

13. With the highlight bar on *Device #0*, press Enter to open the information window about that drive. Note that the information window across the screen changes from *file server* information to *hard drive* information.

14. Record the drive type information from the information window across the top of the screen. Record the *type, card number, controller number,* and *drive number* on the chart. Figure 11-7 shows the disk information screen.

15. From the right side of the information window, locate the *Redirection Blocks* statistic. Record this information on the chart.

16. The next statistic to record is *Redirected Blocks*. Enter this information on the chart.

17. Press Escape once to return to the System Disk Drives window. If your system has more than one hard disk, repeat Steps 13 through 16 for each drive.

18. Press Escape one more time to return to the Available Options menu. Move the highlight bar to the *Resource Utilization* option and press Enter. This will open two new windows, entitled *Server Memory Statistics* and *Tracked Resources*. Figure 11-8 displays the two new open windows.

**Figure 11-7**
Disk Information Screen Dialog Box.

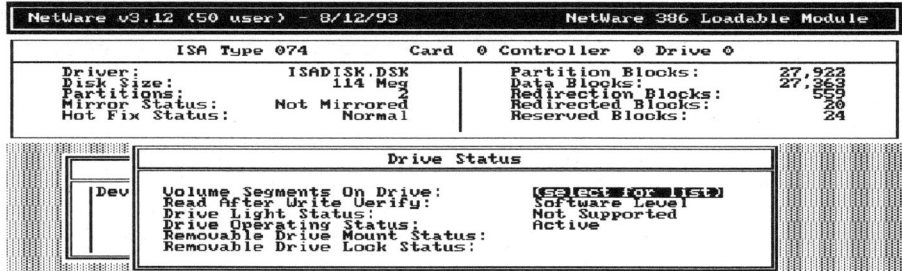

**Figure 11-8**
Server Memory Statistics and Tracked Resources Dialog Box.

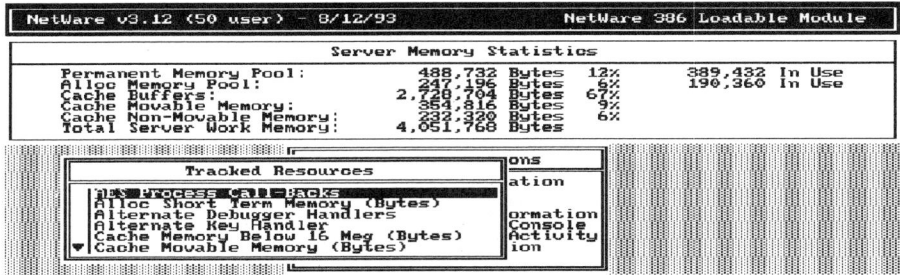

19. From the window across the top of the screen, locate the *Permanent Memory Pool* information. The statistics tracking chart has three columns. Record *bytes* from the first column, the *percentage* from the second column, and the actual number of *bytes in use* from the third column.

20. The next line of statistics is for the *Alloc Memory Pool*. Record the information from the bytes column, percentage column, and bytes in use column on the chart.

21. The third line of information is for *Cache Buffers*. Enter the bytes and percentage information on the chart.

22. Following the Cache Buffers line is *Cache Movable Memory*. Enter the bytes and percentage figures on the chart.

23. The next line shows the *Cache Non-Movable Memory* statistics. Record the total bytes and percentage values on the chart.

24. The final item to record from this window is *Total Server Work Memory*. Enter the total number of bytes on the chart.

25. Press the Escape key twice and answer *Yes* to the Exit Monitor prompt.

This completes filling out the file server statistics tracking chart. Completing this chart on a regular basis* helps you to form good preventive maintenance habits and to create a set of baseline statistics. You can improve the level of information you receive by entering it into a spreadsheet and creating graphs. You can use the graphs to display trends that reflect the health of your file server.

---

*You should complete this chart at least once a week. If you have file servers that you can not allow to be down, or servers that are experiencing problems, complete the tracking chart as a daily procedure.

# NetWare 3.x Advanced Administration

## Performance Tuning

NetWare uses a dynamic memory allocation scheme. It automatically allocates memory and other resources to the areas that need it most. At times the default limitations will be inadequate for your needs. Fortunately, NetWare allows you to set the minimum and maximum resource allocation values. This section shows you how to locate the default settings for your system and make changes to a couple of the settings.

In this section, you'll view and record the setting of four items that often require adjustment: (1) maximum physical receive packet size, (2) minimum packet receive buffers, (3) minimum file cache buffers, and (4) minimum directory cache buffers. You'll then change the default values, restart the file server, and check the status of the new values.

1. From the file server console prompt, type *SET* then press Enter. A list of categories will appear. Press 1, then Enter to view information about communications.

2. The fourth item in this window displays the settings for *Maximum Physical Receive Packet Size*. The first value after the setting name is the system's current setting. Record the current setting for your system.

3. The next setting to view is *Minimum Packet Receive Buffers*. Press Enter once to view the second page of options. The first line of information at the top of the screen is Minimum Packet Receive Buffers. Record the current settings. Press Enter again to view the third page and return the cursor to the prompt.

4. Type the word *SET* again and press Enter to view the configuration categories. This time, press 3 for *File Caching* options, then press Enter. The *Minimum File Cache Buffers* information is on the second page. Press Enter to view page two. The last item on the screen is Minimum File Cache Buffers. Record your current settings.

5. Type *SET* and press Enter to view the configuration categories. Press 4 for *Directory Caching* and press Enter. Press Enter again to view the second page of information. The last item of this category shows the settings for *Minimum Directory Cache Buffers*. Record your system's current setting.

6. In the next set of steps, you will modify the AUTOEXEC.NCF and the STARTUP.NCF files to change the settings of these four parameters. Type *LOAD INSTALL* and press Enter.

7. Move the highlight bar to *System Options* and press Enter.

8. The fourth option of the Available System Options menu is *Edit AUTOEXEC.NCF File*. Move the highlight bar to this option and press Enter.

9. Move the cursor to end of the file by pressing Page Down, then pressing End. With the cursor at the end of the last line, press Enter to add a blank line.

10. With the cursor at the beginning of new blank line, type the following information: *SET MINIMUM FILE CACHE BUFFERS=50*. Press Enter.

11. On the next line type: *SET MINIMUM DIRECTORY CACHE BUFFERS=30* and press Enter. Figure 11-9 shows the two lines added to the original AUTOEXEC.NCF file.

12. Press Escape, then press Enter to Save AUTOEXEC.NCF.

13. Next, move the highlight bar to *Edit STARTUP.NCF File* and press Enter. A dialog box indicating the path to the STARTUP.NCF file appears. Press Enter.

14. Move the cursor to the end of the line of text, then press Enter.

15. With the cursor at the start of a blank line, type *SET MAXIMUM PHYSICAL RECEIVE PACKET SIZE=1514,* and press Enter. The cursor will move to the next line.

16. With the cursor at a blank line, type *SET MINIMUM PACKET RECEIVE BUFFERS=150* and press Enter. Figure 11-10 shows the two lines added to the original STARTUP.NCF file.

17. Press Escape once, then press Enter to save the STARTUP.NCF file.

18. Press Escape twice and answer *Yes* to the Exit Install.

19. You must down the file server and restart it for the changes to take effect. At the file server prompt, type *DOWN* and press Enter. After the file server is down, type *EXIT* and press Enter to return to the DOS prompt.

**Figure 11-9**
Sample AUTOEXEC.NCF File.

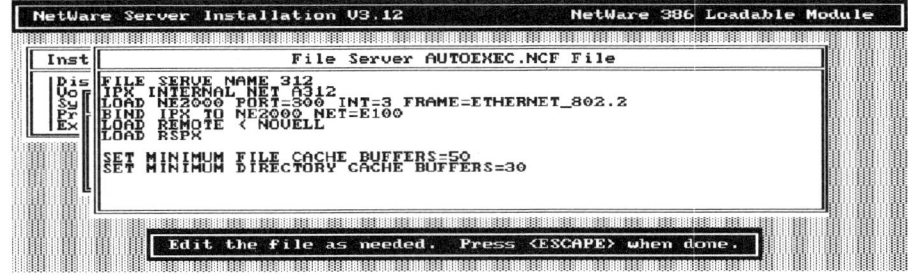

# NetWare 3.x Advanced Administration

**Figure 11-10**
Sample STARTUP.NCF File.

20. Restart the file server by typing *SERVER* and pressing Enter at the DOS prompt.

21. The last step is to verify and record the changes to the system. To verify the new settings repeat Steps 1 through 5. Record the current values and compare them to the original settings.

This completes the performance tuning case study. These settings will help increase the performance of your file server. As you have noticed, there are many other options and configurations that you can use to help optimize your file server.

## Maintenance Procedures

Even with all the preplanning and preventive maintenance, there will always be repairs to make. For example, you may experience problems with the NetWare bindery files and volumes. Novell offers two utilities to correct the problems. This section focuses on the NetWare repair utilities *BINDFIX* and *VREPAIR*.

1. In this exercise you rebuild the NetWare bindery files. The utility to rebuild the bindery file is BINDFIX. Log into the file server as *supervisor*. Change directories to the system subdirectory by typing *CD\SYSTEM* and pressing Enter.

2. Type *BINDFIX* and press Enter to start the bindery repair program.

3. NetWare displays a series of status messages on screen as it rebuilds the bindery files. NetWare will ask if you want to delete the mail directories of users that no longer exist. Press Y to delete the directories.

4. NetWare will then ask if you would like to delete the trustee rights for users that no longer exist. Press Y to delete the trustee rights.

**Figure 11-11**
Display of the SYSTEM>BINDFIX Command Output.

```
F:\SYSTEM>BINDFIX
Rebuilding Bindery.  Please Wait.
Checking object's property lists.
Checking properties to see if they are in an object property list.
Checking objects for back-link property.
Checking set consistency and compacting sets.
Checking Properties for proper order.
Checking user objects for standard properties.
Checking group objects for standard properties.
Checking links between users and groups for consistency.
Delete mail directories of users that no longer exist? (y/n): Y
Checking for mail directories of users that no longer exist.
Checking for users that do not have mail directories.
Delete trustee rights for users that no longer exist? (y/n): Y
Checking volume SYS. Please wait.

Bindery check successfully completed.
Please delete the files NET$OBJ.OLD, NET$PROP.OLD, and NET$VAL.OLD after you
have verified the reconstructed bindery.

F:\SYSTEM>
```

5. NetWare will check the volume and finish creating the new bindery files. Figure 11-11 shows all the messages that BINDFIX displays on screen. Note that BINDFIX displays the message *Bindery Check Successfully Completed.* NetWare saves the original bindery files with an .OLD extension. This last step includes verifying that the new bindery files work properly. To verify the bindery files, check the users, groups, and trustee assignments with SYSCON, then use the system for a week or two. Then, if the users and group accounts are functioning properly, delete the bindery files with the .OLD extension.

6. The next repair utility deals with problems related to NetWare volumes. The VREPAIR utility is an NLM that runs at the file server console. At the file server console prompt, type *LOAD VREPAIR* and press Enter. The VREPAIR menu will appear.

7. Before you can repair a NetWare volume, you must first dismount that volume. To dismount volume SYS, press Alt-Escape to hot key back to the system prompt. At the system prompt, type *DISMOUNT SYS* and press Enter. After dismounting the volume, press Alt-Escape to return to the VREPAIR menu.

8. To start repairing a volume, press 1 for the *Repair a Volume* option, then press Enter. Figure 11-12 shows the VREPAIR status screen. The repair pauses when VREPAIR finds errors on your system;

**Figure 11-12**
Display of the VREPAIR Command Output.

```
Total errors: 0
Current settings:
   Pause after each error
   Do not log errors to a file
Press F1 to change settings

Start 10:59:24 pm
Checking volume SYS

FAT blocks>...........................................................<
Counting directory blocks and checking directory FAT entries .........<
Mirror mismatches>....................................................<
Directories>..........................................................<
Files>................................................................<
Trustees>.............................................................<
Deleted Files>........................................................<
Free blocks>..........................................................<

Done checking volume
Total Time 0:01:29
<Press any key to continue>
```

# NetWare 3.x Advanced Administration

315

strike any key to continue. Press Enter to return to the VREPAIR menu if there are no errors. If your system does have errors, press Y to write the repairs to disk, then press Enter.

9. Press 0, then Enter to exit the VREPAIR utility. Type *MOUNT SYS* and press Enter to remount volume SYS.

This completes the section on maintenance procedures. The BINDFIX and VREPAIR utilities are useful tools that help you maintain your system. Like all repair utilities, you must take care when using them. You should also maintain a current backup of the system.

## Study Questions

1. The primary NetWare operating system file is:
   a. NET$OS.EXE
   b. SERVER.EXE
   c. COMMAND.COM
   d. None of the above

   *b.* The SERVER.EXE file contains the basic code for the NetWare operating system.

2. Before NetWare can communicate with a volume, you must first:
   a. Log into the system.
   b. Bind the protocol to the LAN driver.
   c. Load the disk driver NLM.
   d. Format the drive.

   *c.* The disk driver NLM is the interface between the operating system and the hard disk controller. NetWare can't communicate directly to the hard disk itself.

3. To mount the sales volume, type _____ at the file server prompt.
   a. VOLUME SALES
   b. LOAD SALES
   c. BIND SALES
   d. MOUNT SALES

   *d.* The correct syntax for mounting a volume is to type *MOUNT* followed by the name of the volume.

4. The NetWare configuration files consist of:
   a. AUTOEXEC.NCF and STARTUP.NCF
   b. AUTOEXEC.BAT and CONFIG.SYS
   c. AUTOEXEC.NCF and CONFIG.SYS
   d. SERVER.EXE and AUTOEXEC.NCF

   *a.* The NetWare operating system uses both the AUTOEXEC.NCF and STARTUP.NCF files to configure the way the file server operates.

5. To boot the file server without using the STARTUP.NCF file you:
   a. Delete the AUTOEXEC.BAT file.
   b. Delete the SERVER.EXE file.
   c. Type *SERVER* backwards.
   d. Type *SERVER -NS*.

   *d.* At times, it may be necessary to load NetWare without using the STARTUP.NCF file. The -NS option instructs SERVER.EXE to bypass the existing STARTUP.NCF file.

6. The only way to edit the AUTOEXEC.NCF file is from the INSTALL module.
   a. True
   b. False

   *b.* The INSTALL NLM is only one way of editing the AUTOEXEC.NCF file. AUTOEXEC.NCF is a DOS text that you can edit with any text editor, the EDIT.NLM, or SYSCON.

7. Typing SET at the file server prompt will:
   a. Display a SET configuration menu.
   b. Reset all SET values back to default.
   c. Display how your system is configured.
   d. All of the above.

   *a.* Typing $irSET at the file server displays a menu listing all the categories affected by the SET command. Select a category to obtain a list of items in that category.

8. The default frame type for Ethernet is:
   a. 802.3
   b. Ethernet_II
   c. 802.2
   d. IPX

# NetWare 3.x Advanced Administration

    c. With the release of NetWare 3.x and 4.x, Novell changed the default frame type for Ethernet from 802.3 to 802.2.

9. Each network interface board can support multiple frame types at the same time.
   a. True
   b. False

    *a.* The ODI specifications allow the LAN driver to generically support the NIC. This generic support allows the use of different types of network and transport layer protocols.

10. The acronym *ODI* stands for:
    a. Old DOS Interrupter
    b. Open DOS Interface
    c. Open Data-Link Interface
    d. Open Driver Interface

    *c.* The *Open Data-Link Interface* allows NetWare to access the MAC and the LLC sublayers of the of the Data-Link layer of the OSI model.

11. ODI allows multiple protocols and network boards to exist in a file server or workstation.
    a. True
    b. False

    *a.* The ODI specifications allow for multiple protocol support and for one NIC to appear as other logical NICs.

12. Information displayed by the router tracking screen includes:
    a. SAPS and RIPS
    b. IPX and SPX packets
    c. RIP and IPX packets
    d. None of the above

    *a.* Every file server transmits both SAP (Service Advertisement Protocol) and RIP (Routing Information Protocol) information every minute. The router tracking screen displays both sets of information.

13. To display a list of known network addresses, type _____ at the file server prompt.
    a. DISPLAY SERVERS
    b. SHOW ALL

c. ADDRESSES

d. DISPLAY NETWORKS

*d.* The DISPLAY NETWORKS command reads the information collected by RIP and displays the known network addressees.

14. Streams is an NLM that provides a common interface between NetWare and the communication protocols.
    a. True
    b. False

    *a.* Streams is a common interface that allows the transport protocols to communicate with the NetWare operating system.

15. You can use the CONFIG command to display information about:
    a. The file server name
    b. Loaded LAN drivers
    c. IPX internal network number
    d. All of the above

    *d.* The Config command is internal code that's part of the operating system. Typing *CONFIG* at the file server prompt displays the file server name, the internal IPX address, and LAN driver information.

16. Novell recommends _____ of memory to load the TCP/IP NLMs.
    a. 1 MB
    b. 2 MB
    c. 4 MB
    d. 16 MB

    *c.* The TCP/IP and related support NLMs require approximately 4 MB of RAM and 1 MB of disk space.

17. The Macintosh name space support allows NetWare to store Macintosh files with file names up to 32 characters in length.
    a. True
    b. False

    *a.* NetWare 3.x includes a 5-user version of NetWare for Macintosh that allows Macintosh users to access the NetWare file server. The Macintosh users can store applications and data on the NetWare volume and retain the native Macintosh file information and file names.

# NetWare 3.x Advanced Administration

18. The name space modules bundled with NetWare include:
    a. NFS.NAM
    b. FTAM.NAM
    c. OS2.NAM
    d. All of the above
    e. None of the above

    c. Novell bundles the DOS, OS2, and MACINTOSH name space modules with NetWare. The NFS and FTAM name space modules must be purchased separately.

19. The name space modules require no extra memory.
    a. True
    b. False

    b. Each name space module requires memory for the NLM plus additional memory for the directory table that the name space module uses.

20. To implement name space support, you must load the appropriate NLMs in the _____ file.
    a. AUTOEXEC.NCF
    b. AUTOEXEC.BAT
    c. CONFIG.SYS
    d. STARTUP.NCF

    c. The name space modules add support for the volumes. They're part of the boot process and are added to the STARTUP.NCF file.

21. To view the DOS file name and Macintosh file name for a Macintosh file using the NDIR command, use the _____ option.
    a. /MAC
    b. /BOTH
    c. /LONG
    d. /MAC /DOS

    c. The NDIR option to view both the DOS and Macintosh file name is /LONG. If you want to view only the Macintosh file name you can use the /MAC option.

22. Disk Allocation blocks are _____ in size.
    a. Always 4 K
    b. Can be 4, 8, or 16 K

**c.** Can be 4, 8, 16, 32, or 64 K

**d.** Not larger than the smallest cache buffer

*c.* Disk Allocation blocks are portions of the hard disk that store files. The configuration sizes for these blocks are 4, 8, 16, 32 or 64 K.

23. Directory Table blocks are _____ in size.

    **a.** Only 4 K

    **b.** 4, 8, or 16 K

    **c.** 4, 8, 16, 32, or 64 K

    **d.** Not larger than the smallest cache buffer

    *a.* Regardless of the Disk Allocation block size, the Directory Table block size is always 4 K.

24. Directory Cache Buffers can be _____ in size.

    **a.** Only 4 K

    **b.** 4, 8, or 16 K

    **c.** 4, 8, 16, 32, or 64 K

    **d.** Not larger than the directory table blocks

    *b.* The Directory Cache Buffers are sections of RAM that contain entries from the Directory Table. NetWare places the entries in RAM to provide faster access.

25. As _____ increase, File Cache Buffers decrease.

    **a.** Disk Allocation blocks

    **b.** Directory Cache Buffers

    **c.** The number of users

    **d.** Directory Table blocks

    *b.* The NetWare operating system allocates all unused memory to file caching. The increase in memory for the Directory Cache Buffers will decrease the amount of RAM for file caching.

26. To properly calculate the amount of RAM needed for a file server, you must know:

    **a.** The requirements for the NLMs

    **b.** The volume size

    **c.** The block size

    **d.** All of the above

    *d.* To properly calculate the RAM needed for a file server, you must know something about it. A few of the items to know are how much

RAM the NLMs will use, the size of the volume, and the size of the Disk Allocation blocks.

27. The Semi-Permanent memory pool is used by:
    a. Packet Receive Buffers
    b. Directory tables
    c. LAN drivers
    d. None of the above

    *c.* The Semi-Permanent memory pool is a section for NLMs that usually remain loaded for a long time. These NLMs include the LAN drivers and the Disk drivers.

28. The Alloc Short Term memory pool is used to store:
    a. Drive mappings
    b. User connection information
    c. Open and locked files
    d. All of the above

    *d.* As its name implies, this is memory that's used for only a short time then released. Short-term memory requests include drive mappings, connection information, and file information.

29. The Cache Movable memory is used by:
    a. Tables that grow dynamically
    b. Loadable modules
    c. File caching
    d. None of the above

    *a.* The File Allocation Table and the Directory Table change in size as you create and delete files. NetWare places these tables in Cache Moveable memory so that NetWare can optimize the returned memory as they change.

30. To view the file Server memory statistics, use the _____ option of Monitor.
    a. Processor Utilization
    b. Resource Utilization
    c. System Module Information
    d. Memory Utilization

    *b.* The information about file server memory is available from the Resource Utilization option of the Monitor NLM.

**31.** The Dirty Cache Buffers number isn't a percentage.

　**a.** True

　**b.** False

*a.* The value represented in the Dirty Cache Buffers field is the actual number of memory buffers that have had information changed, but not been written to disk.

**32.** To view the Processor Utilization statistics window, you must:

　**a.** Load MONITOR.

　**b.** Load MONITOR with the P option.

　**c.** Load MONITOR with the PU option.

　**d.** Load MONITOR, then select the Processor Utilization option.

*b.* When loading the Monitor utility, you can place the P option after the word *monitor* to place another option on the menu. Doing this will present an option that displays information about how the different processes on the system are being utilized.

**33.** Both Packet Burst and Large Internet Packet (LIP) are:

　**a.** Loaded on the 3.x server as NLMs

　**b.** Separately purchased items

　**c.** Part of the operating system code

　**d.** EXE files that must be run at the workstations

*c.* With the release of 3.x, Novell incorporated both Packet Burst and Large Internet Packet as part of the operating system code.

**34.** Volume maintenance includes:

　**a.** Backing up the data on the file server.

　**b.** Checking the VOL$LOG.ERR file for system alerts.

　**c.** Using the utilities CHKVOL, CHKDIR, and VOLINO to monitor the growth of directories and files.

　**d.** All of the above.

　**e.** None of the above

*d.* Regular volume maintenance includes backing up the file server, checking the error log, and using the NetWare utilities to monitor the growth of the network.

**35.** The PCONSOLE utility allows you to make permanent and temporary modifications to the printing environment.

　**a.** True

　**b.** False

# NetWare 3.x Advanced Administration

   *a.* You can use the PCONSOLE utility to make temporary changes to the print server and printer while they are running. If you want to make permanent changes to the printing environment, you must change the configuration files and reload the print server software.

## Fun Test

1. Information that NetWare stores in the Alloc Short Term Memory pool is
   - **a.** User Connection information
   - **b.** Open and locked files
   - **c.** Drive Mappings
   - **d.** All of the above

2. The NLM that provides a common interface between NetWare and the communication protocols is Streams.
   - **a.** True
   - **b.** False

3. The size of Directory cache buffers is _____ in size.
   - **a.** Only 4 K
   - **b.** 4, 8, or 16 K
   - **c.** 4, 8, 16, 32, or 64 K
   - **d.** Not larger than the directory table blocks

4. To allow NetWare to store Macintosh files with file names up to 32 characters in length, you must use the Macintosh name space support modules.
   - **a.** True
   - **b.** False

5. The INSTALL module is the only utility to edit the AUTOEXEC.NCF file.
   - **a.** True
   - **b.** False

6. Proper maintenance of a NetWare Volume includes:
   - **a.** Using the utilities CHKVOL, CHKDIR, and VOLINO to monitor the growth of files and directories.
   - **b.** Backing up the data on the file server.
   - **c.** Checking the VOL$LOG.ERR file for system alerts.

d. All of the above.

e. None of the above.

7. NetWare displays both the DOS file name and Macintosh file name when using the _____ option of NDIR to display a Macintosh file.
   a. /LONG
   b. /MAC
   c. /MAC /DOS
   d. /BOTH

8. When loading name space modules, you must add more RAM to the file server.
   a. True
   b. False

9. To make permanent and temporary modifications to the printing environment you use the PCONSOLE utility.
   a. True
   b. False

10. The NetWare volume can not be accessed until you first:
    a. Format the drive.
    b. Log into the system.
    c. Bind the protocol to the LAN driver.
    d. Load the disk driver NLM.

11. The Processor Utilization Statistics window is available if you:
    a. Load MONITOR, then select the Processor Utilization option.
    b. Load MONITOR with the PU option.
    c. Load MONITOR with the P option.
    d. Load MONITOR.

12. When loading the TCP/IP NLMs, your file server should have an additional _____ of RAM.
    a. 1 MB
    b. 2 MB
    c. 4 MB
    d. 16 MB

13. Within the Semi-Permanent memory pool you will find:
    a. Directory Tables
    b. LAN drivers

# NetWare 3.x Advanced Administration

    c. Packet Receive Buffers
    d. None of the above

14. After adding name space support to a NetWare volume, you must load the appropriate NLMs in the _____ file.
    a. CONFIG.SYS
    b. AUTOEXEC.BAT
    c. AUTOEXEC.NCF
    d. STARTUP.NCF

15. From the file server prompt, type _____ to display a list of known network addresses.
    a. DISPLAY NETWORKS
    b. ADDRESSES
    c. DISPLAY SERVERS
    d. SHOW ALL

16. NetWare will _____ by typing SET at the file server prompt.
    a. Reset all SET values back to default.
    b. Display how your system is configured.
    c. Display a SET configuration menu.
    d. All of the above.

17. _____ use Cache Movable memory to store information.
    a. File caching
    b. Loadable modules
    c. Tables that grow dynamically
    d. None of the above

18. To prevent the SERVER.EXE file from accessing the STARTUP.NCF file when booting, you:
    a. Delete the AUTOEXEC.BAT file.
    b. Type *SERVER -NS*.
    c. Delete the SERVER.EXE file.
    d. Type *SERVER* backwards.

19. ODI allows multiple protocols and network boards to exist in a file serve or workstation.
    a. True
    b. False

**20.** File Cache Buffers decrease when _____ increase.
   a. Disk Allocation blocks
   b. The number of users
   c. Directory Table blocks
   d. Directory Cache Buffers

**21.** The _____ file loads into the memory of the file server and becomes the NetWare operating system.
   a. COMMAND.COM
   b. NET$OS.EXE
   c. SERVER.EXE
   d. None of the above

**22.** When calculating how much RAM your file server should have, you need to know:
   a. The memory requirements for each NLM
   b. The volume size
   c. The block size
   d. All of the above

**23.** *ODI* is an acronym that stands for:
   a. Open Driver Interface
   b. Old DOS-Version Interpreter
   c. Open DOS Interface
   d. Open Data-Link Interface

**24.** Large Internet Packet(LIP) and Packet Burst are:
   a. Part of the operating system code
   b. Separately purchased items
   c. Loaded on the 3.x server as NLMs
   d. EXE files that must be run at the workstations

**25.** The Directory Table blocks of each volume are _____ in size.
   a. Only 4 K
   b. 4, 8, or 16 K
   c. 4, 8, 16, 32, or 64 K
   d. Not larger than the smallest cache buffer

**26.** The configuration files for the NetWare operating system are:
   a. AUTOEXEC.NCF and STARTUP.NCF
   b. AUTOEXEC.BAT and CONFIG.SYS

# NetWare 3.x Advanced Administration

    c. AUTOEXEC.NCF and CONFIG.SYS

    d. SERVER.EXE and AUTOEXEC.NCF

27. The Ethernet_II and Ethernet_802.2 frame types can communicate with one network interface board at the same time.

    a. True

    b. False

28. Novell includes which of the following name space modules with NetWare?

    a. OS2.NAM

    b. NFS.NAM

    c. FTAM.NAM

    d. All of the above

    e. None of the above

29. To view the file server's memory statistics screen, you access the _____ option of monitor.

    a. Memory Utilization

    b. Processor Utilization

    c. System Module Information

    d. Resource Utilization

30. The information that the Dirty Cache Buffers option displays as a number is not a percentage.

    a. True

    b. False

31. Using the CONFIG command, NetWare will display information about:

    a. The loaded LAN drivers

    b. The IPX internal network address

    c. The file server name

    d. All of the above

32. If you want to make a NetWare volume available to the network, you must type _____ at the file server prompt.

    a. LOAD SALES

    b. MOUNT SALES

    c. BIND SALES

    d. VOLUME SALES

**33.** With NetWare 3.x, the Ethernet frame type defaults to:
   a. IPX
   b. Ethernet_II
   c. 802.2
   d. 802.3

**34.** When displaying information on the router tracking screen, NetWare displays the _____ and _____.
   a. IPX, SPX packets
   b. RIP, IPX packets
   c. SAPS, RIPS
   d. None of the above

**35.** The available Disk Allocation block size for a volume _____ in size.
   a. Is always 4 K
   b. Can be 4, 8, or 16 K
   c. Can be 4, 8, 16, 32, or 64 K
   d. Cannot be larger than the smallest cache buffer

# Brain Teaser

Getting NetWare installed as we did in the previous chapter is only one step in an ongoing process. Once you have all the workstations and one or more NetWare servers installed, you still need to optimize them for use. The cryptogram in Fig. 11-13 will provide some handy phrases you can rely on to steer you to the best possible NetWare tune-up for both your servers and your workstations. Just in case the idea of working with a symbol-oriented cryptogram is a bit intimidating for you, here's a tip: All spaces really are spaces and all periods are periods. Apostrophes are also what they appear to be. Every other symbol is a replacement for a letter. You'll find the solution for this Brain Teaser in Appendix C, "Brain Teaser Answers."

If you're feeling especially knowledgeable, you can try your hand at the much more difficult cryptogram in Fig. 11-14. This is a server console–related phrase based on one of the questions you answered in the preceding "Fun Test" section. Remember, this second exam will test your knowledge of the NetWare server console, so you need to be prepared for it. Here's a hint about solving this particular puzzle: There are parentheses in the puzzle that are hiding out as letters. If you see some

# NetWare 3.x Advanced Administration

**Figure 11-13**
Server Tuning Cryptogram.

```
!@#!$@  %^&$  *$@($@  )-_^_+  =&<=>*  }$+^_*  <^){  [_#<&$]+$  #%  ){$

%^&$  *$@($@  ^)*$&%  ^_  ){$  %#@¦  #%  *)=)^*)^~*,  ){$_  ¦#($*  #_  )#

]$($&#!¦$_)  #%  =  )-  _^_+  *)@=)$+>.  =&<=>*  }$+^_  ){$  )-_^_+

!@#~$**  }>  &##[^_+  =)  %^&$  *$@($@  ¦$¦#@>  ¦=_=+$¦$_).  #_~$  >#-'($

)-_$]  =  %^&$  *$@($@'*  ¦$¦#@>,  >#-  ~=_  ¦#($  #_  )#  ¦$){#]*  #%

¦=_=+^_+  ){=)  ¦$¦#@>  ¦#*)  $%%^~^$_)&>.
```

| A | | N | |
|---|---|---|---|
| B | | O | |
| C | | P | |
| D | | Q | |
| E | | R | |
| F | | S | |
| G | | T | |
| H | | U | |
| I | | V | |
| J | | W | |
| K | | X | |
| L | | Y | |
| M | | Z | |

letters that look out of place, they might just be those parentheses in disguise.

## Disk Time

Don't forget to spend some time working with the CD-ROM that accompanies this book. It provides valuable, fun-to-use teaching aids that'll

**Figure 11-14**
Server Console Cryptogram.

PGPTW AZRP HPTGPT XTJEHVZXH QKXD HJU ZHPTGZIP JCGPTXZHPVPEX UTKXKIKRF JEC TZU ZTKBXZEY ZEAKTVJXZKE UTKXKIKRF ZEAKTVJXZKE PGPTW VZEBXP. XDP TKBXPT XTJIMZEY HITPPE CZHURJWH QKXD HPXH KA ZEAKTVJXZKE.

| A | | N | |
|---|---|---|---|
| B | | O | |
| C | | P | |
| D | | Q | |
| E | | R | |
| F | | S | |
| G | | T | |
| H | | U | |
| I | | V | |
| J | | W | |
| K | | X | |
| L | | Y | |
| M | | Z | |

help you prepare for your exam. See "Disk Time" in the preface of this book for details about what the disk contains. Make sure you pay special attention to the parts of the Windows help file and the Red Zone game that pertain to this chapter. Also, check out the acronym areas provided in both disk features—they'll help you get up to speed on what's going on in the industry faster.

# CHAPTER 12
# NetWare 3.x Installation and Configuration Workshop

# Introduction

This chapter looks at the requirements for the NetWare 3.x Installation and Configuration Workshop exam. This requirement was added to the original CNE certification program. It seeks to improve the CNE's ability to provide the client with the best installation possible. This exam also parallels the NetWare 4.x requirement by the same name. One of the reasons that Novell added it was so that each CNE specialty would provide a similar level of expertise and receive a similar level of training. There are several discrete sections in this chapter. Each section helps you study for the exam in a different way. You can improve your chances of passing the exam by using the study methods provided in this chapter. In fact, it'll probably help if you study all the sections once and your favorite sections at least twice. Review the study guidelines in Chap. 4 as often as necessary to ensure you that maintain the best possible study atmosphere.

The first section of this chapter is a *case study*. You'll perform some hands-on tasks that help you learn what you need to know to pass the examination. In this case, we look at the requirements for installing NetWare 3.x on a file server and at some of the requirements for installing the client software as well. Even though you'll get a lot more from this section if you perform it on your own network, the inclusion of step-by-step instructions will help you gain something from the section even if you don't have a network.

The second area contains *sample test questions* for this course. We made a special effort to include a variety of NetWare 3.x installation-specific questions, but, as on the real exam, you'll find other types of questions here as well. This section also includes the correct answers to those questions and an explanation of why each answer is correct. Try to answer each question yourself, look at the correct answer, and then determine where you went wrong if you did not answer correctly.

The next section is a *fun test*. As in the sample test questions, we concentrate on NetWare 3.x installation issues, but you'll find a variety of other question types as well. The fun test is an exercise where you'll look at more sample test questions and answer them. The answers appear in App. B at the back of the book. This will help you test what you learned in the previous section. Make sure you save this section of the chapter for last.

The final text section of the chapter is the *brain teaser*. You'll get to have a little fun working on a NetWare 3.x–related puzzle—in this case we'll spend a bit of time looking at some file server installation issues. This chapter provides two cryptograms that should give you some ideas of ways to study for the exam. Obviously, it helps to have a good overall knowledge of NetWare 3.x in this case, since the cryptograms will be easier to solve if you can spot specific patterns in the way they're encrypted. By the way, the cryptograms use different encryption methods, so you'll have to solve each puzzle separately.

Finally, we will spend some time using the *Jeopardy!*-type game named *Red Zone*. This section helps you look at the test from the opposite viewpoint. The game provides you with an answer—you need to come up with the corresponding question. The game awards points for correct answers, and takes points away for incorrect answers. You'll receive a score at the end of the game proclaiming that you either did or did not get your certificate. Make sure you concentrate on the NetWare 3.x–related questions when using the game—they're the ones that'll provide you with the best information about the exams you are about to take. Unlike the specific questions provided in this chapter, Red Zone tests your overall knowledge of Novell products, so be prepared to explore areas that you haven't looked at in the past.

Use all the learning methods that we provide in this chapter to improve your chances of passing the exam. It's a good idea to save the fun test section until you're are almost certain that you possess all the required knowledge. Remember, you can probably go through the fun test only two or three times at most before you'll start to remember the answers without really knowing the material. Obviously, the brain teaser is only good once—after that you'll have all the phrases decrypted.

## Case Study

This case study covers the steps and procedures necessary to install the NetWare 3.x operating system and the workstation software. There are two parts to the case study. The first part installs the *network operating system* and the second part installs the *workstation software*. These are the same two procedures you will need to perform on any network. There's also a floppy disk installation technique. It's a lot like this procedure, but you'll have to swap the floppies a lot as you perform the installation, especially when it comes time to copy the network software to the file server.

### File Server Software Installation

For this demonstration, the installation program will load the necessary files from another file server. The steps and procedures will be the same if you are installing directly from the CD-ROM disk. This procedure also assumes that you are using a clean, nonpartitioned hard drive. Make sure you perform a low-level format, if required, before you start the procedure. Check the installation instructions that came with your file server for additional prerequisites. Some systems will require additional setup steps. For example, an EISA system will require you to run the special EISA setup program that comes with the file server.

1. Configure and install the network interface board, hard disk, and hard disk controller in the new file server. Refer to the procedures in Chap. 3 to learn how to avoid hardware configuration conflicts.

2. Low-level format the drive, if necessary. Use the FDisk utility to create a DOS partition. In most cases 10 MB will provide all the space you need, but installations with newer versions of DOS will require more.

3. Once you create the DOS partition, exit the FDisk utility. The machine will automatically reboot. Use the Format utility to format the DOS partition (use the /S switch to make it bootable).

4. Boot the soon-to-be File Server to DOS and perform any procedures required to access the drive where the NetWare 3.x installation program files reside. If you're installing from a network, log into the file server and map a drive letter to the directory holding the installation program. If you're installing from a CD, load the appropriate drivers for accessing the CD. You may want to create a CONFIG.SYS and AUTOEXEC.BAT file that load all the required drivers for you and reboot the machine.

5. Type the drive letter of the CD-ROM followed by a colon (for example, *E:*) and press Enter. Type *CD \NETWARE.312\ENGLISH* (or the language you are using) and press Enter. Type *INSTALL* and press Enter. You should see the dialog shown in Fig. 12-1.

6. Highlight the *Install new NetWare 3.x* option, and then press Enter. The install program will check your hard disk for existing partitions. It should display a screen similar to the one in Fig. 12-2. Note that you have the option of using the existing partition or creating a new one.

7. Highlight the *Retain Current Partition* option, and then press Enter. You should see the dialog box shown in Fig. 12-3. Enter the new file server name. Select a name that'll be easy for everyone to remember as they log onto the system.

8. In this case, type *FS1* (for the first file server) and Enter. You'll see the dialog shown in Fig. 12-4. This is the screen where you'll enter

# Netware 3.x Installation and Configuration Workshop

**Figure 12-1**
NetWare Installation Selection Dialog.

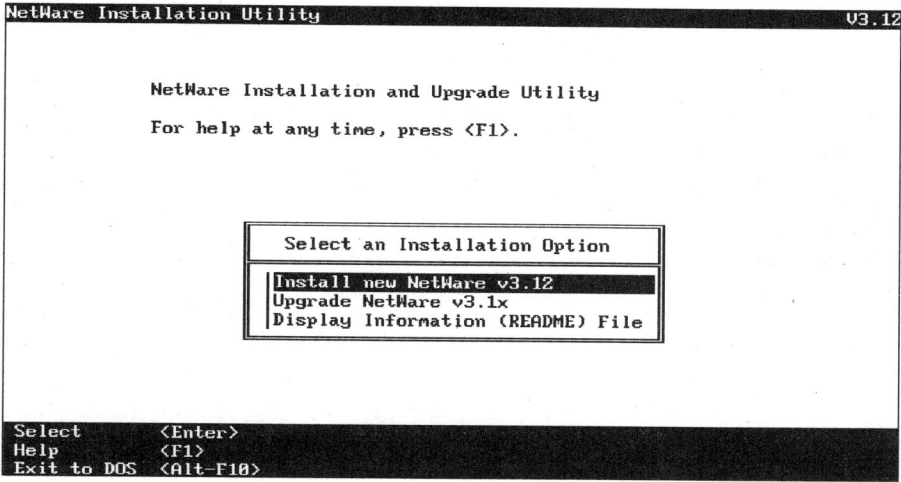

the IPX network number. It's important to use a number that's easy to follow as you track various network resources.

9. Erase the old entry using the Delete key. Type *A312* and press Enter. You'll see the dialog shown in Fig. 12-5. It tells you that the server boot software is ready to install. You'll need to insert the SYSTEM_1 disk in the A drive to start the installation process.

10. Accept the default directories by pressing Enter. The installation utility will begin the installation process. If you didn't place the SYSTEM_1 disk in the A drive, Install will display an error message

**Figure 12-2**
Disk Partition Options Dialog.

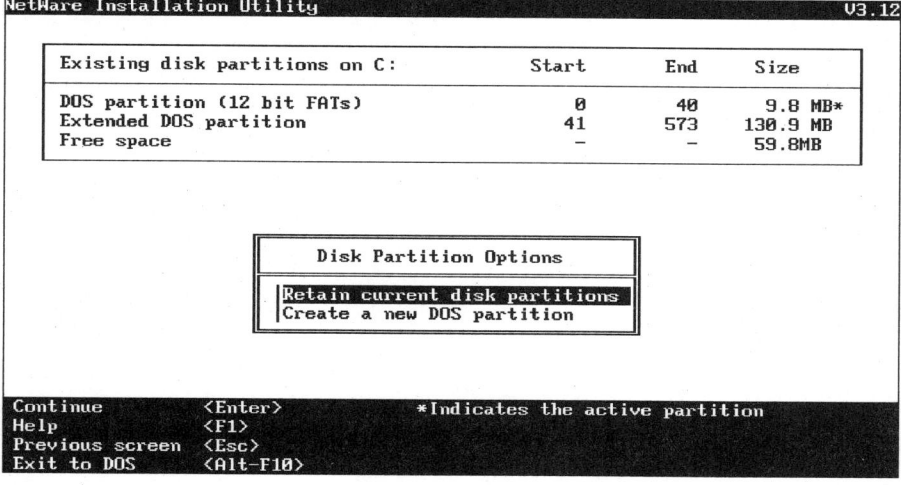

**Figure 12-3**
File Server Name Entry Dialog.

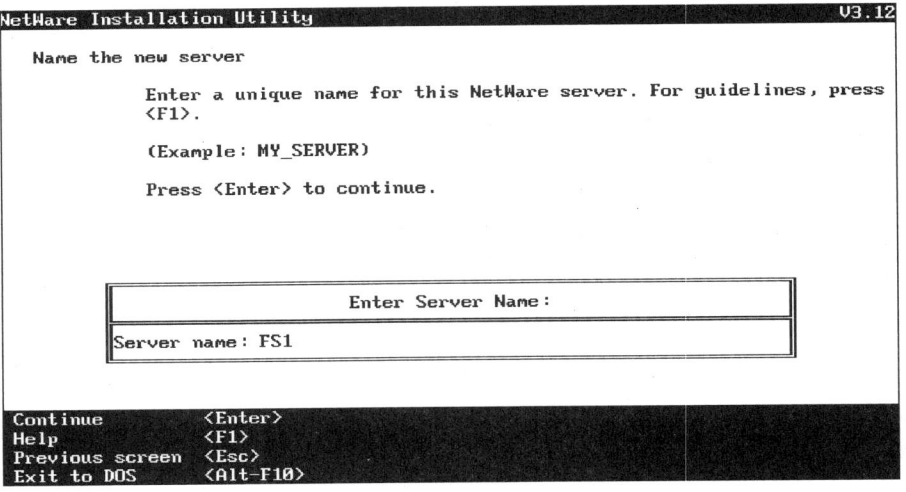

at this point. Insert the disk and press Enter to continue the boot file installation process. A progress indicator at the top of the screen will tell you how the installation is progressing.

11. Once the server boot file installation is complete, you'll see the dialog shown in Fig. 12-6. Accept the default country code, code page, and keyboard mapping entries (unless you need to use a different setting) by pressing F10. You'll see the dialog shown in Fig. 12-7. This dialog allows you to choose between NetWare and standard DOS filenames. Unless you need foreign language support or have

**Figure 12-4**
File Server IPX Network Number Dialog.

# Netware 3.x Installation and Configuration Workshop

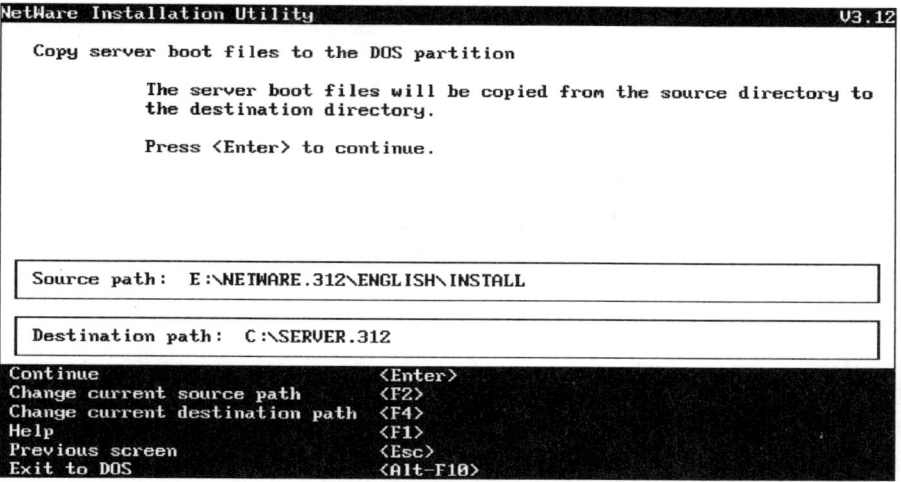

**Figure 12-5**
File Source and Destination Dialog.

other special needs, it's usually better to select the DOS filename support.

12. Accept the default setting of DOS filename format by pressing Enter. Install will display a message that asks if you want to insert any special commands in the STARTUP.NCF file.

13. Press Enter to accept the default value of *NO*. The install program will then ask if you want the AUTOEXEC.BAT file to load SERVER.EXE.

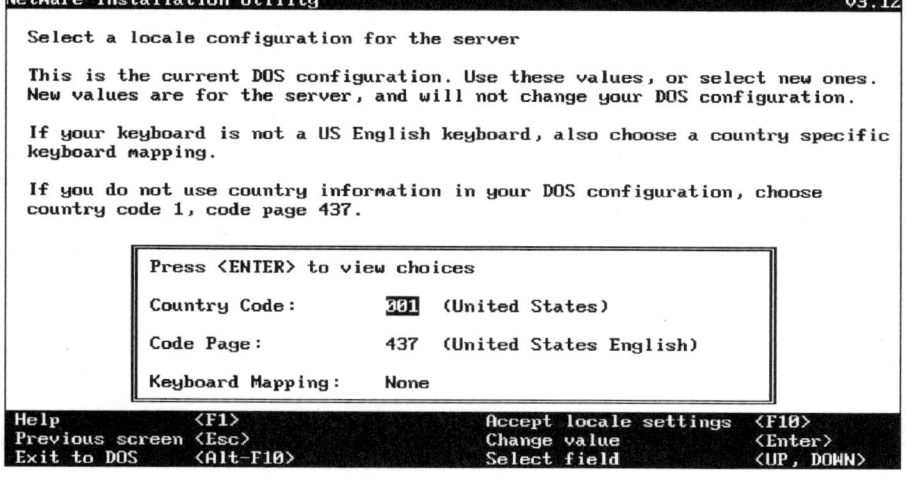

**Figure 12-6**
Country Code, Code Page, and Keyboard Mapping Selection Dialog.

**Figure 12-7**
Filename Format Selection Dialog.

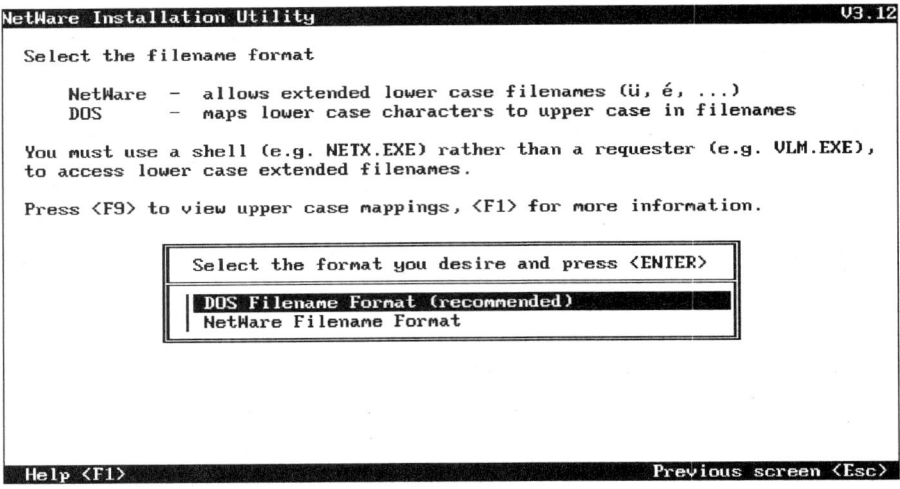

14. Press Enter to accept the default value of *YES*. Press Enter to accept the path to the AUTOEXEC.BAT file. The install program will automatically launch SERVER.EXE to start NetWare on the new server.

15. Load a disk driver so that NetWare can find it's files by typing *LOAD <DISK DRIVER>*. Consult the installation manual for a complete list of disk drivers. Most MFM drives will require the ISADISK driver and most IDE drives will use the IDE driver. Press Enter to load the driver.

16. Type *LOAD INSTALL* to load the installation utility. You should see the NetWare 3.x installation dialog appear.

17. Highlight the *Disk Options* entry and press Enter. Highlight the *Partition Table* entry and press Enter. Install will display a list of the current partitions on your machine. You should see a single partition, the 10 MB partition that holds DOS.

18. Select *Create NetWare Partition* and press Enter. Install will automatically select the rest of the drive for a NetWare partition. For the purposes of this case study, press Escape to accept the default settings. In some cases, you might want to change these settings when creating the drive setup for your own network.

19. Press Escape twice to return to the Installation Options menu. Highlight *Volume Options* and press Enter. You should see a blank list of volumes in the Volumes dialog.

20. Press Insert. You'll see the New Volume Information dialog. This is where you would change the parameters for the way that NetWare

# Netware 3.x Installation and Configuration Workshop

interacts with a partition. Every file server must have volume SYS as the first volume.

21. Press Escape to accept the default settings. Install will ask if you want to create the new volume. Select *Yes* and press Enter. You should now see SYS in the volume listing. Press Escape to close the Volume dialog.

22. Highlight *System Options* and press Enter. Highlight *Copy System and Public Files* and press Enter. Install will tell you that you haven't mounted volume SYS yet. Press Escape to clear the error message. Select *Yes* to mount the volume.

23. Install will now ask you to place the first installation disk in the A drive. Press F6 to override this option. Type in the path to the source files. If you are using a CD-ROM drive, then type *<Drive>:\ NETWARE.312\ENGLISH* and press Enter. Replace *<Drive>* with the actual drive number for your CD-ROM drive. You may need to change the language directory as well, depending on the language you want to install. If you're using a network directory, then type in the path to the network drive and directory that contains the installation files. You'll need to wait while Install copies all the required files to your new NetWare volume. This process could take a while, depending on the speed of your CD-ROM drive or network connection.

24. Once the copying process is complete, Install will display a message stating that *"File Upload is Complete"*. Press Escape to clear the message.

25. Press Escape twice to exit the Install utility. At the console prompt, type *LOAD <LAN DRIVER>* and press Enter. For example, if you had an NE2000 compatible NIC installed, then you would type *LOAD NE2000* and press Enter. You'll need to check the installation manual for a complete list of available drivers.

26. The LAN adapter NLM will load and ask you some questions about the configuration of the NIC. In most cases, this will include the port address and interrupt. You may have to supply other information as well.

27. After you complete all the required NIC configuration information, type *BIND IPX TO <LAN DRIVER>* and press Enter. The LAN DRIVER is the same one you used in the previous steps to access the NIC. If you were using an NE2000 NIC, then you would type *BIND IPX TO NE2000* and press Enter. Now that you have all the

required drivers installed, you need to create an AUTOEXEC.NCF and a STARTUP.NCF file to perform these steps automatically later.

28. Type *LOAD INSTALL* and press Enter. Highlight *System Options* and press Enter. Highlight *Create AUTOEXEC.NCF file* on the Available System Options menu and press Enter. Press Escape to accept the default entries (you may modify the existing entries if needed before pressing Escape). Highlight *Yes* and press Enter when asked if you want to save this file.

29. Highlight *Create STARTUP.NCF file* on the Available System Options menu and press Enter. Press Escape to accept the default entries (you may modify the existing entries if needed before pressing Escape). Highlight *Yes* and press Enter when asked if you want to save this file.

30. Press Escape twice to exit the Installation utility. The file server is now ready for you to log in as SUPERVISOR.

## Workstation Software Installation

After installing the NetWare operating system, you must install the workstation's software. For this example, we connect the CD-ROM to the computer that will be a workstation. The ODI and VLM software will copy from the NetWare 3.12 installation CD to the workstation's hard disk. This case study assumes that you're not using the menu feature of DOS 6.x. You must use a simple CONFIG.SYS and AUTOEXEC.BAT to make the procedure work correctly. (This does not restrict you from loading all the standard drivers and TSRs that you normally load.)

1. Install the CD-ROM drive and appropriate drivers on the workstation.

2. Boot the workstation to DOS and place the NetWare 3.x installation CD in the player. Change drive letters to the CD-ROM drive. For example, if the drive letter for your CD-ROM drive is D, type *D:* and press Enter.

3. At the D:\> prompt, type *CD \CLIENT\DOSWIN* and press Enter. Your prompt will now indicate the past of D:\CLIENT\DOSWIN>. This is the starting directory for the workstation client software.

4. To start the installation program, type *INSTALL* and press Enter. Figure 12-8 shows the NetWare Client installation menu.

**Figure 12-8**
NetWare Client Installation Window (Part 1).

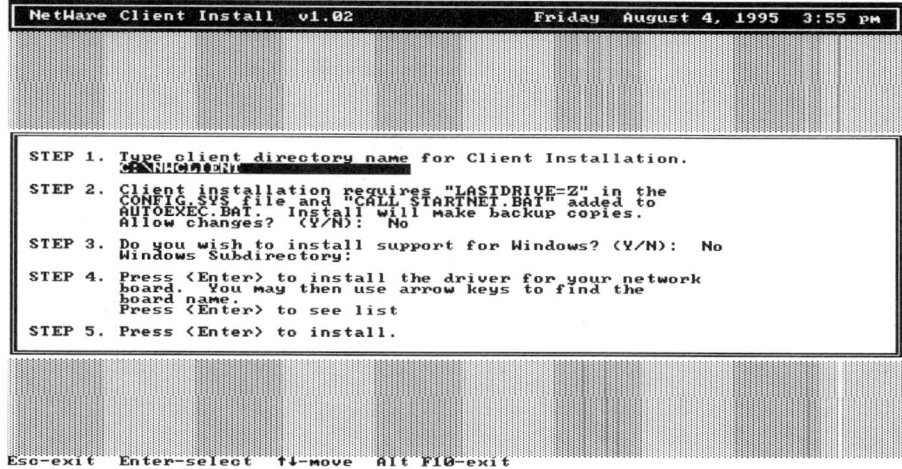

5. The Installation menu is divided into 5 steps. Step 1 shows the path to install the workstation client files. The default path is C:\NWCLIENT; press Enter to accept this path. The cursor will move to Step 2.

6. Step 2 advises you that the client software requires a *LASTDRIVE=Z* statement in your CONFIG.SYS file, and the line *CALL STARTNET.BAT* added to the AUTOEXEC.BAT file. The installation program is asking you in this step if you want the program to make the changes to the files, and create backup copies of your originals. The default value for this step is *NO*. Change the value to *YES* by typing *Y* and pressing Enter.

7. Step 3 is to install the Windows support files. The default for this value is *NO*. Change this to *YES* by typing *Y* and pressing Enter. A path statement to the windows directory will appear. The default path is C:\WINDOWS; press Enter twice to accept the path. If your Windows directory is in another location, type the correct path; then press Enter.

8. Step 4 defines the network interface board and driver for the workstation. Press Enter to view a list of available boards. Using the down arrow key or the Page Down key, scroll through the list until you find the type of board in the workstation, then press Enter. A dialog box will appear listing the default configuration for the network board.

9. Press Escape to accept the values. Figure 12-9 shows the default settings for the Novell/Eagle NE2000 board. Note that the default

**Figure 12-9**
NIC Settings Dialog.

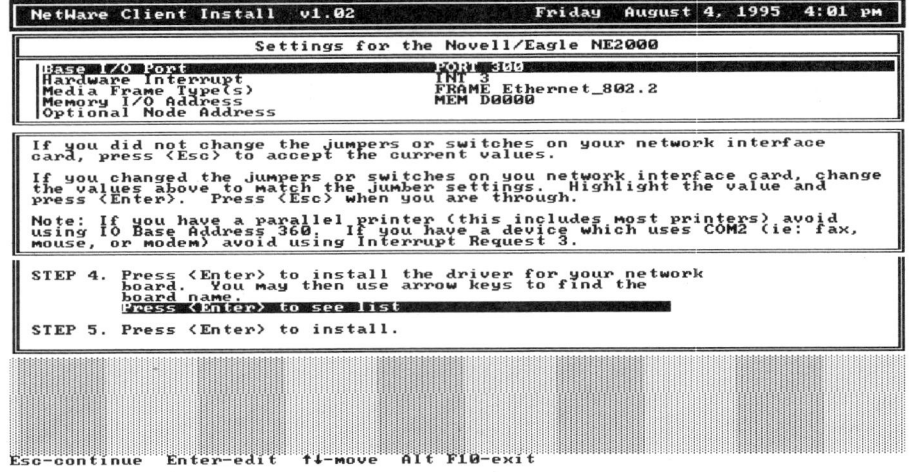

Media Frame Type is Ethernet_802.2. If your network board's not set to the default, make the appropriate changes now.

10. Step 5 is to install the software on the workstation with the specified settings. Compare your screen to Fig. 12-10. Make sure that the first four steps have the correct settings. To continue the installation, press Enter. The system copies the files to the appropriate directories on your hard disk. This process may take several minutes. When the installation program finishes copying the files to your workstation, an information screen will appear. Make note of the information on this screen.

**Figure 12-10**
NetWare Client Installation Window (Part 2).

# Netware 3.x Installation and Configuration Workshop

11. Press Enter to exit the install program. The DOS prompt appears.
12. You must now reboot your workstation, since the CONFIG.SYS file changed. Press CTRL-ALT-DEL to reboot your system. When the system reboots, the new NetWare client software will automatically load and connect you to a file server.

Your workstation is now ready for use on the network. All files necessary to connect the workstation to the file server are now on the workstation's hard disk. The support files for Windows are also on the local workstation. During the installation of the NetWare client software, the install program also created a NetWare Tools program folder in Windows.

## Study Questions

1. Once you complete the file server and workstation software installation, you can log in as:
   a. Admin
   b. Guest
   c. Manager
   d. Supervisor

   *b and d.* The installation software always creates two default accounts for you. The Guest account is meant to be used by visitors to your network and should provide a minimum level of accessibility. The Supervisor account is for the system administrator; it provides the maximum level of accessibility.

2. Before you begin the file server software installation, you must _____.
   a. Install a NIC.
   b. Low-level format the hard drive.
   c. Test the software for bugs.
   d. Both *a* and *b*.
   e. All of the above.

   *d.* Every node on the network requires a NIC to take care of any communication requirements. In addition, you must prepare your hard drive for use before starting the procedure. Fortunately, most modern drives, like IDE and SCSI, do not require you to perform this task.

3. The first NetWare volume always bears this name:
   a. SYS
   b. SYSTEM
   c. FIRST
   d. NOVELL

   *a.* You must always name the first volume on a NetWare 3.x server SYS.

4. When installing a NIC on either a workstation or server, you need at least three pieces of configuration information in most cases: _____, _____, and _____.
   a. Port address, DMA address, and manufacturer
   b. Vendor name, port address, and driver name
   c. IRQ, port address, and DMA address
   d. IRQ, port address, and product type

   *c.* In most cases, you'll need the IRQ, DMA address, and port address. A *port address* allows applications and the operating system to send data to the card. The *DMA address* (when enabled) allows the card to work faster by using direct memory access (DMA) transfers instead of using the processor. The *IRQ* (interrupt) allows the card to notify the processor when it needs some type of service or has data to transfer.

5. What instruction must you execute to complete the LAN driver loading sequence, assuming that you are using an NE2000 NIC?
   a. LOAD NE2000
   b. LOAD <DISK DRIVER>
   c. BIND NE2000 TO IPX
   d. BIND IPX TO NE2000

   *d.* You must always bind the LAN driver to the desired protocol before the file server can actually use the NIC.

6. The default directory for installing the workstation files is:
   a. C:\NET
   b. C:\NWCLIENT
   c. C:\NETWORK
   d. C:\

# Netware 3.x Installation and Configuration Workshop

    *b.* The default path for installing the workstation files is C:\NWCLIENT. During the installation program, you can specify an alternate path if you want.

7. You should always use a complex set of letters and numbers to identify your file server, making it harder for someone to break into your system.

    **a.** True

    **b.** False

    *b.* You should always use an easy-to-remember name for the file servers on your network. Many people use FS1 as the first or central file server. Other people use descriptive names like CENTRAL or RESEARCH.

8. Newer versions of NetWare 3.x provide the _____ online help viewer in place of the _____ online help viewer provided in previous versions.

    **a.** Windows Help, ElectroText

    **b.** ElectroText, DynaText

    **c.** DynaText, ElectroText

    **d.** DynaText, Windows Help

    *c.* The newer versions of NetWare come with the DynaText viewer. This new viewer provides an easier to use interface while reducing the size of the help files. You can't interchange the help files used by the two viewers.

9. NetWare 3.x provides a maximum addressable volume size of _____ and a maximum addressable file size of _____.

    **a.** 255 MB, 255 MB

    **b.** 4 GB, 255 MB

    **c.** 32 TB, 255 MB

    **d.** 32 TB, 4 GB

    *d.* One of the advantages of using NetWare 3.x over NetWare 2.x is the larger volume and file sizes that it allows.

10. The installation program creates these default directories:

    **a.** LOGIN, MAIL, SYSTEM, and PUBLIC

    **b.** LOGIN, SYSTEM, PUBLIC, and PRIVATE

c. LOGIN, MAIL, SYSTEM, and PRIVATE

d. LOGIN, MAIL, PUBLIC, and PRIVATE

*a.* The four default directories are: LOGIN, MAIL, SYSTEM, and PUBLIC. A system administrator will also need to create other application- and user-specific directories before the installation is complete.

11. NetWare 3.x provides optional name space support for the following operating systems:
    a. DOS and Windows
    b. Macintosh
    c. UNIX
    d. FTAM
    e. OS/2

*a, b, c, d, and e.* The latest version of NetWare 3.x provides name space support for all of these operating systems, making it compatible with a wide variety of working environments.

12. NetWare provides a default first network drive statement of F in the _____ file.
    a. CONFIG.SYS
    b. NET.SYS
    c. STARTNET.BAT
    d. NET.CFG

*d.* All of the network-specific configuration information appears in the NET.CFG file. This includes the NIC settings like port address, IRQ, and frame type.

13. The VLM acronym means:
    a. Vital Loadable Module
    b. Virtual Loadable Module
    c. Variable Loadable Module
    d. Virtual Loadable Method

*b.* The Virtual Loadable Module (VLM) has replaced the many TSRs that previous versions of NetWare employed to access the network and load network-specific services. All of them are serviced through the VLM.EXE file, the only TSR now needed to access the network. A list of VLMs always appears in the NET.CFG file.

# Netware 3.x Installation and Configuration Workshop

14. When logging into the network, you must:
    a. Specify the context of the user object.
    b. Enter a user name.
    c. Load the workstation software.
    d. All of the above.

    *b and c.* To log into the network, you must first load the workstation software to communicate to the file server. Then you need to enter a file server name, a backslash, and a user name. The user object context only applies to NetWare 4.x that uses NDS.

15. To unload the VLM client software from memory, type _____ at the prompt.
    a. VLM /?
    b. VLM /D
    c. VLM /E
    d. VLM /U

    *d.* As long as there are no other TSRs loaded in the workstation memory above the VLMs, you can remove the VLMs from memory by typing *VLM /U.* Typing *VLM /?* at the prompt will display a set of help screens.

16. You may use the following disk block sizes with the current version of NetWare 3.x:
    a. 4 K
    b. 8 K
    c. 16 K
    d. 32 K
    e. 64 K

    *a, b, c, d, and e.* You may request any of these disk block sizes when creating a NetWare volume. The choice you make is based on the anticipated size of the files that the volume will store. A large size is more speed-efficient with large files, since NetWare will need to manage fewer blocks in memory. A small size is more space-efficient when storing many small files.

17. OS/2 ODI drivers have the same filenames as DOS ODI drivers, except they have a .SYS extension instead of a .COM extension.
    a. True
    b. False

*a.* Using the same driver names across operating systems makes it easier for someone familiar with the DOS version of the product to make the transition to OS/2.

18. You will find the OS/2 workstation installation software in the _____ directory of the CD.
    a. \CLIENT\DOSWIN
    b. \NETWARE.312\<LANGUAGE>\CLIENT\DOSWIN
    c. \CLIENT\OS2
    d. \NETWARE.312\<LANGUAGE>\CLIENT\OS2

    *c.* You will find the OS/2 specific version of the client software in the \CLIENT\OS2 directory. The DOS- and Windows-specific versions of the product appear in the \CLIENT\DOSWIN directory.

19. The program used to install the NetWare operating system is:
    a. SETUP
    b. SERVER
    c. STARTNET
    d. INSTALL

    *d.* The installation program for the NetWare 3.x operating system is INSTALL.BAT. When installing from the CD-ROM disk, the INSTALL.BAT file is in the \NETWARE.312\<LANGUAGE> directory (where <LANGUAGE> is a supported language like English).

20. The OS/2 version of the NetWare client uses search drives, just like the DOS version.
    a. True
    b. False

    *b.* The OS/2 version of the client software does not use search drives like the DOS version does. It uses the search functionality provided by the OS/2-specific PATH, LIBPATH, and DPATH statements in the CONFIG.SYS file as a replacement. This allows you to better use features provided by OS/2 to find NetWare utilities and other files.

21. You will find the following protocols provided with the NetWare Workstation for OS/2 kit:
    a. SPX
    b. TCP/IP

# Netware 3.x Installation and Configuration Workshop

     **c.** NetBIOS emulation

     **d.** Named Pipes

     **e.** NetBEUI

    *a, c, and d.*   The most current version of NetWare 3.x provides support for the SPX, NetBIOS, and Named Pipes protocols. NetWare uses these protocols to support OS/2 clients and servers on a distributed application network. It also uses SPX to support some NetWare printing utilities.

22. NetWare allows you to modify the default login script.

     **a.** True

     **b.** False

    *b.*   NetWare will not allow you to modify the default script. You must create system or user scripts instead.

23. NetWare 3.x will remember _____ previous passwords of each user.

     **a.** 6

     **b.** 8

     **c.** 10

     **d.** 12

    *b.*   NetWare will remember the last 8 passwords of each user that were used 1 day or longer. If you have the Require Unique Passwords option set to *yes* for your user, NetWare will reject the use of the last 8 passwords.

24. The minimum hardware required to install NetWare 3.x on a file server includes:

     **a.** 386 or 486 (SX or DX) equipped PC

     **b.** 4 MB of RAM

     **c.** 50 MB of hard drive space

     **d.** Ethernet card

    *a, b, and c.*   You can use any supported NIC with NetWare. This includes both ArcNET and Token Ring, as well as other options.

25. The acronym *UPS* stands for:

     **a.** United Parcel Service

     **b.** Unimpeded processor service

     **c.** Uninterruptible power service

     **d.** Uninterruptible power supply

d. You'll normally want to connect your file server to an uninterruptible power supply (UPS) to make sure your data remains intact during a power outage.

26. A file server name may contain the following elements:
    a. Any name from 2 to 47 characters long
    b. Alphanumeric characters, hyphens, and underscores
    c. Periods
    d. Spaces

    *a and b.* You can create a file server name 2 to 47 characters long. The name must begin with a letter or number. It can include hyphens and underscores, but not periods or spaces.

27. The three types of login script include: _____, _____, and _____.
    a. System, user, and supervisor
    b. User, supervisor, and private
    c. System, user, and default
    d. User, default, and supervisor

    *c.* The three types of login script are default, user, and system. The *system* script executes first; it sets the overall system options. The *user* script contains commands for a specific user. The *default* script is executed whenever someone logs in who does not have a user script (this assumes there is no EXIT command at the end of the system login script).

28. Once you create a DOS partition on your file server hard drive using FDisk, you must:
    a. Reboot the system so the change can take effect.
    b. Start the NetWare installation process.
    c. Update the CMOS settings.
    d. All of the above.
    e. None of the above.

    *a.* You need to reboot the machine so that DOS can recognize the new partition. Once you complete this task, you can format the partition, then start preparing it for the NetWare installation.

29. Login script command lines cannot exceed _____ characters in length.
    a. 64
    b. 100

c. 150
d. 255

*c.* NetWare doesn't allow command lines within a login script to exceed 150 characters. Comments lines can be as long as needed.

30. The file used to start the NetWare client software is:
    a. SERVER
    b. STARTNET
    c. INSTALL
    d. NETWARE

    *b.* The file to start the NetWare client software is STARTNET.BAT. You can easily modify this file to meet any special needs. Use the DOS CALL command to access this file automatically from AUTOEXEC.BAT.

31. The NetWare module for the network interface board has a _____ extension.
    a. .NIB
    b. .LAN
    c. .NLM
    d. .DSK

    *b.* All network interface board NLMs on the NetWare 3.x and 4.x file servers have a .LAN extension.

32. You must add the _____ command to AUTOEXEC.BAT prior to using the DynaText online help viewer.
    a. SET NWLANGUAGE=ENGLISH
    b. SET LANGUAGE=ENGLISH
    c. USE NWLANGUAGE=ENGLISH
    d. SET NWLANGUAGE=<LANGUAGE>

    *d.* You would select this generic answer in this case because it is the most correct. NetWare is designed to work with more than one language. You need to substitute the <LANGUAGE> variable with the name of the language you want to use (for example, ENGLISH).

33. NetWare allows up to _____ %n parameter variables in a login script.
    a. 1
    b. 2

c. 9

d. 10

*d.* You may use any parameter variable from %0 through %9 within a login script. The SHIFT command allows you to grab additional parameters from the command line by shifting old parameters to the left. In other words, the %8 variable becomes the %7 variable, and so on.

**34.** You can upgrade a 2.x server to a 3.x server using the _____ utility.
   a. NetWare Upgrade
   b. NetWare Migration
   c. NetWare Installation
   d. NetWare Conversion

*b.* The NetWare Migration utility allows you to convert a 2.x server into a 3.x server. You can also use the utility to upgrade a 3.x server to the current version of the software.

**35.** Optimizing your file server performance can include modifying or upgrading any of the following components:
   a. Memory
   b. Communications subsystem
   c. File system and cache
   d. Processor

*a, b, c, and d.* Adding more memory usually results in some type of performance improvement. There are a number of items within the communication subsystem that affect performance: packet size, communication buffers, Packet Burst protocol, SAP traffic, and network boards. The amount of caching you provide for the file system can greatly affect the performance of applications such as database managers. As with any computer, the system processor and the type of bus used almost always determine the performance you can expect to receive.

**36.** The three NetWare 3.x memory pools are: _____, _____, and _____.
   a. Allocated cache buffer, permanent memory, and file cache buffer
   b. Semipermanent memory, permanent memory, and file cache buffer
   c. File cache buffer, permanent memory, and allocated short-term memory
   d. File cache buffer, cache movable, and cache nonmovable.

# Netware 3.x Installation and Configuration Workshop 353

*c.* NetWare uses these three memory pools to allocate system memory to various system components. The *file cache buffer* contains all the hard disk data reads and writes. NetWare uses the *permanent memory pool* for long-term memory uses like communication buffers and directory cache buffers. It uses the *allocated short-term memory pool* for smaller requirements like drive mappings, SAP and RIP tables, queue manager tables, and user connection information.

**37.** You should always add LASTDRIVE=Z to CONFIG.SYS when using the VLM client software.

  **a.** True
  **b.** False

  *a.* The VLM client software always requires access to 26 drives.

**38.** The NetWare boot up configuration files are:
  **a.** AUTOEXEC.BAT and CONFIG.SYS
  **b.** AUTOEXEC.NCF and CONFIG.NCF
  **c.** AUTOEXEC.NCF and STARTUP.NCF
  **d.** AUTOEXEC.INI and STARTUP.INI

  *c.* The AUTOEXEC.NCF and STARTUP.NCF contain the commands that will customize the operating system for your needs. The STARTUP.NCF and AUTOEXEC.NCF files are NetWare's version of DOS's CONFIG.SYS and AUTOEXEC.BAT.

**39.** The hard disk controller NLM for NetWare file servers will have a .LAN extension.

  **a.** True
  **b.** False

  *b.* The hard disk controller NLM for NetWare file servers will have a .DSK extension.

**40.** An Inherited Rights Mask is:
  **a.** Something you get from NetWare during the installation process
  **b.** Part of the user trustee assignment
  **c.** Automatically assigned to each directory or file when it's created
  **d.** Not automatically assigned to each directory or file when it's created

  *c.* Even though the default Inherited Rights Mask (IRM) includes all rights, this does not mean that users have all rights. It's the combination of the IRM and the users' trustee rights that determine what level of access they have to a file or directory. The owner of a file or directory may also change the IRM for that resource, preventing inadvertent damage to the data the system contains.

## Fun Test

1. Optimizing your file server performance can include modifying or upgrading any of the following components:
   a. Memory
   b. Communications subsystem
   c. File system and cache
   d. Processor

2. NetWare 3.x provides optional Name Space support for the following operating systems:
   a. DOS and Windows
   b. Macintosh
   c. UNIX
   d. FTAM
   e. OS/2

3. NetWare 3.x will remember _____ previous passwords of each user.
   a. 6
   b. 8
   c. 10
   d. 12

4. Login script command lines can't exceed _____ characters in length.
   a. 64
   b. 100
   c. 150
   d. 255

5. The first NetWare volume always bears this name:
   a. SYS
   b. SYSTEM
   c. FIRST
   d. NOVELL

# Netware 3.x Installation and Configuration Workshop

6. An Inherited Rights Mask is:
   a. Something you get from NetWare during the installation process
   b. Part of the user trustee assignment
   c. Not automatically assigned to each directory or file when it's created
   d. Automatically assigned to each directory or file when it's created

7. When logging into the network, you must:
   a. Specify the context of the user object.
   b. Enter a user name.
   c. Load the workstation software.
   d. All of the above.

8. You must add the _____ command to AUTOEXEC.BAT prior to using the DynaText online help viewer.
   a. SET NWLANGUAGE=ENGLISH
   b. SET LANGUAGE=ENGLISH
   c. USE NWLANGUAGE=ENGLISH
   d. SET NWLANGUAGE=<LANGUAGE>

9. Once you complete the file server and workstation software installation, you can log in as:
   a. Admin
   b. Guest
   c. Supervisor
   d. Manager

10. The OS/2 version of the NetWare client uses search drives, just like the DOS version.
    a. True
    b. False

11. A file server name may contain the following elements:
    a. Periods
    b. Alphanumeric characters, hyphens, and underscores
    c. Spaces
    d. Any name from 2 to 47 characters long

12. You should always add LASTDRIVE=Z to CONFIG.SYS when using the VLM client software.
    a. True
    b. False

13. What instruction must you execute to complete the LAN driver loading sequence, assuming that you are using an NE2000 NIC?
    a. LOAD NE2000
    b. LOAD <DISK DRIVER>
    c. BIND NE2000 TO IPX
    d. BIND IPX TO NE2000

14. You may use the following disk block sizes with the current version of NetWare 3.x:
    a. 4 K
    b. 8 K
    c. 16 K
    d. 32 K
    e. 64 K

15. The installation program creates these default directories:
    a. LOGIN, MAIL, SYSTEM, and PUBLIC
    b. LOGIN, SYSTEM, PUBLIC, and PRIVATE
    c. LOGIN, MAIL, SYSTEM, and PRIVATE
    d. LOGIN, MAIL, PUBLIC, and PRIVATE

16. The default directory for installing the workstation files is:
    a. C:\NET
    b. C:\NWCLIENT
    c. C:\NETWORK
    d. C:\

17. The file used to start the NetWare client software is:
    a. SERVER
    b. INSTALL
    c. STARTNET
    d. NETWARE

18. OS/2 ODI drivers have the same filenames as DOS ODI drivers, except they have a .SYS extension instead of a .COM extension.
    a. True
    b. False

# Netware 3.x Installation and Configuration Workshop 357

19. To unload the VLM client software from memory, type _____ at the prompt.
    a. VLM /?
    b. VLM /D
    c. VLM /E
    d. VLM /U

20. The three types of login script include: _____, _____, and _____.
    a. System, user, and supervisor
    b. User, supervisor, and private
    c. System, user, and default
    d. User, default, and supervisor

21. The hard disk controller NLM for NetWare file servers will have a .LAN extension.
    a. True
    b. False

22. Newer versions of NetWare 3.x provide the _____ online help viewer in place of the _____ online help viewer provided in previous versions.
    a. Windows Help, ElectroText
    b. ElectroText, DynaText
    c. DynaText, ElectroText
    d. DynaText, Windows Help

23. The minimum hardware required to install NetWare 3.x on a file server includes:
    a. 386 or 486 (SX or DX) equipped PC
    b. 4 MB of RAM
    c. 50 MB of hard drive space
    d. Ethernet card

24. You can upgrade a 2.x server to a 3.x server using the _____ utility.
    a. NetWare Upgrade
    b. NetWare Migration
    c. NetWare Installation
    d. NetWare Conversion

25. The NetWare module for the network interface board has a _____ extension.
   a. .NIB
   b. .LAN
   c. .NLM
   d. .DSK

26. NetWare 3.x provides a maximum addressable volume size of _____ and a maximum addressable file size of _____.
   a. 32 TB, 4 GB
   b. 32 TB, 255 MB
   c. 4 GB, 255 MB
   d. 255 MB, 255 MB

27. NetWare provides a default first network drive statement of F in the _____ file.
   a. CONFIG.SYS
   b. NET.SYS
   c. STARTNET.BAT
   d. NET.CFG

28. You will find the following protocols provided with the NetWare Workstation for OS/2 kit:
   a. SPX
   b. TCP/IP
   c. NetBIOS emulation
   d. Named Pipes
   e. NetBEUI

29. Before you begin the file server software installation, you must:
   a. Install an NIC.
   b. Low-level format the hard drive.
   c. Test the software for bugs.
   d. Both *a* and *b*.
   e. All of the above.

30. The three NetWare 3.x memory pools are: _____, _____, and _____.
   a. Allocated cache buffer, permanent memory, and file cache buffer
   b. Semipermanent memory, permanent memory, and file cache buffer

c. File cache buffer, permanent memory, and allocated short-term memory
d. File cache buffer, cache movable and, cache nonmovable

31. The *VLM* acronym means _____.
    a. Vital Loadable Module
    b. Virtual Loadable Module
    c. Variable Loadable Module
    d. Virtual Loadable Method

32. You will find the OS/2 workstation installation software in the _____ directory of the CD.
    a. \CLIENT\DOSWIN
    b. \NETWARE.312\<LANGUAGE>\CLIENT\DOSWIN
    c. \CLIENT\OS2
    d. \NETWARE.312\<LANGUAGE>\CLIENT\OS2

33. NetWare allows up to _____ %n parameter variables in a login script.
    a. 1
    b. 2
    c. 9
    d. 10

34. The program used to install the NetWare operating system is:
    a. INSTALL
    b. SERVER
    c. STARTNET
    d. SETUP

35. You should always use a complex set of letters and numbers to identify your file server, making it harder for someone to break into your system.
    a. True
    b. False

36. Once you create a DOS partition on your file server hard drive using FDisk, you must:
    a. Reboot the system so the change can take effect.
    b. Start the NetWare installation process.

c. Update the CMOS settings.
d. All of the above.
e. None of the above.

37. When installing a NIC on either a workstation or server, you need at least three pieces of configuration information in most cases: _____, _____, and _____.
    a. Port address, DMA address, and manufacturer
    b. Vendor name, port address, and driver name
    c. IRQ, port address, and DMA address
    d. IRQ, port address, and product type

38. The acronym *UPS* stands for:
    a. United Parcel Service
    b. Unimpeded processor service
    c. Uninterruptible power service
    d. Uninterruptible power supply

39. NetWare allows you to modify the default login script.
    a. True
    b. False

40. The NetWare boot up configuration files are:
    a. AUTOEXEC.BAT and CONFIG.SYS
    b. AUTOEXEC.NCF and CONFIG.NCF
    c. AUTOEXEC.NCF and STARTUP.NCF
    d. AUTOEXEC.INI and STARTUP.INI

# Brain Teaser

Ready for some challenging puzzles designed to help you pass the certification exam? The cryptogram in Fig. 12-11 is designed to test your knowledge of NetWare file server software installation. Just in case the idea of working with a symbol-oriented cryptogram is a bit intimidating for you, here's a tip: All spaces really are spaces, and all periods are periods. Apostrophes, colons, parentheses, and backslashes are also what they appear to be. Every other symbol is a replacement for a letter or a number (yes,

# Netware 3.x Installation and Configuration Workshop

**Figure 12-11**
File Server Installation Cryptogram.

|~*?~><= ~!+ <+~–*?+ @>]+ |+?}+? ><|~*]]*~>#< >| +*|[. ~[{+ ~!+

$?>}+ ]+~~+? #@ ~!+ &$-?#' @#]]#–+$ %[ * &#]#< (@#? +x*'{]+, +:)

*<$ {?+|¦ +<~+?. ~[{+ &$ \<+~–*?+. ^";\+<=]>|! (#? ~!+ ]*<=u*=+ [#u

*?+ u|><=) *<$ {?+|¦ +<~+?. ~[{+ ><|~*]] *<$ {?+|¦ +<~+?.

| A | | N | | 1 | |
|---|---|---|---|---|---|
| B | | O | | 2 | |
| C | | P | | 3 | |
| D | | Q | | 4 | |
| E | | R | | 5 | |
| F | | S | | 6 | |
| G | | T | | 7 | |
| H | | U | | 8 | |
| I | | V | | 9 | |
| J | | W | | 0 | |
| K | | X | | | |
| L | | Y | | | |
| M | | Z | | | |

there are numbers in this cryptogram). You'll find the solution for this brain teaser in App. C, "Brain Teaser Answers."

If you're feeling especially knowledgeable, you can try your hand at the much more difficult cryptogram shown in Fig. 12-12. This is a NetWare utility-related phrase based on one of the questions you answered in the preceding "Fun Test" section. Remember, Novell can test your ability to use utility programs correctly at any time, so you need to be prepared. Here's a hint about solving this particular puzzle: There are numbers in the puzzle that are spelled out in letters.

**Figure 12-12**
Utility Program Cryptogram.

WSC RCWGFTC VUETFWUBR KWUYUWI FYYBGZ IBK WB

QBROCTW F OCTZUBR WGB ZCTOCT URWB F OCTZUBR

WSTCC ZCTOCT. IBK QFR FYZB KZC WSC KWUYUWI WB

KMETFNC F OCTZUBR WSTCC ZCTOCT WB WSC QKTTCRW

OCTZUBR BJ WSC ZBJWGFTC.

| A | | N | |
|---|---|---|---|
| B | | O | |
| C | | P | |
| D | | Q | |
| E | | R | |
| F | | S | |
| G | | T | |
| H | | U | |
| I | | V | |
| J | | W | |
| K | | X | |
| L | | Y | |
| M | | Z | |

## Disk Time

Don't forget to spend some time working with the disk that accompanies this book. It provides valuable and fun-to-use teaching aids that help prepare you for the exam. See "Disk Time" in the preface of this book for details about what the disk contains.

# CHAPTER 13
# NetWare 3.x to 4.x Update

## Introduction

One of the things that consultants are usually called in for is to update an operating system from one version to the next. In fact, some consultants earn a good living doing just that one task. On the other hand, you may not have to perform very many operating system updates if you work for a company, but it's nice to know where you're headed if you do. Whatever your reason for performing an update, it's important to know what the requirements are before you do so. In addition, you really have to have a good plan in place for both the update and the recovery in case the update doesn't go as planned. It doesn't take too long to figure out why Novell wants to test your ability to perform an update successfully when you consider it in this light.

This chapter helps you understand the requirements for passing the 3.x to 4.x Update exam. It tests your ability to plan and execute the update according to some predefined requirements that reflect those that you'll find in a typical company setting. There are several discrete sections in this chapter. Each section helps you study for the exam in a different way. You can improve your chances of passing the exam by using the study methods provided in this chapter. It'll probably help if you study all the sections once and your favorite sections at least twice. Review the study guidelines in Chap. 4 as often as necessary to ensure that you maintain the best possible study atmosphere.

The first section of this chapter is a *case study*. You'll perform some hands-on tasks that will help you learn what you need to know to pass the examination. This case study involves the Electro Text documentation that Novell provides. We already looked at the process for installing the server and workstation software in Chaps. 11 and 12. However, the ability to research the information you need is one of the requirements that sets the update exam apart from the two administration exams. You need to know what the requirements are for the two operating systems and how they differ before you can perform a successful update, and that's the whole purpose of this chapter. Even though you'll get a lot more from this section if you perform it on your own network, the inclusion of screen shots and step-by-step instructions will help you gain something from the section even if you don't have a network.

The second area contains *sample test questions* for this course. In most cases, you'll find that the questions relate in some way to the process of updating your server from NetWare 3.x to NetWare 4.x. This section also includes the correct answer for each question and an explanation of why that answer is correct. Try to answer each question yourself, look at the correct answer, and then determine where you went wrong if you didn't answer correctly. One word of warning for the test questions: Read each question very carefully before you answer. You're going to find that some questions are worded in such a way that they could apply to either NetWare 3.x or NetWare 4.x—it's the same way on the exam. Make sure you answer the question in a way that takes the operating system into account. In other words, don't provide information for NetWare 3.x when the question is really asking you about NetWare 4.x. The one area where people most often miss questions on this exam is security—make sure you understand the security rules for both NetWare 3.x and NetWare 4.x.

The next section is a *fun test*. The fun test is an exercise where you will look at more sample test questions and answer them. As with the sample test question section, you'll find a mix of NetWare 3.x and NetWare 4.x questions in this section. Make absolutely certain that you read each question completely before you try to answer. The answers for the questions in this section appear in App. B at the back of the book.

The final text section of the chapter is the *brain teaser*. You'll get to have a little fun working on a NetWare 3.x and NetWare 4.x–related puzzle. In this puzzle, you'll need to look for words that we talked about in the case study or in Chap. 12 and 13. Look for NetWare 4.x–related words from Chap. 14 and 15 as well. You may even want to take the opportunity to look these words up in the glossary once you've completed the puzzle.

Finally, we'll spend some time using the *Jeopardy!*-type game named *Red Zone*. This section helps you look at the test from the opposite viewpoint. The game provides you with an answer—you need to come up with the corresponding question. The game awards points for correct answers, and takes points away for incorrect answers. You'll receive a score at the end of the game proclaiming that you either did or did not get your certificate. Make sure you don't concentrate on the NetWare 3.x–related questions when using the game. It's extremely important that you visit all areas of both NetWare 3.x and 4.x when studying for this exam. You must understand both operating systems before you attempt to take the exam.

# Case Study

This case study centers on the use of *Electro Text*, the online documentation program provided with some versions of NetWare. This program replaces all the printed manuals that previously were shipped with the NetWare software. In this case study you will look up and define terms and concepts related to the NetWare 4.x operating system.

**NOTE** *Newer versions of NetWare use the DynaText viewer in place of Electro Text. In fact, you may find that Novell is using some type of HTML- (Internet-) based help by the time you read this text. This chapter does include a DynaText usage section. Simply skip the Electro Text section and use the DynaText section instead. No matter what help system Novell is using when you read this, the principle is the same. You need to know how to find the information required to perform a system update using whatever help Novell provides at the time.*

The first part of the case study introduces you to the basic use of the program. The second part provides step-by-step instructions for locating the terms and concepts we introduce in the first part of the case study. The third portion of the exercise defines a list of terms and concepts for you to look up yourself. The steps for finding each of these definitions is in the final section. Use the definition sheet from the first section while you go through the second, third, and fourth sections of this exercise. This sheet provides you with a handy reference for later use. For example, you could use the definition sheet to help you study for this and the other exams. You may also want to transfer the definitions onto 3 × 5 cards and use them as flash cards.

## Introduction to ET

This portion of the case study provides some simple directions for using Electro Text, the online documentation for the NetWare manuals. We also look at the terms and concepts that you'll use later as part of the exercises in the other sections of the case study.

1. Start Windows and open the NetWare Tools program folder.
2. Open the Electro Text program by double clicking the ET icon.
3. When the Novell Documentation main screen appears, double click on the NetWare 4.0 Manuals icon. This will open a window listing all the Novell manuals. Figure 13-1 shows the NetWare 4.0 manual window.
4. Figure 13-2 contains a list of concepts and terms to look up. Mark this page as you look up the definitions for each of the items in the second section of this case study. Return to this chart and record, in your own words, the meanings or definitions of the items. As an alternative to using this chart, record your findings on a separate note pad or directly on the 3 × 5 flash cards.

# NetWare 3.x to 4.x Update

**Figure 13-1**
NetWare 4.0 Manual Window.

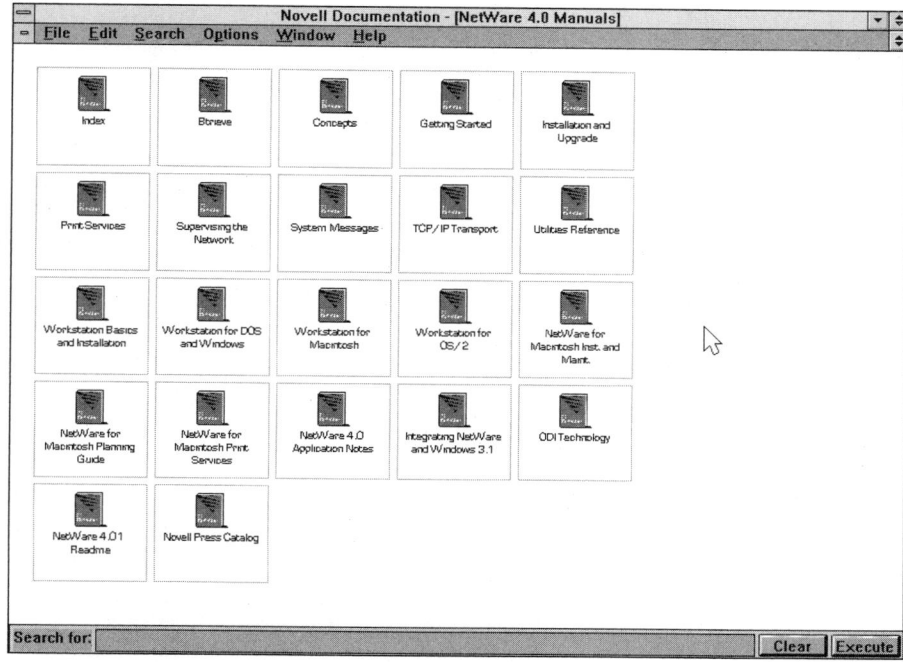

**Figure 13-2**
Definitions of NetWare 4.x Terms and Concepts.

## Definitions of 4.x Terms and Concepts

NDS:_____

_____

_____

_____

_____

NDS Global Database:_____

_____

_____

_____

_____

**Figure 13-2**
(*Continued*).

NDS Object:_____

NDS Property:_____

NDS Property Value:_____

NDS Partitions:_____

NDS Replicas:_____

Object Rights:_____

# NetWare 3.x to 4.x Update

**Figure 13-2**
(*Continued*).

Property Rights:_____

Context:_____

Container Object:_____

Leaf Object:_____

Block Suballocation:_____

File Compression:_____

**Figure 13-2**
(*Continued*).

Storage Management Services: _____
_____
_____
_____
_____

Data Migration: _____
_____
_____
_____
_____

Network Security: _____
_____
_____
_____
_____

IRF: _____
_____
_____
_____
_____

Login Scripts: _____
_____
_____
_____
_____

Using MAP: _____
_____
_____
_____
_____

# NetWare 3.x to 4.x Update

**Figure 13-2**
(*Continued*).

Using CX: _____
_____
_____
_____
_____

Using FLAG: _____
_____
_____
_____
_____

Using NLIST: _____
_____
_____
_____
_____

Using NDIR: _____
_____
_____
_____
_____

Using SEND: _____
_____
_____
_____
_____

The Novell Menu Utility: _____
_____
_____
_____
_____

**Figure 13-2** (*Continued*).

MONITOR: _____

SERVMAN: _____

SBACKUP: _____

NETUSER: _____

ODI: _____

NetWare DOS Requester: _____

# NetWare 3.x to 4.x Update

**Figure 13-2**
(*Continued*).

Virtual Loadable Module (VLM): _____

PCONSOLE: _____

Printing Quick Setup: _____

PSERVER: _____

NPRINTER: _____

Internationalization: _____

**Figure 13-2**
(*Continued*).

Auditing: _____
_____
_____
_____
_____

Memory Protection: _____
_____
_____
_____
_____

Now that you have spent a little time using Electro Text, it's time to define the layout of the Electro Text manuals. Across the top of the window is the *Menu Bar*. On the left side of the window is the *Outline*. On the right side of the window is the *Book Text* and a *Scroll Bar*. Across the bottom of the window is a *Search Field* dialog box. These names will be used for these areas throughout this case study. To expand a view of the Outline, click once on the highlighted *plus* sign (+). To minimize the Outline view, click once on the *minus* sign (–). To open the Book Text side of the window to the desired subject, click once on the topic in the Outline. This is just a brief description of how to use the Electro Text. If you need more information, open the help window by selecting *Help* from the Menu Bar.

## Defining Terms and Concepts

This section is a guided tour through the Electro Text manuals. It uses a slightly different format than the case studies found in the rest of this book. First, we identify the term or concept to look up. This is followed by the steps necessary to find the information. What you need to do is find the meaning for the term and record it on the chart in Fig. 13-2. Compare your definition to the ones we provide in the following paragraphs.

- NDS

    *Steps:* Open the Concepts manual and expand the Outline view by clicking once on the highlighted plus (+) sign next to NNN

# NetWare 3.x to 4.x Update

on the Outline field. Figure 13-3 shows the Electro Text screen, with the arrow pointing to the plus sign. Click once on the *NetWare Directory Services* option. Figure 13-4 shows the window after clicking on the NetWare Directory Services option.

*Definition:* A global database built into NetWare 4.x operating system. The NDS maintains information about every resource on the network. Each resource is an object of the database. The NDS replaces the Bindery of previous versions of NetWare.

- NDS Object

    *Steps:* Expand the NetWare Directory Services option by clicking once on the plus sign, then click on the *Object* option. Figure 13-5 shows the expanded Outline view of the NetWare Directory Services option.

    *Definition:* A category or structure to store information. An object can be physical, such as a User or File Server; logical, such as a Group; or an organizational tool, such as an Organization or Organizational Unit.

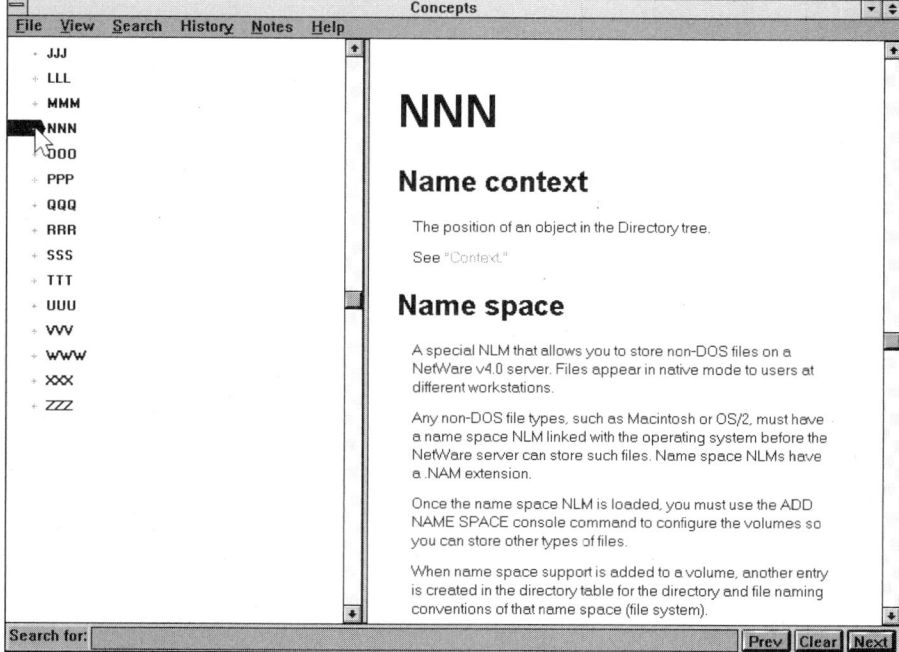

**Figure 13-3**
Electro Text Screen with Arrow Pointing to *Highlighted Plus Sign.*

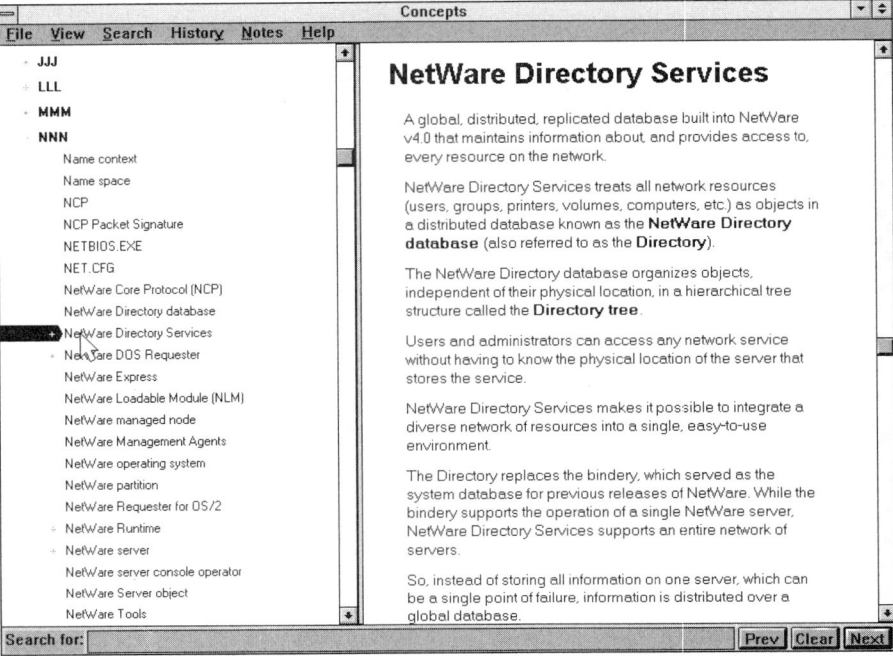

**Figure 13-4**
Window after Selecting NetWare Directory Services Option.

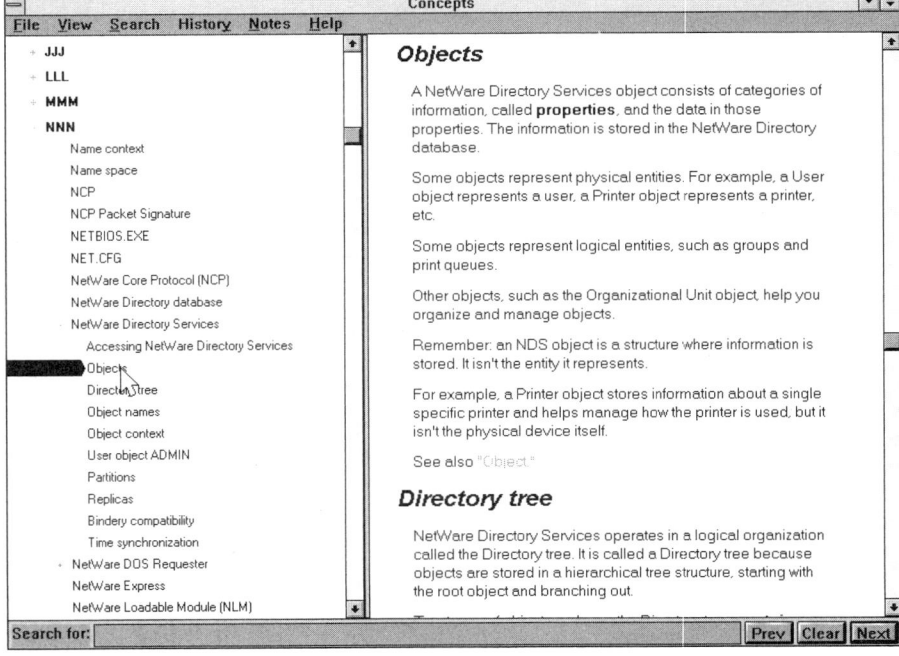

**Figure 13-5**
Expanded Outline View of the NetWare Directory Services Option.

# NetWare 3.x to 4.x Update

- NDS Property

    *Steps:* Minimize the NNN outline option by clicking on the minus sign next to the NNN. Expand the Outline view for the *PPP* option, scroll through the list of options in the outline field until you find the *Property* option, then click it once.

    *Definition:* A characteristic of an Object. These Properties can include information about the user, such as login name, last name, telephone number, and department.

- NDS Property Value

    *Steps:* From the Property information, scroll through the text. Information about the Property value is in this section.

    *Definition:* The actual value of the Property. Such information can include what the login name is, the last name, and the telephone number.

- NDS Partitions

    *Steps:* This time, to find the information about the NDS Partition, use the search feature of Electro Text. At the bottom of the screen is the search dialog box. Type the word *PARTITION* and press Enter. Numbers will appear next to the option in the outline window. Figure 13-6 shows the result. The numbers represent how many times the word *PARTITION* is in the corresponding Book Text. Since the term to look up is *NDS Partition,* and the word *PARTITION* is in the NNN section six times, click on the *NNN Outline* option and expand the view. Figure 13-7 shows the expanded Outline view and the word *hits* next to the NetWare Directory Services option. Click once on this option to expand the Outline view. The word *PARTITION* is in the Partitions options of NetWare Directory Services six times. Click once on this option to view the results. Figure 13-8 shows the results of the word search and the expanded views of the outline options.

    *Definition:* The partition is a small portion of the NDS database, allowing it to be more manageable. Partitions consist of Containers, Objects, and their Properties and Values.

- NDS Replicas

    *Steps:* From the Outline window of the last search, click once on the *Partitions* option to select it.

    *Definition:* A replica is a copy of the partition. The replica can be on as many servers as you would like. The purpose of having

**Figure 13-6**
Using the Search Feature to Find the Word PARTITION in Book Text.

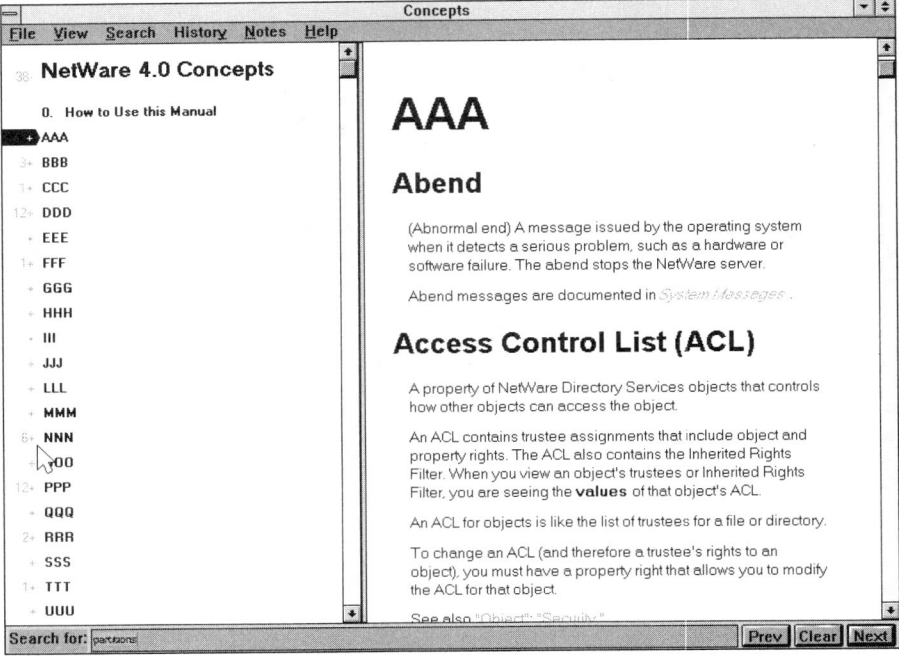

**Figure 13-7**
Expanded NNN Outline View During Word Search.

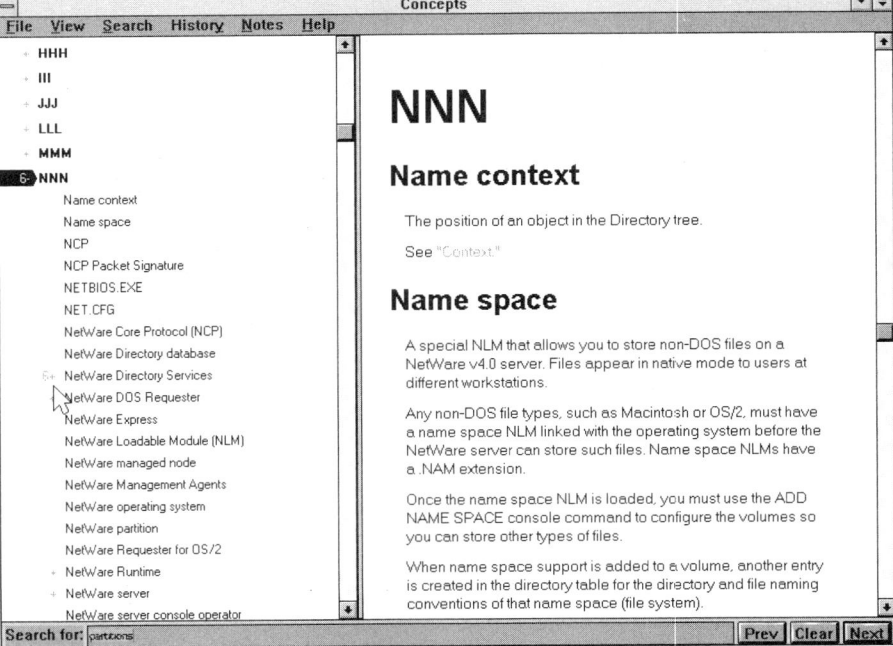

# NetWare 3.x to 4.x Update

**Figure 13-8**
Results of the Word Search.

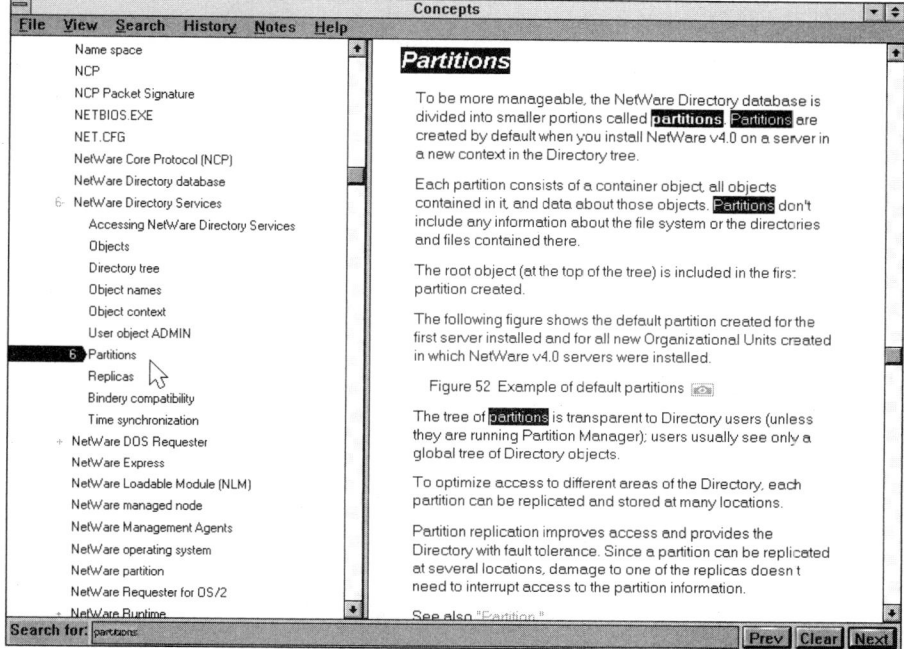

replicas is to provide faster access to the resources over a WAN and to eliminate a single point of failure with the NDS database partition.

- Object Rights

    *Steps:* This time, conduct a search for Object Rights through all the 4.x manuals. Exit the Concepts manual by double clicking the *close* icon in the upper left corner of the screen. This will return you to the Novell Documentation screen. In the search field at the bottom of the screen, type *OBJECT RIGHTS* and click on the Execute button. This will start a search for Object Rights through all manuals. Figure 13-9 shows the results of the global search. Note the numbers next to the manuals. These indicate how many times the search found each item in the manual.

    The Index manual had four hits; double click on the Index manual. Expand the window by clicking on the up arrow button in the upper right of the window. Figure 13-10 shows where the four hits are in the Index manual.

    Since you're looking for information about Object Rights, expand the Outline view of the OOO option by clicking on the plus sign. When the OOO Index option expands, click once on *Object Rights Overview*. The Book Text portion of the screen will tell you what book the information is in. The topic of Object Rights Overview is in the Getting Started Manual. Double click the symbol next to *Getting Started* to open that manual. Figure 13-11 shows the Index and the Book Text screen, showing where to find the Object Rights Overview.

The manual will open to the page that has the information about Object Rights Overview. Figure 13-12 shows the final results and the definition of Object Rights.

*Definition:* A set of rights identifying what a trustee can do with an object. The rights apply only to the object and not to the information values of that object.

## Practice Session

To complete this practice session exercise, finish looking up the terms and concepts from Fig. 13-2. Spend some time getting acquainted with the

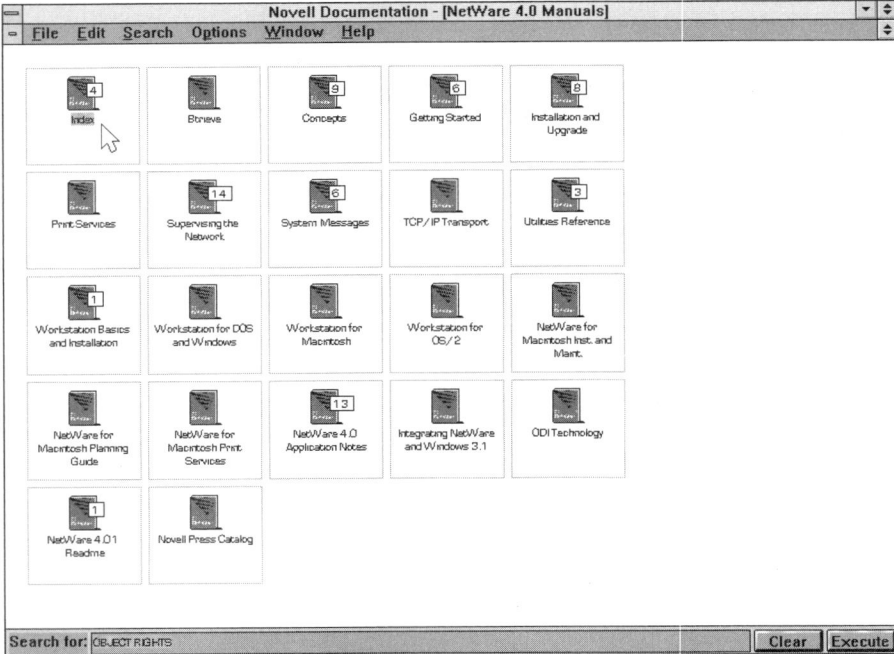

**Figure 13-9**
Result of the Global Search for Object Rights through All Manuals.

# NetWare 3.x to 4.x Update

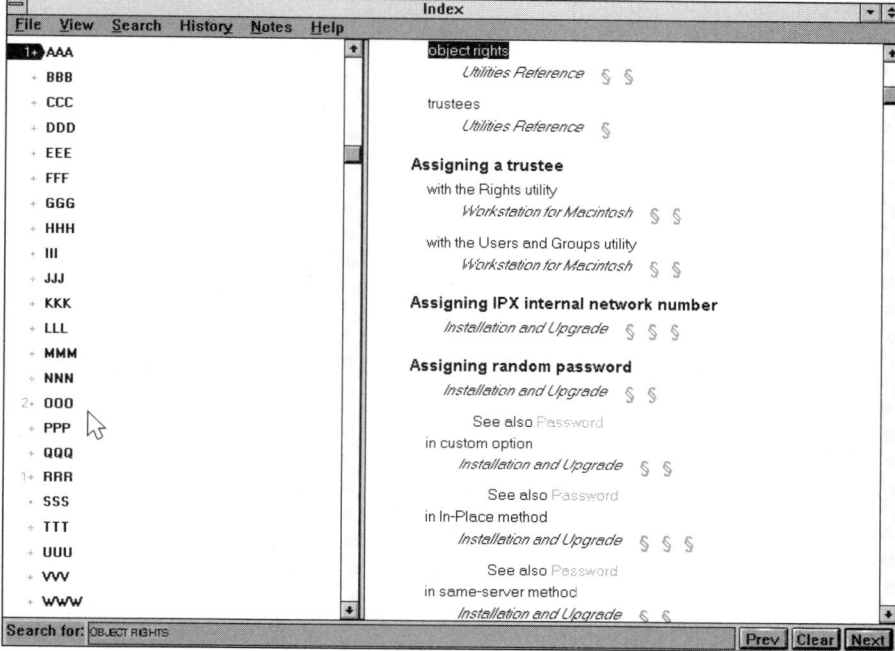

**Figure 13-10**
Index Manual Window Showing Four Hits.

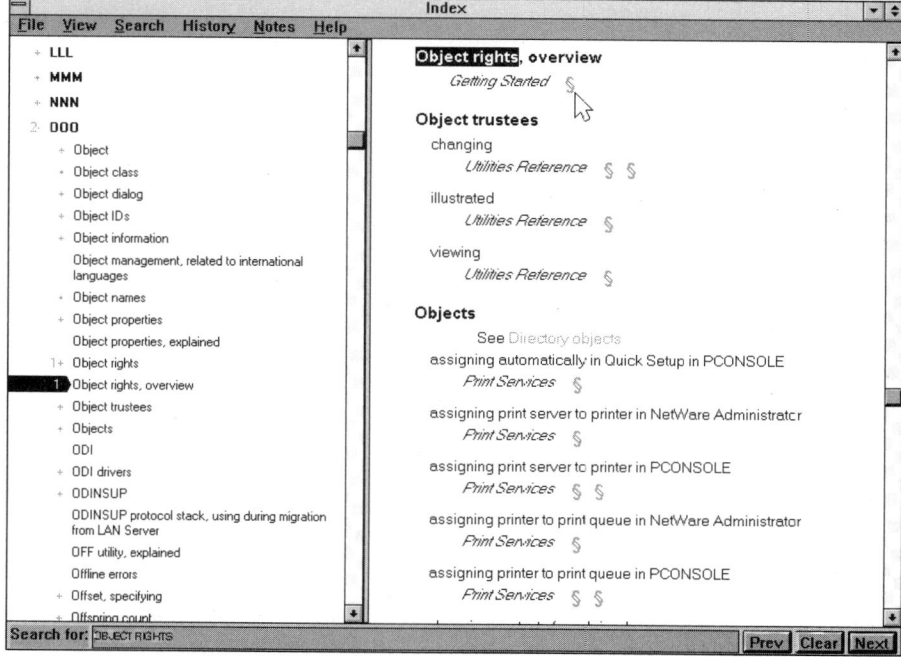

**Figure 13-11**
Index and Book Text Screen Showing Location of Object Rights Overview.

**Figure 13-12**
Screen Showing Definition of Object Rights.

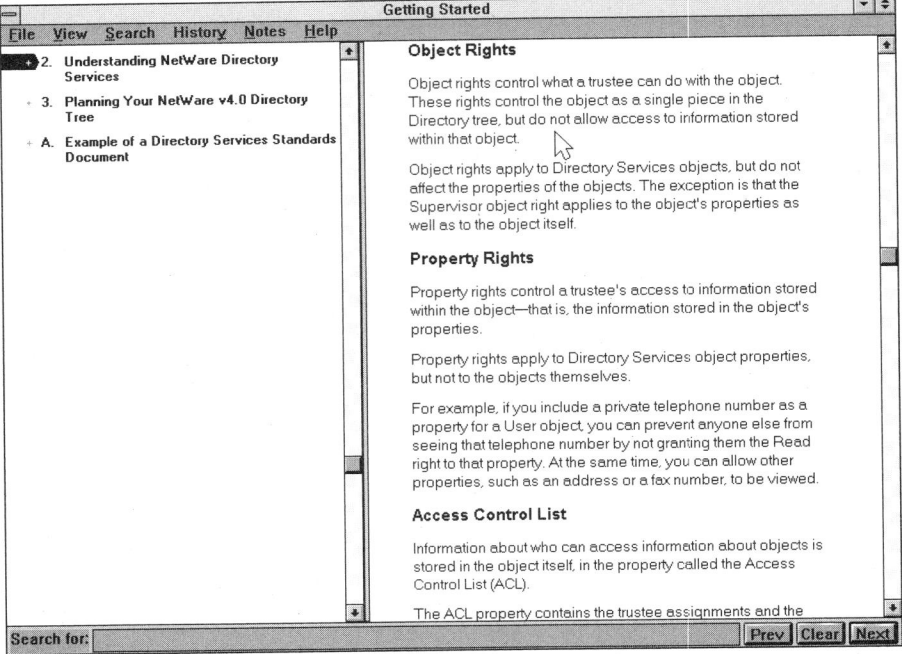

contents of the different manuals. Try looking up the terms and concepts using the search feature from the Novell Documentation screen and the individual manuals. Also, look up the information using the outline page of the manuals. After you finish defining each of the terms or concepts, continue on to the next section. The next section will provide you with the steps necessary to find the topic. If you want to learn this information thoroughly, *do not* continue on to the next section until you complete the entire definition chart.

## Answers to Terms and Concepts

*Property Rights.*   Open the Getting Started manual and expand the Understanding NetWare Directory Services options. Expand the Outline view for Objects in NetWare Directory Services, then expand the Outline view for Object and Property Rights option. Click once on the Property Rights option to display the definition.

*Context.*   Open the Concepts manual, expand the Outline view of CCC and locate the Context option. Click once on the Context option to view the information on this topic.

*Container Object.* Open the Concepts manual, expand the Outline view for the CCC option, and locate the Container Object option. Click once on the option to view the information.

*Leaf Object.* Open the Concepts manual and expand the Outline view for the OOO option. When the Outline view expands, expand the Outline view for Object, then click once on Leaf Objects to view the information.

*Block Suballocation.* Open the Concepts manual and expand the Outline view for BBB. Locate the option for Block Suballocation and click on it once to view the information.

*File Compression.* Open the Concepts manual and expand the Outline view for the FFF option. Locate and click once on the File Compression option to view the information.

*Storage Management Services.* Open the Concepts manual and expand the Outline view for the SSS option. Locate the Storage Management Services (SMS) option and click on it once. This will give you a brief explanation of the topic. If you want more information, expand the Storage Management Services option Outline view and select the additional topics.

*Data Migration.* Open the Getting Started manual and expand the Outline view for the New Features in NetWare v4.0 option. Locate the Data Migration option and click on it to view the information.

*File System Security.* This topic has two good sources of information. For the first source, open the Workstation Basics and Installation manual and expand the Outline view for Understanding Networking Basics. Locate and expand the Outline view for Understanding Network Security, then click once on this option to view the information about security. The second source for information on security is the Concepts manual. Open the Concepts manual and expand the CS option. Locate the Security option and expand the Outline view, then click once on the Security option to open the manual to the information.

*IRF.* Open the Getting Started manual and expand the Outline view for the Understanding NetWare Directory Services option. Next, expand the Outline view for Objects in NetWare Directory Services, then expand Object and Property Rights. Click once on the Inherited Rights Filter option to view the information.

*Login Scripts.* Open the Supervising the Network manual and expand the Outline view for Creating Login Scripts and Menus. Next, expand the Outline view for the About Login Scripts option.

Click once on About Login Scripts to view the information in the Book Text section of the window.

*Using MAP.*   Open the Utilities Reference manual and expand the Outline view for the Using Text Workstation Utilities option. Next, expand the Outline view for MAP, then click once on the Using MAP option to view the information.

*Using CX.*   Open the Utilities Reference manual and expand the Outline view for the Using Text Workstation Utilities option. Next, expand the Outline view for CX, then click once on the Using CX option to view the information.

*Using FLAG.*   Open the Utilities Reference manual and expand the Outline view for the Using Text Workstation Utilities option. Next, expand the Outline view for FLAG, then click once on the Using FLAG option to view the information.

*Using NLIST.*   Open the Utilities Reference manual and expand the Outline view for the Using Text Workstation Utilities option. Next, expand the Outline view for NLIST, then click once on the Using NLIST option to view the information.

*Using NDIR.*   Open the Utilities Reference manual and expand the Outline view for the Using Text Workstation Utilities option. Next, expand the Outline view for NDIR, then click once on the Using NDIR option to view the information.

*Using SEND.*   Open the Utilities Reference manual and expand the Outline view for the Using Text Workstation Utilities option. Next, expand the Outline view for SEND, then click once on the Using SEND option to view the information.

*The Novell Menu Utility.*   Open the Supervising the Network manual and expand the view for the Creating Login Scripts and Menus option. Click once on the Creating, Converting, and Modifying Menu Programs option to see an explanation of the menu program.

*MONITOR.*   Open the Utilities Reference manual and expand the Outline view for the Using Server Utilities option. Expand the Outline view for the MONITOR option, then click once on MONITOR for information about MONITOR. If you need additional information, click an option from the Outline section.

*SERVMAN.*   Open the Utilities Reference manual and expand the Outline view for the Using Server Utilities option. Expand the Outline view for the SERVMAN option, then click once on SERVMAN for information about SERVMAN. If you need additional information, click an option from the Outline section.

# NetWare 3.x to 4.x Update

*SBACKUP.* Open the Utilities Reference manual and expand the Outline view for the Using Server Utilities option. Expand the Outline view for the SBACKUP option, then click once on SBACKUP for information about SBACKUP. If you need additional information, click an option from the Outline section.

*NETUSER.* Open the Utilities Reference manual and expand the Outline view for the Using Text Workstation Utilities. Locate and expand the Outline view of NETUSER. Click once on the NETUSER option for information. To see more information about NETUSER, double click on the icon for the Figure in the Book Text window.

*ODI.* Open the ODI Technology manual and expand the Open Data-Link Interface (ODI) option. Click once on the Open Data-Link Interface (ODI) option for information about ODI.

*NetWare DOS Requester.* Open the Concepts manual and expand the Outline view for the NNN option. Locate the NetWare DOS Requester option and expand the Outline view. Click once on the NetWare DOS Requester option for information. If you need additional information, select another option from the outline.

*Virtual Loadable Module (VLM).* Open the Concepts manual and expand the Outline view for the VVV option. Locate the Virtual Loadable Module (VLM) option and expand the Outline view. Click once on the Virtual Loadable Module (VLM) option for information. If you need additional information, select another option from the outline.

*PCONSOLE.* Open the Print Services manual and expand the Outline view for Setting Up Printing Using Text Utilities. Locate and expand the Outline view for Modifying NetWare Print Services. Click once on the Modifying NetWare Print Services option.

*Printing Quick Setup.* Open the Print Services manual and expand the Outline view for the Setting Up Printing Using Text Utilities option. Click on the Quick Path for Setting Up Printing option for information.

*PSERVER.* Open the Print Services manual and expand the Outline view for Overview of NetWare Printing. Expand the Outline view for Printing on a Network, then click once on the Print Server option to view information about the Print Server and PSERVER.NLM.

*NPRINTER.* Open the Print Services manual and expand the Outline view for Overview of NetWare Printing. Expand the Outline view for Printing on a Network, then click once on the Printer option to view information about the Printer and NPRINTER.

*Internationalization.* Open the Concepts manual and expand the Outline view for the III option. Locate and click on the International use of NetWare v4.0 option to view the information about Internationalization.

*Auditing.* Open the Concepts manual and expand the Outline view for the AAA option. Locate the Auditing option and click on it to view information about the topic.

*Memory Protection.* Open the Concepts manual and expand the Outline view for the MMM option. Locate the Memory Protection option and click on it once to view information about the topic.

This completes the case study for using the Electro Text on line documentation—the next section looks at its *DynaText* counterpart, which is essentially a different viewer for the same information. Throughout this exercise, you learned many terms and concepts concerning the NetWare 4.x operating system and how to use Electro Text. This program is an excellent source of information, tips, ideas, and suggestions to help you maintain a network. The information in this program will also help you prepare yourself for the exams. As you have probably noticed, there's more than one way to look up the different topics and more than one source for the information. The key to finding the information you're looking for is to use the program over and over until you are familiar with the location of the topics.

## A Look at the DynaText Viewer

The goal when using the DynaText viewer is no different than the one you had when using Electro Text—you're still trying to find information that you need. Only the method of delivering that information has changed. In fact, you'll see more of a difference in the interface used to find the information than in anything else. DynaText provides better search capabilities than Electro Text (though some people will most certainly disagree with this assessment), and it provides a newer interface.

The previous sections showed you the basics of using Electro Text to find information. You'll still need to find that same information using the DynaText viewer, so nothing has changed in this regard. What have changed are a few of the techniques. The following steps will help you get acquainted with the DynaText viewer. Once you're acquainted with the

# NetWare 3.x to 4.x Update

viewer, take time to find the words listed in Fig. 13-2 and describe them in your own words.

1. Start Windows and open the NetWare Tools program folder.
2. Open the DynaText program by double-clicking on the DynaText icon.
3. When the NetWare 4.1 Collection screen appears, you'll see a window listing all the Novell manuals. Figure 13-13 shows the NetWare 4.1 manual window. The next thing we need to do is find something.
4. Type *NDS* in the Find field, and then press Enter. DynaText will show you the number of *hits*, or places that you'll find NDS in each of the books, as shown in Fig. 13-14. Let's find a specific reference.
5. Double click on the Installation book. DynaText will open this book up to its very first page.
6. You'll see two arrows on the toolbar; click on the right-pointing one. DynaText will take you to the first occurrence of NDS in the Installation book, as shown in Fig. 13-15. Note that the acronym *NDS* is highlighted each time it appears in the text.

**Figure 13-13**
NetWare 4.1 Manual Window.

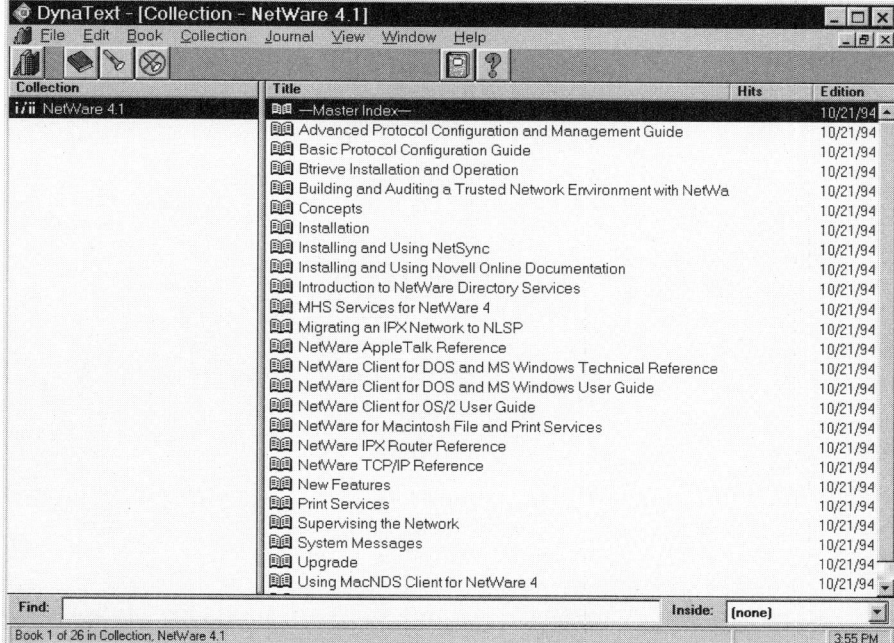

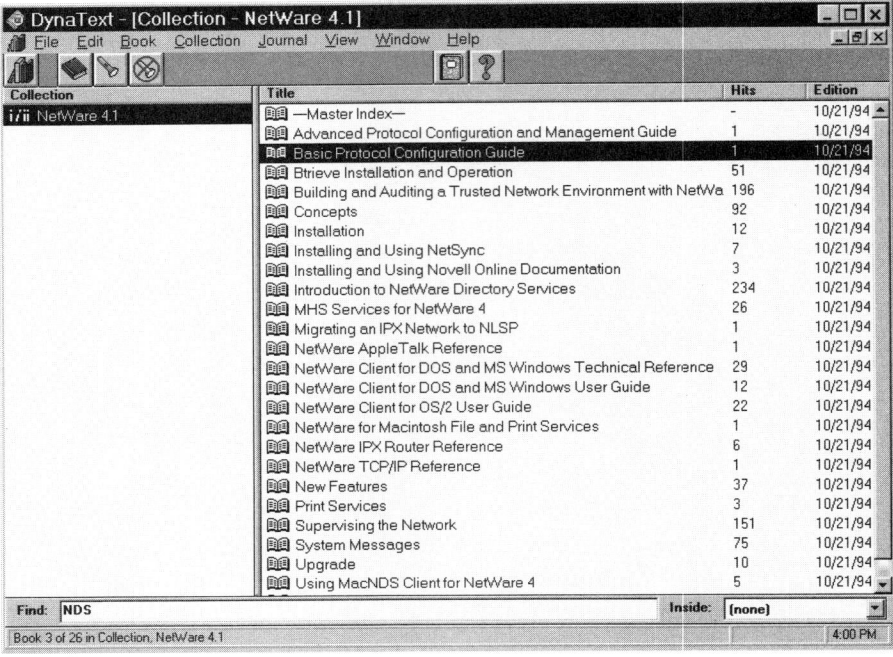

**Figure 13-14**
Find Field Showing Hits for NDS.

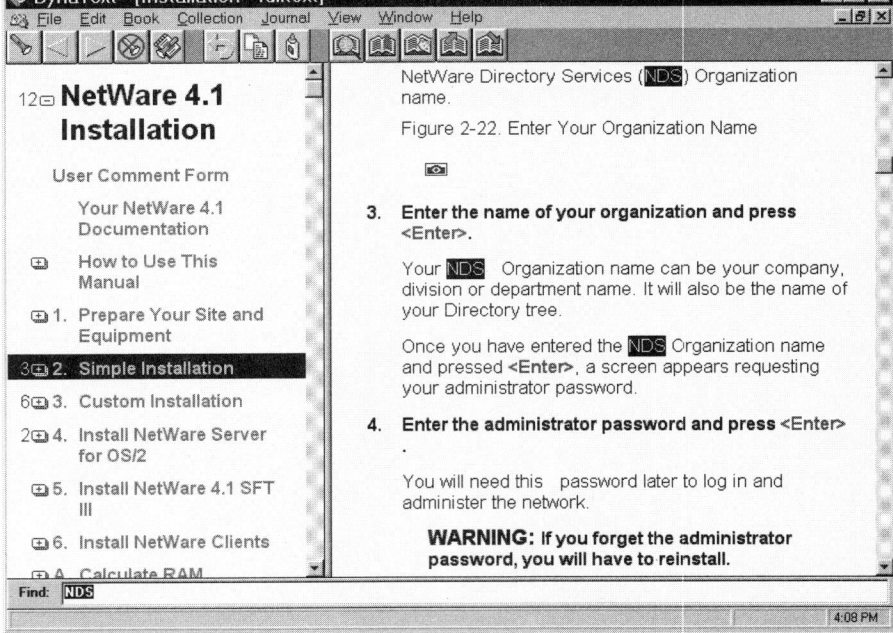

**Figure 13-15**
Screen Showing Occurrences of NDS in the Installation Book.

# NetWare 3.x to 4.x Update 389

7. Click on the Close box of the window or use the File Close command to close it.

8. Repeat Steps 4 through 7 for all of the other words in Fig. 13-2. Make sure you write down the meaning for each in your own words.

It doesn't take long to see that DynaText does provide a much faster and easier-to-use front end than Electro Text does, but you get the same result. The left side of the screen shows a hierarchical format of the book you're looking at; the right side of the screen shows the detail for the current selection. To expand a view of the outline, click once on the highlighted *plus* sign (+). To minimize the Outline view, click once on the *minus* sign (–). To open the Book Text side of the window to the desired subject, click once on the *topic* in the Outline. This is just a brief description of how to use DynaText. If you need more information, open the help window by selecting *Help* from the Menu Bar.

## Study Questions

1. The NetWare 4.x NDS provides bindery emulation for older versions of NetWare.
    a. True
    b. False

    *a.* The NetWare 4.x operating system provides a bindery emulation, making it compatible with previous versions.

2. You can create partitions and replicas of the NDS with which utility?
    a. PARTMGR
    b. NetWare Administrator
    c. DSREPAIR
    d. Both *a* and *b*
    e. All of the Above

    *d.* NetWare provides two utilities capable of creating partitions and replicas of the NDS: PARTMGR and NetWare Administrator.

3. The NDS Object Rights control the management of:
    a. Objects
    b. Properties

c. The NDS
d. All of the above

*a.* The NDS Object Rights control the objects, which include Users, Printers, and Organizational Units.

4. Which of the following are NDS Object rights?
    a. Supervisory, Read, and Write
    b. Supervisory, Create, and Delete
    c. Browse, Write, and Delete
    d. Browse, Create, and Rename

    *d.* The NDS Object Rights include Browse, Create, and Rename. The other Object Rights are Supervisor, Delete, and Modify.

5. Which of the following are NDS Property rights?
    a. Supervisory, Read, and Write
    b. Compare, Write, and Add Self
    c. Read, Add Self, and Modify
    d. All of the above

    *b.* The rights for the properties are Compare, Write, and Add Self. Other property rights include Supervisor, Read, and Delete Self.

6. If the trustee's directory assignment for subdirectory TEMP is [RWCF] and the IRF for subdirectory TEMP is [REF], what are the trustee's effective rights for subdirectory TEMP?
    a. Read, Write, Copy, and File Scan
    b. Read, Erase, and File Scan
    c. Read, Write, Create, Erase, and File Scan
    d. Read, Write, Create, and File Scan

    *d.* The trustee's effective rights for the directory are Read, Write, Create, and File Scan. Whenever a trustee is assigned rights to a directory or file, the effective rights equal the trustee rights.

7. Which of the following can assign rights to users for the file system?
    a. NetWare Administrator
    b. NETADMIN
    c. FILER
    d. RIGHTS
    e. *a, b,* and *d*

# NetWare 3.x to 4.x Update 391

    **f.** All of the above

    *f.* Any of these utilities will assign trustee rights assignments.

**8.** The IRF rights always supersede all other rights.
   - **a.** True
   - **b.** False

    *b.* The IRF acts as a filter to restrict rights from flowing into the directory or file. A trustee's explicit rights to a directory or file will supersede the IRF only at the point of assignment.

**9.** IF the Organizational Unit Sales has a trustee assignment of [RF] to the APPS\DB directory, user Mark has a trustee assignment of [ ] to the APPS\DB directory, the APPS\DB IRF is [SRWCEMFA], and user Mark is a Leaf Object of Sales, what are Mark's effective to the APPS\DB directory?
   - **a.** Read and File Scan
   - **b.** All rights [SRWCEMFA]
   - **c.** None, you cannot assign trustee rights to the Organizational Unit.
   - **d.** None of the above

    *a.* As a Leaf object of the Organizational Unit Sales, Mark inherits the same rights as the Organizational Unit.

**10.** The NetWare 4.x auditing feature tracks which of the following?
   - **a.** User actions
   - **b.** Resource usage
   - **c.** File system security
   - **d.** All of the above

    *d.* The NetWare Auditing feature tracks User actions, Resource usage, and the File system security.

**11.** The utility used for Auditing a NetWare 4.x File Server is:
   - **a.** Auditor
   - **b.** Auditcon
   - **c.** Auditmon
   - **d.** NetWare Administrator

    *b.* Auditcon is the text-based menu utility to manage and monitor the auditing features of NetWare.

12. What is the name of the NetWare backup and restore program?
    a. NetWare Administrator
    b. NBACKUP
    c. SERVMAN
    d. SBACKUP

    *d.* SBACKUP is the user interface for backing up the network data.

13. At a DOS ODI workstation, the files load in what order?
    a. VLM.EXE, IPXODI.COM, NE2000.COM, and LSL.COM
    b. NE2000.COM, LSL.COM, IPXODI.COM, and VLM.EXE
    c. LSL.COM, NE2000.COM, and TCPIP.EXE
    d. None of the above

    *c.* The workstation must load the LLC software first, then the MLID, then the transport protocol. These files are the LSL.COM, NE2000.COM, and TCPIP.EXE files.

14. The _____ file provides the workstation with backwards compatibility to previous versions of NetWare.
    a. NETX.EXE
    b. NETX.VLM
    c. VLM.EXE
    d. IPXODI.COM

    *b.* The NETX.VLM provides backwards compatibility to previous versions of NetWare.

15. To specify which VLMs will load when you execute the VLM.EXE program, edit the _____ file.
    a. VLM.INI
    b. SHELL.CFG
    c. NET.CFG
    d. VLM.CFG

    *c.* The NET.CFG file has a section for specifying which VLMs load and in what order.

16. The NetWare TCP/IP NLMs require at least _____ of RAM, plus at least _____ of disk space.
    a. 1 MB, 1 MB
    b. 1 MB, 3 MB

# NetWare 3.x to 4.x Update

      c. 3 MB, 1 MB

      d. 5 MB, 3 MB

   *a.* Novell recommends that when using the TCP/IP NLMs, the system have an additional 1 MB of RAM and 1 MB of hard disk space.

17. With block suballocation, NetWare can divide a data block into units of what size?

    a. 512 bytes

    b. 1 K

    c. 4 K

    d. Any multiple of 4 K up to 64 K

    *a.* NetWare divides the disk allocation blocks into 512-byte units. Instead of wasting the entire disk block, a small file will only use a 512-byte piece of the original.

18. By default, NetWare will not compress a file unless there is at least a _____ percent savings of disk sectors.

    a. 80

    b. 63

    c. 20

    d. 2

    *d.* NetWare will not compress a file unless it can reduce the number of sectors the file uses by 2 percent.

19. To load the DOS requester in extended memory at the workstation, which command would you use?

    a. VLM –x

    b. VLM +x

    c. VLM /me

    d. VLM /mx

    *d.* The common acronym for extended memory in the computer industry is XMS. The /MX refers to memory extended.

20. The NetWare graphical utility to manage users and groups is:

    a. SYSCON

    b. NETCON

    c. NETWARE ADMINISTRATOR

    d. NETADMIN

*c.* The NetWare Administrator is a graphical utility that requires windows. In the NetWare Tools folder, it's listed as NWADMIN.

21. The NetWare NDS regulates which of the following types of services?
    a. Printers
    b. Volumes
    c. Files
    d. All of the above
    e. None of the above

    *d.* The NDS database regulates all resources of the network. This includes managing printers, volumes, and trustee assignments to files.

22. The property information for a User object in NDS includes:
    a. Telephone number
    b. Password
    c. Supervisor
    d. None of the above

    *a.* NetWare offers an Identification option for the user. One of the fields lets you record the user's telephone number.

23. Three types of Container objects are:
    a. Volumes, Directories, and Files
    b. Country, Organization, and Organizational Units
    c. Organizational Role, Print Queue, and [Root]
    d. All of the above

    *b.* Containers are objects that can hold other NDS objects. They may contain other containers or leaf objects.

24. The term *Leaf object* in NDS services refers to the:
    a. Real network resource
    b. Property of the object
    c. Top of the NDS structure
    d. Files in the directory

    *a.* All resources connected to the network are part of the NDS. The NDS manages the resources that include Users, Groups, Volumes, File Servers, Printers, and any other resource a user might want to use.

# NetWare 3.x to 4.x Update

25. Leaf objects use the attribute of:
    a. LF
    b. OU
    c. CN
    d. LO

    *c.* The acronym *CN* refers to common name. You must use a common name to refer to a network resource such as a printer or user that are leaf objects.

26. The _____ object in NDS best describes the Sales department.
    a. Organizational Group
    b. Organizational Unit
    c. Leaf
    d. [Root]

    *b.* The Sales department of a company will likely have printers, file servers, users, and other resources. The Organizational Unit object will hold these resources.

27. The File Server is a(n) _____ object in NDS.
    a. Leaf
    b. Container
    c. Organizational Unit
    d. None of the above

    *a.* The File Server falls into the Leaf object classification. As a Leaf object it does not contain other NDS objects.

28. The NetAdmin DOS text menu utility manages the:
    a. NDS database
    b. Files
    c. Print services
    d. All of the above

    *a.* The NetAdmin is a DOS text menu utility that will view, modify, and manage objects of the NDS database.

29. The windows based utility NetWare Administrator manages the:
    a. NDS database
    b. File system

c. Use of printers
d. All of the above

*d.* NetWare Administrator is a Windows-based graphical utility that manages the NDS database objects. It also manages the trustee rights to the file system and access to the printer objects.

30. To change locations in the NDS structure use the _____ command.
    a. CD
    b. CX
    c. CL
    d. MOVE

*b.* Your current position in the NDS structure is your Context. The command to change your current Context is CX (Change Context).

31. The NetWare utility to view how much disk space is in use and how much is available is:
    a. NDIR
    b. VOLUME
    c. SPACE
    d. VOLSPACE

*a.* NDIR with the /volume option will display statistics about the volume.

32. NetWare 4.x makes _____ drive letters available for regular drive pointers to every workstation.
    a. 10
    b. 16
    c. 26
    d. Unlimited

*c.* NetWare only allows a single letter as a drive pointer. All 26 letters of the alphabet are available for drive pointers.

33. The correct syntax for creating a drive mapping is:
    a. MAP H:=VOL_SYS.SALES.NS:USERS\CYNDIE
    b. MAP F=SYS:USERS\CYNDIE
    c. MAP K:=.401.NS.SALES.VOL_SYS:USERS\JOHN
    d. None of the above

# NetWare 3.x to 4.x Update 397

    *a.* When creating a drive mapping, first specify the path to the volume object of NDS, then the path to the directory.

**34.** The NetWare Administrator utility allows you to:
    **a.** Manage objects.
    **b.** Salvage deleted files.
    **c.** Purge files.
    **d.** All of the above.

    *d.* The NetWare Administrator utility manages NDS services and the file and directory system, allowing you to salvage or purge deleted files.

**35.** A Trustee file or directory assignment can be made to a:
    **a.** User
    **b.** Group
    **c.** Container object
    **d.** Both *a* and *b*
    **e.** All of the Above

    *e.* Container objects, Users, and Groups are all NDS objects. You can make any NDS object a trustee of a file or directory.

**36.** The combination of user rights minus the rights revoked by the directory equal your _____ rights.
    **a.** Trustee
    **b.** Directory
    **c.** Effective
    **d.** NDS

    *c.* Effective rights are the rights that you can actually use in the file or directory.

**37.** The _____ will track and display the network statistics.
    **a.** SYSCON
    **b.** FCONSOLE
    **c.** MONITOR
    **d.** TRACK ON

    *c.* The Monitor NLM will track and display information and statistics about the file server—user connections, disk drives, memory, and LAN drivers, to name a few.

## Fun Test

1. The NDS database is created and replicated with what utility?
   a. NetWare Administrator
   b. DSREPAIR
   c. PARTMGR
   d. Both *a* and *c*
   e. All of the above

2. Which of the following are NDS Object rights?
   a. Supervisory, Create, and Delete
   b. Browse, Create, and Rename
   c. Browse, Write, and Delete
   d. Supervisory, Read, and Write

3. The program that manages users and groups with a graphical interface is:
   a. NETCON
   b. SYSCON
   c. NETWARE ADMINISTRATOR
   d. NETADMIN

4. The NetWare TCP/IP NLMs require at least _____ of RAM, and at least _____ of disk space.
   a. 1 MB, 1 MB
   b. 1 MB, 3 MB
   c. 3 MB, 1 MB
   d. 5 MB, 3 MB

5. NDS includes _____ as property information for User objects.
   a. Telephone number
   b. Password
   c. Supervisor
   d. None of the above

6. To set up and audit the services of a 4.x file server, you must use the _____ program.
   a. Auditor
   b. Auditcon

c. NetWare Administrator
d. Auditmon

7. Edit the _____ file to identify the VLMs you want to load when the VLM.EXE executes.
   a. VLM.CFG
   b. VLM.INI
   c. NET.CFG
   d. SHELL.CFG

8. Within the NDS services, the term *Leaf object* refers to the:
   a. Property of the object
   b. Real network resource
   c. Files in the directory
   d. Top of the NDS structure

9. To provide the 4.x workstations with backwards compatibility to previous versions of NetWare, you must load _____ on the workstation.
   a. NETX.EXE
   b. NETX.VLM
   c. IPXODI.COM
   d. VLM.EXE

10. The rights that users actually have in a file or directory are their _____ rights.
    a. NDS
    b. Effective
    c. Trustee
    d. Directory

11. NDS defines the File Server as what type of object?
    a. Organizational Unit
    b. Container
    c. Leaf
    d. None of the above

12. The NDS object rights control the management of:
    a. Properties
    b. Objects
    c. The NDS
    d. All of the above

13. Which of the following commands will force the DOS requester to load into extended memory at the workstation?
    a. VLM –x
    b. VLM +x
    c. VLM /me
    d. VLM /mx

14. The NetWare Administrator utility allows you to:
    a. Manage objects.
    b. Salvage deleted files.
    c. Purge files.
    d. All of the above.

15. Use the _____ program to assign trustee rights to a file or directory.
    a. RIGHTS
    b. NetWare Administrator
    c. NETADMIN
    d. FILER
    e. *a, b* and *c*
    f. All of the above

16. Which of the following services does NDS regulate?
    a. Printers
    b. Volumes
    c. Files
    d. All of the above
    e. None of the above

17. The NetWare 4.x NDS provides bindery emulation for older versions of NetWare.
    a. True
    b. False

18. NetWare provides a backup and restore program. What is its name?
    a. SBACKUP
    b. NetWare Administrator
    c. SERVMAN
    d. NBACKUP

# NetWare 3.x to 4.x Update

19. NetAdmin is the DOS text menu utility that manages the:
    a. Print services
    b. NDS database
    c. File system
    d. All of the above

20. The Auditing feature of NetWare 4.x tracks which of the following?
    a. Resource usage
    b. File system security
    c. User actions
    d. All of the above

21. Block suballocation divides the data blocks into what size?
    a. 512 bytes
    b. 1 K
    c. 4 K
    d. Any multiple of 4 K up to 64 K

22. Leaf objects use the attribute of _____.
    a. LO
    b. CN
    c. LF
    d. OU

23. To map a drive letter to Cyndie's home directory, which of the following is the correct syntax?
    a. MAP K:=.401.NS.SALES.VOL_SYS:USERS\CYNDIE
    b. MAP F=SYS:USERS\CYNDIE
    c. MAP H:=VOL_SYS.SALES.NS:USERS\CYNDIE
    d. None of the above

24. Which of the following are NDS Property rights?
    a. Compare, Write, and Add Self
    b. Read, Add Self, and Modify
    c. Supervisory, Read, and Write
    d. All of the above

25. Within the NDS services, the classification for Sales department is as what type of object?
    a. Organizational Unit
    b. [Root]

c. Organizational Group

d. Leaf

26. To change locations in the NDS structure use the _____ command.

    a. CL
    b. CD
    c. MOVE
    d. CX

27. A Trustee file or directory assignment can be made to a:

    a. User
    b. Group
    c. Container object
    d. Both *a* and *b*
    e. All of the above

28. The windows graphical utility, NetWare Administrator manages the:

    a. File system
    b. Use of Printers
    c. NDS database
    d. All of the above

29. The NetWare utility to view how much disk space is in use and how much is available is:

    a. NDIR
    b. VOLUME
    c. SPACE
    d. VOLSPACE

30. NetWare provides the _____ utility to track and display information about the network statistics.

    a. TRACK ON
    b. FCONSOLE
    c. SYSCON
    d. MONITOR

31. When calculating the effective rights of the NDS or file system, the IRF rights always equal your effective rights.

    a. True
    b. False

# NetWare 3.x to 4.x Update

32. Every workstation on a NetWare 4.x network has _____ drive letters available for regular drive pointers.
    a. 10
    b. 16
    c. 26
    d. Unlimited

33. If user Mark has a trustee assignment of [ ] to the APPS\DB directory, Organizational Unit Sales has a trustee assignment of [RF] to the APPS\DB directory, the APPS\DB IRF is [SRWCEMFA], and user Mark is a Leaf Object of Sales, what are Mark's effective rights to the APPS\DB directory?
    a. All rights [SRWCEMFA].
    b. None, you cannot assign trustee rights to the Organizational Unit.
    c. Read and File Scan.
    d. None of the above.

34. When loading the ODI files at your workstation, what is the load order?
    a. LSL.COM, NE2000.COM, and TCPIP.EXE
    b. VLM.EXE, IPXODI.COM, NE2000.COM, and LSL.COM
    c. NE2000.COM, LSL.COM, IPXODI.COM, and VLM.EXE
    d. None of the above

35. If the trustee's directory assignment for subdirectory TEMP is [RWCF] and the IRF for subdirectory TEMP is [REF], what are the trustee's effective rights for subdirectory TEMP?
    a. Read, Erase, and File Scan
    b. Read, Write, Create, and File Scan
    c. Read, Write, Copy, and File Scan
    d. Read, Write, Create, Erase, and File Scan

36. Which of the following are Container objects?
    a. Organizational Role, Print Queue, and [Root]
    b. Country, Organization, and Organizational Units
    c. Volumes, Directories, and Files
    d. All of the above

**Figure 13-16**
NetWare 3.x/4.x Term Word Search.

```
N D S L Z F G R O T I N O M E P O T
O Y T R E P O R P N X P A M N R C C
S N O W I A B Y A O I R T A E B E P
N A R O G G F S R C T W S N W C A I
A T A D A I H E T T Q U I A L O S P
Y E G I L K P T I E T A R G I M E L
R X E E F L P B T N T R F E D P C N
O T X S I S C L I N E E M M I R U A
M E T C E J B O O D N A M E T E R M
E A A R A N K C N I G O L N T S I V
M L V I N E S K I T Z H D T E S T R
G E T P S Y R A I N E I C N F I Y E
R A G T S B I N S R R X D F L O W S
O R B S U B A L L O C A T I O N L Z
U R L I R M P C O N S O L E W O X K
P O U L E R E I K R E Q U E S T E R
V E I N L F R E S U T E N W E E D S
S E R V I C E S V N P R I N T E R X
```

*Term List*

1. Block
2. Compression
3. Container
4. Context
5. Data
6. DynaText
7. File
8. Flag
9. Group
10. IRF
11. Leaf
12. Login
13. Management
14. Map
15. Memory
16. Migrate
17. Monitor
18. NDir
19. NDS
20. NetCon
21. NetUser
22. NETX
23. NList
24. NLM
25. NOS
26. NPrinter
27. Object
28. ODI
29. Partition
30. PConsole
31. Property
32. PServer
33. Repair
34. Replica
35. Requester
36. Right
37. SBackup
38. Script
39. Security
40. Send
41. Services
42. ServMan
43. SNA
44. Storage
45. Suballocation
46. SYS
47. SysCon
48. System
49. TCP/IP
50. VLM

NetWare 3.x to 4.x Update    405

## Brain Teaser

Ready for some challenging puzzles designed to help you pass the certification exam? The word-search puzzle in Fig. 13-16 will test your knowledge of terms associated with NetWare 3.x and 4.x. All you need to do is find the term in the letter grid. Make sure you look forward, backward, diagonally, and vertically since the terms could be hidden in any of those positions. You'll find the solution for this brain teaser in App. C, "Brain Teaser Answers."

You'll want to spend some time looking these terms up, using either Electro Text or DynaText, once you complete the word-search puzzle. It's important to know the terms associated with each operating system. Of course, learning the terms should also provide food for thought. For example, do you really know what the various IRM terms mean? How do they differ from NetWare 3.x to NetWare 4.x? It's questions like these that Novell is going to ask, so you'd better be prepared to provide the answers. You may also want to design your own word-search puzzle for terms. Looking for terms with this kind of puzzle really embeds them in your mind.

## Disk Time

Don't forget to spend some time working with the disk that accompanies this book. It provides valuable and fun-to-use teaching aids that help prepare you for the exam. See "Disk Time" in the preface of this book for details about what the disk contains.

CHAPTER 14

# NetWare 4.x Administration

## Introduction

This chapter looks at what you'll need to know to pass the NetWare 4.x Administration exam. Remember that this first exam will cover some of the simpler tasks that you'll perform with NetWare, but don't be too surprised if you see an occasional hard question—Novell can test any area of NetWare 4.x Administration that it chooses. There are several discrete sections in this chapter. Each section helps you study for the exam in a different way. You can improve your chances of passing the exam by using the study methods provided in this chapter. In fact, it'll help if you study all the sections once and your favorite sections at least twice. Review the study guidelines in Chap. 4 as often as necessary to ensure that you maintain the best possible study atmosphere.

The first section of this chapter is a *case study*. You'll perform some hands-on tasks that will help you learn what you need to know about the NetWare 4.x operating system to pass the examination. In this chapter, we look at what you need to do to set up a workstation. Make sure you study all areas of the case study, because you can't assume that Novell will only test you on the latest technology. Even though you'll get a lot more from this section if you perform it on your own network, the inclusion of screen shots and step-by-step instructions will help you gain something from the section even if you don't have a network.

The second area contains *sample test questions* for this course. Most of the questions are NetWare 4.x Administration–specific, but you'll see questions on other topics, like acronyms, as well. The sample questions section also includes the correct answers and an explanation of why each answer is correct. Try to answer each question yourself, look at the correct answer, and then determine where you went wrong if you didn't answer correctly.

The next section is the *fun test*. This is an exercise where you'll look at some sample test questions and answer them—this time without the aid of having the answers right below the questions. The answers appear in App. B at the back of the book. This will help you test what you learned in the sample questions section. Since you'll only get to use this section once (or twice at the most), you'll want to save it for the end of your study session. Consider the fun test a final check of your new skills before you take the exam.

The final text section of the chapter is the *brain teaser*. You'll get to have a little fun working on a NetWare 4.x Administration–related puzzle. In this case, you'll need to look for words covered in the case study. Look for NetWare 4.x–related words from Chap. 15 as well. You may even

# NetWare 4.x Administration

want to take the opportunity to look these words up in the glossary once you've completed the puzzle itself. Make absolutely certain that you take the time to get everything you can out of the list of words in this word search—even though the puzzle is meant to be fun, it's also meant to teach you something important about your certification.

Finally, we'll spend some time using a *Jeopardy!*-type game named *Red Zone* (for the obvious reasons). This section helps you look at the test from the opposite viewpoint. The game provides you with an answer—you need to come up with the corresponding question. The Red Zone awards points for correct answers and takes points away for incorrect answers. You'll receive a score at the end of the game proclaiming that you either did or did not get your certificate. Make sure you concentrate on the NetWare 4.x questions if time becomes a problem and you want to get the most from the Red Zone game.

Use all the learning methods that we provide in this chapter to improve your chances of passing the exam. It's a good idea to save the fun test section until you're almost certain that you possess all the required knowledge. Remember, you can probably go through the test only one or two times at most before you'll start to remember the answers without really knowing the material. Everyone who wants a NetWare 4.x certification needs to learn the material in this chapter. Make sure you pass this exam before you go on to the other chapters.

## Case Study

In this case study you will set up the NetWare Directory Services (NDS) for a small company. The network will be set up as follows:

- There are four users. All of them are experts in their respective fields, but they have very little network experience.
- There are four different applications, consisting of a word processor, database, spreadsheet, and an accounting package.
- One of the users will use all the applications. The other three users will use the spreadsheet, word processor, and database applications.
- Security is at a moderate level.

Once you obtain information about the company you can start to configure the network. In the following sections you'll go through the necessary steps to make this network functional. Note the logical organization of the procedure. This is the most efficient method of configuring any network.

## Setting Up the Directory Structure

The first step is to create the directory structure for the users and applications. For this exercise you'll create three directories off the root of volume SYS called APPS, DATA, and USERS. The *APPS* directory will contain subdirectories for the applications that the users need. The *DATA* directory will contain subdirectories to store the users' data from each application. Each network user will also have a personal directory under the *USERS* directory. Log into the network as user ADMIN to perform the tasks ahead.

1. Change directories to the root by typing *CD \* and pressing Enter.
2. Once you are at the root of volume SYS, type *MD APPS* and press Enter.
3. Next, move into the APPS directory and create the individual directories for each application. At the F:\> prompt, type *CD APPS* and press Enter.
4. Your prompt now indicates F:\APPS>. Create a directory for the spreadsheet application by typing *MD SS* and press Enter.
5. Now, create directories for the word processing, database, and accounting applications. Repeat Step 4, replacing SS with *WP, DB,* and *ACCT.*
6. Return to the root of volume SYS. Type *CD \* and press Enter.
7. Now, make a DATA directory. From the root of SYS, type *MD DATA* and press Enter.
8. Move to the DATA directory and create individual data directories for each of the applications. At the F:\> prompt, type *CD \DATA* and press Enter.
9. Your prompt now indicates F:\DATA>. Create a data directory for the spreadsheet. Type *MD SS* and press Enter.
10. Create directories for the word processing, database, and accounting applications. Repeat Step 9, replacing SS with *WP, DB,* and *ACCT.*
11. Return to the root of volume SYS by typing *CD \* and pressing Enter. Create the users' home directories. Type *MD USERS* and press Enter. NetWare will automatically create each user's directory in a later step.
12. Use the Novell LISTDIR utility to view your directory structure. At the F:\> prompt, type *LISTDIR APPS /A* to produce a listing of the applications directory, then type *LISTDIR DATA /A* to produce a listing of the data directory. Figure 14-1 displays the directory structure that you have just created.

# NetWare 4.x Administration

**Figure 14-1**
Display Showing Completed Directory Structure.

```
F:\>listdir apps /a

The subdirectory structure of 401/SYS:APPS
Date       Time    Inherited    Effective    Directory
--------------------------------------------------------
3-19-94    5:59a   [SRWCEMFA]   [SRWCEMFA]   ->SS
3-19-94    5:59a   [SRWCEMFA]   [SRWCEMFA]   ->DB
3-19-94    5:59a   [SRWCEMFA]   [SRWCEMFA]   ->WP
3-19-94    5:59a   [SRWCEMFA]   [SRWCEMFA]   ->ACCT
4 subdirectories found

F:\>listdir data /a

The subdirectory structure of 401/SYS:DATA
Date       Time    Inherited    Effective    Directory
--------------------------------------------------------
3-19-94    5:59a   [SRWCEMFA]   [SRWCEMFA]   ->SS
3-19-94    5:59a   [SRWCEMFA]   [SRWCEMFA]   ->WP
3-19-94    6:00a   [SRWCEMFA]   [SRWCEMFA]   ->ACCT
3-19-94    6:00a   [SRWCEMFA]   [SRWCEMFA]   ->DB
4 subdirectories found

F:\>
```

## Creating Organizational Units, Users, and Groups

Once you have created the directory structure, the next step is to create the users and group objects. The NetWare graphical utility used to create the user and group objects is NWADMIN.

1. Log into the file server as user ADMIN.
2. Start Windows on your workstation and double-click the NetWare Tools group folder in program manager. Figure 14-2 shows the NetWare Tools folder. Double-click on the NWADMIN icon[*] to start the graphical utility titled *NetWare Administration*.
3. Click once on the Organization object[†] NS to highlight the object. With the pointer on the NS Organization object, press the right mouse button to display an option menu.
4. From the menu, click once on the Create option to open the New Object window. Figure 14-3 shows the New Object window, with the Organization object highlighted.
5. Locate the Organizational Unit object icon in the New Object window and double-click on it. This will open a dialog box.

---

[*]Depending on how you set Windows up on your system, the NWADMIN icon may be in a different group folder.

[†]For this demonstration the File Server name is *401* and the Organization is *NS*. For the remainder of this case study, any references to the File Server or Organization will use these names.

**Figure 14-2**
NetWare Tools Folder.

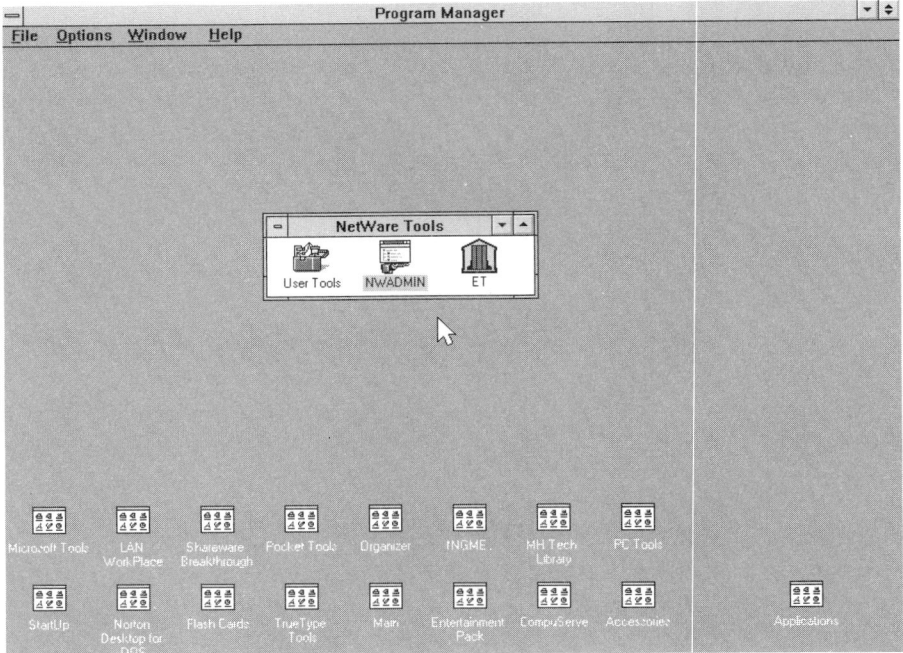

6. In the Create Organizational Unit dialog box, type *Accounting* in the name field, then click the CREATE button.

7. Repeat Steps 3 through 6, this time using the name *Sales* in place of Accounting. Figure 14-4 shows the NDS structure after creating the two Organizational Units.

**Figure 14-3**
New Object Window with the Organization Object Highlighted.

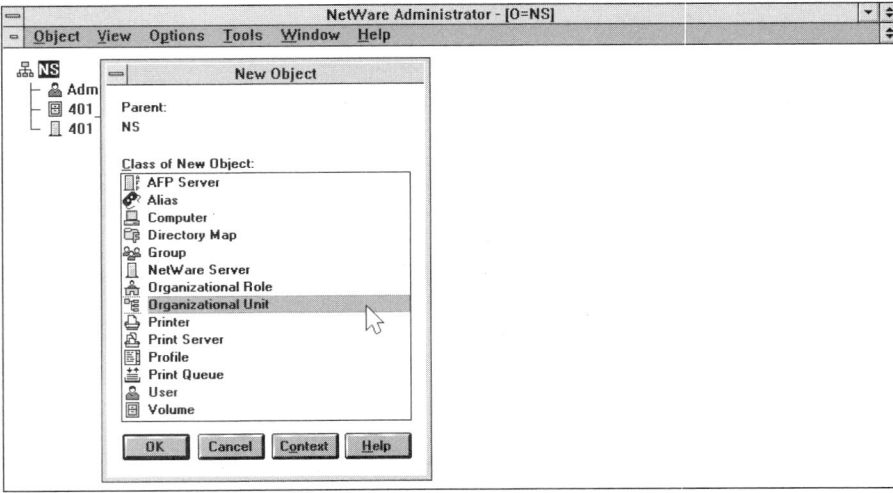

# NetWare 4.x Administration

**Figure 14-4**
NDS Structure after Creating Two Organizational Units.

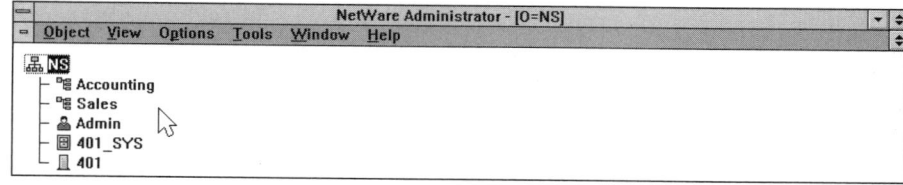

8. In the next few steps you will create the users and groups, set up their accounts, and assign file system rights to them. Click once on the Sales Organizational Unit object with the right mouse button to open an action menu, then click once on the Create option with the left button.

9. In the New Object window, point to the User object icon and double-click it. When the Create New User dialog box appears, type the first and last name of the user in the appropriate fields. Use the name *Rebecca Eastwood*. After typing the name, click on the Create Home Directory option. Specify a path for the home directory by clicking once on the Browser icon to open the Select Object dialog window. Double-click the up arrow icon in the Directory Context field, then double-click on the 401_SYS Volume object icon. This will list the contents of volume SYS in the Files and Directories section of the window. At the Files and Directories window, double-click the USERS directory folder. This will return you to the Create User dialog box and put the path to create the home directory. Now, click the Create button at the bottom of the dialog box to create the user. An empty Create User dialog box will then return to the screen.

10. Repeat Steps 8 and 9, using the names *John Clemens* and *Cyndie Welch*. After creating the two users, click the Cancel button on the bottom of the Create User dialog box.

11. Set up the account for user Paul by repeating Steps 8 and 9, using the *Accounting Organizational Unit* object in place of Sales and using the name *Paul Adams*.

12. Next, create a group in the Sales Organizational Unit. Point and click once on the Sales Organizational Unit object. Press the right mouse button once to open the option menu. Click once on the Create option, then double-click on the Group object. When the dialog box opens, type *Sales-Group* in the name field, then click on the Create button.

13. To view your additions to the NDS structure you must expand the field of view of the NetWare Administrator window. Double-click on the following objects to expand the view: Accounting, Sales, and the 401_SYS Volume objects. After expanding the Volume, double-click

the USERS, APPS, and DATA folders. Figure 14-5 shows the expanded NDS context view.

## User and Group Definitions

After creating the user and group objects, set up their accounts by defining the properties and values. This portion of the case study requires you to define each user and group separately. The purpose is to give you the most hands-on experience possible.

1. Start the NWADMIN program from Windows. Expand the field of view by double-clicking the Sales Organizational Unit object. Double-click on the User object Cyndie to open the user definition window.

2. The first dialog box identifies the user. Type the following information for user Cyndie and compare it to Fig. 14-6.

```
Title: South West Sale Rep.
Description: Sales rep for the South Western US.
Department: Sales
Telephone: 555-1212 x-269
```

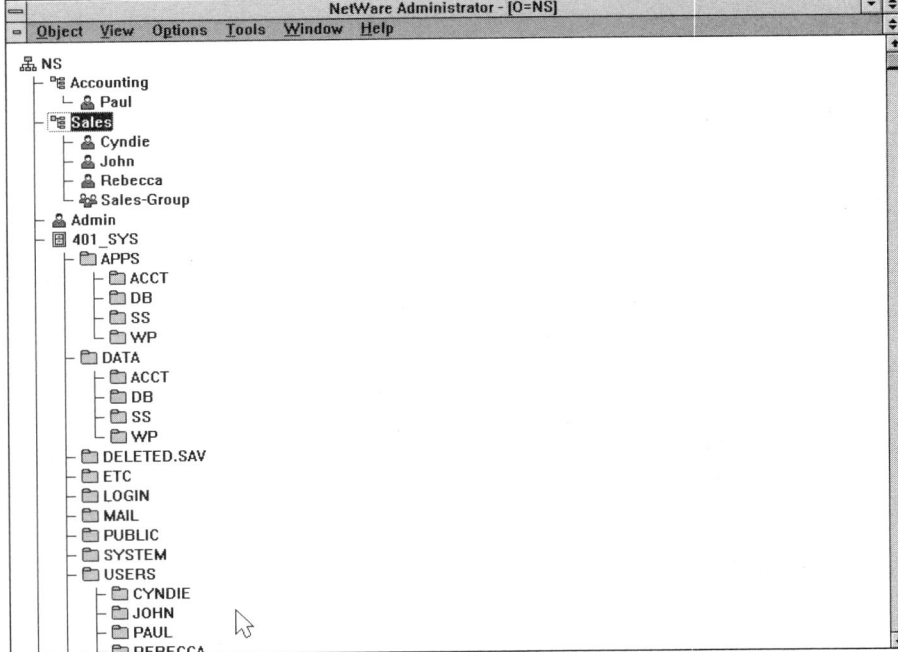

**Figure 14-5**
Expanded NDS Context View.

## NetWare 4.x Administration

**Figure 14-6**
User Identification Dialog Box.

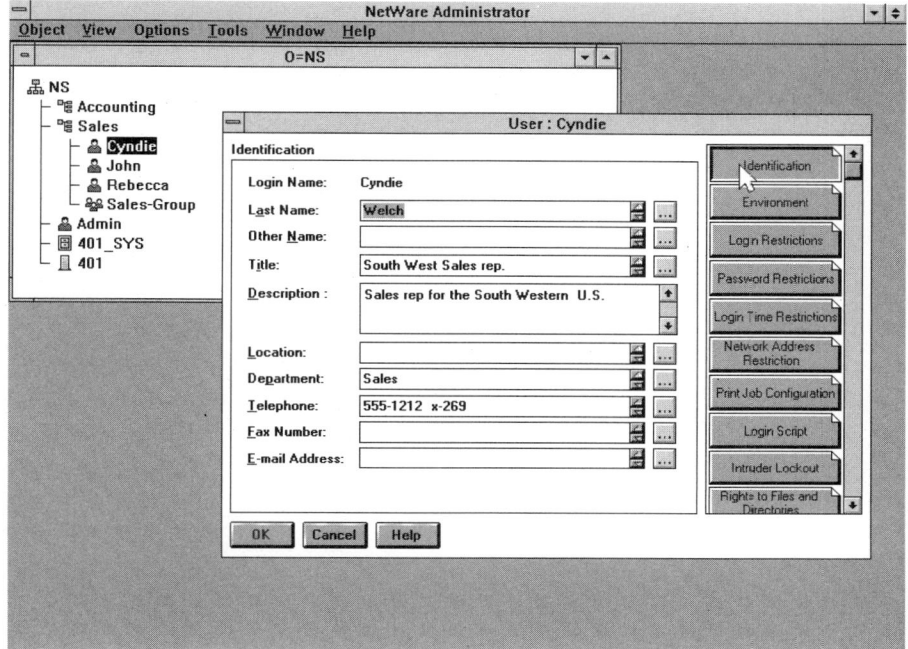

3. Click the Login Restrictions page button on the right side of the dialog box. In the dialog box, click the box to Limit Concurrent Connections and verify that the Maximum Connections value defaults to 1.

4. Click on the Password Restrictions page button to define the user password information. In the dialog box, click the Require a Password option box. Next, click the Minimum Password Length box and leave the default value of 5 characters for the length. Next, click the box for Force Periodic Password Changes, and leave the default value of 40 days. Next click the Require Unique Password box, then the Limit Grace Logins box. Set both Grace Logins Allowed and Remaining Grace Logins to 3. Click on the Change Password button and type *NOVELL* in the New Password field, then press Tab and retype the password. Figure 14-7 shows the changes to the Password Restrictions dialog box.

5. The next area to define is the user Login Time Restrictions. Click on the corresponding page button. Move the pointer to the grid box to Monday 6:00 A.M. Click and hold the left mouse button. Move the pointer to Friday 6:00 P.M., then release the button. Figure 14-8 shows the blocked area allowing the user to login.

**Figure 14-7**
Password Restrictions Dialog Box after Modifications.

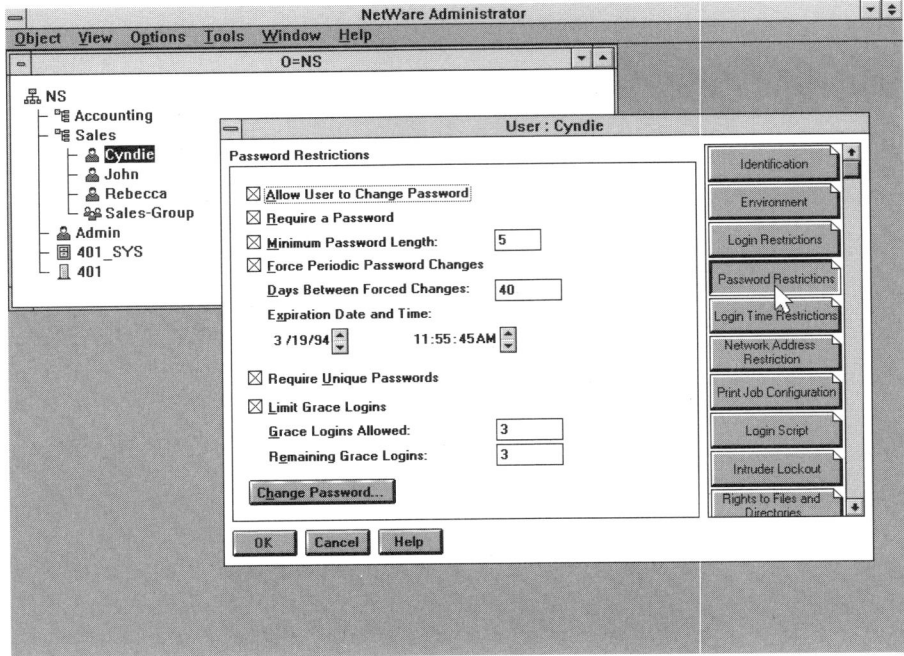

**Figure 14-8**
Login Time Restrictions Showing Allowed Access Times.

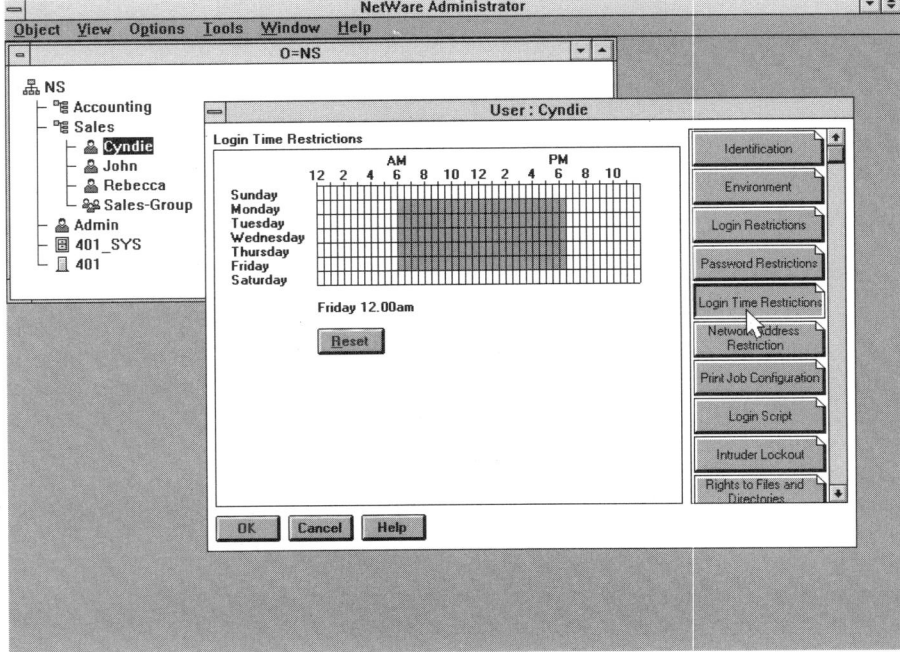

# NetWare 4.x Administration

6. Now, define the directory rights for user Cyndie by pressing the Rights to Files and Directories page button. First, define the volume where the files or directories are. Click on the Show button, then double-click on the up arrow in the Directory Context box. This will display the 401_SYS Volume object in the Volumes window; double-click on it. The Volumes window now displays the 401_SYS.NS Volume object and the Files and Directories windows displays the USERS\CYNDIE directory. Click once on the directory USERS\CYNDIE to select this path and to make the Rights window active. Remove the Supervisor, Modify, and Access Control rights by clicking in the boxes next to those rights. Figure 14-9 shows the Rights to Files and Directories window after completing the changes. Click once on the OK button in the bottom left corner of the window to save all modifications to the account.

7. Using Steps 1 to 6 define the user accounts for Rebecca, John, and Paul.* Substitute the names and Organizational Unit when necessary to make the accounts unique for each user. Use the following information when defining the Identification fields:

*It is possible to create templates defining default settings that the system will assign to the user upon creation. For the purpose of learning the 4.x system and to aid in passing the exam, set up each user account individually.

**Figure 14-9**
Rights to Files and Directories Window after Modifications in Step 6.

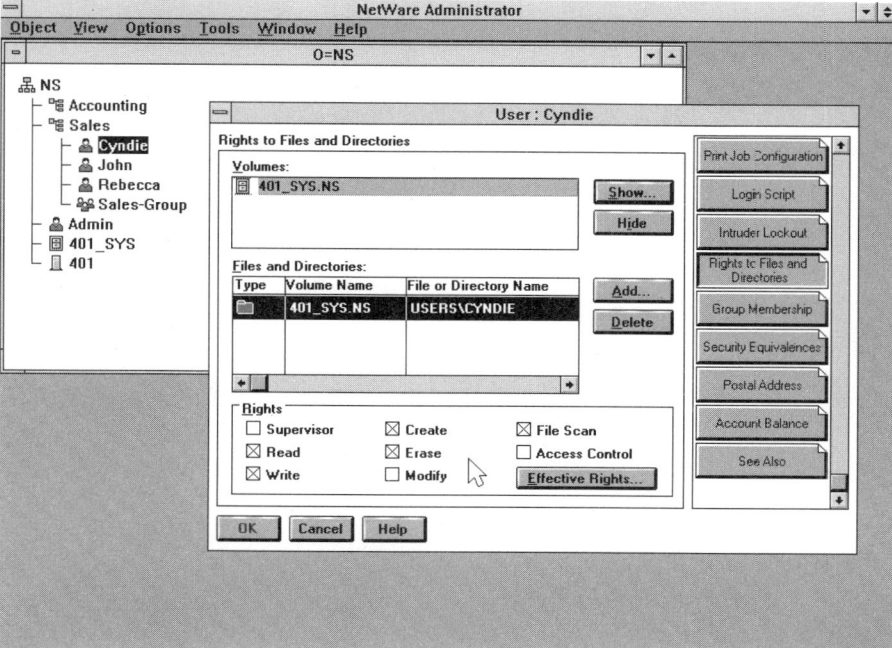

```
User Object: Rebecca Eastwood
Title: North East Sale Rep.
Description: Sales rep for the North Eastern US.
Department: Sales
Telephone: 555-1212 x-123

User Object: John Clemens
Title: Senior Sale Rep.
Description: Sales rep for the North Western, South East and
  Points between.
Department: Sales
Telephone: 555-1212 x-321

User Object: Paul Adams
Title: Controller
Description: Responsible for all accounting.
Department: Accounting
Telephone: 555-1212 x-469
```

**NOTE**  *After completing Step 6 for Paul, don't leave the dialog box; go on to Step 8.*

8. Assign user Paul rights to the APPS directory. Click once on the Add button, then double-click on the Volume object in the Directory Context dialog box. This will display the files and directories in the Files and Directories dialog box. Locate and double-click on the APPS directory. NetWare will assign Paul as a trustee of this directory with Read and File Scan rights. Figure 14-10 shows the Rights to Files and Directories page after making the assignments.

9. Add Paul to the DATA directory by clicking on the Add button, and then double-click the DATA folder icon in the File and Directories window. Add more rights to Paul for DATA directory by clicking the boxes next to Write, Create, and Erase. Figure 14-11 shows the added trustee directory assignment and rights.

10. Click once on the OK button at the bottom left corner of the window to save the changes to Paul's account.

11. Double-click on the Sales Organizational Unit object to expand the field of view, then click once with the right mouse button on the Sales-Group Group object. Click once on the Details option when the menu appears.

12. After the Group dialog box opens, click once on the Members page button. A dialog box will appear showing the members of this group. Since this is a new group, the box is empty. To view a list of users

# NetWare 4.x Administration

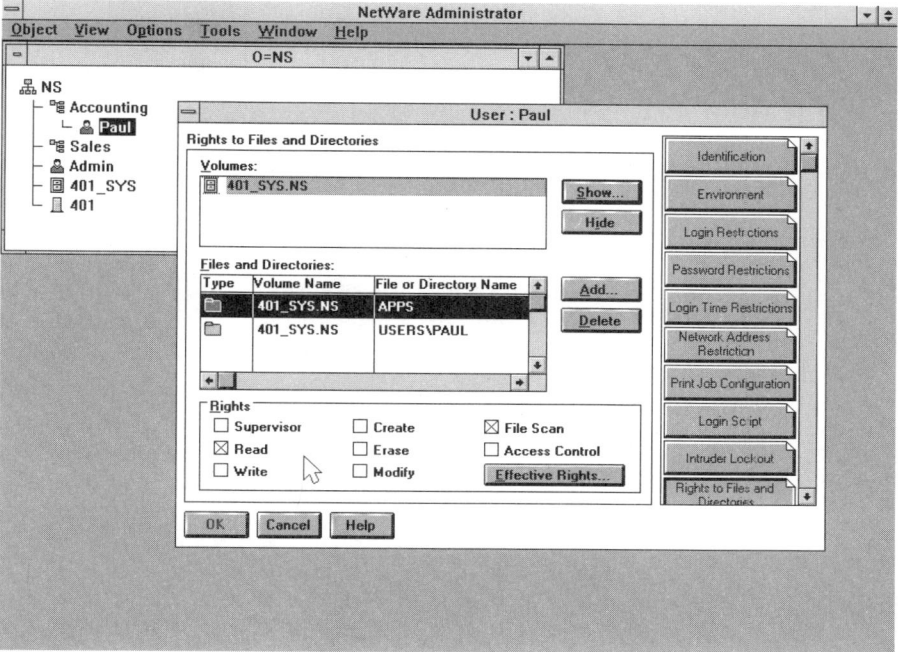

**Figure 14-10**
Rights to Files and Directories Window after Assigning APPS Rights in Step 8.

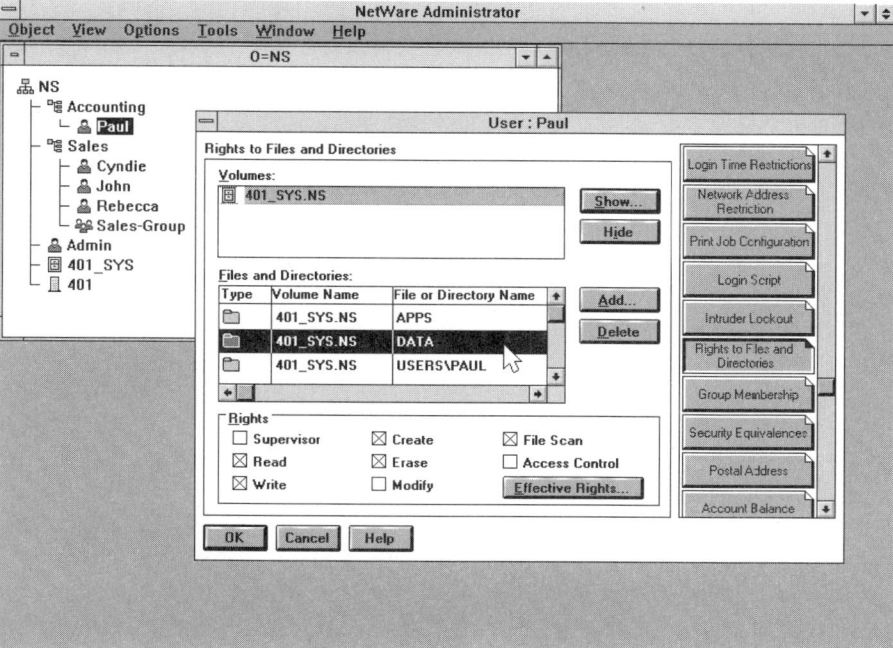

**Figure 14-11**
Rights to Files and Directories Window after Assigning DATA, Write, Create, and Erase Rights in Step 9.

from the Sales Organizational Unit, click the Add button once. The Select Object window will appear and list the users in the Sales Organizational Unit. Hold the Shift key down and then use the left mouse button to select each of the users. As you hold the Shift key down and click on the users, NetWare will highlight their names. After you highlight all the names, press the OK button. This will add all three users to the group at once. Figure 14-12 shows the users added to the group.

13. Click on the Rights to Files and Directories page button. When the Files and Directories dialog box opens, double-click the Show button. When the Select Object dialog box opens, double-click the up arrow icon in the Directory Context window. Double-click on the 401_SYS Volume object in the Volumes dialog box. Click on the Add button next to the Files and Directories dialog box, and then double-click the 401_SYS Volume object in the Directory Context dialog box. This will display a list of the files and directories of volume SYS. Double-click on the APPS icon to display a list of subdirectories. Hold the Shift key down and click on the directories DB, SS, and WP in the Files and Directories window to mark them. Figure 14-13 shows the

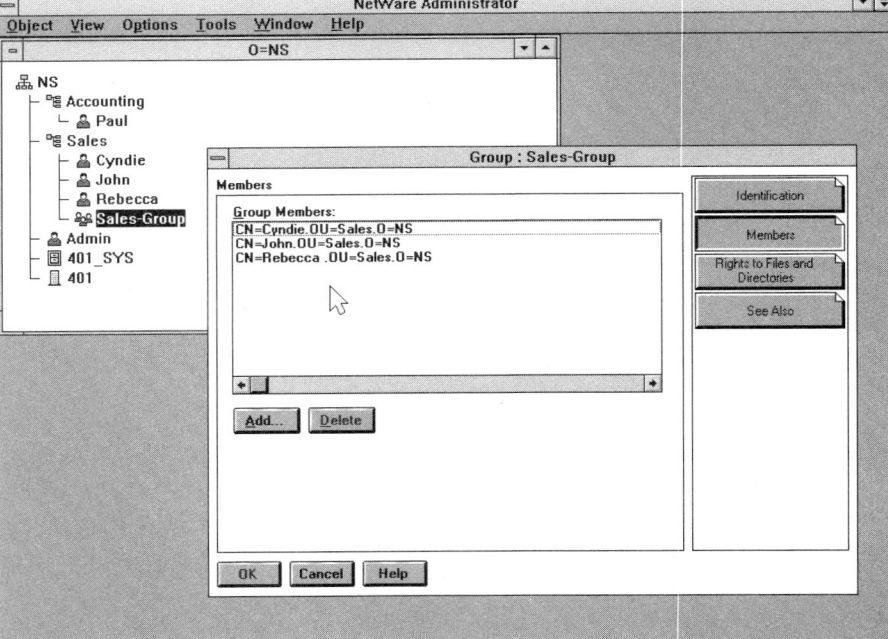

**Figure 14-12**
Members Dialog Box after Adding Users to Sales-Group in Step 12.

# NetWare 4.x Administration

**Figure 14-13**
Files and Directories Window after Marking Directories in Step 13.

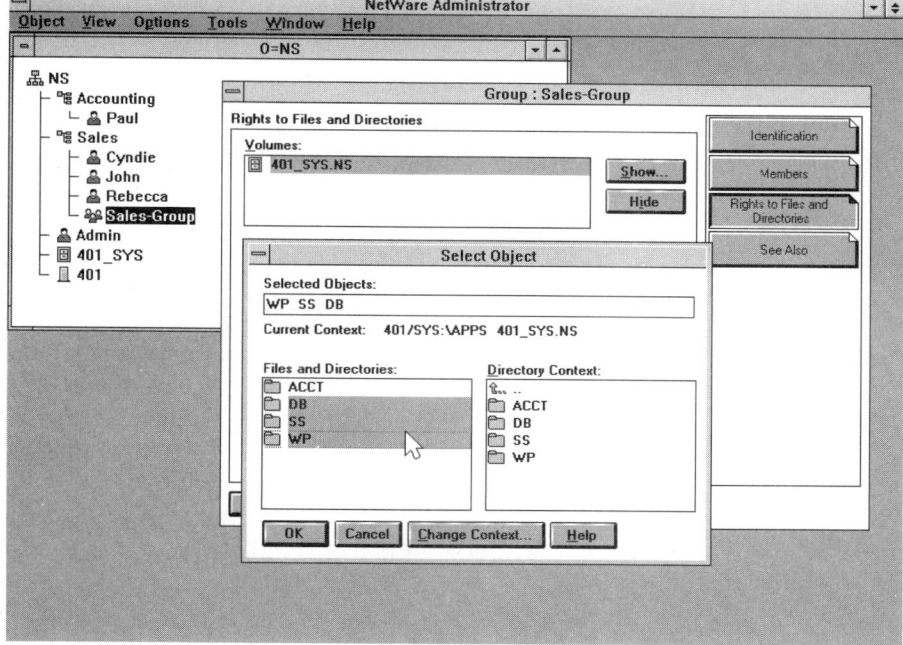

window with the directories marked. After marking the three directories, release the Shift key and click once on the OK button. This will add the group Sales-Group as a trustee to the directories and will assign the Read and File Scan rights to them. Figure 14-14 shows the directories and rights assigned to the group.

14. While in the Rights to Files and Directory dialog box, add the group to the trustee list for the DB, SS, and WP directories under DATA. Click once on the Add button, then double-click on the DATA folder icon. Hold the Shift key and click on the DB, SS, and WP directory folders in the Files and Directories window to mark them, then click once on the OK button. Assign the Write, Create, and Erase rights by clicking the boxes next to those rights. This will assign the group as a trustee to the directories and will grant the Read, Write, Create, Erase, and File Scan rights to them.

15. To save the modifications to the Sales-Group, click once on the OK button in the bottom left corner of the window.

16. Close the NetWare Administration window utility by double-clicking the minus sign in the upper left corner of the window.

**Figure 14-14**
Rights to Files and Directories Window Showing Assignments Made in Step 13.

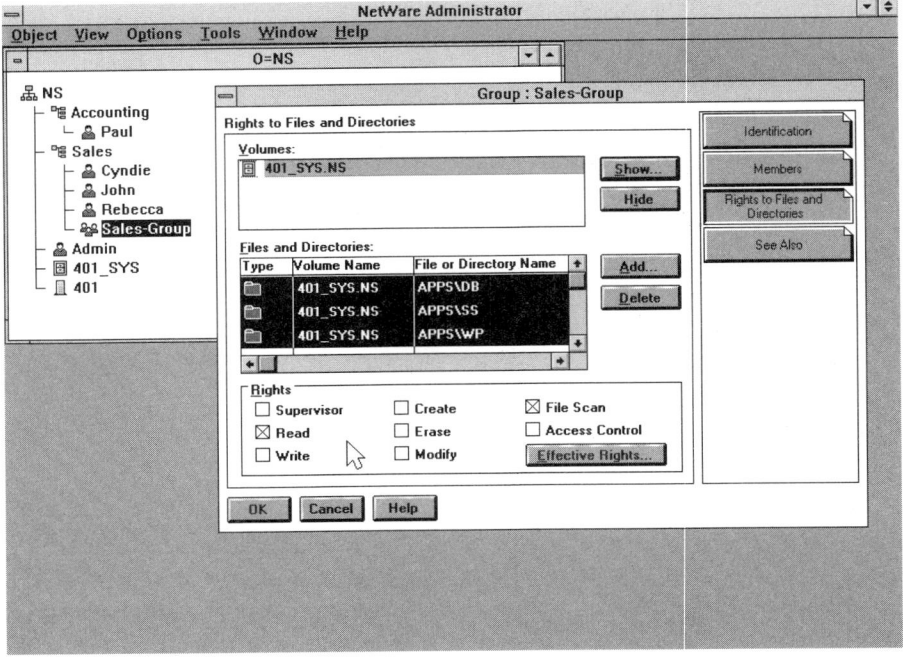

## Testing the Setup

The next step is to make sure that your configurations are set up as planned and work properly. As you complete a group of setup configurations, test them. This will help you isolate problem areas. Before any of the users power up their workstations and log into the network, you must test each of the users' accounts.

1. Using the chart in Fig. 14-15 as checklist, mark the box under the user name and next to the task that you verify as working properly.
2. Log into the network as user *Paul*. Check each item on the checklist that pertains to the previous steps of this case study.
3. Make any necessary changes or modifications on items that did not work properly.
4. Repeat Steps 1 to 4 for users Rebecca, Cyndie, and John.

This completes the case study for NetWare 4.x Administration. The steps in this exercise have helped you build an understanding of how to use the NetWare Administration utility. While there are many more options and tools within the NWADMIN, you now know the fundamentals

# NetWare 4.x Administration

| Activity | Paul | Rebecca | Cyndie | John |
|---|---|---|---|---|
| Password required? | | | | |
| Asked for new password? | | | | |
| Errors during login? | | | | |
| Display Greeting? | | | | |
| Did Screen Pause? | | | | |
| Display Mapping? | | | | |
| Did Screen Pause? | | | | |
| Did Windows start? | | | | |
| Exit Windows—do you have access to the network? | | | | |
| Change to each of the APPS directories, type RIGHTS—are they correct? | | | | |
| Change to each of the DATA directories, type RIGHTS—are they correct? | | | | |
| Will each of the APPS start? | | | | |
| Can you save data from the APPS? | | | | |
| Can you print from all the APPS? | | | | |
| Can you return to Windows? | | | | |
| Can you logout properly? | | | | |
| Other: | | | | |
| Other: | | | | |
| Other: | | | | |
| Other: | | | | |

**Figure 14-15**
Workstation Setup Checklist.

of the program. As you spend time practicing with the network software and adding your own information, complete the checklist in Fig. 14-15. Even though the case study shown is for a small company, you can use the same concepts and practices for a worldwide company having hundreds of file servers and thousands of users. Since this case study covers the fundamentals of NetWare 4.x, you should spend extra hours using NWADMIN until you are comfortable with it. Using this case study, spending extra time practicing on the system, and studying the sample questions section will help prepare you for the exams.

## Setting Up the Windows 95 Client

More and more people are installing Windows 95 on their machines, which means working with 32-bit clients when working with Novell. This product won't necessarily be part of the package you receive from Novell right now, but expect it to be available sometime in the near future. Needless to say, as a CNA/CNE candidate, you'll still be tested on your ability to use these new clients.

The previous subsections on this case study take a very deliberate approach to configuring the workstation. That approach works fine under DOS where you can expect a certain amount of consistency in network use and machine configuration. This subsection takes a more conversational approach to make you aware of configuration options—there are a lot of them. However, we won't provide a blow-by-blow procedure because there isn't any way that we can anticipate your configuration needs. In other words, Windows 95 makes things a lot more complicated for the network administrator, a fact that you'll have to learn to deal with.

Getting Client 32 installed on your machine is fairly easy when compared to the DOS installation. You download the required software from http://support.novell.com/Ftp/Updates/nwos/nc32w952/Date0.html or from CompuServe. Once you download and unpack the software, double-click on the Setup icon. You'll see a dialog box similar to the one shown in Fig. 14-16.

Click on Yes if you agree to the license terms. You'll see a dialog box like the one in Fig. 14-17. Just click on Start and the Setup program takes care of all the details for you.

The first thing Setup does is to remove your old client (the default Microsoft client for NetWare in most cases). I mention this because you may want to run the installation from a local drive instead of from the network. While Setup doesn't actually disconnect you from the server, at this point a failure that requires a reboot could leave you without any client at all (making the file server inaccessible).

Once the old client is removed, Setup installs a few new files in the Windows INF folder. At this point, it forces Windows 95 to rebuild its drivers list, based on the contents of the new INF file. Setup automatically selects the new client for you and gets it installed. You'll see another rebuild of the driver list after the new client is installed.

# NetWare 4.x Administration

**Figure 14-16**
License Agreement for Client 32 Installation.

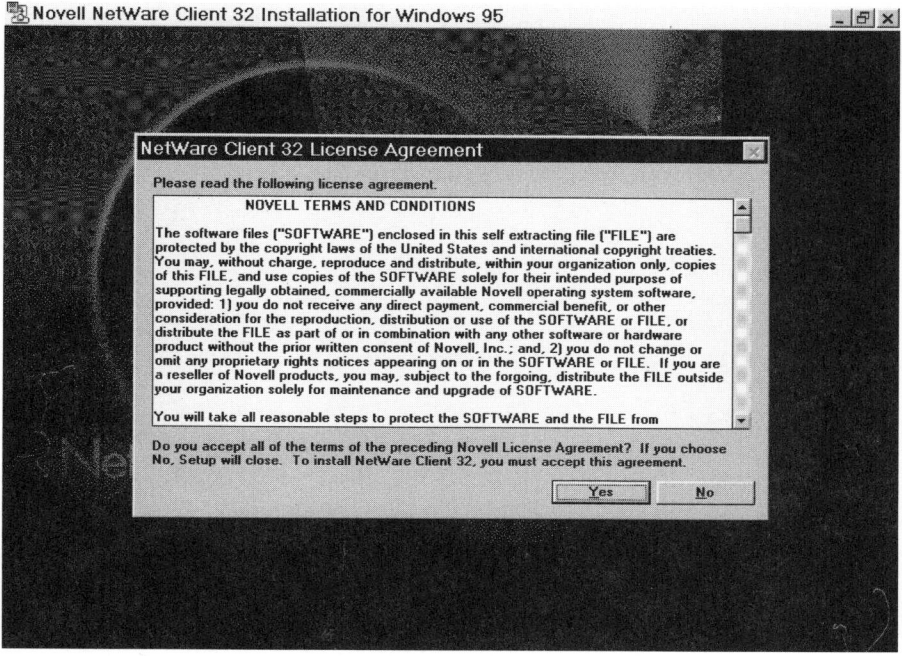

**Figure 14-17**
Setup Dialog Box for Client 32 Installation.

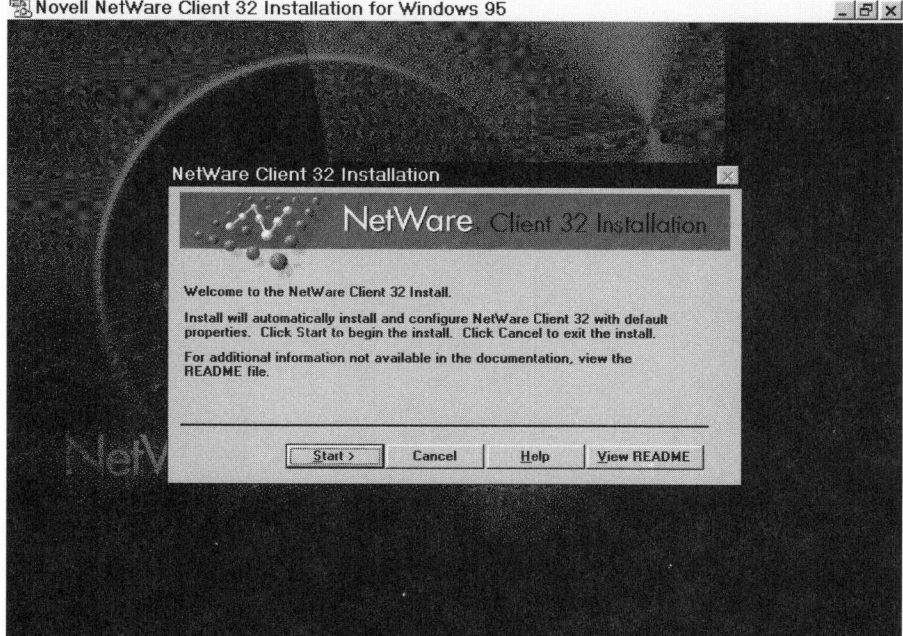

**Chapter Fourteen**

After all the files are copied and Setup performs a basic setup, you'll be asked to reboot your machine. When you restart your machine, you'll be using the new client. At this point you'll need to configure the new client, which may be a little different for each machine depending on how you plan to use it, the machine's location on the network, and the hardware/software options you have installed in Windows 95.

**NOTE** *Make sure that you know your current context and NDS tree. You'll need this information the first time you restart your machine with the Novell client installed. The preferred tree and context information is recorded so that you don't have to enter it again.*

Configuring Novell's Client 32 is much like configuring any other network-related driver under Windows 95. You begin by opening the *Network Properties* dialog box (right-click Network Neighborhood and select Properties from the context menu). Select the Novell NetWare Client 32 entry in the components list shown on the *Configuration* page, and then click the Properties button. You'll see a Novell NetWare Client 32 Properties dialog box similar to the one shown in Fig. 14-18.

As you'll notice, the *Client 32* page of this dialog box contains four fields. Note that the *Preferred Server* field is blank. You need to leave it

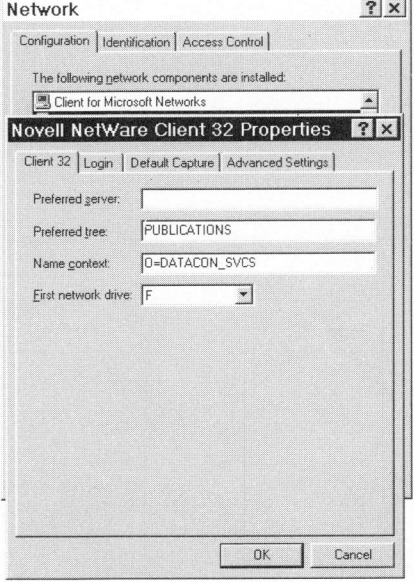

**Figure 14-18**
Properties Dialog Box for Configuring the Client.

# NetWare 4.x Administration

blank unless you want a bindery connection in place of an NDS connection. The *Preferred Tree* field contains the name of the tree that you want the client to search for your name. The *Name Context* text box normally contains the names of your organization and workgroup. (Figure 14-18 shows only the organization name.) Finally, you need to select the *first network drive*. Unlike the Microsoft client, you can actually select a drive below F if you want to. For example, you may have only a hard drive and CD-ROM installed on your machine. Selecting E as the first network connection saves one drive letter.

The *Login* page appears in Fig. 14-19. Normally, when you log into the network, you see a single page login similar to the one used by the Microsoft client. This page allows you to enter a user name and your password. It works fine if you have only one user, who uses the same network configuration each day, working with a machine. However, if you have a user with special needs, you'll want to modify one or more of these settings.

There are three additional page types that you can configure on the Login page of the Novell NetWare Client 32 Properties dialog box. The *Display Connection Page* option tells Client 32 that you want to see the page for selecting a preferred server, tree, and context each time you log in. This allows you to change the default server you use each day and provides some added flexibility for those times when you have to log in as the net-

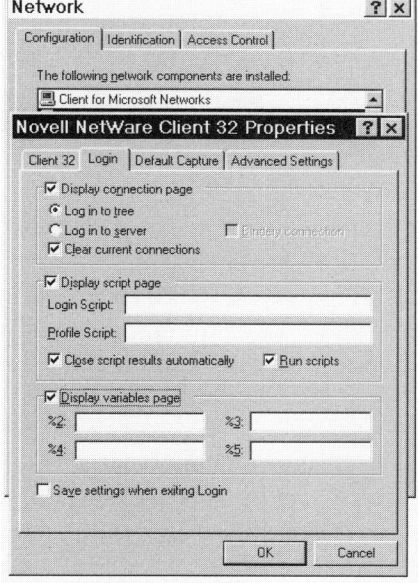

**Figure 14-19**
Login Page for Modifying Login Dialog Box.

work administrator rather than as a regular user. This group includes two additional options. The first clears all the connection information each time you log in. It's normally a good idea to uncheck this selection, because most people use the same server each day unless they're doing something special, like performing administrative duties. However, you'll probably want to keep it checked for security reasons if several users use the same machine. Using this feature enables you to keep a hidden server hidden. The other check box isn't highlighted in this case. If you select the Log in to Server option, you'll enable the Bindery Connection check box. This check box forces a bindery rather than a NDS connection to the server.

Normally, the administrator assigns a default set of scripts to each user on the network. These scripts set up any drive mappings or other essential network configurations. Client 32 allows you to select one of the NDS scripts by using the *Display Script Page* option during log in. That's what the second section of the Login page is all about. Note that there are two separate fields for script names—one for the *login script* and another for the *profile script*. You can choose NDS script objects or a simple batch file on your machine—Client 32 will work with either one. There are two check boxes that affect the way the scripts are run. The first automatically closes the script window when it's complete. In most cases, you'll want to keep this checked. Unchecking the check box allows you to observe the results of a script during debugging. The second check box, Run Scripts, tells Client 32 to run the scripts you've selected. You can uncheck the box if you don't want to run any scripts during the login process.

The third section of the Login page relates to scripts as well. The *Display Variables Page* option displays a third additional page during the login process. You can use the fields on this page to pass variable information to your scripts. This is especially handy if you want to build one script file to serve a number of purposes.

Printing is another major problem in some situations. The *Default Capture* page of the Novell NetWare Client 32 Properties dialog box allows you to get around some of them. Figure 14-20 shows this page. If you've worked with printers under Windows 95 before, you should recognize this page as a generic form of the one normally used within Windows 95. The thing to remember is that these settings affect the network printers as a whole. They won't affect the settings of printers you have already installed—Windows 95 overrides any settings you may make on this page.

The final page in the Novell NetWare Client 32 Properties dialog box is the *Advanced Settings* page shown in Fig. 14-21. In most cases, you'll never have to adjust these settings. However, some of the settings can help you fine-tune the way Client 32 works. For example, the *Delay Writes* setting can help in situations where an application repeatedly opens and

# NetWare 4.x Administration

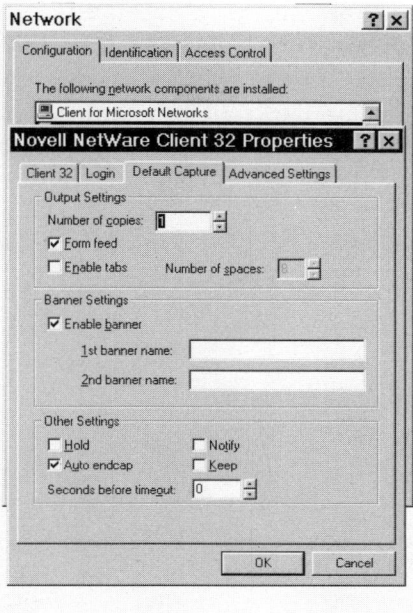

**Figure 14-20**
Default Capture Page for Changing New Network Printer Default Settings.

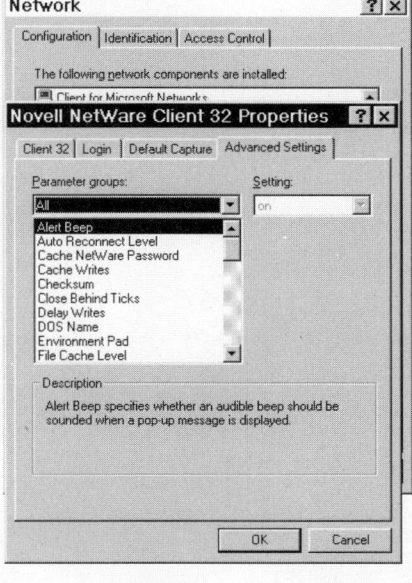

**Figure 14-21**
Advanced Settings Page for Fine-Tuning Client 32 Settings.

closes files on the server (such as overlays). The client will hold the file write for a given number of clock ticks to ensure that the application actually wants to write the information. In essence, this setting works as a disk cache. One of the handier troubleshooting aids is the *Log File* setting. You can tell Client 32 to generate a log of any errors it encounters. The *Log File Size* setting allows you to keep the file size under control.

## Study Questions

1. To load the DOS requester in extended memory at the workstation, which command would you use?
   a. VLM –x
   b. VLM +x
   c. VLM /me
   d. VLM /mx

   *d.* The common acronym for extended memory in the computer industry is *XMS*. The /mx refers to memory extended.

2. The NetWare graphical utility to manage users and groups is:
   a. SYSCON
   b. NETCON
   c. NETWARE ADMINISTRATOR
   d. NETADMIN

   *c.* The NetWare Administrator is a graphical utility that requires windows. In the NetWare Tools folder, it's listed as NWADMIN.

3. The NetWare windows utilities provide context-sensitive help.
   a. True
   b. False

   *a.* The NetWare help files take advantage of this windows feature, as well as the indexing and standard windows help keys.

4. When using the DOS text utilities, modify an entry by pressing the _____ key.
   a. F3
   b. Enter
   c. Insert
   d. F4

# NetWare 4.x Administration

    *a.*   The F3 function key provides a way of modifying an entry in a NetWare menu. This feature dates back to previous versions of NetWare.

5. The NetWare NDS regulates which of the following types of services?
   a. Printers
   b. Volumes
   c. Files
   d. All of the above
   e. None of the above

    *d.*   The NDS database regulates all resources of the network. This includes managing printers, volumes, and trustee assignments to files.

6. The property information for a User object in NDS includes:
   a. Telephone number
   b. Password
   c. Supervisor
   d. None of the above

    *a.*   NetWare offers an Identification option for the user. One of the fields lets you record the user's telephone number.

7. The three categories for NDS objects are:
   a. Users, Groups, and Trustees
   b. File servers, Volumes, and Directories
   c. Physical, Logical, and Virtual
   d. [Root], Container, and Leaf

    *d.*   As with all things, there's a beginning, middle, and end. The [Root] is the beginning of the NDS, Container objects are the middle, and Leaf objects are the ending point.

8. You can create a new [Root] object at any time.
   a. True
   b. False

    *b.*   During the installation process of NetWare 4.x, the install program creates the [Root] object.

9. You can have more than one [Root] object per tree.
   a. True
   b. False

*b.* Each network tree can have only one [Root] object. It is possible to merge the roots of different systems to form one central [Root].

10. Three types of Container objects are:
    a. Volumes, Directories, and Files
    b. Country, Organization, and Organizational Units
    c. Organizational Role, Print Queue, and [Root]
    d. All of the above

    *b.* Containers are objects that can hold other NDS objects. They may contain other containers or leaf objects.

11. The term *Leaf object* in NDS services refers to the:
    a. Real network resource.
    b. The property of the object.
    c. The top of the NDS structure.
    d. Files in the directory.

    *a.* All resources connected to the network are part of the NDS. The NDS manages the resources that include Users, Groups, Volumes, File Servers, Printers, and any other resource a user might want to use.

12. Leaf objects use the attribute of:
    a. LF
    b. OU
    c. CN
    d. LO

    *c.* The acronym *CN* refers to common name. You must use a common name to refer to network resources, such as a printer or user, that are leaf objects.

13. The _____ object in NDS best describes the Sales department.
    a. Organizational Group
    b. Organizational Unit
    c. Leaf
    d. [Root]

    *b.* The Sales department of a company will likely have printers, file servers, users, and other resources. The Organizational Unit object will hold these resources.

# NetWare 4.x Administration

**14.** The File Server is a(n) _____ object in NDS.
  **a.** Leaf
  **b.** Container
  **c.** Organizational Unit
  **d.** None of the above

  *a.* The File Server falls into the Leaf object classification. As a Leaf object it does not contain other NDS objects.

**15.** The NDS is an actual directory and file system on the file server.
  **a.** True
  **b.** False

  *b.* The NDS is a database that resembles a directory structure. It is a group of files on the NetWare volume.

**16.** The NetAdmin DOS text menu utility manages the:
  **a.** NDS database
  **b.** File system
  **c.** Print services
  **d.** All of the above

  *a.* The NetAdmin is a DOS text menu utility that will view, modify, and manage objects of the NDS database.

**17.** The Windows-based utility NetWare Administrator manages the:
  **a.** NDS database
  **b.** File system
  **c.** Use of Printers
  **d.** All of the above

  *d.* NetWare Administrator is a Windows-based graphical utility that manages the NDS database objects. It also manages the trustee rights to the file system and access to the printer objects.

**18.** To change locations in the NDS structure, use the _____ command.
  **a.** CD
  **b.** CX
  **c.** CL
  **d.** MOVE

  *b.* Your current position in the NDS structure is your Context. The command to change your current Context is CX (Change Context).

19. When creating a new user with NetWare Administrator, the _____ is mandatory.
    a. Password
    b. Login script
    c. Last name
    d. Home directory
    e. None of the above

    *c.* NetWare 4.x requires both a first and last name when you create a new user account. The first name value is the login name and the last name value is for reference and uniquely identifies the user.

20. NDS allows you to create two users with the same login name as long as you create them in different containers.
    a. True
    b. False

    *a.* The NDS database does not hold the user names in a central location. NDS holds the User objects within Container objects. Since the system can have many Container objects, you must specify the context or location of the User object that you want to log in as.

21. When logging in to NetWare 4.x, NDS services search the _____ for your user object.
    a. Current context
    b. Entire database
    c. [Root] and Organization objects
    d. All of the above

    *a.* NDS searches only your current context for the User object that you are logging in as. If your User object in not in your current context, you must change contexts or specify the path to the User object.

22. Which of the following is the correct syntax for a complete name?
    a. .CN=CYNDIE.OU=SALES.O=NS
    b. CN=CYNDIE.OU=SALES.O=NS
    c. .CYNDIE.NS.SALES
    d. .CYNDIE.SALES.NS

    *a.* NetWare identifies the complete context name by the leading period, followed by the abbreviation of the object type.

# NetWare 4.x Administration

23. To view a list of user objects for a container, type _____ at the prompt.
    a. NDIR
    b. USERLIST /ALL
    c. NLIST "USER"
    d. CX /ALL

    *c.* The NLIST command will view, among other things, the User objects of a container. NLIST will also display information about the User objects.

24. NetWare supports which of the following as volumes?
    a. Off line tape drives
    b. Floppy drives
    c. CD-ROMs
    d. None of the above

    *c.* NetWare supports the use of CD-ROMs as a read only volume. The CD-ROM player can hold a single CD or multiple CDs in a juke-box system.

25. When NetWare is first installed, the following directories are automatically created:
    a. PUBLIC
    b. NLS
    c. QUEUES
    d. All of the above

    *d.* NetWare automatically creates the PUBLIC, NLS, and QUEUES directories during installation. PUBLIC holds the NetWare external commands, NLS contains the language support files, and the QUEUES directory will hold the print queues.

26. The NetWare utility to view how much disk space is in use and how much is available is:
    a. NDIR
    b. VOLUME
    c. SPACE
    d. VOLSPACE

    *a.* NDIR with the /volume option will display statistics about the volume.

27. NetWare 4.x makes _____ drive letters available for regular drive pointers to every workstation.
   a. 10
   b. 16
   c. 26
   d. Unlimited

   *c.* NetWare only allows a single letter as a drive pointer. All 26 letters of the alphabet are available for drive pointers.

28. The correct syntax for creating a drive mapping is:
   a. MAP H:=VOL_SYS.SALES.NS:USERS\CYNDIE
   b. MAP F=SYS:USERS\CYNDIE
   c. MAP K:=.401.NS.SALES.VOL_SYS:USERS\JOHN
   d. None of the above

   *a.* When creating a drive mapping, specify the path to the volume object of NDS, then the path to the directory.

29. The NetWare Administrator utility allows you to:
   a. Manage objects.
   b. Salvage deleted files.
   c. Purge files.
   d. All of the above.

   *d.* The NetWare Administrator utility manages NDS services and the file and directory system, allowing you to salvage or purge deleted files.

30. A Trustee file or directory assignment can be made to a:
   a. User
   b. Group
   c. Container object
   d. Both *a* and *b*
   e. All of the above

   *e.* Container objects, Users, and Groups are all NDS objects. You can make any NDS object a trustee of a file or directory.

31. To block rights at the file or directory level, remove the rights from the:
   a. IRF (Inherited Rights Filter)
   b. IRM (Inherited Rights Mask)

c. MRF (Maximum Rights Filter)
d. MRM (Maximum Rights Mask)

*a.* The IRF will filter or restrict rights from flowing to the next level.

32. The combination of user rights minus the rights revoked by the directory equal your _____ rights.
    a. Trustee
    b. Directory
    c. Effective
    d. NDS

*c.* Effective rights are the rights that you can actually use in the file or directory.

33. Object rights of the NDS include:
    a. Read
    b. Browse
    c. Write
    d. Both *a* and *c*

*b.* NetWare 4.x has rights for the file system, NDS objects, and NDS properties. The Browse right applies to NDS objects.

34. The Supervisor NDS Object right can be blocked at a level below the initial assignment.
    a. True
    b. False

*a.* Unlike the Supervisor right of the file system, you can block the Object right of Supervisor.

35. The NDS Property rights include the following:
    a. Add or Delete self
    b. Compare
    c. Supervisor
    d. Read
    e. All of the above

*e.* The Property rights include Supervisor, Compare, Read, Write, and Add or Delete self.

**Chapter Fourteen**

36. Every object has a trustee list or ACL property. The Acronym *ACL* means:
    a. Access Control List
    b. Access Common List
    c. All Control Lines
    d. None of the above

    *a.* The ACL is a list of trustees to an NDS object.

37. To implement Object and Property security, you use the _____ utility.
    a. SYSCON
    b. FILER
    c. NETWARE ADMINISTRATOR
    d. AUDITCON

    *c.* The NetWare Administrator utility manages all aspects of the NDS, including the file system security and the NDS security.

38. NetWare 4.x provides four category types of console commands. They are:
    a. Name, LAN, Disk, and NLM
    b. Command Line, Text Menu, Graphical Interface, and Dynamic
    c. Load, Bind, Add, and Mount
    d. Screen Display, Installation, Maintenance, and Configuration

    *d.* Novell groups the file server commands into four categories: Screen Display, Installation, Maintenance, and Configuration. Each category has a set of commands related to that category.

39. The _____ will track and display the network statistics.
    a. SYSCON
    b. FCONSOLE
    c. MONITOR
    d. TRACK ON

    *c.* The Monitor NLM will track and display information and statistics about the file server—user connections, disk drives, memory, and LAN drivers, to name a few.

40. The order of execution for the 4.x login scripts is:
    a. System, User, and Default
    b. System, Profile, User, and Default

### NetWare 4.x Administration

c. Default, User, and System
d. System, User, Profile, and Default

*b.* NetWare executes the login scripts in the following order: System, Profile, User, and Default. You can create and edit all the scripts except Default, code for which is contained in the LOGIN.EXE file.

## Fun Test

1. The program that manages users and groups with a graphical interface is:
   a. NETWARE ADMINISTRATOR
   b. NETADMIN
   c. SYSCON
   d. NETCON

2. The _____ command displays a list of User objects for your current NDS context.
   a. USERLIST /ALL
   b. CX /ALL
   c. NDIR
   d. NLIST "USER"

3. Which of the following are Container objects?
   a. Organizational Role, Print Queue, and [Root]
   b. Country, Organization, and Organizational Units
   c. Volumes, Directories, and Files
   d. All of the above

4. NDS includes _____ as property information for User objects.
   a. Supervisor
   b. Telephone number
   c. Password
   d. None of the above

5. NetWare 4.x requires a first name and a _____ when creating a new user on the system.
   a. Login script
   b. Home directory
   c. Password
   d. Last name
   e. None of the above

6. NetWare automatically creates which of the following directories during installation?
   a. PUBLIC
   b. QUEUES
   c. NLS
   d. All of the above

7. Within the NDS services, the classification for Sales department is as what type of object?
   a. Organizational Unit
   b. [Root]
   c. Organizational Group
   d. Leaf

8. To map a drive letter to Cyndie's home directory, which of the following is the correct syntax?
   a. MAP F=SYS:USERS\CYNDIE
   b. MAP H:=VOL_SYS.SALES.NS:USERS\CYNDIE
   c. MAP K:=.401.NS.SALES.VOL_SYS:USERS\CYNDIE
   d. None of the above

9. The NDS database contains the physical directories and files of a volume.
   a. True
   b. False

10. To view a volume's total disk space and available disk space, type _____ at the workstation prompt.
    a. SPACE
    b. VOLUME SYS
    c. VOLSPACE
    d. NDIR /VOLUME

# NetWare 4.x Administration

11. NetWare provides the _____ utility to track and display information about the network statistics.
    a. TRACK ON
    b. FCONSOLE
    c. SYSCON
    d. MONITOR

12. The NDS services search the _____ for your user object when you log into the 4.x file server to authenticate services.
    a. Entire database
    b. [Root] and Organization objects
    c. Current context
    d. All of the above

13. Which of the following commands will force the DOS requester to load into extended memory at the workstation?
    a. VLM /me
    b. VLM /mx
    c. VLM +x
    d. VLM −x

14. When defining the path for an NDS object, the correct syntax for a complete name is:
    a. .CYNDIE.NS.SALES
    b. CN=CYNDIE.OU=SALES.O=NS
    c. .CYNDIE.SALES.NS
    d. .CN=CYNDIE.OU=SALES.O=NS

15. NDS defines the File Server as what type of object?
    a. Leaf
    b. Container
    c. Organizational Unit
    d. None of the above

16. Every file server on the network will have its own [Root] object connecting to the same network tree.
    a. True
    b. False

17. NetWare supports which of the following as volumes?
    a. CD-ROMs
    b. Offline tape drives
    c. Floppy drives
    d. None of the above

18. The NetWare 4.x operating system executes login scripts in the following order:
    a. System, User, and Default
    b. Default, User, and System
    c. System, User, Profile, and Default
    d. System, Profile, User, and Default

19. The rights that users actually have in a file or directory are their _____ rights.
    a. Trustee
    b. Effective
    c. Directory
    d. NDS

20. Within the NDS services, the term *Leaf object* refers to the:
    a. Files in the directory
    b. Top of the NDS structure
    c. Real network resource
    d. Property of the object

21. NetAdmin is the DOS text menu utility that manages the:
    a. File system
    b. Print services
    c. NDS database
    d. All of the above

22. Every workstation on a NetWare 4.x network has _____ drive letters available for regular drive pointers.
    a. 10
    b. 16
    c. 26
    d. Unlimited

# NetWare 4.x Administration

23. NetWare 4.x divides the file server console commands into the four following categories:
    a. Load, Bind, Add, and Mounting
    b. Screen Display, Installation, Maintenance, and Configuration
    c. Command Line, Text Menu, Graphical Interface, and Dynamic
    d. Name, LAN, Disk, and NLM

24. The Windows graphical utility NetWare Administrator manages the:
    a. File system
    b. Use of Printers
    c. NDS database
    d. All of the above

25. _____ manages the NDS security for Properties and Objects.
    a. NETWARE ADMINISTRATOR
    b. AUDITCON
    c. FILER
    d. SYSCON

26. The NetWare Administrator utility allows you to:
    a. Manage objects.
    b. Salvage deleted files.
    c. Purge files.
    d. All of the above.

27. The files of the NWADMIN and ELECTRO TEXT utilities provide context-sensitive help.
    a. True
    b. False

28. When using the DOS text utilities, press the _____ key to modify an entry.
    a. F4
    b. F3
    c. Enter
    d. Insert

29. The _____ will block rights from passing to the level of the structure.
    a. MRM (Maximum Rights Mask)
    b. MRF (Maximum Rights Filter)

c. IRM (Inherited Rights Mask)

d. IRF (Inherited Rights Filter)

30. Which of the following services does NDS regulate?
    a. Printers
    b. Volumes
    c. Files
    d. All of the above
    e. None of the above

31. NDS objects include:
    a. Physical, Logical, and Virtual
    b. [Root], Container, and Leaf
    c. File servers, Volumes, and Directories
    d. Users, Groups, and Trustees

32. It is possible to block the Supervisor NDS OBJECT right below the assigned level.
    a. True
    b. False

33. To view your current context in the NDS structure, type _____ at the workstation prompt.
    a. CL
    b. CD
    c. MOVE
    d. CX

34. Property rights for the NDS Property include the following:
    a. Read
    b. Supervisor
    c. Add or Delete self
    d. Compare
    e. All of the above

35. You can create a new [Root] object at any time.
    a. True
    b. False

36. Which of the following are NDS Object rights?
    a. Read
    b. Write

    c. Browses
    d. Both *a* and *b*
37. Leaf objects use the attribute of _____.
    a. LF
    b. OU
    c. CN
    d. LO
38. NDS allows you to create two users with the same login name as long as you create them in different containers.
    a. True
    b. False
39. The Acronym *ACL* is short for:
    a. Access Common List
    b. All Control Lines
    c. Access Control List
    d. None of the above
40. A Trustee file or directory assignment can be made to a:
    a. User
    b. Group
    c. Container object
    d. Both *a* and *b*
    e. All of the above

# Brain Teaser

Ready for a challenging puzzle designed to help you pass the certification exam? The word-search puzzle in Fig. 14-22 will test your knowledge of terms associated with NetWare 4.x—especially those terms associated with network administration. (There are a few terms from the Windows 95 Client 32 section of the chapter as well, so make sure you read that section if you haven't already.) All you need to do is find each term in the letter grid. Make sure you look forward, backward, diagonally, and vertically since the terms could be hidden in any of those positions. You'll find the solution for this brain teaser in App. C, "Brain Teaser Answers."

**Figure 14-22**
NetWare 4.x Administration Word Search.

```
R  N  Z  A  C  C  O  U  N  T  S  G  N  R  I  P  X  A
D  I  R  E  C  T  O  R  I  E  S  I  F  I  Q  U  R  Y
N  M  D  O  S  C  R  I  P  T  G  W  C  U  S  T  E  N
S  D  N  T  F  R  E  D  R  O  W  S  S  A  P  T  S  K
R  A  U  I  S  O  D  S  L  H  A  G  P  F  U  W  A  D
E  W  A  D  M  I  N  I  S  T  R  A  T  I  O  N  R  O
S  N  O  V  E  L  L  O  R  T  N  O  C  B  R  I  E  W
U  R  I  O  Q  U  Z  E  Y  S  F  V  J  L  G  R  C  N
J  A  M  L  F  A  E  L  E  P  T  E  F  H  A  O  B  L
C  X  S  U  N  I  T  I  R  E  C  F  T  N  N  Y  D  O
L  P  T  M  G  O  T  H  J  T  E  S  N  T  I  M  C  A
R  C  R  E  K  R  O  W  T  E  N  E  E  T  Z  L  L  D
O  E  I  C  E  F  B  A  W  L  R  X  W  R  A  T  I  X
O  A  V  P  R  I  S  N  O  I  T  C  I  R  T  S  E  R
T  N  O  I  D  E  N  T  I  F  I  C  A  T  I  O  N  B
A  R  B  N  R  L  A  Z  P  X  R  E  B  O  O  T  T  C
P  R  I  N  T  D  K  T  T  E  N  R  E  T  N  I  E  L
H  G  C  O  M  P  U  S  E  R  V  E  R  Z  N  F  P  V
```

*Term List*

1. Access
2. Accounts
3. Administration
4. ASCII
5. Client
6. CompuServe
7. Context
8. Control
9. Create
10. Directories
11. Download
12. Driver
13. Erase
14. Field
15. File
16. Groups
17. Identification
18. INF
19. Internet
20. IPX
21. ISO
22. Leaf
23. LISTDIR
24. Login
25. MSAU
26. NAEC
27. NDS
28. Network
29. NIST
30. Novell
31. NWADMIN
32. Object
33. Online
34. Organization
35. Password
36. Print
37. Properties
38. Reboot
39. Restrictions
40. Rights
41. Root
42. SAP
43. Script
44. Server
45. Tree
46. Unit
47. Users
48. Volume
49. WAN
50. Write

You'll want to spend some time looking up these terms in either the glossary or in App. A after you complete the word-search puzzle. You'll also want to see how these terms are used in context by looking them up in the chapter again. Of course, learning the terms should also provide food for thought. For example, do you really know what the term *IRM* means? It's questions like this that Novell is going to ask, so you'd better be prepared to provide the answers. You may also want to design your own word-search puzzle of terms. Looking for terms in this kind of puzzle really embeds them in your mind.

## Disk Time

Don't forget to spend some time working with the disk that accompanies this book. It provides valuable and fun-to-use teaching aids that help prepare you for the exam. See "Disk Time" in the preface of this book for details about what the disk contains. Make sure you focus on the NetWare 4.x and Acronym questions if you're running out of time when playing the Red Zone game.

# CHAPTER 15
# NetWare 4.x Advanced Administration

# Introduction

This chapter looks at the requirements for the NetWare 4.x Advanced Administration exam. Remember that the NetWare 4.x Administration exam tested your knowledge of simpler procedures and concentrated on the workstation and server setup rather than on the server console. In this exam you can count on being extensively tested by Novell on your knowledge of NetWare procedures—especially those related to console operation. (In fact, Novell has actually increased the intensity of console-related questions since introducing IntranetWare.) You'll need to be especially careful of questions that could have more than one correct answer. For many of you, this test will represent the last step in the certification process, and Novell has to be able to vouch for your levels of knowledge.

There are several discrete sections in this chapter. Each section helps you study for the exam in a different way. You can improve your chances of passing the exam by using all of the study methods provided in this chapter at least once and your favorite sections at least twice. Review the study guidelines in Chap. 4 as often as necessary to ensure that you maintain the best possible study atmosphere.

The first section of this chapter is a *case study*. You'll perform some hands-on tasks that will help you learn what you need to know to pass the examination. In this chapter, we concentrate on some of the more complicated tasks that you might perform. You'll learn how to work with printers, repair the NDS database, and check a volume for errors. We also take a short look at what you'd need to do to install long filename support on a server, which is one of the tasks that many of you will need to perform as companies switch to workstation operating systems like Windows 95. Even though you'll get a lot more from this section if you perform it on your own network, the inclusion of screen shots and step-by-step instructions will help you gain something from the section even if you don't have a network.

The second area contains *sample test questions* for this course. The main emphasis of many of the questions is on server-related activities, especially those you have to perform at the server console. We cover some other areas as well, but most of the workstation-related material is covered in detail in Chap. 14. This section also includes the correct answers and an explanation of why each answer is correct. It's important to understand why a particular answer is correct so that you can get into the Novell way of thinking about the network. Try to answer each question yourself, look at the correct answer, and then determine where you went wrong if you did not answer correctly.

# Netware 4.x Advanced Administration

The next section is the *fun test*. As with the study questions section, you'll find a number of server-related questions—especially ones that deal with the server console. This is an exercise where you'll answer some sample test questions. The answers appear in App. B at the back of the book. This will help you test what you learned in the previous section.

The final text section of the chapter is the *brain teaser*. You'll get to have a little fun working on a NetWare 4.x Advanced Administration–related puzzle. In this case, you'll get to pit your skills against a crossword puzzle specially designed to test your NetWare knowledge. This crossword puzzle uses Chaps. 14 to 16 as its main sources of information, though you'll find acronyms in it as well. Make sure you really understand the meaning behind each word you put into the crossword puzzle, even if you get it by default when you add the surrounding words. You may even want to take the opportunity to look these words up in the glossary after you've completed the puzzle itself. Make absolutely certain that you take the time to get everything you can out of the list of words in this crossword puzzle—even though the puzzle's meant to be fun, it's also meant to teach you something important about your certification.

Finally, you'll spend some time using the *Jeopardy!*-type game. This section helps you look at the test from the opposite viewpoint. The game provides you with an answer—you need to come up with the corresponding question. The game awards points for correct answers, and takes points away for incorrect answers. You'll receive a score at the end of the game proclaiming that you either did or did not get your certificate.

Since this will be your final exposure to NetWare 4.x before the exam, make sure you spend plenty of time studying the chapter. It's an especially good idea to save the fun test section until you're almost certain that you possess all the required knowledge. Remember, you can probably go through the fun test only two or three times at most before you'll start to remember the answers without really knowing the material.

## Case Study

This case study covers the process of setting up the printing environment, repairing the NDS database, and repairing the NetWare volume. We also spend some time adding long filename support to a server, though this knowledge isn't absolutely required for the exam. (Novell could always start testing for this information, but as of this writing they haven't.) While these topics are unrelated, they're essential components of setting up and maintaining the health of your network. Each topic covers the fundamentals; you'll need to practice on your network to get the details down pat. Remember, the better your knowledge base, the better your chances of passing the exams. Of course, this knowledge base will also help you apply yourself in the marketplace.

The printing portion of the case study walks you through the steps required to create the print queue objects, printer objects, and print server objects in the NDS database. In this portion of the case study you use the NetWare Administrator utility to create a print queue object for the Accounting and Sales users. The print queues will send print jobs to printers located in the accounting office and in the sales bullpen. Each printer will connect to a workstation in the associated areas. One print server will service both print queues and the print server software will load on the file server. Once you create the print objects, the exercise will instruct you how to link the print queue to the printer and link the printer to the print server. In the final print section, you install the print server software on the file server and install the remote printer software on the workstation.

The next two sections of the case study show you how to use two of NetWare's repair utilities to fix problems with the NDS database and the NetWare volume. The repair utilities are *DSREPAIR* and *VREPAIR*. You use DSREPAIR to fix NDS, and VREPAIR to repair the volume. Both of these utilities are NLMs that run on the file server. Make sure you study these sections especially well—you'll definitely see questions related to one or both utilities on the test since they perform such important functions.

The final section of the case study shows you the fastest, most efficient method for adding long filename support to your NetWare 4.x server. We assume a couple of things in this section; first of all, that you're actually using a NetWare 4.x server. IntranetWare servers may use different names for some of the drivers you'll need. As a result, even though the procedure is the same, you'll need to modify filenames in our instructions slightly if you're using IntranetWare. Second, we assume that you plan to use long filename support with Windows 95. You can also use this support with OS/2—the console part of the picture doesn't change one bit. However, all of the instructions are slanted toward use with Windows 95 and you may need to change some of the workstation-related steps if you're using OS/2 instead. Finally, we assume that by the time you reach this part of the case study you'll be somewhat proficient at working with NetWare. Don't attempt to perform this section of the case study first—build up to it by looking at the other sections.

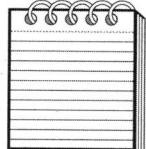

**NOTE** *This case study assumes that you have completed the case study in Chap. 14. You must complete that case study or have a machine available that uses approximately the same setup or the procedures in this chapter won't work. It's also important that you understand the procedures in Chap. 14 before you start working on this chapter, since we build on the knowledge you learned previously.*

## Print Queue Setup

The first step in setting up the printing environment for a network is to create a *print queue*. In the following steps you create a print queue for the Accounting users and another print queue for the Sales users. The print queues are in the Accounting and Sales Organizational Unit objects, respectively.

1. Log into the file server as user *Admin*.
2. Start Windows, open the NetWare Tools folder, and open the NWADMIN utility.
3. Double-click on the Accounting and Sales Organizational Unit objects to expand the view.
4. Click once with the right mouse button on the Accounting Organizational Unit object to open an action menu. When the menu opens, click once on the Create option.
5. When the New Object window opens, double-click on the Print Queue object to select it. A dialog box will open. In the Print Queue Name field type *ACCOUNTING-Q* and press Tab to move the cursor to the next Print Queue Volume field. Move the pointer to the Browser button and click it once. When the Select Object dialog box opens, double-click on the up arrow icon from the Directory Context window to change the context. From the Objects window double-click on the 401_SYS Volume object; this will return you to the Create Print Queue dialog box. Click once on the Define Additional Properties option. Figure 15-1 shows the completed Create Print Queue dialog box. When your screen matches the figure, click once on the Create button. This will create the print queue and open a details window.
6. This step documents the Print Queue. The first screen shows the Identification dialog box. In the Other Names field, type *PQ-1* and press Tab. In the Description field, type *PRINT QUEUE FOR*

**Figure 15-1**
Create Print Queue Dialog Box.

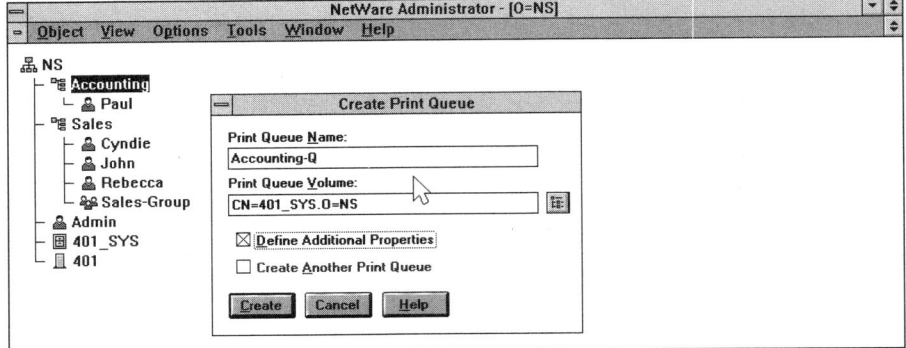

ACCOUNTING and press Tab twice. In the Department field, type ACCOUNTING. Compare your screen to the one in Fig. 15-2. When the screens match, click once on the OK button to save the information.

7. Create a print queue for Sales. Click once on the Sales Organizational Unit object with the right mouse button. When the menu opens, click once on Create. Repeat Steps 5 and 6 using the following information:

```
Print Queue Name: Sales-Q
Print Queue Volume: CN=401_SYS.O=NS
Other Names: PQ-2
Description: PRINT QUEUE FOR SALES
Department: SALES
```

**Figure 15-2**
Identification Dialog Box after Filling Description and Department Fields.

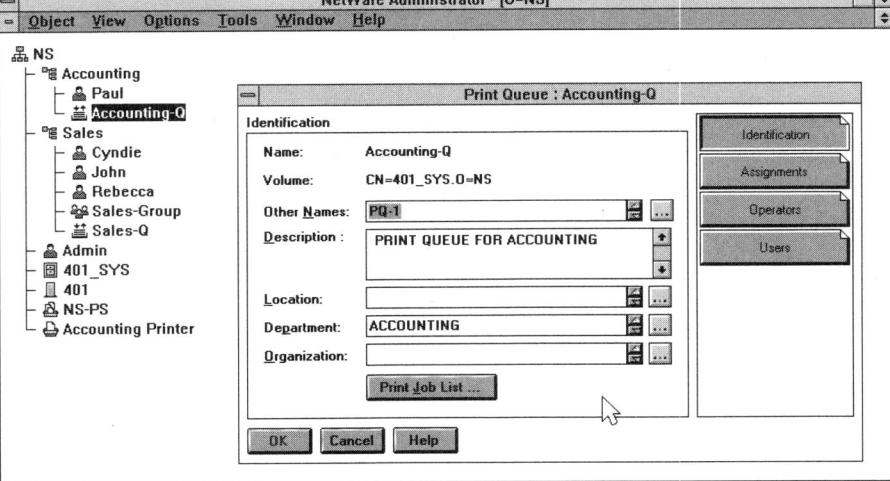

## Print Server Setup

The second step in setting up the printing environment is to create the *print servers*. You'll create one Print Server object during this exercise. The Print Server object is part of the NS Organization for ease of management. Both the Accounting and Sales print queues will use the same print server.

1. If you haven't done so, open the NetWare Tools folder and double click the NWADMIN icon to open the NetWare Administrator utility.
2. Point to the NS Organization object and click once with the right mouse button to open an action menu. After the menu appears, click once on the Create option to open the Create New Object window.
3. When the Create New Object window opens, point to the Print Server Object and double-click on it. In the Print Server Name field, type *NS-PS*. Next, mark the Define Additional Properties field by pointing to and clicking once on that field. After defining the Print Server name and selecting the Define Additional Properties field, click once on the Create button. A detail window will appear after NetWare creates the Print Server object.
4. By default, the Information dialog box is the first screen to appear. Move the cursor to the Other Names field, type *NS-PRINT SERVER* and press Tab twice to move the cursor to the Description field. Type *PRINT SERVER FOR ACCOUNTING AND SALES* and press Tab. Next, edit the Location field—type *NLM ON FILE SERVER 401* and press Tab, then type *ACCOUNTING AND SALES* in the Department field. Figure 15-3 shows the completed Information dialog box. After editing the Information dialog box, click once on the OK button to save the information.

## Printer Setup

The third step in setting up the printing environment is to create the *printer object*. The Printer Objects for this exercise are part of the NS Organization object. You'll create two Printer objects, one for Accounting and the other for Sales. The Print Queue objects must then link to the appropriate printers.

1. If you haven't done so, open the NetWare Tools folder and double-click the NWADMIN icon to open the NetWare Administrator utility.

**Figure 15-3**
Completed Identification Dialog Box for Print Server Setup.

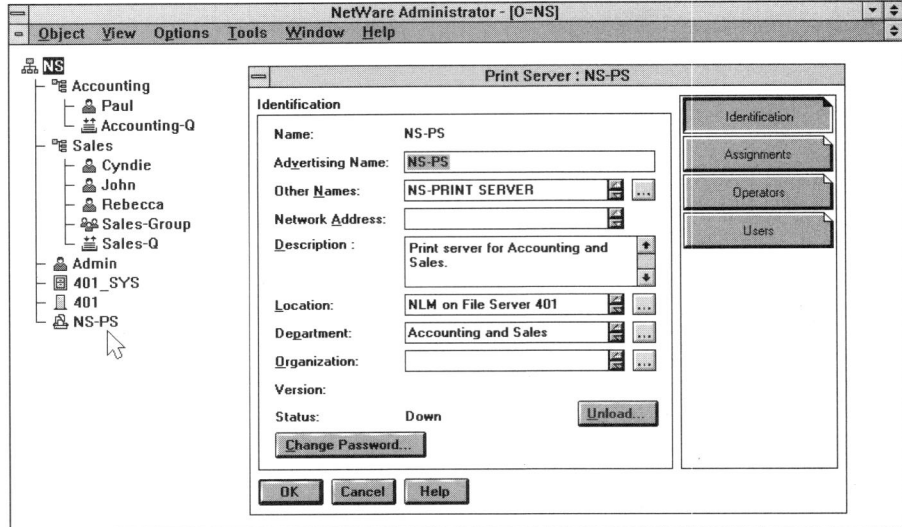

2. Move the pointer to the NS Organization object and click the right mouse button once to open an action menu. From the menu, click once on the Create Option to open the Create New Object window.

3. When the Create New Object window opens, create the Printer Object by double-clicking on it. In the Printer Name field, type *ACCOUNTING PRINTER*. Next, mark the Define Additional Properties field by pointing to and clicking once on that field. After defining the Printer name and selecting the Define Additional Properties field, click once on the Create button. A detail window will appear after NetWare creates the Printer object.

4. By default, the Information dialog box is the first screen to appear. Move the cursor to the Other Names field, type *PRINTER-0* and press Tab once to move the cursor to the Description field. Type *PRINTER FOR USE BY ACCOUNTING* and press Tab twice. The next fields to edit are Location and Department. Type *PAUL'S OFFICE* in the Location field and press Tab. Type *ACCOUNTING* in the Department field. Figure 15-4 shows the completed Information dialog box.

5. The next step is to link the printer to the print queue. Click once on the Assignments page button. When the Assignments window opens, click the Add button once to open the Select Object window. In the Directory Context window, select the Accounting Organizational Unit object by pointing to and double-clicking on it. When the

# Netware 4.x Advanced Administration

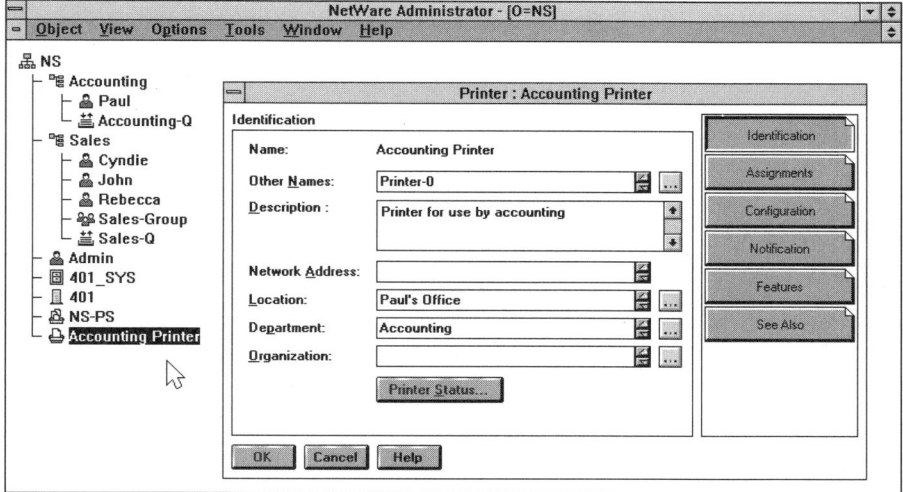

**Figure 15-4**
Completed Identification Dialog Box for Printer Setup.

Accounting-Q object appears in the Objects window, double-click it. The Assignments window will return to the screen. Figure 15-5 shows the completed Assignments window. Notice that the Print Server field is blank. NetWare will automatically fill this field in later.

6. Define the method that the printer will use to communicate to the print server by clicking once on the Configuration page button. When the dialog box opens, click once on the Communication button.

**Figure 15-5**
Completed Assignments Window for Printer Setup.

Change the Connection Type from the Auto Load (Local to Print Server) option to Manual Load (Remote from Print Server) option by clicking on the Manual Load line. Figure 15-6 shows the new settings. When your screen looks like the figure, click the OK button to save the changes.

7. Create the Printer Object for sales. Repeat Steps 2 to 5 and use the name *SALES PRINTER* for this Printer Object. Use the Sales-Q Print Queue object in the Sales Organizational Unit object when linking the Printer Object to the Print Queue Object. Use the following information when defining the Identification page. Figure 15-7 shows the completed Identification dialog box for the Sales Printer Object.

```
Identification:
Printer Name: Sales Printer
Other Names: Printer-1
Description: Printer for use by Sales
Location: Sales Bull-Pen
Department: Sales
Configuration/Communication:
Port: LPT1
Interrupts: Polled
Connection Type: Manual Load (Remote From Print Server)
```

8. The next few steps will link the printers to the print server. From the NetWare Administrator window, click once on the NS-PS object with the right mouse button. When the action menu appears, click the Details option once.

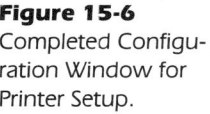

**Figure 15-6**
Completed Configuration Window for Printer Setup.

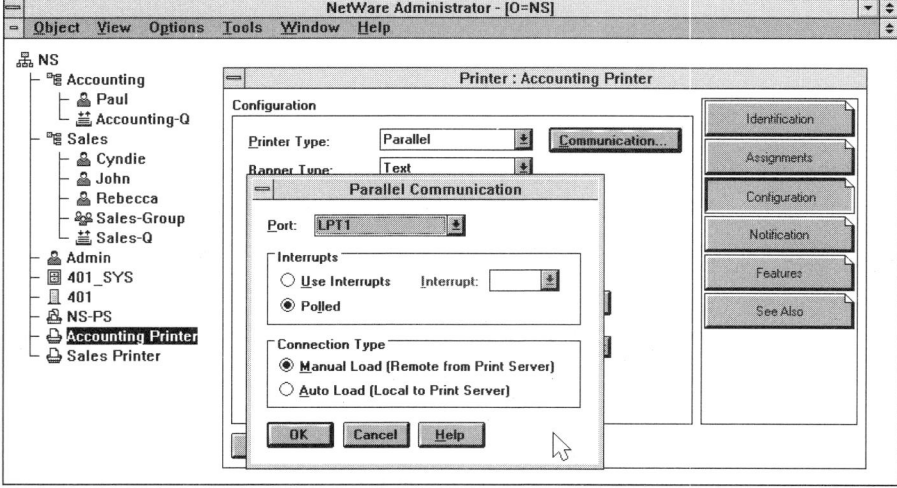

# Netware 4.x Advanced Administration

**Figure 15-7**
Completed Identification Dialog Box for the Sales Printer Object.

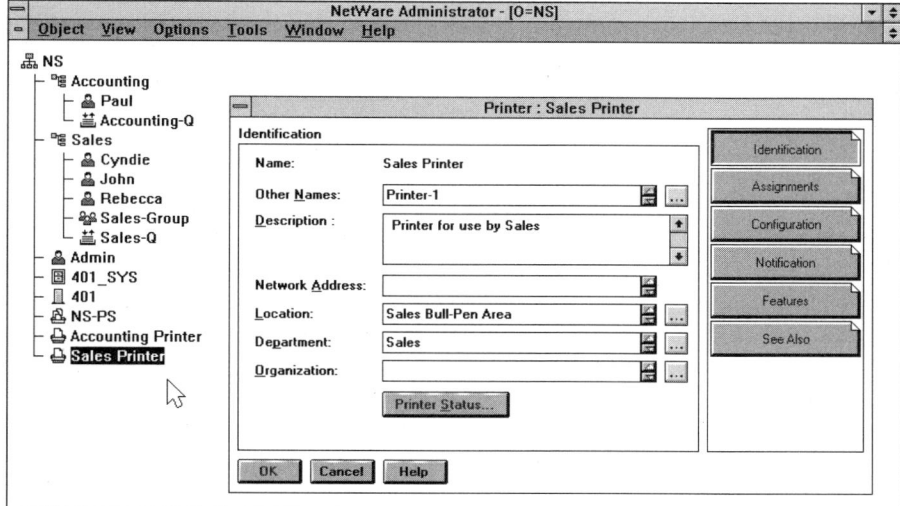

9. When the Details dialog box opens, click once on the Assignments page button. The Assignments dialog box will open. Click once on the Add button; this will open a Select Objects window. Since the Accounting Printer object and Sales Printer objects are in the same context as the Print Server object, they automatically show up in the Object window. Shift-click once on each Printer object to mark them. After marking both objects, click the OK Button once. This will assign both printers to the print server. Figure 15-8 shows the Printer objects added to the Print Server object. After comparing Fig. 15-7 with your screen, click once on the OK button to save the changes.

10. This step verifies the link between the Printer object and the Print Server object. From the NetWare Administrator window click on the Accounting Printer object with the right mouse button. Click on the Select Details menu option. Click on the Assignment page button. Since the Printer and Print Server objects have a link to one another, the Print Server object and path appear in the Print Server field. Figure 15-9 shows the dialog box with the Print Server field now complete.

## Printing Software Installation

This section covers the steps necessary to set up the print server. For this case study, the print server software will load on the file server as an

460                                                                    **Chapter Fifteen**

**Figure 15-8**
Assignments Window Showing Printer Objects Added to Print Server Object.

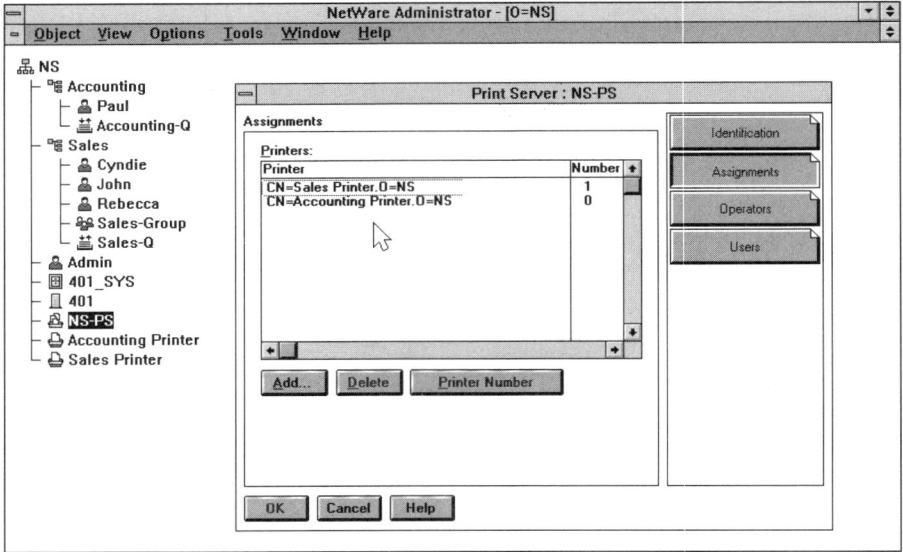

NLM. The workstations with the printers attached will load the remote printer software.

1. At the File Server prompt type *LOAD SERVER NS-PS* and press Enter. This will load the Print Server NLM into the file server memory. Figure 15-10 shows the Print Server management screen.

**Figure 15-9**
Assignments Window with Completed Print Server Field.

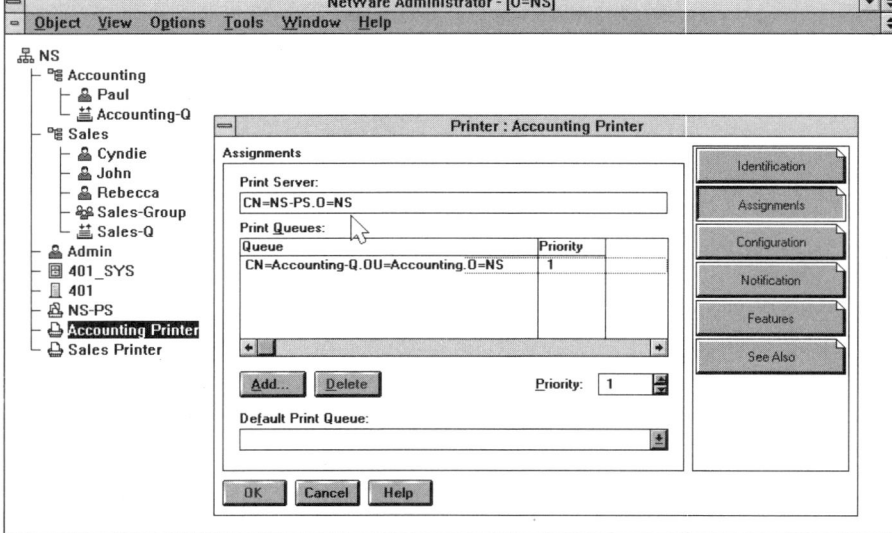

# Netware 4.x Advanced Administration

**Figure 15-10**
Print Server Management Screen.

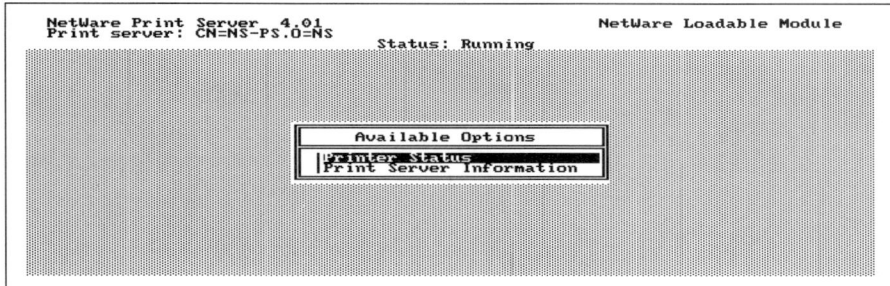

2. Go to the workstation with the printer connected to it and log into the File Server. Type *NPRINTER* and press Enter to start the remote printer software.* NPRINTER displays a menu listing the Available Print Servers on the network. Figure 15-11 shows the list of available Print Servers. Move the highlight bar to the NS-PS Print Server and press Enter. A list of predefined remote Printers will appear.

3. Highlight the Accounting Printer, then press Enter. Figure 15-12 shows the list of available remote printers. Move the highlight bar to the ACCOUNTING PRINTER and press Enter. The NPRINTER software will load as a TSR, unload the menu screen, and display a message stating that the software is in memory.

4. The workstations must issue the capture statement to redirect printing from their local LPT port to the appropriate print queue. Type one of the following capture statements at the workstation prompt. You can add this statement to a batch file or to the login script. In the following example, the first line is the capture statement for the Accounting users and the second line is for the Sales

---

*You can bypass the menu selections by typing the full command at the prompt. The full syntax is *NPRINTER (PRINT SERVER) (PRINTER NUMBER)*.

**Figure 15-11**
Available Print Servers Screen.

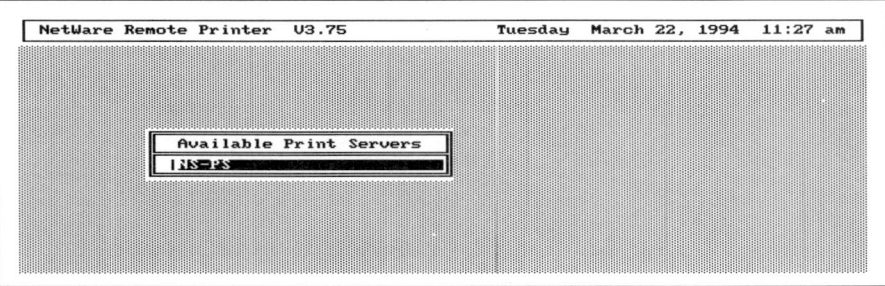

**Figure 15-12**
Available Print Servers Screen Showing Available Remote Printers.

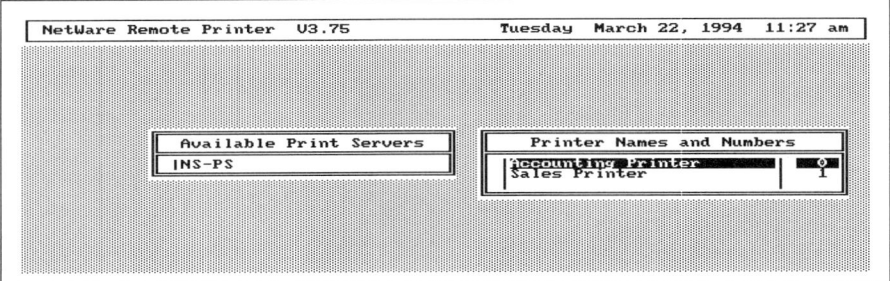

users. After executing one of the following commands, send a print job from that workstation to the printer.

```
CAPTURE Q=ACCOUNTING-Q NT NB NFF TI-10
CAPTURE Q=SALES-Q NT NB NFF TI-10
```

This completes the printing setup. Keep in mind that this represents only one way with one utility of setting up your network printers. Regardless of the utility you decide to use, the concepts and many of the steps are the same. You should practice this setup several times with the different utilities until you can complete the process without looking at the case study. As you practice setting up the printing environment, make sure that you familiarize yourself with the different options and windows. The more you know about the different options, the better your chances are of passing the exams.

## DSREPAIR

Like other databases, the NDS database can occasionally become corrupt. The DSREPAIR utility attempts to repair these problems. NetWare locks the NDS when you run the DSREPAIR utility. It's a good idea to run the utility after hours when the users are off the system. Another good precaution is to have a current backup of the NDS in case any unrecoverable problems should arise. This case study walks you through using the DSREPAIR utility.

1. At the File Server prompt, type *LOAD DSREPAIR* and press Enter. This will load the DSREPAIR utility into the file server memory. A menu will then list the available options of DSREPAIR. Figure 15-13 shows the main menu of DSREPAIR.

2. To start the DSREPAIR repair process for the NDS, press option 2. The repair process will immediately start repairing the NDS struc-

**Figure 15-13**
DSREPAIR Main Menu.

```
Netware 4.01 Directory Services Repair Utility

Options:
        1. Select Options
        2. Begin Repair
        3. Exit

        Enter your choice:
```

ture. DSREPAIR displays a status screen showing the area it is checking as it checks the different areas of the database. Figure 15-14 shows the status screen after DSREPAIR finishes checking the system. A message at the bottom of the screen instructs you to press any key to continue. Press Enter to return to the main menu.

3. Type 3 to exit when the DSREPAIR utility is complete. When the DSREPAIR.NLM unloads from the file server memory, the last thing it does is unlock the NDS database. This allows users to use the services again.

# VREPAIR

From time to time the NetWare volumes may experience problems with FAT tables, directory tables, and files. The VREPAIR utility will attempt to repair these problems. Make sure that you have a good backup of the system just in case VREPAIR cannot make the repairs. It's a good idea to run the VREPAIR utility after working hours when the users are off the system unless it is an emergency. In this case study, you'll use the VREPAIR utility to repair volume SYS.

**Figure 15-14**
DSREPAIR Status Screen after Completion of System Check.

```
Netware 4.01 Directory Services Repair Utility Status Screen
Total errors: 1
Press F1 to change settings
Start 1:00:03 pm
STRUCTURE>.................................................<
SCHEMA>...................................................<
Generating Schema Cache
MASTER     : [Root]
EXTERNAL REFERENCES>......................................<
INITIAL STATES>...........................................<
TRUSTEE SYS>
Purging invalid trustees from volume SYS
Checking mail directories
Checking stream syntax files
Repair process completed, total errors found = 1
<WARNING: Directory files are LOCKED until you exit DSREPAIR>
Finish 1:00:18 pm
Total Time 0:00:16
<Press any key to continue>
```

1. At the File Server prompt, type *LOAD VREPAIR* and press Enter. This will load the VREPAIR utility into the file server memory. VREPAIR will display a menu listing the available options. Figure 15-15 shows the VREPAIR main menu.

2. To use VREPAIR on a volume, you must first dismount the volume. At the file server prompt, press the hot-key combination of Alt-Escape to return to the console prompt. At the File Server prompt, type *DISMOUNT SYS* and press Enter. This will dismount the volume and make it available for repairs.

3. Using the Alt-Escape hot-key combination, switch back to the VREPAIR utility. To start repairing the volume, type *1* and press Enter. The VREPAIR will start repairing the volume. It displays a status screen as it checks the volume.

4. After VREPAIR finishes repairing the volume, it displays a status screen showing how many errors it found on the volume (Fig. 15-16). A message at the bottom of the screen instructs you to press any key to continue. Press Enter to return to the main menu.

5. Press 0 to exit the utility. After returning to the File Server prompt, remount the volume by typing MOUNT SYS, then press Enter. After the volume mounts, all services of that volume are available again.

## Adding Long Filename Support

Windows 95 provides a feature that Windows probably should have provided a long time ago—long filename support. Using long filenames for files allows you to find what you need more quickly, and you don't have to come up with those interesting short names for files. Unfortunately, NetWare doesn't support long filenames unless you do a little extra work. The

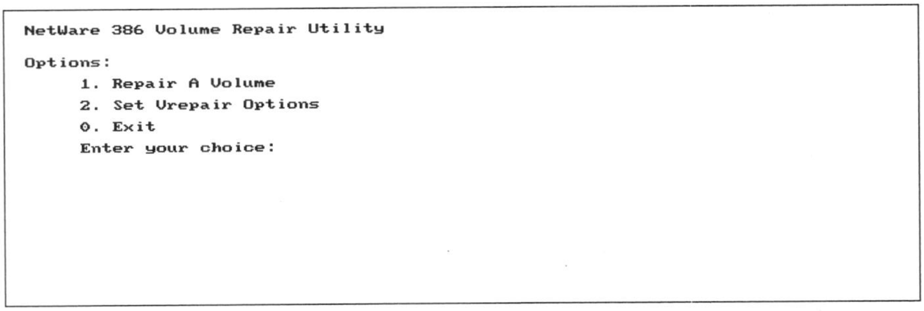

**Figure 15-15**
VREPAIR Main Menu.

```
NetWare 386 Volume Repair Utility

Options:
    1. Repair A Volume
    2. Set Vrepair Options
    0. Exit
Enter your choice:
```

# Netware 4.x Advanced Administration

**Figure 15-16**
VREPAIR Status Screen after Completion of Volume Repair.

```
Total errors: 0
Current settings:
   Pause after each error
   Do not log errors to a file
Press F1 to change settings

Start  2:23:19 pm
Checking volume SYS

FAT blocks>.....
Counting directory blocks and checking directory FAT entries ................ <
Mirror mismatches>.............................................................<
Directories>..................................................................<
Files>........................................................................<
Trustees>.....................................................................<
Deleted Files>................................................................<
Free blocks>..................................................................<

Done checking volume
Total Time  0:00:12
<Press any key to continue>
```

following procedure tells you how to install long filename support. It's the fastest, most efficient way to do so.

**NOTE**  *You'll need to down your server to implement this change, so you'll probably want to do it on a weekend. Since this procedure won't take you more than a few minutes per server to perform, you won't need to take the network offline for a long period of time*

1. Make sure you have the most current OS2.NAM name space file. You can download the most current drivers from Novell's Internet site at http://www.novell.com or from their CompuServe forum. (You can always check the status of the patches on your server and workstations by looking at the Minimum OS, NLM, and File Updates site at http://support.novell.com/search/patlst.htm.)

2. Once you get the needed driver, copy it from a local drive to the \SYSTEM directory on the server. There are two console commands you'll need to use to install name space support (at the server, not at your workstation).

3. Load name space support for long filenames by typing *LOAD OS2.NAM* at the file server console. Once the name space is loaded, you'll need to tell NetWare to use it.

4. Type *ADD NAME SPACE OS2 TO <Volume Name>* to tell NetWare which volume to use long filename support on. For example, if you wanted to add long filename support to volume SYS, then you'd type *ADD NAME SPACE OS2 TO SYS*. You need to add long filename support to each volume separately.

5. Down the server.

6. Add the OS2.NAM file to the DOS directory containing the rest of your server software.
7. Restart the server. The long filename support should be installed automatically as the server boots. (The message may pass too quickly for you to actually see it, so you'll have to actually test the installation to be sure that the long filename support was loaded.)
8. Check the long filename support from a Windows 95 workstation. You should be able to create a file or folder containing a long filename. Don't try to change the name of an existing file—use a blank file or folder for the purpose of testing long filename support.

## Study Questions

1. The NetWare 4.x NDS provides bindery emulation for older versions of NetWare.
   a. True
   b. False

   *a.* The NetWare 4.x operating system provides a bindery emulation, making it compatible with previous versions.

2. A distinct unit of data in the NDS services forms a:
   a. Partition
   b. Directory
   c. Leaf Object
   d. Bindery

   *a.* NetWare 4.x divides the NDS database into manageable partitions.

3. _____ are copies of an NDS partition.
   a. Files
   b. Organizational Units
   c. Replicas
   d. Images

   *c.* Replicas are copies of the NDS database partitions. These replicas are most often on other file servers.

# Netware 4.x Advanced Administration

4. You can create partitions and replicas of the NDS with which utility?
   a. PARTMGR
   b. NetWare Administrator
   c. DSREPAIR
   d. Both *a* and *b*
   e. All of the above

   *c.* NetWare provides two utilities capable of creating partitions and replicas of the NDS: PARTMGR and NetWare Administrator.

5. The NDS Object Rights control the management of:
   a. Objects
   b. Properties
   c. The NDS
   d. All of the above

   *a.* The NDS Object Rights control the objects, which include Users, Printers, and Organizational Units.

6. Which of the following are NDS Object rights?
   a. Supervisory, Read, and Write
   b. Supervisory, Create, and Delete
   c. Browse, Write, and Delete
   d. Browse, Create, and Rename

   *d.* The NDS Object Rights include Browse, Create, and Rename. The other Object Rights are Supervisor, Delete, and Modify.

7. Property rights determine how a user can access information about:
   a. An Object
   b. A Property
   c. A Directory
   d. A File

   *a.* Property rights determine how a user can access information about an object. The objects (users, printers, and so on) have properties such as names, phone numbers, or descriptions. The property rights determine what a user can do with these properties.

8. Which of the following are NDS Property rights?
   a. Supervisory, Read, and Write
   b. Compare, Write, and Add Self

c. Read, Add Self, and Modify
d. All of the above

*b.* The rights for the properties are Compare, Write, and Add Self. Other property rights include Supervisor, Read, and Delete Self.

9. If the trustee's directory assignment for subdirectory TEMP is [RWCF] and the IRF for subdirectory TEMP is [REF], what are the trustee's effective rights for subdirectory TEMP?
   a. Read, Write, Copy, and File Scan
   b. Read, Erase, and File Scan
   c. Read, Write, Create, Erase, and File Scan
   d. Read, Write, Create, and File Scan

   *d.* The trustee's effective rights for the directory are Read, Write, Create, and File Scan. Whenever a trustee is assigned rights to a directory or file, the effective rights equal the trustee rights.

10. Which of the following can assign rights to users for the file system?
    a. NetWare Administrator
    b. NETADMIN
    c. FILER
    d. RIGHTS
    e. *a, b,* and *d*
    f. All of the above

    *f.* Any of the above utilities will assign trustee rights assignments.

11. The IRF rights always supersede all other rights.
    a. True
    b. False

    *b.* The IRF acts as a filter to restrict rights from flowing into the directory or file. A trustee's explicit rights to a directory or file will supersede the IRF only at the point of assignment.

12. If the Organizational Unit Sales has a trustee assignment of [RF] to the APPS\DB directory, user Mark has a trustee assignment of [ ] to the APPS\DB directory, the APPS\DB IRF is [SRWCEMFA], and user Mark is a Leaf Object of Sales, what are Mark's effective rights to the APPS\DB directory?
    a. Read and File Scan.
    b. All rights [SRWCEMFA].

**Netware 4.x Advanced Administration**

   c. None; you cannot assign trustee rights to the Organizational Unit.

   d. None of the above.

   *a.* As a Leaf object of the Organizational Unit Sales, Mark inherits the same rights as the Organizational Unit.

13. The NetWare 4.x auditing feature tracks which of the following?
    a. User actions
    b. Resource usage
    c. File System security
    d. All of the above

   *c.* The NetWare Auditing feature tracks User actions, Resource usage, and the File System security.

14. The utility used for Auditing a NetWare 4.x File Server is:
    a. Auditor
    b. Auditcon
    c. Auditmon
    d. NetWare Administrator

   *b.* Auditcon is the text-based menu utility to manage and monitor the auditing features of NetWare.

15. A single Print Server can service up to _____ printers.
    a. 16
    b. 26
    c. 256
    d. Unlimited

   *c.* The NetWare 4.x print server now manages up to 256 printers on the network.

16. You may have multiple print queues per printer, but not multiple printers per print queue.
    a. True
    b. False

   *b.* NetWare printing supports both multiple print queues per printer and multiple printers per print queue.

**Chapter Fifteen**

17. To check the status of the network printers, which of the following utilities would you use?
    a. PSERVER
    b. PCONSOLE
    c. NetWare Administrator
    d. All of the above

    *d.* The PSERVER, PCONSOLE, and NetWare Administrator are all utilities to check the status of network printers.

18. The acronym *SMS* is short for:
    a. System Management Services
    b. System Maintenance Scheme
    c. Storage Migration Server
    d. Storage Management Services

    *d.* Storage Management Services (SMS) refers to keeping a backup copy of your data.

19. The NetWare Storage Management Services provides NetWare with what service?
    a. Hard disk access
    b. CD-ROM compatibility
    c. Backup and restore functions
    d. All of the above

    *c.* The NetWare SMS provides the services for backing up and restoring your network data.

20. What is the name of the NetWare backup and restore program?
    a. NetWare Administrator
    b. NBACKUP
    c. SERVMAN
    d. SBACKUP

    *d.* SBACKUP is the user interface for backing up the network data.

21. When using the NetWare backup program, the tape drive is attached to the:
    a. File Server
    b. Workstation
    c. Bridge
    d. Either *a* or *b*

# Netware 4.x Advanced Administration

*a.* When using the NetWare backup program, the tape drive attaches directly to a file server.

22. At a DOS ODI workstation, the files load in what order?
    a. VLM.EXE, IPXODI.COM, NE2000.COM, and LSL.COM
    b. NE2000.COM, LSL.COM, IPXODI.COM, and VLM.EXE
    c. LSL.COM, NE2000.COM, and TCPIP.EXE
    d. None of the above

    *c.* The workstation must load the LLC software first, then the MLID, then the transport protocol. These files are the LSL.COM, NE2000.COM, and TCPIP.EXE files.

23. The _____ file provides the workstation with backwards compatibility to previous versions of NetWare.
    a. NETX.EXE
    b. NETX.VLM
    c. VLM.EXE
    d. IPXODI.COM

    *b.* The NETX.VLM provides the backwards compatibility to previous versions of NetWare.

24. To specify which VLMs will load when you execute the VLM.EXE program, edit the _____ file.
    a. VLM.INI
    b. SHELL.CFG
    c. NET.CFG
    d. VLM.CFG

    *c.* The NET.CFG file has a section for specifying which VLMs load and in what order.

25. The NetWare requester for OS/2 workstations supports:
    a. Named Pipes
    b. NLMs
    c. UNIX applications
    d. All of the above

    *a.* The NetWare requester provides the OS/2 workstation with full Named Pipes support. This means that OS/2 applications are fully supported without modifications.

26. By adding OS/2 name space support to a NetWare volume, you can store OS/2 files with names up to _____ characters long.
    a. 11
    b. 32
    c. 64
    d. 255

    *d.* By adding the name space support to a NetWare volume, you can store OS/2 files in their native name format, with all the information and attributes as well.

27. The NetWare TCP/IP NLMs require at least _____ of RAM, plus at least _____ of disk space.
    a. 1 MB, 1 MB
    b. 1 MB, 3 MB
    c. 3 MB, 1 MB
    d. 5 MB, 3 MB

    *a.* Novell recommends that when using the TCP/IP NLMs, the system have an additional 1 MB of RAM and 1 MB of hard disk space.

28. The WSUPDATE utility is used for what?
    a. Updating files at the workstation
    b. Updating the Date and Time at the workstation to match the File Server
    c. Updating the CMOS settings in the workstation
    d. Updating users about changes to the network

    *a.* The WSUPDATE utility will update files at a workstation by comparing the name and time stamp of the new file with the name and time stamp of the old file.

29. For NetWare to support filenames of operating systems other than DOS, you must:
    a. Load a name space module and add the name space to the volume.
    b. Load the name space protocol and directly connect that type of workstation to the File Server.
    c. Load another LAN card and bind a protocol to it.
    d. Copy the operating system on to the File Server and Map a drive letter to it.

# Netware 4.x Advanced Administration

    *a.* The NetWare operating system must have an additional name space NLM loaded to support file formats from other operating system. The volume must also create a special Directory Table for the non-DOS operating system.

**30.** Which utility monitors and configures the NetWare operating system?

    **a.** INSTALL
    **b.** MONITOR
    **c.** NetWare Administrator
    **d.** SERVMAN

    *d.* New to NetWare is the SERVMAN NLM. This utility will monitor and configure the NetWare operating system.

**31.** With block suballocation, NetWare can divide a data block into what size units?

    **a.** 512 bytes
    **b.** 1 K
    **c.** 4 K
    **d.** Any multiple of 4 K up to 64 K

    *a.* NetWare divides the disk allocation blocks into 512-byte units. Instead of wasting the entire disk block, a small file will now only use a 512-byte piece of the original.

**32.** Block suballocation can be enabled or disabled at any time.

    **a.** True
    **b.** False

    *b.* Only during the installation process can you enable or disable block suballocation.

**33.** By default, NetWare won't compress a file unless there's at least a(n) _____ percent savings of disk sectors.

    **a.** 80
    **b.** 63
    **c.** 20
    **d.** 2

    *d.* NetWare won't compress a file unless it can reduce the number of sectors the file uses by 2 percent.

34. To prevent NetWare from compressing a file, you need to:
    a. Copy the file to volume SYS.
    b. Flag the file with the attribute DC.
    c. Grant trustee rights to the file.
    d. Flag the file with the attribute NSRW.

    *b.* The DC (don't compress) flag will prevent a file from being compressed on the volume.

35. When viewing the Cache Utilization statistics in Monitor, the Long Term Cache Hits statistics should not fall below:
    a. 20 percent
    b. 50 percent
    c. 80 percent
    d. 90 percent

    *d.* Novell recommends that the Long Term Cache Hits shouldn't fall below 90 percent.

## Fun Test

1. Within NDS there are Objects and Properties. Which of the following are Object rights?
    a. Browse, Write, and Delete
    b. Browse, Create, and Rename
    c. Supervisory, Create, and Delete
    d. Supervisory, Read, and Write

2. To store OS/2 files on a NetWare volume with their original file names and attributes, you must:
    a. Load the name space protocol and directly connect that type of workstation to the File Server.
    b. Copy the operating system on to the File Server and Map a drive letter to it.
    c. Load another LAN card and bind a protocol to it.
    d. Load a name space module and add the name space to the volume.

# Netware 4.x Advanced Administration

3. The Auditing feature of NetWare 4.x tracks which of the following?
   a. Resource usage
   b. File system security
   c. User actions
   d. All of the above

4. The Storage Management Services of NetWare provides what service?
   a. Backup and restore functions
   b. Hard disk access
   c. CD-ROM compatibility
   d. All of the above

5. When calculating the effective rights of the NDS or file system, the IRF rights always equal your effective rights.
   a. True
   b. False

6. When using OS/2 as an operating system at the workstation, you must use the OS/2 requester that supports:
   a. UNIX applications
   b. Named Pipes
   c. NLMs
   d. All of the above

7. If user Mark has a trustee assignment of [ ] to the APPS\DB directory, Organizational Unit Sales has a trustee assignment of [RF] to the APPS\DB directory, the APPS\DB IRF is [SRWCEMFA], and user Mark is a Leaf Object of Sales, what are Mark's effective rights to the APPS\DB directory?
   a. All rights [SRWCEMFA].
   b. None; you cannot assign trustee rights to the Organizational Unit.
   c. Read and File Scan.
   d. None of the above.

8. When loading the ODI files at your workstation, what is the load order?
   a. LSL.COM, NE2000.COM, and TCPIP.EXE
   b. VLM.EXE, IPXODI.COM, NE2000.COM, and LSL.COM

c. NE2000.COM, LSL.COM, IPXODI.COM, and VLM.EXE

d. None of the above

9. The NetWare TCP/IP NLMs require at least _____ of RAM, and at least _____ of disk space.

   a. 1 MB, 1 MB
   b. 1 MB, 3 MB
   c. 3 MB, 1 MB
   d. 5 MB, 3 MB

10. The 4.x Print Server will service a maximum of _____ printers.

    a. 16
    b. 26
    c. 256
    d. Unlimited

11. The definition of the acronym *SMS* is:

    a. Storage Migration Server
    b. Storage Management Services
    c. System Maintenance Scheme
    d. System Management Services

12. Edit the _____ file to identify the VLMs you want to load when the VLM.EXE executes.

    a. VLM.CFG
    b. VLM.INI
    c. SHELL.CFG
    d. NET.CFG

13. NetWare provides a backup and restore program. What is its name?

    a. NBACKUP
    b. SERVMAN
    c. SBACKUP
    d. NetWare Administrator

14. The NDS database is created and replicated with what utility?

    a. NetWare Administrator
    b. DSREPAIR
    c. PARTMGR
    d. Both *a* and *c*
    e. All of the above

15. Attach the tape backup unit to the _____ before using the using the NetWare backup program.
    a. Bridge
    b. Workstation
    c. File Server
    d. Either *b* or *c*

16. Property rights determine how a user can access information about:
    a. A Property
    b. A File
    c. A Directory
    d. An Object

17. When _____, use the WSUPDATE utility.
    a. Updating users about changes to the network
    b. Updating files at the workstation
    c. Updating the CMOS settings in the workstation
    d. Updating the Date and Time at the workstation to match the File Server

18. You can enable or disable the NetWare Block suballocation at any time.
    a. True
    b. False

19. A distinct unit of data in the NDS services forms a:
    a. Leaf Object
    b. Directory
    c. Bindery
    d. Partition

20. To provide the 4.x workstations with backwards compatibility to previous versions of NetWare, you must load _____ on the workstation.
    a. IPXODI.COM
    b. NETX.EXE
    c. NETX.VLM
    d. VLM.EXE

21. _____ to prevent NetWare from compressing a file on the volume.
    a. Flag the file with the attribute DC
    b. Flag the file with the attribute NSRW

c. Grant trustee rights to the file

d. Copy the file to volume SYS

22. The NetWare 4.x NDS provides bindery emulation for older versions of NetWare.

   a. True
   b. False

23. Use the _____ program to assign trustee rights to a file or directory.

   a. RIGHTS
   b. NetWare Administrator
   c. NETADMIN
   d. FILER
   e. *a, b,* and *c*
   f. All of the above

24. The Long Term Cache Hits statistics should not fall below _____; this information is in the Cache Utilization statistics screen of Monitor.

   a. 20 percent
   b. 50 percent
   c. 80 percent
   d. 90 percent

25. To setup and audit the services of a 4.x file server, you must use the _____ program.

   a. Auditcon
   b. Auditmon
   c. NetWare Administrator
   d. Auditor

26. To monitor and configure the NetWare operating system after installation, you will use what program?

   a. SERVMAN
   b. NetWare Administrator
   c. INSTALL
   d. MONITOR

27. NetWare print services support multiple printers per print queue, but not multiple print queues per printer.

   a. True
   b. False

28. Block suballocation divides the data blocks into what size units?
    a. 512 bytes
    b. 1 K
    c. 4 K
    d. Any multiple of 4 K up to 64 K

29. If the trustee's directory assignment for subdirectory TEMP is [RWCF] and the IRF for subdirectory TEMP is [REF], what are the trustee's effective rights for subdirectory TEMP?
    a. Read, Erase, and File Scan
    b. Read, Write, Create, and File Scan
    c. Read, Write, Copy, and File Scan
    d. Read, Write, Create, Erase, and File Scan

30. With the appropriate support on the file server, filenames up to _____ characters by an OS/2 workstation are possible on the volume.
    a. 11
    b. 32
    c. 64
    d. 255

31. The NDS object rights control the management of:
    a. The NDS
    b. Objects
    c. Properties
    d. All of the above

32. By default, there must be a _____ percent savings of disk sectors before NetWare will compress a file.
    a. 2
    b. 20
    c. 63
    d. 80

33. Which of the following are NDS Property rights?
    a. Supervisory, Read, and Write
    b. Compare, Write, and Add Self
    c. Read, Add Self, and Modify
    d. All of the above

**Chapter Fifteen**

34. Which of the following utilities would you use to check the status of the network printers?
    a. PSERVER
    b. PCONSOLE
    c. NetWare Administrator
    d. All of the above

35. When you make copies of the NDS partitions, they're known as:
    a. Files
    b. Replicas
    c. Organizational Units
    d. Images

## Brain Teaser

Are you ready to perform advanced installation and configuration procedures with NetWare? The crossword puzzle in Fig. 15-17 may not test your ability to actually perform a variety of procedures on both the workstation and server console, but it's a fun way to test your advanced NetWare knowledge. Just work it as you would any other crossword. The clues appear in two columns, one for *down* and another for *across*. If you find that you have a hard time completing the crossword, you may want to take another look at the case study in this chapter. As in most crosswords, you'll find a lot of acronyms. Make sure you check out App. A and the glossary if you're having trouble figuring out one of the acronyms in the crossword puzzle. We also use some fairly obscure common-knowledge clues just to make the puzzle more interesting. You'll find the solution for this brain teaser in App. C, "Brain Teaser Answers."

## Disk Time

Don't forget to spend some time working with the CD-ROM that accompanies this book. It provides valuable, fun-to-use teaching aids that'll help you prepare for your exam. See "Disk Time" in the preface of this book for details about what the disk contains. Make sure you pay special attention to the parts of the Windows help file and the Red Zone game that pertain to this chapter. Most important of all are the console-related questions, but the workstation-related questions are important as well. Also, check out the acronym areas provided in both disk features—they'll help you get up to speed on what's going on in the industry faster. If you find yourself running out of time when playing Red Zone, then you probably aren't ready for this exam—remember that Novell will fully test your knowledge of NetWare 4.x.

**Figure 15-17**
Advanced NetWare Crossword Puzzle.

## Across

**1.** Entry point for server commands

**7.** NDS utility for fixing errors

**14.** Every entity within NDS

**15.** What you'll need to pass the exam

**16.** Standards group responsible for the RS-232 port

**18.** A city in western France, it's southeast of Nantes

**19.** Resolutely courageous, fearless

**21.** Novell's answer to device drivers

**22.** Recreational vehicle (abbreviation)

**23.** Not off

**24.** Computer's mimicking of the human brain

**25.** The unconscious part of the psyche

**26.** Programmer's batch file

**27.** Older than another

**30.** A separately executing part of the main program

**33.** Fourteenth letter of the Greek alphabet

**34.** Topmost NDS level

**36.** Egyptian god of the sun during the reign of Akhenaton

**37.** Novell certified individuals

**39.** Type of Service (abbreviation)

**41.** You'll need to pass one or more of these to get your certification

**43.** Eastern Rumanian city, north-northeast of Bucharest

**45.** Long filename and associated characteristics support mechanism (abbreviation)

**47.** Lowest level software on a network (abbreviation)

**49.** Plant related to the onion

**50.** Elemental symbol for gallium

**51.** Advanced Network Training Center (abbreviation)

**54.** Conclusive

**57.** Computer used to preprocess information for a mainframe (abbreviation)

**58.** To run with a steady, easy gait

**59.** Dialog box control

**61.** Hard drive host adapter standard

**64.** Seventh note of the diatonic scale

**66.** Retired warrior's assistance organization (abbreviation)

67. Either of two small American flycatchers (genus *Contopus*)
68. Spoken
69. Uneasy or troubled condition
72. Singer's cry
73. Someone on vacation
75. In addition
76. Simple instructions for encrypting data
77. Elevated in rank or age
78. Initials of Novell's older help system for NetWare
80. An imitation or substitute
85. Daytime
87. Group normally responsible for computers in a large corporation (abbreviation)
88. Measurement of the external surface of a cylinder (abbreviation)
90. Accomplished in scientific pursuits, but less than adequate socially
92. A sudden, violent display of emotion
94. A distinctive band of color on the bend of a bird's wing
96. Up in the air
97. Elemental symbol for aluminum
98. Either of two main surface veins in the leg
99. Harass or annoy

102. Group enjoying superior intellectual, social, or financial status
103. Internet search engine
104. Special mental abilities
105. Not from

## Down

1. Object NDS Location
2. A wide sash fastened in the back with a large flat bow
3. Nordic god of wealth and ships
4. Allows file and print sharing
5. Eight (German)
6. Light (abbreviation)
7. Storage medium that relies on relational theory
8. Macro instructions for logging into the server
9. Route (abbreviation)
10. The act of spying
11. Computer chip manufacturer
12. NDS object right
13. Field in the Identification dialog: Other _____
15. Function (abbreviation)
17. Type or kind
19. Adding operating system feature support
20. Interdialog Gap (abbreviation)

26. Printer connection method: _____ Load
28. Large carnivorous feline mammal
29. Fish eggs
31. A thief's job
32. Electronic manufacturing giant
35. A bovine mammal
38. NetWare password utility
40. Computer instructions
42. Myself
44. DOS and OS/2 print redirection utility
46. Flying expert
48. Internet location (node)
52. Company you're working with to get your certification
53. Highest ranking church leader of an archdiocese or region (abbreviation)
55. The cognitive process
56. American standards group (abbreviation)
57. DOS-based disk management utility
60. A tributary of the Ubangi river in northern Zaire
61. Beginning of a network transmission (abbreviation)
62. Monitor component
63. Rude and disrespectful

65. Not out
70. Elemental symbol for radium
71. A good term for your computer if you don't have a surge suppressor
74. Software or hardware that allows access from one computer system to another
76. An NDS object right
79. VREPAIR works with both directory and FAT _____.
81. User privilege granted by the network administrator
83. Elemental symbol for zirconium
84. The Windows interface is one.
86. Twelfth letter of the Greek alphabet
87. Small island
89. The front of a watch
91. To move quickly
92. An annual calendar containing instructions for the Mass
93. Standard backup media
94. A small, usually unwelcome, mammal
95. A honey of an insect
100. Naval police
101. Not writeable (abbreviation)

# CHAPTER 16
# NetWare 4.x Installation and Configuration Workshop

## Introduction

This chapter looks at the requirements for the NetWare 4.x Installation and Configuration Workshop exam. There are several discrete sections in this chapter. Each section helps you study for the exam in a different way. You can improve your chances of passing the exam by using the study methods provided in this chapter. In fact, it'll probably help if you study all the sections once and your favorite sections at least twice. Review the study guidelines in Chap. 4 as often as necessary to ensure that you maintain the best possible study atmosphere.

The first section of this chapter is a *case study*. You'll perform some hands-on tasks that will help you learn what you need to know to pass the examination. Even though you'll get a lot more from this section if you perform it on your own network, the inclusion of screen shots and step-by-step instructions will help you gain something from the section even if you don't have a network.

The second area contains *sample test questions* for this course. It also includes the correct answers and an explanation of why those answers are correct. Try to answer each question yourself, look at the correct answer, then determine where you went wrong if you didn't answer correctly.

The next section is a *fun test*. This is an exercise where you'll look at more sample test questions and answer them. The answers appear in App. B at the back of the book. This will help you test what you learned in the previous section.

The final text section of the chapter is the *brain teaser*. You'll get to have a little fun working on a NetWare 4.x–related puzzle. This chapter provides two cryptograms that should give you some ideas of ways to study for the exam. Obviously, it helps to have a good overall knowledge of NetWare 4.x in this case, since the cryptograms will be easier to solve if you can spot specific patterns in the way they're encrypted. By the way, the cryptograms use different encryption methods, so you'll have to solve each puzzle separately.

Finally, you'll spend some time using the *Jeopardy!*-type game. This section helps you look at the test from the opposite viewpoint. The game provides you with an answer—you need to come up with the corresponding question. The game awards points for correct answers, and takes points away for incorrect answers. You'll receive a score at the end of the game proclaiming that you either did or did not get your certificate.

Use all the learning methods that we provide in this chapter to improve your chances of passing the exam. It's a good idea to save the fun test sec-

# NetWare 4.x Installation and Configuration Workshop

tion until you're are almost certain that you possess all the required knowledge. Remember, you can probably go through the test only two or three times at most before you'll start to remember the answers without really knowing the material.

## Case Study

This case study covers the steps and procedures necessary to install the NetWare 4.x operating system and the workstation software. For this demonstration, the installation program will load the necessary files from another file server. The steps and procedures will be the same if you are installing directly from the CD-ROM disk. This procedure also assumes that you are using a clean, nonpartitioned hard drive. Make sure you perform a low-level format, if required, before you start the procedure.

1. Configure and install the network interface board, hard disk, and hard disk controller in the new file server. Refer to the procedures in Chap. 3 to learn how to avoid hardware configuration conflicts.

2. Boot the soon-to-be File Server to DOS and perform any procedures required to access the drive where the NetWare 4.x installation program files reside.*

3. At workstation prompt, type *CD \NETWARE.40\ENGLISH* and press Enter.

4. To start the installation program, type *INSTALL* and press Enter. The installation program will load and display the NetWare Installation Utility. Figure 16-1 shows the opening screen of the installation utility.

5. Highlight the *Install new NetWare v4.x* option, then press Enter. The install program will check your hard disk for existing partitions. If you don't have a DOS partition on your hard disk, the installation program will create one for you. If you don't want to use the NetWare utility to create a partition, cancel the installation program and create a 5-MB DOS partition now.

---

* If you are installing from a network, log into the file server and map a drive letter to the directory holding the installation program. If you are installing from a CD, load the appropriate drivers for accessing the CD.

**Figure 16-1**
NetWare Installation Utility Screen.

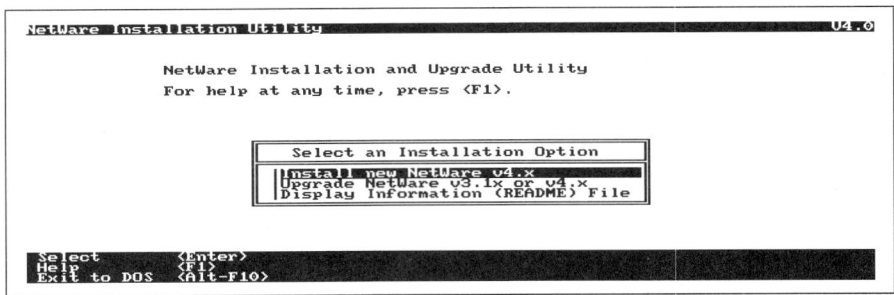

6. For this case study, the installation program will create the partition. Press Enter at the partition information screen. A screen will appear asking how big to make the partition. By default, the installation program selects a partition size of 5 MB. Press Enter to accept the default partition size. The system will restart at this point.

7. When the computer restarts, repeat Steps 2 to 4. When you restart the installation program, the program will go directly to the format option. Enter the source path to the location of *FORMAT.COM* and press Enter. FORMAT will format the drive.

8. When format is complete, select *Install new NetWare v4.x* from the installation menu. This will display the current hard disk partitions. At this point you should see a 5-MB DOS partition on the drive. The rest of the disk is free space. Figure 16-2 shows the list of partitions. Highlight the *Retain Current disk partitions* option, then press Enter. The installation utility displays a screen asking for the file server name.

9. Type *401* and press Enter. The installation utility displays a dialog box for the Internal Network Number.

10. Using the delete key, delete the default internal network number. Type *A401* and press Enter. Figure 16-3 shows the dialog box with

**Figure 16-2**
Installation Utility Screen Showing Disk Partition Options.

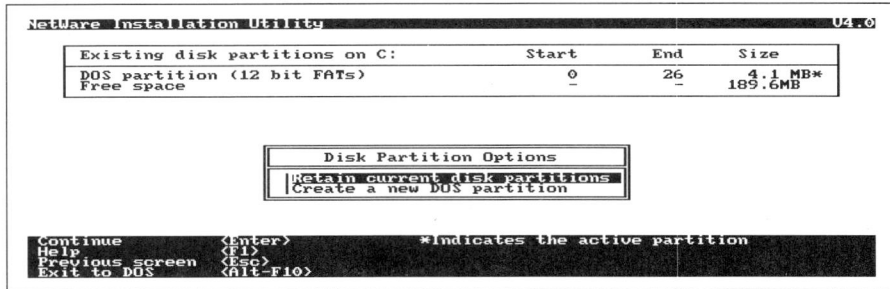

# NetWare 4.x Installation and Configuration Workshop

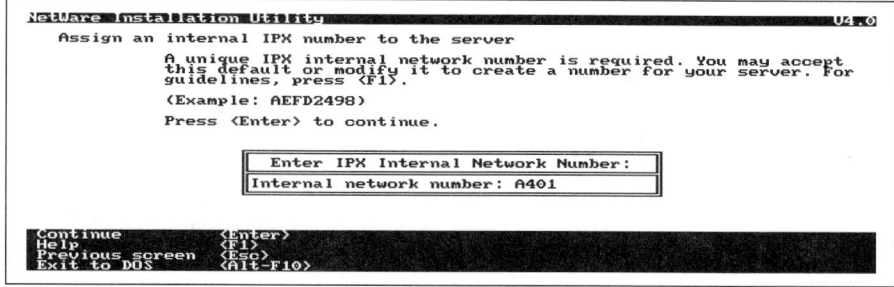

**Figure 16-3**
Installation Utility Dialog Box Showing Internal Network Number.

the new internal network number of A401. The installation utility displays a dialog box, which asks for the source and destination paths for the boot files.

11. Figure 16-4 shows the source path to our files and the destination path of C:\SERVER.40. To continue the installation process, press Enter. NetWare will copy some files to the DOS partition. After NetWare copies the files to the DOS partition, a dialog box appears showing the Country Code, Code Page, and Keyboard Mapping.

12. Press F10 to accept the default Country Code, Code Page, and Keyboard Mapping values. A dialog box will then appear asking you to select a file naming format.

13. Novell recommends the DOS Filename Format. Press Enter to accept the recommended value. The installation utility displays a screen asking if you would like to add any special commands to the Startup file.

14. Press Enter to accept the default value of *NO*. The install program will then ask if you want the AUTOEXEC.BAT file to load SERVER.EXE.

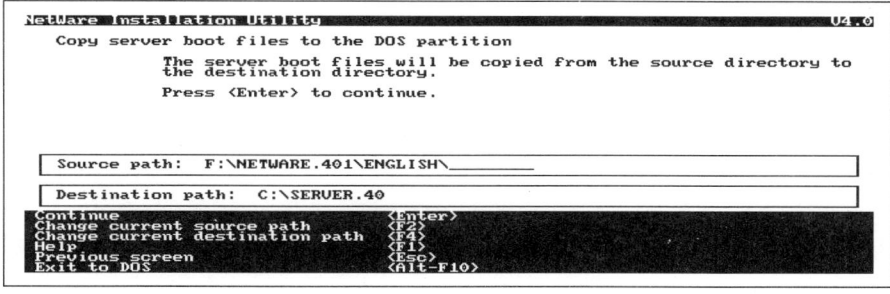

**Figure 16-4**
Installation Utility Screen Showing Source Path and Destination Path.

**Figure 16-5**
Installation Utility Screen Showing NetWare Installation Path.

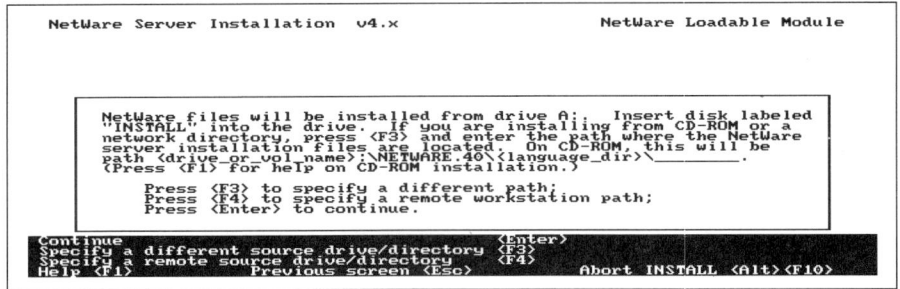

15. Press Enter to accept the default value of *YES*. Press Enter to accept the path to the AUTOEXEC.BAT file. The install program will automatically launch SERVER.EXE to start NetWare on the new server. A screen will appear that tells you which path NetWare will search for the source files. The screen will also display information about how to copy the files if you are using a CD-ROM. Figure 16-5 shows this screen.

16. Press Enter to continue. A list of available hard disk controller drivers appears.

17. Move the highlight bar to the appropriate driver, then press Enter. For our file server, the selection is ISADISK.DSK. Figure 16-6 shows the list of available controllers. A dialog box will then appear listing the parameters for configuring the controller.

18. Make any necessary changes to the hard disk controller configuration, then press F10 to exit the configuration form and load the driver. After the driver loads, press Enter when the *Strike any Key to Continue* message appears. A new menu will appear in the center of the screen, asking you to select an action.

19. Move the highlight bar to the *Continue with Installation* option, then press F10. The next screen asks if you want NetWare to auto-

**Figure 16-6**
Dialog Box Showing Controller Configuration Parameters.

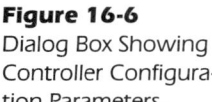

# NetWare 4.x Installation and Configuration Workshop

matically create the NetWare partition. By default, the highlight bar is on the option to automatically create the partition.

20. Press Enter to continue. NetWare will create the partition. Once it creates the partition, NetWare displays a message showing the partition size and volume name.

21. Press Enter to continue. Another screen will then appear showing you the volume and its size.

22. Press F10 to save volume changes and continue, then answer *YES* to the Save Volume Changes confirmation window. NetWare will mount the volume. The install program displays a message stating that it needs the LICENSE diskette containing the SERVER.MLS file.

23. Insert the license diskette in drive A, then press Enter. The program will read the information from the diskette and display a message stating that the license was successfully installed.

24. Press Enter to continue. NetWare will display another message indicating the installation path. The message will also display information about loading the files from a CD-ROM.

25. Press Enter to continue. The next screen lists the different utilities NetWare will copy to the file server. Figure 16-7 shows the list of options. By default, NetWare will install all items.

26. Press F10 to accept the marked options and continue. The installation utility displays a confirmation window.

27. Press Enter on *YES*. NetWare will copy the files and utilities to volume SYS. This process will take several minutes depending upon where the files are being copied from and the speed of your device. When NetWare finishes copying the files, it'll display a message stating that the file copying is complete.

28. Press Enter to continue. The install program scans the computer for a network interface board and a matching LAN driver. When this is

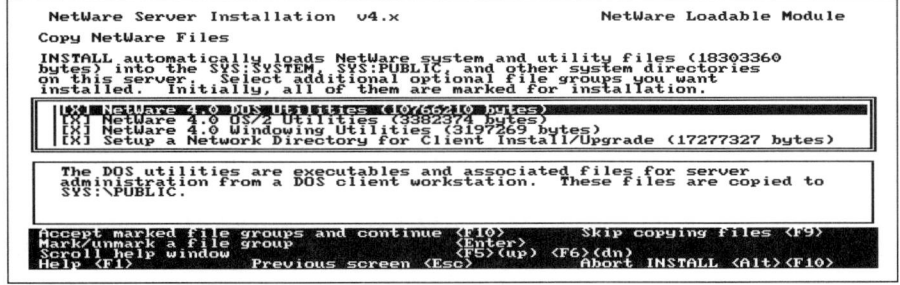

**Figure 16-7**
Dialog Box Showing Utilities NetWare Will Install.

**Figure 16-8**
LAN Driver Screen Showing Selections.

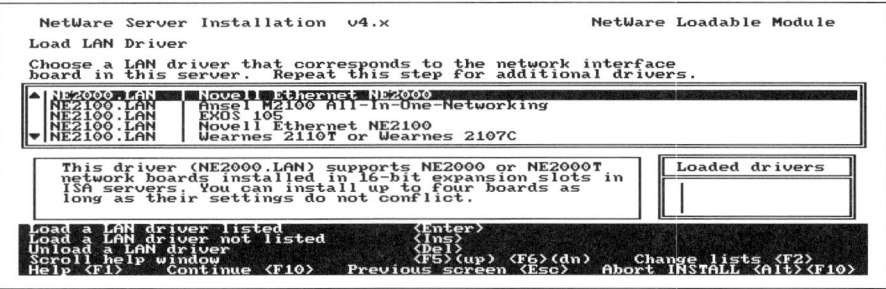

complete, NetWare displays the LAN driver list and automatically highlights the one it determined is best for your NIC. Figure 16-8 shows the selections on the LAN driver screen.

29. Press Enter to copy the LAN file to your system. A screen showing the setup parameters will appear.

30. Make the appropriate changes to match your hardware. When you reach the Frame type field, press Enter. By default, NetWare marks both Ethernet_802.3 and Ethernet_802.2 frame types. For this exercise, deselect the Ethernet_802.3 frame type by pressing Enter with the highlight bar on the Ethernet_802.3 option. Figure 16-9 shows the possible frame type selections. Note that the only selected frame type is Ethernet_802.2. Press Escape to save the frame type and return to the previous screen.

31. After you return to the LAN driver parameters window, press F10 to exit the form and load the driver. As the software loads, it scans the system looking for existing protocols and network addresses. If NetWare doesn't find the network information, a dialog box will appear prompting you to supply one. If NetWare identifies a matching protocol during the scan, it assigns that address to the network. A screen will appear listing information about the Ethernet_802.2 frame type.

**Figure 16-9**
Screen Showing Frame Type List.

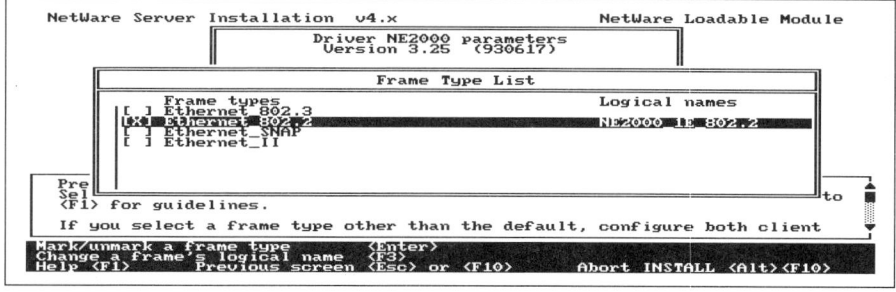

# NetWare 4.x Installation and Configuration Workshop

**Figure 16-10**
Screen Showing Ethernet_802.2 Frame Type Information.

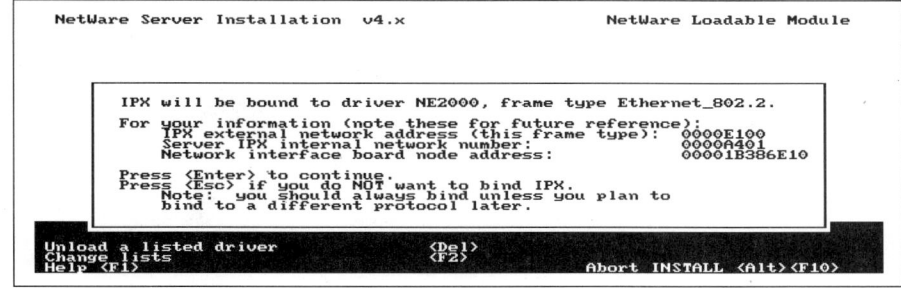

Figure 16-10 shows this information. If this is a single server network, type the network IPX number in the appropriate field. When the message appears stating that the driver loaded successfully, press Enter. The final menu for the LAN driver information will appear, asking if you want to load another driver or continue with the installation.

32. Press Enter to continue the installation. NetWare will examine the network for directory services. Since NetWare finds no other servers with directory services, a message appears stating that fact.

33. Move the highlight bar to *Yes* (this is the First Directory server) option, then press Enter. Figure 16-11 shows the message and the menu. NetWare displays a screen which asks for the name of the new directory tree.

34. Type *NS* and press Enter. A screen will appear asking you to choose a time zone for your server.

35. Move the highlight bar to the appropriate time zone, then press Enter. Figure 16-12 shows the Time Zone selection screen. A screen will then appear showing the default time configuration for this server.

36. Press F10 to accept the default time configuration, then press Enter at the confirmation window. NetWare displays a dialog box asking you to specify a context for this server and its objects.

**Figure 16-11**
Dialog Box for Selecting Directory Server.

**Figure 16-12**
Time Zone Selection Screen.

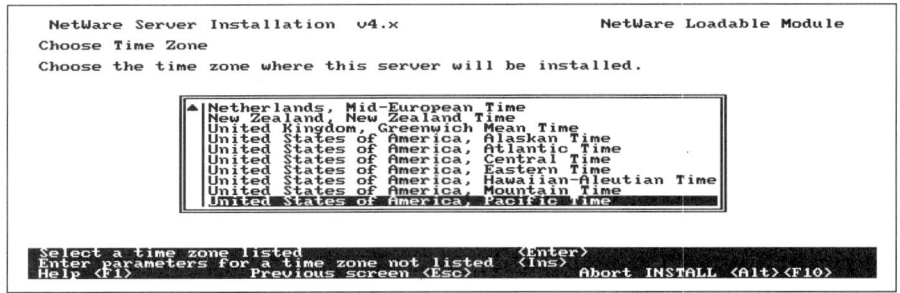

37. In the Company or Organization field, type *NS* and press Enter. This will fill in the *Company or Organization* field, the *Server Context* field, and the *Administrator Name* field. The only other option to complete in this window is assigning a password to the user Admin. Move the highlight bar to the *Password* field, type *NOVELL* and Enter, then type *NOVELL* again. Figure 16-13 shows the screen after filling in the Company or Organization field and typing the password the first time. When complete, press F10 to save and continue. NetWare will then continue to create the directory services on the server. This may take several minutes. A message will also inform you of how many volumes are in the directory.

38. Press Enter to continue. A second information screen will appear listing the name of the directory tree, directory context, and the name and context for the administrator. Figure 16-14 shows the information about the Directory Service. Document this information for future reference.

39. Press Enter to continue. NetWare then displays the contents of the STARTUP.NCF file.

40. If you need to make any changes to this file make them now. Press F10 to save the file, and press Enter at the confirmation window. NetWare displays the contents of the AUTOEXEC.NCF file.

**Figure 16-13**
Dialog Box for Specifying Server and Objects Context.

# NetWare 4.x Installation and Configuration Workshop

**Figure 16-14**
Screen Showing Directory Service Installation.

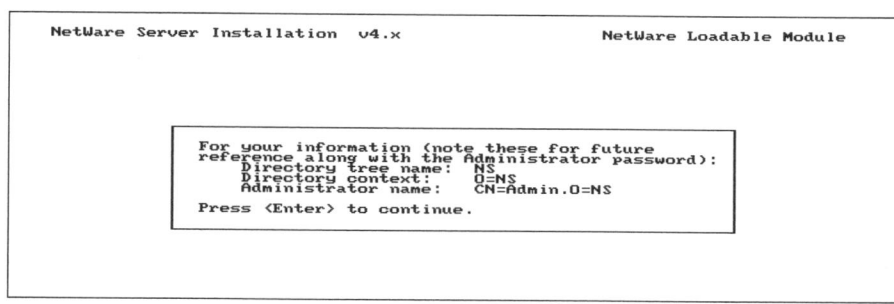

41. Review the contents of the file and make notes for your future reference. Figure 16-15 shows the special commands that NetWare 4.x adds to the file. To save the file, press F10, then press Enter at the confirmation window. NetWare displays an *Other Installation Options* dialog box.

42. Scroll through this window, shown in Fig. 16-16, to become familiar with the options. Press F10 to continue with the installation. NetWare displays a message that the 4.x installation is complete.

43. Press Enter to continue and exit install. NetWare will then end the installation process and return you to the console prompt. The file server is now operational and ready for you to log in as user Admin.

**Figure 16-15**
Screen Showing AUTOEXEC.NCF File Special Commands.

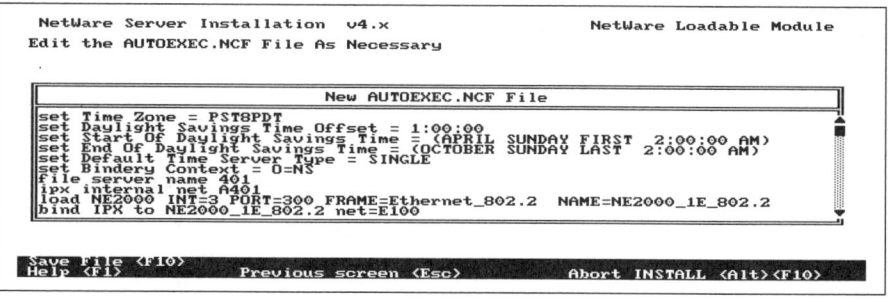

**Figure 16-16**
Other Installation Options Dialog Box.

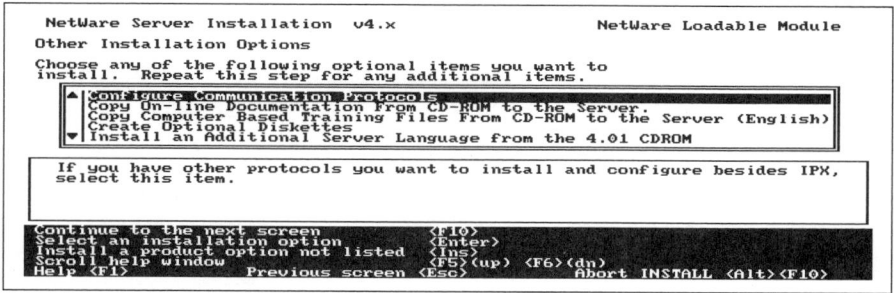

## Install the Workstation ODI/VLM Software

After installing the NetWare operating system, you must install the workstation's software. For this example, we connected the CD-ROM to the computer that will be a workstation. The ODI and VLM software will copy from the NetWare 4.01 installation CD to the workstation's hard disk. This case study assumes that you are not using the menu feature of DOS 6.x. You must use a simple CONFIG.SYS and AUTOEXEC.BAT to make the procedure work correctly. (This does not restrict you from loading all the standard drivers and TSRs that you normally load.)

**NOTE** *If you want to find out how to install the Novell Client 32 software for Windows 95, then look at the "Setting Up the Windows 95 Client" section in Chap. 14. Here we assume that you're using DOS and you want to use the DOS client to access NetWare. It's never a good idea to install the DOS client if you're going to use Windows 95 because the DOS client is 16-bit and can cause problems for you in the Windows 95 32-bit environment. However, since Novell will test your ability to use both clients, you'll still need to go through this section and learn the procedure for the exam.*

1. Install the CD-ROM drive and appropriate drivers on the workstation.
2. Boot the workstation to DOS and place the NetWare 4.x installation CD in the player. Change drive letters to the CD-ROM drive. For example, if the drive letter for your CD-ROM drive is D, type *D:* and press Enter.
3. At the D:\> prompt, type *CD \CLIENT\DOSWIN* and press Enter. Your prompt will now indicate the past of D:\CLIENT\DOSWIN>. This is the starting directory for the workstation client software.
4. To start the installation program, type *INSTALL* and press Enter. Figure 16-17 shows the NetWare Client installation menu.

**Figure 16-17**
NetWare Client Installation Menu.

5. The installation menu is divided into 5 steps. Step 1 shows the path to install the workstation client files. The default path is C:\NWCLIENT; press Enter to accept this path. The cursor will move to Step 2.

6. Step 2 advises you that the client software requires a *LASTDRIVE=Z* statement in your CONFIG.SYS file, and the line *CALL STARTNET.BAT* added to the AUTOEXEC.BAT file. The installation program is asking you in this step if you want the program to make the changes to the files, and create backup copies of your originals. The default value for this step is *NO*. Change the value to *YES* by typing *Y* and pressing Enter.

7. Step 3 is to install the Windows support files. The default for this value is *NO*. Change this to *YES* by typing *Y* and pressing Enter. A path statement to the windows directory will appear. The default path is C:\WINDOWS, press Enter twice to accept the path.*

8. Step 4 defines the network interface board and driver for the workstation. Press Enter to view a list of available boards. Using the down arrow key or the Page Down key, scroll through the list until you find the type of board in the workstation, then press Enter. A dialog box will appear listing the default configuration for the network board.

9. Press Escape to accept the values. Figure 16-18 shows the default settings for the Novell/Eagle NE1000 board. Note that the default Media Frame Type is Ethernet_802.2. If your network board's not set to the default, make the appropriate changes now.

---

* If your Windows directory is in another location, type the correct path, then press Enter.

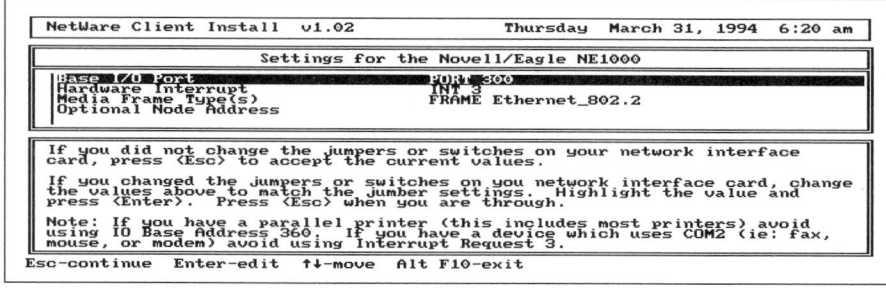

**Figure 16-18**
Default Settings for the Novell/Eagle NE1000 Board.

**Figure 16-19**
Screen Showing Correct Settings for Workstation Software Installation.

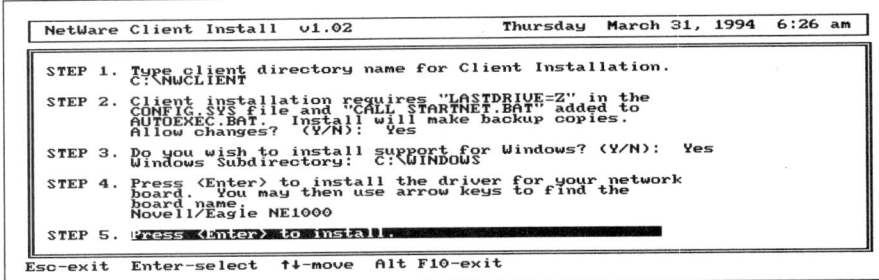

10. Step 5 is to install the software on the workstation with the specified settings. Compare your screen to Fig. 16-19. Make sure that the first 4 steps have the correct settings. To continue the installation, press Enter. The system copies the files to the appropriate directories on your hard disk. This process may take several minutes. When the installation program finishes copying the files to your workstation, an information screen will appear. Make note of the information on this screen.

11. Press Enter to exit the install program. The DOS prompt appears.

12. You must now reboot your workstation, since the CONFIG.SYS file changed. Press CTRL-ALT-DEL to reboot your system. When the system reboots, the new NetWare client software will automatically load and connect you to a file server.

Your workstation is now ready for use on the network. All files necessary to connect the workstation to the file server are now on the workstation's hard disk. The support files for Windows are also on the local workstation. During the installation of the NetWare client software, the install program also created a NetWare Tools program folder in Windows.

## Study Questions

1. The Ethernet LAN drivers for NetWare 4.x default to the _____ frame type.
   a. Ethernet_snap
   b. Ethernet_802.3
   c. Ethernet_802.2
   d. Ethernet_II

# NetWare 4.x Installation and Configuration Workshop

      *c.* The default Ethernet frame type for NetWare 4.x and 3.12 is now Ethernet_802.2. This is to provide greater compatibility with the OSI model.

2. The default directory for installing the workstation files is:
   a. C:\NET
   b. C:\
   c. C:\NETWORK
   d. C:\NWCLIENT

      *d.* The default path for installing the workstation files is C:\NWCLIENT. During the installation program, you can specify an alternate path if you want.

3. When installing the workstation software, you have the choice of installing the Windows support files.
   a. True
   b. False

      *a.* The NetWare 4.x workstation files include Windows support. During the installation, NetWare presents you with the option of installing these files.

4. To start the workstation installation program, type _____ from the WSDOS_1 diskette.
   a. SETUP
   b. INSTALL
   c. WSDOS
   d. None of the above

      *b.* The name of the workstation installation program is INSTALL.

5. If the workstation installation program modifies the AUTOEXEC.BAT and CONFIG.SYS files, NetWare saves the original files with a _____ extension.
   a. .OLD
   b. .BAK
   c. .NET
   d. .BNW

      *d.* Before changing your original files, NetWare saves the backup files with the .BNW extension.

**Chapter Sixteen**

6. When using the 4.x workstation files, the Lastdrive statement in the CONFIG.SYS file needs to be set to:
   a. LASTDRIVE=E
   b. LASTDRIVE=Z
   c. LASTDRIVE=F
   d. LASTDRIVE=C

   *b.* The NetWare VLMs require a Lastdrive statement of Z in the CONFIG.SYS file. NetWare then uses a first network drive statement of F in the NET.CFG file.

7. To change your current context to the ROOT, type:
   a. CX
   b. CX /R
   c. ROOT
   d. CD \

   *b.* To view or change your NDS context, the command is CX. By placing the /R after the command, NetWare will change your context to the ROOT.

8. To view the NDS structure, type:
   a. NDIR
   b. DIR
   c. CX /T
   d. TREE

   *c.* To view or change your NDS context, use the CX command. By appending the /T to the command, the display will include any container objects.

9. To view your current NDS context, type:
   a. CX
   b. PROMPT $P$G
   c. PWD
   d. NDIR

   *a.* The CX (Change ConteXt) command will show your current context within the NDS database.

10. When logging into the network, you must:
    a. Specify the context of the user object.
    b. Enter a user name.

# NetWare 4.x Installation and Configuration Workshop

   c. Load the workstation software.

   d. All the above.

   *d.* To log into the network, you must first load the workstation software to communicate to the file server. Then you must specify the location in the NDS database of the user and the name of the user.

11. To unload the VLM client software from memory, type _____ at the prompt.

   a. VLM -U

   b. LOGOUT

   c. EXIT

   d. VLM

   *a.* As long as there are no other TSRs loaded in the workstation memory above the VLMs, you can remove the VLMs from memory by typing *VLM -U.* Typing *VLM /?* at the prompt will display a set of help screens.

12. The program used to install the NetWare operating system is:

   a. SETUP

   b. INSTALL

   c. STARTNET

   d. SERVER

   *b.* The installation program for the NetWare 4.x operating system is INSTALL.BAT. When installing from the CD-ROM disk, the INSTALL.BAT file is in the \NETWARE.40\ENGLISH directory.

13. The NetWare 4.x operating system installation program will automatically create the NDS structure.

   a. True

   b. False

   *a.* Part of the installation program is to create the NDS database. This option will appear toward the end of the installation.

14. NetWare 4.x will remember _____ previous passwords of each user.

   a. 8

   b. 10

   c. 6

   d. 12

*a.* NetWare will remember the last 8 passwords of each user that were used 1 day or longer. If you have the Require Unique Passwords set to *yes* for your user, NetWare will reject the use of the last 8 passwords.

15. When using SBACKUP, the tape drive must be attached to the:
    a. Workstation
    b. Backbone
    c. File server
    d. Any of the above

    *c.* The SBACKUP (server backup) utility requires the backup device to attach directly to a file server.

16. The user interface for SBACKUP can be run from:
    a. The file server
    b. A workstation
    c. A UNIX host
    d. Both *a* and *b*

    *d.* The user interface to the SBACKUP program is an NLM that's run at the file server. If a workstation is using the RCONSOLE program, the users can access all NLMs from the workstation just as if they're at the file server console.

17. To back up data from a NetWare 4.x file server, use SBACKUP; to restore data to the file server, use:
    a. SRESTORE
    b. SBACKUP
    c. NRESTORE
    d. INSTALL.NLM

    *b.* The NetWare SBACKUP utility will back up and restore data on the network.

18. The SBACKUP program will only back up NetWare file servers.
    a. True
    b. False

    *b.* The SBACKUP program will back up not only the file server with the backup device attached, but can also back up other systems on the network, including other servers (3.x and 4.x), DOS workstations, OS/2 workstations, and NDS databases.

# NetWare 4.x Installation and Configuration Workshop

19. For the menu utility to view and set the NetWare operating system SET parameters, type _____ at the file server prompt.
    a. LOAD INSTALL
    b. LOAD MONITOR
    c. LOAD SERVMAN
    d. SETS

    *c.* The SERVMAN utility provides an easy-to-use interface that will allow you to view and change the configuration of the operating system's settable parameters. This program will also modify the STARTUP.NCF and AUTOEXEC.NCF automatically for you.

20. If you make changes to the Maximum Physical Receive Packet Size, you must:
    a. Have the users log out of the network.
    b. Down the server, then restart it.
    c. Load the MONITOR.NLM to confirm that the setting is the proper value.
    d. Do nothing else; changes will take effect immediately.

    *b.* When changing the set parameter for Maximum Physical Receive Packet Size, edit the STARTUP.NCF file. Before the changes will take effect, you must down then restart the file server.

21. If you suspect a problem with the NDS, use the _____ utility to fix the NDS database.
    a. NDSREPAIR
    b. VREPAIR
    c. DSREPAIR
    d. COMPSURF

    *c.* The DSREPAIR (directory service repair) is an NLM that will attempt to repair problems with the NDS database. It is the NetWare 4.x version of the 3.x Bindfix utility.

22. To load NLMs into a protected ring, you must:
    a. Load the DOMAIN.NLM.
    b. Type *MODULES* at the file server prompt.
    c. Load the RING.NLM.
    d. Load the PROTECT.NLM.

*a.* The DOMAIN.NLM is the primary support for loading NLMs into protected rings. The DOMAIN.NLM must load from the first line in the STARTUP.NCF file.

23. To enable the NetWare 4.x file compression feature, you must:
    a. Load the file compression NLM.
    b. Load the INSTALL.NLM and set file compression to *on*.
    c. Edit the STARTUP.NCF to load the COMPRESS.NLM during bootup, then reboot the system.
    d. Load the COMPRESS.NAM module and type *ADD COMPRESS TO VOLUME SYS*.

    *b.* File compression can be enabled only when setting up a new volume and be completely disabled by removing the volume. The INSTALL.NLM will create and setup a new volume on the file server.

24. Novell supplies what utility to move a NetWare 3.x server information to a 4.x server?
    a. FSUPDATE
    b. UPGRADE
    c. MIGRATE
    d. MOVE

    *c.* The MIGRATE utility will move the 3.x server information to the 4.x file server. The MIGRATE utility files do not automatically copy to the 4.x file server during installation. You must manually copy them from the \CLIENT_____\ENGLISH directory on the CD-ROM to your file server.

25. To partition a NetWare 4.x NDS database, you can use the _____ utility.
    a. PARTMGR.NLM
    b. PARTMGR.EXE
    c. NWADMIN.EXE
    d. Either *b* or *c*

    *d.* NetWare provides two utilities to manage the NDS partitions: PARTMGR.EXE and NWADMIN.EXE. PARTMGR is a DOS-based program, and NWADMIN is the Windows-based program. Using either utility will produce the same results.

# NetWare 4.x Installation and Configuration Workshop

26. After completing the 4.x installation program, you must:
    a. Call Novell and register your NDS tree name.
    b. Cold-boot the computer.
    c. Type *ENABLE LOGIN* to allow the users to log into the file server.
    d. Do nothing; the file server is ready for user ADMIN to log in.

    *d.* After completing the NetWare 4.x installation program, the file server setup is complete. You must log in as user *ADMIN* and complete the installation by setting up the directory structure, loading applications, and setting up the NDS structure for users, printers, and other resources.

27. The NetWare module for the network interface board has a _____ extension.
    a. .NIB
    b. .LAN
    c. .NLM
    d. .DSK

    *b.* All network interface board NLMs on the NetWare 3.x and 4.x file servers have a .LAN extension.

28. The NetWare module for the hard disk controller will have a _____ extension.
    a. .HDC
    b. .LAN
    c. .NLM
    d. .DSK

    *d.* The hard disk controller NLM for NetWare file servers will have a .DSK extension.

29. The file used to start the NetWare operating system is:
    a. SERVER
    b. STARTNET
    c. INSTALL
    d. NETWARE

    *a.* The file to start the NetWare operating system is SERVER.EXE.

**30.** The NetWare boot up configuration files are:
  a. AUTOEXEC.BAT and STARTUP.NCF
  b. AUTOEXEC.NCF and STARTUP.NCF
  c. SERVER.EXE and STARTUP.NCF
  d. AUTOEXEC.BAT and SERVER.EXE

  *b.* The AUTOEXEC.NCF and STARTUP.NCF contain the commands that will customize the operating system for your needs. The STARTUP.NCF and AUTOEXEC.NCF files are NetWare's version of DOS's CONFIG.SYS and AUTOEXEC.BAT.

**31.** The maximum size of a NetWare 4.x volume is 4 GB.
  a. True
  b. False

  *b.* The maximum size of a NetWare volume is 32 TB. The maximum amount of RAM NetWare can address is 4 GB.

**32.** To aid users in logging into the network, add which of the following lines to the NET.CFG file?
  a. SET CONTEXT = <PATH>
  b. NAME CONTEXT = <PATH>
  c. NDS CONTEXT = <PATH>
  d. LOG IN CONTEXT = <PATH>

  *b.* By setting the NAME CONTEXT = <PATH> statement in the NET.CFG file, users will not need to enter the context path to the login statement.

**33.** The name of the superuser on NetWare 4.x is:
  a. SUPERVISOR
  b. ROOT
  c. ADMIN
  d. SUPERUSER

  *c.* The user ADMIN is the superuser on the NetWare 4.x system—the equivalent of the 3.x SUPERVISOR, in that this user initially has complete access rights to the entire system.

**34.** User Paul has trustee rights from the Sales Organization object of [RCEF] to the DATA directory. From the Northern Organizational

Unit object, which is below Sales, Paul has [RF] to the DATA directory. As a user, Paul has explicit trustee rights of [RWF] to the DATA directory. What are Paul's effective rights to the DATA directory?
a. Read, Create, Erase, and File Scan
b. Read and File Scan
c. Read, Write, and File Scan
d. Read, Write, Create, Erase, and File Scan

*c.* The rights granted at the Leaf Object level supersede any previous rights granted at the Container level.

35. If user Paul is a member of the SALES group that has a trustee assignment of [RWCF] to the DATA directory, and as a user has a trustee assignment of [RWEF] to the DATA directory, what are Paul's effective rights to the DATA directory?
a. Read, Write, Create, and File Scan.
b. Read, Write, Erase, and File Scan.
c. Read, Write, Erase, Create, and File Scan.
d. It depends upon the IRF at the DATA directory.

*c.* The rights Paul has as a user and the rights he has as a member of a group combine to form his effective rights.

## Fun Test

1. To install the NetWare operating system, use the _____ program.
   a. SERVER
   b. SETUP
   c. STARTNET
   d. INSTALL

2. The _____ program located on the WSDOS_1 diskette will prepare the workstation to connect to the file server.
   a. INSTALL
   b. SETUP
   c. WSGEN
   d. None of the above

3. To back up data from a NetWare 4.x file server, use SBACKUP; to restore data to the file server use:
   a. SRESTORE
   b. INSTALL.NLM
   c. SBACKUP
   d. NRESTORE

4. Add the _____ line to the NET.CFG file to set the users context in the NDS.
   a. NAME CONTEXT = <PATH>
   b. LOG IN CONTEXT = <PATH>
   c. SET CONTEXT = <PATH>
   d. NDS CONTEXT = <PATH>

5. At the file server prompt, type _____ to load the menu utility for setting the operating system's SET parameters.
   a. SET
   b. LOAD INSTALL
   c. LOAD MONITOR
   d. LOAD SERVMAN

6. The command to remove the NetWare client files from the workstation memory is:
   a. VLM -U
   b. LOGOUT
   c. EXIT
   d. VLM

7. The user interface for SBACKUP can be run from:
   a. The file server
   b. A workstation
   c. A UNIX host
   d. Both *a* and *b*

8. As soon as you finish installing the 4.x operating system, you must:
   a. Cold-boot the computer.
   b. Type *ENABLE LOGIN* to allow the users to log into the file server.
   c. Do nothing; the file server is ready for user ADMIN to log in.
   d. Call Novell and register your NDS tree name.

# NetWare 4.x Installation and Configuration Workshop

9. The SBACKUP program will only backup NetWare file servers.
   a. True
   b. False

10. The tape drive must be attached to the _____ if you are using the SBACKUP program supplied by Novell.
    a. File server
    b. Workstation
    c. Backbone
    d. Any of the above

11. User Paul has trustee rights from the Sales Organization object of [RCEF] to the DATA directory. From the Northern Organizational Unit object, which is below Sales, Paul has [RF] to the DATA directory. As a user, Paul has explicit trustee rights of [RWF] to the DATA directory. What are Paul's effective rights to the DATA directory?
    a. Read, Write, Create, Erase, and File Scan
    b. Read, Write, and File Scan
    c. Read, Create, Erase, and File Scan
    d. Read and File Scan

12. When using an Ethernet NIC, NetWare defaults the LAN drivers to what frame format?
    a. Ethernet_802.3
    b. Ethernet_II
    c. Ethernet_snap
    d. Ethernet_802.2

13. The _____ utility will partition the NetWare 4.x NDS database.
    a. PARTMGR.EXE
    b. NWADMIN.EXE
    c. PARTMGR.NLM
    d. Either A or B

14. To change from your current context to the ROOT, type:
    a. CD \
    b. CX /R
    c. ROOT
    d. CX

15. 256 MB is the maximum size of a NetWare 4.x volume.
    a. True
    b. False

16. If you want to look at the NDS structure in a tree layout, type _____ at the command line.
    a. NDIR
    b. CX /T
    c. TREE
    d. DIR

17. NetWare supplies you with the _____ utility to correct problems with the NDS database.
    a. VREPAIR
    b. NDSREPAIR
    c. COMPSURF
    d. DSREPAIR

18. When loading NLMs into a protected ring for testing, you must:
    a. Load the RING.NLM.
    b. Load the PROTECT.NLM.
    c. Type *MODULES* at the file server prompt.
    d. Load the DOMAIN.NLM.

19. File compression on the file server is set up using which of the following?
    a. Loading the COMPRESS.NAM module and typing *ADD COMPRESS TO VOLUME SYS*
    b. Loading the INSTALL.NLM and setting file compression to *on*
    c. Editing the STARTUP.NCF to load the COMPRESS.NLM during bootup, then rebooting the system
    d. Loading the file compression NLM

20. When upgrading a NetWare 3.x server to a NetWare 4.x server, you would use the _____ utility.
    a. UPGRADE
    b. MIGRATE
    c. FSUPDATE
    d. MOVE

21. The NetWare operating system uses two configuration files. They are:

# NetWare 4.x Installation and Configuration Workshop

   a. AUTOEXEC.BAT and STARTUP.NCF
   b. AUTOEXEC.NCF and STARTUP.NCF
   c. SERVER.EXE and STARTUP.NCF
   d. AUTOEXEC.BAT and SERVER.EXE

22. If user Paul is a member of the SALES group that has a trustee assignment of [RWCF] to the DATA directory, and as a user has a trustee assignment of [RWEF] to the DATA directory, what are Paul's effective rights to the DATA directory?
   a. Read, Write, Create, and File Scan.
   b. Read, Write, Erase, and File Scan.
   c. Read, Write, Erase, Create, and File Scan.
   d. It depends upon the IRF at the DATA directory.

23. The NLM for the network interface board has an extension of:
   a. .NLM
   b. .NIB
   c. .DSK
   d. .LAN

24. By default, the workstation installation program will install the files in the _____ directory on the workstation.
   a. C:\NWCLIENT
   b. C:\NET
   c. C:\NETWORK
   d. C:\

25. The _____ command will display your current NDS context.
   a. NDIR
   b. PROMPT $P$G
   c. CX
   d. PWD

26. When NetWare installs the workstation files, it modifies the AUTOEXEC.BAT and CONFIG.SYS files and saves the original files with an extension of:
   a. .OLD
   b. .BAK
   c. .NET
   d. .BNW

27. To load the NetWare operating system into memory and turn a workstation into a file server, type _____ at the prompt.
    a. SERVER
    b. INSTALL
    c. NETWARE
    d. STARTNET

28. When installing NetWare, the installation program won't automatically create the NDS structure.
    a. True
    b. False

29. The name of the superuser on NetWare 4.x is:
    a. ADMIN
    b. SUPERVISOR
    c. ROOT
    d. SUPERUSER

30. The NetWare 4.x operating system requires which of the following before you are able to access the system?
    a. Load the workstation.
    b. Enter a user name.
    c. Specify the context of the user object software.
    d. All of the above.

31. When making modifications to the Maximum Physical Receive Packet Size, you must:
    a. Have the users log out of the network.
    b. Down the server, then restart it.
    c. Load the MONITOR.NLM to confirm that the setting is the proper value.
    d. Do nothing else; changes will take effect immediately.

32. The workstation installation program won't allow you to install the Windows support files.
    a. True
    b. False

33. When using unique passwords, NetWare 4.x will remember the previous _____ passwords of each user.

# NetWare 4.x Installation and Configuration Workshop 513

      a. 6
      b. 8
      c. 10
      d. 12

34. When using the 4.x workstation files, the Lastdrive statement in the CONFIG.SYS file needs to be set to:
      a. LASTDRIVE=E
      b. LASTDRIVE=Z
      c. LASTDRIVE=F
      d. LASTDRIVE=C

35. The NLM file for the hard disk controller will have a _____ extension.
      a. .HDC
      b. .LAN
      c. .NLM
      d. .DSK

## Brain Teaser

Installing NetWare as we did in this chapter is only one step in an ongoing process. Once you have all the workstations and one or more NetWare servers installed, you still need to optimize them for use. The cryptogram in Fig. 16-20 provides you with a handy phrase you can rely on to steer you to the best possible NetWare tune-up for both your servers and your workstations. You'll find the solution for this brain teaser in App. C, "Brain Teaser Answers."

    If you're feeling especially knowledgeable, you can try your hand at the much more difficult cryptogram in Fig. 16-21. This is a server console–related phrase based on one of the questions you answered in the preceding fun test section. Remember that this exam will test your knowledge about the NetWare server console, so you need to be prepared for it. Just in case the idea of working with a symbol-oriented cryptogram is a bit intimidating for you, here's a tip: All spaces really are spaces and all periods are periods. Apostrophes are also what they appear to be. Every other symbol replaces a letter.

**Figure 16-20**
Workstation Tuning Cryptogram.

EXMEVY CPKPKIPC HDEH E 32-IQH AZPCEHQJR YVYHPK

CPOSQCPY E 32-IQH JPHMACU NXQPJH BAC AZHQKSK

ZPCBACKEJNP. SYQJR JAFPXX'Y NXQPJH NI NXQPJH MDPJ

MACUQJR MQHD MQJTAMY QP BAC IPYH ZPCBACKEJNP.

| A | | N | |
|---|---|---|---|
| B | | O | |
| C | | P | |
| D | | Q | |
| E | | R | |
| F | | S | |
| G | | T | |
| H | | U | |
| I | | V | |
| J | | W | |
| K | | X | |
| L | | Y | |
| M | | Z | |

## Disk Time

Don't forget to spend some time working with the CD-ROM that accompanies this book. It provides valuable, fun-to-use teaching aids that'll help you prepare for the exam. See "Disk Time" in the preface of this book for details about what the disk contains. Make sure you pay special attention to the parts of the Windows help file and the Red Zone game that pertain to this chapter. Also, check out the acronym areas provided in both disk features—they'll help you get up to speed on what's going on in the industry faster.

# NetWare 4.x Installation and Configuration Workshop

**Figure 16-21**
Server Volume Cryptogram.

+@(? *=])/?##@=~ *%~ =~(< [? ?~%[(?! &;?~ #?{{@~> _) % ~?&

\=(_]? %~! *=])(?{?(< !@#%[(?! [< /?]=\@~> {;? \=(_]?. {;? @~#{%((.~(]

&@(( */?%{? %~! #?{_) % ~?& \=(_]? =~ {;? +@(? #?/\?/.

| | | | |
|---|---|---|---|
| ! | | { | |
| @ | | } | |
| # | | [ | |
| $ | | ] | |
| % | | < | |
| ^ | | > | |
| & | | ! | |
| * | | \ | |
| ( | | / | |
| ) | | ? | |
| _ | | ~ | |
| + | | : | |
| = | | ; | |

CHAPTER 17

# GroupWise System Administration

## Introduction

This chapter looks at the requirements for the GroupWise System Administration exam. This is part of the new GroupWise CNE certification route that Novell has recently made available. This chapter is the first step toward learning to use GroupWise. You'll begin by learning to install both the administration and the client workstation software. We also look at some basic usage requirements in the case study portion of the chapter.

This exam also parallels the NetWare 3.x and 4.x requirements by the same name. The study questions portion of the chapter provide the same overall view that the exam provides. Of course, the actual operating system will be completely different depending on which version of the product you select. There are both UNIX and Windows version of the product. We concentrate on the Windows version of the product since it's more likely that you'll use that product. The two product versions are about the same (except for the differences between operating systems) so UNIX users can benefit from this chapter as well.

One of the reasons that Novell has added the GroupWise System Administration exam is so that each CNE specialty provides a similar level of expertise and receives a similar level of training. There are several discrete sections in this chapter. Each section helps you study for the exam in a different way. You can improve your chances of passing the exam by using the study methods provided in this chapter. In fact, it'll probably help if you study all the sections once and your favorite sections at least twice. Review the study guidelines in Chap. 4 as often as necessary to ensure that you maintain the best possible study atmosphere.

**NOTE** *This chapter assumes that you have already bought the version of GroupWise required for your operating system. You need an intimate knowledge of the operating system that you plan to use with GroupWise, as well. This chapter also assumes that you have a minimal setup of one server and one workstation available to fully utilize the case study and exercises. You can still benefit from this chapter if you don't have a network. Make sure you become familiar with the GroupWise manuals before starting this chapter, as well.*

The first section of this chapter is a case study. You will perform some hands-on tasks that will help you learn what you need to know to pass the examination. In this case, we look at what you need to do to get GroupWise installed on a Windows workstation. We then concentrate on one of the

# GroupWise System Administration 519

ways that you can set up GroupWise once you get it installed. Even though you'll get a lot more from this section if you perform it on your own network, the inclusion of step-by-step instructions and screen shots will help you gain something from the section even if you don't have a network.

The second area contains *sample test questions* for this course. We make a special effort to include a variety of GroupWise setup- and administration-specific questions; but, as on the real exam, you'll find other types of questions, as well. It would not be too unrealistic to expect a few UNIX-, Windows-, and NetWare-specific questions. You need to have at least a cursory knowledge of the operating systems that you don't use and an in-depth knowledge of the ones that you do. This section also includes the correct answers to those questions and an explanation of why each answer is correct. Try to answer each question yourself, look at the correct answer, then determine where you went wrong if you did not answer correctly.

The next section is a *fun test*. This is an exercise where you'll look at more sample test questions and answer them. The answers appear in App. B at the back of the book. This will help you test what you learned in the previous section.

The final text section of the chapter is the *brain teaser*. You'll get to have a little fun working on a GroupWise-related puzzle. This chapter provides two cryptograms that should give you some ideas of ways to study for the exam. Obviously, it helps to have a good overall knowledge of GroupWise in this case, since the cryptograms will be easier to solve if you can spot specific patterns in the way they're encrypted. By the way, the cryptograms use different encryption methods, so you'll have to solve each puzzle separately.

Finally, we'll spend some time using the *Jeopardy!*-type game named *Red Zone*. Unlike most sections of this book, there are only two GroupWise categories included with the game: *Administration* and *Remote Connections*. You need more than just GroupWise knowledge to pass the exam, so the lack of GroupWise categories shouldn't present any problems. Playing the Red Zone game helps you look at the test from the opposite viewpoint. The game provides you with an answer—you need to come up with the corresponding question. The game awards points for correct answers, and takes points away for incorrect answers. You'll receive a score at the end of the game proclaiming that you either did or did not get your certificate. Make sure you concentrate on the GroupWise-related questions when using the game; they are the ones that will provide you with the best information about the exams you are about to take. Unlike the specific questions provided in this chapter, Red Zone tests your overall knowledge of Novell products, so be prepared to explore areas that you haven't looked at in the past.

Use all the learning methods that we provide in this chapter to improve your chances of passing the exam. It's a good idea to save the fun test section until you're almost certain that you possess all the required knowledge. Remember, you can probably go through the fun test only two or three times at most before you'll start to remember the answers without really knowing the material.

## Case Study

Passing the administrator exam requires you to have a good understanding both of GroupWise and of the operating system that you'll use it with. This is a two-part case study. The first part looks at the requirements for installing GroupWise on a Windows workstation. The second part looks at actually using GroupWise to set up a domain and post office. This includes setting up users and security. Going through this case study will give you the GroupWise-specific knowledge that you need to pass the exam; you should also spend some time learning your operating system(s) completely.

Since much of the installation process is automated, you won't easily be able to exit the procedure and start it up again. We have broken the procedure into five sections. Exiting the program at one of these points will enable you to pick up where you left off in the case study. (The GroupWise installation utility will detect that it isn't completely set up and will prompt you to restart the installation process.)

We look at the Novell-recommended way to perform this task. That's what you will see on the exam, so it really pays to spend a lot of time on this section of the chapter if you normally use alternate installation strategies.

### GroupWise Installation on a Windows Workstation

Before you can start to administer GroupWise, you have to get both the administration and client software installed. We use the floppy disk installation method for this case study. You can look at the NetWare 3x Installation and Configuration Workshop in Chap. 12 for an example of a CD-ROM installation (of course, that procedure won't help you install

# GroupWise System Administration

GroupWise; it'll simply give you an idea of what a CD-ROM installation looks like, in contrast to the floppy installation we show here). The selection of features and what to install is the same in both installations, but the CD-ROM installation is more convenient. The following steps will help you get the administration and client software set up.

1. Insert the *Admin 1* disk into a floppy drive. Switch to the installation drive by typing the drive letter and a colon and then pressing Enter.

2. Type *Install* and press Enter. You will see the initial installation screen shown in Fig. 17-1. Novell suggests that you complete the setup worksheet before proceeding. In most cases, this is a good idea. Since we're performing a simple setup, we'll skip the worksheet for right now.

3. Type *Y*. You'll see the first setup screen. This is where you would enter the information from the worksheet.

4. Type *T* to select the *Install To* field. Type a drive letter and path. We chose E:\DOMAIN for our domain directory, but you could use any directory name you want. Press Enter. Type *Y* when asked if you want to create the directory.

5. Type *I* to display the *Files to Install* dialog. You must select, at minimum, the Administration software and one type of Client software during the initial installation. Users of Perfect Office 3.1 will also need to select the Office 3.1 Compatibility software. In this case we chose to install only the administration software and the Windows client, as shown in Fig. 17-2.

6. Press F10 to complete the selection process. Your display should look similar to the one shown in Fig. 17-3. Note that we have a source

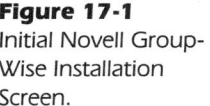
**Figure 17-1**
Initial Novell Group-Wise Installation Screen.

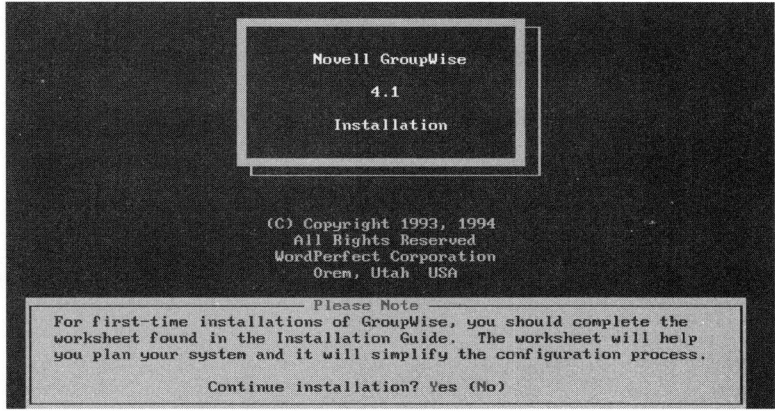

**Figure 17-2**
Files to Install Dialog Box Showing Selection of Administration and Windows Client Software.

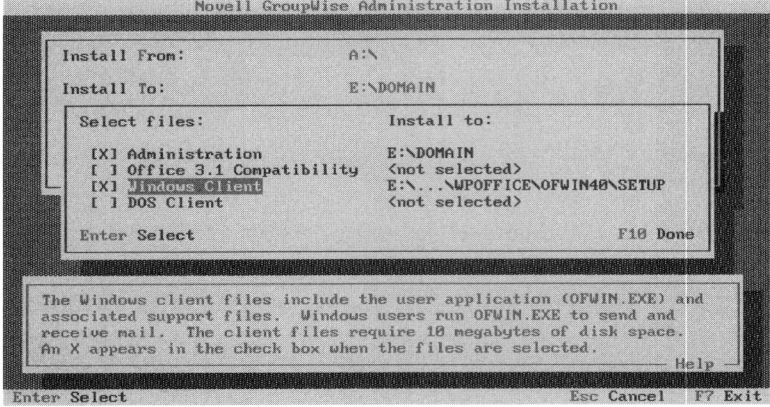

directory, a destination directory, and the software we want to install. The installation program will automatically select the next entry on the list, *Start Installation*.

7. Press Enter to start the installation. The installation program will display a dialog box similar to the one in Fig. 17-4. This gives you one last chance to abort the installation before proceeding.

8. Type *Y* to accept the installation parameters. If you are using a CD-ROM drive for installation, then you can sit back and relax for a while. Otherwise, you'll need to swap floppies for a while. You'll see a display similar to the one in Fig. 17-5 each time the installation program needs another floppy.

9. Press Enter to get past the final installation dialog once you have completed the installation. Install displays this final dialog to show you what it installed.

**Figure 17-3**
Display after Selecting Software in Fig. 17-2.

# GroupWise System Administration

**Figure 17-4**
Dialog Box for Proceeding with GroupWise Administration Installation.

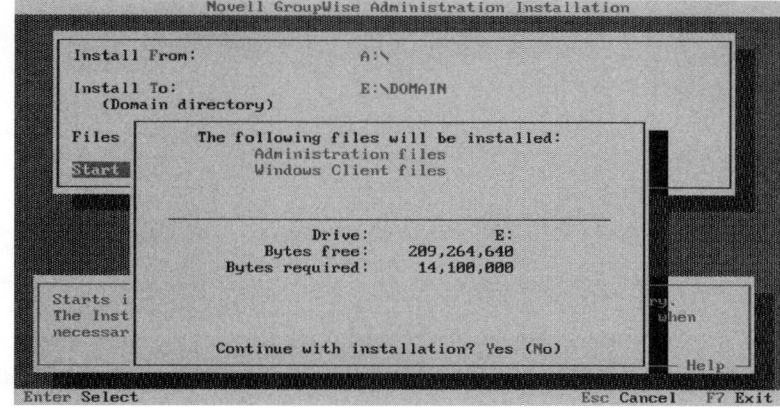

10. Type *N* to bypass reading the README file right now. Normally, you would view this file to see if there are any changes to the printed documentation. You'll also find this file on disk, so you can easily read it later using any text editor. Install will display a message telling you to press Enter to start the AD.EXE program.

11. Press Enter. You'll see the opening GroupWise setup screen shown in Fig. 17-6. This program will guide you through the four steps required to create a basic GroupWise setup (as described in the bulleted list shown in the figure).

12. GroupWise is installed. Click on Exit to leave the case study now and return later. Otherwise, go to the next section to perform the setup process.

**Figure 17-5**
Message Requesting Next Floppy for Installation Program.

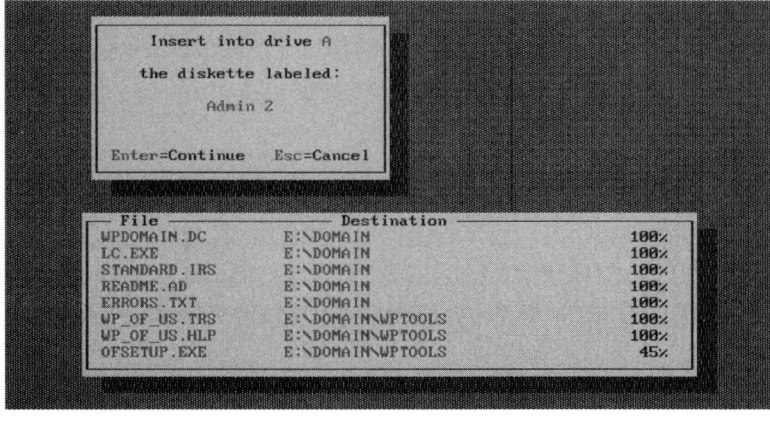

**Figure 17-6**
Opening GroupWise Setup Screen.

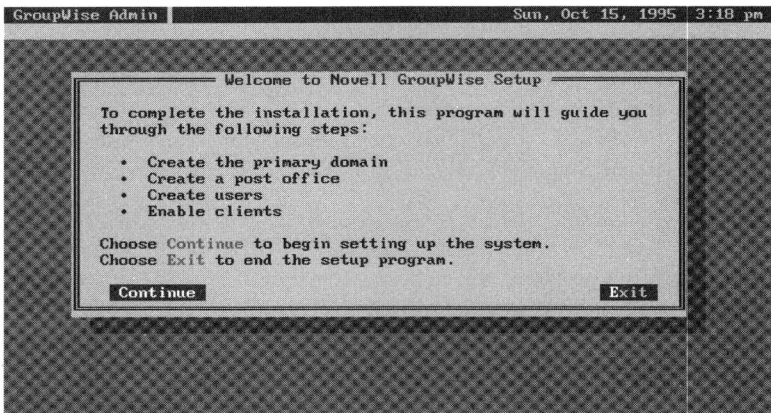

## Creating a Post Office and Setting Up Users

In this section of the case study you will prepare GroupWise for use in a small company. There are four users in our company and one of them will be the administrator when you leave. We will create a single post office to meet all our needs. This particular company uses a peer-to-peer network instead of a central file server.

**CREATING A DOMAIN.** The first step in setting up a post office is creating a domain. That's what we'll do in the next few steps of our case study. You can skip these steps if you already have a domain in place (or you can simply follow the written steps without actually doing them on your network).

1. Whether you continued from the previous section of the case study or simply typed *AD* in the DOMAIN directory, you should see the opening dialog in Fig. 17-6. Click on Continue to continue the case study. GroupWise Admin will display a dialog that asks if you can see your mouse. If you can't see your mouse, perform the mouse setup; otherwise, click on Continue. You'll see the Domain dialog shown in Fig. 17-7.

**NOTE** *You'll need to move your mouse around to see it. There are some places on the dialog where the mouse cursor won't show up. Moving your mouse around ensures that you don't run the mouse setup unless you really need to.*

2. Type a domain name in the dialog box shown in Fig. 17-7. This is the name of your domain and usually reflects a location or other identi-

# GroupWise System Administration

**Figure 17-7**
Primary Domain Dialog Box.

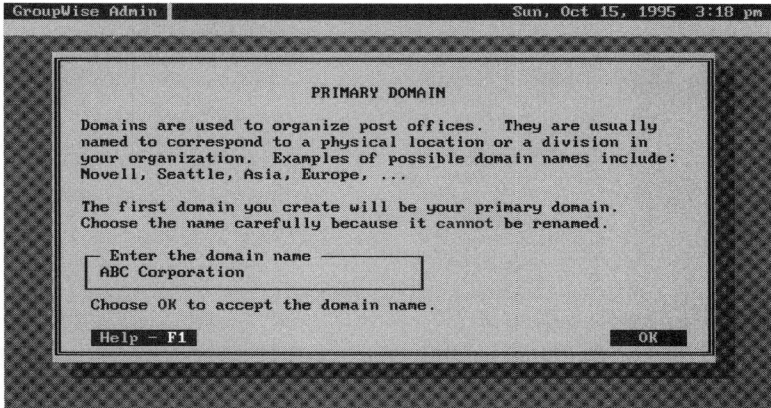

fying information. We used the name of our example company, *ABC Corporation,* as shown in Fig. 17-7.

3. Click on OK. You will see a Select Time Zone dialog box like the one shown in Fig. 17-8. This dialog isn't too important for small businesses, but does synchronize events for a worldwide company.

4. Select the right time zone from the list and click on Select. GroupWise Admin will ask if you are in an area that uses daylight savings time.

5. Click on Yes or No depending on your area. If you select *yes,* then GroupWise Admin will display a dialog box asking for the starting and ending dates for daylight savings time. Select the required dates and click on OK. GroupWise Admin will display the Language and Network dialog box shown in Fig. 17-9. Note that this dialog box

**Figure 17-8**
Select Time Zone Dialog Box.

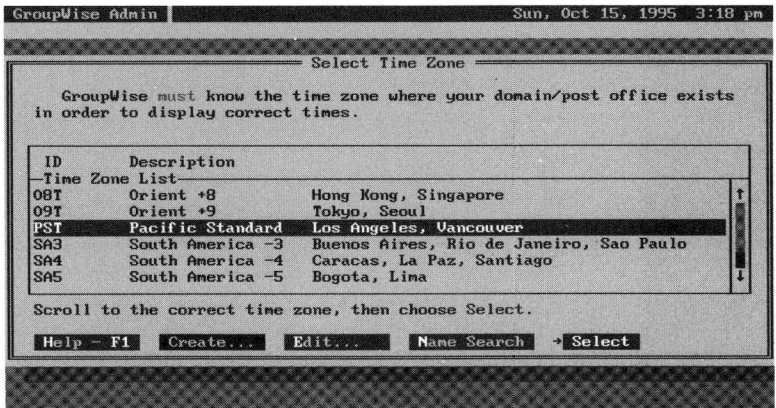

**Figure 17-9**
Language and Network Dialog Box.

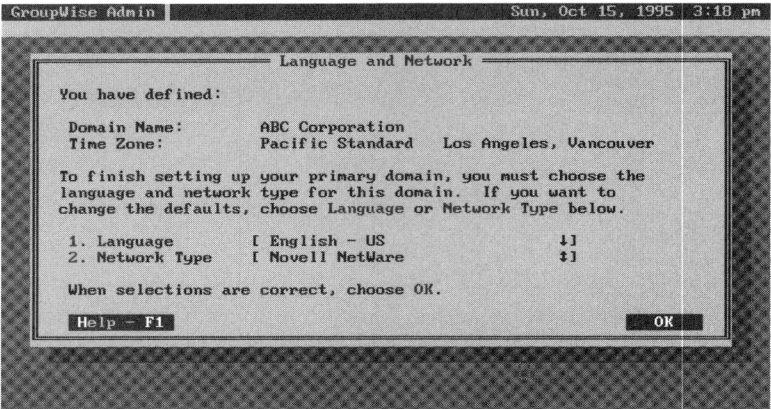

displays our current domain name and the time zone information for our post office.

6. Select a language. In our case, we chose English.

7. Select a network. Since this is a peer-to-peer network, we chose *Other*. The only peer-to-peer network that GroupWise supports directly is *LANtastic*. Choose the network that you're using.

8. Click on OK to complete the network and language selections. GroupWise Admin will display the reminder dialog box shown in Fig. 17-10. Make sure you record this information so that you won't forget it. The AD.EXE program will be executed from the domain directory that you choose.

9. Click on Continue. GroupWise will display a dialog like the one shown in Fig. 17-11. Note that we can now see the domain for our company.

**Figure 17-10**
Domain Reminder Dialog Box.

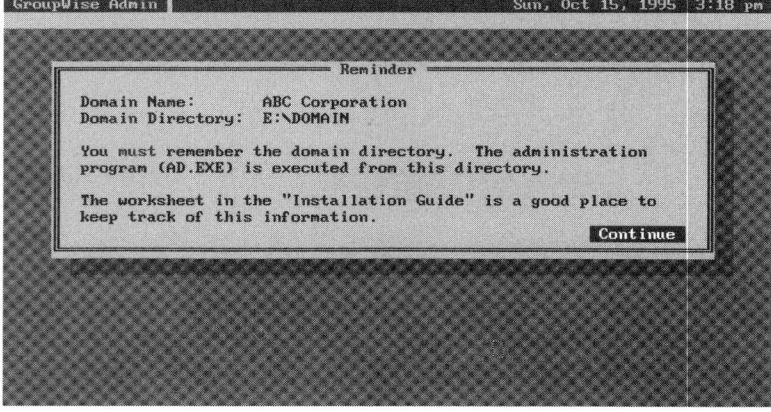

# GroupWise System Administration

**Figure 17-11**
Domain Progress Report Dialog Box.

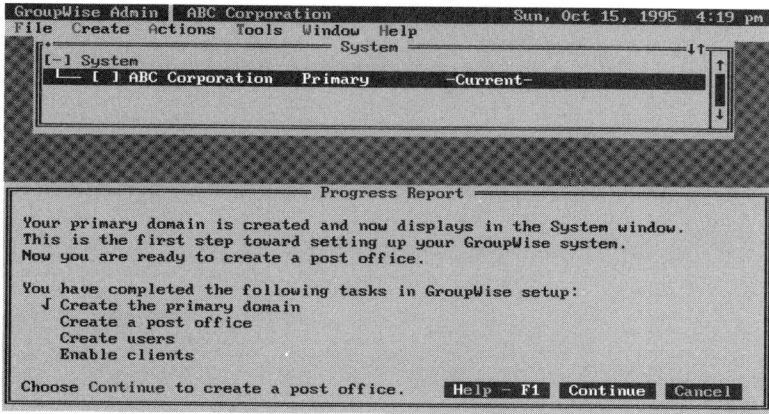

10. This completes the domain setup. Click on Cancel, then on Exit to leave the case study now and return later. Otherwise, go to the next section to perform the post office setup process.

**CREATING A POST OFFICE.** Once you complete the setup of a domain, you can create a post office. While a domain groups people together, the post office acts as a database to store messages from a particular group of users. For example, you might create a domain for an entire satellite office. That domain might contain separate post offices for accounting, engineering, and other departments. The following steps show you how to set up a post office.

1. Start at Step 2 if you're continuing from the previous section. If you started this procedure by typing *AD* at the DOS prompt in the DOMAIN directory, then you'll need to click on Continue at the Partial Setup Detected dialog. You'll see the Progress Report dialog box shown in Fig. 17-11.

2. Click on Continue. You will see the Creating a Post Office dialog box shown in Fig. 17-12.

3. Type the name of your post office. A post office normally reflects a specific group of people, such as a department. Since this is a small company, we decided to create one central post office called *Everyone,* as shown in Fig. 17-12. Note that we used an 8-character name. The advantage of doing this is that the post office name and the directory path can be the same.

4. Click OK to create the post office. GroupWise Admin will display the dialog box shown in Fig. 17-13. Note that the Post Office Directory dialog has a default name based on the post office name.

**Figure 17-12**
Creating a Post Office Dialog Box.

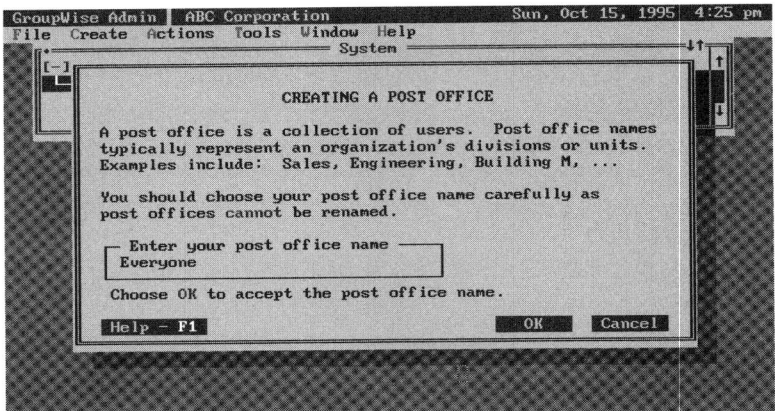

5. Click on OK to accept the default directory name (unless you want to use something else). In the case of our example post office, we simply accepted the default directory of E:/EVERYONE. GroupWise will copy some default files to your new post office directory, then display the dialog box shown in Fig. 17-14. Note that GroupWise Admin automatically selects the Windows client since this is the only one we installed. You would see the other options enabled if you had installed those clients.

6. Click on OK to accept the Windows client. GroupWise Admin will copy some software to the post office directory, then display the reminder dialog box shown in Fig. 17-15. Make sure you record this information so that you won't forget it. Every user without access to the domain directory will need to start the client software from the post office directory shown in this reminder.

**Figure 17-13**
Post Office Directory Dialog Box.

# GroupWise System Administration

**Figure 17-14**
Copy Software to Post Office Dialog Box.

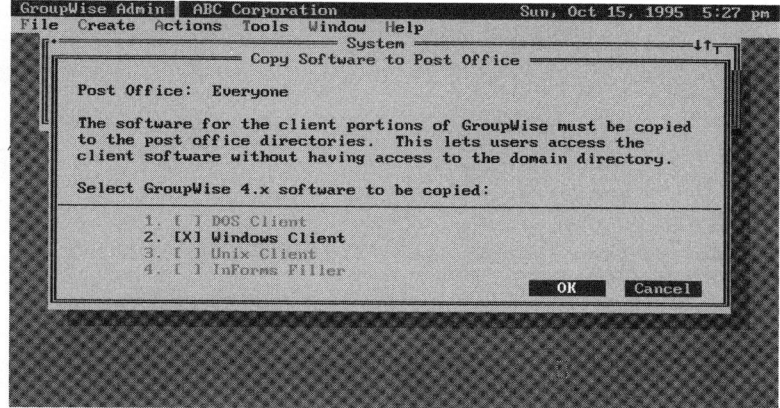

7. Click on Continue. GroupWise will display a dialog box like the one shown in Fig. 17-16. Note that we can now see the post office for our company.

8. This completes the post office setup. Click on Cancel, then on Exit to leave the case study now and return later. Otherwise, go to the next section to perform the user setup process.

**CREATING AND ENABLING USERS.** Creating a domain and a post office gives you a place to store data. Now you have to create some users, the people who will actually use the post office to get work done. The following paragraphs show you the generic setup for creating four users. Obviously, you can modify this procedure as needed for your network.

**Figure 17-15**
Post Office Reminder Dialog Box.

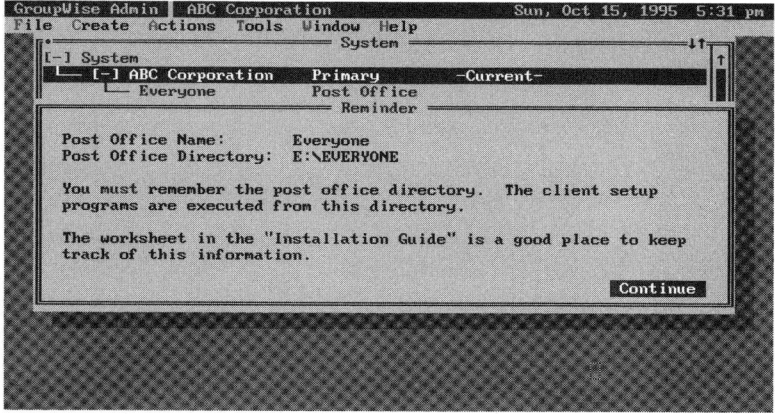

**Figure 17-16**
Post Office Progress Report Dialog Box.

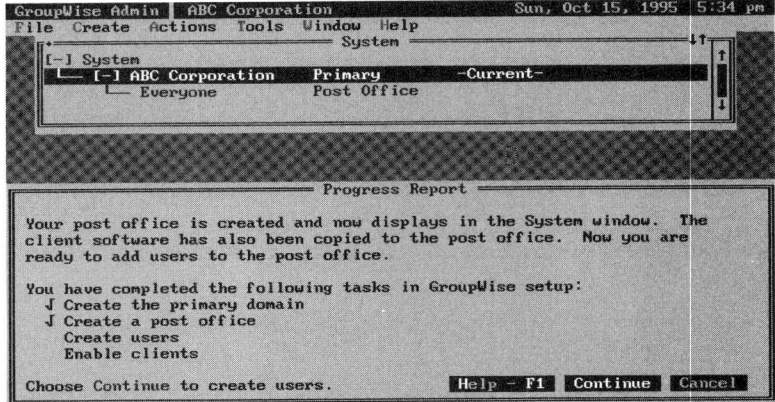

1. Start at Step 2 if you're continuing from the previous section. If you started this procedure by typing *AD* at the DOS prompt in the DOMAIN directory, then you'll need to Click on Continue at the Partial Setup Detected dialog. You'll see the Progress Report dialog box shown in Fig. 17-16.
2. Click on Continue. You'll see the Add User dialog box shown in Fig. 17-17.
3. Type the name of the first user, preferably the network administrator. Using the user's login name will reduce confusion later. In this case we used the name *John*.
4. Click on OK to accept the user name. GroupWise Admin will display a User Attributes dialog box like the one shown in Fig. 17-18. You can use same the settings that we did in the figure or come up with

**Figure 17-17**
Add User Dialog Box.

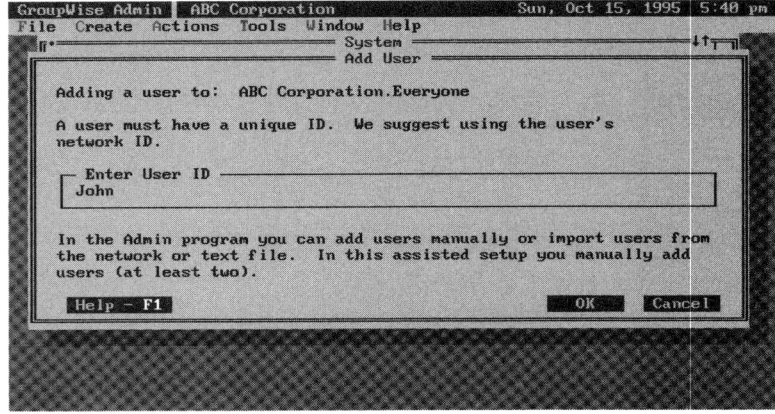

# GroupWise System Administration

**Figure 17-18**
User Attributes Dialog Box.

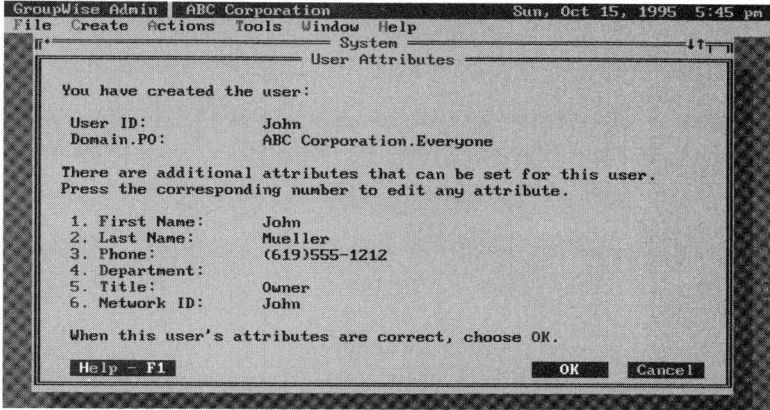

some of your own. GroupWise does not require you to provide any of the optional attributes; you can simply accept the default settings.

5. Click on OK when you are satisfied with the user attributes. Group-Wise will display an Add Users dialog box like the one shown in Fig. 17-19. In this case, you select whether or not you want to create additional users. Note that we can see the first user in the Users dialog.

6. Click on Add User to create another user. (Don't click on Add User after you have added all four users; skip to Step 8 instead.)

7. Perform Steps 3 to 6 for users *Rebecca, Cindy,* and *Bob.*

8. Click on Continue. You'll see the Progress Report dialog box shown in Fig. 17-20. Note that we can see at least three of our four users (you might see more).

**Figure 17-19**
Add Users Dialog Box.

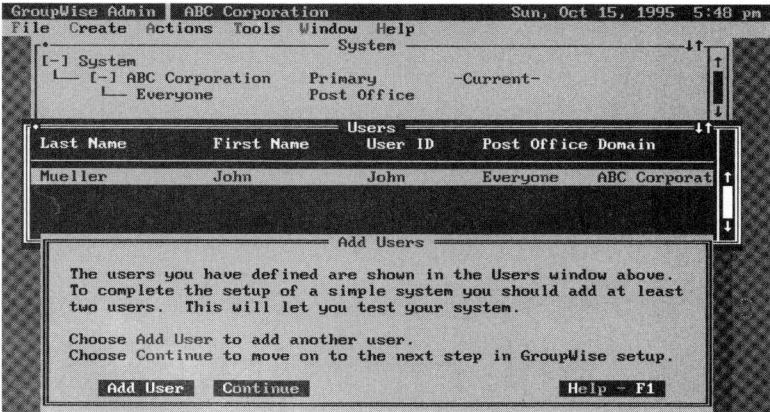

**Figure 17-20**
User Creation Progress Report Dialog Box.

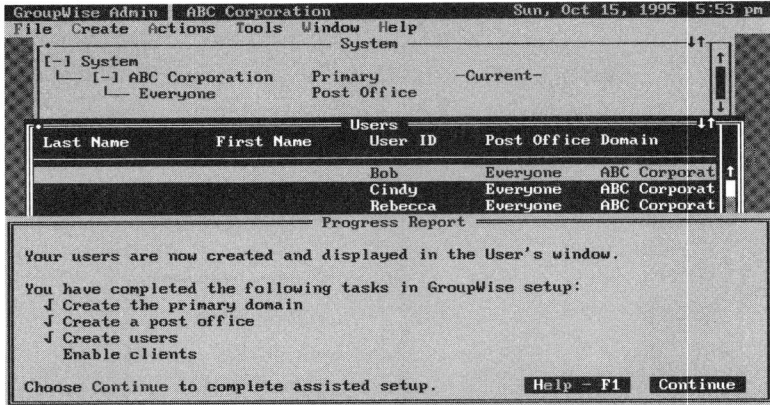

9. Click on Continue to clear the Progress Report dialog. You will see the Enable Clients dialog box shown in Fig. 17-21. Note that you have to perform this step manually. However, GroupWise Admin does provide a SUMMARY.TXT file to assist you. This file contains the information that you should have placed on your worksheet, so you can refer to it if the worksheet gets lost.

10. Click on Done to exit the GroupWise Admin program. You will see a DOS prompt.

**SETTING UP THE WORKSTATION.** GroupWise is ready to go now, but your users still can't access it. You have to add a shortcut to the client software in either Program Manager (Windows 3.x) or the Start Menu (Windows 95). There are two phases to this process. The administrator has to perform some setup first. The setup creates a common set of files

**Figure 17-21**
Enable Clients Dialog Box.

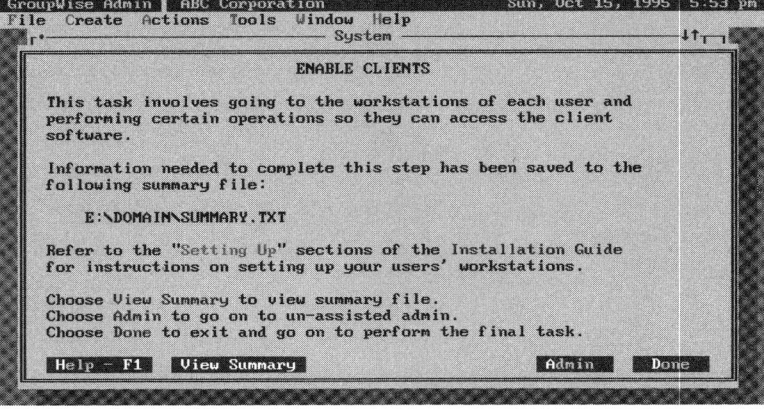

# GroupWise System Administration 533

on the shared drive. The users can then add GroupWise to their workstations using the files that the administrator created. The following example shows you how to add the required shortcut to a Windows 3.x or Windows 95 workstation. (Any differences between Windows 3.x and Windows 95 appear in parentheses.)

1. Perform any steps needed to start Windows on a workstation (preferably the network administrator's workstation) and log into the network.

2. Use the File | Run command in Program Manager (*Run* on the Start menu) to start the SETUPWIN /A command from the post office directory on the network (in our case, *EVERYONE*). Using the /A switch starts the program in administrator mode. You'll see a dialog box similar to the one shown in Fig. 17-22.

3. Click the Standard Install pushbutton. GroupWise will ask you which drive to use for the shared files using a dialog box similar to the one shown in Fig. 17-23.

4. Select the appropriate network drive, then click on OK. In this case we chose drive H. The workstation installation program normally displays the same drive as your post office as a default. You'll see a progress indicator as the GroupWise Server Install program completes its task.

5. A final dialog will ask if you want to read the README files. You'd normally say yes, but click on *No* for the purposes of this example. You'll see the dialog box shown in Fig. 17-24.

6. Click on OK. The administrator portion of the workstation installation is complete.

7. Perform any steps needed to start Windows on one of the client workstations and log into the network.

**Figure 17-22**
GroupWise Server Install Dialog Box.

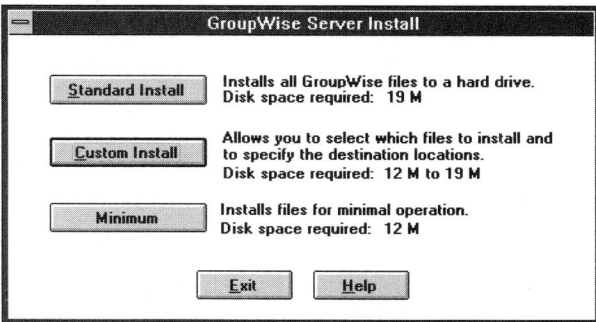

**Figure 17-23**
Select Drive Dialog Box.

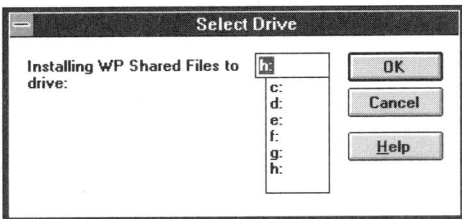

8. Use the File ¦ Run command in Program Manager (*Run* on the Start menu) to start the SETUPWIN command from the post office directory on the network (in our case, *EVERYONE*). Don't use the /A switch this time since you don't want to run the program in administrator mode. You'll see a dialog box similar to the one shown in Fig. 17-25.

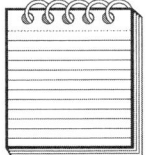

**NOTE** *If GroupWise Install won't allow you to select the Workstation pushbutton in the next step, you need to have the administrator perform the GroupWise Server Install portion of this procedure (Steps 1 to 6) on the affected machine.*

9. Click on the Workstation pushbutton. The first three options are used with a floppy disk installation. This fourth option was enabled when we performed the administrator setup in Steps 1 to 6. You'll see a System Initialization dialog, then the Set Up Program Manager Group dialog box shown in Fig. 17-26.

10. Click OK to select the default group of GroupWise. The installation program will create the new Program Manager group shown in Fig. 17-26. Once it completes this step, the installation program will ask if you want to read the README files.

11. Normally you would click on Yes to read the latest information about GroupWise. Click on *No* for the purposes of this example. You will see a Quick Tour dialog box.

12. Normally you would want to take the quick tour to learn how to use GroupWise (it takes 15 minutes). For the purposes of this example,

**Figure 17-24**
GroupWise Installation Complete Dialog Box.

# GroupWise System Administration

**Figure 17-25**
GroupWise Install Dialog Box.

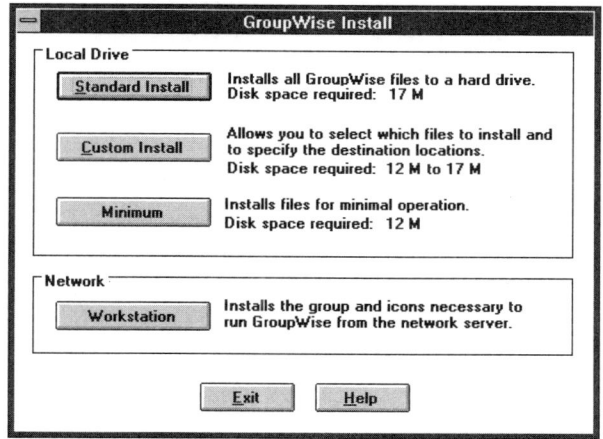

click on *No.* The GroupWise Install program will display an installation complete dialog like the one shown in Fig. 17-27.

13. Click on OK to complete the installation. The GroupWise Installation program will end.
14. Perform Steps 8 to 13 for all remaining workstations. Once you complete the installation on all workstations, the GroupWise installation is complete.
15. As a final step, you must set the rights for each user on the network. Make sure you give regular users access to only the post office directory. Administrators will require access to both the post office and the domain directories.

## The Final Test

The final step is to make sure that everything you set up works properly. You need to ensure that the users can receive messages from you first. Then, try communications the other way. See if the users can send a message to you. It probably isn't necessary to test every link on the entire

**Figure 17-26**
Set Up Program Manager Group Dialog Box.

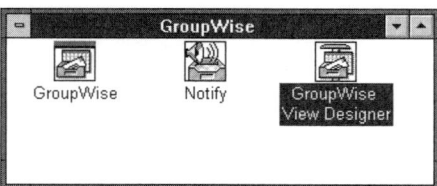

**Figure 17-27**
GroupWise Installation Complete Dialog Box.

network, but you should try a few. The following procedure shows one way to test the GroupWise setup. Of course, this isn't the only way, but it probably is the fastest.

1. Using the chart in Fig. 17-28 as guideline, create a chart of all the users for your network.
2. Log into the network as the first user. In our example, this is user *John*.
3. Verify that you can access both the post office (*EVERYONE* in our example) and the domain (*DOMAIN* in our example) directory if this is an administrator account. Verify that you cannot access the domain directory if this is a user account, but that the post office directory is still accessible. Repeat this step for each user on the network.
4. Send a message to each user individually, then to all the users as a group. Place a check mark next to each user's name as you receive a reply. Make sure you get an individual reply for each message since there are error conditions that will affect one, but not the other, type of message.
5. If you didn't get a reply from a particular user, verify that your messages were received. If they were, then there's a problem with either the user's rights to the post office directory or some part of the installation. Check the user rights first, then try to reinstall the software to correct the problem.

**Figure 17-28**
GroupWise Workstation Setup Checklist.

| Activity | John | Rebecca | Cyndie | Bob |
|---|---|---|---|---|
| Directory rights assigned | | | | |
| Single message sent | | | | |
| Group message sent | | | | |
| Single message response | | | | |
| Group message response | | | | |

# Study Questions

1. A GroupWise user normally has access to the _____ directory, but not the _____ directory.
   a. Mail, post office
   b. Domain, post office
   c. Post office, domain
   d. Public, private

   *a.* A user must have access to the post office directory to access mail and the working copy of the client software. They don't need access to the domain directory because the administrator software and a copy of the client software are stored there.

2. The GroupWise Windows client requires _____ of disk space for a full installation.
   a. 11 MB
   b. 12 MB
   c. 17 MB
   d. 19 MB

   *c.* A minimum installation requires 12 MB. To get all the GroupWise client features, you need to allocate 17 MB. The server installation requires 19 MB of hard drive space.

3. What are the three types of views you can use with GroupWise?
   a. Public, Private, and Calendar
   b. Group, Personal, and Calendar
   c. Group, Personal, and EMail
   d. Public, Private, and EMail

   *b.* The *group* view allows you to send mail messages, appointments, tasks, notes, or phone messages to other users. The *personal* view allows you to create appointments, tasks, or notes for your own use. The *calendar* view displays all your scheduled items. It includes the date they are scheduled and when they are due.

4. Granting proxy rights to your GroupWise mailbox allows anyone in your group to access your messages.
   a. True
   b. False

b. You have to grant proxy rights to a specific person. The designated individual can answer your mail and other items on your behalf. This is a handy feature to use if you intend to be away from the office for an extended period of time.

5. The Admin program is available for the _____ operating system(s).
    a. DOS
    b. Windows
    c. Macintosh
    d. UNIX

    *a and d.* The client software is available for all four operating systems, but the administration software will only run under DOS and UNIX.

6. An undeleted item appears in the _____ folder if the folder the item was deleted from no longer exists.
    a. Out Box
    b. Main
    c. Root
    d. In Box

    *c.* The undeleted item will appear in the root folder of either the In Box or the Out Box, depending on which folder it was deleted from, if the user has removed the original folder.

7. The three types of domain links that GroupWise provides include _____, _____, and _____.
    a. Mail, post office
    b. Domain, post office
    c. Post office, domain
    d. Direct, indirect, gateway

    *d.* The three link types are direct, indirect, and gateway. You can create both *direct* and *indirect* links using the base product. The *gateway* link requires additional message server and gateway software.

8. GroupWise scripts contain _____ pairs of _____ and _____ fields.
    a. 16, When given, Respond with
    b. 32, When given, Respond with
    c. 16, input, output
    d. 16, Get information, Send information

# GroupWise System Administration

    *a.* There are 16 pairs of fields in each script. The *When given* fields can contain 17 characters each. The *Respond with* fields can contain 49 characters each.

9. GroupWise allows you to create _____ primary domain(s) on your system.
   a. 1
   b. 2
   c. 4
   d. Unlimited

    *a.* You can only create one primary domain. All other domains that you create are called *secondary* domains. The primary domain acts as a central distribution point and sends information to all secondary domains.

10. You can get step-by-step GroupWise usage instructions from _____.
    a. Quick Tour
    b. Cue Cards
    c. Coach
    d. How Do I

    *c.* The Coach will provide step-by-step instructions for performing many tasks. You can also use the How Do I help option to get explanations of how to perform common tasks.

11. GroupWise directly supports which of the following networks?
    a. Banyan Street Talk
    b. IBM LAN Server
    c. Microsoft LAN Manager
    d. Artisoft LANtastic

    *a, b, c, and d.* GroupWise directly supports all the networks in this list in addition to Novell NetWare. You must choose the *Other* option during setup if you are using a peer-to-peer network other than LANtastic.

12. You will find the AD.EXE program in the _____ directory.
    a. Mail
    b. Domain
    c. Post office
    d. Administrator

b. The administrator program, AD.EXE, is always found in the domain directory. (The actual directory name depends on the directory you specified during installation.)

13. The Busy Search feature of GroupWise allows you to determine when other people are busy.
    a. True
    b. False

    *a.* All you need to do is select the people you want to have a meeting with, then click on the Busy icon to use the Busy Search feature.

14. Which of the following commands will start the Windows client software installation on a workstation?
    a. SETUP
    b. SETUPWIN
    c. INSTALL
    d. SETUP /A

    *b.* You use the SETUPWIN command to start the installation process. Adding the /A switch will start the setup software in the administrator mode.

15. GroupWise allows you to import user names from which of the following?
    a. Novell NetWare
    b. Banyan VINES
    c. IBM LAN Server
    d. Microsoft LAN Manager
    e. ASCII text file

    *a, b, c, d, and e.* GroupWise allows you to import user names from any of these sources. You may also import them from WordPerfect Office Notebook. Of course, you can always create the user names manually.

16. _____ link domains together in a multiple domain GroupWise setup.
    a. Leased lines
    b. MODEMs
    c. Gateways
    d. Message servers

# GroupWise System Administration

    *d.* Two or more message servers create the links between multiple domains. Each primary domain requires its own message server.

17. To connect a GroupWise with WP Office, the GroupWise setup must have a _____ and the WP Office setup must have a _____.
    a. Gateway, message server
    b. Connection server, connection server
    c. Message server, connection server
    d. Message server, message server

    *c.* The GroupWise setup must have a message server, while the WP Office setup uses a connection server. You add the WP Office's hosts to GroupWise under the External Office domain, then define the GroupWise post offices as route hosts.

18. GroupWise administration tasks that you cannot perform through a gateway include:
    a. Creating a domain
    b. Modifying objects
    c. Copying software to the domain
    d. Modifying the message server configuration settings

    *a and c.* GroupWise won't allow you to create a domain or copy software to the domain through a gateway. Other tasks that you can't perform include creating the domain's post offices and merging or releasing domains.

19. You will find a list of WP Office post offices in the _____ file. The AD utility allows you to convert them into a GroupWise format and add them to your regular GroupWise post office list.
    a. USERID.NB
    b. HOSTID.NB
    c. RESOURCE.NB
    d. HOSTID.DB

    *b.* The HOSTID.DB file contains the list of WP Office hosts. The AD utility converts them to post offices for use under GroupWise.

20. Each GroupWise domain owns the following object types:
    a. Users, resources, groups, and nicknames
    b. Gateways, resources, groups, and users

c. Message servers, gateways, users, and groups

d. Groups, users, resources, and clients

*a.* Each GroupWise domain owns one or more user, resource, group, and nickname objects.

21. GroupWise uses _____ files to store configuration information.
    a. INI
    b. CFG
    c. TXT
    d. BIF

*d.* The latest version of GroupWise (the one you'll be tested on) uses the BIF file, not the INI file for configuration storage.

22. An attachment is a _____ which may contain text, graphics, applications, sounds, or movies.
    a. Task
    b. OLE object
    c. File
    d. Note

*b and c.* GroupWise allows you to attach OLE objects or files to notes and mail messages. Sending attachments makes it easier for coworkers to find the resources they need to get a job done.

23. You use the _____ program in the _____ directory to install GroupWise Remote from the network.
    a. RMSETUP.EXE, \post office\OFWIN40
    b. AD.EXE, domain
    c. RMSETUP.EXE, \WPC20
    d. SETUPUS.EXE, \post office\OFWIN40

*a.* You would use the RMSETUP utility to install GroupWise Remote from the network. You can also install it from floppies using the standard SETUP program found on the Client 1 disk.

24. The @B[#] script command _____.
    a. Sends # beep signals to the host computer
    b. Sets the machine up for binary transfer mode
    c. Changes the display mode to black and white
    d. Sends a break signal # milliseconds long

# GroupWise System Administration

    *d.* The break signal is used for a variety of purposes, like gaining the attention of the host computer after you connect.

25. You can retract _____ whether or not the recipient has opened them.
    a. Mail
    b. Appointments
    c. Tasks
    d. Phone messages
    e. Notes

*b, c, and e.* GroupWise allows you to retract any appointments, tasks, or notes you send to someone else, even if they've already opened them. You cannot retract mail and phone messages once the recipient has opened them.

26. You must add the users contained in the _____ file and the resources contained in the _____ file from a WP Office setup before you can convert it.
    a. USERID.DB, RESOURCE.DB
    b. USER5K1.DB, USERLCO.DB
    c. USERID.NB, RESOURCE.NB
    d. USER.NB, RESOURCE.NB

*c.* You use the File | Convert command of the AD utility to convert the user identification information in USERID.NB and the resource information in RESOURCE.NB.

27. The _____ utility allows you to detect errors in a GroupWise database using batch file commands.
    a. AD
    b. OFCHECK
    c. OFSETUP
    d. LC

*d.* You can use batch commands with the OFCHECK utility by specifying the BATCH command line switch. You also have to supply an options filename and one or more command line switches that tell the name and location of the post office you want to check.

28. GroupWise supports the _____ external domain(s).
    a. Primary
    b. Office 3.1

    **c.** GroupWise 4.x

    **d.** Secondary

*b and c.* You would use the Office 3.1 option to connect to WP Office 3.1 systems. The GroupWise 4.x allows you to connect to external GroupWise domains.

29. You would use a _____ to link two or more remote GroupWise sites together.

    **a.** Leased line

    **b.** MODEM

    **c.** Gateway

    **d.** Message server

    *c.* A gateway will allow you to create remote connections. Novell supports a variety of connection types like X.400 and Async.

30. The text descriptions of notes, tasks, and appointments remain italicized in your Calendar until you accept or decline them.

    **a.** True

    **b.** False

    *a.* Using an italic font helps you find new items in your Calendar quickly. If you accept an item, the font changes to normal and GroupWise informs the sender of your acceptance. Otherwise, GroupWise removes the entry from your Calendar and tells the sender you declined.

31. GroupWise Remote requires a minimum of _____ extended memory and _____ disk space.

    **a.** 4 MB, 17 MB

    **b.** 8 MB, 17 MB

    **c.** 4 MB, 13 MB

    **d.** 8 MB, 13 MB

    *c.* You must have a minimum of 4 MB of extended memory and 13 MB of disk space to install GroupWise Remote. However, Novell recommends 8 MB or more of RAM for optimum performance. You'll also need 17 MB of disk space if you want to install all the GroupWise features.

# GroupWise System Administration

32. You can add resources to GroupWise using which of the following as a source?
    a. Novell NetWare
    b. Banyan VINES
    c. IBM LAN Server
    d. Microsoft LAN Manager
    e. ASCII text file

    *e.* The only source you can use to import resources from this list is the ASCII text file. You can also import resources from WordPerfect Office Notebook or create them manually.

33. You can use the _____ Database option of the GroupWise administration program to correct physical post office problems as well as to update incorrect database information.
    a. Update
    b. Recover
    c. Fix
    d. Rebuild

    *d.* The *Rebuild Database* option allows you to correct physical problems and update the database information. However, this can be a very time consuming process. Use the *Recover Database* option if you only need to correct physical problems in the database.

34. The standard GroupWise setup uses the _____ key to access help.
    a. Escape
    b. F1
    c. F2
    d. F3

    *b.* Normally, F1 is the help key in GroupWise. However, you can change this to F3 by selecting the Keyboard (F1 = Cancel, F3 = Help) option in the Setup dialog box.

35. The GroupWise Windows Client files appear in the _____ directory.
    a. WPINFF
    b. OFUNIX40
    c. OFWIN40
    d. OFFILES

c. The Windows Client files appear in the OFWIN40 directory. You'll find the UNIX Client files in the OFUNIX40 directory and the WordPerfect InForms Filler files in the WPINFF directory.

36. GroupWise Remote requires one of which of the following gateways?
    a. X.400
    b. X.25
    c. Telephone Access Server
    d. Async

    *b and d.* You need a message server and either an Async or X.25 gateway to use GroupWise remote. GroupWise Remote can also use a direct network connection if you don't have a gateway installed, but you still need a message server.

37. When creating a single domain, multiple post office setup, all the post offices have to appear on the same server.
    a. True
    b. False

    *b.* You may place all the post offices on a single server, but this isn't a requirement. One of the reasons for creating a multiple post office setup is if the network users can't all access the same file server.

38. You send a carriage return using the _____ GroupWise script command.
    a. ^J
    b. ^I
    c. ^[
    d. ^M

    *d.* The ^M command is the same as sending a carriage return. You normally use ^M to end a command.

39. You can use the _____ utility found in the _____ directory to edit GroupWise BIF files.
    a. AD, domain
    b. BIFED20, WPC20
    c. AD, OFFILES
    d. BIFED20, OFWIN40

    *b.* The BIF Edit utility allows you to make changes to a GroupWise configuration file.

# GroupWise System Administration

40. You can undelete or accept a declined item in your GroupWise Calendar until you _____.
    a. End the current session.
    b. Tell GroupWise to send the results to the sender.
    c. Empty your Trash box.
    d. Move the item to the Trash box.

    *c.* GroupWise automatically places any items you delete or decline in the Trash box. All you need to do to reinstate the item so that you can accept it is undelete it. You can access the Trash box by double clicking on the Trash icon.

## Fun Test

1. The text descriptions of notes, tasks, and appointments remain italicized in your Calendar until you accept or decline them.
   a. True
   b. False

2. GroupWise directly supports which of the following networks?
   a. Banyan Street Talk
   b. IBM LAN Server
   c. Microsoft LAN Manager
   d. Artisoft LANtastic

3. You will find a list of WP Office post offices in the _____ file. The AD utility allows you to convert them into a GroupWise format and add them to your regular GroupWise post office list.
   a. USERID.NB
   b. HOSTID.NB
   c. RESOURCE.NB
   d. HOSTID.DB

4. You can add resources to GroupWise using which of the following as a source?
   a. Novell NetWare
   b. Banyan VINES
   c. IBM LAN Server

d. Microsoft LAN Manager

e. ASCII text file

5. What are the three types of views you can use with GroupWise?

   a. Public, Private, and Calendar

   b. Group, Personal, and Calendar

   c. Group, Personal, and EMail

   d. Public, Private, and EMail

6. You must add the users contained in the _____ file and the resources contained in the _____ file from a WP Office setup before you can convert it.

   a. USERID.DB, RESOURCE.DB

   b. USER5K1.DB, USERLCO.DB

   c. USERID.NB, RESOURCE.NB

   d. USER.NB, RESOURCE.NB

7. _____ link domains together in a multiple domain GroupWise setup.

   a. Leased lines

   b. MODEMs

   c. Gateways

   d. Message servers

8. You use the _____ program in the _____ directory to install GroupWise Remote from the network.

   a. RMSETUP.EXE, \post office\OFWIN40

   b. AD.EXE, domain

   c. RMSETUP.EXE, \WPC20

   d. SETUPUS.EXE, \post office\OFWIN40

9. An attachment is a(n) _____ which may contain text, graphics, applications, sounds, or movies.

   a. Task

   b. OLE object

   c. File

   d. Note

10. The GroupWise Windows client requires _____ of disk space for a full installation.

    a. 11 MB

    b. 12 MB

# GroupWise System Administration

    c. 17 MB
    d. 19 MB

11. GroupWise Remote requires one of which of the following gateways?
    a. X.400
    b. X.25
    c. Telephone Access Server
    d. Async

12. GroupWise allows you to create _____ primary domain(s) on your system.
    a. 1
    b. 2
    c. 4
    d. Unlimited

13. Each GroupWise domain owns the following object types:
    a. Users, resources, groups, and nicknames
    b. Gateways, resources, groups, and users
    c. Message servers, gateways users, and groups
    d. Groups, users, resources, and clients

14. You can retract _____ whether or not the recipient has opened them.
    a. Mail
    b. Appointments
    c. Tasks
    d. Phone messages
    e. Notes

15. Granting proxy rights to your GroupWise mailbox allows anyone in your group to access your messages.
    a. True
    b. False

16. You can use the _____ Database option of the GroupWise administration program to correct physical post office problems as well as update incorrect database information.
    a. Update
    b. Recover
    c. Fix
    d. Rebuild

17. GroupWise scripts contain _____ pairs of _____ and _____ fields.
    a. 16, When given, Respond with
    b. 32, When given, Respond with
    c. 16, input, output
    d. 16, Get information, Send information

18. GroupWise allows you to import user names from which of the following?
    a. Novell NetWare
    b. Banyan VINES
    c. IBM LAN Server
    d. Microsoft LAN Manager
    e. ASCII text file

19. You can undelete or accept a declined item in your GroupWise Calendar until you _____.
    a. End the current session
    b. Tell GroupWise to send the results to the sender
    c. Empty your Trash box
    d. Move the item to the Trash box

20. The Admin program is available for the _____ operating system(s).
    a. DOS
    b. Windows
    c. Macintosh
    d. UNIX

21. The _____ utility allows you to detect errors in a GroupWise database using batch file commands.
    a. AD
    b. OFCHECK
    c. OFSETUP
    d. LC

22. You can get step-by-step GroupWise usage instructions from _____.
    a. Quick Tour
    b. Cue Cards
    c. Coach
    d. How Do I

# GroupWise System Administration

23. To connect a GroupWise with WP Office, the GroupWise setup must have a _____ and the WP Office setup must have a _____.
    a. Gateway, message server
    b. Connection server, connection server
    c. Message server, connection server
    d. Message server, message server

24. A GroupWise user normally has access to the _____ directory, but not the _____ directory.
    a. Mail, post office
    b. Domain, post office
    c. Post office, domain
    d. Public, private

25. The @B[#] script command _____.
    a. Sends # beep signals to the host computer
    b. Sets the machine up for binary transfer mode
    c. Changes the display mode to black and white
    d. Sends a break signal # milliseconds long

26. You can use the _____ utility found in the _____ directory to edit GroupWise BIF files.
    a. AD, domain
    b. BIFED20, WPC20
    c. AD, OFFILES
    d. BIFED20, OFWIN40

27. GroupWise administration tasks that you can't perform through a gateway include:
    a. Creating a domain
    b. Modifying objects
    c. Copying software to the domain
    d. Modifying the message server configuration settings

28. An undeleted item appears in the _____ folder if the folder the item was deleted from no longer exists.
    a. Out Box
    b. Main
    c. Root
    d. In Box

29. Which of the following commands will start the Windows client software installation on a workstation?
    a. SETUP
    b. SETUPWIN
    c. INSTALL
    d. SETUP /A

30. You send a carriage return using the _____ GroupWise script command.
    a. ^J
    b. ^I
    c. ^[
    d. ^M

31. The Busy Search feature of GroupWise allows you to determine when other people are busy.
    a. True
    b. False

32. The three types of domain links that GroupWise provides include _____, _____, and _____.
    a. Mail, post office
    b. Domain, post office
    c. Post office, domain
    d. Direct, indirect, gateway

33. GroupWise supports the _____ external domain(s).
    a. Primary
    b. Office 3.1
    c. GroupWise 4.x
    d. Secondary

34. When creating a single domain, multiple post office setup, all the post offices have to appear on the same server.
    a. True
    b. False

35. GroupWise uses _____ files to store configuration information.
    a. INI
    b. CFG
    c. TXT
    d. BIF

# GroupWise System Administration

36. GroupWise Remote requires a minimum of _____ extended memory and _____ disk space.
    a. 4 MB, 17 MB
    b. 8 MB, 17 MB
    c. 4 MB, 13 MB
    d. 8 MB, 13 MB

37. The GroupWise Windows Client files appear in the _____ directory.
    a. WPINFF
    b. OFUNIX40
    c. OFWIN40
    d. OFFILES

38. You will find the AD.EXE program in the _____ directory.
    a. Mail
    b. Domain
    c. Post office
    d. Administrator

39. You would use a _____ to link two or more remote GroupWise sites together.
    a. Leased line
    b. MODEM
    c. Gateway
    d. Message server

40. The standard GroupWise setup uses the _____ key to access help.
    a. Escape
    b. F1
    c. F2
    d. F3

# Brain Teaser

Installing GroupWise as we did in this chapter is only one step in an ongoing process. Keeping the mail secure once users start generating messages is another problem you'll have to solve. In fact, GroupWise requires just as much, if not more, security precautions than other applications on your server. The cryptogram in Fig. 17-29 provides you with a

**Figure 17-29**
GroupWise Security Cryptogram.

APVGUBXI BA D TDNQU JUQMYPT QW TDWI WPXRQUHA, MGX IQG VDW VQWXUQY BX MI VQWXUQYYBWK FDXD DVVPAA. UPTPTMPU XSDX D GAPU TGAX SDOP DVVPAA XQ XSPBU JQAX QZZBVP FBUPVXQUI XQ DVVPAA XSPBU TDBY DWF XSP RQUHBWK VQJI QZ XSP VYBPWX AQZXRDUP. XSPI FQW'X WPPF DVVPAA XQ XSP FQTDBW FBUPVXQUI MPVDGAP XSP DFTBWBAXUDXQU AQZXRDUP DWF D VQJI QZ XSP VYBPWX AQZXRDUP DUP AXQUPF XSPUP.

| A | | N | |
| --- | --- | --- | --- |
| B | | O | |
| C | | P | |
| D | | Q | |
| E | | R | |
| F | | S | |
| G | | T | |
| H | | U | |
| I | | V | |
| J | | W | |
| K | | X | |
| L | | Y | |
| M | | Z | |

# GroupWise System Administration

**Figure 17-30**
GroupWise Troubleshooting Cryptogram.

```
}:\:)^   ^#=<*{:(!  *#=%$!>( _!)  %!  /!#&  ?:>!  _=)(<>:)^  :}  &=<

;=)'?  }=$$={  ?+!  #:^+?  *#=_!;<#!.  ?+!  #!%<:$;  ;¦?¦%¦(!  =*?:=)

¦$$={(  &=<  ?=  _=##!_?  %=?+  *+&(:_¦$  *#=%$!>( ¦);  <*;¦?!  ?+!

;¦?¦%¦(! :)}=#>¦?:=).  <(! ?+!  #!_=/!#  ;¦?¦%¦(!  =*?:=) :}  &=<  =)$&

)!!;  ?=  _=##!_?  *+&(:_¦$  *#=%$!>( :)  ?+!  ;¦?¦%¦(!.
```

| | | | |
|---|---|---|---|
| ! | | { | |
| @ | | } | |
| # | | [ | |
| $ | | ] | |
| % | | < | |
| ^ | | > | |
| & | | ¦ | |
| * | | \ | |
| ( | | / | |
| ) | | ? | |
| _ | | ~ | |
| + | | : | |
| = | | ; | |

handy phrase that you can rely on to help you set up security on your GroupWise setup. You'll find the solution for this brain teaser in App. C, "Brain Teaser Answers."

If you're feeling especially knowledgeable, you can try your hand at the much more difficult cryptogram in Fig. 17-30. This is a GroupWise troubleshooting-related phrase based on one of the questions you answered in the preceding fun test section. Remember that this exam will test your knowledge of how to fix GroupWise-related errors as well as of managing GroupWise as a whole, so you need to be prepared for it. Just in case the idea of working with a symbol-oriented cryptogram is a bit intimidating for you, here's a tip: All spaces really are spaces and all periods are periods. Apostrophes are also what they appear to be. Every other symbol replaces a letter.

## Disk Time

Don't forget to spend some time working with the disk that accompanies this book. It provides valuable and fun-to-use teaching aids that will help prepare you for the exam. See "Disk Time" in the preface of this book for details about what the disk contains.

# CHAPTER 18
## GroupWise 4.x Asynchronous Gateway and Remote Client Support

## Introduction

This chapter looks at the requirements for the GroupWise 4.x Asynchronous Gateway and Remote Client Support exam. It's one of the exams for the new GroupWise CNE certification route that Novell has recently made available. Novell will test your ability to install and use the message server software. You will also need to show that you can use the message server both in stand-alone mode and with a gateway. Novell provides several different gateways, but this exam will concentrate on your knowledge of the asynchronous gateway normally used by off-site employees. You'll also be called upon to demonstrate your ability to perform advanced administrative tasks. The majority of the administration questions you will see will center around the message server itself, not GroupWise installation or user and resource administration topics. You may still see some installation and usage related questions, but they will be the exception rather than the rule.

There's no NetWare route exam that parallels this one. Since there are a variety of versions of this product, including NLM, OS/2, UNIX, and Windows, you'll need to take special care when studying for the exam. Novell could (and probably will) ask you questions centered on any of these product versions. We concentrate on the DOS version of the product in the case study since it's more likely that you'll use that product in a small network setup. (The other major version is the NLM version, which we cover extensively in the question and answer section.)

This exam covers a special requirement for using GroupWise efficiently in a corporate setting. You have to know how to communicate to use GroupWise to its fullest possible potential. There are several discrete sections in this chapter. Each section helps you study for the exam in a different way. You can improve your chances of passing the exam by using the study methods provided in this chapter. In fact, it'll probably help if you study all the sections once and your favorite sections at least twice. Review the study guidelines in Chap. 4 as often as necessary to ensure that you maintain the best possible study atmosphere.

**NOTE** *This chapter assumes that you have already bought the version of GroupWise required for your operating system and installed it using the default settings. We'll use a single domain, single post office setup as a starting point for the case study in this chapter. (You can follow the case study in Chap. 17 to create a standard setup if you need to.) You can still benefit from this chapter if you don't have a network by reading through the case study.*

# GroupWise 4.x Asynchronous Gateway/Remote Client Support

The first section of this chapter is a *case study*. You will perform some hands-on tasks that will help you learn what you need to know to pass the examination. This is a two-part case study. The first section looks at one of the ways that you can setup your GroupWise message server. We look at the DOS version of the product in the case study. Unfortunately, this will limit its appeal to those of you who have either installed the DOS version already or plan to use one of the other versions. Even if you do fall into this category, you can still follow along to learn a little more about the DOS version of the message server.

The second part of the case study talks about using the message server once you get it installed. Everyone should be able to follow this part of the case study, no matter which version of the message server you have installed. Even though you'll get a lot more from this section if you perform it on your own network, the inclusion of step-by-step instructions and screen shots will help you gain something from the section even if you don't have a network.

The second area contains *sample test questions* for this course. We make a special effort to include a variety of GroupWise administration-specific questions; but, as on the real exam, you'll find other types of questions as well. This section also includes the correct answers to those questions and an explanation of why each answer is correct. Try to answer each question yourself, look at the correct answer, then determine where you went wrong if you did not answer correctly.

The next section is a *fun test*. This is an exercise where you'll look at more sample test questions and answer them. The answers appear in App. B at the back of the book. This will help you test what you learned in the previous section.

The final text section of the chapter is the *brain teaser*. You'll get to have a little fun working on a NetWare 3.x- and NetWare 4.x-related puzzle. In this case, you'll need to look for words that we talked about in the case study or within Chaps. 12 and 13. Look for NetWare 4.x-related words from Chaps. 14 and 15 as well. You may even want to take the opportunity to look these words up in the glossary once you've completed the puzzle itself.

Finally, we'll spend some time using the *Jeopardy!*-type game named *Red Zone*. Unlike most sections of this book, there are only two GroupWise categories included with the game: *Administration* and *Remote Connections*. You need more than just GroupWise knowledge to pass the exam, so the lack of GroupWise categories shouldn't present any problems. Playing the Red Zone game helps you look at the test from the opposite viewpoint. The game provides you with an answer—you need to come up with the corresponding question. The game awards points for correct answers, and takes points away for incorrect answers. You'll receive a score at the end of the game proclaiming that you either did or did not get your certificate. Make sure you concentrate on the GroupWise-related questions when using the game; they're the ones that will provide you with the best information about the exams you are about to take. Unlike the specific questions provided in this chapter, Red Zone tests your overall knowledge of Novell products, so be prepared to explore areas that you haven't looked at in the past.

Use all the learning methods that we provide in this chapter to improve your chances of passing the exam. It's a good idea to save the fun test section until you're almost certain that you possess all the required knowledge. Remember, you can probably go through the fun test only two or three times at most before you'll start to remember the answers without out really knowing the material.

## Case Study

There are four separate procedures in this case study. The first two help you get the DOS version of the message server installed. The second two help you use the message server once you get it installed. Try to follow all four sections in sequence. Even if you aren't using the DOS version of the message server, you can at least read the procedure to see how our message server is set up. Here's an overview of this section of the chapter:

- Installing the GroupWise Message Server
- Configuring the GroupWise Message Server
- Creating Links Between Domains
- Checking Your Installation

The overall goal of this case study is to learn how to use the message server in a variety of ways. We concentrate on the message server because that is the most important part of creating a remote communication setup. The gateway shouldn't present much of a problem since most of them present about the same interface to the administrator. (Obviously, they are completely different from a communication point of view.)

# Installing the GroupWise Message Server

Before you can use a message server, you have to install it. This part of the case study shows you how to install the DOS version of the GroupWise Message Server software. You'll need a copy of the software and a dedicated workstation to actually complete the installation. If you lack either of these items, you can still follow along to see how we perform the installation.

**NOTE** *You must install and set up a domain and post office using the GroupWise administration product before you can install a message server. The message server software allows you to create links between two or more post offices. You also need to install it prior to installing a gateway*

1. Place the message server disk in a floppy drive. Change drives to the floppy drive. Type *Install* and press Enter. You'll see the initial installation dialog.
2. Type *T* to select the *Install To* field. Type *E:\DOMAIN* (or the path to your domain directory), then press Enter. The installation program will automatically select the *Files to Install* field for you.
3. Press Enter to open the software selection dialog box shown in Fig. 18-1.
4. Highlight the *Message Server* field and press Enter. Press F10 to complete the action. (You may also need to select the Office Compatibility option, but we don't need it for this example.) The installation

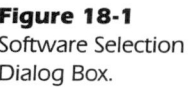
**Figure 18-1**
Software Selection Dialog Box.

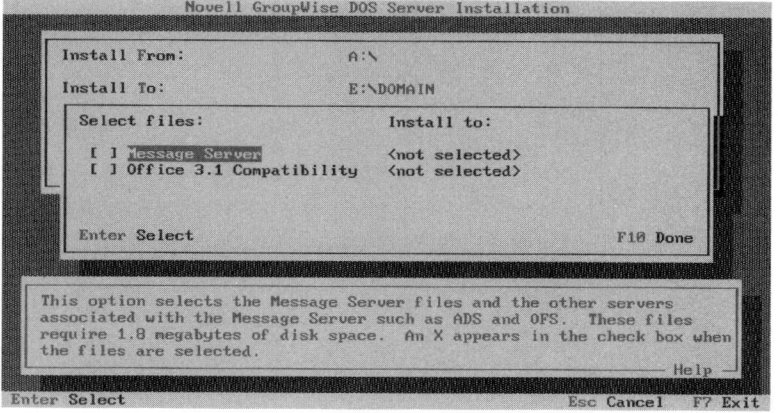

**Figure 18-2**
Main Installation Dialog Box.

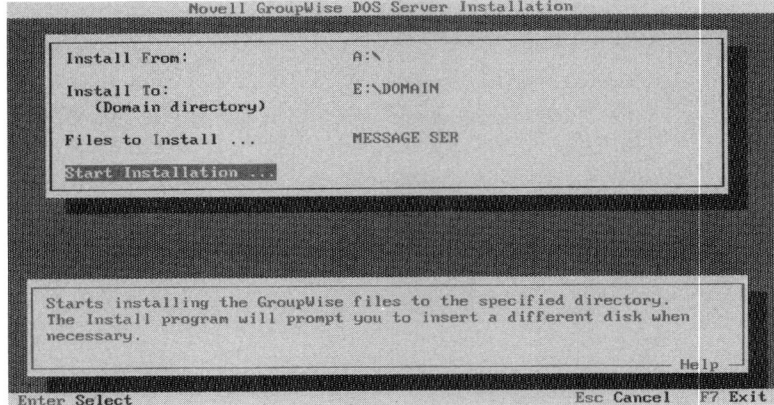

program will return you to the main installation dialog. Your dialog box should look similar to the one shown in Fig. 18-2.

5. Press Enter to start the message server installation. The installation program will display a last dialog box like the one shown in Fig. 18-3 asking if you want to accept the current setup.

6. Type Y to accept the parameters and begin the installation. The installation program will display some messages as it copies files to the hard drive. Once it completes the copying process, you'll see the success dialog box shown in Fig. 18-4. Note that the dialog tells you which software elements the installation program has installed.

7. Press Enter. The installation program will ask if you want to see the README file. Normally you would select Y at this dialog to see the most current message server information.

**Figure 18-3**
Continue Installation Message Dialog Box.

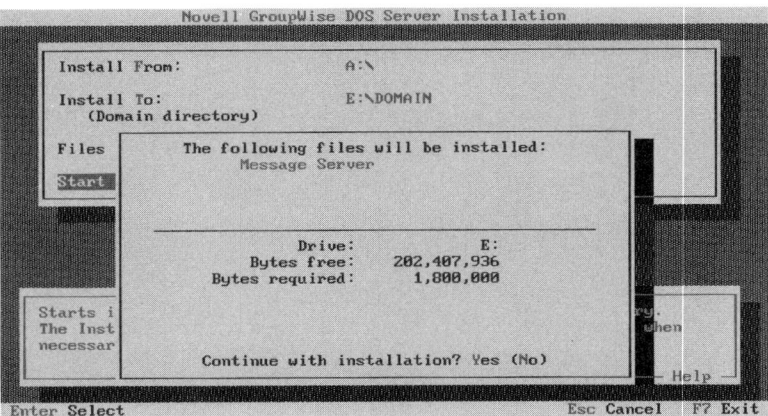

# GroupWise 4.x Asynchronous Gateway/Remote Client Support 563

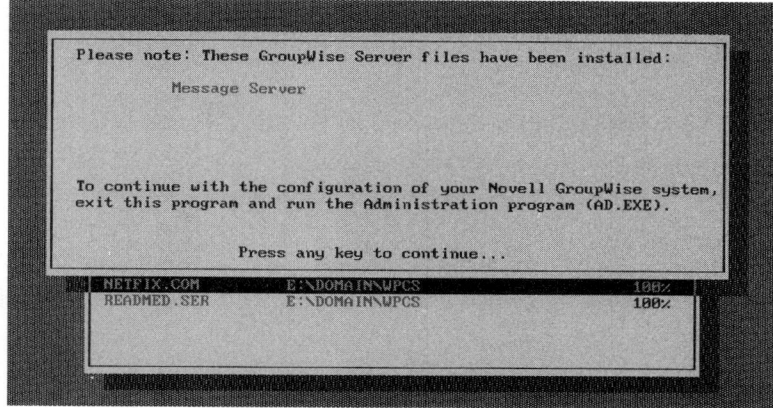

**Figure 18-4**
Installation Success Message Dialog Box.

8. Type *N* to bypass the README file for this example. The installation program will tell you to press Enter to exit the program.

9. Press Enter. You have successfully installed the message server software. Now that we have the message server software installed, we need to tell the GroupWise installation about it. We also need to configure the message server for use.

## Configuring the GroupWise Message Server

This part of the case study takes you through the steps of configuring your GroupWise domain to use a message server. Unlike some areas of this case study, you can use the same procedure no matter which version of the message server you install. The following procedure continues from the previous subsection of the case study. You can begin here if you already have the GroupWise software and a message server installed. This procedure also comes in handy when you want to reconfigure your message server. For example, you may need to add another domain and then configure it to use the message server as the size of your company increases.

1. Change directories to your domain directory (the \\*DOMAIN* directory in our case). Type *AD* and press Enter to start the administrator utility. You will see an initial system screen like the one in Fig. 18-5.

2. Highlight the primary domain (*ABC Corporation* for our example), then use the Actions ¦ Edit command or press the F6 key to display

**Figure 18-5**
Initial Administrator Utility Screen.

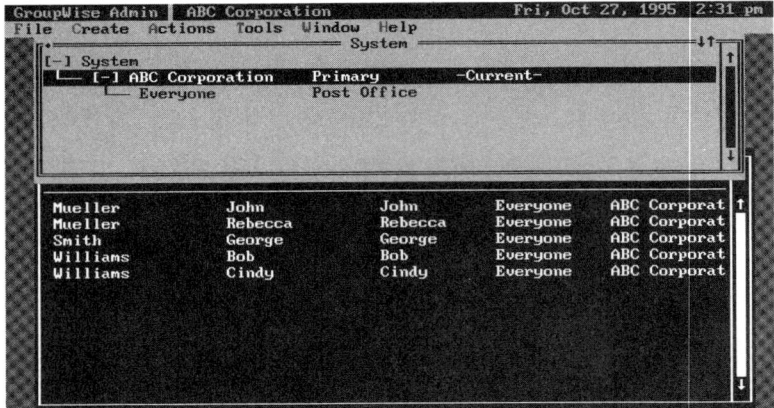

the Domain Information dialog box shown in Fig. 18-6. (You can also right-click on the domain entry and select Edit from the context menu.) Your display may differ slightly depending on your domain setup.

3. Click on the *Message Server Configuration* field (or type *M*) to display the Message Server Configuration dialog box shown in Fig. 18-7. This is where you'll configure GroupWise to use the message server. The first thing we need to do is turn the message server on.

4. Click on the *Message Delivery* field (or type *3*, then *5*). Highlight the *Use App Thresholds* option and press Enter.

5. Click on OK (or press Enter) to accept the message server configuration. GroupWise Admin will display a few messages as it updates your configuration.

**Figure 18-6**
Domain Information Dialog Box.

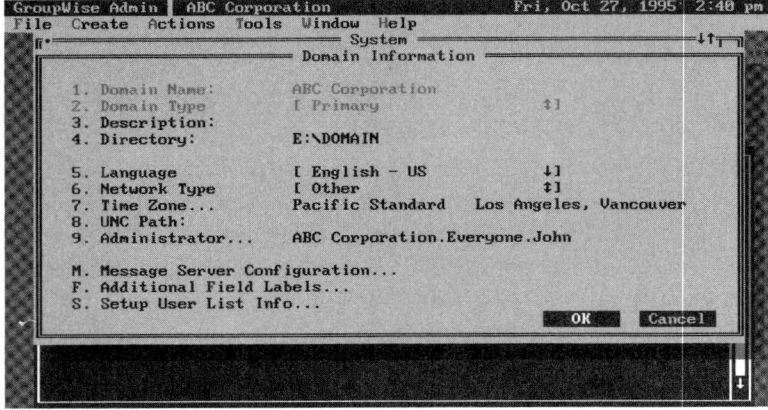

# GroupWise 4.x Asynchronous Gateway/Remote Client Support 565

**Figure 18-7**
Message Server Configuration Dialog Box.

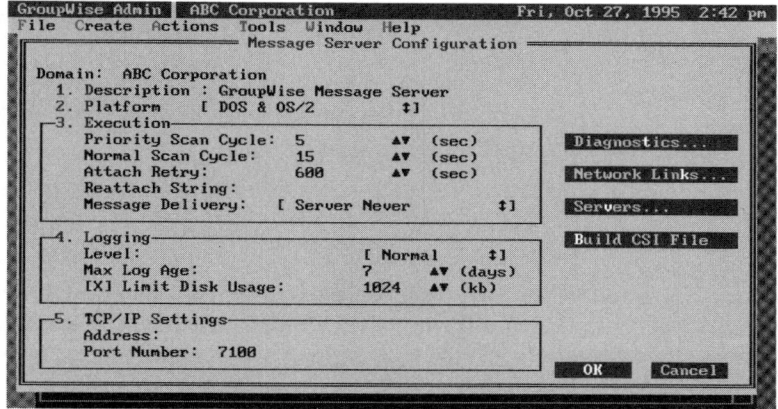

6. Click on OK in the Message Server Configuration dialog box to complete the action.

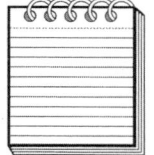

**NOTE** *You must have another domain with at least one post office installed to complete the next step. Use the procedure in Chap. 17 to create another domain if you need to. Once you complete this step, you can create a link between the two domains using the procedure in the next section.*

## Creating Links Between Domains

One of the reasons for using a Message Server is to create links between a primary and secondary (or other type) of domain. The message server provides two-way communication between the two domains, allowing them to talk to each other. The following procedure shows you how to create links between two domains. The same principles hold true for creating other types of links as well. Skip Steps 1 to 3 in this procedure if you already have a secondary domain with at least one post office installed on your machine. You must at least create a secondary domain before you proceed. We called our secondary domain *Satellite Office 1;* you can use any name you want. Just make the appropriate name and directory substitutions in the procedure.

1. Change directories to your secondary domain directory (the \*SAT01* directory in our case). Type *AD* and press Enter to start the administrator utility. You'll see an initial system screen like the one in Fig. 18-5.

2. Add a new post office named Managers to the secondary domain using the procedure found in Chap. 17. Once you complete this task, exit the GroupWise Admin program and continue with the next step. Now that we have two domains with at least one post office each, it's time to start the message server.

3. Change directories to your message server directory (the \*DOMAIN*\\*WPCS* directory in our case). Type *CS /PH-E: \DOMAIN /PC-E:\TEMP* and press Enter to start the Message Server. (Change the path as needed to fit your particular installation.) You'll see an initial Message Server status screen like the one shown in Fig. 18-8.

**NOTE** *You can run the Message Server in a DOS box under Windows 95 in most cases (it may also work in some cases under Windows 3.x). If this does work on your machine, you could start two DOS sessions—one for the message server and another for the GroupWise Admin utility. Make certain you keep track of any error messages on the Message Server if you do this. Novell recommends running the Message Server on a stand-alone machine.*

4. Type 5 to keep the message server running and exit to the DOS prompt. (You do not need to perform this step if you're running the GroupWise Admin utility in a separate session under Windows 95 or Windows 3.x.) We need to perform some additional work in the GroupWise Admin program before the setup is complete.

5. Change directories to your domain directory (the \*DOMAIN* directory in our case). Type *AD* and press Enter to start the administra-

**Figure 18-8**
Message Server Status Screen.

# GroupWise 4.x Asynchronous Gateway/Remote Client Support

tor utility. You'll see an initial system screen like the one in Fig. 18-5.

6. Highlight the *Satellite Office 1* entry in the System window. Use the Tools | Database Management | Sync Primary with Secondary command to synchronize the two domains. You should see the primary domain, *ABC Corporation,* with one post office named *Everyone.* The window should also include the secondary domain, *Satellite Office 1,* with a post office named *Managers.*

7. Highlight the primary domain (*ABC Corporation* for our example), then use the Actions | Edit command or press the F6 key to display the Domain Information dialog box shown in Fig. 18-6. (You can also right-click on the domain entry and select Edit from the context menu.) Your display may differ slightly depending on your domain setup.

8. Click on the *Message Server Configuration* field (or type *M*) to display the Message Server Configuration dialog box shown in Figure 18-7.

9. Click on the *Network Links* pushbutton (or type *K*) to display the Network Links dialog box shown in Fig. 18-9. This is where we'll define the communication links between domains. The first thing we'll need to do is define the appropriate link types.

10. Highlight the *Satellite Office 1* entry. Click on the *Edit Link* pushbutton (or type *E*) to display the Define Domain Connection dialog box shown in Fig. 18-10. Note that there are four different connection types: *Direct, Indirect, Gateway,* and *None.* You need to install

**Figure 18-9**
Network Links Dialog Box.

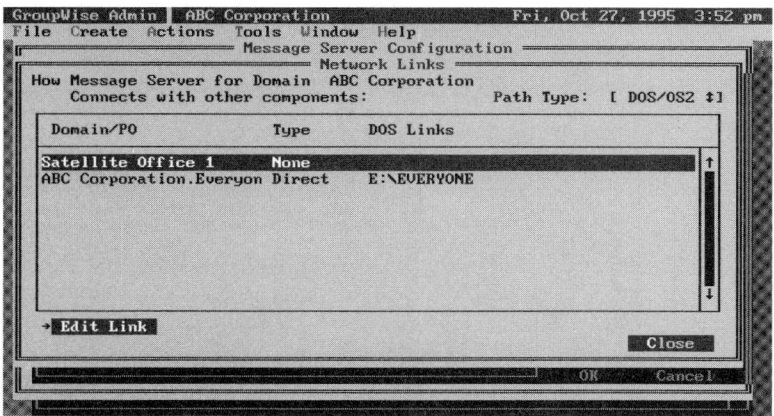

**Figure 18-10**
Define Domain Connection Dialog Box.

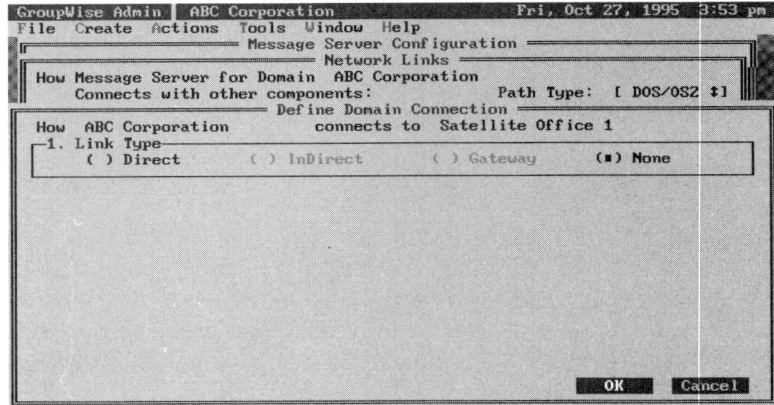

gateway software before GroupWise Admin will highlight the Gateway option. Your system must contain at least three domains before you can create an indirect link.

11. Click on the *Direct* radio button (or type *L,* then *D*). GroupWise will change the Define Domain Connection dialog as shown in Fig. 18-11. The only two settings that you need to verify for right now are the *Protocol* and the *Link Address.* Make sure the Protocol is set to *Mapped* and that the Link Address contains the path to the secondary domain.

12. Click on OK (or highlight *OK* and press Enter) to complete the action. You'll return to the Network Links dialog. You should see a Direct link for the Satellite Office 1 entry along with the appropriate

**Figure 18-11**
Define Domain Connection Dialog Box after Step 11.

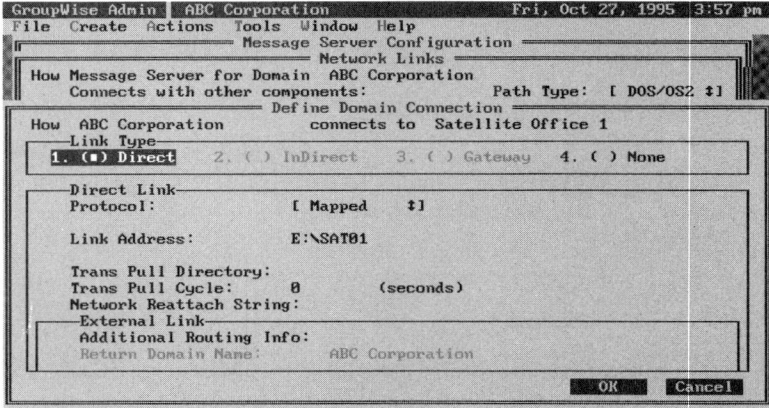

# GroupWise 4.x Asynchronous Gateway/Remote Client Support

**Figure 18-12**
Define Direct Post Office Connection Dialog Box.

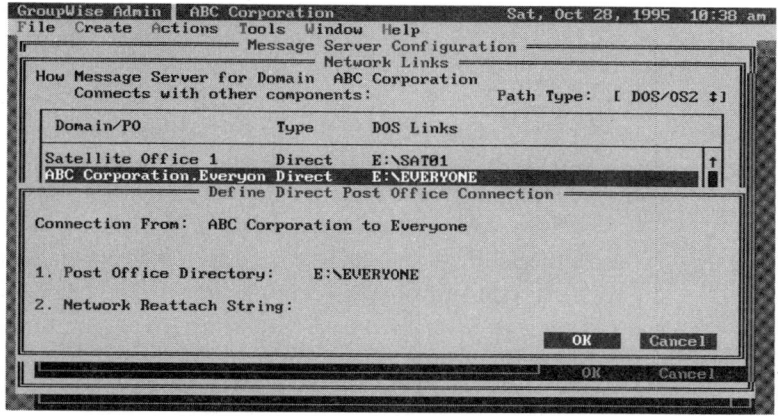

path entry. You should also see a direct link for the Everyone post office.

13. Highlight the *Everyone* post office entry. Press Enter to edit it. You will see a dialog box similar to the one in Fig. 18-12. In this case, the Post Office Directory field contains the correct information, so we don't need to change it.

14. Click on OK (or highlight *OK* and Press Enter) to complete the action. You'll return to the Network Links dialog. Both the post office and domain links are now verified. Normally you would verify each post office and domain separately, but we only have one of each for this example.

15. Click on Close (or press C) to close the Network Links dialog. Click on OK (or press Enter) to close the Message Server Configuration dialog. Click on OK (or press Enter) to close the Domain Information dialog. You should see the System window containing the list of post offices and domains for our GroupWise configuration. This completes the link configuration process for the primary domain.

16. Log into another machine on the network as an administrator. You need to have two machines, one for each message server. We'll use the message server software installed on the host machine for this second message server, so there's no need to install the server software again.

17. Use the "Configuring the GroupWise Message Server" procedure in this chapter to configure the Satellite Office 1 domain. Make sure you substitute the correct paths during the configuration process.

We used a path of H:\SAT01. Your path will probably differ, depending on your network setup.

18. Use Steps 3 to 10 to create the necessary links in the secondary domain. The GroupWise Admin program will register an error when you start it since the post office drive mapping will be incorrect. This problem will go away by the time you complete the procedure. Make certain you provide the correct path information and take the required network drive mappings into account. You'll definitely need to change the Link Address field of the Define Domain Connection dialog in Step 11. The Post Office Directory field in Step 13 will also require change.

19. Change the Directory field entry in both the Post Office Information and the Domain Information dialogs so they reflect the current setup. This is the step that'll clear the error message you saw when starting the GroupWise Admin utility. The current directory settings reflect the settings we originally used to create the domain and post office. We need to change them to reflect the new drive mapping on the second machine.

20. Check both Message Server status screens. (You'll need to exit the GroupWise Administrator, type *Exit,* then Press Enter to see the Message Server on both the primary and secondary domain if you didn't use multiple DOS sessions under Windows 95.) Both displays should contain some update messages. You shouldn't see any blocked entries in the *Blocked* column of the Status area of the screen (upper left corner). This completes the link configuration for both the primary and secondary domain Message Server.

## Checking Your Installation

Now that we have two fully functional message servers, it's time to check them out. This process isn't too involved. It can be broken down into three steps: (1) primary to secondary domain administration, (2) primary to secondary domain message handling, and (3) secondary to primary domain message handling. You should always try to check out every connection (both post office and domain) at least once, so the testing process for a multiple domain, multiple post office setup could get to be time-consuming. This simple procedure shows the basics you'll need to perform on a more complex system. Of course, the fact that we only have two domains and two post offices will greatly reduce the complexity of the task for this example. You may skip the first step if you are continuing this procedure from the previous section of the case study and used the multiple DOS session method under Windows 95.

1. Change directories to your domain directory (the \*DOMAIN* directory in our case). Type *AD* and press Enter to start the administrator utility. You will see an initial system screen like the one in Fig. 18-5. The first thing we need to do is create a user in our secondary domain. GroupWise allows you to add users to a secondary domain post office from the primary domain, but you can't do anything to a primary domain post office from the secondary domain.

2. Select the *Managers* post office in the Satellite Office 1 domain. Use the Adding a New User procedure in Chapter 17 to create a new user called *Henry* (or any other name you like). This process will require the use of the Message Server since we don't have a direct link to the Managers post office from the ABC Company domain. You'll see a dialog box similar to the one in Fig. 18-13. This dialog simply informs you that GroupWise Admin has requested a new user for the secondary post office.

3. Click on OK (or press Enter) to clear the message. You'll see a new user added to the Managers post office. Now that we've added the new user, let's look at the two message server status screens to see how it happened.

4. Look at the *Satellite Office 1* Message Server display. You should see three new log entries like the ones shown at the bottom of Fig. 18-14. These log entries tell you that the Message Server added a new user named Henry to the Managers post office.

**Figure 18-13**
Remote Management Message Sent Dialog Box.

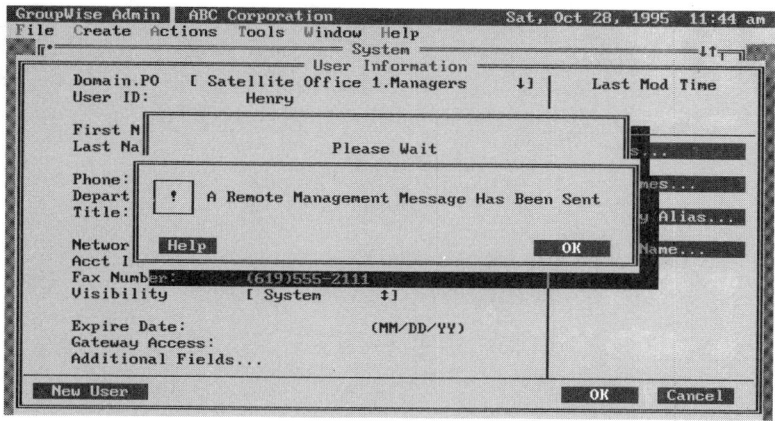

**Figure 18-14**
Sattelite Office 1 Message Server Display.

```
Satellite Office 1      GroupWise Message Server 4.1      10-28-95  11:48:58
┌──── Status ──────────────┐┌──────── Statistics ──────────────────────────┐
│         Active  Blocked  ││                        Total      10 Minutes │
│Post Offices  1     0     ││Messages routed           8            8      │
│Gateways      0     0     ││Undeliverable             0            0      │
│Applications  4     0     ││Corrupted                 0            0      │
│Domains       2     0     ││                                              │
│Log       cslog.4         ││Busy                     11%          11%     │
│Screen: Low  Disk: Low    ││Uptime            0:05:18                     │
└──────────────────────────┘└──── Messages ────────────────────────────────┘
11:28:25 ads: Result: Completed
11:28:27 ads: Object: Satellite Office 1.Managers
11:28:27 ads: Operation: Update object in Post Office database - Post Office
11:28:27 ads: Result: Completed
11:28:30 ofs: Processing message a0927644.003
11:28:30 ofs: Processing admin message
11:28:30 ofs: Processing admin task delete
11:28:30 ofs: Delete user/resource: Henry
11:28:38 ofs: Admin task completed: OK
11:28:38 ofs: Admin message processed: OK
11:48:41 ads: Object: Satellite Office 1.Managers.Henry
11:48:41 ads: Operation: Add User
11:48:41 ads: Result: Completed

1-Log; 2-Stats; 3-Status; 4-Control; 5-Go to DOS; ↑↓ Logfile; F7-Exit
```

5. Look at the *ABC Corporation* Message Server display. You'll see three new log entries here as well (Fig. 18-15). These messages tell the primary domain to update its replication database. In short, these messages are synchronizing the primary and secondary domain databases.

**NOTE** *Depending on how you set up your machines for this case study, you may need to log onto another machine as any user in the primary domain at this point.*

6. Open GroupWise as any primary domain user (we logged in as user *John* for this example). Send a test message to user Henry. This

**Figure 18-15**
ABC Corporation Message Server Display.

```
ABC Corporation         GroupWise Message Server 4.1      10-28-95  11:57:11
┌──── Status ──────────────┐┌──────── Statistics ──────────────────────────┐
│         Active  Blocked  ││                        Total      10 Minutes │
│Post Offices  1     0     ││Messages routed          17            1      │
│Gateways      0     0     ││Undeliverable             0            0      │
│Applications  4     0     ││Corrupted                 0            0      │
│Domains       2     0     ││                                              │
│Log       cslog.1         ││Busy                      7%           7%     │
│Screen: Low  Disk: Low    ││Uptime            2:22:59                     │
└──────────────────────────┘└──── Messages ────────────────────────────────┘
10:44:29 ads: Result: Completed
11:28:50 ads: Object: Satellite Office 1
11:28:50 ads: Operation: Update replica Domain
11:28:50 ads: Result: Completed
11:28:51 ads: Object: Satellite Office 1.Managers
11:28:51 ads: Operation: Update replica Post Office
11:28:51 ads: Result: Completed
11:28:51 ads: Object: Satellite Office 1.Managers.Henry
11:28:51 ads: Operation: Delete replica User
11:28:52 ads: Result: Completed
11:49:05 ads: Object: Satellite Office 1.Managers.Henry
11:49:05 ads: Operation: Update replica User
11:49:05 ads: Result: Completed

1-Log; 2-Stats; 3-Status; 4-Control; 5-Go to DOS; ↑↓ Logfile; F7-Exit
```

# GroupWise 4.x Asynchronous Gateway/Remote Client Support

tests the ability of GroupWise to send a message from the primary domain to the secondary domain. Now it's time to see if user Henry received the message.

**NOTE** *Depending on how you set up your machines for this case study, you may need to log onto another machine as any user in the secondary domain at this point.*

7. Open GroupWise as any secondary domain user (we logged in as user *Henry* since this is our own secondary domain user for this example). Check for the test message sent by user John (or the user that you logged on as in Step 6). If the message didn't get from John to Henry, make sure both Message Servers are online and that there aren't any blocked objects. Now that we know the message has arrived, let's see what the Message Servers had to do to get it from John to Henry.

8. Look at the *Satellite Office 1* Message Server display. You should see four new log entries like the ones shown at the bottom of Fig. 18-16. There are two sections to this group of messages. The first section tells you that the Message Server received a message and processed it. The second section tells you that the Message Server successfully routed the message (placed it in the user's mailbox).

9. Look at the *ABC Corporation* Message Server display. You should see three new log entries like the ones shown at the bottom of Fig. 18-17. The first message tells you that the Message Server processed John's message. The second tells you that the Message Server

**Figure 18-16**
Sattelite Office 1 Message Server Display Showing New Log Entries.

**Figure 18-17**
ABC Corporation Message Server Display Showing New Log Entries.

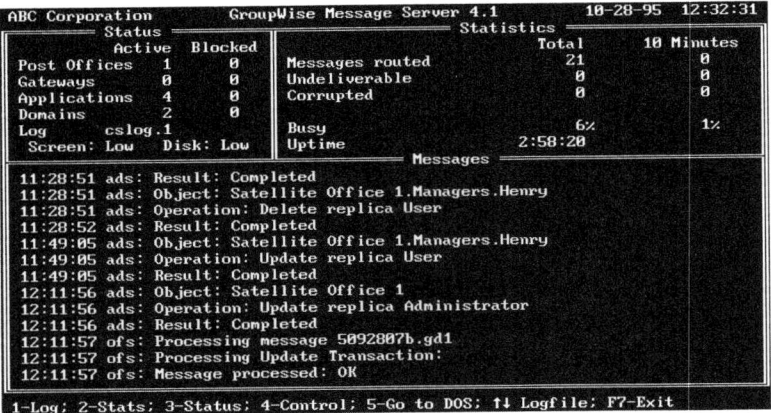

received and updated a transaction from the secondary domain Message Server. In other words, the other Message Server received the message. The third line tells you that the secondary Message Server successfully processed the message.

10. Perform Steps 6 to 9 using Henry as the sender and John as the receiver to test the connection from the secondary server to the primary server. You'll see the opposite results on the primary and secondary server displays. Now we need to perform one last test. We need to verify that we can update our primary GroupWise Admin diagnostics display from the secondary server.

11. Change directories to your domain directory (the \*DOMAIN* directory in our case). Type *AD* and press Enter to start the administrator utility. You'll see an initial system screen like the one in Fig. 18-5.

12. Highlight the primary domain (*ABC Corporation* for our example), then use the Actions ¦ Edit command or press the F6 key to display the Domain Information dialog box shown in Fig. 18-6. (You can also right-click on the domain entry and select Edit from the context menu.) Your display may differ slightly, depending on your domain setup.

13. Click on the *Message Server Configuration* field (or type *M*) to display the Message Server Configuration dialog box shown in Fig. 18-7.

14. Click on the *Diagnostics* pushbutton (or press *T*). This is the display where you can monitor the current status of your Message Server.

# GroupWise 4.x Asynchronous Gateway/Remote Client Support

**Figure 18-18**
Message Server Diagnostics Dialog Box.

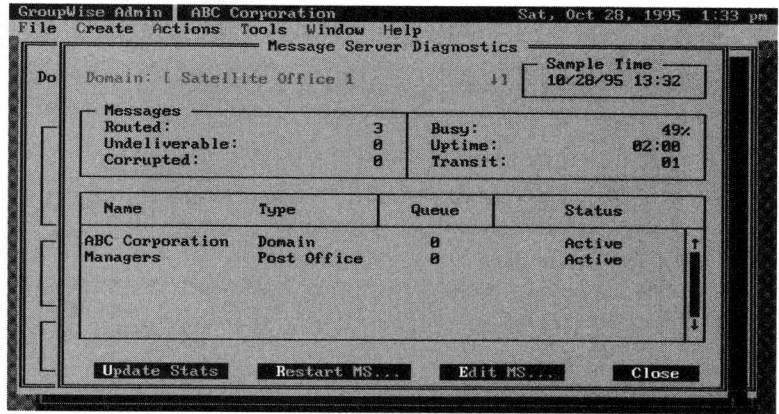

Each domain tracks its own Message Server, so you'll need to select each one individually.

15. Click on the *Update Stats* pushbutton (or press *U*). GroupWise Admin will display some messages as it updates its status from the secondary domain. Once it completes the task, you should see a display similar to the one in Fig. 18-18. Compare these readings to those on the secondary Message Server. They should match (make sure you take any message traffic into account when there are differences between the two displays). This completes the procedure for checking your installation.

## Study Questions

1. You need to install a message server _____.
   a. Any time you install GroupWise
   b. When your setup requires two or more domains
   c. When your setup requires two or more post offices
   d. If you require access to a gateway

   *b and d.* While you can administer multiple GroupWise post offices without installing a message server, you do need one to administer multiple domains. The message server creates the links between the domains. It performs the same function when you need access to a gateway.

2. GroupWise supports the following Message Server protocols:
   a. Mapped and TCP/IP
   b. IPX and NetBEUI
   c. X.25, X.400, and TCP/IP
   d. Direct, indirect, and gateway

   *a.* You will normally use the mapped connection with GroupWise. It's the option to use if you want to create a link between two domains on the same network using a drive mapping.

3. When modifying an object, the GroupWise Message Server always displays three messages in order consisting of a _____, a _____, and a _____ status.
   a. Operation, Object, Result
   b. Object, Processing, Result
   c. Message, Routing, Complete
   d. Object, Operation, Result

   *d.* The Message Server initially tells you that it is going to perform an operation on a specific object like a user or a post office. It then tells you what that operation is. For example, it might need to update the replica Administrator record. Finally, it tells you the result of the operation. In most cases this is a simple *Complete*.

4. The Message Server launches the Post Office Server _____ and the Administration Server _____ during message delivery.
   a. AD.EXE, OFS.EXE
   b. OFCHECK.EXE OFSETUP.EXE
   c. OFS.EXE, ADS.EXE
   d. ADS.EXE, OFS.EXE

   *c.* The Message Server launches these applications each time it has a message to process, which may be hundreds of times per day. Because these files are so important, it's usually better to locate the Message Server software on the local hard drive rather than a network drive.

5. The default minimum processing time that each application under the Message Server receives is _____.
   a. 15 seconds
   b. 30 seconds

# GroupWise 4.x Asynchronous Gateway/Remote Client Support

    **c.** 45 seconds
    **d.** 60 seconds

    *b.* The Message Server gives the ADS.EXE, OFS.EXE, and the MFC.EXE applications 30 seconds to complete a message processing task. This is usually enough time. However, you may want to increase the time if you see an unusually high number of corrupted messages and all the network data links are working properly.

**6.** The /ATS Message Server switch allows you to change the _____.
    **a.** Automatic time slice
    **b.** Automated testing sequence
    **c.** Automatic transmission sequence
    **d.** Arithmetic time slice

    *d.* Every application that the message server runs competes for computer processing time. The Message Server normally uses a message-priority formula for determining the size of the time slice (the amount of time each application gets to perform its work). The /ATS switch tells the Message Server to use an arithmetic time slice method instead.

**7.** If you are using an external or foreign domain with a message server, then you will need the _____ utility to perform the required message conversion to GroupWise format.
    **a.** AD
    **b.** MFC
    **c.** OFS
    **d.** ADS

    *b.* You would need the message file conversion (MFC) utility to perform the required work. GroupWise doesn't install this file (unless you tell it you need the Office 3.1 Compatibility option) if you are using the Message Server with a secondary domain.

**8.** The acronym *VDM* stands for:
    **a.** Virtual Data Management
    **b.** Vital Data Mode
    **c.** Virtual DOS Machine
    **d.** Vital Document Management

*c.* OS/2 uses a virtual DOS machine to run the Message Server. You must specify the /OS2 switch when running the message server in that environment. This switch reduces CPU usage levels.

9. GroupWise requires a minimum of _____ domains to setup an indirect link.

    **a.** 1
    **b.** 2
    **c.** 3
    **d.** 4

    *c.* GroupWise requires a minimum of 3 domains for an indirect link. You must always create a direct link between two of the domains. The third link can then be an indirect link. This enables you to create a variety of message transmission paths, including a ring. One Message Server passes any messages on to the next server in line.

10. The message server software comes in which of the following platform versions?

    **a.** DOS
    **b.** OS/2
    **c.** UNIX
    **d.** NLM

    *a, b, c, and d.* You can get the message server software in any of these configurations. The DOS and OS/2 versions are convenient if you are running a peer-to-peer network. Use the UNIX and NLM versions for maximum performance.

11. The default app threshold for GroupWise is _____.

    **a.** 0
    **b.** 1
    **c.** 5
    **d.** 10

    *a.* Using the default value of 0 means that the Message Server delivers the message to all recipients. Setting a threshold allows you to take part of the load off the message server by having the client software deliver some of the messages.

12. You would need to select the _____ option during message server installation if you needed to connect your GroupWise 4.x setup to a WP Office 3.1 setup.

# GroupWise 4.x Asynchronous Gateway/Remote Client Support

    **a.** Message Server
    **b.** WP Office
    **c.** Office 3.1 Compatibility
    **d.** GroupWise 4.x Compatibility

    *c.* The only time you need to install the Office 3.1 Compatibility software is if you currently have a WP Office 3.1 installation. This additional software allows you to create external links with the Message Server.

**13.** GroupWise allows you to add users to a secondary domain post office from the primary domain, but you can't do anything to a primary domain post office from the secondary domain.
    **a.** True
    **b.** False

    *a.* You can't even edit the primary post office information from a secondary domain. GroupWise will display a message saying that you don't have the proper rights if you try to do so. However, you can at least display various types of primary domain information, including post offices and users.

**14.** You must create separate reattach batch files for each Message Server in a multidomain system.
    **a.** True
    **b.** False

    *a.* Since each message server has different requirements, you must create a different batch file to restart it.

**15.** Using a priority scan cycle with the Message Server allows you to scan for priority messages at a faster rate than standard messages. Which of the following messages are priority messages?
    **a.** Message Server reboot or reconfiguration requests
    **b.** GroupWise Gateway reboot or reconfiguration requests
    **c.** Busy Search requests
    **d.** GroupWise Remote requests
    **e.** Directory Synchronization requests

    *a, b, c, d, and e.* All of these messages are on the priority list. The default scan cycle for priority messages is 5 seconds. The default setting for standard messages is 15 seconds. Using a shorter scan cycle reduces message server response time. Using a longer scan cycle reduces network traffic.

16. A Post Office Server requires a minimum _____ of conventional memory, _____ of extended memory and _____ of hard disk space.
   a. 500 K, 4 MB, 40 MB
   b. 640 K, 4 MB, 40 MB
   c. 640 K, 2 MB, 40 MB
   d. 500 K, 2 MB, 40 MB

   *d.* A Post Office Server takes some of the load off the Message Server by completing delivery of messages to the recipient's mailbox. Normally, the Message Server launches the Post Office Server as needed and shares time with it. You should always run the Post Office Server on a dedicated machine containing an 80386 processor at minimum.

17. The Message Server gives corrupted messages a _____ extension and places them in the _____ directory of the domain or post office.
   a. DB, PROBLEM
   b. CS, PROBLEM
   c. DB, OFMSG
   d. CS, OFMSG

   *b.* When the Message Server can't recognize the format of a particular message, it considers it to be corrupted. Placing these messages in a special place allows you to look at them to see what the problem is or send them to customer support for analysis. The Message Server automatically deletes corrupted messages after 7 days unless you specify a different interval using the /CI startup option.

18. The Message Server takes a snapshot of the current statistics and outputs it to a log file every _____ minutes.
   a. 10
   b. 15
   c. 30
   d. 60

   *c.* Viewing the log can help you determine the precise time an error occurred or give you an overall picture of the Message Server's usage rate during the day. You can reset the log using the Stats ¦ Reset command. The Stats ¦ Last command allows you to view the last 30-minute snapshot. Use the up and down arrows to view all the snapshots that the log contains.

# GroupWise 4.x Asynchronous Gateway/Remote Client Support

19. The _____ propagates the administration message created by GroupWise Admin every time you make a change to the domain information.
    a. Message Server
    b. Post Office Server
    c. Message File Conversion Utility
    d. Administration Server

    *d.* In a multidomain system, the Administration Server makes sure that any domain information changes get sent to all domains. Changes are stored in the domain database and all post office databases in the affected domain. The Administration Server also sends these changes to any post offices that are closed to GroupWise Admin.

20. Both Message Servers involved in a particular action will always display status messages when the Log setting is set to *Low*.
    a. True
    b. False

    *b.* Some actions, like a status update of the secondary domain Message Server from the primary GroupWise Admin display, will only appear on the primary server. Only actions that require some processing at the Message Server will appear on the Message Server display.

21. The message server software must be installed in the _____ directory.
    a. Domain
    b. Post Office
    c. \WPC20
    d. \WPCNET

    *a.* The message server software gets installed in the \WPCS subdirectory of your domain directory. It contains all the Message Server executable files.

22. You start the DOS version of the Message Server by typing _____ at the command prompt and pressing Enter.
    a. CS /PC-<POST OFFICE PATH> /PH-<SWAP FILE PATH>
    b. CS /PC-<DOMAIN PATH> /PH-<SWAP FILE PATH>
    c. CS /PH-<POST OFFICE PATH> /PC-<SWAP FILE PATH>
    d. CS /PH-<DOMAIN PATH> /PC-<SWAP FILE PATH>

*d.* You use the CS command to start the Message Server. The domain path always reflects the domain, not the post office path. You'll normally use a local swap file directory even if the domain is located on a network drive to improve the Message Server's response time.

23. The default reattach retry interval for a Message Server is _____.
    a. 120 seconds
    b. 300 seconds
    c. 600 seconds
    d. 900 seconds

    *c.* The default retry interval is 600 seconds (10 minutes). However, you can select any interval between 0 and 999 seconds. You can change the interval by changing the Attach Retry field of the Message Server Configuration dialog.

24. Setting the Logging Level field of the Message Server Configuration dialog to *Verbose* would tell the Message Server to display which of the following message types?
    a. Error Messages
    b. Application Activity
    c. Message Movement Between Post Offices
    d. Gateway Activity
    e. Message Movement Between Domains

    *a, b, and d.* The *Verbose* level of logging tracks these three types of information. There are four levels of logging: Off, Normal, Verbose, and Diagnostic. The *Off* level tells the Message Server not to log anything. The *Normal* level only logs error messages. You'll see all of these information types tracked when using the *Diagnostic* level of logging.

25. If you wanted to suspend user messages going to a particular domain or post office, but didn't want to suspend administrative messages, you'd select the _____ entry for that particular post office or domain.
    a. Ads
    b. Ofs
    c. Post Office or Domain
    d. Application

    *b.* You can suspend processing at the gateway, post office, or domain level if you want to stop sending any information to that

# GroupWise 4.x Asynchronous Gateway/Remote Client Support

particular gateway, post office, or domain. However, the *Ofs* and *Ads* application entries allow you to suspend specific message types instead of all messages. (Suspended messages show up as delayed in the Post Office Server screen.)

**26.** You have to rebuild the CSI file after making a domain setup change when using the NLM version of the Message Server.
   **a.** True
   **b.** False

   *b.* Only the DOS and OS/2 versions of the Message Server use the CSI file. The NLM and UNIX versions update their information directly from the domain database.

**27.** The Message Server's log files and local work files appear in the _____ directory.
   **a.** CSLOCAL
   **b.** CSHOLD
   **c.** CSWORK
   **d.** CSTEMP

   *a.* You will find all of these other directories under the CSLOCAL directory. They contain the Message Server's work files. The log files appear in the /CSLOCAL directory using the name CSLOG.*XXX*, where *XXX* is a number between 001 and 999. Fortunately, these log files are plain ASCII text, so you can view them using a standard text editor.

**28.** You would use the _____ switch if you wanted to suspend delivery to post offices, gateways, and domains the first time that the Message Server is started.
   **a.** /DWN
   **b.** /ZAR
   **c.** /ZAR1
   **d.** /XOFS

   *c.* The /ZAR switch allows you to suspend delivery to all post offices, domains, and gateways no matter how often you restart the Message Server. You can unblock them using the Control ¦ Resume Facility command at the Message Server. The /ZAR1 switch only suspends delivery the first time you start the Message Server. Restarting it using the Control ¦ Restart Message Server command will resume all message processing.

29. You will see _____ next to any suspended facilities in the Message Server Status dialog.
    a. An asterisk (*)
    b. A question mark (?)
    c. A dash (-)
    d. Suspended

    *d.* The Control ¦ Suspend Facility displays a dialog that shows all of the objects under the Message Server's control. As you select objects to suspend, the Message Server will display asterisks next to the item. The same holds true in the Resume Facility display. The word *Suspend* appears to the right of any suspended objects in the Message Server Status, Suspend Facility, and Resume Facility dialogs.

30. You can use the _____ switch with the Post Office Server to redirect its temporary files to a RAM drive and speed up processing.
    a. /D
    b. /PC
    c. /PL
    d. /LG

    *a.* The /D parameter allows you to redirect the Post Office Server's temporary files to a RAM drive. You should only take this step on a machine with a large amount of memory (at least 4 MB) since using a RAM drive on a memory-starved machine will actually reduce overall Post Office Server performance.

31. The Message File Conversion utility's temporary files appear in the _____ directory.
    a. CSS
    b. CSHOLD
    c. CSWORK
    d. CSTEMP

    *d.* The Message File Conversion uses the CSTEMP directory for its temporary files, while the Message Server uses the CSWORK directory.

32. The Control menu of the Message Server screen allows you to _____.
    a. Suspend Facility
    b. Resume Facility
    c. Go To DOS
    d. Restart Message Server

# GroupWise 4.x Asynchronous Gateway/Remote Client Support 585

*a, b, and d.* Temporarily suspending a facility allows you to concentrate the Message Server's processing power on a single domain, post office, or gateway. This comes in handy if the object was blocked for an extended amount of time and has a lot of messages to process. The *Go To DOS* option appears as a separate main menu option.

33. Which of the following modes enable the message server in the Message Server Configuration dialog?
    a. Server Never
    b. Use App Thresholds
    c. Server Always
    d. Use Server Thresholds

    *b and c.* Selecting the Server Never option always turns the Message Server off. The standard delivery mode is *Use App Thresholds*. It uses a threshold that you set to determine when it should deliver a message. The default threshold value is 0. The Server Always mode tells the Message Server to always deliver the messages.

34. One way to detect malfunctioning links is to look at the _____ column of the _____ section of the Message Server screen.
    a. Status, Messages
    b. Undeliverable and Corrupted, Statistics
    c. Blocked, Status
    d. Active, Status

    *c.* If an object is blocked, it usually means there is some type of configuration error or a damaged link. Once you complete the GroupWise installation and have it working, there's no reason for a configuration error. The only alternative is a damaged link in most cases.

35. Assume that the name of the reattach batch file for a particular Message Server is *REATTACH.BAT* and that it resides in the root directory of the C drive. The Reattach String field of the Message Server Configuration dialog would contain _____.
    a. Execute C:\REATTACH
    b. Call C:\REATTACH
    c. C:\REATTACH.BAT
    d. Call C:\REATTACH.BAT
    e. None of the above

    *d.* You must use the command Call, followed by the name of the reattach batch file.

36. The Post Office Server message statistics include:
    a. Corrupted
    b. Delivered
    c. Delayed
    d. Undeliverable

    *b, c, and d.* Only the Message Server displays the number of corrupted messages. In addition to these three statistics, the Post Office Server also displays the Total Messages it has received.

37. You can use _____ to enable the Message Server to mask critical errors during message processing when running NetWare 3.1x.
    a. NETFIX.COM
    b. CS.EXE
    c. ADS.EXE
    d. NETFIX.EXE

    *a.* Running the NETFIX.COM program will allow the Message Server to mask critical (Abort, Retry, or Fail) errors. In essence, this will allow it to keep running even when an error occurs.

38. The GroupWise Message Server always displays statistics for the following message intervals:
    a. Total
    b. 5 minutes
    c. 10 minutes
    d. 15 minutes

    *a and c.* The Message Server always tells you the total number of messages it has processed along with the number it has processed in the last 10 minutes. This includes routed, undeliverable, and corrupted messages.

39. There's always a minimum of two message servers in a GroupWise multiple domain configuration: one for the domain and another for the post office.
    a. True
    b. False

    *b.* Message Servers only work with domains. You need two Message Servers: one for the primary domain and another for the other domain (secondary, foreign, or external).

**40.** You must select the _____ platform option when using the DOS version of the Message Server.
   a. DOS
   b. NLM
   c. UNIX
   d. DOS & OS/2

   *d.* The DOS and OS/2 versions of the Message Server use the same platform setting. The other versions require a separate setting.

## Fun Test

**1.** You have to rebuild the CSI file after making a domain setup change when using the NLM version of the Message Server.
   a. True
   b. False

**2.** The default app threshold for GroupWise is _____.
   a. 0
   b. 1
   c. 5
   d. 10

**3.** One way to detect malfunctioning links is to look at the _____ column of the _____ section of the Message Server screen.
   a. Status, Messages
   b. Undeliverable and Corrupted, Statistics
   c. Blocked, Status
   d. Active, Status

**4.** You must select the _____ platform option when using the DOS version of the Message Server.
   a. DOS
   b. NLM
   c. UNIX
   d. DOS & OS/2

5. Setting the Logging Level field of the Message Server Configuration dialog to *Verbose* would tell the Message Server to display which of the following message types?
   a. Error Messages
   b. Application Activity
   c. Message Movement Between Post Offices
   d. Gateway Activity
   e. Message Movement Between Domains

6. When modifying an object, the GroupWise Message Server always displays three messages in order consisting of a _____, a _____, and a _____ status.
   a. Operation, Object, and Result
   b. Object, Processing, and Result
   c. Message, Routing, and Complete
   d. Object, Operation, and Result

7. You would use the _____ switch if you wanted to suspend delivery to post offices, gateways, and domains the first time that the Message Server is started.
   a. /DWN
   b. /ZAR
   c. /ZAR1
   d. /XOFS

8. Using a priority scan cycle with the Message Server allows you to scan for priority messages at a faster rate than standard messages. Which of the following messages are priority messages?
   a. Message Server reboot or reconfiguration requests
   b. GroupWise Gateway reboot or reconfiguration requests
   c. Busy Search requests
   d. GroupWise Remote requests
   e. Directory Synchronization requests

9. You can use _____ to enable the Message Server to mask critical errors during message processing when running NetWare 3.1x.
   a. NETFIX.COM
   b. CS.EXE
   c. ADS.EXE
   d. NETFIX.EXE

10. The default minimum processing time that each application under the Message Server receives is _____.
    a. 15 seconds
    b. 30 seconds
    c. 45 seconds
    d. 60 seconds

11. GroupWise allows you to add users to a secondary domain post office from the primary domain, but you can't do anything to a primary domain post office from the secondary domain.
    a. True
    b. False

12. Which of the following modes enable the message server in the Message Server Configuration dialog?
    a. Server Never
    b. Use App Thresholds
    c. Server Always
    d. Use Server Thresholds

13. GroupWise supports the following Message Server protocols:
    a. Mapped and TCP/IP
    b. IPX and NetBEUI
    c. X.25, X.400, and TCP/IP
    d. Direct, indirect, and gateway

14. You start the DOS version of the Message Server by typing _____ at the command prompt and pressing Enter.
    a. CS /PC-<POST OFFICE PATH> /PH-<SWAP FILE PATH>
    b. CS /PC-<DOMAIN PATH> /PH-<SWAP FILE PATH>
    c. CS /PH-<POST OFFICE PATH> /PC-<SWAP FILE PATH>
    d. CS /PH-<DOMAIN PATH> /PC-<SWAP FILE PATH>

15. The Message Server launches the Post Office Server _____ and the Administration Server _____ during message delivery.
    a. AD.EXE, OFS.EXE
    b. OFCHECK.EXE OFSETUP.EXE
    c. OFS.EXE, ADS.EXE
    d. ADS.EXE, OFS.EXE

16. The message server software comes in which of the following platform versions?
    a. DOS
    b. OS/2
    c. UNIX
    d. NLM

17. Assume that the name of the reattach batch file for a particular Message Server is *REATTACH.BAT* and that it resides in the root directory of the C drive. The Reattach String field of the Message Server Configuration dialog would contain _____.
    a. Execute C:\REATTACH
    b. Call C:\REATTACH
    c. C:\REATTACH.BAT
    d. Call C:\REATTACH.BAT
    e. None of the above

18. Both Message Servers involved in a particular action will always display status messages when the Log setting is set to *Low*.
    a. True
    b. False

19. GroupWise requires a minimum of _____ domains to setup an indirect link.
    a. 1
    b. 2
    c. 3
    d. 4

20. You must create separate reattach batch files for each Message Server in a multidomain system.
    a. True
    b. False

21. The default reattach retry interval for a Message Server is _____.
    a. 120 seconds
    b. 300 seconds
    c. 600 seconds
    d. 900 seconds

# GroupWise 4.x Asynchronous Gateway/Remote Client Support 591

22. A Post Office Server requires a minimum _____ of conventional memory, _____ of extended memory, and _____ of hard disk space.
    a. 500 K, 4 MB, 40 MB
    b. 640 K, 4 MB, 40 MB
    c. 640 K, 2 MB, 40 MB
    d. 500 K, 2 MB, 40 MB

23. The GroupWise Message Server always displays statistics for the following message intervals.
    a. Total
    b. 5 minutes
    c. 10 minutes
    d. 15 minutes

24. You need to install a message server _____.
    a. Any time you install GroupWise
    b. When your setup requires two or more domains
    c. When your setup requires two or more post offices
    d. If you require access to a gateway

25. The Message File Conversion utility's temporary files appear in the _____ directory.
    a. CSS
    b. CSHOLD
    c. CSWORK
    d. CSTEMP

26. The _____ propagates the administration message created by GroupWise Admin every time you make a change to the domain information.
    a. Message Server
    b. Post Office Server
    c. Message File Conversion Utility
    d. Administration Server

27. There is always a minimum of two message servers in a GroupWise multiple domain configuration: one for the domain and another for the post office.
    a. True
    b. False

28. The message server software must be installed in the _____ directory.
   a. Domain
   b. Post office
   c. \WPC20
   d. \WPCNET

29. The /ATS Message Server switch allows you to change the _____.
   a. Automatic time slice
   b. Automated testing sequence
   c. Automatic transmission sequence
   d. Arithmetic time slice

30. The Message Server takes a snapshot of the current statistics and outputs it to a log file every _____ minutes.
   a. 10
   b. 15
   c. 30
   d. 60

31. The Control menu of the Message Server screen allows you to _____.
   a. Suspend Facility
   b. Resume Facility
   c. Go To DOS
   d. Restart Message Server

32. If you are using an external or foreign domain with a message server, then you will need the _____ utility to perform the required message conversion to GroupWise format.
   a. AD
   b. MFC
   c. OFS
   d. ADS

33. If you wanted to suspend user messages going to a particular domain or post office, but didn't want to suspend administrative messages, you'd select the _____ entry for that particular post office or domain.

# GroupWise 4.x Asynchronous Gateway/Remote Client Support 593

    a. Ads
    b. Ofs
    c. Post Office or Domain
    d. Application

34. The acronym *VDM* stands for:
    a. Virtual Data Management
    b. Vital Data Mode
    c. Virtual DOS Machine
    d. Vital Document Management

35. The Post Office Server message statistics include:
    a. Corrupted
    b. Delivered
    c. Delayed
    d. Undeliverable

36. You can use the _____ switch with the Post Office Server to redirect its temporary files to a RAM drive and speed up processing.
    a. /D
    b. /PC
    c. /PL
    d. /LG

37. You would need to select the _____ option during message server installation if you needed to connect your GroupWise 4.x setup to a WP Office 3.1 setup.
    a. Message Server
    b. WP Office
    c. Office 3.1 Compatibility
    d. GroupWise 4.x Compatibility

38. The Message Server gives corrupted messages a _____ extension and places them in the _____ directory of the domain or post office.
    a. DB, PROBLEM
    b. CS, PROBLEM
    c. DB, OFMSG
    d. CS, OFMSG

**39.** The Message Server's log files and local work files appear in the _____ directory.
   a. CSLOCAL
   b. CSHOLD
   c. CSWORK
   d. CSTEMP

**40.** You will see _____ next to any suspended facilities in the Message Server Status dialog.
   a. An asterisk (*)
   b. A question mark (?)
   c. A dash (-)
   d. Suspended

# Brain Teaser

Ready for some challenging puzzles designed to help you pass the certification exam? The word-search puzzle in Fig. 18-19 will test your knowledge of terms associated with GroupWise. You'll also find some acronyms and a few terms associated with NetWare 4.x. All you need to do is find the terms in the letter grid. Make sure you look forward, backward, diagonally, and vertically since the terms could be hidden in any of those positions. You'll find the solution for this brain teaser in App. C, "Brain Teaser Answers."

You'll want to spend some time looking these terms up in the glossary, App. A, or this chapter after you complete the word-search puzzle. (You'll find any NetWare 4.x terms in Chaps. 14 to 16.) It's important to know the terms associated with GroupWise and how they relate to the various environments you'll work in. Of course, learning the terms should also provide food for thought. For example, do you really know how to set up and configure a post office? How can you repair any problems you find with your GroupWise database? It's questions such as these that Novell is going to ask, so you'd better be prepared to provide the answers. You may also want to design your own word-search puzzle of terms. Looking for terms using this kind of puzzle really embeds them in your mind.

# GroupWise 4.x Asynchronous Gateway/Remote Client Support 595

**Figure 18-19**
GroupWise Asynchronous Gateway and Remote Client Support Word Search.

```
G A T E W A Y A D Y D A T A B A S E
R X S N E T W O R K Y T I L I T U V
O A Z Y Q I E O P N D I A R O U T E
U N I X N U T T P R O T O C O L A R
P S 2 D F C C Y I N D I R E C T N
W I O A E L H V T L Y L S E K G S O
I W B R S I E R P I T F R V D M 2 I
S Z I X C E H J O Y T T U R Q B D T
E D N X P N X C N N B M A E S L E A
H R E M O T E L G R O U P S O O L R
E G A S S E M T L T Y U E H T C I T
T T 2 R T U V I W F P C S O W K V S
R C D D O S D S I A O E O C E E I
O E E X F D K T F R R B B V R D R N
R J C R F N R Z P H E E N T M L Y I
R B Q F I E L D T R R Z D E P P A M
E O U L C D R E S U L T N I A M O D
C O N N E C T I O N S 2 T Y U M K A
```

*Term List*

1. Administration
2. ANSI
3. Asynchronous
4. Blocked
5. Certify
6. Client
7. CNE
8. Connections
9. Database
10. Delivery
11. Direct
12. Directory
13. Domain
14. DOS
15. Drive
16. Error
17. FCC
18. FDDI
19. Field
20. Gateway
21. Groups
22. GroupWise
23. Indirect
24. Links
25. Mapped
26. Message
27. NetWare
28. Network
29. NLM
30. NOS
31. NTFS
32. Object
33. OS/2 (OS2)
34. Postoffice
35. Process
36. Protocol
37. RAID
38. Reboot
39. Remote
40. Result
41. Route
42. Satellite
43. Server
44. Status
45. Threshold
46. UNIX
47. User
48. Utility
49. VDM
50. Windows

## Disk Time

Don't forget to spend some time working with the disk that accompanies this book. It provides valuable and fun-to-use teaching aids that will help prepare you for the exam. See "Disk Time" in the preface of this book for details about what the disk contains.

CHAPTER 19

# GroupWise 4.x Advanced System Administration

# Introduction

This chapter looks at the requirements for the GroupWise 4.x Advanced System Administration exam. It's the second administration exam for the new GroupWise CNE certification route that Novell has recently made available. Novell will test your ability to perform advanced administrative tasks. You'll still see some installation- and usage-related questions, but the exam will concentrate on the particulars of performing tasks like creating multiple domains.

You'll find that this exam also parallels the NetWare 3.x and 4.x requirements of the same name. Of course, the actual operating system is completely different. There are both UNIX and Windows versions of this product (along with various clients for other platforms). We'll concentrate on the Windows version of the product since it's more likely that you'll use that product. The two product versions are about the same (except for the differences between operating systems), so UNIX users can benefit from this chapter as well.

One of the reasons that Novell has added this certification is so that each CNE specialty provides a similar level of expertise and receives a similar level of training. There are several discrete sections in this chapter. Each section helps you study for the exam in a different way. You can improve your chances of passing the exam by using the study methods provided in this chapter. In fact, it'll probably help if you study all the sections once and your favorite sections at least twice. Review the study guidelines in Chap. 4 as often as necessary to ensure that you maintain the best possible study atmosphere.

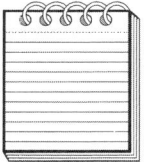

**NOTE**  *This chapter assumes that you have already bought the version of GroupWise required for your operating system and installed it using the default settings. We'll use a single domain, single post office setup as a starting point for the case study in this chapter. (You can follow the case study in Chap. 17 to create a standard setup if you need to.) You can still benefit from this chapter if you don't have a network by reading through the case study.*

The first section of this chapter is a *case study*. You'll perform some hands-on tasks that will help you learn what you need to know to pass the examination. In this case, we look at one of the ways that you can set up your GroupWise installation once you get it installed. We'll look at some user management tasks, the steps required to setup additional post offices, and what you need to do to create multiple domains. (The case study uses the same Windows peer-to-peer network used in Chap. 17, but any network setup should work with minor changes.) Even though you'll get a lot more from this section if you perform it on your own network, the inclusion of step-by-step instructions and screen shots will help you gain something from the section even if you don't have a network.

The second area contains *sample test questions* for this course. We make a special effort to include a variety of GroupWise administration specific questions; but, as on the real exam, you'll find other types of questions as well. This section also includes the correct answers to those questions and an explanation of why each answer is correct. Try to answer each question yourself, look at the correct answer, then determine where you went wrong if you did not answer correctly.

The next section is a *fun test*. This is an exercise where you'll look at more sample test questions and answer them. The answers appear in App. B at the back of the book. This will help you test what you learned in the previous section.

The final text section of the chapter is the *brain teaser*. You'll get to have a little fun working on a GroupWise-related puzzle. In this case, we concentrate on an advanced topic. This chapter provides two cryptograms that should give you some ideas of ways to study for the exam. Obviously, it helps to have a good in-depth knowledge of GroupWise in this case, since the cryptograms will be easier to solve if you can spot specific patterns in the way they're encrypted. By the way, the cryptograms use different encryption methods, so you'll have to solve each puzzle separately.

Finally, we'll spend some time using the *Jeopardy!*-type game named *Red Zone*. Unlike most sections of this book, there are only two GroupWise categories included with the game: *Administration* and *Remote Connections*. You need more than just GroupWise knowledge to pass the exam, so the lack of GroupWise categories shouldn't present any problems. Playing the Red Zone game helps you look at the test from the opposite viewpoint. The game provides you with an answer—you need to come up with the corresponding question. The game awards points for correct answers, and takes points away for incorrect answers. You'll receive a score at the end of the game proclaiming that you either did or did not get your certificate. Make sure you concentrate on the GroupWise-related questions when using the game; they're the ones that will provide you with the best information about the exams you are about to take. Unlike the specific questions provided in this chapter, Red Zone tests your overall knowledge of Novell products, so be prepared to explore areas that you haven't looked at in the past.

Use all the learning methods that we provide in this chapter to improve your chances of passing the exam. It's a good idea to save the fun test section until you're almost certain that you possess all the required knowledge. Remember, you can probably go through the Fun Test only two or three times at most before you'll start to remember the answers without really knowing the material.

## Case Study

GroupWise is a complex product. There isn't any way for us to show you everything that it can do in the space of three chapters. What this means is that you'll need to spend time working with the GroupWise manuals and trying different setups on your own. This case study shows you the principles of managing your setup; it'll give you the broadest possible overview of what GroupWise is like and what you need to do to manage it. We'll look at some of the more detailed topics in this chapter, things you didn't learn in Chap. 17. The areas of study include:

- Adding a New User
- Changing a User Setup
- Adding New Post Offices
- Adding New Domains
- Merging Domains
- Performing Database Maintenance

Fortunately, unlike the case study in Chap. 17, you could probably perform this case study in any order you wanted using some fake entries in your company post office (which you would need to delete later). We'll use the same post office and setup as in Chap. 17 for those of you who followed that case study on your own network.

The end goal for this case study is learning some of the more common management techniques for a GroupWise installation. You should spend the time required to really learn the material in this case study, because you can count on being tested on these types of skills during the exam. Of course, you'll want to branch out a little from this case study as well. Try several different approaches to getting these tasks done on your network. It's important to have a thorough knowledge of these advanced management tasks before you take the exam.

# Adding a New User

The task of adding a new user (and deleting old ones, for that matter) is so basic to GroupWise that everyone needs to know how to do it. We looked at the automated approach to performing this task in Chap. 17. However, once you get past the original installation, you'll have to perform this task using the tools provided with the administrator utility. That's what this section of the case study looks at—the requirements for adding a new user to a post office. (Deleting a user is very easy by comparison, so we don't cover that task specifically in this chapter.)

**NOTE** *To delete a user object that you no longer need, simply highlight the name in the user list, then press Delete. GroupWise Admin will ask you if you're sure that you want to delete the name. Click on No or Yes as appropriate.*

1. Change directories to your domain directory (the \*DOMAIN* directory in our case). Type *AD* and press Enter to start the administrator utility. You'll see an initial system screen like the one in Fig. 19-1.

2. Click on the *Create* | User command (or press *Ctrl-U*). You will see a User Information dialog box similar to the one in Fig. 19-2. (This is the same dialog that is used to edit a user's information.) We haven't really looked at this dialog before, because we used the automatic user creation method in Chap. 17. (This method uses all defaults for the many fields displayed on this dialog and simply defines the minimum of a new user name.)

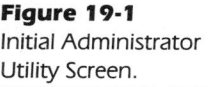

**Figure 19-1**
Initial Administrator Utility Screen.

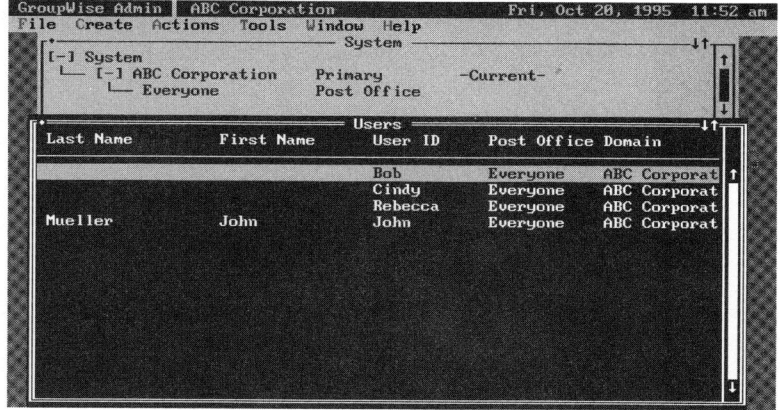

**Figure 19-2**
User Information Dialog Box.

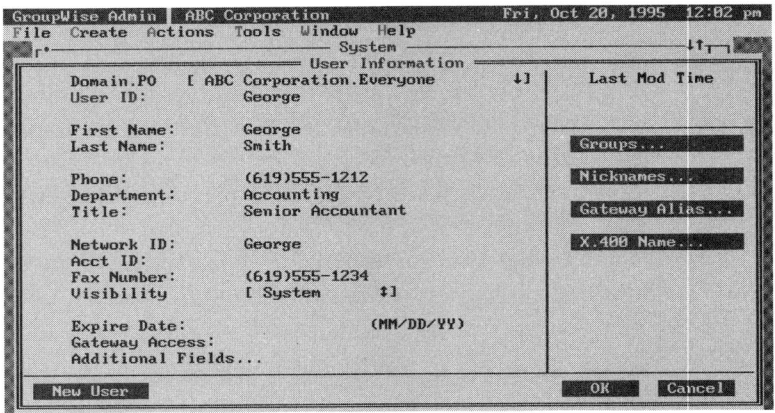

3. Fill in the new user details as shown in Fig. 19-2. Most of the fields are self-explanatory. Several fields do deserve a special mention. The *Expiration Date* field is useful when entering temporary employees. Using this field ensures that their access to the network ends on their last day of work. The *Visibility* field comes in handy for maintaining group integrity if you use multiple post offices. You can restrict access to a particular person by restricting their visibility to the domain or post office level. A user can still access this person if they know the correct address, but not having that address does add a certain level of security. See Chap. 18 for information on the *Acct ID* and *Gateway* fields.

4. Click on the *Additional Fields* entry. You will see a dialog box similar to the one in Fig. 19-3. Note that this is a list of 10 user-defined fields. We used one of these fields to display the user's network location. Of course, you can use them for any need you might have.

5. Fill in the first user defined field as shown in Fig. 19-3, then click on OK. The GroupWise Admin utility will return you to the User Information dialog.

6. Click on OK to complete adding our new user *George*. Note that George's name appears at the end of the list and that his name is highlighted. You can exit the GroupWise Admin utility now or continue with the next section of the case study.

## Changing a User Setup

Creating users is only one part of the task of administering them. You will need to make account changes as your company grows or the users' needs

# GroupWise 4.x Advanced System Administration

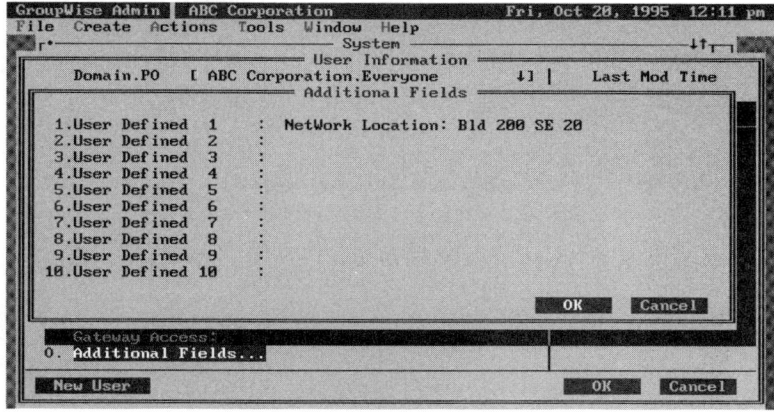

**Figure 19-3**
Additional Fields Dialog Box.

change. There are also other changes that take place. For example, you might need to add users from a group or add them to a new group. The process of adding and removing resources is also a user setup change since one of the users must own the resource. This section of the case study looks at how to modify a user's account. (Skip the first step if you're continuing from the previous section.)

1. Change directories to your domain directory (the \DOMAIN directory in our case). Type *AD* and press Enter to start the administrator utility. You'll see an initial system screen like the one in Fig. 19-1. We didn't complete setting our users up in Chap. 17, so let's take care of that now.

2. Double-click on user Bob's account entry (or highlight the account and press Enter or F6). You'll see a User Information dialog box similar to the one in Fig. 19-2. Note the differences between this dialog and the new user dialog shown in the figure. The first thing you should notice is that the *Domain.PO* and *User ID* fields are grayed out. You can't edit either of these fields since GroupWise uses them to index the database. The second thing you should notice is that there's a *Last Mod Time* entry in the upper right corner of the dialog.

3. Type entries into the same fields that we did for Fig. 7-2. You can use values similar to the ones we used for user George.

4. Repeat Steps 2 and 3 for users *Rebecca, Cindy,* and *John*. Once you complete this step, let's take a look at creating some groups for our users to belong to.

5. Use the *Create* | Group command to display the Group Information dialog shown in Fig. 19-4. (You can also press *Ctrl-G* to display the dialog.)

**Figure 19-4**
Group Information Dialog Box.

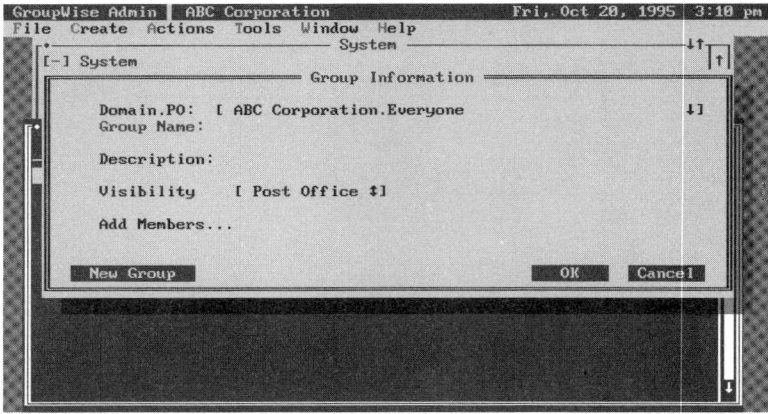

6. Type *Managers* in the Group Name field, then press Tab to move to the Description field.

7. Press Enter. GroupWise Admin will display the Group Information Description dialog box shown in Fig. 19-5. Note that we have already added a description to the field.

8. Press Tab or F7 to complete the action. GroupWise Admin will automatically select OK as the next button to select. However, we want to add members of our post office to the group right away. Defining the users first, then the groups, allows us to group the users a lot faster. It also provides us with a list we can use during the creation process so that no one gets left out.

9. Double click on the *Edit Members* field (or press 5). GroupWise Admin will display the dialog shown in Fig. 19-6. This is where we

**Figure 19-5**
Group Information Description Dialog Box.

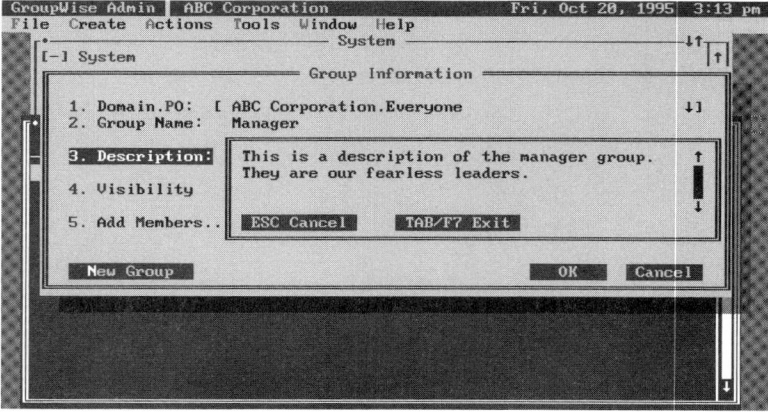

# GroupWise 4.x Advanced System Administration

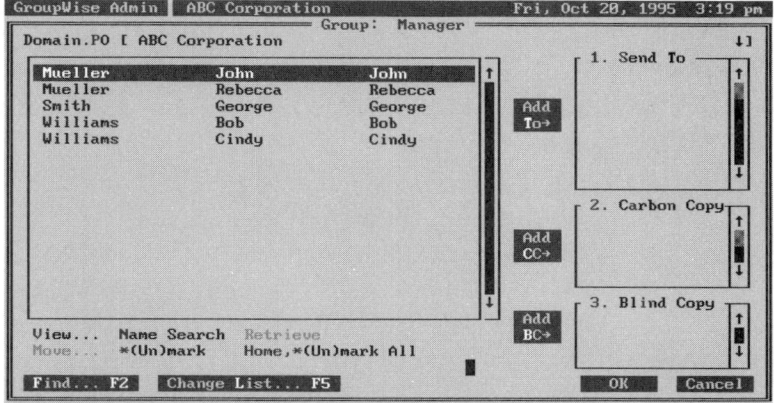

**Figure 19-6**
Group Dialog Box.

tell GroupWise whom to send group messages addressed to Managers to. We can also choose to send some people (like administrative assistants) carbon copies or blind copies.

10. Double-click on user John. (You can also highlight user John and press Enter.) Note that GroupWise Admin adds John to the *Add To* list.

11. Add user Bob to the Add To list as well.

12. Highlight Cindy's name and either click on the *Add CC* field or type C. GroupWise Admin will add Cindy to the Add CC field. Your Group dialog should look like the one in Fig. 19-7.

13. Click on OK to complete the action. GroupWise Admin will take you back to the Group Information dialog.

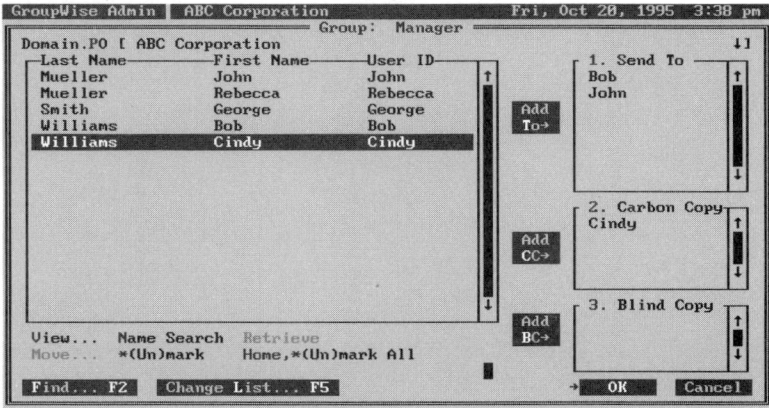

**Figure 19-7**
Group Dialog Box after Step 12.

14. Click on OK or press Enter to exit the Group Information dialog. We have now defined one group, managers. You can define other groups using the same technique. Now that we have defined a group and added some users to it, let's see how this has modified an individual user's record.

15. Double-click on John in the Users list (or highlight his name and press Enter). Click on *Groups* (or press *G*). You should see a dialog box similar to the one shown in Fig. 19-8. Note that we defined this part of the user record without even entering it. What if you need to see who else is on this list?

16. Click on *View* (or type *V*). You'll see a dialog box similar to the one in Fig. 19-9. This list allows you to quickly see who else is a member of a particular group.

17. Press Escape three times to clear the current screens. (You could also click on Cancel three times to accomplish the same task.) Now that we have a group for our users to belong to, let's give the users some resources to share.

18. Use the *Create | Resource* command (or press *Ctrl-R*) to display the Resource Information dialog box shown in Fig. 19-10. Now we have to describe the resource and assign it an owner.

19. Type *Green Ford Pickup* in the Resource ID field and press Tab. This is the way that GroupWise will display the resource when we need to request it in something like a meeting entry.

20. Press Enter at the Owner ID field (you could also double-click on it). GroupWise Admin will display a list of users who could own the resource, as shown in Fig. 19-11.

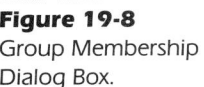

**Figure 19-8**
Group Membership Dialog Box.

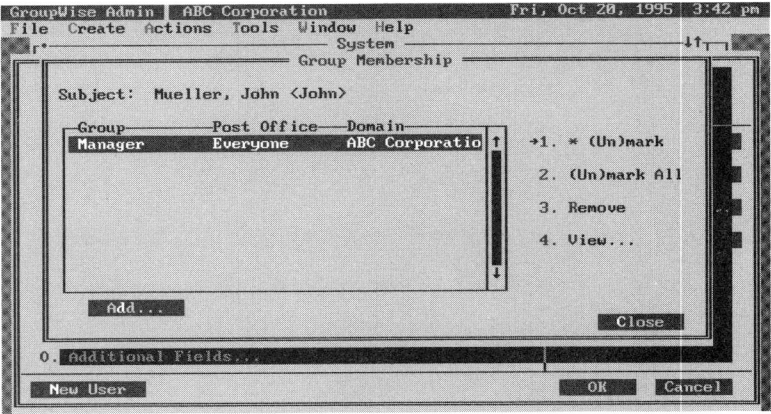

# GroupWise 4.x Advanced System Administration

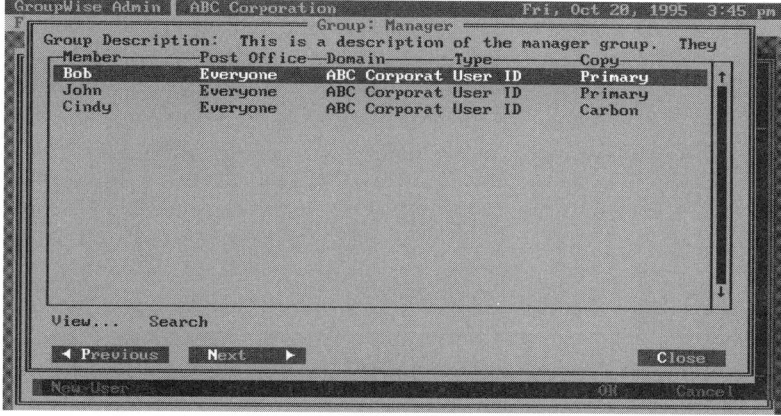

**Figure 19-9**
Group Description Dialog Box.

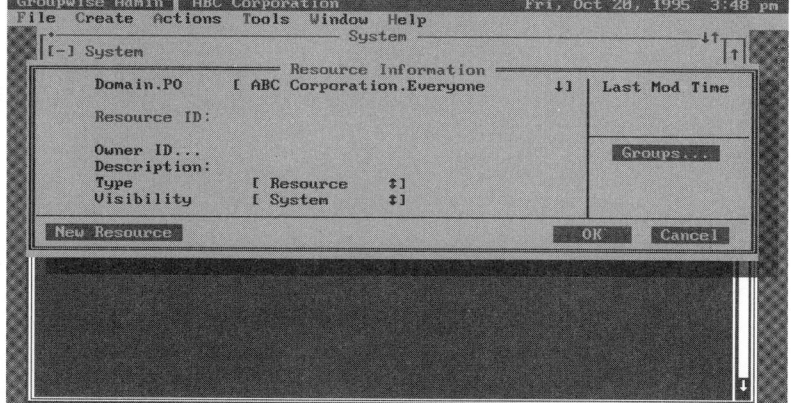

**Figure 19-10**
Resource Information Dialog Box.

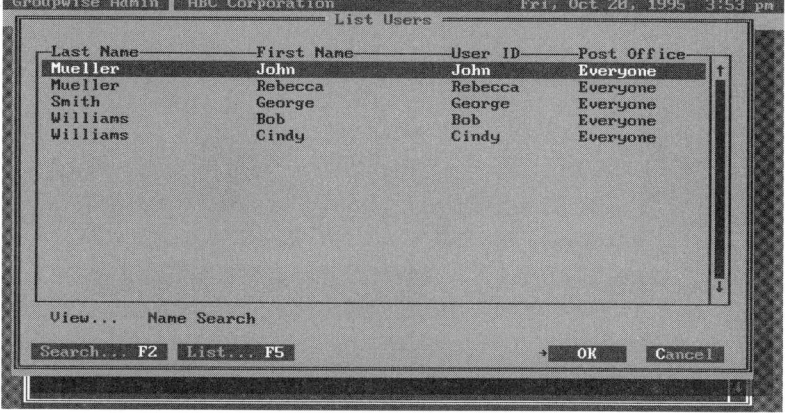

**Figure 19-11**
List Users Dialog Box.

21. Double-click on George (or highlight his name and press Enter). GroupWise Admin will take you back to the Resource Information dialog.

22. Click on OK (or press Enter) to complete the action. Now it's time to see how this has affected George's record.

23. Highlight *George* in the User list. Use the *Actions | Information* command to display George's User Information dialog box, like the one shown in Fig. 19-12. (You can also right-click on his entry and select Info from the menu.) Note that it shows that George owns one resource, but doesn't tell us which one.

24. Press Escape to clear the User Information dialog. Now, let's see how we can determine who owns specific resources.

25. Use the *Window | Resources* command (or press *Alt-3*) to display the Resources window, as shown in Fig. 19-13. Note that this window displays the resource, but not the owner's name.

26. Double-click on the Green Ford Pickup entry (or highlight it and press Enter). You'll see the Resource Information dialog box shown in Fig. 19-14. Note that this dialog will also allow you to change the owner's name or add new information about the resource.

27. Press Escape (or click on Cancel) to close the Resource Information dialog. You can exit the GroupWise Admin utility now or continue with the next section of the case study.

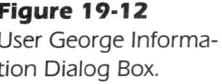

**Figure 19-12**
User George Information Dialog Box.

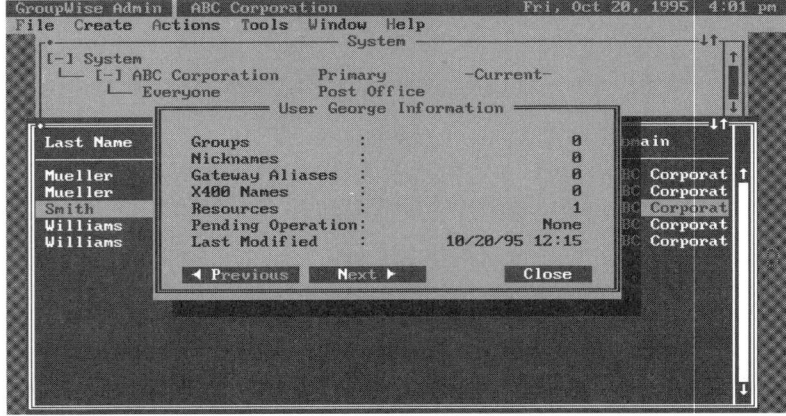

# GroupWise 4.x Advanced System Administration

**Figure 19-13**
Resources Window.

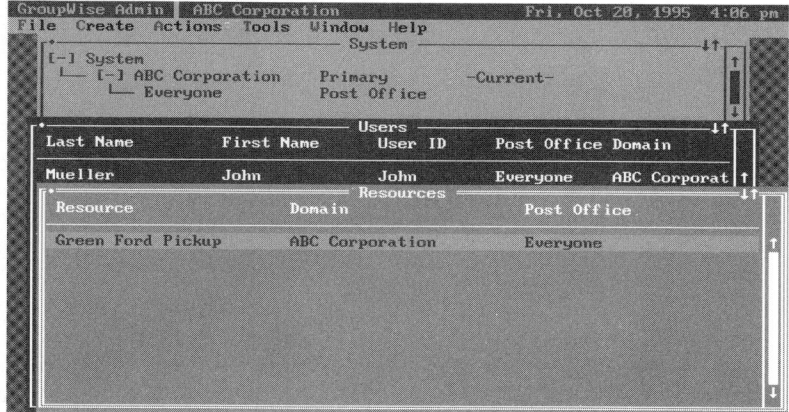

## Adding New Post Offices

Once you get past adding, deleting, and changing user objects, you have to start thinking about the other parts of GroupWise. Post offices are one part of GroupWise that you probably won't need to change a lot once you get them set up unless the company grows or changes in some other way. However, you'll probably need to add a new post office or remove an old one from time to time as the needs of the company change. For example, your boss might create a special research group to complete a specific project. This group may need its own post office, which you'll create at the beginning of the project and delete at its end. The following case study shows one method for performing this task. (Skip the first step if you're continuing from the previous section.)

**Figure 19-14**
Resource Information Dialog Box.

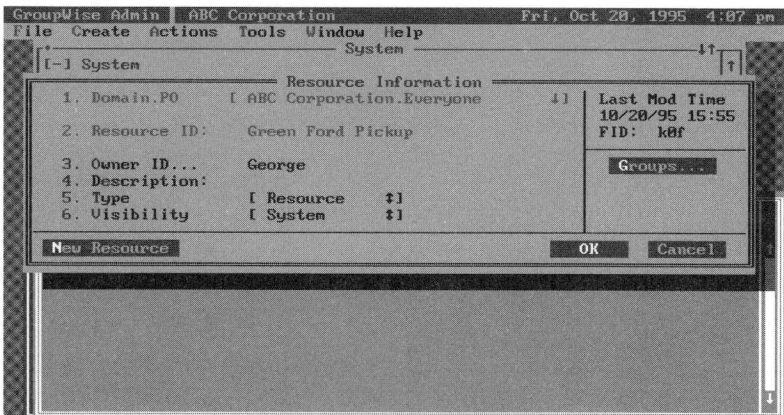

1. Change directories to your domain directory (the \*DOMAIN* directory in our case). Type *AD* and press Enter to start the administrator utility. You will see an initial system screen like the one in Fig. 19-1. The first thing we need to do is close any excess Windows so that we can concentrate on the System window (the one containing the domain and post office information).

2. Close any unneeded windows by clicking on the diamond in the upper left corner. You can also close it by selecting the window by pressing Alt-<window number> (where 2 is the Users window and 3 is the Resources window), then pressing Ctrl-F4.

3. Resize the System window as needed by dragging the lower right corner or pressing Ctrl-F3 to display the Window dialog. Now that we have a window that we can work with, let's add a post office to it. Two of the most common reasons for adding a new post office include adding a new company workgroup and adding a new file server that you want to use for a post office.

4. Use the *Create | Post Office* command to display the Create Post Office dialog box shown in Fig. 19-15. The managers have requested their own post office so they can discuss private company matters using GroupWise. This new post office will reflect those requirements.

5. Type *Managers* in the Post Office Name field, then press Tab.

6. Press Enter in the Description field. You'll see a dialog similar to the one shown in Fig. 19-16. Note that we have already added a description to this dialog. Add a similar description to your dialog. Descrip-

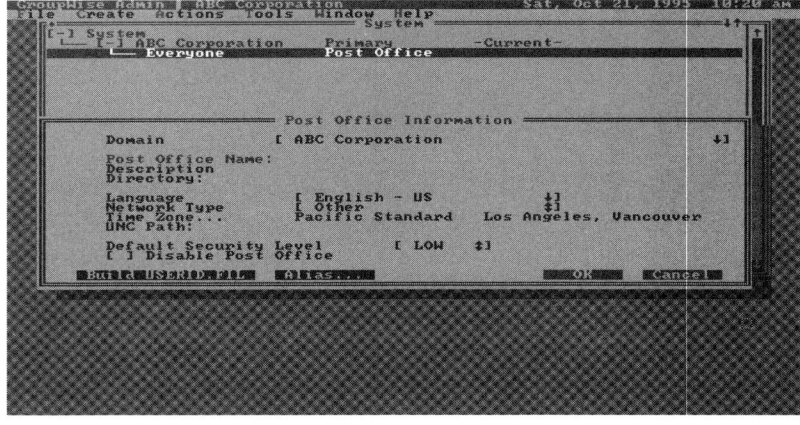

**Figure 19-15**
Create Post Office Dialog Box.

# GroupWise 4.x Advanced System Administration

**Figure 19-16**
Post Office Information Dialog Box.

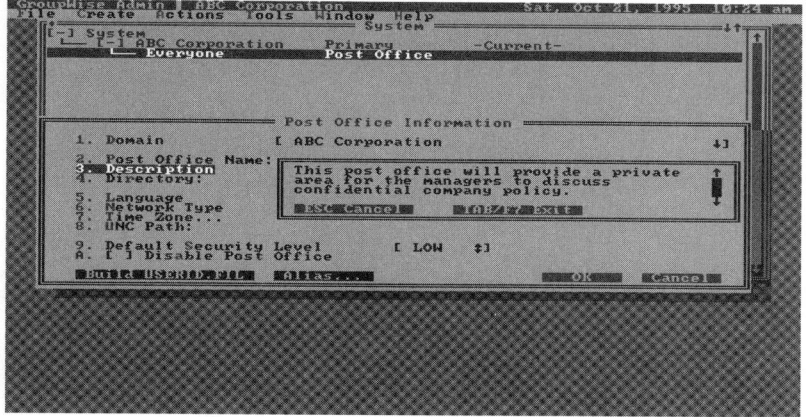

tions are an important part of the documentation process for a GroupWise installation, especially if there is more than one person administering the installation.

7. Press F7 or Tab to complete the action. At this point GroupWise Admin appears willing to create the post office because it highlights the OK button, but you need to add a directory (at a minimum) to complete the process. Our post office also needs some special security features. First, we'll use a different directory for this post office so we can protect it at the network operating system (NOS) level.

8. Type *R* to access the Directory field. Type the name of a directory (we chose E:\MANAGERS, but you could use any other name you like).

9. Press F7 or Tab to complete the action. Now that we have a special directory assigned, let's further increase security by changing the GroupWise security level.

10. Type *S* to select the Default Security Level field. GroupWise Admin will display a list box like the one shown in Fig. 19-17. Note that there are only two security levels: low and high.

11. Highlight the *High* option, then press Enter. Your post office dialog box should look like the one shown in Fig. 19-18. Note especially the directory and security settings. These two entries form the basis for the enhanced security offered by this post office. Of course, the precise level of security that you'll get depends as much on the NOS you use as it does on GroupWise.

**Figure 19-17**
Post Office Information Dialog Box after Step 10.

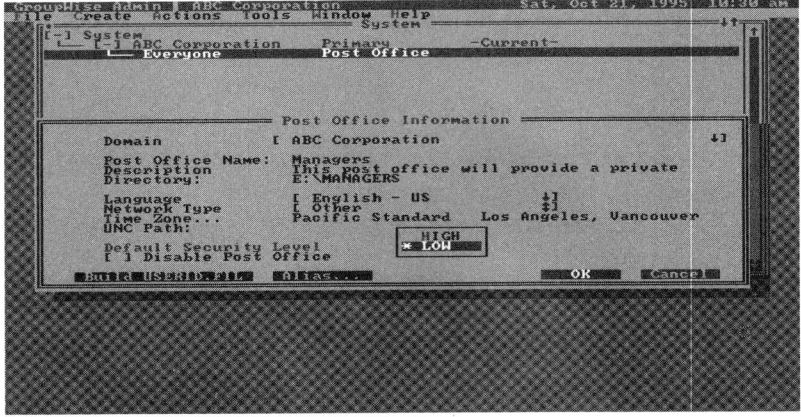

**Figure 19-18**
Post Office Information Dialog Box after Step 11.

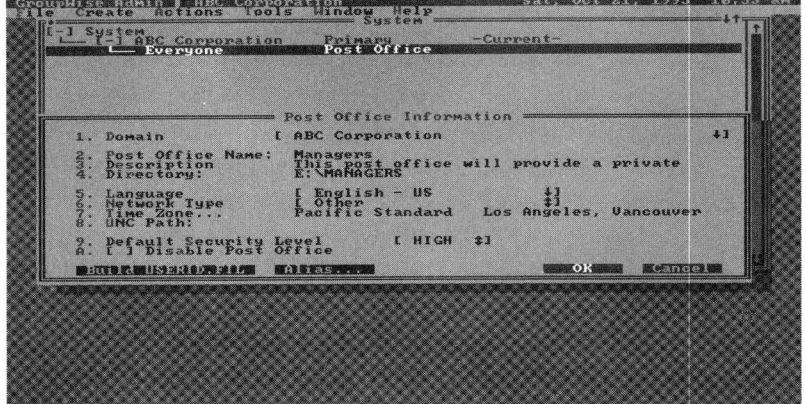

12. Click on OK (or highlight the OK pushbutton and press Enter) to accept the new post office settings. GroupWise Admin will copy some files to the new post office, then display the Copy Software to Post Office dialog box shown in Fig. 19-19. This is where you select the client to use with the post office. Since we have only the Windows client installed, that's the one we'll select.

13. Select the Windows client by clicking on the check box next to it or typing 2. (This entry should be checked by default, so you may not need to perform this step.)

14. Click on OK (or highlight OK and press Enter) to complete the action. GroupWise Admin will copy the client software to the new Managers post office. It'll then display instructions for installing the new client on your user's workstation, as shown in Fig. 19-20. Note that you

# GroupWise 4.x Advanced System Administration

**Figure 19-19**
Copy Software to Post Office Dialog Box.

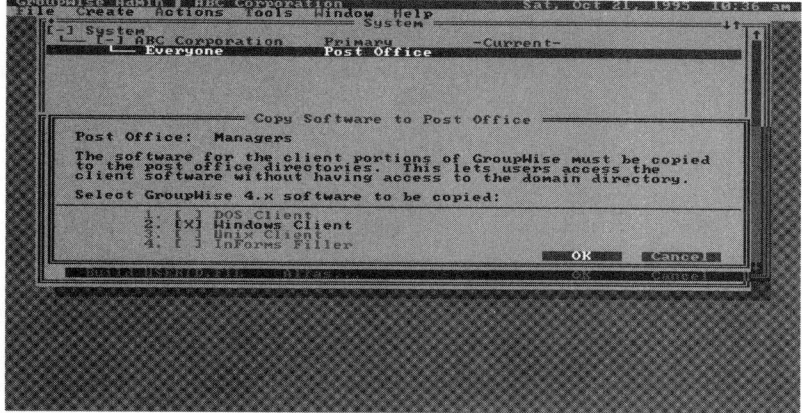

**Figure 19-20**
Setting Up the Windows Client Display.

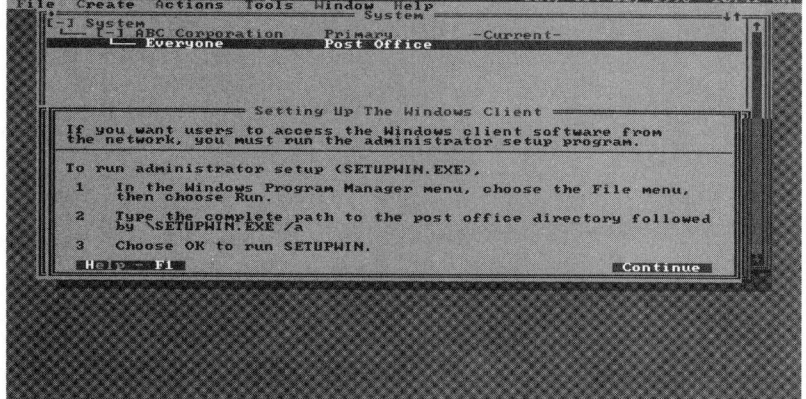

must run SETUPWIN using the /A switch to complete this task. (We also covered this process in Chap. 17, so we won't cover it again here.)

15. Press Enter to continue the post office installation process. You will see a new post office added to the System window, as shown in Fig. 19-21. Note that both post offices appear below the ABC Corporate domain.

16. Before we can use our new post office, we need to add some users to it. You can follow the procedure at the beginning of this chapter to do that. Make sure you only add the people you want to access that post office. It's also important to give them a post office level visibility.

17. To completely secure the Manager post office, you would need to hide it from everyone but the managers in your company using the

**Figure 19-21**
System Window Showing New Post Office.

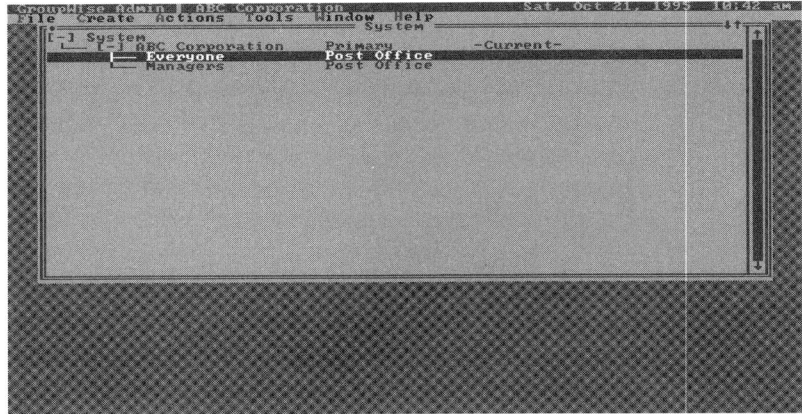

security features of your particular NOS. When using Novell NetWare, you'd need to give the Manager group trustee rights to this new directory, but exclude everyone else.

18. Once you completely secure the post office directory, you can use the procedures we covered in Chap. 17 to give the managers access to it. You can exit the GroupWise Admin utility now or continue with the next section of the case study.

## Adding New Domains

A growing company often needs to add a domain somewhere along the way for performance reasons. The Novell documentation states that a typical domain contains anywhere from 3 to 6 post offices, a reasonable limit. You might also need to add a domain if you add another file server. It makes sense to create a new domain for that file server so that all its post offices can appear in one place. The following case study shows one method for performing this task. (Skip the first step if you're continuing from the previous section.)

1. Change directories to your domain directory (the \*DOMAIN* directory in our case). Type *AD* and press Enter to start the administrator utility. You'll see an initial system screen like the one in Fig. 19-1. The first thing we need to do is close any excess Windows so that we can concentrate on the System window (the one containing the domain and post office information).

2. Close any unneeded windows by clicking on the diamond in the upper left corner. You can also close it by selecting the window by pressing Alt-<window number> (where 2 is the Users window and 3 is the Resources window), then pressing Ctrl-F4.

3. Resize the System window as needed by dragging the lower right corner or pressing Ctrl-F3 to display the Window dialog. Now that we have a System window that we can work with, let's add a new domain to it. We'll add a secondary domain to meet the needs of our growing company.

4. Type the domain name in the Domain Name field (we used Satellite Office 1), then press Tab to select the Domain Type field. Since this field already contains the value we want, we can press Tab again to bypass it. GroupWise does support four domain types in addition to the Primary domain: *Secondary, External GroupWise 4.x, External Office 3.1,* and *Foreign.* (Note that the foreign domain type is for non-GroupWise systems like Microsoft Mail or CC:Mail.)

5. Press Enter in the Description field. You'll see a dialog box similar to the one shown in Fig. 19-22. Note that we have already added a description to this dialog. Add a similar description to your dialog. Descriptions are an important part of the documentation process for a GroupWise installation, especially if there's more than one person administering the installation.

6. Press F7 or Tab to complete the action. At this point GroupWise Admin appears willing to create the new domain because it highlights the OK button, but you need to add a directory (at a minimum) to complete the process.

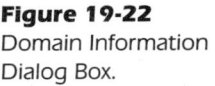
**Figure 19-22**
Domain Information Dialog Box.

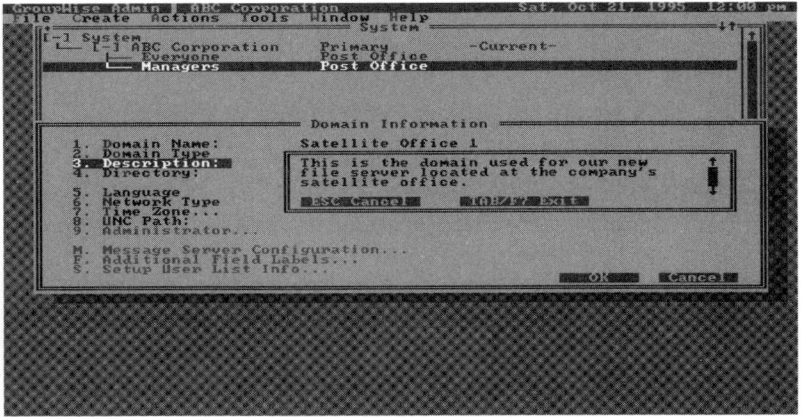

7. Type *R* to access the Directory field. Type the name of a directory (we chose E:\SAT01, but you could use any other name you like).

8. Press F7 or Tab to complete the action. Your new domain screen should look similar to the one in Fig. 19-23.

9. Click on OK (or highlight OK and press Enter) to complete the action. GroupWise Admin will copy the domain software to the new Satellite Office 1 domain. GroupWise will display the Copy Software to Domain dialog box shown in Fig. 19-24. Note that the Administration software (option 2) isn't selected. Since you can administer a secondary domain from your primary domain, there's no reason to copy the administration software (unless you plan to have an assistant help you manage the installation from the secondary domain's directory).

10. Accept the default settings by pressing Enter. GroupWise will copy the software you selected to the new domain directory. It'll then redisplay the System window showing the new domain. Your System window should look similar to the one in Fig. 19-25. Now that we have a new secondary domain, we have to perform some additional work to get the primary and secondary domain to work together.

11. Double-click on the Satellite Office 1 entry in the System window (you can also highlight it and press Enter). You've selected the secondary domain so we can do some work with it.

12. Use the *Tools | Database Management | Sync Primary with Secondary* command to create some links between the primary and secondary domain. You'll see the dialog box shown in Fig. 19-26.

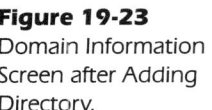

**Figure 19-23**
Domain Information Screen after Adding Directory.

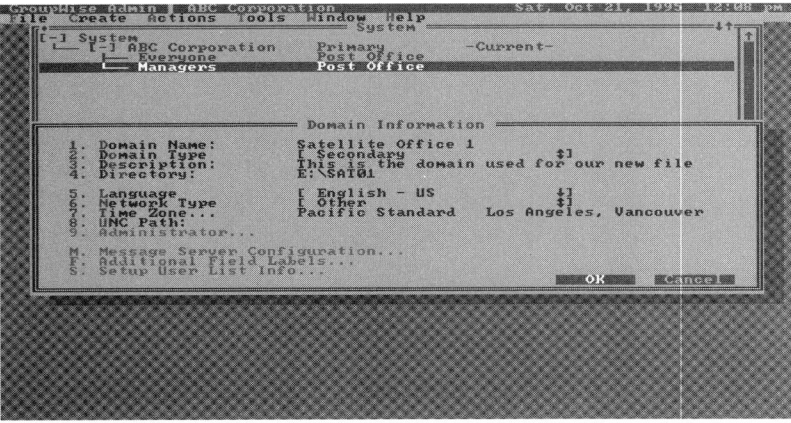

# GroupWise 4.x Advanced System Administration

**Figure 19-24**
Copy Software to Domain Dialog Box.

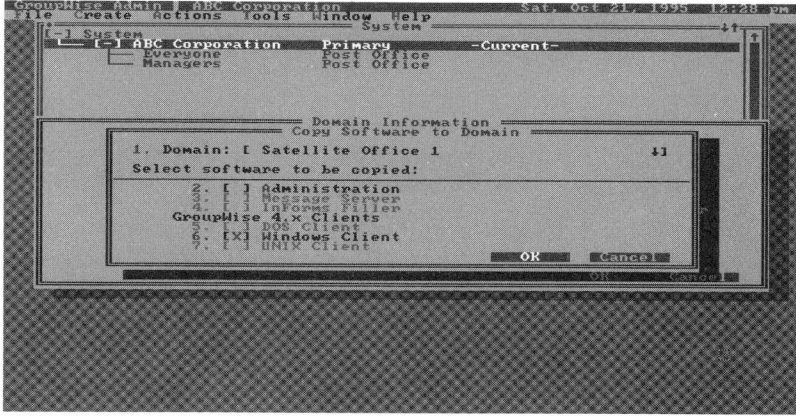

**Figure 19-25**
System Window Showing New Domain.

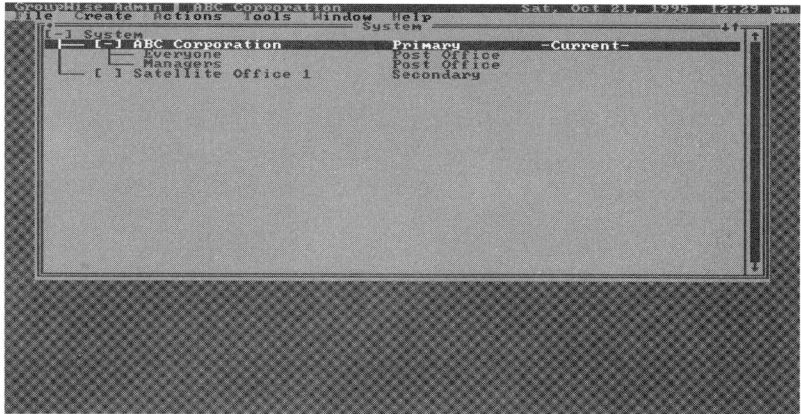

**Figure 19-26**
Synchronize with Secondary Domain Dialog Box.

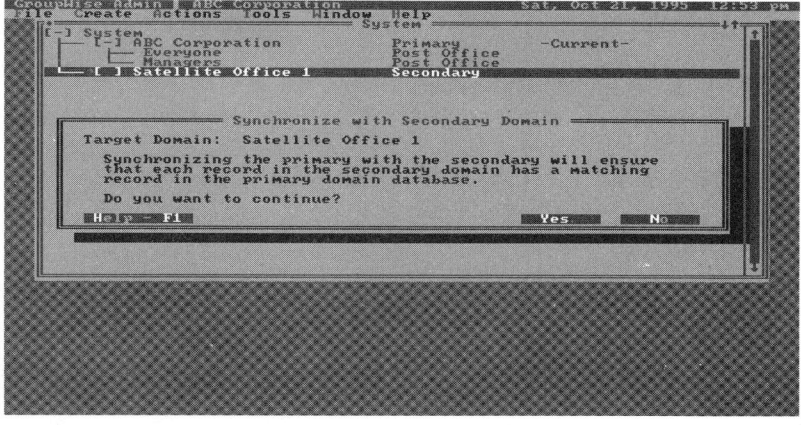

**Chapter Nineteen**

13. Press Enter to select *Yes*. GroupWise Admin will display the dialog box shown in Fig. 19-27. It asks you to provide the secondary domain path, but usually provides the correct path as a default.

14. Press Enter to accept the default path. GroupWise will make some new entries in the primary domain's database, then display the success message shown in Fig. 19-28.

15. Press Enter to clear the success dialog. You have successfully added a secondary domain to your GroupWise setup.

**NOTE**  *GroupWise Admin will display an error message when you exit the administration utility stating that you haven't started the message server if you try to create a secondary domain without first installing a message server. You can safely ignore the message for the purposes of this example since we aren't going to actually use the secondary domain. Chap. 18 shows how to install a message server. Use the procedures in that chapter to install a message server before you create a secondary domain that you intend to actually use.*

16. You'd need to add some post offices, users, and resources to complete the secondary domain creation process. We cover all those procedures in other segments of the case study, so we won't cover them again here. You can exit the GroupWise Admin utility now or continue with the next section of the case study.

**NOTE**  *You have to exit GroupWise Admin, change directories to the secondary domain directory, then restart GroupWise Admin to add new post offices to the domain. Once you add post offices, you can perform all other activities from the primary domain directory.*

**Figure 19-27**
Enter Path to Database Dialog Box.

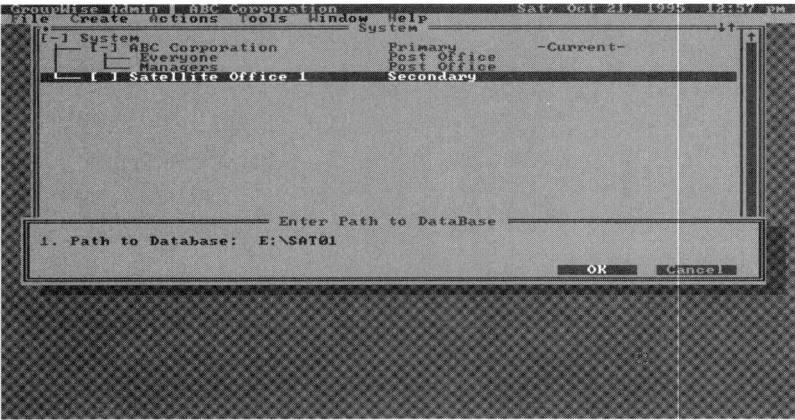

# GroupWise 4.x Advanced System Administration

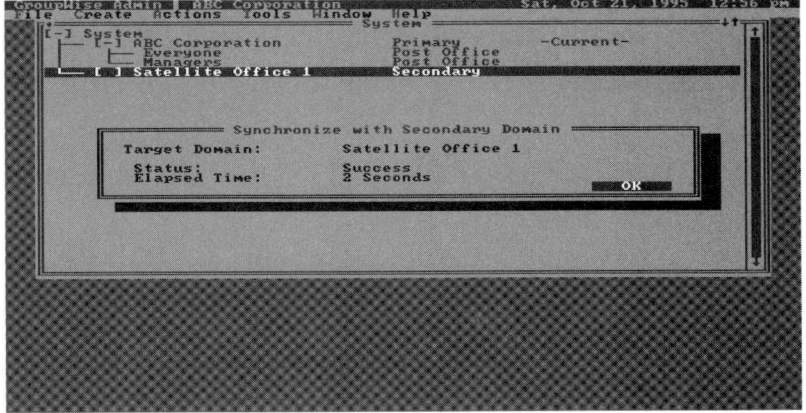

**Figure 19-28**
Synchronize with Secondary Domain Success Message.

## Merging Domains

There are more than a few reasons for merging domains. One of the biggest reasons is that you have an older WordPerfect Office setup that you recently converted to GroupWise. You can merge the old data with the new data in your existing setup. Merging allows you to administer the entire GroupWise setup from the primary domain directory—you gain the benefits of centralized management using this technique. Some GroupWise administrators will need to do this as they move one segment of a company at a time from WordPerfect Office to GroupWise.

Another common reason for merging domains is that your company is downsizing or consolidating existing departments. What happens when a research and development group gets combined with the rest of the company? How about the satellite office that your company recently closed due to a lack of sales in that particular location? All of these scenarios usually provide a reason for merging domains in your GroupWise setup. Maintaining separate e-mail systems made sense in the past, but there's no longer a need to do so.

**NOTE** *This procedure requires you to create links between the primary and secondary domains. We examine the technique for doing this in Chap. 18. You'll get a* link record missing *error in Step 16 if you attempt to do it without creating the required links first.*

The following procedure shows how to merge two domains together. (Skip the first step if you're continuing from the previous section.) What we'll actually do is two procedures. The first releases the secondary

**Chapter Nineteen**

domain from the primary domain. The second merges the two separate domains back together again. This part of the case study assumes that you created the secondary domain in the previous subsection of this case study, but you can easily use the procedure in other situations as well with a few changes to the procedure we provide. You'll most likely want to start at Step 11 if your only goal is to merge an external domain with your current primary GroupWise domain.

1. Change directories to your domain directory (the \*DOMAIN* directory in our case). Type *AD* and press Enter to start the administrator utility. You'll see an initial system screen like the one in Fig. 19-1. The first thing we need to do is close any excess Windows so that we can concentrate on the System window (the one containing the domain and post office information).

2. Close any unneeded windows by clicking on the diamond in the upper left corner. You can also close it by selecting the window by pressing Alt-<window number> (where 2 is the Users window and 3 is the Resources window), then pressing Ctrl-F4.

3. Resize the System window as needed by dragging the lower right corner or pressing Ctrl-F3 to display the Window dialog. Now that we have a System window that we can work with, let's merge the secondary domain we created in the previous procedure with the primary domain.

4. Double-click on the *Satellite Office 1* domain (or highlight it and press Enter.) This selects the domain for editing.

5. Use the *Action | Edit* command (or press F6) to display the Domain Information dialog box shown in Fig. 19-29. Note that the Domain

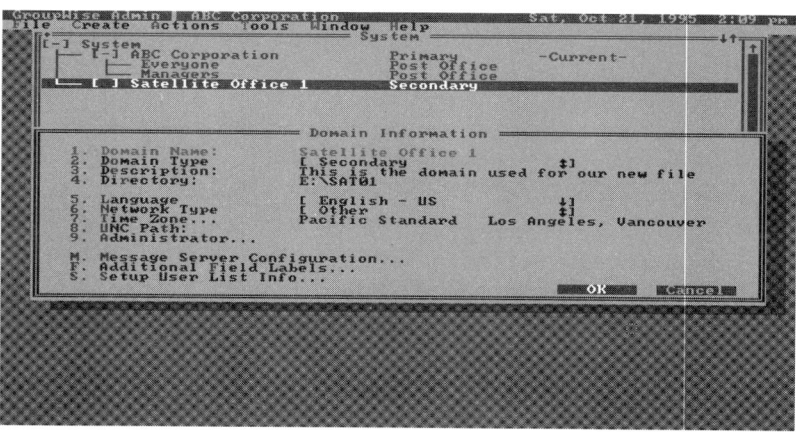

**Figure 19-29**
Domain Information Dialog Box.

# GroupWise 4.x Advanced System Administration

Name field is grayed out, but that all other fields are accessible for editing. The field that we are concerned with is the Domain Type field.

6. Click on the *Domain Type* field (or press 0) to select it.
7. Click on the *External GroupWise 4.x* entry (or highlight it and press Enter). GroupWise Admin will display the dialog box shown in Fig. 19-30, which asks if you want to release the Satellite Office 1 domain from the primary domain.
8. Press Enter to select *Yes*. GroupWise Admin will display a Domain Path and Password dialog. If our domain had a password, we would enter it here. The default path is normally correct, but you may want to check it to be sure.
9. Press Enter to accept the default path and password settings. GroupWise Admin will display some messages as it releases the domain, then the success message shown in Fig. 19-31.

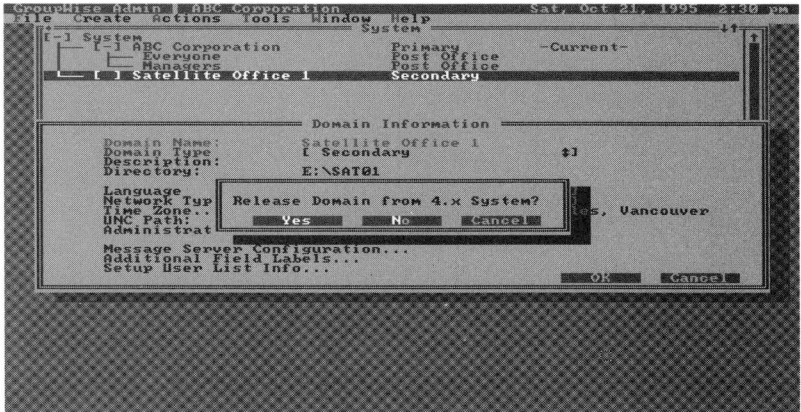

**Figure 19-30**
Release Domain Dialog Box.

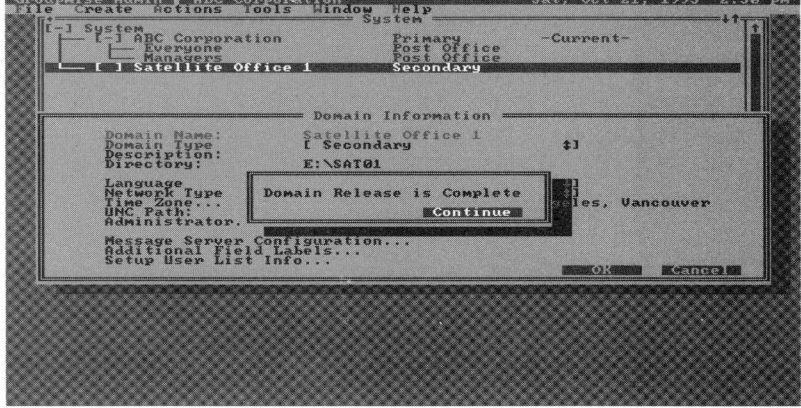

**Figure 19-31**
Domain Release Success Message.

# Chapter Nineteen

10. Press Enter to clear the success message. The Satellite Office 1 domain is now an external GroupWise installation. You can't manage it from the primary domain directory anymore. Now we'll merge it with the primary domain again.

11. Double-click on the *Satellite Office 1* domain (or highlight it and press Enter) to select it for editing.

12. Use the *Action | Edit* command (or press F6) to display the Domain Information dialog box shown in Fig. 19-29.

13. Click on the *Domain Type* field (or press 0) to select it.

14. Click on the *Secondary* entry (or highlight it and press Enter). GroupWise Admin will display the dialog box shown in Fig. 19-32, which asks if you want to merge the Satellite Office 1 domain into the primary domain.

15. Press Enter to select *Yes*. GroupWise Admin will display a Domain Path and Password dialog. If our domain had a password, we would enter it here. The default path is normally correct, but you may want to check it to be sure.

16. Press Enter to accept the default path and password settings. GroupWise Admin will display some messages as it merges the Satellite Office 1 domain into the ABC Corporation domain, then a success message similar to the one shown in Fig. 19-33.

17. Press Enter to clear the success message. The Satellite Office 1 domain is now a secondary domain under the ABC Corporation primary domain.

**Figure 19-32**
Merge Domain Dialog Box.

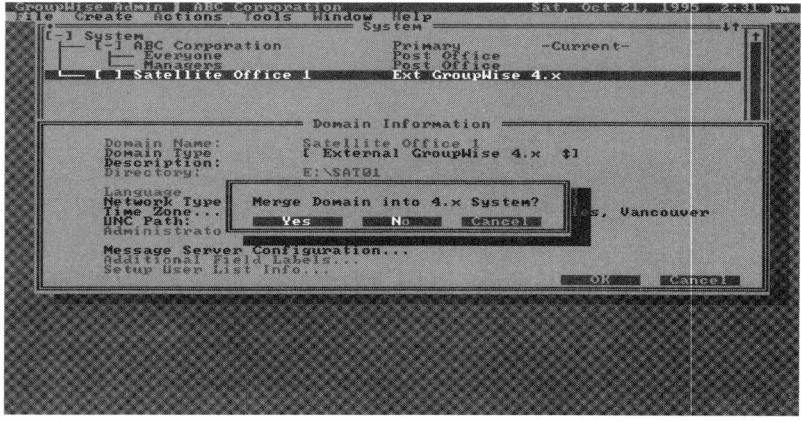

# GroupWise 4.x Advanced System Administration 623

**Figure 19-33**
Domain Merge
Success Message.

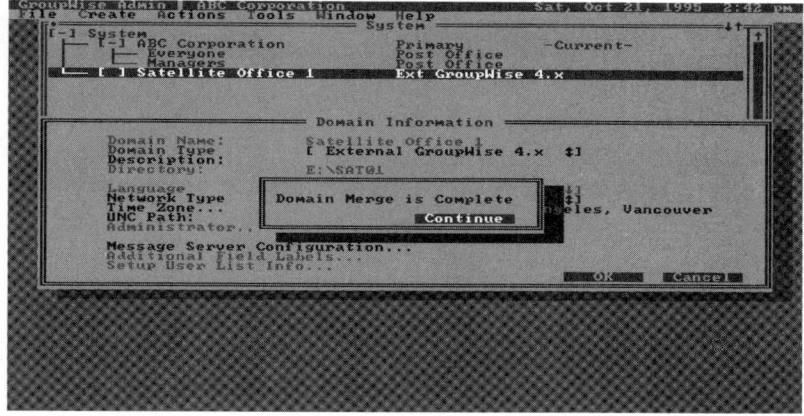

## Performing Database Maintenance

The more you use GroupWise, the more often you need to maintain it. The types of maintenance you need to do are fairly simple, though they can take a while to perform. In most cases, you'll only need to check the database for errors and make sure the lines of communication between various objects remain open. The following procedure takes a quick tour of the database management utilities that GroupWise provides. (Skip the first step if you're continuing from the previous section.)

**WARNING:** Log everyone out of GroupWise before you perform this procedure. Always perform diagnostics with the database closed and everyone logged off.

1. Change directories to your domain directory (the \*DOMAIN* directory in our case). Type *AD* and press Enter to start the administrator utility. You'll see an initial system screen like the one in Fig. 19-1. The first thing we'll want to do is verify that we have clean communications. One way to do this is to check the message server statistics.

2. Use the *Tools | Diagnostics* command (or press F11) to display the Message Server Diagnostics dialog box (Fig. 19-34). This is the place where you'll see whether there are problems with the current communication setup. The *Undeliverable* and *Corrupted* fields should remain at 0. Anything higher indicates an error condition that you need to take care of.

**Figure 19-34**
Message Server Diagnostics Dialog Box.

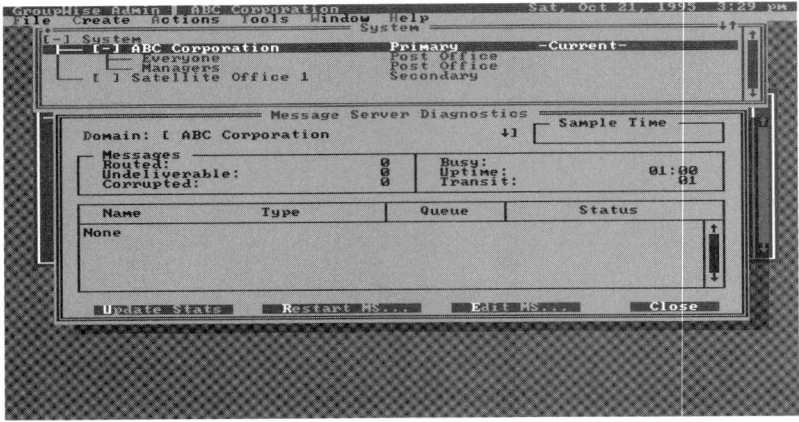

3. Click on Close (or press Enter) to remove the dialog. Now we need to check on the status of the database itself.

4. Select one of the domains in the System window by double-clicking on it (or highlighting it and pressing Enter). The domain you select is the one whose database you'll check. You must check each database individually.

5. Use the *Tools | Database Management | Validate Database* command to display the Database Validate dialog box shown in Fig. 19-35.

6. Press Enter to start the validation process. You should see a dialog box similar to the one in Fig. 19-36 if the database is error free. Otherwise, you'll need to rebuild or recover the database to correct the errors.

**Figure 19-35**
Validate Database Dialog Box.

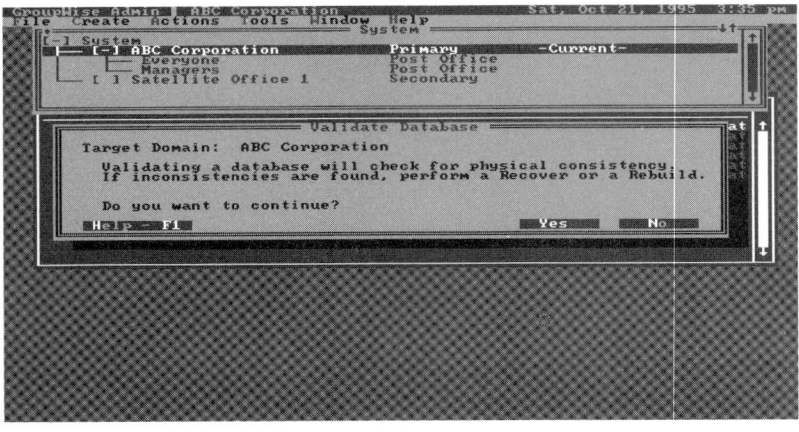

# GroupWise 4.x Advanced System Administration

**Figure 19-36**
Validate Database Success Message.

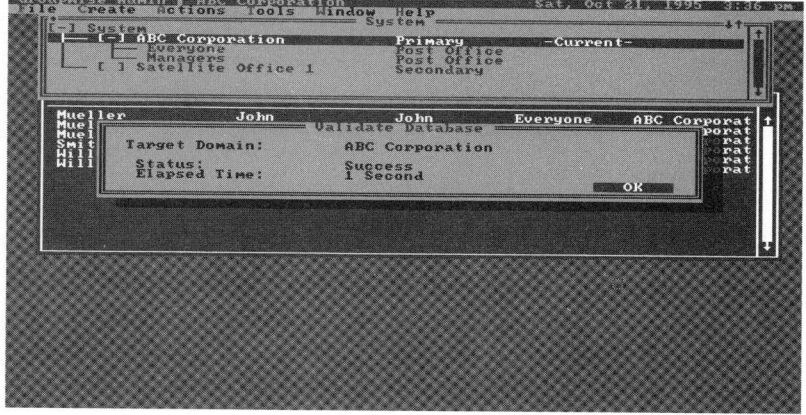

7. Press Enter to clear the dialog. Now that we have ensured that the database is error free, let's optimize it for speed.

8. Use the *Tools | Database Management | Reclaim Unused Database Space* command to display the Reclaim Unused Database Space dialog box shown in Fig. 19-37.

9. Press Enter to select *Yes*. Once GroupWise Admin completes the compression process, it'll display the success dialog shown in Fig. 19-38.

10. Press Enter to clear the success dialog. The final step in our maintenance process is to reindex the database.

11. Use the *Tools | Database Management | Rebuild Listing Indexes* command to display the dialog shown in Fig. 19-39.

**Figure 19-37**
Reclaim Unused Database Space Dialog Box.

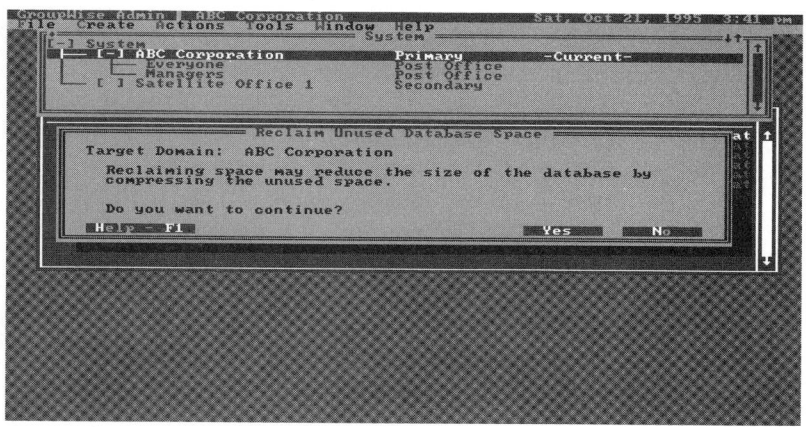

**Figure 19-38**
Reclaim Unused Database Space Success Message.

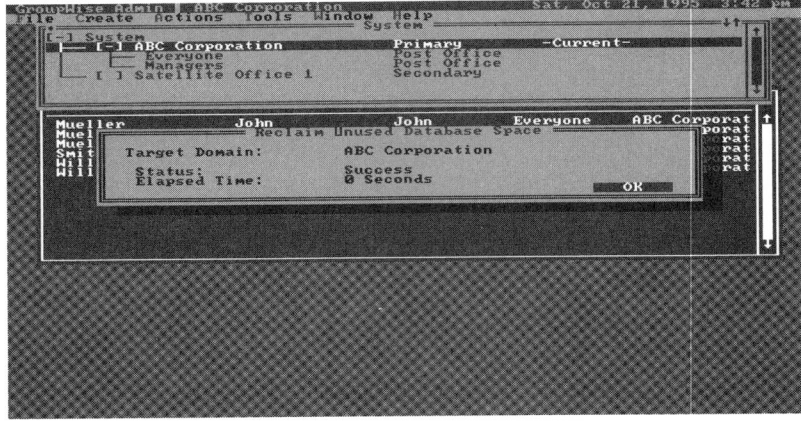

**Figure 19-39**
Rebuild Listing Indexes Dialog Box.

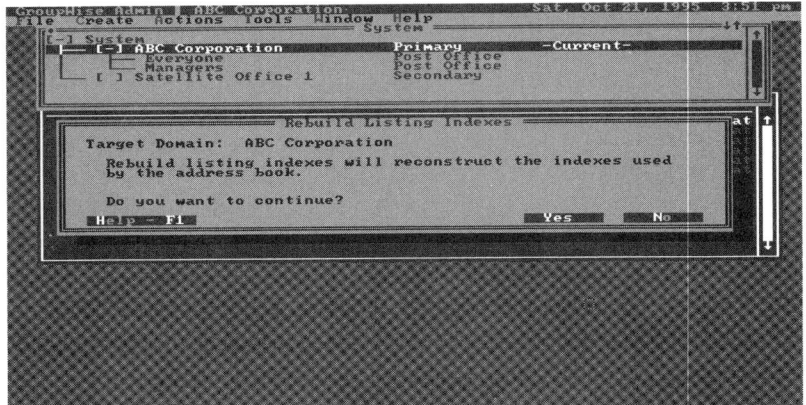

12. Press Enter to select *Yes*. GroupWise Admin will rebuild the indexes, then display a success dialog similar to the ones we've seen before.
13. Press Enter to clear the success dialog.
14. Performs Steps 4 to 12 on the rest of the domains in your GroupWise setup. Once you complete these steps for all the domains that you maintain, you have checked GroupWise for most errors and optimized it for best performance.

# Study Questions

1. The GroupWise User Information dialog provides space for _____ user-defined entries.
   a. 5
   b. 10
   c. 15
   d. 20

   *b.* You get 10 user-defined entries. GroupWise lets you put any kind of information needed here. For example, you could use a user-defined entry to specify the user's actual network location.

2. The two levels of post office security are:
   a. High and low
   b. Read/write and read-only
   c. Public and private
   d. Visible and hidden

   *a.* The two levels of security that GroupWise provides for post offices are high and low. A high level of security restricts anyone from logging into a post office that they aren't supposed to access (unless the user has assigned the post office a password and the second user knows it). GroupWise detects who is trying to access an account by checking the name they used to log into the network.

3. Which of the following domain types does GroupWise support?
   a. Primary
   b. Secondary
   c. External GroupWise 4.x
   d. External GroupWise 3.1
   e. Foreign

   *a, b, c, and e.* At first glance it might appear that all the answers are correct. However, answer *d* should be External Office 3.1.

4. GroupWise restricts you to using _____ links when creating a link to a secondary domain.
   a. Indirect
   b. Direct

c. Gateway

d. None

*a, b, c, and d.* There isn't any limitation as long as you have the correct software and the proper setup. The *direct* and *none* link types are automatically enabled. You must have three or more domains to create an *indirect* link. Obviously, the *gateway* option requires you to have a gateway installed on your system.

5. The _____ Database Management command in GroupWise Admin removes excess space in your GroupWise databases.

   a. Rebuild Listing Indexes
   b. Validate Database
   c. Reclaim Unused Database Space
   d. Rebuild Database

   *c.* Removing the excess space from a GroupWise database is one step in optimizing it for optimum performance. You'll also want to purge expired records and rebuild the listing indexes.

6. You cannot recover the secondary post office database in the secondary domain by using the Recover Database command in the primary domain.

   a. True
   b. False

   *a.* You can recover the primary domain database, the post office databases in the primary domain, and any secondary domain database from the primary domain. The only databases you cannot recover are the secondary post office databases.

7. The three types of message transmission that you can specify in the Group dialog of the GroupWise Admin utility include: _____, _____, and _____.

   a. Direct, Public, and Private
   b. Add To, Add Private, and Add Public
   c. Add To, Add CC, and Add BC
   d. Add All, Add Public, and Add None

   *c.* You can send a message directly to someone (Add To), send them a carbon copy (Add CC) or send them a blind copy (Add BC).

# GroupWise 4.x Advanced System Administration

8. Merging an external GroupWise domain with a primary domain allows you to _____.
   a. Get rid of the extra domain.
   b. Manage both domains from the primary domain's directory.
   c. Circumvent the other domain's security.
   d. Modify the other domain's Domain Name field.

   *b.* One of the major benefits of merging two domains is that you can garner the benefits of centralized management. You could also save some disk space by removing the administration software from the new secondary domain.

9. The DOS client software requires a minimum of _____ hard disk space, _____ of conventional memory, and _____ of expanded or extended memory.
   a. 6.5 MB, 500 K, 4 MB
   b. 40 MB, 500 K, 2 MB
   c. 12 MB, 450 K, 4 MB
   d. 0 MB, 450 K, 0 MB

   *d.* If you run the DOS client from a network directory, you can get by with these minimal requirements. However, Novell recommends that you have 6.5 MB of hard disk space to copy the client files locally, 500 K or more of conventional memory, and 4 MB or more of expanded or extended memory.

10. To create a new group, you'd press _____ at the Main Screen.
    a. Alt-G
    b. Alt-4
    c. Ctrl-G
    d. Ctrl-4

    *c.* Pressing Ctrl-G at the Main Screen will display the Group Information dialog.

11. You'd use the _____ command line switch of AD.EXE to prevent it from using expanded memory.
    a. /NE
    b. /DU
    c. /DX
    d. /NX

*a.* The /NE switch prevents the administration program from using expanded memory. You can also disable the use of upper memory block using the /DU switch and extended memory using the /NX switch.

12. A Group Name must be unique and can't contain which of the following characters?

    **a.** WordPerfect Character Set 1

    **b.** At Sign (@)

    **c.** Colon (:)

    **d.** Underscore (_)

    *b and c.* Besides the at sign and the colon, you cannot use the following characters in a group name: ASCII characters 0 through 31, braces, comma, double quote, parentheses, period, and WordPerfect character sets 3 to 7. These same restrictions hold true with other types of address and identification fields (like the Resource ID field in the Resource Information dialog.

13. The Build USERID.FIL option of the Post Office Information dialog allows you to create this file that's used by:

    **a.** GroupWise 4.x

    **b.** WP Office 2.0

    **c.** WordPerfect 5.1

    **d.** WP Office 3.1

    *b, c, and d.* GroupWise doesn't need this file. However, it's used by a variety of WordPerfect network products below the 6.x level. For example, you would need to generate this file for WordPerfect 5.1, but not for WordPerfect 6.0.

14. You'll find the DOS Message Server update information in the _____ file.

    **a.** WPDOMAIN.DC

    **b.** WPDOMAIN.CSI

    **c.** WPHOST.DC

    **d.** WPDOMAIN.DB

    *b.* The administration program sends a message to the Message Server each time you change its configuration. The OS/2, NLM, and UNIX Message Servers update their configuration directly from the domain database. Only the DOS Message Server requires a separate WPDOMAIN.CSI file.

# GroupWise 4.x Advanced System Administration

**15.** User visibility options in GroupWise include _____.
   **a.** Domain
   **b.** Post Office
   **c.** System
   **d.** None

*a, b, c and d.* You can define any one of these four visibility levels. A visibility level affects which address lists receive the user's name and address. Limiting a user's visibility can restrict the average user's access to them. However, this doesn't prevent someone who knows the user's address from sending them a message.

**16.** You must install a _____ before you can use a secondary domain.
   **a.** File server
   **b.** Post office
   **c.** Client
   **d.** Message server

*d.* A message server allows you to send messages between domains by creating links between them. GroupWise won't prevent you from creating a secondary domain if you don't have a message server installed, but you won't be able to communicate with it.

**17.** During a database rebuild, GroupWise Admin renames the database to _____.
   **a.** WPDOMAIN.DB
   **b.** CREATING.DDB
   **c.** RECOVER.DDB
   **d.** REBUILD.DDB

*c.* The administration program renames the current WPDOMAIN.DB file to RECOVER.DDB. It then adds records from RECOVER.DDB to the CREATING.DDB file. If the rebuild is successful, the administration program renames the CREATING.DDB file to WPDOMAIN.DB and erases the RECOVER.DDB file.

**18.** GroupWise provides _____ priority subdirectories in the WPCSIN directory that determines the order in which messages get processed.
   **a.** 5
   **b.** 6

**c.** 7
   **d.** 8

   *d.* There are eight levels of message processing. The directories are numbered from 0 to 7. GroupWise processes the messages in the 0 directory first and the 7 directory last.

19. The administration program uses LC.EXE to launch various external programs like OFSETUP and OFCONV.
    **a.** True
    **b.** False

    *a.* AD.EXE uses these external programs to perform a variety of tasks. The use of external applications also allows the administrator to use some of them (like OFCHECK) in a batch processing mode.

20. Three communication specific statistics that the Message Server Diagnostics dialog provides are: _____, _____, and _____.
    **a.** Routed, Undeliverable, and Transmission Errors
    **b.** Sent, Undeliverable, and Transmission Errors
    **c.** Routed, Undeliverable, and Corrupted
    **d.** Sent, Undeliverable, and Corrupted

    *c.* The Routed field tells you how many messages were sent. The other two fields tell you how many errors there were and their type. You should see a value of 0 in both the Undeliverable and Corrupted fields if there aren't any communication problems.

21. You can give two users the same User ID as long as they appear in different post offices.
    **a.** True
    **b.** False

    *b.* The first thing you'll notice if you do this is that both users will experience problems logging in. GroupWise will eventually tell you that there is a duplicate name in the database, but this usually won't happen immediately. The best policy is to run database maintenance whenever you see some type of problem with your GroupWise setup.

22. You can view which resources a user owns by looking at the _____ in the GroupWise Admin utility.
    **a.** Resources window
    **b.** User List dialog

# GroupWise 4.x Advanced System Administration

    **c.** User Information dialog

    **d.** Resource Information dialog

*d.* The Resource Information dialog accessed from the Resources window will tell you who owns a specific resource. The Resources window itself only lists the resources. Likewise, the User Information dialog only tells how many resources the user owns, not which resources they are.

23. One way to start the GroupWise domain merge process is to change the Domain Type field entry from _____ to _____.
    **a.** External GroupWise 4.x, Secondary
    **b.** Primary, Secondary
    **c.** Secondary, External GroupWise 4.x
    **d.** External Office 3.1, Secondary

*a and d.* The GroupWise Admin utility will help you merge either external domain type into a primary domain by simply changing its Domain Type field and following the prompts. It's also possible to change the current primary domain into a secondary domain and the specified secondary domain into a primary domain using this method. Remember that there's only one primary domain for any GroupWise installation.

24. The user mailbox information is stored in the _____ file.
    **a.** USER*XXX*.DB
    **b.** WPDOMAIN.DB
    **c.** MSG*XX*.DB
    **d.** WPHOST.DB

*a.* Each user gets a separate mailbox. The *XXX* portion of the filename is the same as the user's File ID (you can see the File ID in the upper right corner of the User Information dialog).

25. You can insert characters from the WordPerfect character sets into a text field by pressing Ctrl-2, typing the character set number, adding a comma, typing the number of the character you want, and then pressing Enter.
    **a.** True
    **b.** False

*a.* There are 14 different character sets provided with GroupWise. You can use any of them in most text fields. You cannot use character sets 3 to 7 (symbols) in an address field like Domain Name, Post Office Name, WP Name, User ID, Resource ID, Group Name, or Nickname.

26. Access denied errors, undelivered messages, the user being unable to execute the Client program, and the Message Server displaying blocked domains, post offices, or gateways are all symptoms of what type of problem?
    a. Corrupted Client program installation
    b. Insufficient network rights
    c. Corrupted domain database files
    d. A malfunctioning NIC (network interface card)

    *b.* A user has to have the proper level of rights to the post office and mailbox directories to prevent this type of problem. Only administrators need access to the domain directory.

27. Novell recommends that you back up the user and message databases at least _____.
    a. Once a day.
    b. Once a week.
    c. Once every other week.
    d. Once a month.

    *b.* You should back up all the USER*XXX*.DB and MSG*XX*.DB files at least once a week. Backing them up more often than that will certainly reduce the level of loss if some type of error occurs.

28. GroupWise Admin allows you to change the length of the various User Information dialog fields within the _____ dialog.
    a. Setup
    b. Environment
    c. User Information
    d. Setup List Users

    *d.* You can access the Setup List Users dialog by clicking on the Setup User List Info field (option S) in the Domain Information dialog box.

29. The _____ and _____ files contain entries which enable MAPI support in GroupWise.
    a. WINFILE.BIF, WPCMAPI.BIF
    b. WIN.INI, SYSTEM.INI

# GroupWise 4.x Advanced System Administration

    **c.** WINFILE.INI, WPCMAPI.INI
    **d.** OFVIEWUS.INI, WPCMAPI.INI

*c.* The WINFILE.INI and WPCMAPI.INI files contain entries that enable the Windows messaging application programming interface (MAPI) support.

30. You must fill in which fields of the Post Office Information dialog to create a default post office setup?
    **a.** Post Office Name
    **b.** Description
    **c.** Directory
    **d.** Default Security Level

*a and c.* GroupWise Admin automatically fills some fields in with default values. The Default Security Level field defaults to a low security level. You must tell the administration program the post office name and the directory you want to use for it at a minimum. The Description field is a must from a documentation point of view, but you don't necessarily have to fill it in.

31. The Expire Date field of the User Information dialog in the GroupWise Admin utility allows you to _____.
    **a.** Specify the date when a user's access will end.
    **b.** Specify the date when GroupWise will remove the account.
    **c.** Enhance security by limiting temporary employee access.
    **d.** Modify the date when GroupWise updates the account.

*a and c.* The main function of the Expire Date field is to tell GroupWise when to end users' access to their accounts. However, this has the effect of enhancing security when used to limit a temporary employee's access to the system.

32. You cannot edit either the Domain.PO or the User ID fields of the User Information dialog (once you create the user) since GroupWise uses them to index the database.
    **a.** True
    **b.** False

*a.* GroupWise Admin always grays these fields out when you edit a user's record. The only way to change either field is to create a new user record and then erase the old one.

## Chapter Nineteen

33. You can import user information from NetWare 4.x into GroupWise 4.1 when using _____.
    a. Multiple post offices
    b. An external domain
    c. NDS
    d. Bindery emulation

    *d.* GroupWise doesn't currently support NetWare Directory Services (NDS), but it does support bindery emulation.

34. All of the Message Server files appear in the _____ directory.
    a. WPTOOLS
    b. WPOFFICE
    c. WPCS
    d. WPCSIN

    *c.* The GroupWise Message Server installation program will create the WPCS directory for you during setup.

35. You can change the order in which GroupWise Admin displays the user names by changing the Sort By field of the Setup List Users dialog.
    a. True
    b. False

    *a.* GroupWise only allows you to sort the list using the Last Name or First Name fields.

36. If you can't import a file exported from the UNIX administration program, then you should check for the following:
    a. A corrupted UNIX domain database
    b. A corrupted UNIX post office database
    c. UNIX end of line character [LF][CR] converted into the DOS equivalent [LF]
    d. UNIX end of line character [LF] converted into the DOS equivalent [LF][CR]

    *d.* You need to convert the end of line characters in the UNIX file before you can use them with the DOS administration program. Performing a binary transfer will take care of this problem.

37. The Recover Database option of the Database Management menu allows you to:
    a. Correct physical database problems.
    b. Compress the database.
    c. Rebuild the database indexes.
    d. Update incorrect database information.

    *a.* The Recover Database option is the fastest and most convenient method of quickly correcting physical problems in your GroupWise database. However, you'll need to use the Rebuild Database option if you also need to update incorrect database information.

38. The acronym *UNC* stands for:
    a. Unidentified Network Connection
    b. Universal Naming Convention
    c. Universal Network Connection
    d. Unidentified Naming Convention

    *b.* Using a UNC path provides an absolute network path and eliminates the need for drive letters or mappings.

39. You cannot create which of the following secondary domain objects from the primary domain?
    a. Post office
    b. User
    c. Resource
    d. Group

    *a.* GroupWise will allow you to manage every other secondary domain aspect from the primary domain directory once you set up the appropriate post offices.

40. Pressing _____ at the ancillary input dialogs, like the Group Information Description dialog, will complete the current action.
    a. F5
    b. Enter
    c. F7
    d. Tab

    *c and d.* Pressing either F7 or Tab will complete an action in most ancillary input dialogs. GroupWise Admin normally provides a hint within the dialog telling you which keys are available.

## Fun Test

1. One way to start the GroupWise domain merge process is to change the Domain Type field entry from _____ to _____.
   a. External GroupWise 4.x, Secondary
   b. Primary, Secondary
   c. Secondary, External GroupWise 4.x
   d. External Office 3.1, Secondary

2. User visibility options in GroupWise include _____.
   a. Domain
   b. Post Office
   c. System
   d. None

3. You cannot edit either the Domain.PO or the User ID fields of the User Information dialog (once you create the user) since GroupWise uses them to index the database.
   a. True
   b. False

4. The DOS client software requires a minimum of _____ hard disk space, _____ of conventional memory, and _____ of expanded or extended memory.
   a. 6.5 MB, 500 K, 4 MB
   b. 40 MB, 500 K, 2 MB
   c. 12 MB, 450 K, 4 MB
   d. 0 MB, 450 K, 0 MB

5. During a database rebuild, GroupWise Admin renames the database to _____.
   a. WPDOMAIN.DB
   b. CREATING.DDB
   c. RECOVER.DDB
   d. REBUILD.DDB

6. The GroupWise User Information dialog provides space for _____ user-defined entries.
   a. 5
   b. 10

# GroupWise 4.x Advanced System Administration

   c. 15
   d. 20

7. You cannot create which of the following secondary domain objects from the primary domain?
   a. Post office
   b. User
   c. Resource
   d. Group

8. Three communication specific statistics that the Message Server Diagnostics dialog provides are: _____, _____, and _____.
   a. Routed, Undeliverable, and Transmission Errors
   b. Sent, Undeliverable, and Transmission Errors
   c. Routed, Undeliverable, and Corrupted
   d. Sent, Undeliverable, and Corrupted

9. The Build USERID.FIL option of the Post Office Information dialog allows you to create this file that is used by:
   a. GroupWise 4.x
   b. WP Office 2.0
   c. WordPerfect 5.1
   d. WP Office 3.1

10. You can import user information from NetWare 4.x into GroupWise 4.1 when using:
    a. Multiple post offices
    b. An external domain
    c. NDS.
    d. Bindery emulation

11. All of the Message Server files appear in the _____ directory.
    a. WPTOOLS
    b. WPOFFICE
    c. WPCS
    d. WPCSIN

12. You can insert characters from the WordPerfect character sets into a text field by pressing Ctrl-2, typing the character set number, adding

a comma, typing the number of the character you want, and then pressing Enter.

   a. True
   b. False

13. Which of the following domain types does GroupWise support?

    a. Primary
    b. Secondary
    c. External GroupWise 4.x
    d. External GroupWise 3.1
    e. Foreign

14. Access denied errors, undelivered messages, the user being unable to execute the Client program, and the Message Server displaying blocked domains, post offices, or gateways are all symptoms of what type of problem?

    a. Corrupted Client program installation
    b. Insufficient network rights
    c. Corrupted domain database files
    d. A malfunctioning NIC (network interface card)

15. A Group Name must be unique and can't contain which of the following characters?

    a. WordPerfect Character Set 1
    b. At Sign (@)
    c. Colon (:)
    d. Underscore (_)

16. The Recover Database option of the Database Management menu allows you to:

    a. Correct physical database problems.
    b. Compress the database.
    c. Rebuild the database indexes.
    d. Update incorrect database information.

17. You must install a _____ before you can use a secondary domain.

    a. File server
    b. Post office
    c. Client
    d. Message server

# GroupWise 4.x Advanced System Administration

18. The _____ and _____ files contain entries that enable MAPI support in GroupWise.
    a. WINFILE.BIF, WPCMAPI.BIF
    b. WIN.INI, SYSTEM.INI
    c. WINFILE.INI, WPCMAPI.INI
    d. OFVIEWUS.INI, WPCMAPI.INI

19. GroupWise restricts you to using _____ links when creating a link to a secondary domain.
    a. Indirect
    b. Direct
    c. Gateway
    d. None

20. You can give two users the same User ID as long as they appear in different post offices.
    a. True
    b. False

21. Pressing _____ at the ancillary input dialogs, like the Group Information Description dialog, will complete the current action.
    a. F5
    b. Enter
    c. F7
    d. Tab

22. The two levels of post office security are:
    a. High and low
    b. Read/write and read-only
    c. Public and private
    d. Visible and hidden

23. You must fill in which fields of the Post Office Information dialog to create a default post office setup?
    a. Post Office Name
    b. Description
    c. Directory
    d. Default Security Level

24. You will find the DOS Message Server update information in the _____ file.
    a. WPDOMAIN.DC
    b. WPDOMAIN.CSI
    c. WPHOST.DC
    d. WPDOMAIN.DB

25. GroupWise provides _____ priority subdirectories in the WPCSIN directory that determine the order in which messages get processed.
    a. 5
    b. 6
    c. 7
    d. 8

26. You can change the order in which GroupWise Admin displays the user names by changing the Sort By field of the Setup List Users dialog.
    a. True
    b. False

27. The Expire Date field of the User Information dialog in the GroupWise Admin utility allows you to:
    a. Specify the date when a user's access will end.
    b. Specify the date when GroupWise will remove the account.
    c. Enhance security by limiting temporary employee access.
    d. Modify the date when GroupWise updates the account.

28. Merging an external GroupWise domain with a primary domain allows you to:
    a. Get rid of the extra domain.
    b. Manage both domains from the primary domain's directory.
    c. Circumvent the other domain's security.
    d. Modify the other domain's Domain Name field.

29. Novell recommends that you back up the user and message databases at least _____.
    a. Once a day
    b. Once a week
    c. Once every other week
    d. Once a month

# GroupWise 4.x Advanced System Administration

30. You cannot recover the secondary post office database in the secondary domain by using the Recover Database command in the primary domain.
    a. True
    b. False

31. If you can't import a file exported from the UNIX administration program, then you should check for the following:
    a. A corrupted UNIX domain database
    b. A corrupted UNIX post office database
    c. UNIX end of line character [LF][CR] converted into the DOS equivalent [LF]
    d. UNIX end of line character [LF] converted into the DOS equivalent [LF][CR]

32. You would use the _____ command line switch of AD.EXE to prevent it from using expanded memory.
    a. /NE
    b. /DU
    c. /DX
    d. /NX

33. The acronym *UNC* stands for:
    a. Unidentified Network Connection
    b. Universal Naming Convention
    c. Universal Network Connection
    d. Unidentified Naming Convention

34. The _____ Database Management command in GroupWise Admin removes excess space in your GroupWise databases.
    a. Rebuild Listing Indexes
    b. Validate Database
    c. Reclaim Unused Database Space
    d. Rebuild Database

35. The user mailbox information is stored in the _____ file.
    a. USER*XXX*.DB
    b. WPDOMAIN.DB
    c. MSG*XX*.DB
    d. WPHOST.DB

**Chapter Nineteen**

36. You can view which resources a user owns by looking at the _____ in the GroupWise Admin utility.
    a. Resources window
    b. User List dialog
    c. User Information dialog
    d. Resource Information dialog

37. The three types of message transmission that you can specify in the Group dialog of the GroupWise Admin utility include: _____, _____, and _____.
    a. Direct, Public, and Private
    b. Add To, Add Private, and Add Public
    c. Add To, Add CC, and Add BC
    d. Add All, Add Public, and Add None

38. GroupWise Admin allows you to change the length of the various User Information dialog fields within the _____ dialog.
    a. Setup
    b. Environment
    c. User Information
    d. Setup List Users

39. The administration program uses LC.EXE to launch various external programs like OFSETUP and OFCONV.
    a. True
    b. False

40. To create a new group, you'd press _____ at the Main Screen.
    a. Alt-G
    b. Alt-4
    c. Ctrl-G
    d. Ctrl-4

# Brain Teaser

This chapter looked at activities that you're bound to perform on a more than occasional basis, like database maintenance or adding or deleting a user from the database. You'll find that GroupWise is a lot more complex

# GroupWise 4.x Advanced System Administration

```
48 08 46 18 25 29 31 01 11 53 25 08 46 38 31 30 11 01 53 47 19 15 32 53 24 11
19 28 18 08 11 01 53 32 46 18 53 47 19 32 53 15 46 28 53 15 46 28 31 37 11 53
19 28 53 24 31 08 01 28 53 16 31 09 11 53 18 01 11 08 53 30 11 24 31 15 11 30
53 11 15 28 08 31 11 01 54 53 04 46 18 53 02 11 28 53 28 11 15 53 18 01 11 08
53 30 11 24 31 15 11 30 53 11 15 28 08 31 11 01 54 53 48 08 46 18 25 29 31 01
11 53 16 11 28 01 53 32 46 18 53 25 18 28 53 19 15 32 53 09 31 15 30 53 46 24
53 31 15 24 46 08 47 19 28 31 46 15 53 15 11 11 30 11 30 53 51 11 08 11 54 53
21 46 08 53 11 22 19 47 25 16 11 55 53 32 46 18 53 37 46 18 16 30 53 18 01 11
53 19 53 18 01 11 08 53 30 11 24 31 15 11 30 53 11 15 28 08 32 53 28 46 53 01
25 11 37 31 24 32 53 28 51 11 53 18 01 11 08 56 01 53 19 37 28 18 19 16 53 15
11 28 13 46 08 09 53 16 46 37 19 28 31 46 15 54 53 17 19 09 11 53 19 49 01 46
16 18 28 11 16 32 53 37 11 08 28 19 31 15 53 28 51 46 18 02 51 53 28 51 19 28
53 32 46 18 53 18 01 11 53 28 51 11 53 11 15 28 08 31 11 01 53 37 19 08 11 24
18 16 16 32 53 49 32 53 01 11 16 11 37 28 31 15 02 53 30 19 28 19 53 28 51 19
28 53 13 31 16 16 53 19 25 25 16 32 53 28 46 53 47 46 01 28 55 53 31 24 53 15
46 28 53 19 16 16 55 53 46 24 53 32 46 18 08 53 18 01 11 08 01 54
```

| A | | N | | a | | n | | | |
|---|---|---|---|---|---|---|---|---|---|
| B | | O | | b | | o | | . | |
| C | | P | | c | | p | | , | |
| D | | Q | | d | | q | | ' | |
| E | | R | | e | | r | | | |
| F | | S | | f | | s | | | |
| G | | T | | g | | t | | | |
| H | | U | | h | | u | | | |
| I | | V | | i | | v | | | |
| J | | W | | j | | w | | | |
| K | | X | | k | | x | | | |
| L | | Y | | l | | y | | | |
| M | | Z | | m | | z | | | |

**Figure 19-40**
GroupWise User-Defined Entry Cryptogram.

**Figure 19-41**
GroupWise Preventative Maintenance Cryptogram.

;{_{(!; ;{#{ =+ {%*{$+ { &\[)%!_ ][\ {~$ {&&%=^{#=[~, !?!~

(\[¦&*=+!. $[¦ +}[¦%; ){^: ¦& {%% #}! ¦+!\>>>.;) {~; _+(>>.;)

]=%!+ {# %!{+# [~^! { *!!:. ){^:=~( #}!_ ¦& _[\! []#!~ #}{~

#}{# *=%% ^!\#{=~%$ \!;¦^! #}! %!?!% [] %[++ =] +[_!

#$&! [] !\\[\ [^^¦\+.

| | | | |
|---|---|---|---|
| ! | | { | |
| @ | | } | |
| # | | [ | |
| $ | | ] | |
| % | | < | |
| ^ | | > | |
| & | | ¦ | |
| * | | \ | |
| ( | | / | |
| ) | | ? | |
| _ | | ~ | |
| + | | : | |
| = | | ; | |

in some areas than it looks when you first open the package. One of the ways that you can help yourself is to keep good notes about your GroupWise setup. In fact, GroupWise provides user-defined entries that you can use for this very purpose. The cryptogram in Fig. 19-40 provides you with a handy phrase that you can rely on to help you use those user-defined entries effectively to manage your GroupWise setup. This puzzle also uses a new numeric method for encrypting the phrase. Uppercase characters use a different code than lowercase characters. And, in case you haven't noticed, all punctuation and spaces are encoded as well (which should

# GroupWise 4.x Advanced System Administration

make it a bit more interesting to solve this cryptogram). As for the details of the phrase, I'll let you find out about them on your own. You'll find the solution for this brain teaser in App. C, "Brain Teaser Answers."

If you're feeling especially knowledgeable, you can try your hand at the much more difficult cryptogram in Fig. 19-41. This is a GroupWise preventative maintenance–related phrase based on one of the questions you answered in the preceding fun test section. Remember that this exam will test your knowledge of how to fix GroupWise related errors as well as of managing GroupWise as a whole, so you need to be prepared for it. Just in case the idea of working with a symbol-oriented cryptogram is a bit intimidating for you, here's a tip: All spaces really are spaces and all periods are periods. Apostrophes are also what they appear to be. Every other symbol replaces a letter.

## Disk Time

Don't forget to spend some time working with the disk that accompanies this book. It provides valuable and fun-to-use teaching aids that will help prepare you for the exam. See "Disk Time" in the preface of this book for details about what the disk contains.

CHAPTER 20

# NetWare Service and Support

# Introduction

This chapter looks at the requirements for the NetWare Service and Support exam. Of all the exams, this one requires the greatest amount of hands-on work on your part. Novell can draw upon a vast pool of hardware-related topics when preparing questions. *Hardware* can include items like diagnostic aids and virus checkers. It can even include such items as knowing where you need to go to get help maintaining your network. Even the manuals for the course related to this exam are larger than usual. The one thing that Novell won't test is your knowledge of current technology—something that happened just yesterday. You only need to worry about the material in the manual, which might make studying a little easier, but only a little. It pays to remember these facts as you study.

There are several discrete sections in this chapter. Each section helps you study for the exam in a different way. You can improve your chances of passing the exam by using two or more of the study methods provided in this chapter. It'll probably help if you study all the sections once and your favorite sections at least twice. Remember to review the study guidelines in Chap. 4 as required to ensure that you maintain the best possible study atmosphere.

The first section of this chapter is a *case study*. You'll perform some hands-on tasks that will help you learn what you need to know to pass the examination. Even though the case study provides you with screen shots, there's little chance that you'll get anything from it if you don't actually perform the steps. You don't need a network to perform the case study, but it helps. This is a hands-on study area and you need to treat it as such.

The second area contains *sample Novell questions* for this course. It also includes the correct answers and an explanation of why each answer is correct. Try to answer each question yourself, look at the correct answer, then determine where you went wrong if you didn't answer correctly.

The next section is a *fun test*. This is an exercise where you'll look at some sample test questions and answer them. The answers appear in App. B at the back of the book. This will help you test what you learned in the previous section.

The final text section of the chapter is the *brain teaser*. You'll get to have a little fun working on a hardware-related puzzle. In this case, we concentrate on both preventative maintenance and hazard recognition. This chapter provides two cryptograms that should give you some ideas of ways to study for the exam. Obviously, it helps to have a good in-depth knowledge of hardware in this case, since the cryptograms will be easier to solve if you can spot specific patterns in the way they're encrypted. You won't

# NetWare Service and Support

have to know anything more than what you'll normally find in the Novell manuals to solve the cryptograms, since that's what you'll be tested on. It's always a good idea, however, to keep current on the latest technology trends, including hardware. By the way, the cryptograms use different encryption methods, so you'll have to solve each puzzle separately.

Finally, we'll spend some time using the *Jeopardy!*-type game. This section helps you look at the test from the opposite viewpoint. The game provides you with an answer—you need to come up with the corresponding question. The game awards points for correct answers, and takes points away for incorrect answers. You'll receive a score at the end of the game proclaiming that you either did or didn't get your certificate.

By the time you finish this chapter, you should have all the knowledge required to pass the NetWare Service and Support exam. Use all the learning methods that we provide in this chapter to improve your chances of passing the exam. It's a good idea to save the fun test section until you're almost certain that you possess all the required knowledge. Remember, you can probably go through the test only two or three times at most before you'll start to remember the answers without really knowing the material.

Anyone, CNE candidate or above, who wants a certification needs to learn the material in this chapter; there are no exceptions. Candidates pursuing a CNA certification do not need to take this exam. The chapter provides you with an in-depth look at hardware that affects all the other courses of study in this book. Since this exam is hardware-oriented instead of software-oriented, you can actually wait to take it last.

## Case Study

This case study doesn't pursue many hardware repair or installation-specific topics. We look at these topics in depth in Chap. 9. It also doesn't cover the installation and use of DOS for the same reason. Make sure you understand Chap. 9 before you pursue this case study. It'll also help if you have some understanding of the NOS itself, but this isn't mandatory.

This case study looks at a variety of other hardware-related topics that every network administrator needs to know. The first section looks at how you access *CompuServe* to get answers to your questions. This very important online help can provide you with more answers in a shorter length of time than any other medium. The reason is simple: Not only do you tap the resources that Novell has to offer, but the knowledge possessed by your fellow network administrators, as well. CompuServe also provides the fastest method for obtaining patches and other files needed to maintain your network. You need a MODEM, a CompuServe account, and an installed copy of the Windows version of CompuServe Information Manager (WinCIM) to participate in this part of the case study.

The second section takes a look at *viruses* and how to prevent them. A virus attack is every network administrator's nightmare, and you need to know how to deal with them. We look at several different things you need to do to prevent a virus attack, although this section is not a complete tutorial. Let's call the case study an appetizer designed to pique your interest instead. You will want to enhance your knowledge about virus protection before you get a network up and running.

The final section takes a look at the *NetWare Support Encyclopedia* (*NSE*). This is such an important source of information that you may want to dedicate an entire CD drive to its use. Every CNE candidate receives a free limited-time subscription to the *NSE* upon completing the requirements, so it really pays to know how to use this tool.

## CompuServe

CompuServe represents one of the most dynamic methods you can use to keep up to date on NetWare and the technologies available to maintain your network. Novell maintains the NetWire forum for that very reason. Of course, this is only the tip of the iceberg. This case study looks at some of the things that you can do on CompuServe. Make sure you have a MODEM, a CompuServe account, and a copy of WinCIM installed before you start. You need to install WinCIM correctly and enter all the information that appears under the *Special* menu. Test the connection before starting the case study. We'll use the 1.2 version of WinCIM, so your screens may vary somewhat from the ones presented here.

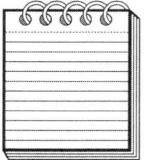

**NOTE** *Novell does maintain an Internet presence. You can contact their home page at http://www.novell.com. The Novell Web site includes all kinds of information, like course catalogs (http://db.netpub.com/nov_edu/x/qsearch.pl) and product guides (http://www.novell.com/products/). You'll also find a general education page at http://education.novell.com/. As of this writing, though, there aren't any Novell-supported newsgroups on the Internet. (There are a few newsgroups supported by third parties that cater to Novell products—like comp.groupware.groupwise, which talks about GroupWise—that you should look at if you have Internet-only access to an online service.) What all this means is that if you want direct support from someone at Novell, you have to use CompuServe. That's why we cover CompuServe instead of the Internet in this section.*

1. Double-click the WinCIM icon in Presentation Manager. Open the Favorite Places dialog box by clicking the Heart icon on the toolbar. Your display should look similar to the one in Fig. 20-1.
2. Click the Add button. The dialog box in Fig. 20-2 should appear. Type the information shown, then press Enter (or click the OK button).
3. Double-click the new NetWire entry in Favorite Places. WinCIM will check the MODEM, dial CompuServe, and take you to the *NetWire* menu shown in Fig. 20-3.
4. Double-click on the *What's New* menu entry. WinCIM will take you one menu dialog down to show three options: New Novell Files, New NetWare Services, and Upcoming Trade Shows/Conferences/Events. Double-click on New Novell Files. Your display should look like the one in Fig. 20-4. Note that the menu appears on the left side of the display, while the file summaries appear on the right.
5. Several important pieces of information are provided in the file summaries. The first thing you'll see is the user identifier (UID) of the person who uploaded the file. This is the person you should contact if you have any problems with the file after you download it. The next item is the name of the file (you'll need this to download it) and the file type. Most of the files that you need are binary files. You can read text files while online rather than download them. The next four items provide file statistics including file size, the number of people who downloaded the file, the date the originator uploaded the

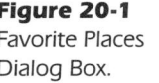

**Figure 20-1**
Favorite Places Dialog Box.

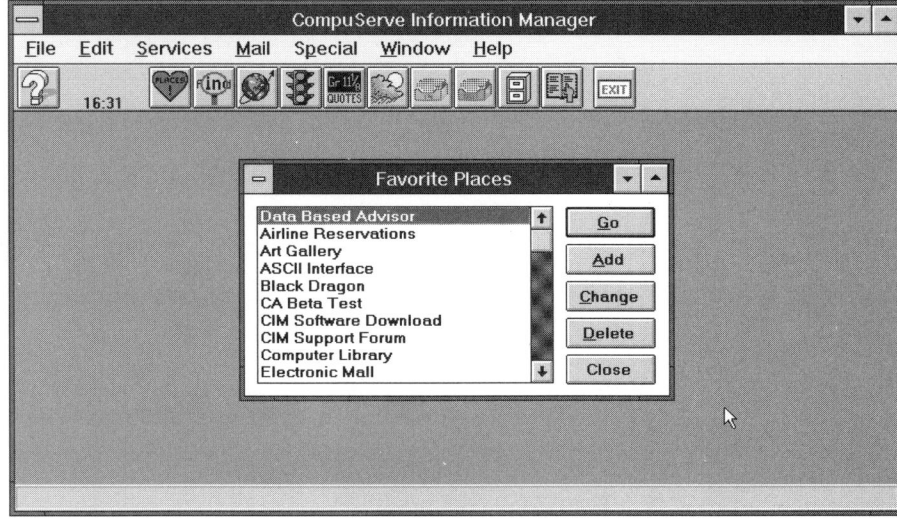

**Figure 20-2**
Add to Favorite Places Dialog Box.

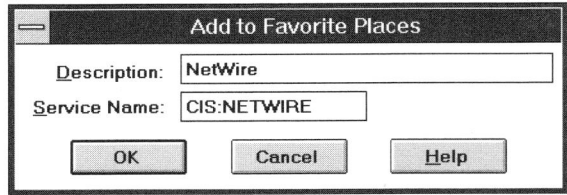

**Figure 20-3**
NetWire Main Menu.

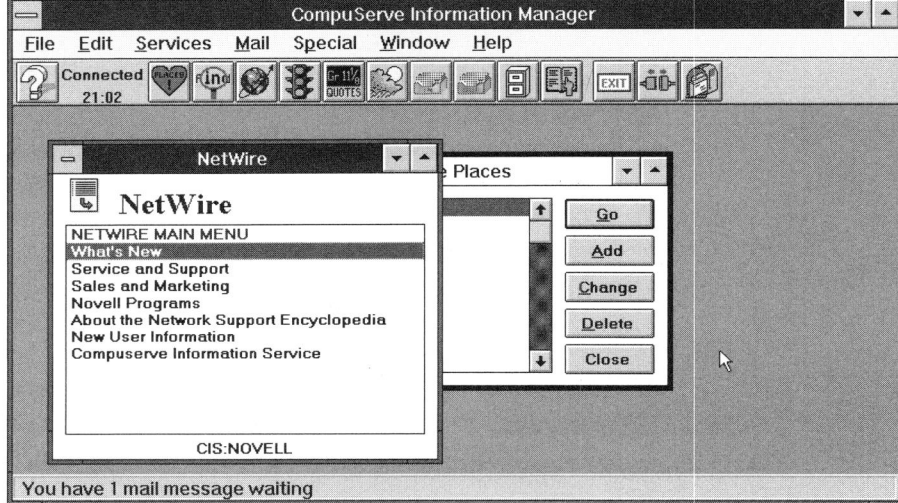

**Figure 20-4**
What's New and New Novell Files Dialog Boxes.

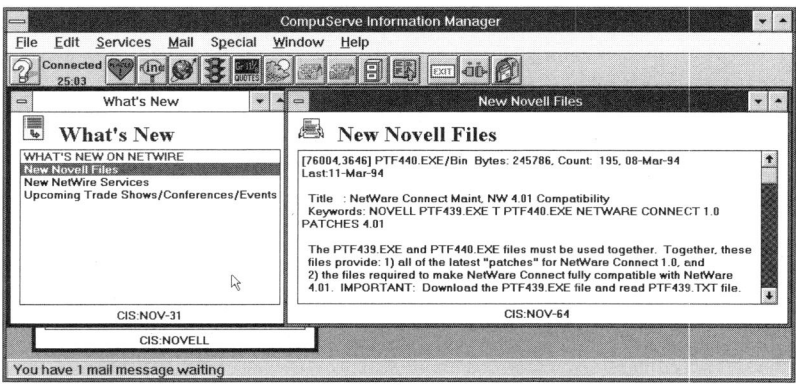

# NetWare Service and Support

file, and the date that someone last downloaded the file. The next three sections tell you the file title, keywords you can use to search for it, and a description of its contents. It's important to keep this information in mind because you'll need it later.

6. Double-click on the hyphen in the upper left corner of the dialog box to close it. Double-click on New NetWare Services. You should see a dialog box similar to the New Novell Files dialog. It contains information about new services that you'll find on NetWire.

7. Double-click on the hyphen in the upper left corner of the New NetWare Services dialog box to close it. Double-click on the hyphen in the upper left corner of the What's New menu dialog box to close it. This will take you back to the original NetWire menu.

8. Now we get to the really interesting part of NetWire. Double-click on *Service and Support.* Figure 20-5 shows the services you can expect to find in this part of NetWire. Note that there are a variety of entries to meet all your information needs, hardware-related or not.

9. Double-click on *Messages.* You should see a list of available forums, as shown in Fig. 20-6. Each forum takes care of a different networking need. Note that each forum is followed by a *GO* word. You can add these GO words to your Favorite Places dialog box as needed.

10. Double-click on *Novell NetWare 3.x Forum.* Users new to a forum always see the initial screen shown in Fig. 20-7. This screen allows you to join, leave, or visit a forum. Your rights as a visitor are extremely limited, so it pays to join the forum in most cases. Note the icons at the right side of the display. These icons allow you to use the forum services. Refer to your WinCIM manual or online help for a complete summary of their use.

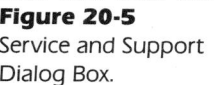
**Figure 20-5**
Service and Support Dialog Box.

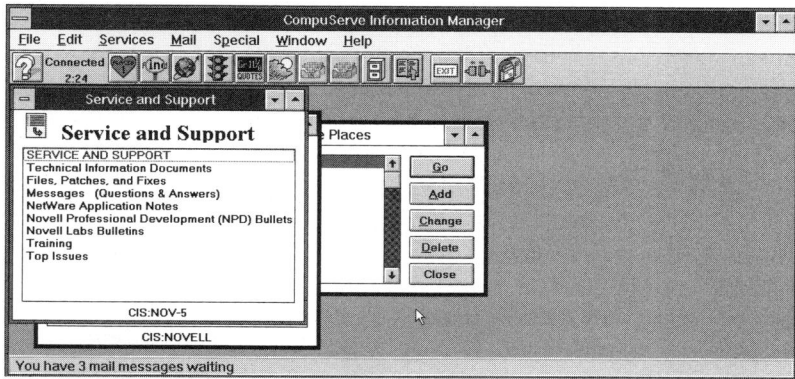

**Figure 20-6**
Messages Dialog Box.

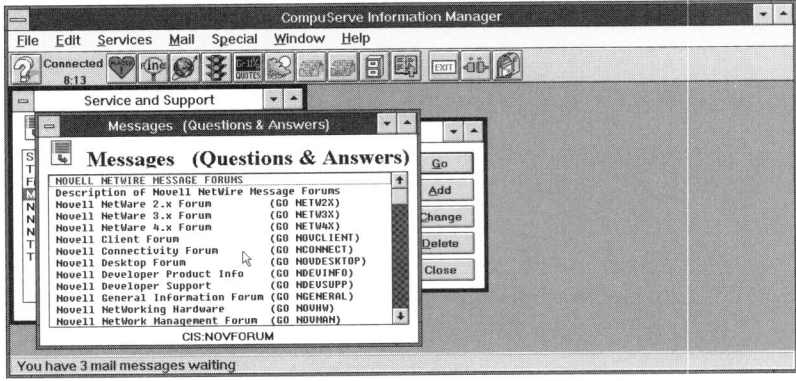

**Figure 20-7**
NetWare 3.x Forum Initial Screen.

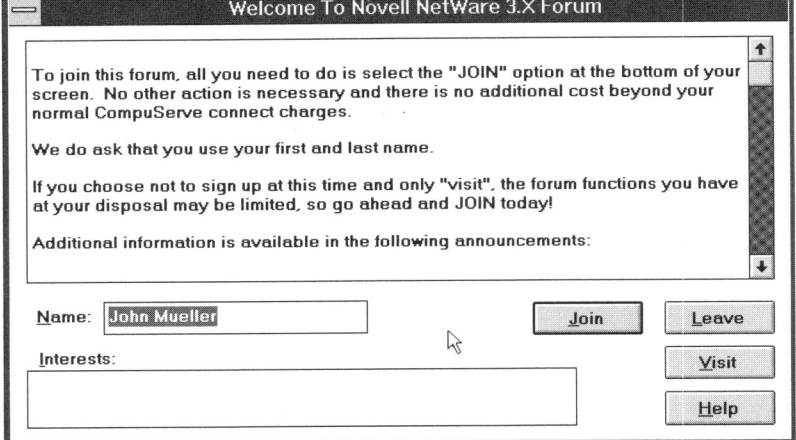

11. Verify that your name is correct, then press Tab. This takes you to the Interests field of the dialog box. Type in your interests. Separate each interest with a space. Other members can search on this information; providing it makes it easier for other members with similar interests to find you. Click on Join to complete the process.

12. You may or may not see a *News Flash* when you enter the forum. If you do see a News Flash, read it, then click on OK. You should see a blank window (or the default dialog you chose during the WinCIM setup).

13. Click on the Messages icon. WinCIM displays the message sections of the forum that you can access. Double-click on the *NetWare Utilities* section of the forum. Your screen should look similar to the

# NetWare Service and Support

one in Fig. 20-8. WinCIM provides a lot of information about the forum in the two dialogs. The top of the first dialog tells you the date and time of the oldest message you haven't seen. The section dialog provides information on the number of messages and topics (threads). You can view the individual message headers (subjects). Each thread entry is followed by the number of messages it contains.

14. Each section and thread title is preceded by a box. Clicking this box allows you to download as little or much information as you want and read it offline (saving online time and your pocketbook in the process). Click on one or two of the message boxes. Click on the *Messages* menu, then the *Retrieve Marked* option. WinCIM displays the dialog box shown in Fig. 20-9.

15. Click on *Get All*. WinCIM displays a dialog that keeps you informed of the download process. Downloading files is essentially the same process as downloading messages, so we won't go into that process here.

16. Click on the Filing Cabinet icon. Double-click on the Novell NetWare 3.x entry. You should see the messages you downloaded from the forum, as shown in Fig. 20-10.

17. Double-click on one of the message entries. As you can see, the message box allows you to perform a plethora of activities, including responding to the message, saving the CIS UID of the sender or receiver, or navigating to other messages in the thread.

18. Double-click on the upper left corner of WinCIM to close the application. This concludes the case study of this product.

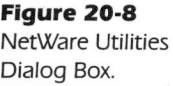

**Figure 20-8**
NetWare Utilities Dialog Box.

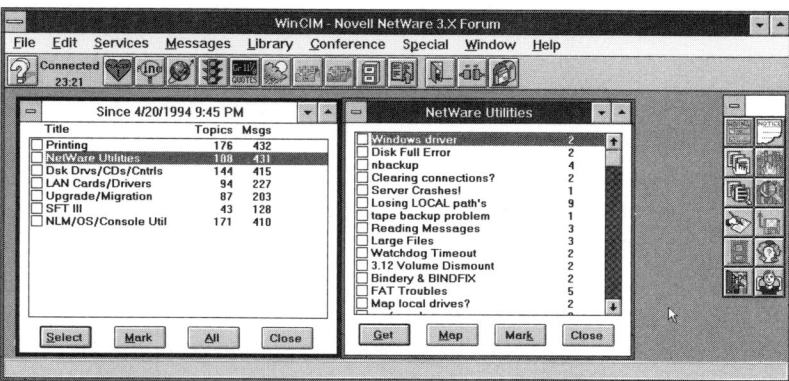

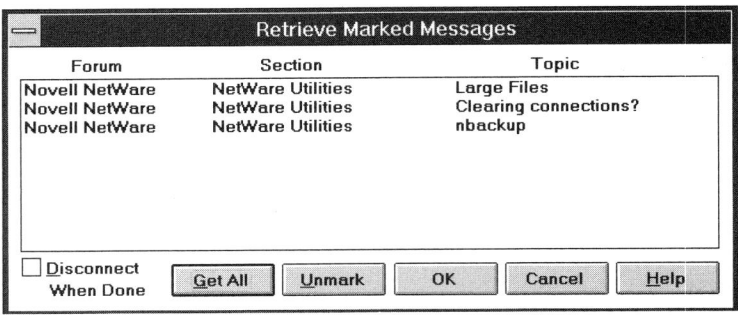

**Figure 20-9**
Retrieve Marked Messages Dialog Box.

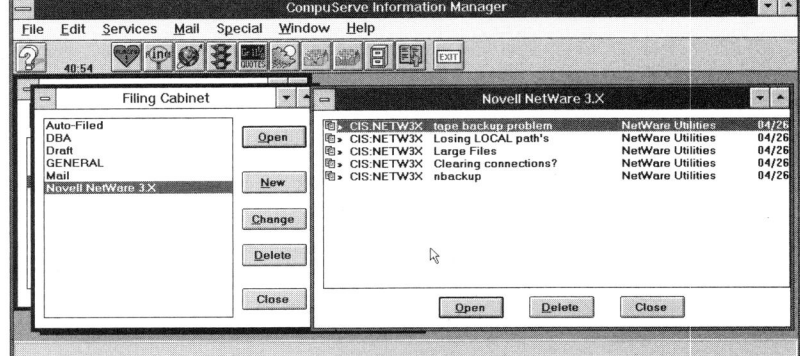

**Figure 20-10**
Filing Cabinet Dialog Box.

## Virus Protection

Protecting your network from a virus attack is one of the most important things you can do. Cleaning it up after an attack is a messy and error-prone procedure that you won't want to do. This case study obviously won't tell you everything there is to know about this important topic, but it will give you a start. Make sure you take the time to investigate the topic further before you start working with your LAN.

This case study takes you through some basic steps required to keep your LAN virus free. We look at three essential parts of any virus protection scheme: *disk scanning, drive scanning,* and *active virus detection.* We also show you how to create a simple clean-up disk that you can enhance to meet your particular needs.

There are a number of virus detection products on the market, but this case study focuses on the virus scanners provided by McAfee Associates. You can download the shareware version of these products from CompuServe. Simply GO VIRUSFORUM and download the files for VShield,

NetShield, and VirusScan from Library 1. The names of these files change as the version number for the product changes, so we can't provide specific filenames here. *VShield* is a TSR that actively protects a workstation from virus attack. *NetShield* provides the same type of protection for your file server. There are separate versions of the product for NetWare 3.x and 4.x, so make sure you download the right one. *VirusScan* allows you to check floppies, network drives, and local hard drives for virus infection.

**NOTE** *McAfee and other virus protection program vendors do have Windows versions of their products. In fact, many of these vendors have Windows 95 versions of their products that are both safe and easy to use. The only problem with many of these products is that they assume you can actually start Windows, which may not always be the case. Needless to say, Windows doesn't copy very well to a floppy disk, so you can't easily make yourself an emergency disk that relies on a Windows product. For that reason this case study looks at the time-proven DOS-based utilities that you can copy to a single floppy disk and boot as needed. Even though an emergency disk is critical for your network, you'll want to avail yourself of the easier-to-use Windows products whenever possible.*

We assume that you are using the 2.x version of VirusScan and VShield for this case study. We also assume that you have the products installed in the SCAN and VSHIELD directories, respectively. Change the directory and drive designations as required for your machine configuration.

1. Type *CD\SCAN* and press Enter. Type *SCAN /ADL /ADN* and press Enter to start scanning your drives. This process will take quite a while; the actual time depends on the size of your drives. The /ADL parameter scans the local drives while the /ADN parameter scans the network drives. VirusScan will check itself, then your computer's RAM, then all the files on the drive. When it finishes checking everything, you should see a display similar to Fig. 20-11.

2. Type *SCAN /?* and press Enter. VirusScan displays a help screen, as shown in Fig. 20-12, which explains some of the command line switches available for your use. This doesn't represent a complete list, merely the most common switches. Make sure you take the time to read the manual provided with the product.

3. Type *CD\* and press Enter. Type *EDIT AUTOEXEC.BAT* and press Enter. Use the cursor to go to the very end of the file. Press End, then Enter to make a new entry. Type *C:\VSHIELD\VSHIELD*. (Substitute the appropriate drive and directory. Press Alt-F, then type *S* to save the file. Press Alt-F, then type *X* to exit the editor. Press

**Figure 20-11**
VirusScan Report Screen.

```
D:\SCAN>SCAN /ADL /ADN
Scan version 2.0.0 Copyright (c) McAfee, Inc. 1994.  All rights reserved.
(408) 988-3832
Virus data file    V2.0.200 created Tue Apr 19 18:12:34 1994
No viruses found in memory.
Scanning C:

Summary report on C:

File(s)
         Analyzed: ...............        213
         Scanned: ................        156
         Possibly Infected: ......          0
Master Boot Record(s): .........            1
         Possibly Infected: ......          0
Boot Sector(s): ................            1
         Possibly Infected: ......          0

Scanning D:

Summary report on D:

File(s)
         Analyzed: ...............       5267
         Scanned: ................       2926
         Possibly Infected: ......          0
Master Boot Record(s): .........            1
         Possibly Infected: ......          0
Boot Sector(s): ................            1
         Possibly Infected: ......          0

Scanning E:

Summary report on E:

File(s)
         Analyzed: ...............        924
         Scanned: ................        846
         Possibly Infected: ......          0
Boot Sector(s): ................            1
         Possibly Infected: ......          0

Scanning F:

Summary report on F:

File(s)
         Analyzed: ...............       2083
         Scanned: ................       1369
         Possibly Infected: ......          0

Time: 924.79 sec.
D:\SCAN>
```

**Figure 20-12**
VirusScan Help Screen.

```
D:\SCAN>scan /?
Scan version 2.0.0 Copyright (c) McAfee, Inc. 1994.  All rights reserved.
(408) 988-3832

Usage: SCAN [object1] [object2...] [option1] [option2...]
Options:
 /?                         Display this help screen.
 /ADL                       Scan all local drives.
 /ADN                       Scan all network drives.
 /AF        <filename>      Store validation codes for all files into <filename>.
 /ALERT     <server>        Alert <server> on infected files.
 /APPEND                    Append to report file rather than overwriting.
 /AV                        Add validation code to executable files.
 /BOOT                      Scan boot sector and master boot record only.
 /CF        <filename>      Check validation codes stored in <filename> by /AF.
 /CLEAN                     Clean viruses from infected files and system areas.
 /CV                        Check validation codes added to files by /AV.
 /DEL                       Delete infected files.
 /EXCLUDE   <filename>      Do not add validation codes to file listed in <filename>.
 /FAST                      Faster scanning (may miss some infections)
 /HELP                      Display this help screen.
 /LISTEN    <server>        Load SCAN and wait for command from <server>.
 /LOAD      <filename>      Load options from file.
 /LOG                       Save date and time of the current scan to the log file.
 /MOVE      <directory>     Move infected files into <directory>, preserving path.
 /NOBREAK                   Disable Ctrl-C / Ctrl-Brk during scanning
 /NOMEM                     Do not scan memory for viruses.
 /PAUSE                     Pause at end of each screen page.
 /PLAD                      Preserve Last Access Dates on Novell NetWare drives.
 /REPORT    <filename>      Report names of viruses found into <filename>.
 /RF        <filename>      Remove validation codes from <filename> created by /AF.
 /RPTCOR                    Include corrupted files in /REPORT file.
 /RPTERR                    Include errors in /REPORT file.
 /RPTMOD                    Include modified files in /REPORT file.
 /RV                        Remove validation codes added to files by /AV.
 /SHOWLOG                   Display date and time information from the log file.
 /STD                       Scan standard extensions only.
 /SUB                       Scan subdirectories
 /VIRLIST                   Display virus list.

D:\SCAN>
```

# NetWare Service and Support

Ctrl-Alt-Del to reboot the computer and install the resident virus protection. During startup, VShield will check itself, check the system memory, then check the system files and boot sector for viruses.

4. Place a floppy in drive A. Type *FORMAT A: /S* and press Enter. This creates a floppy with a copy of the operating system. Type *COPY SCAN.EXE A:* and press Enter. Type *COPY SCAN.DAT A:* and press Enter. Type *COPY CLEAN.DAT A:* and press Enter. Type *COPY NAMES.DAT A:* and press Enter.

5. Type *CD\DOS* (substitute the name of your DOS directory if necessary) and press Enter. Type *COPY FORMAT.\* A:* and press Enter. Type *COPY SYS.\* A:* and press Enter. Type *COPY FDISK.\* A:* and press Enter. Type *COPY DEBUG.\* A:* and press Enter. Type *COPY CHKDSK.\* A:* and press Enter. If you own DOS version 6.x, type *COPY SCANDISK.\* A:* and press Enter.

6. Type *A:* and press Enter. You should see the A:\> prompt. Type *MD INIFILES* and press Enter. Type *CD INIFILES* and press Enter. Type *COPY C:\AUTOEXEC.BAT* and press Enter. *Type COPY C:\CONFIG.SYS* and press Enter. If you use Windows, type *COPY C:\WINDOWS\\*.INI* and press Enter. (Change the drive and directory for Windows as needed.)

7. Once you get all these files copied to the disk, you need to create a simple AUTOEXEC.BAT and CONFIG.SYS. Type *COPY CON AUTOEXEC.BAT* and press Enter. Type the following lines. Make sure you press Enter at the end of each line.

    ```
    @ECHO OFF
    PROMPT $P$G
    ```

8. Press F6 to place a ^Z at the end of your file. Press Enter to save the new AUTOEXEC.BAT.

9. Type *COPY CON CONFIG.SYS* and press Enter. Type the following lines and press Enter at the end of each line.

    ```
    FILE=30
    BUFFERS=30
    ```

10. Press F6 to place a ^Z at the end of the file. Press Enter to save the file.

11. Type *C:* and press Enter. Type *CD\SCAN* and press Enter. Remove your virus-free boot floppy from the drive and write-protect it. You do this by covering the write-protect notch on 5.25-in disks or opening the write-protect notch on 3.5-in disks.

12. Place a floppy in drive A. Type *SCAN A:\*.\* /SUB* and press Enter. Even though you use different command switches, the display will look similar to Fig. 20-11. The major difference is that this procedure checks the contents of drive A only.

## *NetWare Support Encyclopedia*

Every CNE gets a one-year subscription to the *NetWare Support Encyclopedia Professional Edition* (*NSEPro*). (Graduates of earlier CNE programs may have gotten the standard edition instead, so we cover both in this chapter.) This CD-ROM-based product provides you with a full reference library and all the patches required (as of the date of release) to maintain your network.

The following case study goes through some of the things you can do with the *NSE* (standard edition) and *NSEPro*. Simply use the instructions that apply to your version of the product. Of course, you'll want to spend a lot of time looking through the vast amount of information on this disk. You'll need a computer equipped with a CD-ROM drive and a copy of the *NSE* to perform this case study. Since you're not a CNE right now, you may need to check with a friend who is.

1. Type *CD\NSEPRO* (or *CD\NSESTD* if you have the standard version) and press Enter. This takes you to the *NSE* directory.

2. Type *NSEPRO* (or *NSESTD* if you have the standard version) and press Enter. You should see the initial program screen shown in Fig. 20-13. The main menu provides you with a variety of entry points into the database, including product information and the patches you need to keep your network current.

3. Press Tab four times. The cursor should appear under the *Service and Support* entry. Note the triangle at the beginning of this entry. You can get further information about any topic preceded by this symbol.

**Figure 20-13**
NSEPro Main Menu.

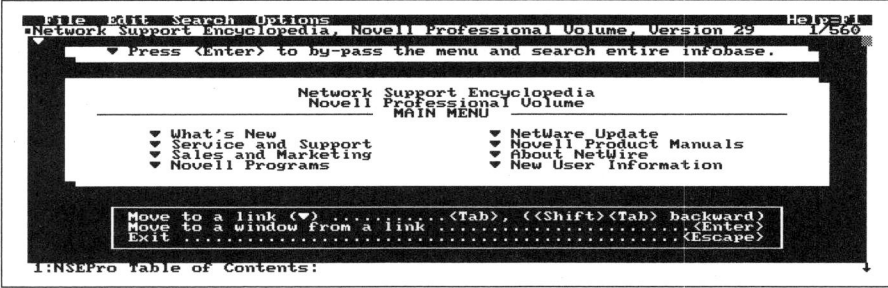

# NetWare Service and Support

4. Press Enter. *NSE* displays the Service and Support menu (Fig. 20-14).

5. Press Tab twice to select the *Technical Information Documents* option. Press Enter. *NSE* displays the first technical information document in the database, as shown in Fig. 20-15. Note that the bulletin provides you with a quick description of the problem, a full description of the problem, and a solution.

6. Press Escape twice. *NSE* returns you to the main menu. There are other ways to search for information than the orderly level-by-level approach we just saw.

7. Press Alt-S. *NSE* displays the *Search* menu (Fig. 20-16). Note that every menu entry is followed by a hot-key combination. You can use these hot keys to perform quicker searches of the database.

8. Press down arrow, then Enter, to select Search. *NSE* displays the query dialog box shown in Fig. 20-17. Let's search for any information about print servers that does not relate to NetWare version 2.2.

9. Type *PRINT* and press Ctrl-A. Type *SERVER* and press Ctrl-N. Type *2.2*. Note that *NSE* updates the display every time you type something. This allows you to follow the search as it progresses and

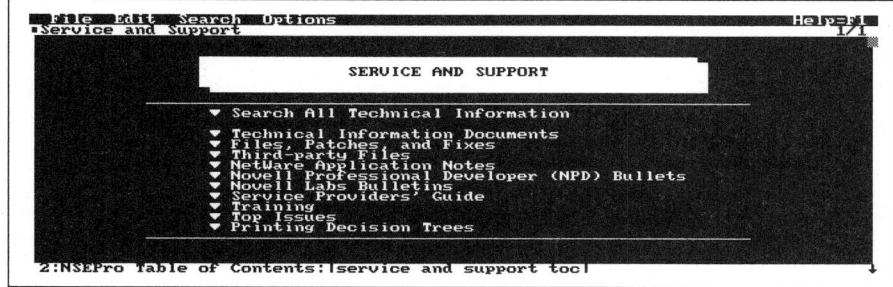

**Figure 20-14**
NSEPro Service and Support Menu.

**Figure 20-15**
NSEPro Technical Bulletin.

**Figure 20-16**
NSEPro Search Menu.

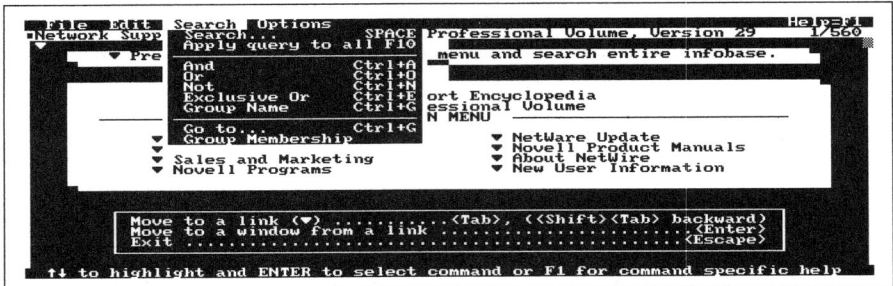

**Figure 20-17**
NSEPro Query Dialog Box.

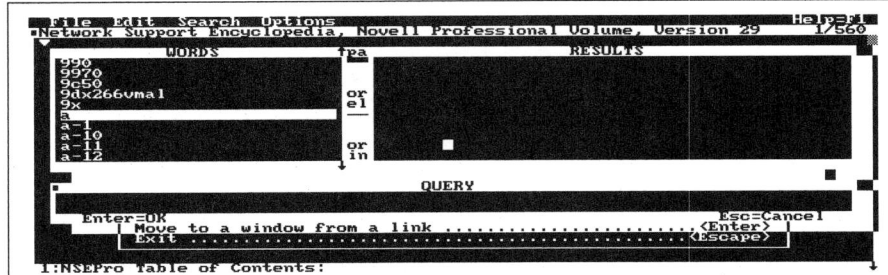

reduces the chances that you won't find what you need. Figure 20-18 shows the results of this search.

10. **Press Enter, then PgDn twice.*** *NSE* takes you to the first search result as shown in Fig. 20-19. Note that it also highlights the search term that you requested. This allows you to find the pertinent information within a large amount of text quickly.

---

*You may need to press PgDn to find the first incidence of a search in some cases. In other cases you will see the search word immediately. *NSE* displays the search result from the beginning of the document it appears in.

**Figure 20-18**
NSEPro Query Results.

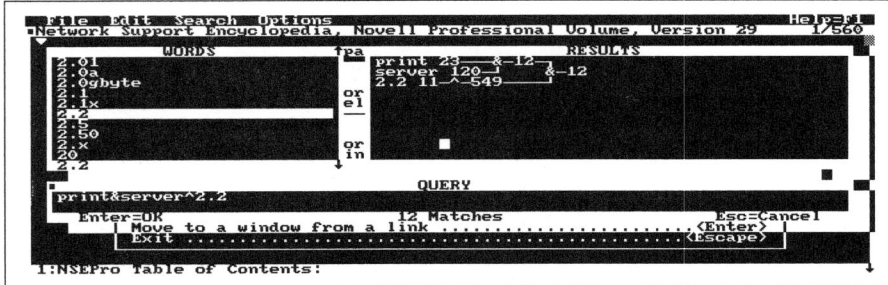

# NetWare Service and Support

**Figure 20-19**
NSEPro Search Results.

```
 File   Edit   Search   Options                                    Help F1
 NetWare Application Notes                                          1 12
   ▼ August 1993
     ▼ NetWare for Macintosh 3.xx Print Services: A Configuration Tutorial
     ▼ Exploring Hard Disk Compression
     ▼ NACS 3.0 and NetWare Access Services 1.3 Integration
     ▼ NetNotes
     ▼ Research Index
   ▼ July 1993
     ▼ Using NetAdmin to Create and Administer NDS Objects
     ▼ A Test Workload Analysis of LANQuest Lab's Application Benchmark
     ▼ Multi-Segment LAN Imaging Implementations: Four-Segment Ethernet
     ▼ A NetWare Interface for Visual Basic
     ▼ Understanding Relational Theory
     ▼ NetNotes
     ▼ Research Index

                                                (PgDn for more titles)
 1:NSEPro Table of Contents:print&server^2.2
```

11. Press Escape to return to the Main menu. Press Escape. You should see the DOS prompt.

As you can see, the *NSE Professional Edition* provides you with a very fast and efficient method of finding information. Of course, this case study doesn't provide everything you need to know about the product. It's best if you spend some time looking around and seeing what is available. Every release contains the most up-to-date information available at the time that Novell produced the CD. This is an important consideration, since even the *NSE* may be a little out of date. You need to maintain good contact with Novell by using online services like NetWire to supplement the *NSE* information.

## Study Questions

The Service and Support test covers an extremely broad range of topics. Part of the exam will retest the material you learned in Chap. 9, but at a higher level. It includes everything from network protocols to troubleshooting printing problems. Make sure you fully understand the material in this chapter, in Chap. 9, and anything found in the chapters specific to your operating system before you attempt to take the exam. Studying this section alone won't provide you with enough information to pass.

1. Steps that you can take to prevent damage to your LAN include:
   a. Arrange the physical setup and location of the LAN to minimize the possibility of problems caused by environmental factors.
   b. Use appropriate record keeping to keep the LANs running smoothly and to support troubleshooting.

c. Use a stepwise troubleshooting model to analyze and act on problems.

d. Store all your system backups on site in a fireproof safe.

*a, b, and c.* Just about the fastest way to destroy your LAN is to allow environmental factors to get in the way. This even includes things that some people do not associate with the environment, like heat from poor air circulation, people with inadvertent access to cables or other components, and dust. Records are essential to any LAN maintenance plan.* Using the correct troubleshooting strategy always reduces maintenance time and increases the chances that you'll find the problem the first time around.

2. The four areas of security that every LAN administrator must think about include:
   a. Communications, personal, environmental, and regional
   b. Communications, environmental, human resources, and regional
   c. Communications, environmental, human resources, and organizational
   d. Personal, environmental, human resources, and organizational

   *c.* A LAN administrator must monitor all four areas to create a security net for the LAN.

3. The seven layers of the OSI model include:
   a. Application, Presentation, Session, Transport, Network, Data Link, and Physical
   b. Application, Preparation, Session, Transport, Network, Data Link, and Physical
   c. Program, Presentation, Session, Transport, Network, Data Link, and Physical
   d. Program, Preparation, Session, Transport, Network, Data Link, and Physical

   *a.* A good way to remember the initial letters of the layers and their order of appearance is to use the phrase "All people seem to need data processing." The order of layers is every bit as important as the actual names for the purpose of the test.

---

*Get the author's book *The Hands-On Guide to Network Management* (McGraw-Hill, ISBN 0-8306-4439-3) if you want complete details on the records you should keep.

4. Novell's online service is called:
   a. NovTerm
   b. NetStats
   c. NetWire
   d. NovWire

   *c.* You access the online service through CompuServe. The *GO* word for this service is *NetWire*.

5. The *NSEPro* contains which of the following information aids?
   a. The Most Up-To-Date Files, Patches, and Fixes
   b. Technical Information Documents
   c. NetWare Application Notes
   d. Service Provider's Guide

   *b, c, and d.* The *NSEPro* contains all this and much more. It's one of the most valuable tools that a CNE will receive. It doesn't contain the most up-to-date files, patches and fixes, but it does contain the most recent release at the time of production. You need to visit the NetWire forum on CompuServe to get the most up-to-date files, patches, and fixes.

6. You use a time domain reflectometer (TDR) to:
   a. Find cabling problems like shorts, breaks, and crimps.
   b. Troubleshoot NICs.
   c. Determine where a protocol error occurs.
   d. Analyze network transmission speed.

   *a.* A TDR allows you to locate a variety of cabling problems. It can even help you determine where a cable break occurred.

7. A Token Ring network can use wiring concentrators known as _____ or _____ to create the ring.
   a. Multisection Access Units (MSAUs), Central Access Units (CAUs)
   b. Multistation Access Units (MSAUs), Controlled Access Units (CAUs)
   c. Multisection Access Units (MSAUs), Central Access Units (CAUs)
   d. Multistation Access Units (MSAUs), Controlled Access Units (CAUs)

   *b.* You can use a passive MSAU or a powered CAU to create the ring in a Token Ring LAN. The powered CAU is an intelligent concentrator that can assist in the physical part of network management.

8. The SET MAXIMUM PACKET RECEIVE BUFFERS command allows you to:
   a. Force the file server to allocate a specific number of packet receive buffers on startup.
   b. Reduce the memory used by other memory intensive processes.
   c. Increase overall system performance by making more packet buffers available.
   d. Avoid excessive allocation of communication buffers.

   *d.* Peaks in server usage can needlessly increase the number of communication buffers that NetWare allocates. These extra buffers reduce the memory available for other tasks, reducing overall system performance.

9. Jumpers are _____.
   a. A form of dress worn with a blouse
   b. Plastic-covered clips used to complete circuits on a PCB
   c. People who wish to commit suicide
   d. A form of electric spark that damages circuits by burning them

   *b.* You use jumpers to configure an add-on board like a NIC. Options usually include the I/O port, IRQ number, and DMA address. Other options depend on the type of board you want to configure.

10. The initials *FDDI* stand for:
    a. Fiber Distributed Data Interface
    b. Fabricated Digital Data Interface
    c. Fiberoptic Distributed Data Interface
    d. Focused Data Distribution Internetwork

    *a.* The Fiber Distributed Data Interface (FDDI) is a fiberoptic LAN. Another form of FDDI using copper cable is CDDI. Both LAN types use two rings: one for data and the other to perform backups and other services.

11. The initials *NEMA* stand for:
    a. National Electrical Monitoring Association
    b. National Electronic Monitoring Association

# NetWare Service and Support

    **c.** National Electrical Manufacturers Association
    **d.** National Electronic Manufacturers Association

    *c.* The National Electrical Manufacturers Association helps create specifications for cabling and other electrical needs. For example, they helped define the requirements for Level 4 UTP cable.

12. Sources of RFI include:
    **a.** Light switches
    **b.** Furnaces
    **c.** Radar
    **d.** Microwaves

    *b and d.* Furnaces and microwaves both act as sources of RFI (radio frequency interference). Light switches and radar produce EMI (electromagnetic interference). It is very important to know the difference between these two sources of noise.

13. The IEEE 802.4 standard specifies the characteristics of _____.
    **a.** Ethernet LANs
    **b.** Token Ring LANs
    **c.** ARCnet LANs
    **d.** The logical link control (LLC)

    *c.* The IEEE 802.4 standard specifies the characteristics of an ARCnet LAN. You would use the 802.3 standard for Ethernet and 802.5 standard for Token Ring. The 802.1 and 802.2 standards are for network management and logical link control, respectively.

14. Autotuning is NetWare's ability to dynamically alter the configuration of the following parameters to accommodate changing workloads on the network:
    **a.** Service Processes
    **b.** Minimum Packet Receive Buffers
    **c.** Cache Buffer Size
    **d.** Directory Caching

    *a and d.* Attempting to manually adjust some OS parameters proves difficult at best. In some cases, there is no best value, just a value that works best for a given circumstance. That's why NetWare automatically adjusts some parameters to accommodate changing workloads.

**15.** Type 2 Token Ring Cables consist of _____.
   **a.** Four shielded twisted pairs of #22 AWG telephone conductor
   **b.** Two shielded twisted pairs of #22 AWG telephone conductor
   **c.** Four unshielded twisted pairs of #22 AWG telephone conductor
   **d.** Fiberoptic conductors.

   *a.* You use this type of cable for the interconnection of terminal devices located in work areas and distribution panels located in wiring closets. Shielded cable is less susceptible to noise and crosstalk. It also allows longer runs than unshielded cable.

**16.** The session layer of the OSI model _____.
   **a.** Ensures data reliability
   **b.** Moves information across multiple segments of an internetwork
   **c.** Transforms data into a format that can be understood by each application and the computers they run on
   **d.** Maintains the dialog between communicating applications

   *d.* The session layer maintains the dialog between communication applications.

**17.** CheckIt Pro allows you to perform all the following tasks except:
   **a.** Check for viruses.
   **b.** Modify partition table information.
   **c.** Perform repetitive testing for system burn-in and acceptance testing.
   **d.** Check the alignment of floppy drives.

   *b.* CheckIt Pro won't allow you to modify your partition table information. You'd need a utility like Central Point's PC Tools to perform this task.

**18.** Pressing the Ctrl-A key combination while in the search dialog box of the *NSEPro* produces _____.
   **a.** An *or Boolean* search
   **b.** An exclusive *or Boolean* search
   **c.** An *and Boolean* search
   **d.** A *not Boolean* search

   *c.* The *and Boolean* search symbol means that *NSEPro* must find both the first and second criteria to satisfy the requirement. Likewise, the *or Boolean* search symbol means that finding either the first or the second criteria will satisfy the requirement.

# NetWare Service and Support

19. Asynchronous Transfer Mode (ATM) is a _____.
    a. Packet-switching technology that looks a similar to a high-speed telephone switch
    b. Serial cable technology that offers low-cost data transmission
    c. New WAN solution that allows data transfer during off-peak hours
    d. Fiberoptic cabling strategy that offers characteristics similar to Ethernet

    *a.* ATM is one of the newest technologies for increasing network bandwidth. Most ATM installation will support multimedia applications for high-end clients.

20. You can use a VOM to check which of the following?
    a. Networks for invalid packets
    b. Cables for broken connections
    c. Terminators for improper impedance levels
    d. Ground wires for improper connections

    *b and d.* A volt-ohm meter can perform a variety of tasks, like checking outlets for the proper line voltage, as well. It can't, however, see the signal going through the cable. As a result, you can't use it for packet analysis. In addition, you can't use a VOM to check impedance (a different measurement than resistance).

21. You need special tools to tune your NetWare 3.x network for optimum performance.
    a. True
    b. False

    *b.* The MONITOR.NLM provided with NetWare 3.x can help you perform a variety of network optimization tasks. This isn't to say that MONITOR.NLM is as easy to use as many third-party products, but you can use it.

22. An Attached Resource Computer Network (ARCnet) LAN has which of the following characteristics?
    a. Uses a hierarchy of active and passive hubs
    b. Token bus runs at 5 Mbps
    c. Invented at Datapoint
    d. Uses RG-62 (93-$\Omega$) coaxial cable, UTP, or fiberoptic media.

*a, b, and d.* ARCnet has all these characteristics. It transmits your data at 2.5 Mbps. Datapoint developed this LAN type in 1977. Current installations should adhere to the ANSI 878.1 standard.

23. To minimize the risk from noise you should not:
    a. Run cables near fluorescent lights.
    b. Use equipment without checking the FCC rating for noise emissions first.
    c. Use equipment that isn't properly grounded.
    d. None of the above.
    e. All of the above.

    *e.* All the recommended precautions will help you avoid noise in the LAN environment.

24. A computer virus is _____.
    a. A biological organism that feeds on electronic components and eventually destroys them
    b. An application that affects the monitor frequency and causes you to feel ill
    c. An application that destroys data on your hard disk
    d. A biological organism that only makes computer users feel ill

    *c.* A computer virus can infect your boot sector, applications, and even the operating system. You need to scan your system, every disk, and anything you download for viruses.

25. You would use Level 3 UTP cable for _____.
    a. Intermediate level telephone and data connections with speeds less than 4 Mbps
    b. high-speed data connections and LANs with speeds less than 16 Mbps
    c. Extended distance and/or high-speed data LAN with speeds less than 20 Mbps
    d. 150-$\Omega$ data-grade media LAN applications

    *b.* You can use level 3 cable for high-speed LANs. Level 3 UTP cable conforms to the ICEA (Insulated Cable Engineers Association) S-80-5776, UL (Underwriter's Laboratories) 444, and EIA/TIA (Electronics Industry Association/Telecommunications Industry Association) 568 specifications.

# NetWare Service and Support

26. You can use the PATCHMAN.NLM utility to apply dynamic, semi-static, and static patches.
    a. True
    b. False

    *a.* The PATCHMAN.NLM utility allows you to enhance system performance and correct problems by patching system files. You can download the patches from *NSEPro* or NetWire. Always check the patch description first to see if you actually need it.

27. Which of the following are Ethernet frame types?
    a. Ethernet_802.3 (raw)
    b. Ethernet_802.2
    c. Ethernet_SNAP
    d. Ethernet_II

    *a, b, c, and d.* A frame provides a container to hold the data the network transmits from one node to the next.

28. A router affects the _____ layers of the OSI model.
    a. Physical
    b. Data-link and physical
    c. Network, data-link, and physical
    d. Transport, network, data-link, and physical

    *c.* A router provides more speed and less functionality than a gateway. Using a router instead of a bridge can offer performance benefits since the router can determine the best routing path through the internetwork based on current load conditions. However, it does take the bridge less time to actually process a signal.

29. Standard ST-506 drive types include _____.
    a. ESDI
    b. SCSI
    c. MFM
    d. RLL

    *c and d.* The MFM (modified frequency modulation) drive was originally pioneered by Seagate. It provides a 5-Mbps transfer rate. The RLL (run length limited) version provides higher data densities (26 versus 17 sectors per track) and a 7.5-Mbps transfer rate.

**30.** The physical layer of the OSI model defines the mechanical and electrical specifications of the network medium and network interface hardware.

   **a.** True
   **b.** False

   *a.* The physical layer determines how you physically connect various parts of the network together. For example, it defines what type of cables and NICs you use. It also helps determine the speed at which you communicate across the network.

**31.** A protocol analyzer can help you perform which of the following tasks?

   **a.** Monitor network performance.
   **b.** Troubleshoot network errors.
   **c.** Optimize the LAN.
   **d.** Plan for growth.
   **e.** All of the above.

   *e.* A protocol analyzer is a powerful tool that can help you perform a wide variety of network-related tasks. Some of the better analyzers use a combination of hardware and software. However, you can still perform quite a few tasks with a software-only version.

**32.** You should periodically test the integrity of your backups by copying files from a backup to their standard network locations, then checking the files for errors.

   **a.** True
   **b.** False

   *b.* You should never copy files from the backup into their standard network locations. Always copy the files into a temporary directory and test their integrity there. Otherwise, you could copy faulty data from the backup over the good data on your network drive.

**33.** Burst mode allows the client to issue a single read or write request for blocks of data up to _____ in size without intermediate acknowledgment of individual packets.

   **a.** 16 K
   **b.** 32 K
   **c.** 64 K
   **d.** 128 K

# NetWare Service and Support

c. Burst mode optimizes transactions on a WAN by reducing the dead time between acknowledgments. Normally, each packet sent by the sender requires an acknowledgment by the receiver before the next packet gets sent.

34. WinCIM is a _____.
    a. Windows product that allows you to communicate with intermediate speed media
    b. Windows product that provides online help
    c. Windows communications program that allows you to access NetWire and other CompuServe forums
    d. Windows communications program that only allows you to access NetWire

    c. WinCIM is a communications program specially designed to make your sessions easier and more productive. A special Novell version of the product contains all the extra materials required to make your NetWire visits even easier. Either version will allow you to visit any of the forums that CompuServe has to offer.

35. Running all your applications from the local workstation and using the file server for data storage isolates the network from virus infection.
    a. True
    b. False

    b. A virus can attack your network in a variety of ways. All it takes is a connection from the workstation to the file server. You can never exercise too much caution when it comes to viruses.

36. Disk duplexing involves:
    a. Using one controller and hard disk in pairs. Each drive set duplicates the other's data.
    b. Using one controller and three or more hard drives. Data gets striped across two or more drives at the bit level. This system uses a dedicated parity drive.
    c. Using controllers and hard disks in pairs. Each drive set duplicates the other's data. Each drive in the set uses a different controller.
    d. Using one controller and three or more hard drives. Data and parity information get striped across all the drives at the block level.

*c.* Disk duplexing provides redundant controllers and disks. If either a controller or a disk in one set stops working, the other controller and disk take over. This allows the LAN administrator to make repairs during off-peak hours.

37. Two users on an ARCnet installation complain about intermittent access problems depending on the time of day that they log into the network. You discover that both users generally arrive at work at about the same time. The probable cause of this problem is:

    **a.** A faulty passive hub.

    **b.** That the users have a vivid imagination.

    **c.** There is some sort of software configuration problem.

    **d.** The cards in both machines have the same address.

    *d.* Setting the addresses of two ARCnet NICs the same will cause many intermittent problems since the network will never know whom to send messages to. It is the same problem that you would have if you shared an address with someone else—your mail service would prove intermittent, at best. Always keep a record of the address of every card in your network to avoid this problem.

38. The acronym CSMA/CD stands for _____.

    **a.** Collision Sense Multiple Access/Carrier Detect

    **b.** Carrier Sense Machine Access/Collision Detect

    **c.** Collision Sense Machine Access/Carrier Detect

    **d.** Carrier Sense Multiple Access/Collision Detect

    *d.* Ethernet uses this media access protocol to provide an equitable method of arbitrating cable access. When a node wants to transmit it listens to see if anyone else is transmitting, transmits the data, then checks for collision. Each node waits an arbitrary amount of time before attempting to retransmit the data when a collision occurs.

39. The Micro House Technical Library (MTL) provides the following features:

    **a.** Hard disk drive parameters

    **b.** Main board criteria

    **c.** NIC specifications

    **d.** Articles on how to more effectively use NetWare

    *a, b and c.* The Micro House Technical Library contains a vast array of information about the hardware used on your LAN. It won't

# NetWare Service and Support

677

help you answer any NetWare specific questions (or any other software questions, for that matter).

40. What is the one thing you should never do while observing ESD rules?
   a. Allow someone to touch you while you work on a board containing ICs.
   b. Ground yourself and your equipment with proper wrist strap and mat before working on any device containing a printed circuit board.
   c. Transport and store boards and ICs in static-shielding bags.
   d. Test your grounds daily to make sure they haven't become loose or intermittent.

   *a.* Never allow someone to touch you while you work on an electrosensitive device (ESD).

## Fun Test

1. You should periodically test the integrity of your backups by copying files from a backup to their standard network locations, then checking the files for errors.
   a. True
   b. False

2. The *NSEPro* contains which of the following information aids?
   a. The Most Up-To-Date Files, Patches, and Fixes
   b. Technical Information Documents
   c. NetWare Application Notes
   d. Service Provider's Guide

3. Type 2 Token Ring Cables consists of _____.
   a. Four shielded twisted pairs of #22 AWG telephone conductor
   b. Two shielded twisted pairs of #22 AWG telephone conductor
   c. Four unshielded twisted pairs of #22 AWG telephone conductor
   d. Fiberoptic conductors

4. To minimize the risk from noise you should not:
   a. Run cables near fluorescent lights.
   b. Use equipment without checking the FCC rating for noise emissions first.

c. Use equipment that isn't properly grounded
d. None of the above.
e. All of the above.

5. Standard ST-506 drive types include _____.
   a. ESDI
   b. SCSI
   c. MFM
   d. RLL

6. The IEEE 802.4 standard specifies the characteristics of _____.
   a. Ethernet LANs
   b. Token Ring LANs
   c. ARCnet LANs
   d. The logical link control (LLC).

7. Steps that you can take to prevent damage to your LAN include:
   a. Arrange the physical setup and location of the LAN to minimize the possibility of problems caused by environmental factors.
   b. Use appropriate record keeping to keep LANs running smoothly and to support troubleshooting.
   c. Use a stepwise troubleshooting model to analyze and act on problems.
   d. Store all your system backups on site in a fireproof safe.

8. Burst mode allows the client to issue a single read or write request for blocks of data up to _____ in size without intermediate acknowledgment of individual packets.
   a. 16 K
   b. 32 K
   c. 64 K
   d. 128 K

9. The initials *FDDI* stand for:
   a. Fiber Distributed Data Interface
   b. Fabricated Digital Data Interface
   c. Fiberoptic Distributed Data Interface
   d. Focused Data Distribution Internetwork

10. An Attached Resource Computer Network (ARCnet) LAN has which of the following characteristics?
    a. Uses a hierarchy of active and passive hubs
    b. Token bus runs at 5 Mbps
    c. Invented at Datapoint
    d. Uses RG-62 (93-Ω) coaxial cable, UTP, or fiberoptic media.

11. The four areas of security that every LAN administrator must think about include:
    a. Communications, personal, environmental, and regional
    b. Communications, environmental, human resources, and regional
    c. Communications, environmental, human resources, and organizational
    d. Personal, environmental, human resources, and organizational

12. Pressing the Ctrl-A key combination while in the search dialog box of the NSEPro produces _____.
    a. An *or Boolean* search.
    b. An exclusive *or Boolean* search.
    c. An *and Boolean* search.
    d. A *not Boolean* search.

13. The acronym *CSMA/CD* stands for:
    a. Collision Sense Multiple Access/Carrier Detect
    b. Carrier Sense Machine Access/Collision Detect
    c. Collision Sense Machine Access/Carrier Detect
    d. Carrier Sense Multiple Access/Collision Detect

14. A Token Ring network can use wiring concentrators known as _____ or _____ to create the ring.
    a. Multisection Access Units (MSAUs), Central Access Units (CAUs)
    b. Multistation Access Units (MSAUs), Controlled Access Units (CAUs)
    c. Multisection Access Units (MSAUs), Central Access Units (CAUs)
    d. Multistation Access Units (MSAUs), Controlled Access Units (CAUs)

15. Which of the following are Ethernet frame types?
    a. Ethernet_802.3 (raw)
    b. Ethernet_802.2

c. Ethernet_SNAP

d. Ethernet_II

16. Sources of RFI include:
    a. Light switches
    b. Furnaces
    c. Radar
    d. Microwaves

17. The seven layers of the OSI model include:
    a. Application, Presentation, Session, Transport, Network, Data Link, and Physical
    b. Application, Preparation, Session, Transport, Network, Data Link, and Physical
    c. Program, Presentation, Session, Transport, Network, Data Link, and Physical
    d. Program, Preparation, Session, Transport, Network, Data Link, and Physical

18. CheckIt Pro allows you to perform all the following tasks except:
    a. Check for viruses.
    b. Modify partition table information.
    c. Perform repetitive testing for system burn-in and acceptance testing.
    d. Check the alignment of floppy drives.

19. What is the one thing you should never do while observing ESD rules?
    a. Allow someone to touch you while you work on a board containing ICs.
    b. Ground yourself and your equipment with proper wrist strap and mat before working on any device containing a printed circuit board.
    c. Transport and store boards and ICs in static-shielding bags.
    d. Test your grounds daily to make sure they haven't become loose or intermittent.

20. A protocol analyzer can help you perform which of the following tasks?
    a. Monitor network performance.
    b. Troubleshoot network errors.

# NetWare Service and Support

      c. Optimize the LAN.
      d. Plan for growth.
      e. All of the above.

21. You can use a VOM to check which of the following?
    a. Networks for invalid packets
    b. Cables for broken connections
    c. Terminators for improper impedance levels
    d. Ground wires for improper connections

22. Novell's online service is called _____.
    a. NovTerm
    b. NetStats
    c. NetWire
    d. NovWire

23. A computer virus is _____.
    a. A biological organism that feeds on electronic components and eventually destroys them
    b. An application that affects the monitor frequency and causes you to feel ill
    c. An application that destroys data on your hard disk
    d. A biological organism that only makes computer users feel ill

24. Running all your applications from the local workstation and using the file server for data storage isolates the network from virus infection.
    a. True
    b. False

25. You can use the PATCHMAN.NLM utility to apply dynamic, semi-static, and static patches.
    a. True
    b. False

26. The SET MAXIMUM PACKET RECEIVE BUFFERS command allows you to:
    a. Force the file server to allocate a specific number of packet receive buffers on startup.
    b. Reduce the memory used by other memory intensive processes.

c. Increase overall system performance by making more packet buffers available.

d. Avoid excessive allocation of communication buffers.

27. The Micro House Technical Library (MTL) provides the following features:
    a. Hard disk drive parameters
    b. Main board criteria
    c. NIC specifications
    d. Articles on how to more effectively use NetWare

28. The session layer of the OSI model _____.
    a. Ensures data reliability
    b. Moves information across multiple segments of an internetwork
    c. Transforms data into a format that can be understood by each application and the computers they run on
    d. Maintains the dialog between communicating applications

29. You would use Level 3 UTP cable for _____.
    a. Intermediate level telephone and data connections with speeds less than 4 Mbps
    b. High-speed data connections and LANs with speeds less than 16 Mbps
    c. Extended distance and/or high-speed data LAN with speeds less than 20 Mbps
    d. 150-$\Omega$ data-grade media LAN applications.

30. Asynchronous Transfer Mode (ATM) is a _____.
    a. Packet-switching technology that looks a similar to a high-speed telephone switch
    b. Serial cable technology that offers low-cost data transmission
    c. New WAN solution that allows data transfer during off-peak hours.
    d. Fiberoptic cabling strategy that offers characteristics similar to Ethernet

31. Two users on an ARCnet installation complain about intermittent access problems depending on the time of day that they log into the network. You discover that both users generally arrive

at work at about the same time. The probable cause of this problem is:
   a. A faulty passive hub.
   b. That the users have a vivid imagination.
   c. There is some sort of software configuration problem.
   d. The cards in both machines have the same address.

32. Jumpers are _____.
   a. A form of dress worn with a blouse
   b. Plastic-covered clips used to complete circuits on a PCB
   c. People who wish to commit suicide
   d. A form of electric spark that damages circuits by burning them

33. Autotuning is NetWare's ability to dynamically alter the configuration of the following parameters to accommodate changing workloads on the network:
   a. Service Processes
   b. Minimum Packet Receive Buffers
   c. Cache Buffer Size
   d. Directory Caching

34. The physical layer of the OSI model defines the mechanical and electrical specifications of the network medium and network interface hardware.
   a. True
   b. False

35. Disk duplexing involves:
   a. Using one controller and hard disks in pairs. Each drive set duplicates the other's data.
   b. Using one controller and three or more hard drives. Data gets striped across two or more drives at the bit level. This system uses a dedicated parity drive.
   c. Using controllers and hard disks in pairs. Each drive set duplicates the other's data. Each drive in the set uses a different controller.
   d. Using one controller and three or more hard drives. Data and parity information get striped across all the drives at the block level.

36. You use a time domain reflectometer (TDR) to:
    a. Find cabling problems like shorts, breaks, and crimps.
    b. Troubleshoot NICs.
    c. Determine where a protocol error occurs.
    d. Analyze network transmission speed.

37. You need special tools to tune your NetWare 3.x network for optimum performance.
    a. True
    b. False

38. WinCIM is a _____.
    a. Windows product that allows you to communicate with intermediate speed media
    b. Windows product that provides online help
    c. Windows communications program that allows you to access NetWire and other CompuServe forums
    d. Windows communications program that only allows you to access NetWire.

39. The initials *NEMA* stand for:
    a. National Electrical Monitoring Association
    b. National Electronic Monitoring Association
    c. National Electrical Manufacturers Association
    d. National Electronic Manufacturers Association

40. A router affects the _____ layers of the OSI model.
    a. Physical
    b. Data-link and physical
    c. Network, data-link, and physical
    d. Transport, network, data-link, and physical

# Brain Teaser

Now that you have a better idea of the kinds of hardware-related questions you might see on your exam, it's time for a little fun. The cryptogram in Fig. 20-20 gives you some tips that you can use to reduce your LAN maintenance time. Hardware maintenance is the one issue that you'll

# NetWare Service and Support

PER GEVROCRERQC VW ER CWWCROVEP UEYO AL CSCYI QRC'W NAJ. NKWO EJAKO OTC LEWOCWO MEI OA XCWOYAI IAKY PER VW OA EPPAM CRSVYARGCROEP LEQOAYW PVBC UAAY EVY QVYQKPEOVAR STCEOM, UCAUPC MVOT VREXSCYOCRO EQQCWW OA QEJPCW AY AOTCY QAGUARCROW, GAVWOKYC, ERX XKWO OA ZCO VR OTC MEI. YCQAYXW EYC CWWCROVEP OA ERI PER GEVROCRERQC UPER. KWVRZ OTC QAYYCQO OYAKJPCWTAAOVRZ WOYEOCZI EPMEIW YCXKQCW GEVROCRERQC OVGC ERX VRQYCEWCW OTC QTERQC OTEO IAK'PP LVRX OTC UYAJPCG OTC LVYWO OVGC EYAKRX.

| A | | N | |
|---|---|---|---|
| B | | O | |
| C | | P | |
| D | | Q | |
| E | | R | |
| F | | S | |
| G | | T | |
| H | | U | |
| I | | V | |
| J | | W | |
| K | | X | |
| L | | Y | |
| M | | Z | |

**Figure 20-20**
Hardware Maintenance Cryptogram.

**Figure 20-21**
Destructive Environmental Factors Cryptogram.

*>~(;>{ $~^[ =<[@(<[:') :>:#$ ;) ]=: \;[)] )]:& ;> :¦;#;><];>{ ;].

\^[><_:) <>@ #;_[~(<?:) +~]= <_] <) )~^[_:) ~\ [\; ([<@;~ \[:!^:>_$

;>]:[\:[:>_:). ¦;{=] )(;]_=:) <>@ [<@<[ &[~@^_: :#; (:¦:_][~#<{>:];_

;>]:[\:[:>_:. +~]= )~^[_:) ~\ [<@;<];~> _<> _<^): =<[@(<[: &[~+¦:#),

+^] ;> @;\\:[:>] (<$). #<*: )^[: $~^ *>~( <+~^] +~]=.

| ! |   | { |   |
|---|---|---|---|
| @ |   | } |   |
| # |   | [ |   |
| $ |   | ] |   |
| % |   | < |   |
| ^ |   | > |   |
| & |   | ¦ |   |
| * |   | \ |   |
| ( |   | / |   |
| ) |   | ? |   |
| _ |   | ~ |   |
| + |   | : |   |
| = |   | ; |   |

always have to face as a CNE—it really doesn't matter how well vendors eventually enhance the self-diagnostic capabilities of the products they sell, you'll still have to maintain them in some way. In fact, many CNEs find that they spend the vast majority of their time working on hardware-related issues, so anything you can do to reduce maintenance time is a real plus. You'll find the solution for this brain teaser in App. C, "Brain Teaser Answers."

# NetWare Service and Support 687

If you're feeling especially knowledgeable, you can try your hand at the much more difficult cryptogram shown in Fig. 20-21. This is a destructive-environmental-factors-related phrase based on one of the questions you answered in the preceding fun test section. Remember that this exam will test your knowledge of how to prevent hardware problems in the first place as well as of how to fix them when they appear. It's important to understand what kinds of things you need to watch out for when you work with the hardware under your care. Just in case the idea of working with a symbol-oriented cryptogram is a bit intimidating for you, here's a tip: All spaces really are spaces and all periods are periods. Apostrophes are also what they appear to be. Every other symbol replaces a letter.

## Disk Time

Don't forget to spend some time working with the disk that accompanies this book. It provides valuable and fun-to-use teaching aids that will help prepare you for the exam. See "Disk Time" in the preface of this book for details about what the disk contains. Make sure you focus on the NetWare 4.x and Acronym questions if you're running out of time when playing Red Zone.

# CHAPTER 21
# Networking Technologies

# Introduction

This chapter looks at the requirements for the Networking Technologies exam. There are several discrete sections in this chapter. Each section helps you study for the exam in a different way. You can improve your chances of passing the exam by using two or more of the study methods provided in this chapter. It'll probably help if you study all the sections once and your favorite sections at least twice. Remember to review the study guidelines in Chap. 4 as required to ensure that you maintain the best possible study atmosphere.

The first section of this chapter is a *case study*. You'll perform some network theory tasks that'll help you learn what you need to know to pass the examination. This is an especially important part of the exam study process since you'll be tested on your knowledge of network theory, the methods used to transfer data from one node on a network to another. Unlike the other case studies in this book, this case study is best performed away from your network. You'll want the quietest possible environment while studying network theory.

The second area contains *actual Novell questions* for this course. An important consideration for the questions on this exam is the world view of networking. You're going to see a lot of acronyms and non-Novell network-specific questions. Each question also includes the correct answer and an explanation of why that answer is correct. Try to answer each question yourself, look at the correct answer, then determine where you went wrong if you didn't answer correctly.

The next section is a *fun test*. This is an exercise where you'll look at some sample test questions and answer them. The answers appear in App. B at the back of the book. This will help you test what you learned in the previous section.

The final text section of the chapter is the *brain teaser*. You'll get to have a little fun working on a network technology-related puzzle. In this case, you'll need to look for words that we talk about in the case study or fun test sections of this chapter. The word-search puzzle will definitely contain some of the more interesting acronyms from App. A as well, so be prepared to spend a little time searching. You may even want to take the opportunity to look these words up in the glossary once you've completed the puzzle. Remember, Novell is testing your theoretical knowledge during this exam, which means that just about any technology, current or not, will be fair game on the exam.

Finally, we'll spend some time using the *Jeopardy!*-type game. This section helps you look at the test from the opposite viewpoint. The game pro-

# Networking Technologies

vides you with an answer—you need to come up with the corresponding question. The game awards points for correct answers, and takes points away for incorrect answers. You'll receive a score at the end of the game proclaiming that you either did or didn't get your certificate.

By the time you finish this chapter you should have all the knowledge required to pass the Networking Technologies exam. Use all the learning methods that we provide in this chapter to improve your chances of passing the exam. It's a good idea to save the fun test section until you're almost certain that you possess all the required knowledge. Remember, you can probably go through the test only two or three times at most before you'll start to remember the answers without really knowing the material.

Everyone who wants a certification needs to learn the material in this chapter; there are no exceptions. The chapter provides the basics that you will use to learn other computing concepts in this book. Without a firm knowledge foundation, there's no way that you'll fully understand the material in the other chapters. Make sure you pass this exam before you go on.

## Case Study

In this case study we show you how to decode a network packet. We use the Internet (DOD) model packet shown in Fig. 21-1. This helps you build an understanding of how a network actually transmits your data. More important, it helps you learn about the various layers that make up a network protocol. We use the packet shown in Fig. 21-2 as the basis for this case study. Make a copy of the figure so you can follow along with the case study. You do not need a computer to complete the case study.

1. Count off the first 6 bytes of the figure and draw a line. This is the *destination address*.
2. Count off the second 6 bytes of the figure and draw a line. This is the *source address*.
3. Count off 2 more bytes and draw a line. This is the *type* or *length field*. Whether it is a type or length depends on the number you find. The 0800 in our example makes it a *type field* (or a DOD Ethernet_II packet). Novell uses a value of 8137 to represent its Ethernet_II packets. If it were 05DC or less, then it would a *length field* (or an 802.3 packet). These three fields represent the data-link layer. Your

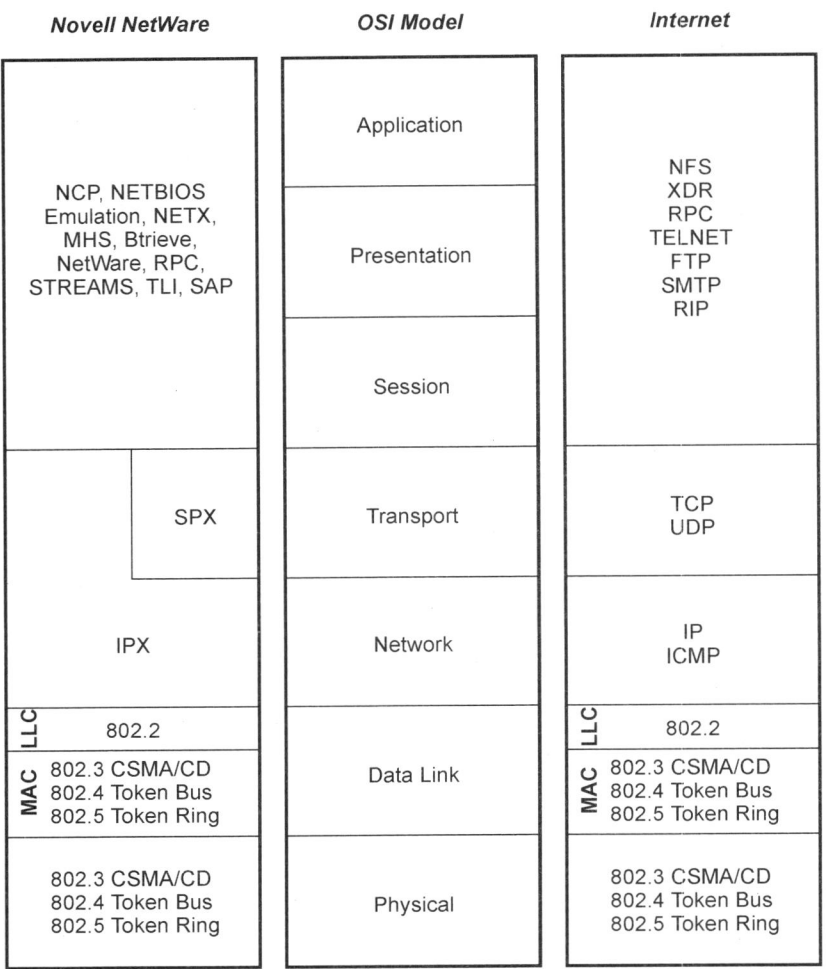

**Figure 21-1**
Protocol Stack Structure Compared to the OSI Model.

figure should look like the one in Fig. 21-3. The 0800 value in the type field tells us a few other things, as well. For one thing, it tells us that this is a TCP/IP packet and that we'll use the IP protocol in the network (internet) layer. You'd normally need a packet decoder at this point, but we'll lead you through the decoding process.

4. Draw a line between the first and the second nibble (4 bits), then another line at the end of the second nibble. The first nibble is the *version number* (4 in our example). The second nibble contains the *IP header length* (IHL). This is the number of long words (4 bytes each) in the header. This is 20 bytes (5 * 4 bytes for each long word) in our example.

# Networking Technologies

**Figure 21-2**
Typical Internet Packet.

```
08 00 14 23 04 27 08 00    14 70 00 13 08 00 45 00

00 29 55 62 00 00 3C 06    41 B5 59 70 00 13 59 12

35 23 11 51 00 17 2D E7    BC 49 3E 6E 1B 0E 50 10

05 B4 1D 52 00 00 50 6E    78 33 35 30
```

**Figure 21-3**
Data Link Layer Entries.

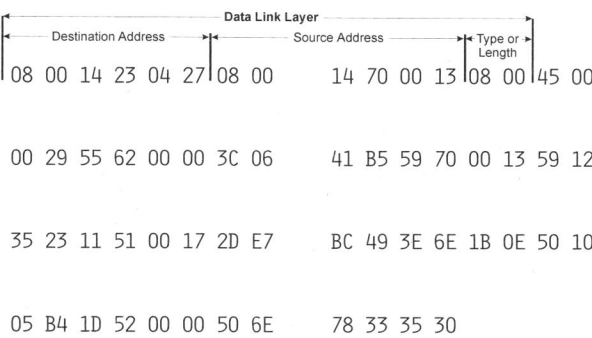

```
00 29 55 62 00 00 3C 06    41 B5 59 70 00 13 59 12

35 23 11 51 00 17 2D E7    BC 49 3E 6E 1B 0E 50 10

05 B4 1D 52 00 00 50 6E    78 33 35 30
```

5. Count out 20 bytes from the end of the data-link layer and draw a line. This is the end of the IHL header (or network layer).

6. Draw a line at the end of the second byte. This byte contains the type of service. This is the *precedence* (or the importance) of the packet. It helps the network prioritize the data it transfers.

7. Count 2 more bytes from the end of the type of service field and draw a line. This is the *total length field*. The total length field tells you how long the entire datagram is. In this case, it's 41 bytes long from the end of the data link layer (29 hex in our example). The extra 5 bytes at the end of our packet is padding. The specification says that the data field has to contain a minimum of 46 bytes, but we only need 41 to get the job done.

8. Count 21 more bytes from the end of the network layer and draw a line. This is the end of our data. We've gone from the end of the network layer to the end of the application layer. You should see the 5 extra bytes shown in the previous step. Your figure should look like the one in Fig. 21-4.

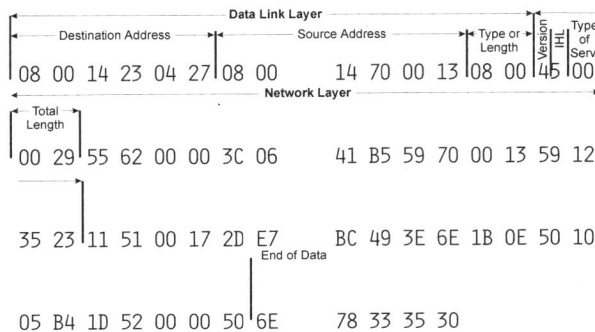

**Figure 21-4**
Network Layer Entries.

9. Count 2 bytes from the end of the total length field and draw a line. This is the *identification field.* It simply identifies the packet to the recipient. For example, what if you had two sessions going at once from a single workstation. The identifier would help the host keep the two sessions straight when it came time to transfer data.

10. Count 2 bytes (one word) and draw a line. There are actually three fields in this section. Bit 15, the last bit in the word, is unused. Bit 14 contains the *Don't Fragment* flag. This flag tells any routers in the path that you don't want to break the packet into smaller pieces for faster transport. Bit 13 contains the *More Fragments* flag. This flag tells the recipient that there are more packets on the way. Bits 0 through 12 contain the *fragment offset.* This tells where the packet will be fragmented. We don't need to fragment the data in this case, so the word contains zeros. Your figure should look like the one in Fig. 21-5.

11. Count 1 byte and draw a line. This is the *time to live* (TTL) field. This essentially tells the network how long you can use the packet

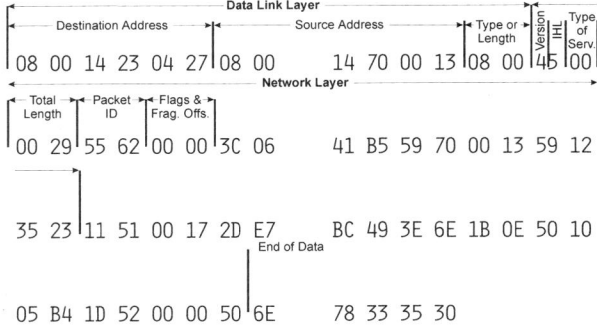

**Figure 21-5**
Network Layer Entries after Step 10.

# Networking Technologies

before the network determines that it can't find the destination address. In this case, we use the default time of 60 seconds.

12. Count 1 byte and draw a line. This is the *protocol field*. It tells whom we'll hand the packet to in the transport (host-to-host) layer. A value of 6 means that we'll hand it off to TCP. A value of 11h would hand it off to UDP instead.

13. Count 2 bytes and draw a line. This is the *header checksum*. It allows us to check the integrity of the packet. If the checksum of the package (a mathematical way of checking the value of the packet) doesn't match this field, then the packet is corrupt. Your figure should match the one in Fig. 21-6.

14. Count 4 bytes and draw a line. This is the *IP source address*. Essentially, this contains the software address of the sender.

15. Count 4 bytes and draw a line. This is the *IP destination address*. Like the IP source address, this contains a software rather than a hardware address. This is the address of the receiver. This ends the network (or Internet) layer. Your figure should match the one in Fig. 21-7.

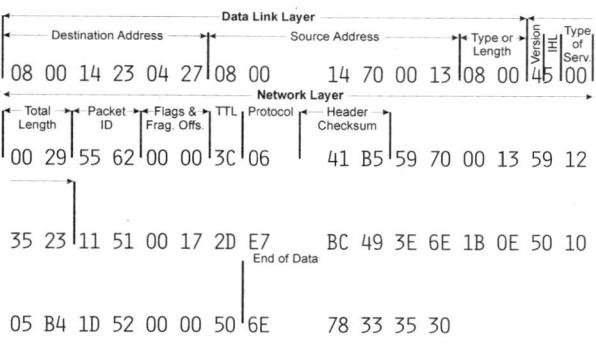

**Figure 21-6**
Network Layer Entries after Step 13.

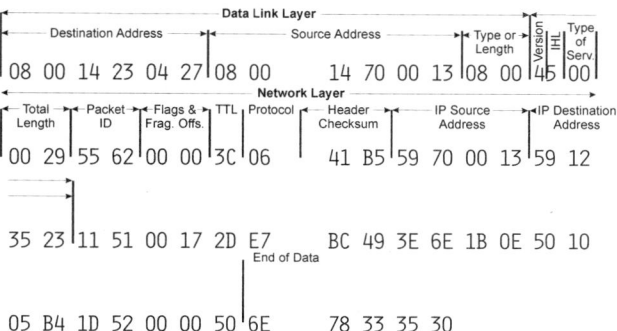

**Figure 21-7**
Network Layer Entries after Step 15.

16. Count 2 bytes and draw a line. This is the *source port*. (We'll see what the source port is all about in the next step.)

17. Count 2 bytes and draw a line. This is the *destination port*. These two ports represent software port addresses. Don't confuse these with the hardware ports on your machine. For example, the value of 23 (17 hex) in our example relates to a Telnet port. There are a variety of predefined ports that the packet will use. These 4 bytes represent both the transport and session (host-to-host) layer.

18. Count 4 bytes and draw a line. This is the *sequence number field*. It identifies which packet this is within a group of packets. The sequence number does not start at any particular value. All that needs to happen is that the source and destination increment the number at the same interval. Essentially, it tells the destination if it missed a packet.

19. Count 4 bytes and draw a line. This is the *acknowledgment number field*. It tells the source that the destination received a certain number of bytes of data.

20. Count 1 nibble and draw a line. This is the *length of the TCP header* in long words. In this case we have a value of 5 or 20 bytes.

21. Count 20 bytes from the end of the IP header and draw a line. This should leave one byte of data, as shown in Fig. 21-8.

22. Count 6 bits (1.5 nibbles) from the end of the TCP header length and draw a line. This is a *reserved field*—it isn't used for anything at the moment.

23. Count 6 bits and draw a line. These 6 bits represent the following flags: urgent, acknowledgment, push, reset, synchronize, and fin-

**Figure 21-8**
Transport Layer Entries.

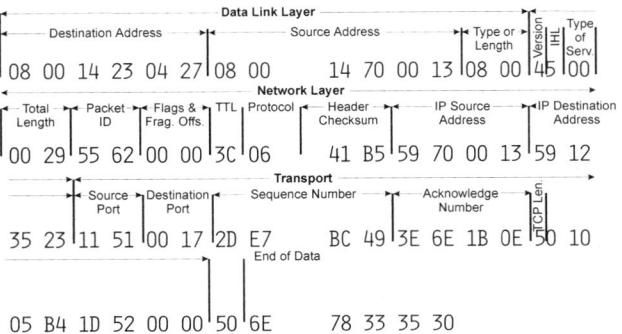

# Networking Technologies

ish. The *urgent* flag tells the recipient that the contents of the urgent field are valid. The *acknowledgment* flag indicates that the acknowledgment field is valid. The *push* flag tells the sending TCP to rush the delivery of data through the rest of the layers. The *reset* flag initializes the connection to a known state after an error occurs. The *synchronize* flag helps two nodes to synchronize their transmissions. The *finish* flag indicates that this is the last packet of data.

24. Count 2 bytes and draw a line. This is the *window field*. It determines the rate at which two nodes can transfer data. Of course, this depends on a lot of factors, including the load on each node.

25. Count 2 bytes and draw a line. This is the *checksum field*. It allows us to check the integrity of the TCP header. If the checksum of the package (a mathematical way of checking the value of the packet) does not match this field, then the packet is corrupt.

26. Count 2 bytes and draw a line. This is the *urgent pointer field*. The receiver counts this number of bytes from the beginning of the sequence number field to the point in the data stream where urgent data exists. Your figure should look like the one in Fig. 21-9.

27. You should have 1 byte of information left at this point. It's a hex value of 50. We went through all this work to transfer the letter *P* from one node to another.

This gives you an overview of one type of packet containing one byte of data. It's not meant to provide an exhaustive reference, but it should get you started. Analyzing packets is an important part of network troubleshooting in some cases. Learning how to do it takes time and patience, but it's well worth the effort.

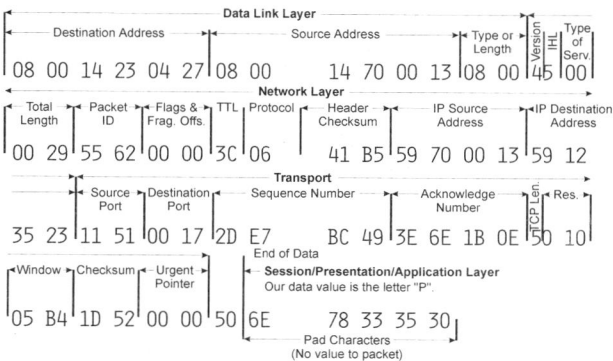

**Figure 21-9**
Session/Presentation/Application Layer Entries.

## Study Questions

1. The seven layers of the OSI model include:
   a. Application, Presentation, Session, Transport, Network, Data Link, and Physical
   b. Application, Preparation, Session, Transport, Network, Data Link, and Physical
   c. Program, Presentation, Session, Transport, Network, Data Link, and Physical
   d. Program, Preparation, Session, Transport, Network, Data Link, and Physical

   *a.* A good way to remember the initial letters of the layers and their order of appearance is to use the phrase "All people seem to need data processing." The order of layers is every bit as important as the actual names for the purpose of the test.

2. Most of the LANs in use today use the Polling access scheme.
   a. True
   b. False

   *b.* False. Many of the older computer systems used the polling access scheme. Today, the most common schemes are *contention* and *token-passing,* used by Ethernet and Token Ring networks.

3. A protocol will never specify more than one layer of OSI model.
   a. True
   b. False

   *b.* False. Protocols may be specific to just one layer of the OSI model, or span multiple layers of the model. Take, for example, the IPX protocol—it spans the network and transport layers.

4. The function of the Network layer is to:
   a. Move information across a network made up of multiple segments.
   b. Run the NetWare software for networking computers together.
   c. Hold the names of the users on the network.
   d. Make a common interface for sharing data.

   *a.* The function of the network layer is to move data across network segments. At this layer the network address for the recipient is added to the header.

# Networking Technologies

5. SDLC, HDLC, and LLC are all protocols that operate at which layer of the OSI model?
   a. Session
   b. Presentation
   c. Network
   d. Data Link

   *d.* SDLC (Synchronous Data Link Control), HDLC (High Level Data Link Control), and LLC (Logical Link Control) are protocols that correspond to the Data Link layer of the OSI model.

6. Every SDLC frame starts and ends with a unique series of bits referred to as the _____.
   a. CRC
   b. Flag
   c. Poll/Final
   d. Start/Stop

   *b.* In the SDLC frame, the unique bits at the start and end of the frame are *flags*. Other protocols label the same basic grouping of bits Start/Stop bits, Sync/End, or SD/ED.

7. The IEEE project 802 is primarily concerned with what layers of the OSI model?
   a. Physical and Data Link
   b. Data Link and Network
   c. Physical and Network
   d. The lower four layers

   *a.* For the most part, the IEEE project 802 handles the lower two layers of the OSI model. However, there are other 802 work groups that cover technology at other layers as well.

8. Ethernet LANs use what type of digital encoding scheme?
   a. Manchester
   b. Differential Manchester
   c. Polar
   d. Nonreturn to zero

   *a.* Two of the most popular digital encoding schemes for LAN's are Manchester and Differential Manchester. While the Ethernet networks use the Manchester encoding, Token Ring uses the Differential Manchester encoding.

9. Both Ethernet and Token Ring networks use what type of switching technique?
   a. Circuit switching
   b. Message Switching
   c. Packet Switching
   d. None of the above

   *c.* Both Ethernet and Token Ring networks use packet switching. The data is broken down into smaller units and packaged as a self-contained unit that is sent across the network.

10. Which layer of the OSI model organizes the one and zero bits into Frames?
    a. Application
    b. Physical
    c. Data Link
    d. Presentation

    *c.* The Data Link layer receives a stream of bits from the physical layer then groups them into Frames. The frames are then passed to the network layer for further decoding.

11. With Asynchronous transmission, the data is _____.
    a. Sent as individual characters surrounded by a start and stop bit.
    b. Sent as a block of data surrounded by a start and stop bit
    c. Very susceptible to transmission errors
    d. Faster than synchronous transmission; that is why it's used on PCs

    *a.* When transmitting data using asynchronous transmission, each character has a start bit and a stop bit added, alerting the receiver when to start and stop sampling the data.

12. The IEEE 802.7 advisory group provides guidance for which technology?
    a. LAN Security
    b. Fiber Optics
    c. Broadband Networks
    d. Integrated Voice and Data Networks

# Networking Technologies

*c.* The IEEE 802.7 advisory group deals with technology for broadband networks. The IEEE 802.10 group covers LAN security, 802.8 covers fiberoptics, and 802.9 covers Integrated Voice and Data Networks. It's a good idea to remember these four IEEE 802 committees for the test.

13. The Ethernet version 2.0 specification was released by whom?
    a. IBM
    b. Xerox
    c. Apple
    d. Digital, Intel, and Xerox

    *d.* The Ethernet specification versions 1.0 and 2.0 were jointly released by Digital, Intel, and Xerox.

14. The IEEE 802.5 token-passing ring networks are patterned after rings researched and developed by _____.
    a. IBM
    b. Digital
    c. WANG
    d. NASA

    *a.* The IEEE used the technology researched and developed by IBM as a model for their 802.5 token passing networks specifications.

15. The function of the Presentation layer is to:
    a. Transform the data into a mutually agreed upon format.
    b. Present a stream of bits to the physical layer for transmitting.
    c. Present the data on the screen for the user to view.
    d. All of the above.

    *a.* One of the functions of the Presentation layer is to transform the data into a mutually agreed upon format by the communicating computers.

16. Repeaters function at what layer of the OSI model?
    a. Physical
    b. Data Link
    c. Network
    d. Any layer above the network layer

    *a.* Repeaters are physical layer devices that regenerate the signal, then pass it on.

17. With the development of the _____, computers became smaller, faster, and less expensive.
    a. 360-K floppy
    b. IC chip
    c. PS2
    d. Apple

    *b.* One of the greatest advancements for computing was the development of the IC (Integrated Circuit) chip. The IC chip allowed computers to become smaller, faster, and less expensive.

18. Wide area networks use which communication mode?
    a. Simplex
    b. Half-duplex
    c. Full-duplex
    d. All of the above

    *c.* Full-duplex allows computers to communicate with each other at a much faster rate than simplex or half-duplex. With full-duplex transmission, both the sending and receiving computers can communicate at the same time.

19. The OSI model serves as a _____.
    a. Functional guideline
    b. Protocol for transmitting data
    c. Governing body that all other organizations report to
    d. Blueprint for building computers

    *a.* The OSI model serves only as a guideline of how data is handled. The actual movement of data must be implemented by a protocol.

20. Any given layer of the OSI model may add a header to the message.
    a. True
    b. False

    *a.* Any layer may add a header to the message as the data is passed through that layer. The headers are control information telling the layer how to handle the data.

21. The physical layer is responsible for what?
    a. Grouping bits into frames
    b. How ones and zeros are sent via electrical or electromagnetic signals across the network

# Networking Technologies

c. Moving the data from on network segment to another

d. Multiplexing signals

*b.* The physical layer deals with issues concerning the actual physical movement of data from one computer to the next. Some of the physical layer issues are media type, such as twisted pair cables or, possibly, infrared transmission.

22. Gateways function at what layer of the OSI model?
    a. Physical
    b. Data Link
    c. Network
    d. Any layer above the network layer

    *d.* Gateways function at any layer above the network layer. The gateway must alter as much of the data above the network layer as necessary to make it compatible with the destination computer system.

23. The acronym *DTE* generally refers to:
    a. The telephone equipment
    b. The device that transmits the data
    c. The device the user interfaces with
    d. All of the above

    *c.* The acronym *DTE* stands for *Data Terminal Equipment*. This is the device that a user will interface with. This piece of equipment is the place of origin for the data or the final destination for the data.

24. It is not possible to connect the send circuit of one computer to the receive circuit of another computer with a null modem cable and move data between the two computers.
    a. True
    b. False

    *b.* Yes, it is possible to connect two computers and send data by crossing their send and receive circuits. Watch for this type of question on the test. If you don't read closely and remember that the word *not* is in the sentence, you'll more than likely choose the wrong answer.

25. Bounded transmission media refers to:
    a. Wires or cables that conduct electricity or light
    b. Wires that are encased in a plastic covering

c. When the bandwidth of the network cabling becomes full and transmission speeds fall below the rated throughput

d. The knot of wires behind every computer

*a.* The term *bounded transmission media* refers to a media that constrains the signal in some type of conduit, such as copper wire or glass cable.

26. When moving data from one computer to another, it's important to remember that:
    a. Both analog and digital signals can carry both analog and digital data.
    b. Only analog data can be transmitted across analog lines.
    c. Only digital data can be transmitted across digital lines.
    d. Both computers must be physically attached to each other.

    *a.* When moving data from one computer to another, the digital data from the computer may be sent via a digital signal or converted and sent via analog signal. It's also possible to convert and send analog data by a digital signal.

27. The function of the Session layer is to:
    a. Convert the data into a series of one and zero bits that the physical layer can understand.
    b. Transform the data into a language that both the sending and receiving computers understand.
    c. Move the data in a reliable manner across the network.
    d. Maintain dialog between communicating applications.

    *d.* A function of the session layer is to establish, maintain, synchronize, and manage the dialog between the communicating applications.

28. Bridges function at what layer of the OSI model?
    a. Physical
    b. Data Link
    c. Network
    d. Any layer above the network layer

    *b.* Bridges operate at the data-link layer of the OSI model. A bridge has access to the hardware MAC address and can segment a network according to that address. Many times a bridge is used to divide a busy network into separate segments.

# Networking Technologies

29. The function of the Application layer isn't to specify the communication interface with the user.
    a. True
    b. False

    *b.* False. The application layer will specify the communication interface with the user. This is another one of those "not" questions.

30. In a network that uses a contention access scheme:
    a. Each device will wait until it possess the correct address of every file server before transmitting data.
    b. Each device may transmit whenever it wants.
    c. Will transmit more data under heavy traffic loads.
    d. The file server will act as a traffic cop, directing each workstation when to transmit data.

    *b.* In a contention access scheme, each device may transmit whenever it wants as long as the channel is available. One of the most common types of contention access schemes is CSMA/CD (Carrier Sense Multiple Access with Collision Detection), used by Ethernet.

31. The development of _____ helped to aid in the networking evolution.
    a. Color monitors
    b. Fiberoptics
    c. Standards
    d. Protocols

    *c.* The development of standards aided greatly in the evolution of networking. Standards form a set of rules specifying the physical and logical handling of the data.

32. Standards that come into common use in spite of law are referred to as:
    a. Proprietary standards
    b. De jure standards
    c. De facto standards
    d. IBM standards

    *c.* Standards that are accepted by the industry without being mandated are referred to as *de facto standards,* whereas mandated standards are known as *de jure* (by law) *standards.*

**33.** Data and Signals can either be:
   a. Analog or digital
   b. Spanish or English
   c. ASCII or EBCDIC
   d. Physical or logical

   *a.* Both data and signals can be represented in either analog or digital formats.

**34.** The point at which the subscriber's responsibility for the telephone wiring ends and the phone company's responsibility starts is known as the:
   a. Demarcation point (demarc)
   b. Central Office (CO)
   c. Regional Bell Holding Companies (RBOC)
   d. Public Switched Telephone Network (PSTN)

   *a.* The demarcation point or *demarc* is the location where the subscriber's responsibility for the telephone wiring ends and the phone company's responsibility begins.

**35.** Routers function at what layer of the OSI model?
   a. Physical
   b. Data Link
   c. Network
   d. Any layer above the network layer

   *c.* Routers function at the network layer of the OSI model connecting the different networks. As such they decode the physical layer, data-link layer and network layer information, then rebuild the data for transmission on another network segment.

**36.** The _____ layer is generally considered to be the heart of the OSI model.
   a. Application
   b. Network
   c. Session
   d. Transport

   *d.* Connecting the upper layer protocols to the lower layer protocols, the transport layer is considered to be the heart of the OSI model.

# Networking Technologies

37. The function of the Transport layer is to:
    a. Carry the data from one application to another.
    b. Move data across multiple cable segments.
    c. Ensure reliable data delivery.
    d. None of the above.

    *c.* Part of the job of the transport layer is to ensure reliable data delivery between systems. The transport layer accomplishes this by establishing logical connections between systems and using packet sequencing and packet acknowledgment to confirm data delivery.

38. Modern computers use _____ signaling.
    a. EMI
    b. Analog
    c. Simplex
    d. Digital

    *d.* Modern computers use digital signaling, thus the term *digital computer*.

39. Multiplexing is the process of combining several low-bandwidth channels into one high-bandwidth channel.
    a. True
    b. False

    *a.* Multiplexing is the process of combining several signals or channels into one signal or channel. This is a more efficient use of the signal or channel since you move more data during each transmission.

# Fun Test

1. What is the name of the unique sequence of bits at the start and end of every SDLC frame?
    a. Flag
    b. CRC
    c. Poll/Final
    d. Start/Stop

2. The job of the OSI model is to serve as a _____.
   a. Blueprint for building computers
   b. Functional guideline
   c. Protocol for transmitting data
   d. Governing body that all other organizations report to

3. The function of the Application layer is to specify the communication interface with the user.
   a. True
   b. False

4. The switching technique used by Ethernet and Token Ring networks is:
   a. Packet Switching
   b. Message Switching
   c. Circuit switching
   d. None of the above

5. What are the seven layers of the OSI model in order from the bottom up?
   a. Application, Presentation, Session, Transport, Network, Data Link, and Physical
   b. Physical, Data Link, Network, Transport, Session, Presentation, and Application
   c. Program, Presentation, Session, Transport, Network, Data Link, and Physical
   d. Program, Preparation, Session, Transport, Network, Data Link, and Physical

6. It is possible to connect the send circuit of one computer to the receive circuit of another computer with a null modem cable and move data between the two computers.
   a. True
   b. False

7. Bounded transmission media refers to:
   a. Wires that are encased in a plastic covering
   b. When the bandwidth of the network cabling becomes full and transmission speeds fall below the rated throughput
   c. The knot of wires behind every computer
   d. Wires or cables that conduct electricity or light

# Networking Technologies

8. The most effective mode of communications for a wide area network is:
   a. Simplex
   b. Half-duplex
   c. Full-duplex
   d. All of the above

9. In a network that uses a contention access scheme:
   a. Each device will wait until it possesses the correct address of every file server before transmitting data.
   b. Each device may transmit whenever it wants.
   c. Will transmit more data under heavy traffic loads.
   d. The file server will act as a traffic cop, directing each workstation when to transmit data.

10. What are the responsibilities of the physical layer?
    a. Multiplexing signals
    b. Grouping bits into frames
    c. Moving the data from one network segment to another.
    d. How ones and zeros are sent via electrical or electromagnetic signals across the network.

11. The function of the Network layer is to:
    a. Run the NetWare software for networking computers together.
    b. Make a common interface for sharing data.
    c. Hold the names of the users on the network.
    d. Move information across a network made up of multiple segments.

12. What's the purpose of the DTE?
    a. It's the telephone equipment.
    b. It's the device that transmits the data.
    c. It's the device the user interfaces with.
    d. All of the above.

13. What's the signaling method used by modern computers?
    a. Digital
    b. EMI
    c. Analog
    d. Simplex

14. Standards that come into common use in spite of law are referred to as:
    a. Proprietary standards
    b. De facto standards
    c. IBM standards
    d. De jure standards

15. Most of the LANs in use today use the Polling access scheme.
    a. True
    b. False

16. The development of _____ helped to aid in the networking evolution.
    a. Protocols
    b. Fiberoptics
    c. Color monitors
    d. Standards

17. The Ethernet version 2.0 specification was released by whom?
    a. Digital, Intel, and Xerox
    b. Apple
    c. IBM
    d. Xerox

18. What is the name of the OSI model layer that is generally considered to be the heart of the model?
    a. Transport
    b. Session
    c. Application
    d. network

19. A protocol will always specify more than one layer of OSI model.
    a. True
    b. False

20. The IEEE 802.5 specification is patterned after networks developed by _____.
    a. NASA
    b. Digital
    c. WANG
    d. IBM

# Networking Technologies

21. Which of the following statements is true when moving data from one computer to another?
    a. Both computers must be physically attached to each other.
    b. Both analog and digital signals can carry both analog and digital data.
    c. Only digital data can be transmitted across digital lines.
    d. Only analog data can be transmitted across analog lines.

22. The IEEE project 802 is primarily concerned with what layers of the OSI model?
    a. The lower four layers
    b. Physical and Network
    c. Physical and Data Link
    d. Data Link and Network

23. At what layer of the OSI model do Bridges function?
    a. Physical
    b. Data Link
    c. Network
    d. Any layer above the network layer

24. The function of the Transport layer is to:
    a. Move data across multiple cable segments.
    b. Ensure reliable data delivery.
    c. Carry the data from one application to another.
    d. None of the above.

25. At what layer of the OSI model do Routers function?
    a. Physical
    b. Data Link
    c. Network
    d. Any layer above the network layer

26. Any given layer of the OSI model may add a header to the message.
    a. True
    b. False

27. Data and Signals can either be:
    a. ASCII or EBCDIC
    b. Physical or logical

c. Spanish or English

d. Analog or digital

28. The function of the Presentation layer is to:
    a. Present a stream of bits to the physical layer for transmitting.
    b. Present the data on the screen for the user to view.
    c. Transform the data into a mutually agreed upon format.
    d. All of the above.

29. At what layer of the OSI model do Gateways function?
    a. Physical
    b. Data Link
    c. Network
    d. Any layer above the network layer

30. Computers became faster, smaller, and less expensive because of the:
    a. Apple computer
    b. 360-K floppy drive
    c. PS2
    d. IC chip

31. With Asynchronous transmission, the data is _____.
    a. Very susceptible to transmission errors
    b. Faster than synchronous transmission; that's why it's used on PCs
    c. Sent as a block of data surrounded by a start and stop bit
    d. Sent as individual characters surrounded by a start and stop bit.

32. What's the name of the digital encoding scheme used by Ethernet LANs?
    a. Polar
    b. Manchester
    c. Differential Manchester
    d. Nonreturn to zero

33. The function of the Session layer is to:
    a. Convert the data into a series of one and zero bits that the physical layer can understand.
    b. Transform the data into a language that both the sending and receiving computers understand.
    c. Move the data in a reliable manner across the network.
    d. Maintain dialog between communicating applications.

# Networking Technologies

34. What's the name for the point that ends the phone company's responsibility for the phone wiring and starts the subscriber's responsibility?
    a. Public Switched Telephone Network (PSTN)
    b. Demarcation point (demarc)
    c. Central Office (CO)
    d. Regional Bell Holding Companies (RBOC)

35. The organization of bits into *Frames* is done at what layer of the OSI model?
    a. Data Link
    b. Presentation
    c. Physical
    d. Application

36. SDLC, HDLC, and LLC are all protocols that operate at which layer of the OSI model?
    a. Data Link
    b. Network
    c. Session
    d. Presentation

37. Repeaters function at what layer of the OSI model?
    a. Physical
    b. Data Link
    c. Network
    d. Any layer above the network layer

38. The IEEE 802.7 advisory group provides guidance for which technology?
    a. Integrated Voice and Data Networks
    b. Broadband Networks
    c. LAN Security
    d. Fiberoptics

39. Multiplexing is the process of combining several high-bandwidth channels into one low-bandwidth channel.
    a. True
    b. False

## Brain Teaser

Ready for some challenging puzzles designed to help you pass the certification exam? The word-search puzzle in Fig. 21-10 will test your knowledge of terms associated with networking technology. Many of these terms refer to theory—you probably won't run into them on a daily basis, but you still need to know what they mean. You'll also find some acronyms, something that Novell is sure to test you on when you take the exam. Completing the puzzle is easy. All you need to do is find each term in the letter grid. Make sure you look forward, backward, diagonally, and vertically since the terms could be hidden in any of those positions. You'll find the solution for this brain teaser in App. C, "Brain Teaser Answers."

You'll want to spend some time looking these terms up in the glossary, in App. A, or in this chapter after you complete the word search puzzle. (You'll find any NetWare 4.x terms in Chap. 14 to 16.) It's important to know the theory terms associated with network technology and how they relate to the various environments you'll work in. Of course, learning the terms should also provide food for thought. For example, what do you really know about the OSI model? How well do you know technologies other than the ones you work with on a daily basis? It's questions like these that Novell is going to ask, so you'd better be prepared to provide the answers. You may also want to design your own word-search puzzle of terms. Looking for terms using this kind of puzzle really embeds them in your mind.

## Disk Time

Don't forget to spend some time working with the disk that accompanies this book. It provides valuable and fun-to-use teaching aids that will help prepare you for the exam. See "Disk Time" in the preface of this book for details about what the disk contains.

# Networking Technologies

**Figure 21-10**
Networking Technologies Word Search.

```
E T H E R N E T O T C A F E D Y R B
A X R E T S E H C N A M Z T N A V R
S P R E S E N T A T I O N H D W F O
W E P H Y S I C A L R T Y D P E O A
I P O L H E A D E R K N I L A T A D
U A L Y I T X E L P M I S C R A I B
F C L D S C M H E G N B M A F G D A
L K I D S O A Q W E X B N E I C E N
A E N R I N A T Z P I S O T O X M D
G T G C N T V B I R P N A B M L A U
S K H G F E F R B O E L R W Q N A P
D E X D R N F G R T N O I S S E S L
C H G E A T J T I O K L T I R T E E
A W L M R I I Q D C R A M E D W D X
M Q E A E O D M G O L A N A F O G H
S U T R D N X T E L A Y E R C R R E
C S N F D Y T I R U C E S N E K O T
S W I T C H I N G R E P E A T E R D
```

*Term List*

1. Analog
2. ANSI
3. Application
4. Bridge
5. Broadband
6. Contention
7. CSMA/CD
(shown as CSMACD)
8. Data
9. Data Link
(shown as DATALINK)
10. Defacto
11. Demarc
12. Digital
13. DTE
14. Duplex
15. EMI
16. Encode
17. Ethernet
18. Flags
19. Frame
20. Gateway
21. HDLC
22. Header
23. IBM
24. IEEE
25. Infrared
26. Intel
27. IPX
28. Layer
29. LLC
30. MAC
31. Manchester
32. Media
33. Network
34. OSI
35. Packet
36. Physical
37. Polling
38. Presentation
39. Protocol
40. RBOC
41. Repeater
42. SDLC
43. Security
44. Segment
45. Session
46. Simplex
47. Switching
48. Token
49. Transport
50. Xerox

# CHAPTER 22
# SoftSolutions 4.x Administration

# Introduction

This chapter looks at the requirements for the SoftSolutions 4.x Administration exam. As with the previous chapters, there are five distinct study-oriented sections in this chapter. Each section helps you study for the exam in a different way.

Don't be surprised if this exam is particularly difficult, since Novell only gets one chance to ask you SoftSolutions administration-related questions. Adding to the complexity is the fact that SoftSolutions is a document management program and Novell has to assume some fairly generic parameters for the test questions as a result. In other words, don't expect questions that reflect your specific document management configuration. Unlike the other administration exams in this book, you'll see a broader range of questions for the SoftSolutions exam.

You can improve your chances of passing the exam by using two or more of the study methods provided in this chapter. It'll probably help if you study all the sections once and your favorite sections at least twice. Remember to review the study guidelines in Chap. 4 as required to ensure that you maintain the best possible study atmosphere.

**NOTE** *This chapter won't help you to prepare for the SoftSolutions Advanced Administration exam (course 348, exams 50-159 and 50-259). It's designed to help those who want to learn about small- to medium-size SoftSolutions setup.*

The first section of this chapter is a *case study*. We look at a variety of SoftSolutions related administrations tasks including a simple product installation. It's important to realize that this case study can't possibly cover every aspect of the product—what you'll get is an overview of the product as a whole. Even though you'll get a lot more from this section if you perform it on your own network, the inclusion of screen shots and step-by-step instructions will help you gain something from the section even if you don't have a network.

The second area contains *actual Novell questions* for this course, including product-specific questions. An important consideration for the questions on this exam is the document management connection that SoftSolutions provides. One of the more common document types is likely to be a database. As a result, you'll see some database-related terms like *ODBC* on the exam as well—make sure you understand database terminology before you enter the exam room, because Novell will certainly test you on it. Each question in the study questions section also includes the

# SoftSolutions 4.x Administration 719

correct answer and an explanation of why that answer is correct. Try to answer each question yourself, look at the correct answer, and then determine where you went wrong if you didn't answer correctly.

The next section is the *fun test*. This is an exercise where you'll look at some sample test questions and answer them. The answers appear in App. B at the back of the book. Try to answer the questions without looking in the appendix first—cheating here will only reduce your chances of passing the exam. This section will also help you test what you learned in the study questions section.

The final text section of the chapter is the *brain teaser*. You'll get to have a little fun working on a network technology-related puzzle. In this case, you'll need to look for words that we talk about in the case study or fun test sections for this chapter. The word-search puzzle definitely contains some of the more interesting acronyms from App. A as well, so be prepared to spend a little time searching. You may even want to take the opportunity to look these words up in the glossary after you've completed the puzzle. Remember, Novell is testing your SoftSolutions administration and database management knowledge with this exam, which means that just about any technology, current or not, is going to be fair game.

Finally, we'll spend some time using the *Jeopardy!*-type game. This section helps you look at the test from the opposite viewpoint. The game provides you with an answer—you need to come up with the corresponding question. The game awards points for correct answers, and takes points away for incorrect answers. You'll receive a score at the end of the game proclaiming that you either did or didn't get your certificate.

By the time you finish this chapter you should have all the knowledge required to pass the SoftSolutions 4.x Administration exam. Use all the learning methods that we provide in this chapter to improve your chances of passing the exam. It's a good idea to save the fun test section until you're almost certain that you possess all the required knowledge. Remember, you can probably go through the test only two or three times at most before you'll start to remember the answers without really knowing the material.

**NOTE**  *We install SoftSolutions 4.x on a Windows 95 machine in the next section. Novell doesn't normally recommend that you do this since SoftSolutions is a Windows 3.x product. However, that's not the main problem. Installing SoftSolutions 4.x on a Windows 95 machine (at least as of this writing) will result in client compatibility problems. The product will work as anticipated in most respects—but you won't be able to use integrations fully and the built-in docu-*

ment viewer may not work properly. Neither of these problems is so serious that you can't use SoftSolutions under Windows 95 to study for the exam. You will, however, want to take these problems into consideration when performing a real-world installation.

## Case Study

There's only one SoftSolutions-related certification exam currently offered by Novell for CNAs (CNEs and MCNEs can also participate in the SoftSolutions Advanced Administration exam). As a result, this case study needs to cover more ground than just about any previous case study. Fortunately, SoftSolutions is a relatively easy program to learn how to use if you have the requisite database and application knowledge.

**NOTE** *This section assumes a familiarity with general database terminology. In essence, SoftSolutions is a specialized DBMS application that helps you keep track of documents and their contents. You'll also need to know about the applications that you want to use with SoftSolutions. The case study uses the Windows 95 version of the Windows operating system. It uses Microsoft Mail, Excel, and Microsoft Word as example applications, though you could easily use the examples with any application that you like.*

This case study looks at a few SoftSolutions administration-related tasks. The next few subsections look at such things as getting SoftSolutions installed and configuring it to work with your system. Obviously, there isn't any way that we can determine what types of documents you'll need to manage, so we'll look at some more generic examples.

### SoftSolutions Installation

This section shows you how to perform a basic installation using the *Custom* setup. We use the custom setup so that you can see the various features it provides. In most cases, you'll use the *Express* installation on a workstation because it's faster and requires less participation on your part. However, you'll need to know what installation features SoftSolutions can provide on the exam—make sure you perform several instalations using the Custom option so that you get a chance to experiment with them all.

# SoftSolutions 4.x Administration

The following procedure assumes that you've already installed Windows 95 (you can also use other versions of Windows with SoftSolutions). It also assumes that you have access to the application programs, like Excel and Word, that you want to use with SoftSolutions. We'll look at the process for a first-time installation since that type of installation covers more SoftSolutions features. This kind of installation also gives you a test platform that you can use for the other sections of this chapter.

1. Place the SoftSolutions CD in your CD-ROM drive. Windows 95 users won't see a screen automatically since SoftSolutions doesn't provide an AUTORUN file on the CD.
2. Use the *Start Menu | Run* command to display the Windows 95 Run dialog.
3. Click on the Browse button and you'll see a standard File Open dialog.
4. Find the *Install* file on the CD for your specific language. For example, English-speaking users would look in the *US* folder, while French-speaking users would look in the *FR* folder.
5. Click Open in the File Open dialog, and then OK in the Run dialog. You'll see a SoftSolutions for Windows Install dialog box similar to the one shown in Fig. 22-1.

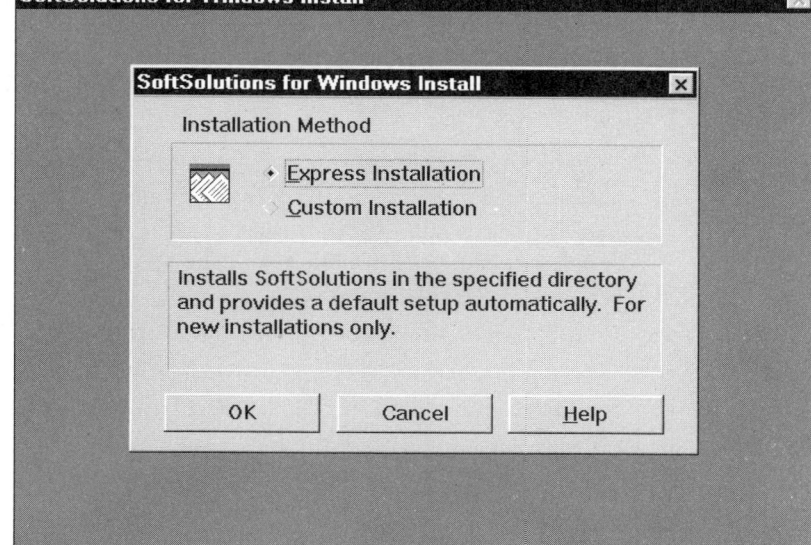

**Figure 22-1**
SoftSolutions for Windows Install Dialog Box.

**Figure 22-2**
Select Install Items Dialog Box.

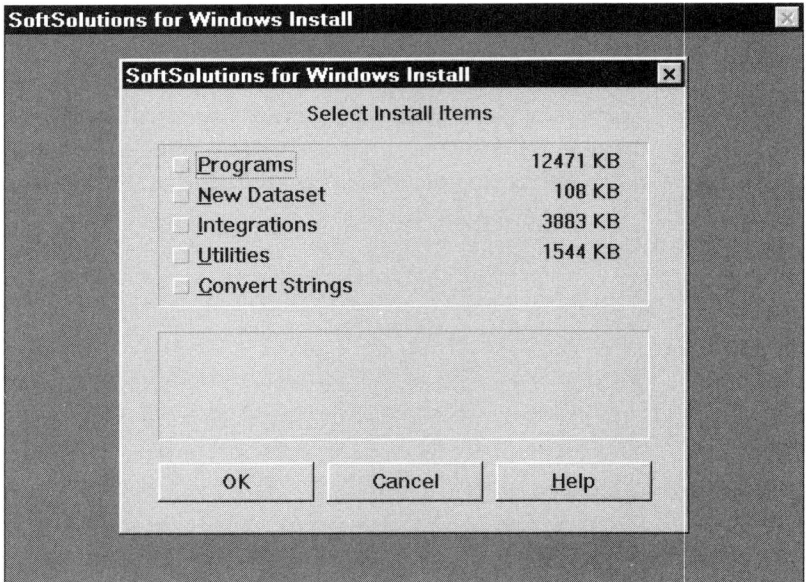

6. Choose the *Custom* option, and then click OK. You'll see the next SoftSolutions for Windows Install dialog, shown in Fig. 22-2. In this dialog you'll need to choose which program features you want to install. Obviously, you'll need to choose the *Programs* option if you want to do anything with SoftSolutions at all. The other features are optional; you'll need to decide whether you actually want to install them on your network. (Note that the installation program displays a description of each program feature in the lower half of the dialog when you click on the feature to select it.)

7. Check the first four options, leaving only the *Convert Strings* option blank, and then click OK. (The Convert Strings feature is only handy if you have the 3.x version of SoftSolutions and you want to perform an upgrade.) You'll see the Installation Directories dialog shown in Fig. 22-3. This is where you choose the location of the various SoftSolutions files on your hard drive.

8. Change the drive part of the destination to a local hard drive, if required. Click on OK. You'll see a third SoftSolutions for Windows Install dialog, like the one shown in Fig. 22-4. This dialog allows you to enter your company name and the serial number of your product.

9. Type your company name and serial number in the appropriate fields, and then click OK. (The serial number is included on the

# SoftSolutions 4.x Administration

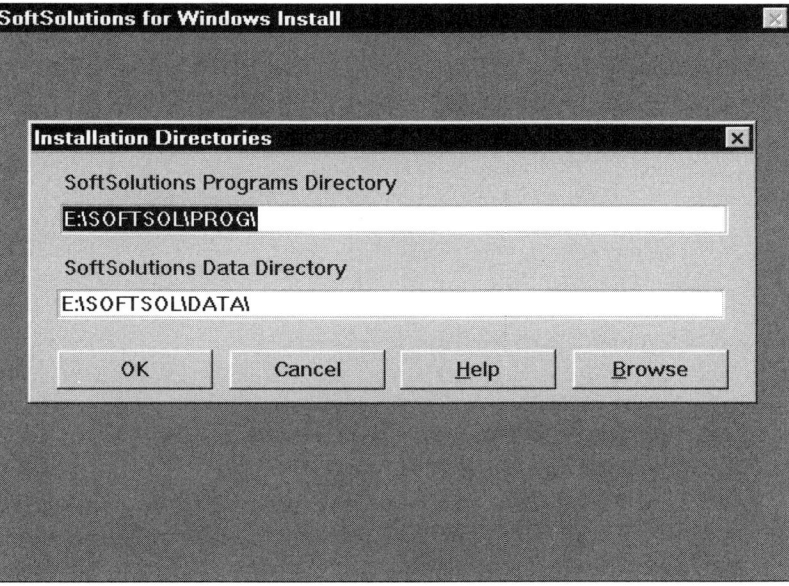

**Figure 22-3**
Installation Directories Dialog Box.

**Figure 22-4**
Registration Information Entry Dialog Box.

product registration card—make sure you place the remainder of the card in a safe place after you mail off the registration part.) You'll see a SoftSolutions for Windows Install dialog like the one shown in Fig. 22-5. This dialog will create a supervisor account for you in SoftSolutions.

**Figure 22-5**
System Manager Creation Dialog Box.

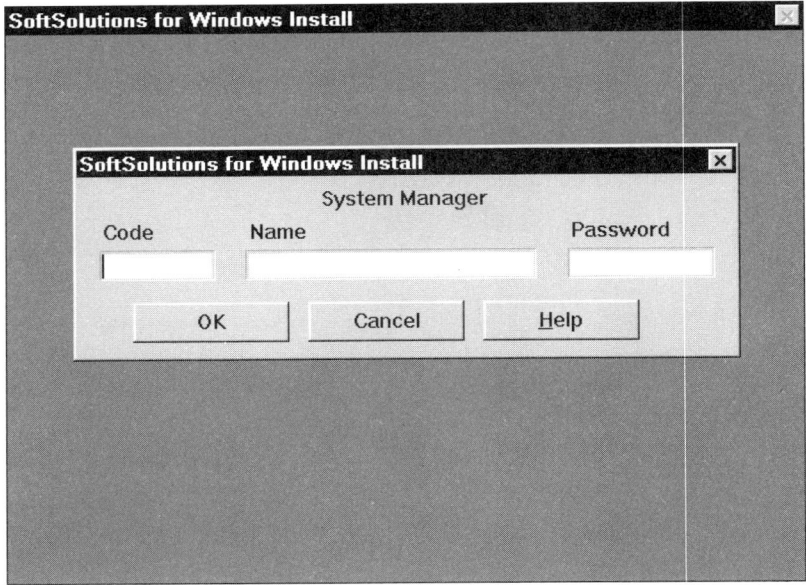

10. Type *A100* in the *Code* field, your name in the *Name* field, and a password in the *Password* field. Click OK. You'll see a SoftSolutions for Windows Install dialog like the one shown in Fig. 22-6.

11. Click OK to accept the default data directory setup. You'll see the Application Integration Installation dialog box shown in Fig. 22-7. This dialog allows you to choose which applications you'll use Soft-Solutions with. We'll be using Excel 5.0, Microsoft Word 6.0, and Microsoft Mail 3.0 for this case study. Obviously, you'll need to choose the applications you actually have installed on your machine.

12. Highlight one or more of the application entries in the *Integrations Available* list. Click the Select button to add them to the Integrations Selected list. You should see one more new entry in the Integrations Selected list every time you highlight an application and press the Select button (unless the Integrations Available list is empty). Highlighting an entry in the Integrations Selected list and clicking Deselect will remove the entry if you make a mistake.

13. Click OK to make the selections permanent. SoftSolutions needs to know the location of each of the applications at this point, so you'll see a dialog box similar to the one shown in Fig. 22-8 for each application you selected in the Application Integration Installation dialog.

# SoftSolutions 4.x Administration

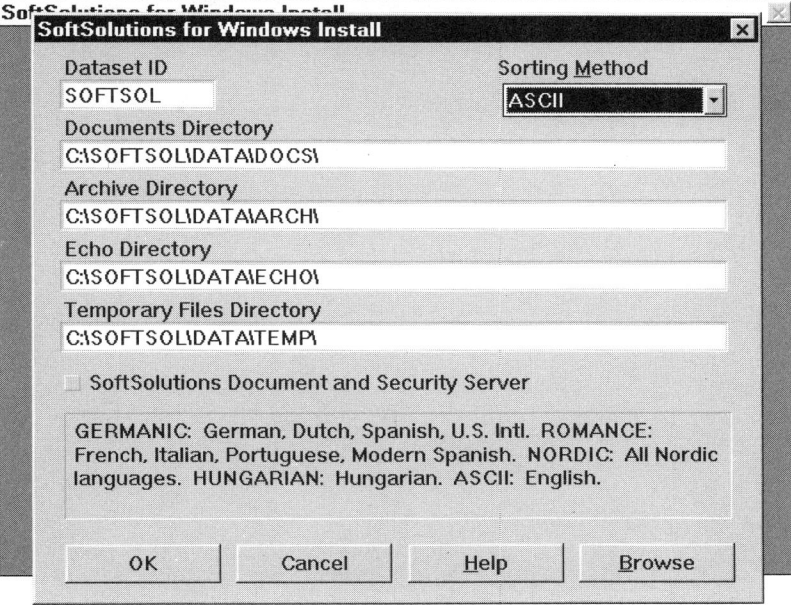

**Figure 22-6**
Default Data Directory Setup Dialog Box.

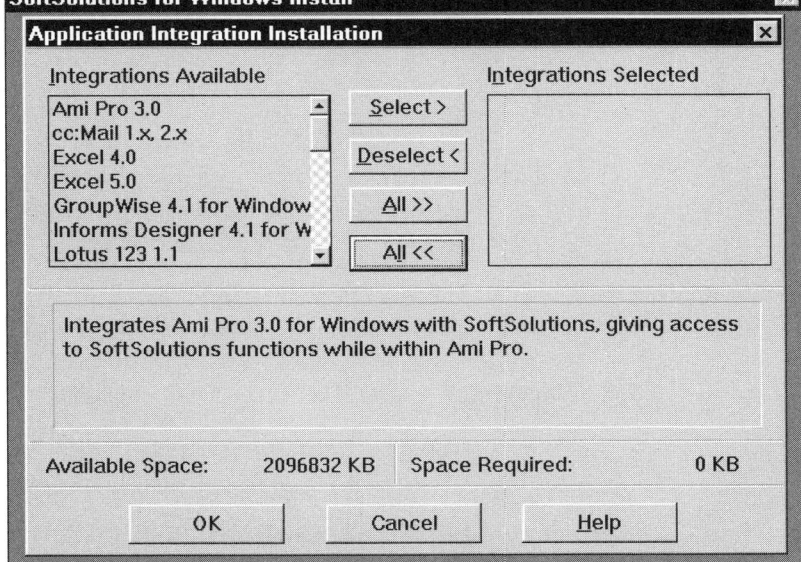

**Figure 22-7**
Application Integration Installation Dialog Box.

**Figure 22-8**
Application Location Dialog Box.

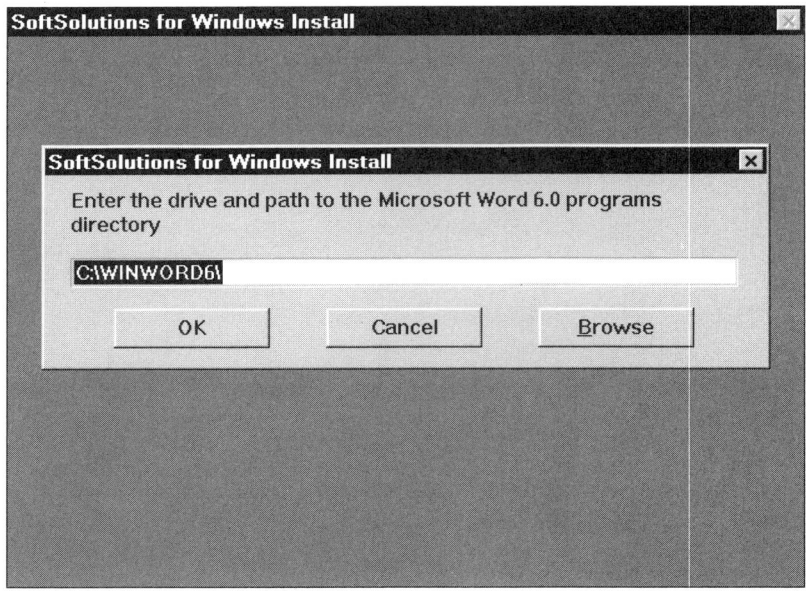

14. Answer each of the directory-related questions by entering a location and then clicking OK. Once you click OK at the last directory dialog, you'll see the Utility Installation dialog box shown in Fig. 22-9.

15. Click OK to select all of the utility programs. At this point, SoftSolutions will copy all of the files required for your installation to the hard drive. You'll see a progress dialog box like the one shown in Fig. 22-10. Once SoftSolutions is installed, you'll see a final dialog saying that the installation was successful. Click OK to clear the dialog.

## Document Desktop Installation

Installing the Document Desktop is relatively easy, but there are a few potential problem areas that you need to consider. We'll cover these areas as we talk about the installation procedure. For right now, all you need to know is that installing the Document Desktop is part of a full SoftSolutions installation. The following procedure tells you about all the details.

# SoftSolutions 4.x Administration

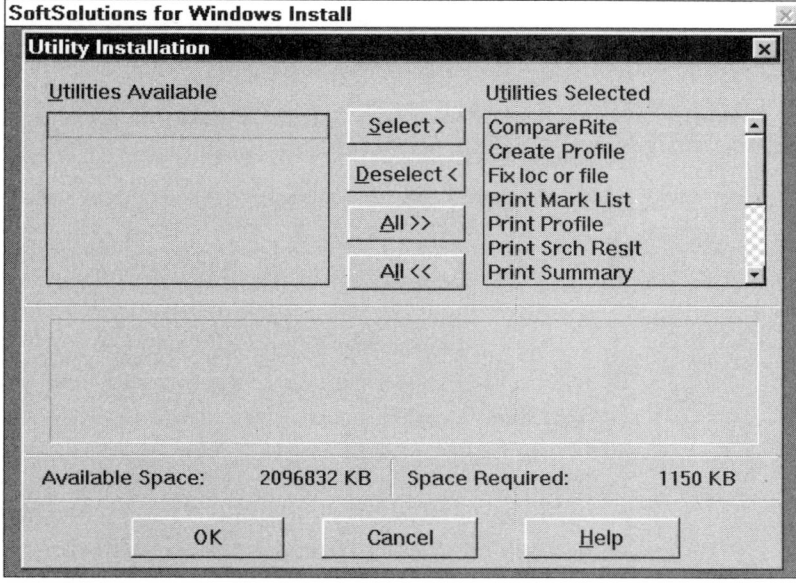

**Figure 22-9**
Utility Installation Dialog Box.

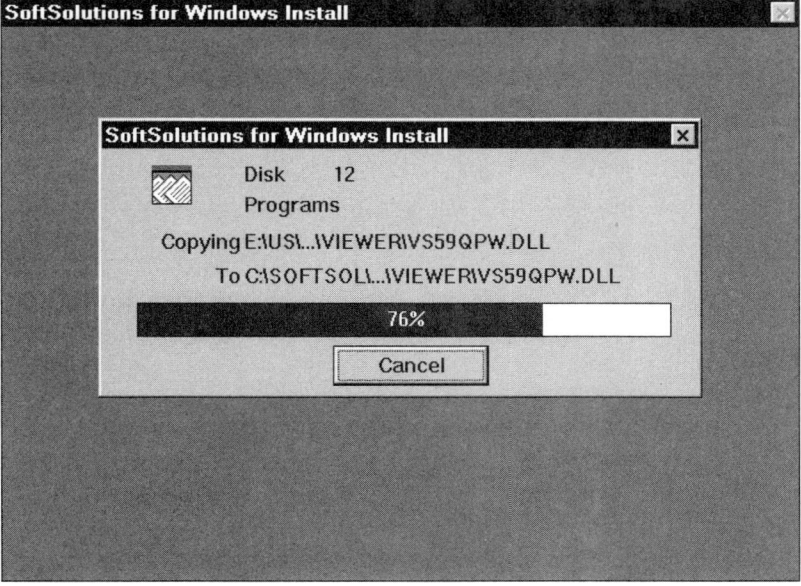

**Figure 22-10**
Progress Dialog Box.

1. Place the SoftSolutions CD in your CD-ROM drive. Windows 95 users won't see a screen automatically since SoftSolutions doesn't provide an AUTORUN file on the CD.
2. Use the *Start Menu | Run* command to display the Windows 95 Run dialog.
3. Click on the Browse button and you'll see a standard File Open dialog.
4. Find the *InstDesk* file on the CD for your specific language. For example, English-speaking users would look in the *US* folder, while French-speaking users would look in the *FR* folder.
5. Click Open in the File Open dialog, and then OK in the Run dialog. You'll see a SoftSolutions Document Desktop Install dialog box similar to the one shown in Fig. 22-11. As you can see, there are two sets of document location directory fields to fill out—one for standard (primary) documents and other for portable document support. You already created the first set of document directories when you installed SoftSolutions (see Fig. 22-3); we'll create the second set in a few moments.

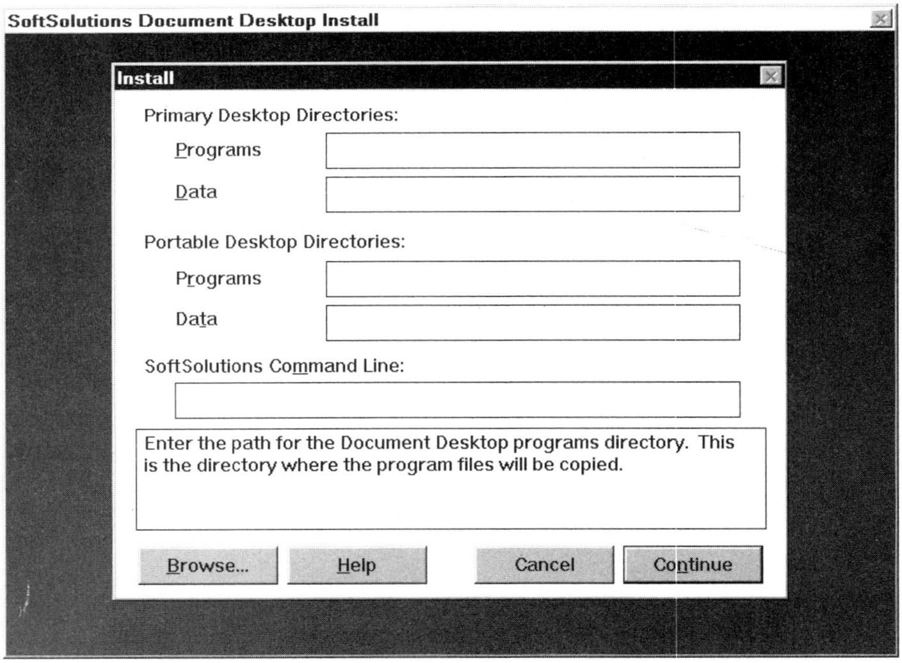

**Figure 22-11**
SoftSolutions Document Desktop Install Dialog Box.

# SoftSolutions 4.x Administration

6. Use the Browse button to find the SoftSolutions program directory. We used *SOFTSOL\PROG\* in the previous subsection. (You should see a standard File Open–type dialog box when you click the Browse button that you can use to find the SoftSolutions program directory. Simply find the directory and then click OK in the File Open–type dialog.)

7. Use the Browse button to find the SoftSolutions data directory. We used *SOFTSOL\DATA\* in the previous subsection. Now we need to define a portable program and data directory. This is where a local copy of SoftSolutions gets stored. You'll use it when you can't access the network copy of the program. For example, you'll find that this option comes in handy when you're on the road using a laptop.

8. Type *C:\PORTABLE\PROG* in the Portable Desktop Directories Program field.

9. Type *C:\PORTABLE\DATA* in the Portable Desktop Directories Data field. Now we need to provide a command line that will automatically start SoftSolutions for us.

10. Type *C:\SOFTSOL\PROG\SOFTSOLW.EXE /DATA=C:\SOFTSOL\DATA /USER=A100* in the SoftSolutions Command Line field. You'll need to change the program and data directories to match your installation; the example command line uses the settings from the previous subsection of this chapter. You may also need to change the user value to match the one you used for the supervisor. (Alternatively, you can use an environment variable to enter the user's name based on who is logged into Windows.) Now we're ready for the next step.

11. Click Continue. The Installation program will copy the required files to your hard drive. Once it's finished, you'll see the completion dialog shown in Fig. 22-12.

12. Click OK to complete the installation process.

## Correcting Database Errors

Anyone who works with a DBMS for very long realizes that you sometimes have to perform certain types of maintenance. For example, if the database becomes corrupted for any reason, you need to know why in

**Figure 22-12**
Completion Dialog Box.

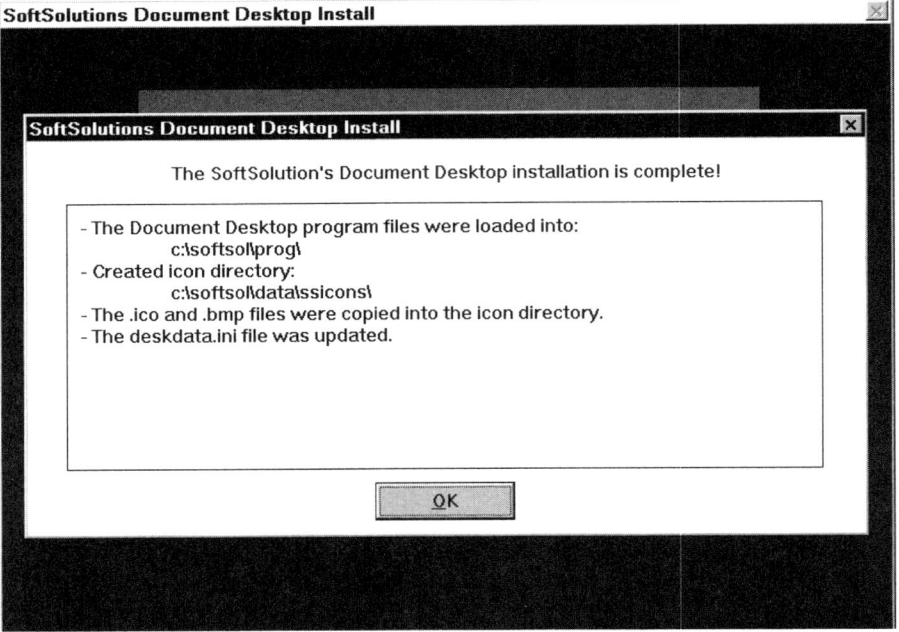

order to prevent the problem from happening in the future. Indexes can also become corrupt, which can prevent you from seeing the data contained in the database in the correct order, or from seeing it at all. Fortunately, SoftSolutions provides an easy-to-use utility program for detecting and repairing potential problems. The following procedure looks at the process for correcting database errors.

1. Open the *Database Reconstruction* utility in your SoftSolutions for Windows folder. You'll see a SoftSolutions 4.x Reconstruction dialog box like the one shown in Fig. 22-13. Note that you must run this utility when no one else is using the database. This means you'll have to have exclusive access to the database. You can achieve exclusive access by working after hours, working after everyone else has finished using the database for the day, or working as we're doing with the test setup, where only one machine has access to the database.

2. Click Continue. You'll see the second screen of the SoftSolutions 4.x Reconstruction dialog, as shown in Fig. 22-14. This is where you

# SoftSolutions 4.x Administration

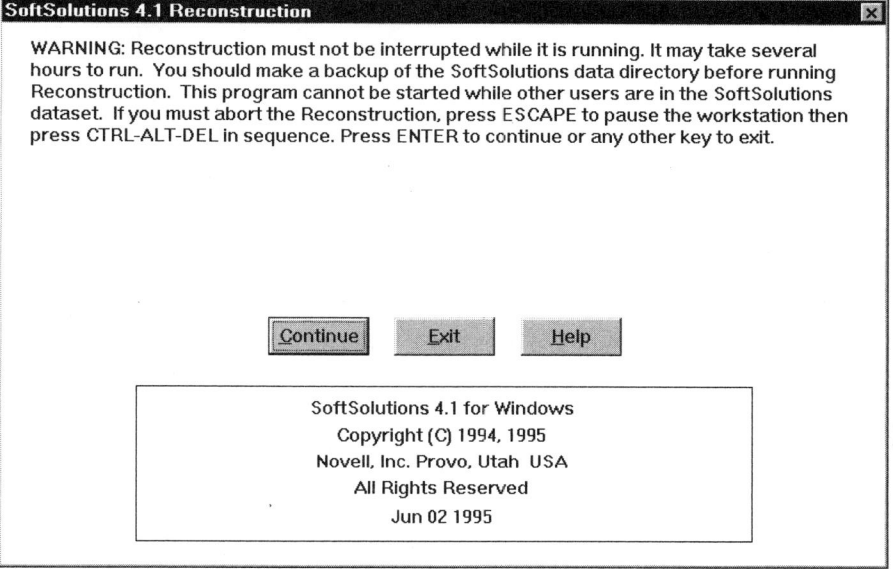

**Figure 22-13**
SoftSolutions 4.1 Reconstruction Dialog Box.

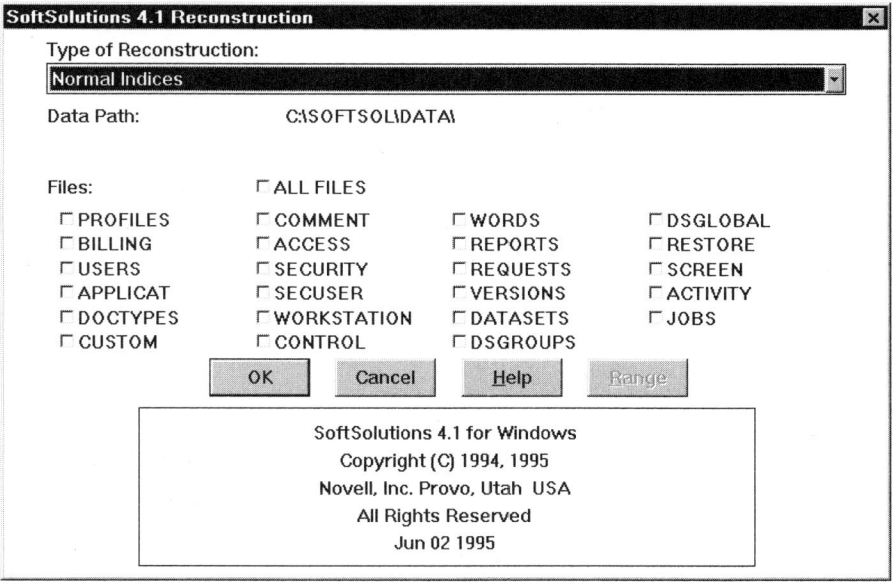

**Figure 22-14**
Reconstruction Level Selection Dialog Box.

**Chapter Twenty-Two**

decide what level of reconstruction to perform. The default selection is the *Normal Indices,* which really don't affect the search capability of SoftSolutions all that much. The indices that do affect searching are the *Speedsearch Indices*. You can perform two levels of reconstruction on them. The *Delta* option only updates the Speedsearch Indices that you've restored from a backup with any new entries you've made. The Speedsearch Indices option performs a more thorough reconstruction by building the indices from scratch. In many cases, you'll simply want to select the *All* option to make sure that every problem gets corrected. Note that you can also choose to reconstruct individual files.

3. Choose the All option in the Type of Reconstruction drop-down list box. Note that the program automatically checks all the files for you.

4. Click OK. The Database Reconstruction utility will automatically reconstruct all of the indices in your SoftSolutions setup. If you're using a test setup, the reconstruction process should take very little time. Once the reconstruction process is complete, you'll see a success message like the one shown in Fig. 22-15.

5. Click Continue to complete the process.

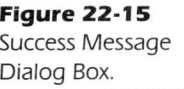

**Figure 22-15**
Success Message Dialog Box.

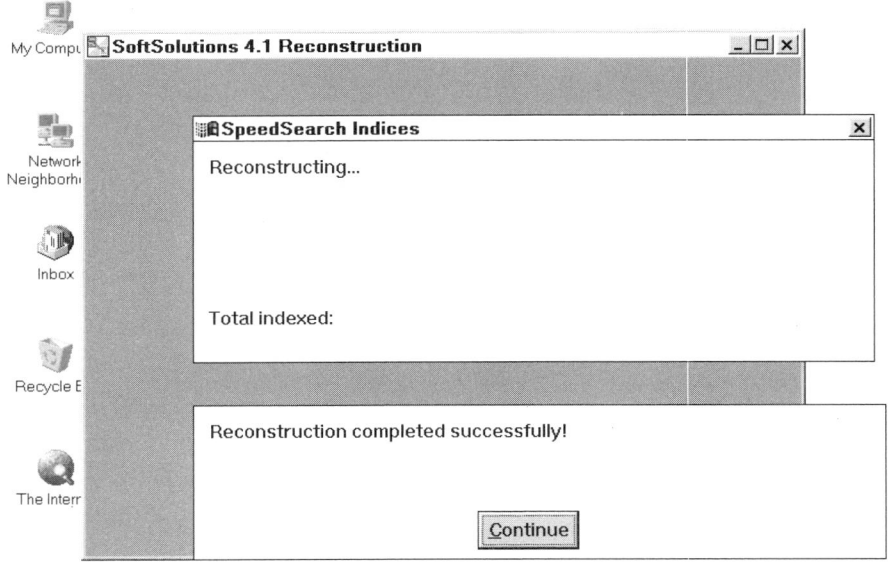

## Index Compaction

The method that SoftSolutions uses to index the records in the various database tables it uses could leave blank spots in the indices. These blank spots normally don't cause any problems, but they do slow the system down a bit. You can improve the performance of your SoftSolutions setup by compacting the indices on a regular basis. As with the Database Reconstruction utility, you'll want to gain exclusive access to your SoftSolutions setup before you try to compact the indices. The following procedure shows you how to compact the indices.

1. Open the *Index Compaction* utility in your SoftSolutions for Windows folder. You'll see a SoftSolutions 4.x Compactor dialog box like the one shown in Fig. 22-16.

2. Click Continue. The Index Compaction utility will take all the blank space out of the indices, then display a success message like the one shown in Fig. 22-17. (This process could take several hours if you're using a standard setup; the test setup will take just a few seconds to complete.)

3. Click Continue to complete the compaction process.

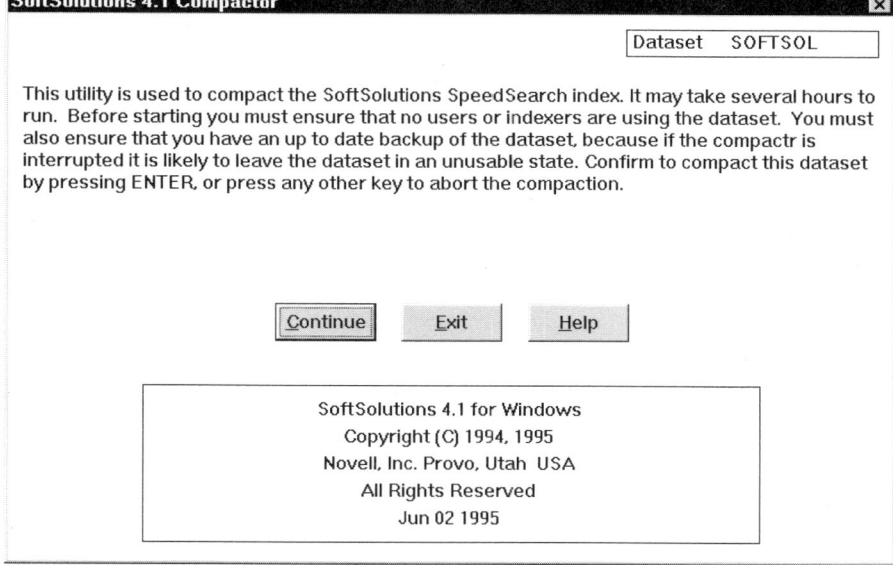

**Figure 22-16**
SoftSolutions 4.1 Compactor Dialog Box.

**Figure 22-17**
Success Message Dialog Box.

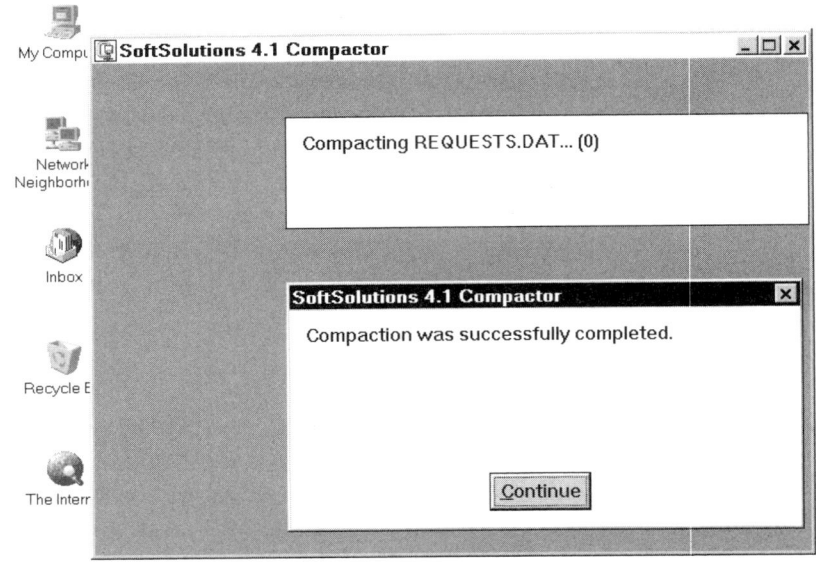

## Study Questions

1. The acronym *OAM* means:
   a. Open address modules
   b. Object access modules
   c. Open access modules
   d. Object address modules

   *b.* OAM is the acronym commonly used for *object access modules*. You'll also see this acronym as a prefix on files used to provide object access in SoftSolutions.

2. You'll normally find the SoftSolutions workstation installation files in the _____ directory on the server.
   a. SOFTWIN
   b. SOFTSOL
   c. PROG
   d. SYSTEM
   e. PUBLIC

# SoftSolutions 4.x Administration

    *c.* The SoftSolutions workstation files normally appear in the PROG directory. The name of the program you'll execute to start the installation process is SOFTWIN. In addition, the SOFTSOLW program gets called during workstation installation.

3. If you don't want to load SoftSolutions automatically each time you start an integrated application, set the AutoLoad= value to No in the _____ section of the SoftSolW.INI file.
    a. [Integration]
    b. [Application]
    c. [AutoLoad]
    d. [Implementation]

    *a.* You'll need to change the AutoLoad= entry in the [Integration] section of the SoftSolW.INI file to No. This file is located in the main Windows directory, not the SoftSolutions directory.

4. You'll use _____ to connect an outside application to your SoftSolutions database.
    a. DAO
    b. ODBC
    c. SQL
    d. DLL
    e. All of the above

    *b and c.* Novell provides ODBC drivers in the form of DLLs to allow access to the SoftSolutions database. SQL is the database language you'll use to query the database (ask it questions).

5. What are the three files not copied when you install SoftSolutions on a stand-alone PC?
    a. LAUNCOAM, PREVIOAM, and ENDOAM
    b. OAM1, OAM2, and OAM3
    c. OAMSUPP, OAMEDIT, and OAMLAUNC
    d. OAMLAUNC, OAMPREVI, and OAMEND

    *d.* You'll be missing the OAMLAUNC, OAMPREVI, and OAMEND files. Don't copy these three files to your network in an effort to gain OAM support. Use the Object Access Modules window in SoftSolutions to add them.

6. Which utility allows you to reconstruct the indices used to search the SoftSolutions database?
   a. RECONSSW.EXE
   b. COMPCTRW.EXE
   c. LOADCSTW.EXE
   d. SSINTMGR.EXE

   *a.* You'd use the RECONSSW.EXE (Database Reconstruction) utility to reconstruct the indices used to search the SoftSolutions database. Either the Delta (with a restored set of indices) or Speedsearch Indices option will work.

7. You should never compact your indices.
   a. True
   b. False

   *b.* Compacting your indices using the Index Compaction utility removes extra space from the index files. This maintenance action reduces search time and the amount of space that each index file takes up on the hard drive.

8. Even though you can run SoftSolutions on less, Novell recommends that you use a _____ equipped PC with _____ of RAM.
   a. 80386SX, 4MB
   b. 80386SX, 8 MB
   c. 80486, 4 MB
   d. 80486, 8 MB

   *d.* Even though you can run SoftSolutions on an 80386SX machine with 4 MB of memory, Novell recommends that you use an 80486 machine with 8 MB of RAM for optimum performance. Of course, a better processor and more memory would enhance performance even more.

9. The default SoftSolutions archive directory is:
   a. C:\SOFTSOL\DATA\DOCS\
   b. C:\SOFTSOL\DATA\ARCH\
   c. C:\SOFTSOL\DATA\ECHO\
   d. C:\SOFTSOL\DATA\TEMP\

   *b.* SoftSolutions uses the special C:\SOFTSOL\DATA\ARCH\ directory to store an archive of your data.

## SoftSolutions 4.x Administration

10. The server software of SoftSolutions is called:
    a. AOM
    b. SEM
    c. TCP
    d. NFS

    *b.* The server software for SoftSolutions is the Server Enhancement Module (SEM). It runs as an NLM under NetWare 4.x.

11. The SoftSolutions client software that runs under DOS and Windows is fully interchangeable for both NetWare and TCP/IP because it provides this feature:
    a. Multiple Router Support
    b. Stacked Protocol Support
    c. Independent Module Support
    d. Multiple Protocol Support

    *d.* The SoftSolutions client provides a Multiple Protocol Support feature that enables you to use one client for either NetWare or TCP/IP installations.

12. SoftSolutions depends on a particular network protocol and topology.
    a. True
    b. False

    *b.* SoftSolutions is designed to work with a variety of network protocols and topologies. The only limitation is that the network must support DOS file sharing and locking.

13. Which of the following networks have SEM support?
    a. NetWare 3.x
    b. NetWare 4.x
    c. SCO Unix
    d. IBM AIX

    *b, c, and d.* There are SEMs for a wide variety of NOS. Unfortunately, NetWare 3.x isn't one of the support NOS for SoftSolutions.

14. The advantages of using a Dedicated Indexer include:
    a. Data searching availability
    b. Lower equipment costs
    c. Loss of power synchronization protection
    d. Improved security

*a and d.* Using a Dedicated Indexer means that new or updated documents are automatically indexed—the system manager won't need to perform a separate indexing cycle at night on a nondedicated machine. In addition, since you can lock a dedicated indexer in a separate room, you'll have fewer security concerns when using one.

15. The /NOVMAP switch allows you to:
    a. Gain access to the data you need without actually creating a MAP to the required drive.
    b. Access data on a NetWare file server using any means possible.
    c. Remove old documents from the SoftSolutions database.
    d. Use dynamic file server attachments to access SoftSolutions data without logging onto all the required servers first.

    *d.* The user still has to be logged onto at least one NetWare file server to use dynamic file server attachments. When users try to access a document on a file server that they aren't attached to, SoftSolutions creates a temporary attachment for them (as long as the server and volume name are provided).

16. All users will need the _____ rights to the SoftSolutions PROG directory.
    a. Read
    b. Write
    c. Execute
    d. File Scan

    *a and c.* The user will have to have the Read and Execute rights to the PROG directory. However, giving the Write right might mean a breach in security since the user could then delete or tamper with the program files.

17. The _____ utility allows you to remove matured (old) documents from the SoftSolutions database.
    a. Database Reconstruction
    b. Janitor
    c. Index Compaction
    d. Database Editor

    *b.* The Janitor utility allows you to remove old documents that you no longer need from the SoftSolutions database.

# SoftSolutions 4.x Administration

18. The _____ window allows you to create new security groups.
    a. Screen Access Groups
    b. Users
    c. Document Security Groups
    d. Task Manager

    c. The Document Security Groups window allows you to create new security groups. Assigning a user to a group allows you to change the security restrictions for an entire group of people without having to change their rights individually.

19. The _____ Screen Access Group provides full access to all the windows, dialog boxes, and options in SoftSolutions.
    a. SEC
    b. PRIVATE
    c. ADMIN
    d. SYSM

    d. The SYSM Screen Access Group allows full access to everything that SoftSolutions has to offer. It's the setting used for the system administrator when you first install SoftSolutions. This setting isn't recommended for most SoftSolutions users.

20. If a field in the Document Profile window requires a valid entry, but one isn't supplied, you'll get a(n) _____ error.
    a. Entry Required
    b. 414
    c. Windows Exclamation
    d. 614

    d. You'll receive a 614 error if you don't provide a valid entry for a particular field in the Document Profile window. The error message will also tell you which field is incorrect or blank. For example, you must provide a value for the Author field.

21. The three types of applications you can define in SoftSolutions are:
    a. Open, Launch, and System
    b. Open, Print, and System
    c. Open, Print, and Edit
    d. System, EXE, and COM

*a.* The default setting is *Open,* which means the application uses documents. A *Launch* application doesn't use documents. For example, Microsoft Mail is an example of a Launch application since it doesn't rely on documents to perform its work. A *System* application refers to the OAMs that the SoftSolutions calls when accessing a document.

22. You can use SoftSolutions on a network as well as on a stand-alone PC.
    **a.** True
    **b.** False

    *a.* SoftSolutions can be installed on a stand-alone PC. However, you may be missing some of the required files should you decide to start using a stand-alone PC on the network.

23. The acronym *ODBC* means:
    **a.** Omni-directional Balanced Connectivity
    **b.** Old Data Buffer Cache
    **c.** Odd Delta Binary Coupling
    **d.** Open Database Connectivity

    *d.* Open Database Connectivity (ODBC) was originally pioneered by Microsoft and is one of the standard methods of accessing a DBMS outside the system. This is the one way that you can couple your SoftSolutions database to another application.

24. You access the various windows in SoftSolutions using the _____ command.
    **a.** Setup
    **b.** View
    **c.** Utilities
    **d.** EZLaunch

    *a.* The Setup command (menu selection) displays a list of windows that you can access using SoftSolutions.

25. The Command Line field in the Applications window is limited to _____ characters.
    **a.** 256
    **b.** 128

# SoftSolutions 4.x Administration

    **c.** 65

    **d.** 64

*c.* You must be able to express the entire command line for the application in 65 characters.

26. The %D parameter allows you to do this when executing an application:
    
    **a.** Pass the Dataset ID of the current dataset to the application.
    
    **b.** Provide the date the current document was created.
    
    **c.** Define the date the current document was opened in the Document Profile window.
    
    **d.** Tell the application that you've defined special parameters for it to use.
    
    *a.* The %D parameter allows you to pass the Dataset ID of the current dataset to the application. The Dataset ID is defined in the Control File window.

27. Which Windows DLLs will SoftSolutions update during installation?
    
    **a.** COMMDLG.DLL
    
    **b.** SHELL.DLL
    
    **c.** LZEXPAND.DLL
    
    **d.** TOOLHELP.DLL
    
    **e.** DDEML.DLL
    
    *b, d, and e.* These aren't the only DLLs that SoftSolutions requires, but they do represent the three common files that it uses. Other applications require these files, so you may experience difficulty using them if SoftSolutions installs versions of the files that are incompatible with the applications you currently use.

28. The acronym *SQL* means:
    
    **a.** Structured Query Language
    
    **b.** Stratified Question Lingo
    
    **c.** Structured Question Language
    
    **d.** Stratified Query Language
    
    *a.* Structured Query Language (SQL) is a standardized database language used to ask any DBMS questions about the data it manages.

29. The Name Service field of the Datasets window can contain which of the following values?

   a. FIL
   b. NWB
   c. DEC
   d. IN
   e. All of the above

   *e.* The default setting is FIL (File Services), which is what you should use if there is no SoftSolutions SEM in use. The other three values are *NWB* for NetWare Bindery, *DEC* for DECnet, and *IN* for Internet.

30. The Primary User field contains the name of the person who is responsible for managing the document security group.

   a. True
   b. False

   *a.* The Primary User field contains the name of the group manager in most cases. Valid entries for this field include the names of users entered in the Users window.

31. The maximum number of concurrent versions allowed for documents is _____.

   a. 1
   b. 32
   c. 64
   d. 99

   *d.* Even though the default setting for the Max Ver field in the Document Types window is 1, you can set it to a maximum limit of 99.

32. The RDS allows you to perform this valuable function:

   a. Send documents to users via e-mail.
   b. Allow searching of documents by people who can't access them in any other way.
   c. Repeat data searches endlessly.
   d. Make SoftSolutions documents available to qualified people who aren't connected to the LAN.

# SoftSolutions 4.x Administration

*a and d.* The Remote Document Server (RDS) allows people who aren't connected to the LAN to access documents. It does this by using e-mail to transfer the document to a remote location. The remote user likewise uses e-mail to transfer commands and document requests to SoftSolutions.

33. The maximum SoftSolutions password length is _____ characters.
    a. 5
    b. 10
    c. 15
    d. 20

    *b.* The maximum password length is 10 characters. No default password is provided and Novell encourages system administrators to allow users to change their password during the first session to ensure the most secure setup.

34. The _____ window allows you to perform maintenance routines automatically.
    a. Workstation
    b. EZLaunch Options
    c. Task Manager
    d. Applications

    *c.* The Task Manager window allows you to schedule any tasks that you want SoftSolutions to perform automatically. You can specify an interval or a specific time and day of the week.

35. When optimizing a Dedicated Indexer's performance you should:
    a. Use at least one 80486- or Pentium-equipped machine for every 100 to 125 workstations.
    b. Not use an 80286 or 80386SX equipped machine unless the number of workstations on the network is small.
    c. Ensure that the file server has plenty of memory.
    d. Use the DOS-based Indexer program.
    e. All of the above.

    *e.* All of these optimizing techniques are valuable. There are also a number of things you shouldn't do—like use more than four or five Dedicated Indexers on one network. The SSTASK.EXE program gets called to perform the actual tasks.

36. Setting the Document Life field to _____ ensures that it never gets archived or deleted.
   a. 0
   b. 99
   c. −1
   d. 128

   *a.* Setting the Document Life field in the Document Profile window to 0 tells SoftSolutions that you don't want to archive or delete it. SoftSolutions will use the Date Opened value as a starting point if you do decide to archive or delete the document after a specific number of days.

37. If you are using a SoftSolutions SEM, you should use the _____ instead of the _____ program to back up the database.
   a. SSBack, SSPause.
   b. SSSemBk, SSBack.
   c. SSPause, SSBack.
   d. Always use the SSBack program.

   *c.* Use the SSPause program when using a SoftSolutions SEM. While the SSBack program ensures that you get an uncorrupted copy of the database locally, the SSPause program also ensures that the SEM is paused before starting the backup process.

38. The RDS server must be both _____ and _____ compliant to provide full e-mail services.
   a. TAPI, MAPI
   b. Internet, TAPI
   c. MAPI, MIME
   d. VIM, MAPI

   *d.* The Remote Data Server (RDS) will work just fine if it is VIM or MAPI compliant. However, to provide the fullest possible email compatibility, it should provide both levels of compliance. (MAPI is the favored e-mail specification for the Windows environment.)

39. SoftSolutions provides which of the following Document Security Groups as a default?
   a. PUBLIC
   b. PRIVATE

## SoftSolutions 4.x Administration

c. GUEST
d. SEMIPRIV
e. All of the above

*a, b, and d.* SoftSolutions provides the *PUBLIC* security group for documents that anyone can access. The *SEMIPRIV* security group would include specialized groups of people, like managers. The *PRIVATE* security group is intended to hold documents that require confidential handling.

40. SoftSolutions only works with Novell applications.
    a. True
    b. False

*b.* SoftSolutions is designed to work with a variety of applications, including those sold by Novell. It's important to remember that SoftSolutions is a document management database designed to meet a wide variety of needs.

# Fun Test

1. The acronym *ODBC* means:
    a. Omni-directional Balanced Connectivity
    b. Old Data Buffer Cache
    c. Odd Delta Binary Coupling
    d. Open Database Connectivity

2. SoftSolutions depends on a particular network protocol and topology.
    a. True
    b. False

3. The default SoftSolutions archive directory is:
    a. C:\SOFTSOL\DATA\DOCS\
    b. C:\SOFTSOL\DATA\ARCH\
    c. C:\SOFTSOL\DATA\ECHO\
    d. C:\SOFTSOL\DATA\TEMP\

4. The RDS allows you to perform this valuable function:
   a. Send documents to users via e-mail.
   b. Allow searching of documents by people who can't access them in any other way.
   c. Repeat data searches endlessly.
   d. Make SoftSolutions documents available to qualified people who aren't connected to the LAN.

5. The _____ window allows you to create new security groups.
   a. Screen Access Groups
   b. Users
   c. Document Security Groups
   d. Task Manager

6. Which Windows DLLs will SoftSolutions update during installation?
   a. COMMDLG.DLL
   b. SHELL.DLL
   c. LZEXPAND.DLL
   d. TOOLHELP.DLL
   e. DDEML.DLL

7. Which utility allows you to reconstruct the indices used to search the SoftSolutions database?
   a. RECONSSW.EXE
   b. COMPCTRW.EXE
   c. LOADCSTW.EXE
   d. SSINTMGR.EXE

8. When optimizing a Dedicated Indexer's performance you should:
   a. Use at least one 80486 or Pentium equipped machine for every 100 to 125 workstations.
   b. Not use an 80286 or 80386SX equipped machine unless the number of workstations on the network is small.
   c. Ensure that the file server has plenty of memory.
   d. Use the DOS-based Indexer program.
   e. All of the above.

# SoftSolutions 4.x Administration

9. The maximum number of concurrent versions allowed for documents is _____.
   a. 1
   b. 32
   c. 64
   d. 99

10. The acronym *OAM* means:
    a. Open address modules
    b. Object access modules
    c. Open access modules
    d. Object address modules

11. All users will need the _____ rights to the SoftSolutions PROG directory.
    a. Read
    b. Write
    c. Execute
    d. File Scan

12. The Primary User field contains the name of the person who is responsible for managing the document security group.
    a. True
    b. False

13. You'll use _____ to connect an outside application to your SoftSolutions database.
    a. DAO
    b. ODBC
    c. SQL
    d. DLL
    e. All of the above

14. The Name Service field of the Datasets window can contain which of the following values?
    a. FIL
    b. NWB
    c. DEC
    d. IN
    e. All of the above

15. If a field in the Document Profile window requires a valid entry, but one isn't supplied, you'll get a(n) _____ error.
    a. Entry Required
    b. 414
    c. Windows Exclamation
    d. 614

16. You'll normally find the SoftSolutions workstation installation files in the _____ directory on the server.
    a. SOFTWIN
    b. SOFTSOL
    c. PROG
    d. SYSTEM
    e. PUBLIC

17. The %D parameter allows you to do this when executing an application:
    a. Pass the Dataset ID of the current dataset to the application.
    b. Provide the date the current document was created.
    c. Define the date the current document was opened in the Document Profile window.
    d. Tell the application that you've defined special parameters for it to use.

18. If you don't want to load SoftSolutions automatically each time you start an integrated application, set the AutoLoad= value to No in the section of the SoftSolW.INI file.
    a. [Integration]
    b. [Application]
    c. [AutoLoad]
    d. [Implementation]

19. If you are using a SoftSolutions SEM, you should use the _____ instead of the _____ program to backup the database.
    a. SSBack, SSPause.
    b. SSSemBk, SSBack.
    c. SSPause, SSBack.
    d. Always use the SSBack program.

# SoftSolutions 4.x Administration

20. You should never compact your indices.
    a. True
    b. False

21. SoftSolutions only works with Novell applications.
    a. True
    b. False

22. The /NOVMAP switch allows you to:
    a. Gain access to the data you need without actually creating a MAP to the required drive.
    b. Access data on a NetWare file server using any means possible.
    c. Remove old documents from the SoftSolutions database.
    d. Use dynamic file server attachments to access SoftSolutions data without logging onto all the required servers first.

23. The Command Line field in the Applications window is limited to _____ characters.
    a. 256
    b. 128
    c. 65
    d. 64

24. The SoftSolutions client software that runs under DOS and Windows is fully interchangeable for both NetWare and TCP/IP because it provides this feature:
    a. Multiple Router Support
    b. Stacked Protocol Support
    c. Independent Module Support
    d. Multiple Protocol Support

25. Setting the Document Life field to _____ ensures that it never gets archived or deleted.
    a. 0
    b. 99
    c. −1
    d. 128

26. Even though you can run SoftSolutions on less, Novell recommends that you use a _____ equipped PC with _____ of RAM.
    a. 80386SX, 4 MB
    b. 80386SX, 8 MB
    c. 80486, 4 MB
    d. 80486, 8 MB

27. The _____ window allows you to perform maintenance routines automatically.
    a. Workstation
    b. EZLaunch Options
    c. Task Manager
    d. Applications

28. The _____ Screen Access Group provides full access to all the windows, dialog boxes, and options in SoftSolutions.
    a. SEC
    b. PRIVATE
    c. ADMIN
    d. SYSM

29. The acronym *SQL* means:
    a. Structured Query Language
    b. Stratified Question Lingo
    c. Structured Question Language
    d. Stratified Query Language

30. Which of the following networks have SEM support?
    a. NetWare 3.x
    b. NetWare 4.x
    c. SCO Unix
    d. IBM AIX

31. You can use SoftSolutions on a network as well as a stand-alone PC.
    a. True
    b. False

32. SoftSolutions provides which of the following Document Security Groups as a default?
    a. PUBLIC
    b. PRIVATE

# SoftSolutions 4.x Administration

    c. GUEST

    d. SEMIPRIV

    e. All of the above

33. What are the three files not copied when you install SoftSolutions on a standalone PC?

    a. LAUNCOAM, PREVIOAM, and ENDOAM

    b. OAM1, OAM2, and OAM3

    c. OAMSUPP, OAMEDIT, and OAMLAUNC

    d. OAMLAUNC, OAMPREVI, and OAMEND

34. The three types of applications you can define in SoftSolutions are:

    a. Open, Launch, and System

    b. Open, Print, and System

    c. Open, Print, and Edit

    d. System, EXE, and COM

35. The maximum SoftSolutions password length is _____ characters.

    a. 5

    b. 10

    c. 15

    d. 20

36. The RDS server must be both _____ and _____ compliant to provide full e-mail services.

    a. TAPI, MAPI

    b. Internet, TAPI

    c. MAPI, MIME

    d. VIM, MAPI

37. The server software of SoftSolutions is called:

    a. AOM

    b. SEM

    c. TCP

    d. NFS

38. The advantages of using a Dedicated Indexer include:

    a. Data searching availability

    b. Lower equipment costs

    c. Loss of power synchronization protection

    d. Improved security

**39.** The _____ utility allows you to remove matured (old) documents from the SoftSolutions database.

　**a.** Database Reconstruction

　**b.** Janitor

　**c.** Index Compaction

　**d.** Database Editor

**40.** You access the various windows in SoftSolutions using the _____ command.

　**a.** Setup

　**b.** View

　**c.** Utilities

　**d.** EZLaunch

## Brain Teaser

Ready for some challenging puzzles designed to help you pass the certification exam? The word-search puzzle in Fig. 22-18 will test your knowledge of terms associated with Novell's SoftSolutions. Quite a few of these terms are database-related since you'll be working with a database as you work with SoftSolutions. You'll also find some acronyms, something that Novell is sure to test you on when you take the exam. Completing the puzzle is easy. All you need to do is find each term in the letter grid. Make sure you look forward, backward, diagonally, and vertically since the terms could be hidden in any of those positions. You'll find the solution for this brain teaser in App. C, "Brain Teaser Answers."

　You'll want to spend some time looking these terms up in the glossary, in App. A, or in this chapter after you complete the word-search puzzle. (You'll find any NetWare 4.x terms in Chaps. 14 to 16.) Of course, learning the terms should also provide food for thought. For example, do you really know what ODBC is all about? How well do you know technologies other than the ones you work with on a daily basis? It's questions like these that Novell is going to ask, so you'd better be prepared to provide the answers. You may also want to design your own word-search puzzle of terms. Looking for terms using this kind of puzzle really embeds them in your mind.

## SoftSolutions 4.x Administration

**Figure 22-18**
SoftSolutions Word Search.

```
S E C U R I T Y Z T E N R E T N I E
P O F G A D A R C H I V E D I L A V
O H F J I D K I L D R O W S S A P I
T Z X T D E M H C R A E S D E E P S
K V T E S A T A D P C V L A U O T U
S I B N N O I T A C I L P P A N M L
E E Q Y O W L Q S K A P S M E S E C
D W D R I T Y U S N C R C M U R U X
C E I D T O P A T A S E U T O S D E
O R L F A G T N E I L C H T T J Y Z
M E O K R T L A Z K O O I O Z X R L
P X C C G V A T B D N N M W E R A A
A E O T E U Y B B U A S S M B D R U
C D T I T O P C A J A T E A L S O N
T N O O N G H L P S D R R P Z N P C
I I R L I A M E X C E U V I M V M H
O U P A S C I I N D I C E S B N E M
N T Y X Y G O L O P O T R I G H T S
```

*Term List*

1. APPC
2. Application
3. Archive
4. ASCII
5. Autorun (File)
6. CBT
7. Client
8. Compaction
9. Custom (Install)
10. Database
11. Dataset
12. DBMS
13. DDE
14. Desktop (Document)
15. DLL
16. Documents
17. Dynamic (File Server Attachment)
18. Email
19. Exclusive (Access)
20. EZLaunch
21. Indexer
22. Indices
23. Integrations
24. Internet
25. Janitor
26. LAN
27. MAPI
28. NLM
29. OAM
30. ODBC
31. Password
32. Protocol
33. RAID
34. RDS
35. Reconstruct
36. Rights
37. Security
38. SEM
39. Server
40. SoftSolutions
41. Speedsearch
42. SQL
43. Task (Manager)
44. TCPIP (TCP/IP)
45. Temporary (Attachment)
46. Topology
47. UPS
48. Valid (Input)
49. Viewer (Document)
50. VIM

## Disk Time

Don't forget to spend some time working with the disk that accompanies this book. It provides valuable and fun-to-use teaching aids that help prepare you for the exam. See "Disk Time" in the preface of this book for details about what the disk contains.

# CHAPTER 23

# InForms 4.x Administration and Form Design

# Introduction

This chapter looks at the requirements for the InForms 4.x Administration and Form Design exam. As with the previous chapters, there are five distinct study-oriented sections in this chapter. Each section helps you study for the exam in a different way.

Don't be surprised if this exam is particularly difficult, since Novell only gets one chance to ask you InForms administration- and form design-related questions. Adding to the complexity is the fact that InForms is a form designer that is designed to work with a variety of application programs. The bottom line is that Novell has to assume some fairly generic parameters for the test questions. In other words, don't expect questions that reflect your specific configuration. Unlike the other administration exams in this book, you'll see a broader range of questions on the InForms exam.

You can improve your chances of passing the exam by using two or more of the study methods provided in this chapter. It'll probably help if you study all the sections once and your favorite sections at least twice. Remember to review the study guidelines in Chap. 4 as required to ensure that you maintain the best possible study atmosphere.

The first section of this chapter is a *case study*. You'll perform some hands-on tasks that'll help you learn what you need to know to pass the examination. For example, you can be sure that Novell is going to test your ability to install the product, so that's one of the tasks that we perform in the case study. Even though the case study provides you with screen shots, there's little chance that you'll get anything from it if you don't actually perform the steps. You don't need a network to perform the case study, but it helps. This is a hands-on study area, and you need to treat it as such.

The second area contains *sample Novell questions* for this course. It also includes the correct answers and an explanation of why each answer is correct. Try to answer each question yourself, look at the correct answer, and then determine where you went wrong if you didn't answer correctly.

The next section is a *fun test*. This is an exercise where you'll look at some sample test questions and answer them. The answers ʻ      ar in App. B at the back of the book. This section will help you test ᴠ.ɴat you learned in the previous section. Try to answer the questions without peeking at the answers in the appendix.

The final text section of the chapter is the *brain teaser*. You'll get to have a little fun working on a couple of InForms-related puzzles. In this case, we concentrate on both form design and administration. This chapter provides two cryptograms that should give you some ideas of ways to study for the exam. Obviously, it helps to have a good in-depth knowledge of InForms in this case, since the cryptograms will be easier to solve if you can spot specific patterns in the way they're encrypted. You won't have to know anything more than what you'll normally find in the Novell manuals to solve the cryptograms since that's what you'll be tested on. By the way, the cryptograms use different encryption methods, so you'll have to solve each puzzle separately.

Finally, we'll spend some time using the *Jeopardy!*-type game. This section helps you look at the test from the opposite viewpoint. The game provides you with an answer—you'll need to come up with the corresponding question. The game awards points for correct answers, and takes points away for incorrect answers. You'll receive a score at the end of the game proclaiming that you either did or didn't get your certificate.

By the time you finish this chapter, you should have all the knowledge required to pass the InForms 4.x Administration and Form Design exam. Use all the learning methods that we provide in this chapter to improve your chances of passing the exam. It's a good idea to save the fun test section until you're almost certain that you possess all the required knowledge. Remember, you can probably go through the test only two or three times at most before you'll start to remember the answers without really knowing the material.

**NOTE** *We install InForms 4.x on a Windows 95 machine in the next section. While InForms is fully functional in the Windows 95 environment, Novell doesn't normally recommend that you do this since InForms is a Windows 3.x product. The major problem you'll face is that InForms will be less stable than your other Windows 95-specific applications since it can't make use of the 32-bit features that the operating system provides. Keep this potential problem in mind if you decide to install InForms in a working Windows 95 environment.*

## Case Study

This case study begins by looking at a few InForms administration-related tasks. The first few subsections look at things like getting InForms installed and configuring it to work with your system. Obviously, there isn't any way that we can determine what types of forms you'll need to create or the applications you'll want to work with, so we'll look at some more generic examples.

Getting the product installed is only the first step. We'll also take a look at what you'll need to know to actually create a form, though we'll only hit the highlights in this case study. You'll want to spend some time working with InForms before you take the exam. Make sure you use it with a variety of applications so that you can see everything that InForms is capable of doing.

## Installation

Before we can do anything else, you need to install InForms (if you haven't done so already). Since we're going to spend some time creating forms and working with the administration tools, you may want to create a test setup for the purpose of studying. After all, you wouldn't want to mess up a working installation that your company depends on to get work done on a daily basis.

**NOTE** *To make the installation a little easier and to allow the maximum number of people to participate in this case study, the installation we'll perform won't use GroupWise. You'll want to keep the GroupWise option in mind if you decide to install InForms in a real-world environment and the company uses GroupWise for e-mail delivery*

1. Place the InForms CD in your CD-ROM drive. Windows 95 users won't see a screen automatically since SoftSolutions doesn't provide an AUTORUN file on the CD.
2. Use the *Start Menu | Run* command to display the Windows 95 Run dialog.
3. Click on the Browse button and you'll see a standard File Open dialog.
4. Find the *Setup* file on the CD for your specific language. For example, English-speaking users would look in the *US* folder, while French-speaking users would look in the *FR* folder.
5. Click Open in the File Open dialog, and then OK in the Run dialog. You'll see an InForms for Windows Setup dialog box similar to the one shown in Fig. 23-1.
6. Click Install. You'll see the Install Type dialog box shown in Fig. 23-2. Normally, you'd need to decide what kind of installation to perform. The *Standard* install places the files you would use most often

# InForms 4.x Administration and Form Design

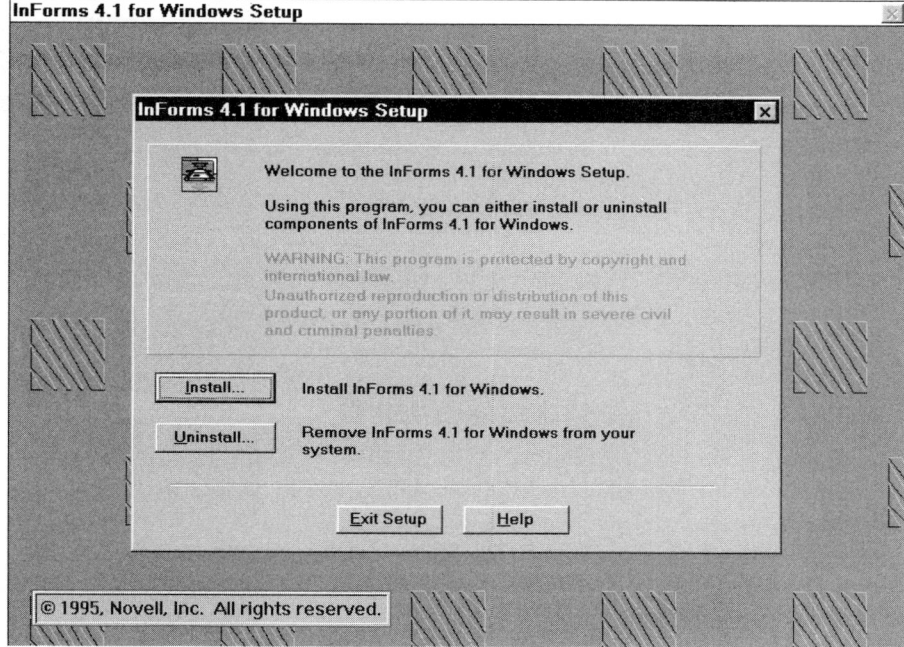

**Figure 23-1**
InForms 4.1 for Windows Setup Dialog Box.

on the local hard drive, while a *Minimum* install places only the files you absolutely have to have on the local hard drive to save disk space. A *Custom* install will allow you to choose which application components you actually want to install. Use the *Network* install if you want to place the program on a network rather than on a local drive. We'll use the custom install to create our test platform since it allows you to see more of the Install program features.

7. Click Custom. You'll see the Custom Installation: InForms dialog box shown in Fig. 23-3. This is where you decide the locations for the various files that the installation program has to copy to the hard drive. This dialog will allow you to select specific components. For example, you don't absolutely have to install the Bitstream True Type fonts that come as part of the Perfect Fit package. You might also decide that you don't want to install the sample forms that come with the main InForms product—especially considering that they consume 3 MB of hard disk space. Since this is a test platform, we'll install everything. This will allow you to check out all of the features that InForms has to offer. Normally, you wouldn't install everything unless you actually needed every feature that InForms provides.

**Figure 23-2**
Installation Type
Dialog Box.

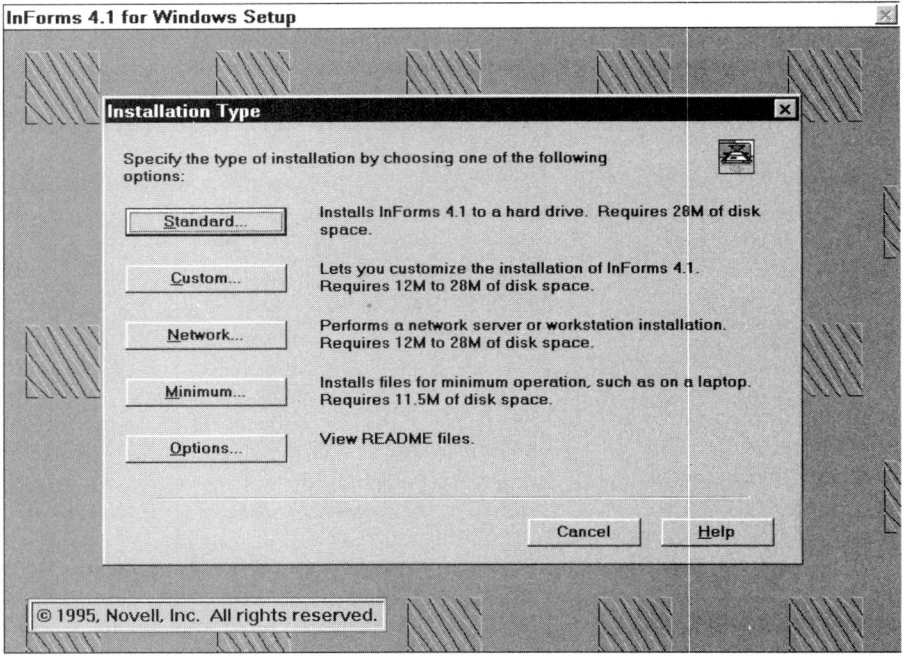

**NOTE** *Our test setup will consume 37.25 MB of hard disk space instead of the 24 MB usually required for a standard installation. Make sure that you have enough hard disk space on your system before you start the installation. If not, you could prune some features, like the sample files, without affecting your ability to study for the exam.*

8. Click Start Installation. You'll see an Install Files dialog box like the one shown in Fig. 23-4. The progress bar will show how much of the Informs product has been copied to your hard drive. Once the install program has placed the required files on your hard disk, it'll display a Set Up Program Manager Group dialog box like the one shown in Fig. 23-5. This is where you decide which program group to use for your InForms programs.

9. Click OK to accept the default setting of InForms. The rest of the case study in this chapter assumes that you chose the default directories and the default Program Manager group (Start Menu folder) for your InForms setup. At this point you'll see the README Files dialog box shown in Fig. 23-6. You can read the files at your leisure later; we'll skip them for right now.

# InForms 4.x Administration and Form Design

**Figure 23-3**
Custom Installation:
InForms Dialog Box.

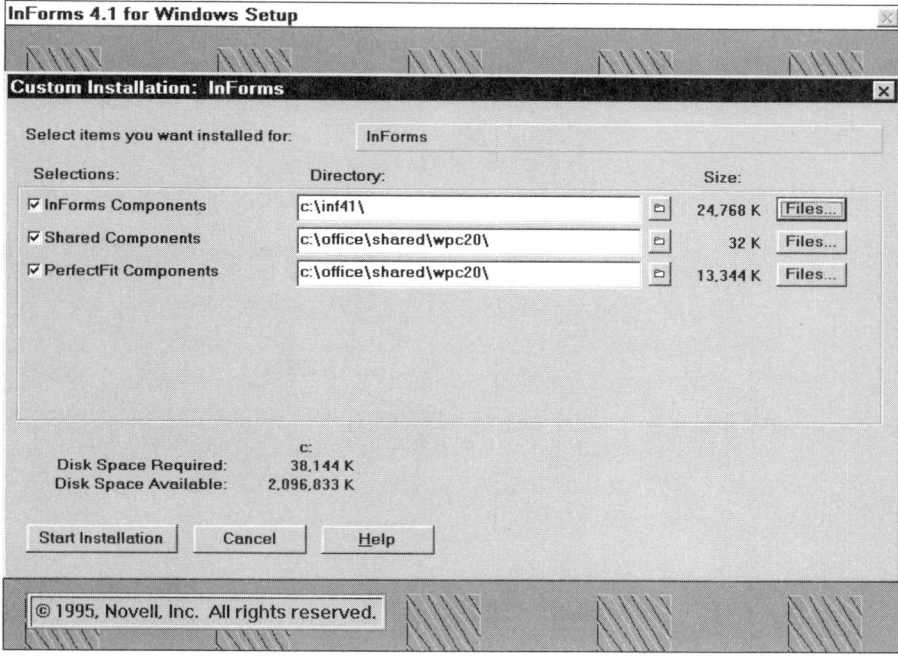

**Figure 23-4**
Install Files Dialog Box.

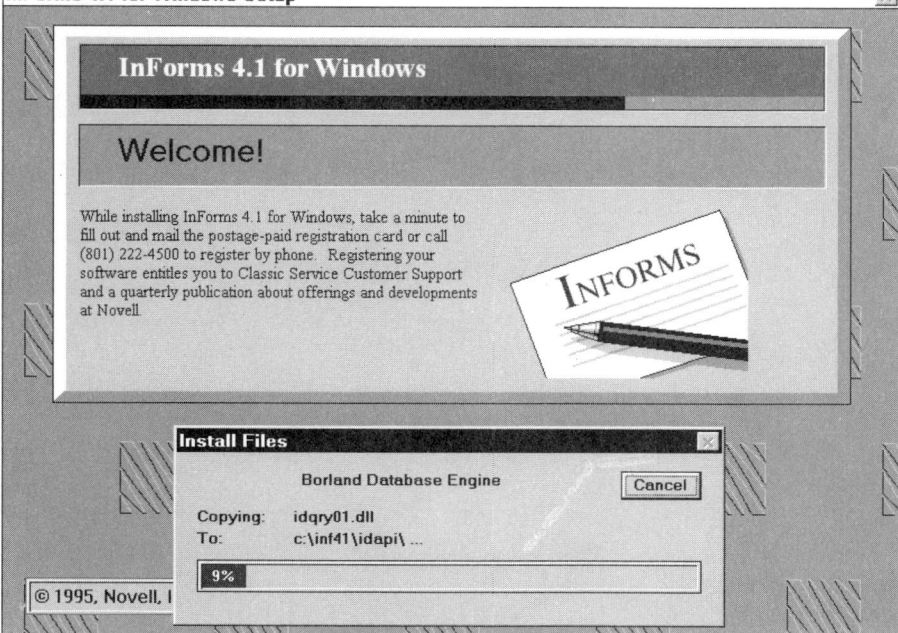

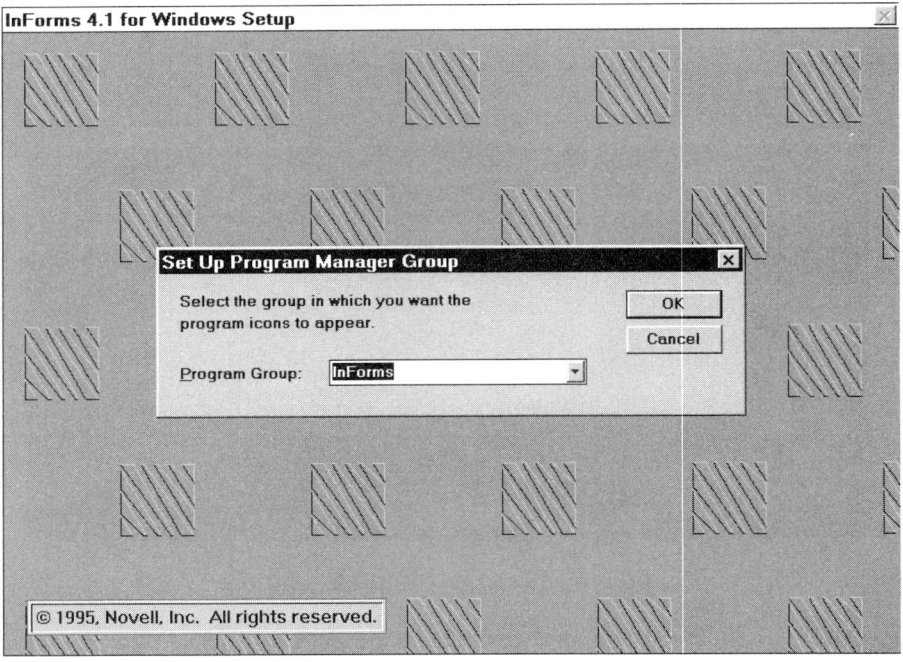

**Figure 23-5**
Set Up Program Manager Group Dialog Box.

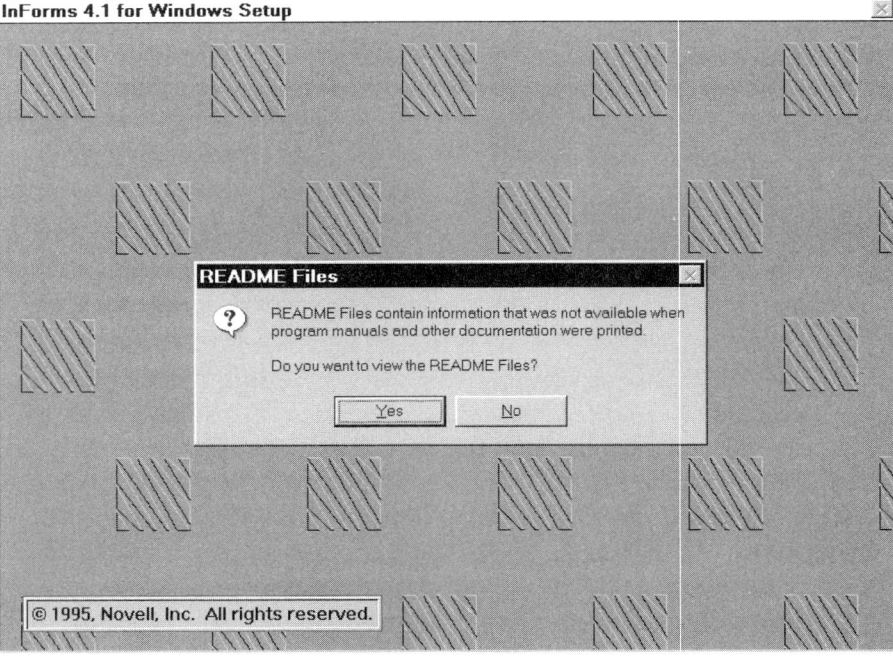

**Figure 23-6**
README Files Dialog Box.

10. Click No. You'll see the success message shown in Fig. 23-7.

11. Click OK. The installation program dialog will disappear. You've successfully installed the test configuration of InForms.

## First Time Configuration

The first time you start InForms after you install it, you'll have to take care of a few configuration details. The following steps cover these configuration items. However, as with most Windows programs, you can customize InForms completely. We won't have time in this chapter to cover every configuration detail—you'll want to take the time to learn about these configuration items after you've completed this case study.

1. Open the *InForms Designer* utility in the InForms folder on the Start menu. You'll see a Serial Number/PIN dialog box like the one shown in Fig. 23-8. This is where you enter the serial number for your copy of InForms (located on the registration card). You probably won't have a PIN; it's OK to leave that field blank.

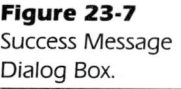

**Figure 23-7**
Success Message Dialog Box.

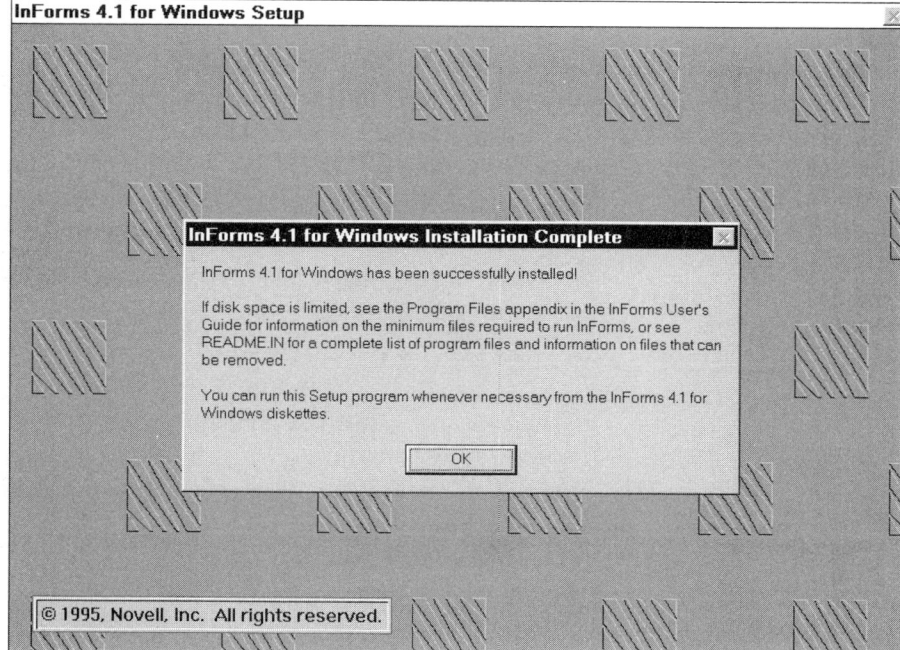

**Figure 23-8**
Serial Number/PIN
Dialog Box.

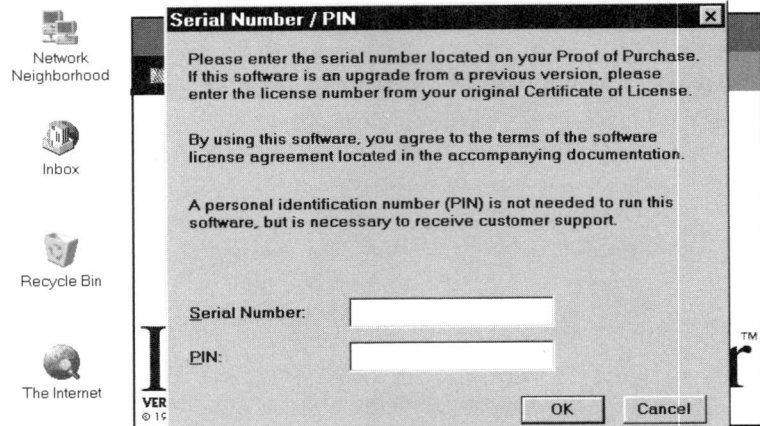

2. Type your InForms serial number in the *Serial Number* field. If this is an upgrade to an older copy of InForms, then use the serial number from the original version.

3. Click OK. You'll see the InForms Designer dialog box shown in Fig. 23-9. Any time InForms detects a new installation, it automatically takes you through the process of performing the essential configuration. If you're a system administrator, you'll want to take care of this step for the users on the network. This means starting InForms up on each machine you install it on (unless you're using a network setup).

4. Click OK. You'll see an InForms Designer dialog box reminding you to restart Microsoft Mail and Windows so that changes to the system configuration can take effect.

5. Click OK to close the dialog. You'll see an InForms Designer dialog box like the one shown in Fig. 23-10. In this case, the program is asking whether you want InForms to use the same mail options as Microsoft Mail.

6. Click Yes. You'll see a Mail Setup is Complete message box.

7. Click OK to clear the dialog. You'll see the InForms Designer window shown in Fig. 23-11. This is where we'll design a form in the next subsection of this case study.

# InForms 4.x Administration and Form Design

**Figure 23-9**
InForms Designer Dialog Box.

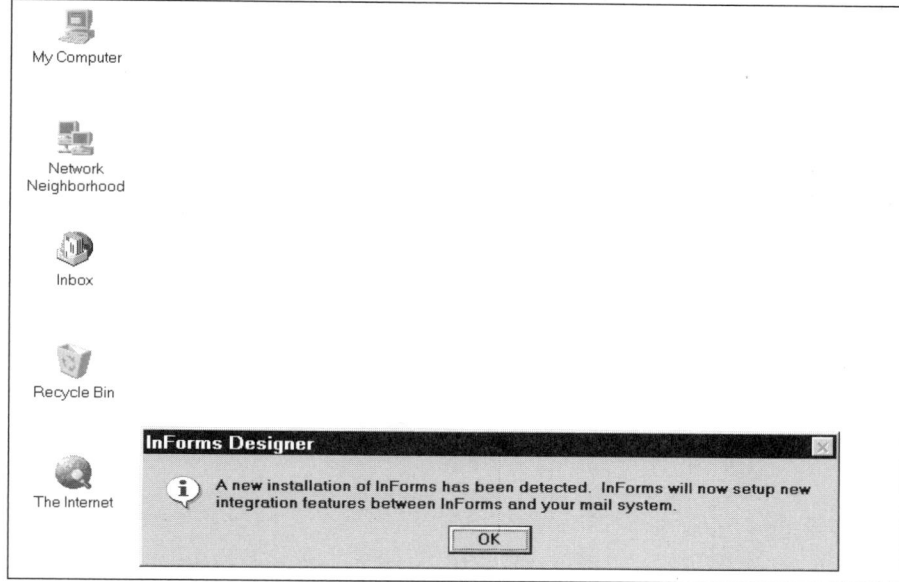

**Figure 23-10**
InForms Designer Dialog Box.

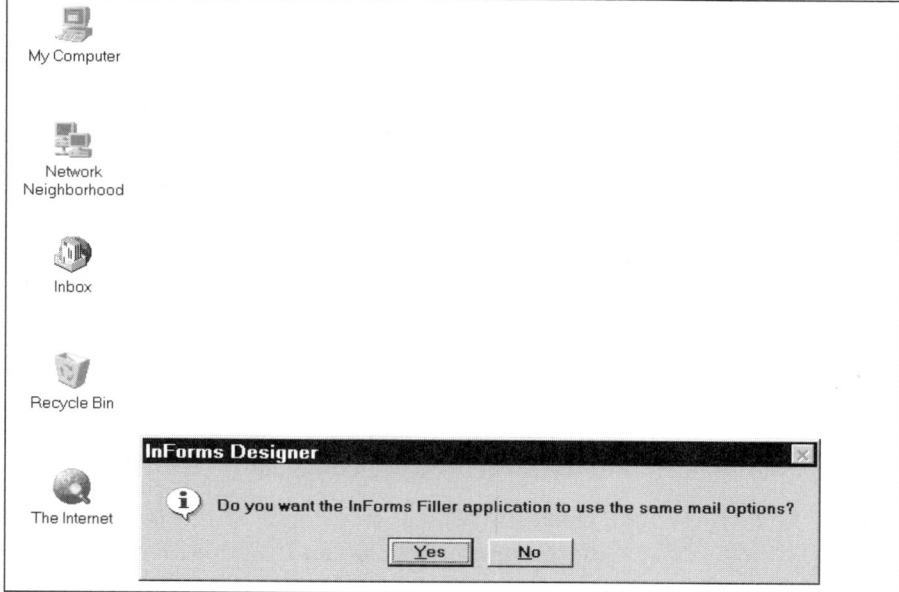

**Figure 23-11**
InForms Designer Window.

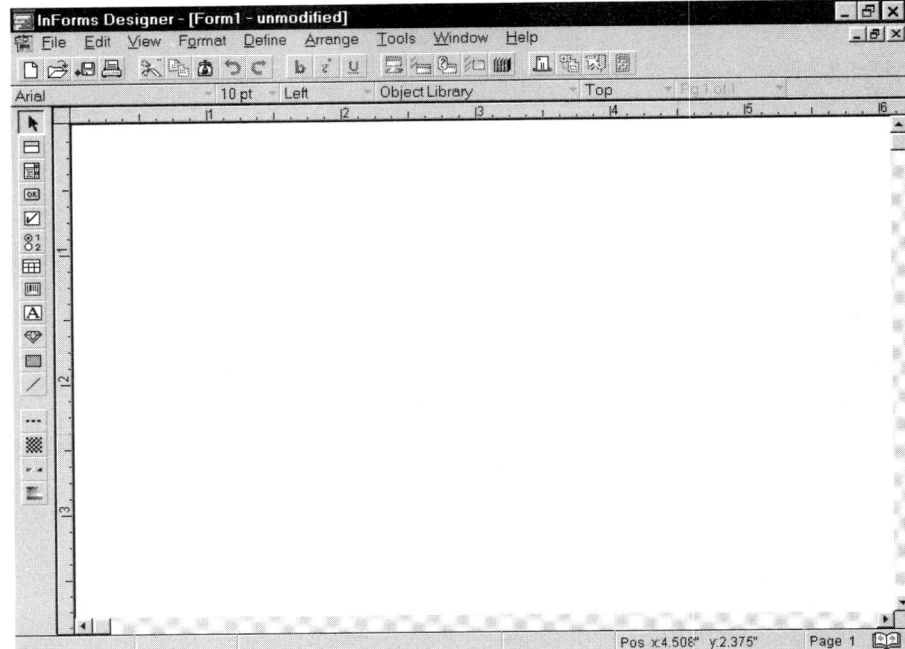

## Designing a Form

Now that you have InForms installed, you're probably anxious to try it out. There are quite a few sample forms you can test—they're all in the InForms folder if you performed a full installation (as we did in the "Installation" subsection of this chapter).

Looking at forms someone else has designed can give you some ideas on what to do and how you want your forms to look. The sample forms will also show you what's possible. However, looking at what someone else has designed and creating your own form are two different matters. This subsection of the case study will give you some first hand experience in designing a form. The form we'll look at is very simple; its only purpose is to give you some much-needed InForms design experience. We'll actually use this form in the next subsection of the case study, so make sure you save the form once you complete it.

1. Open the *InForms Designer* utility found in the InForms folder (if necessary). You'll see an InForms Designer window like the one shown in Fig. 23-11. On the left side of the window is a toolbar, very similar to the ones you've seen in graphics programs like Microsoft

# InForms 4.x Administration and Form Design

Paint. Using InForms Designer is much like using a paint program—with some important differences, most of which we'll cover as the case study progresses. Across the top of the window you'll see a toolbar containing the application tools. For example, this is where you'll find the Save button.

2. Click on the Text Box tool (ninth button on the left side). Draw a text box .5 in from the top and left edges of the form. Make it 2 in long and .25 in high. InForms places a text box of the desired size on the form.

**NOTE** *If you make a mistake positioning or sizing the various controls, like the text box, right-click on the control and choose Position and Size from the context menu. You'll see a Set Object Position & Size dialog, which allows you to change the size and position of the control.*

3. Type *"Type your name and age."* in the text box.
4. Click on the Field tool (second button on the left side). Draw a field 1 in from the top and .5 in from the left edge of the form. Make it 1 in long and .25 in high. When you release the mouse, you'll see a Form Object Name dialog box like the one shown in Fig. 23-12.

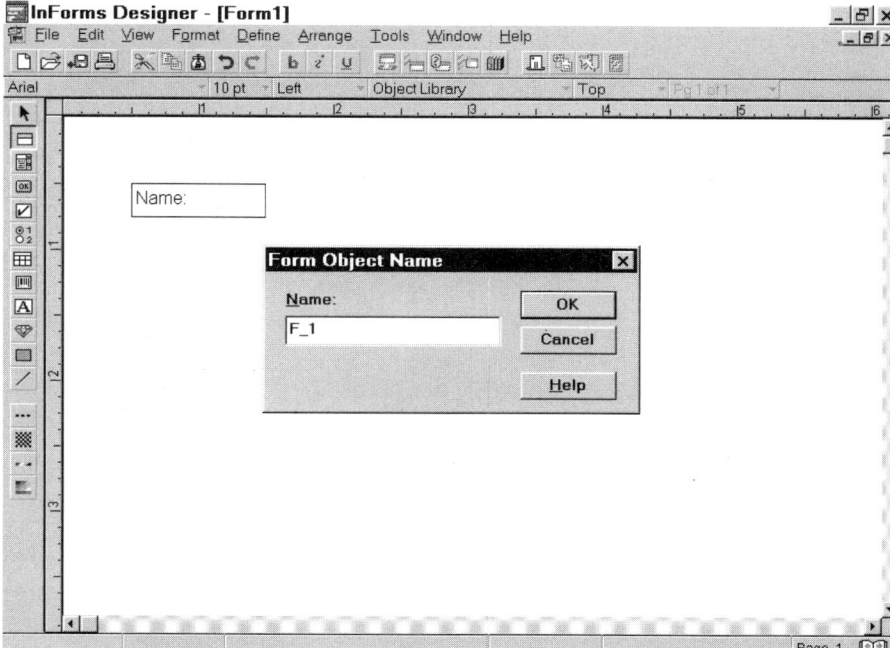

**Figure 23-12**
Form Object Name Dialog Box.

InForms is asking what you want to call the field so that you can process the information it contains later.

5. Type *Name* and click OK. The Form Object Name dialog box will close after it names the field we've just added. Using a field name of Name will make the field easy to identify later.

6. Create an *Age* field using the Field tool, just like we did in Steps 4 and 5. In this case, draw the field 1 in from the top and 1.75 in from the left edge of the form. Since the Age field isn't text, we'll also need to change its definition to make it a numeric field. Assigning the correct type to a field ensures that you can work with it as needed and reduces the chance that the user will enter an incorrect value.

7. Right-click the Age field and choose *Object Definition* from the context menu. You'll see the Entry Field Definition dialog box shown in Fig. 23-13.

8. Change the Data Type field to *Numeric*. Note that the Text group changes to a Numeric group, as shown in Fig. 23-14. Since it's unlikely that anyone will be over 100, set the *Maximum Value* field to 100. You'll also want to set the *Minimum Value* field to 0, since no one can have a negative age.

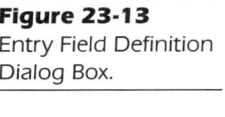

**Figure 23-13**
Entry Field Definition Dialog Box.

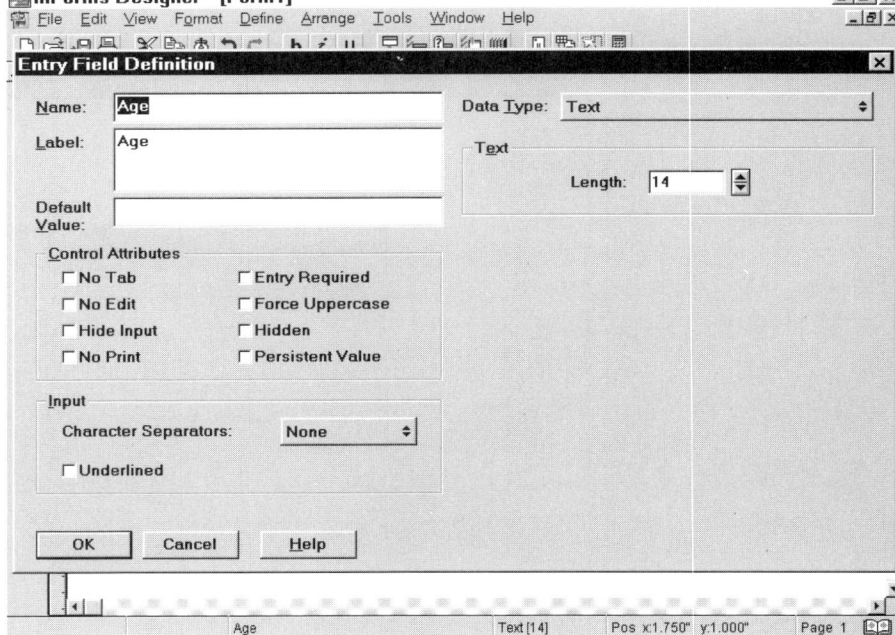

# InForms 4.x Administration and Form Design

**Figure 23-14**
Entry Field Definition Dialog Box Showing Data Type Field Changed to Numeric.

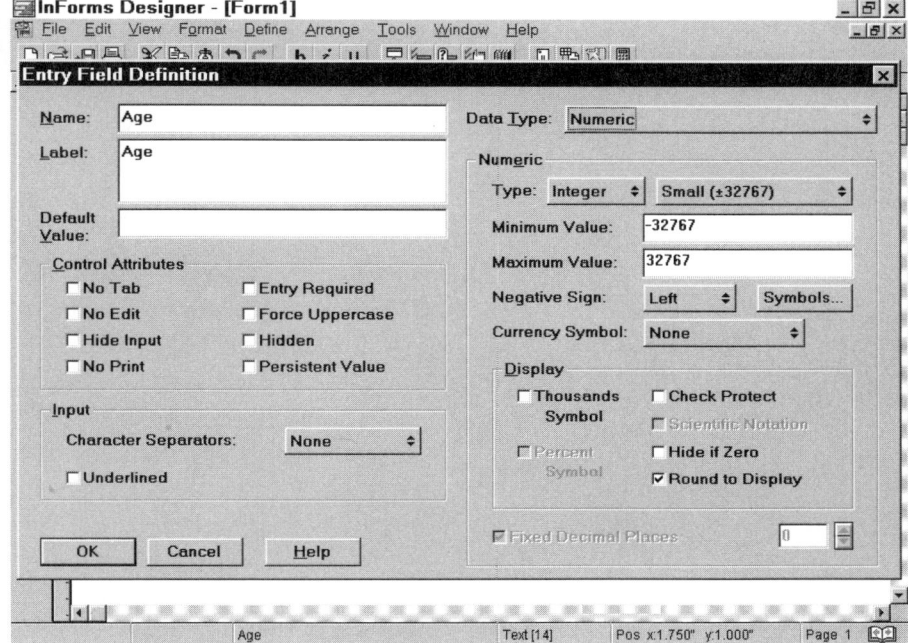

9. Click OK to make the changes permanent. You'll return to the main design window.

10. Click on the Action Button tool (fourth button on the left side). Draw an action button 1.5 in from the top and .5 in from the left edge of the form. Make it 1 in long and .25 in high. When you release the mouse, you'll see a Form Object Name dialog box like the one shown in Fig. 23-12. InForms is asking what you want to call the action button so that you can use it to process information or perform other tasks later.

11. Type *Clear_Form* and click OK. As before, the Form Object Name dialog box will close. Now we need to assign an action to the action button.

12. Right-click on the Clear_Form action button and chose *Formulas* from the context menu. You'll see a Formula Worksheet dialog box like the one shown in Fig. 23-15. This is where you assign a formula (an action) to the various events that the action button supports.

13. Click Create. You'll see a Formula For: window like the one shown in Fig. 23-16.

# 770

**Chapter Twenty-Three**

**Figure 23-15**
Formula Worksheet Dialog Box.

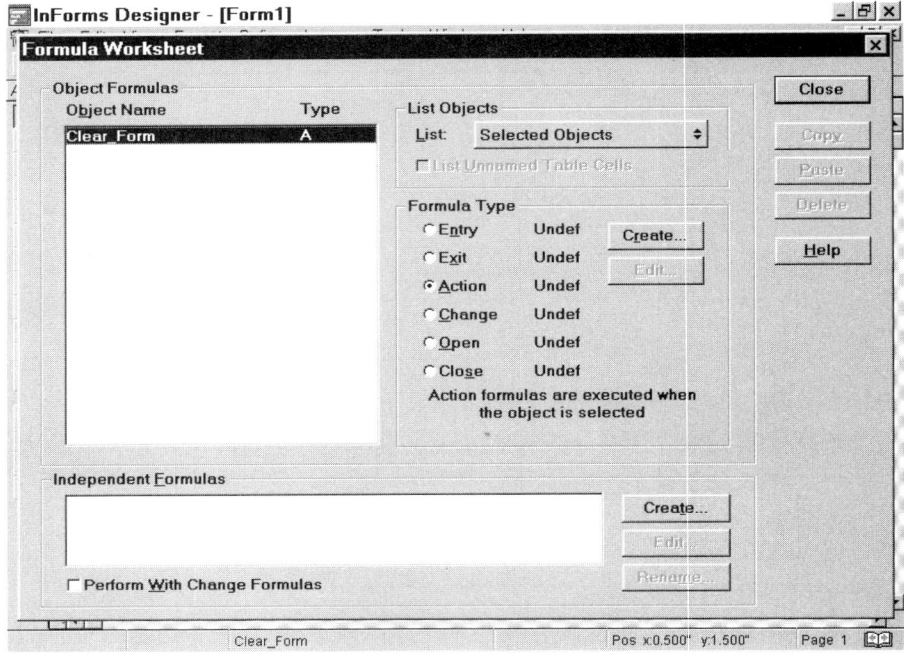

**Figure 23-16**
Formula for: Window.

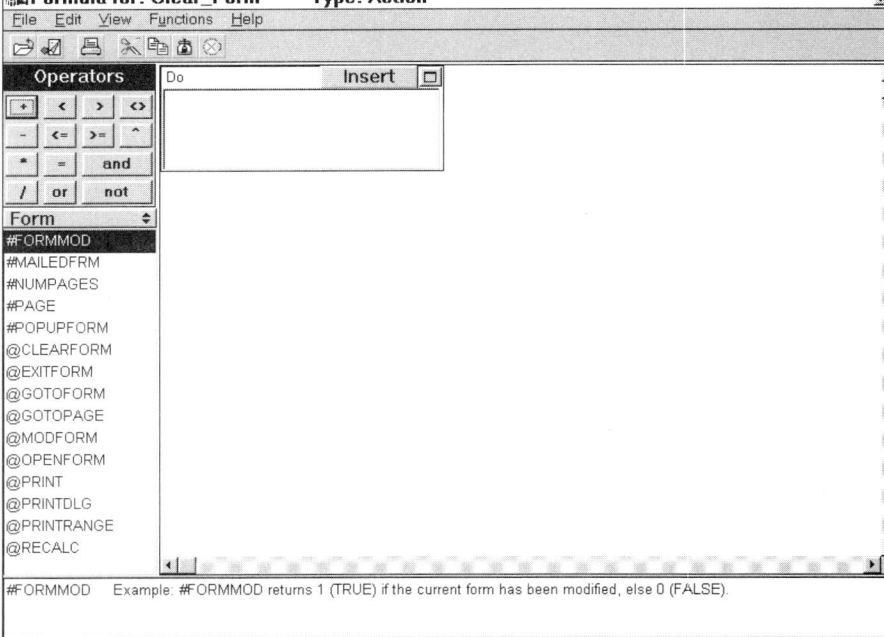

# InForms 4.x Administration and Form Design

14. Choose the *Form* group from the drop-down list box (as shown in Fig. 23-16. Note that there is an entire list of form-related functions you can use, including one to clear the form.
15. Double-click the *@CLEARFORM* function. You'll see it added to the *Do* area of the Formula For: window.
16. Type *TRUE* between the parentheses so that your formula looks like this: @CLEARFORM(TRUE). This clears the form without asking the users if they want to save the form or restore the default values.
17. Click the Save/Close button on the toolbar. The Formula For: window closes and the Formula Worksheet dialog box reappears. Note that there is a *Valid* entry next to the Action entry in the Formula Type group. If you don't see the Valid entry, then the formula you created is incorrect and you should correct it before proceeding.
18. Click Close. You'll return to the main design window.
19. Create another action button. In this case, draw the action button 1.5 in from the top and 1.75 in from the left edge of the form. Name this action button *Check_Age*. Follow Steps 12 and 13 to begin assigning a formula to this action button. However, in this case we'll do something special in the Formula For: window.
20. Choose the *Other* group from the drop-down list box in the Formula For: window. Double-click the *@MESSAGE* function, then type "*Age is equal to or greater than 21.*" between the parentheses.
21. Click the Insert button. Now you should see three boxes. The first box sets a condition. The default condition check is *IF,* but you can also choose *SELECT* (a case statement for those of you who are programmers).
22. Type *Age>=21* in the first box. Type "*Age is less than 21.*" in the Otherwise box. Your Formula For: window should now look like the one shown in Fig. 23-17.
23. Click the Save/Close button on the toolbar, and then click the Close button in the Formula Worksheet dialog. Our sample form is ready to go. Your form should look like the one shown in Fig. 23-18.
24. Click the Save button. You'll see a Save As dialog box (people with SoftSolutions installed will see SoftSolutions start—you'll save your new form in the SoftSolutions database). Save your new form as *Sample1*. Close InForms Designer.

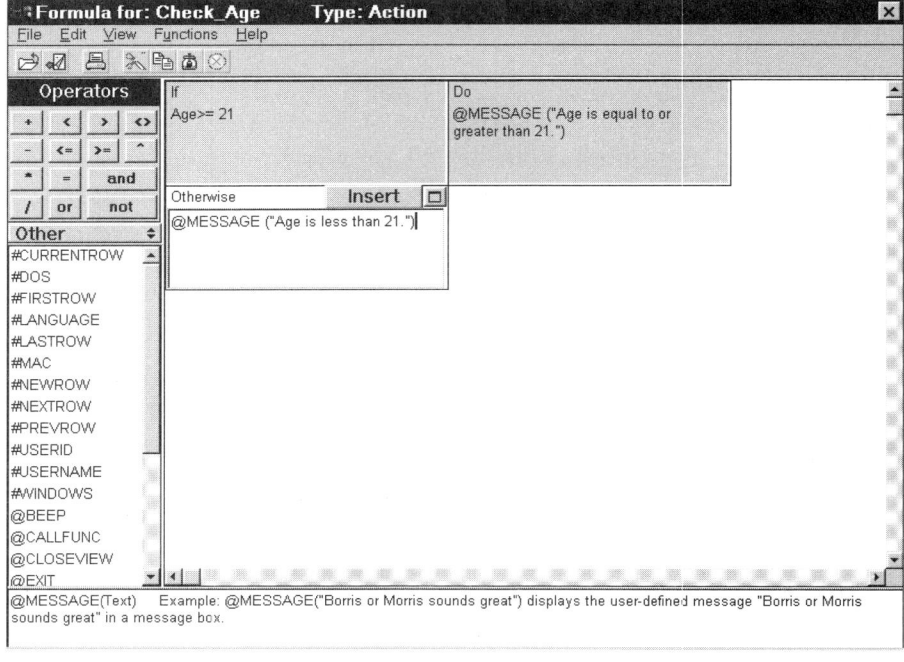

**Figure 23-17**
Formula for: Window after Step 22.

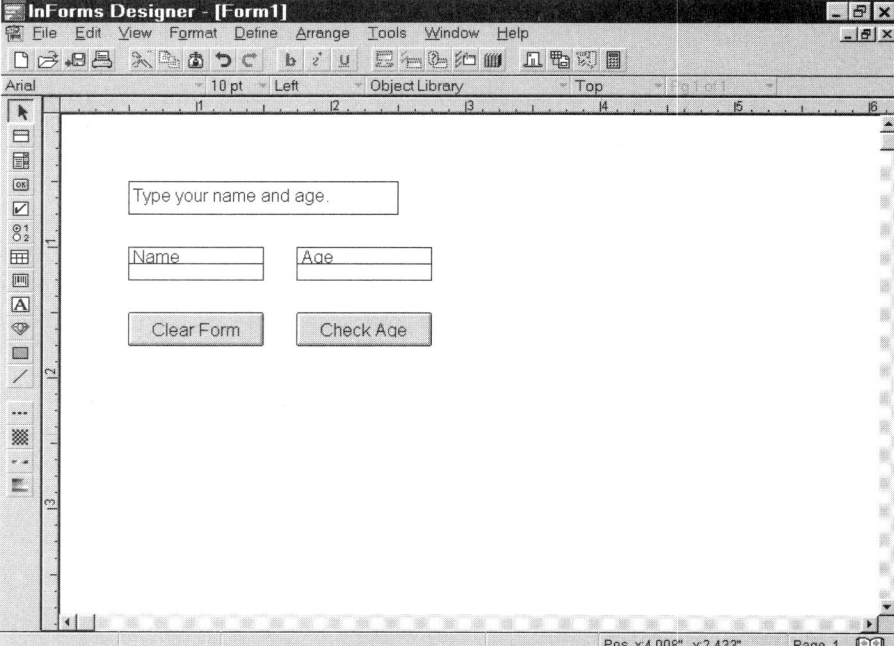

**Figure 23-18**
Display of Completed Sample Form.

# InForms 4.x Administration and Form Design

## Testing a Form

In the previous subsection we created a sample form. Just like in the real world, we have no idea of whether the form will work as intended. This subsection shows you how the user will see your new form. You can also use this process of viewing the form to test its functionality.

1. Open the *InForms Filler* program found in the InForms folder. It should automatically display an Open dialog like the one shown in Fig. 23-19. Note that our sample form from the previous subsection is automatically displayed.
2. Select the *SAMPLE1.WPF* entry, and then click OK to open it. You'll see the sample form we created, as shown in Fig. 21-20. The first thing you should notice is that the data entry fields are too short. You'll need to correct this later.
3. Type your name in the *Name* field and press Enter. The cursor will advance to the *Age* field.
4. Try typing your name in this field as well. Press Enter. InForms Filler will display an Invalid Character message dialog box similar to the one shown in Fig. 23-21.

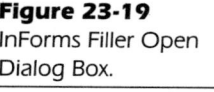

**Figure 23-19**
InForms Filler Open Dialog Box.

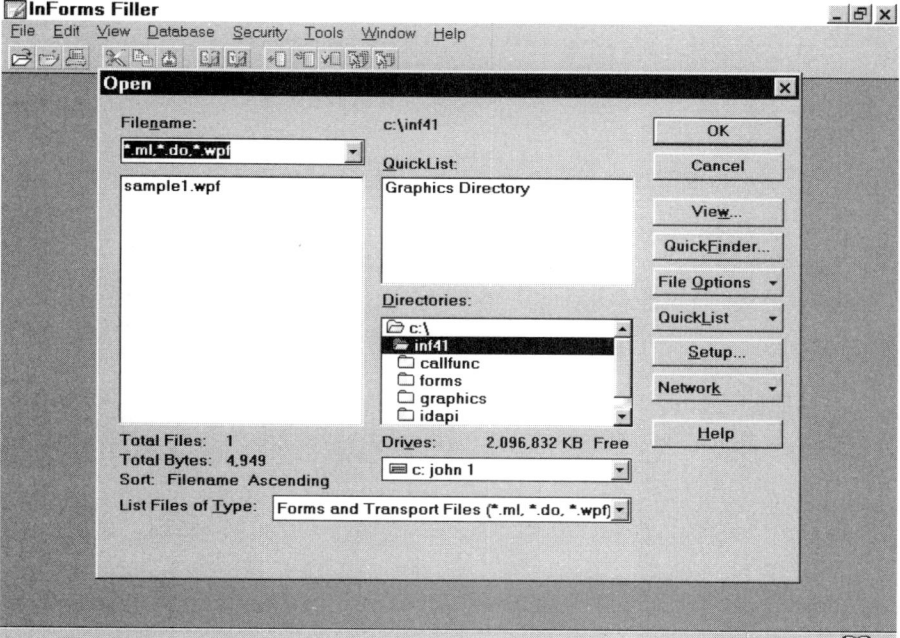

## 774

**Chapter Twenty-Three**

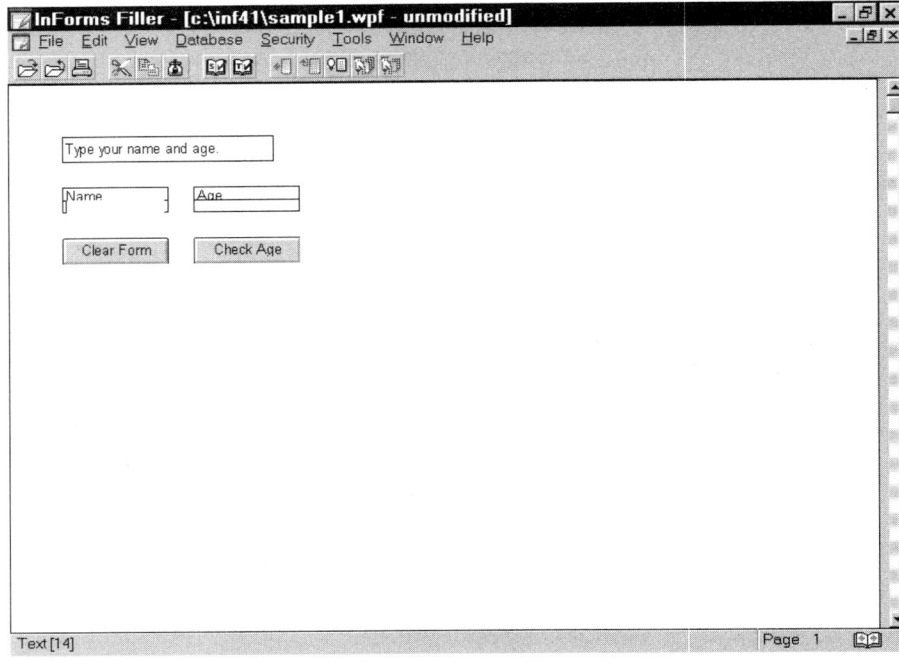

**Figure 23-20**
InForms Filler Window Showing Sample Form.

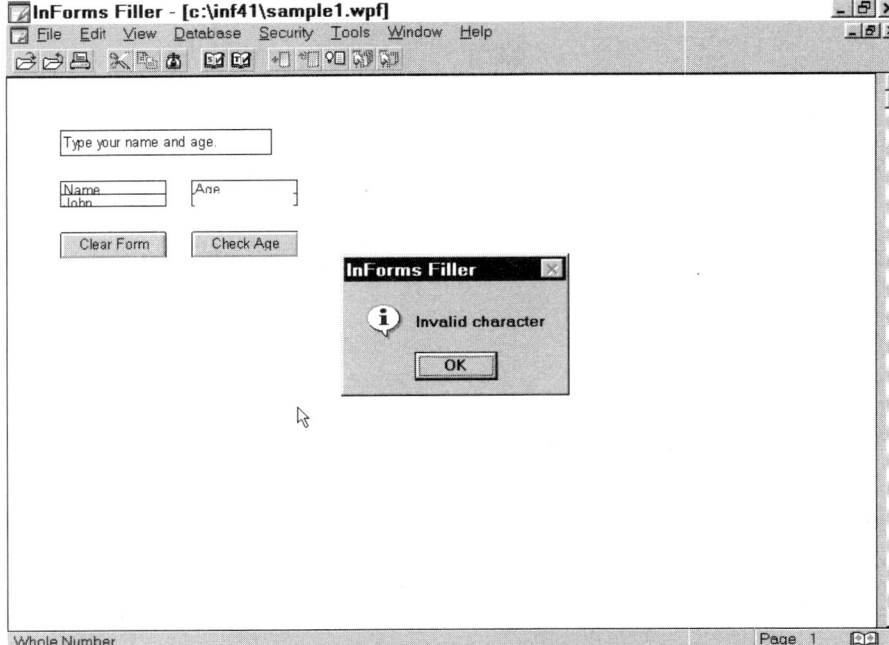

**Figure 23-21**
"Invalid Character" Message.

# InForms 4.x Administration and Form Design

5. Click OK to clear the message box. Type *18* in the Age field, and then click the Check Age button. This time you'll see one of the message boxes we created in the previous subsection (see Fig. 23-22). InForms Filler compared the age we typed with the condition we specified in the Check Age formula. It then displayed the appropriate message.

6. Click OK to clear the message box. Type *21* in the Age field, and then click the Check Age button. We get a different message this time because the Age field matches the criteria we set for it (see Fig. 23-23).

7. Click OK to clear the message box. Click the Clear Form button. The entire form is cleared so that we can start over again.

The form seems to work as intended. We can check the users' age and also allow them to clear the form as needed. The only thing we need to do is fix the problem with the field spacing (which we'll leave as an exercise for the reader).

## Assigning Security

At this point you've seen how to create a basic form. However, a form isn't much good if anyone can fill it out and make changes to it at will. Just

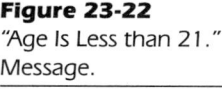

**Figure 23-22**
*"Age Is Less than 21."* Message.

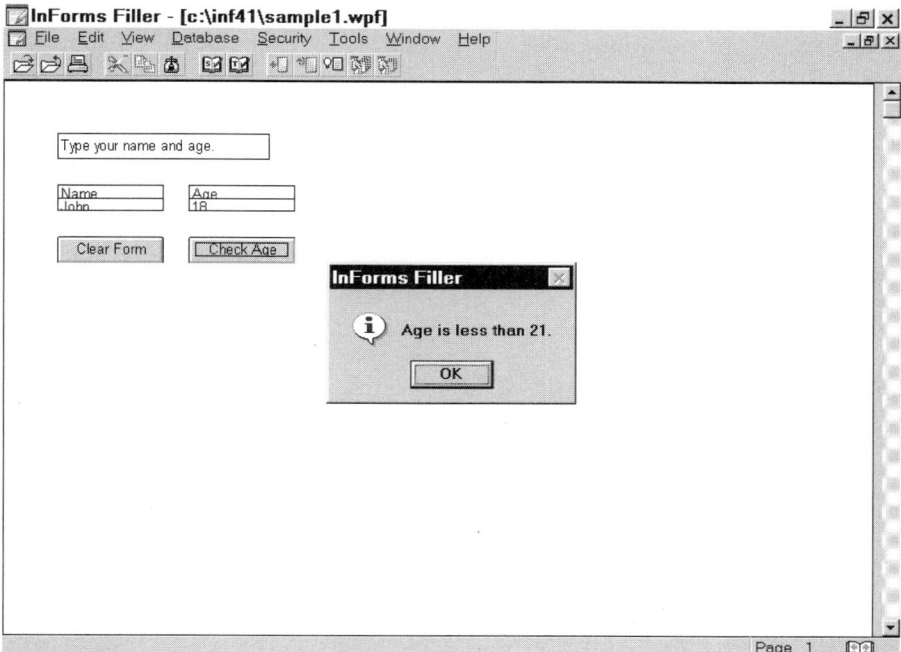

**Figure 23-23**
"Age Is Equal to or Greater than 21." Message.

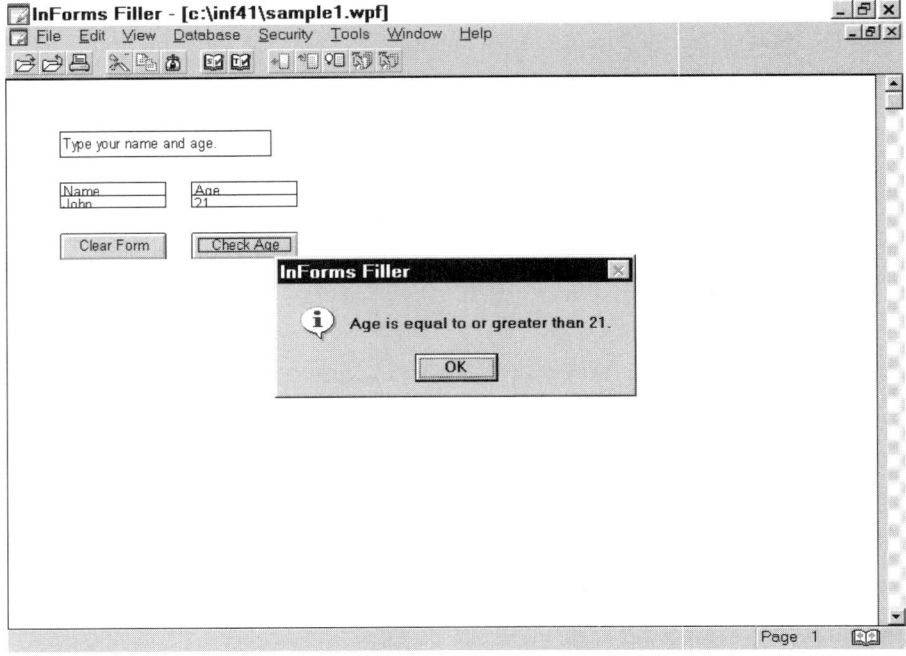

think of the chaos there would be if someone could come along and change a pay-raise form right before it went to personnel. InForms does provide some security mechanisms that allow you to digitally sign a form. This makes it easy to detect any attempt to change the form. We'll look at a simple way to add a signature field to our sample form in this subsection.

**NOTE** *This subsection of the chapter assumes that you created the sample form in the previous section. However, the information applies to any form you might create with InForms. If you decided not to create the sample form in the previous section, simply substitute a form that you've created. We will need to add a signature field to the form, so make sure you use a copy and not the original.*

1. Open the *InForms Security* utility found in the InForms folder.
2. Create a new security database using the *File | New* command. You'll see a Create New Security Database dialog box like the one shown in Fig. 23-24.
3. Type *SAMPLE1* in the *Filename* field, and then click Save to create the new database. You'll see an Administrator Information dialog box like the one shown in Fig. 23-25.

# InForms 4.x Administration and Form Design

**Figure 23-24**
Create New Security Database Dialog Box.

**Figure 23-25**
Administrator Information Dialog Box.

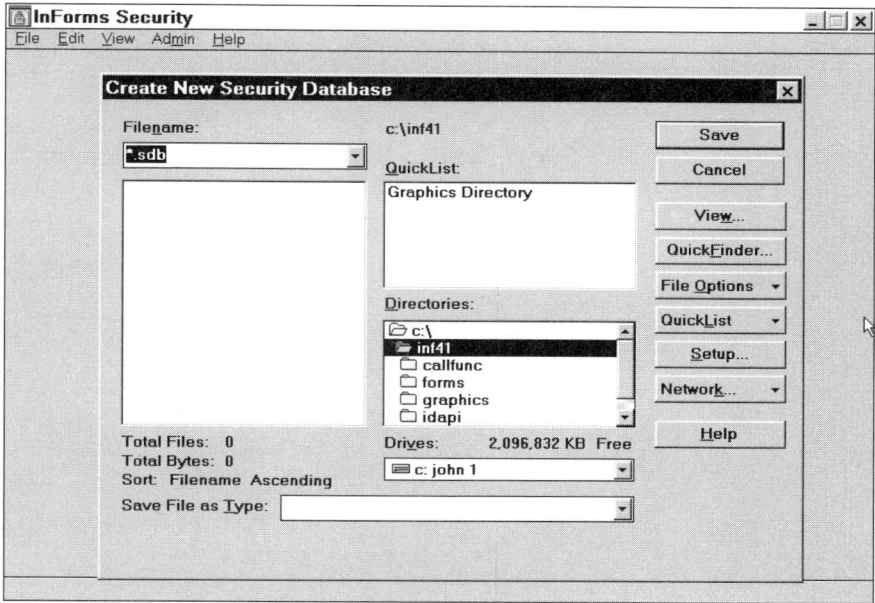

4. Type your name and a password. Make sure you choose a password you can remember since InForms Security will ask for it each time you need to change the security database contents. You'll also need to include a mail address and telephone number, even if they aren't real.

5. Click OK to complete the Administrator Information dialog. InForms will ask you to verify your password.

6. Type the password again, then click OK. You should see a window like the one shown in Fig. 23-26. The first thing we'll need to do is add a user.

7. Type *John* in the *User Name* field. Type *A100* in the *User ID* field. Now we need to add a Department for John to belong to.

8. Click the Department button. You'll see a Departments dialog box like the one shown in Fig. 23-27.

9. Type *Publications* in the *Department Name* field, and then click Add. InForms Security will add the new department to the list of departments stored in the database.

10. Click Close to close the Departments dialog. Choose *Publications* in the Department drop-down list box for user John. Now we need to add a group for John to belong to.

**Figure 23-26**
InForms Security Window.

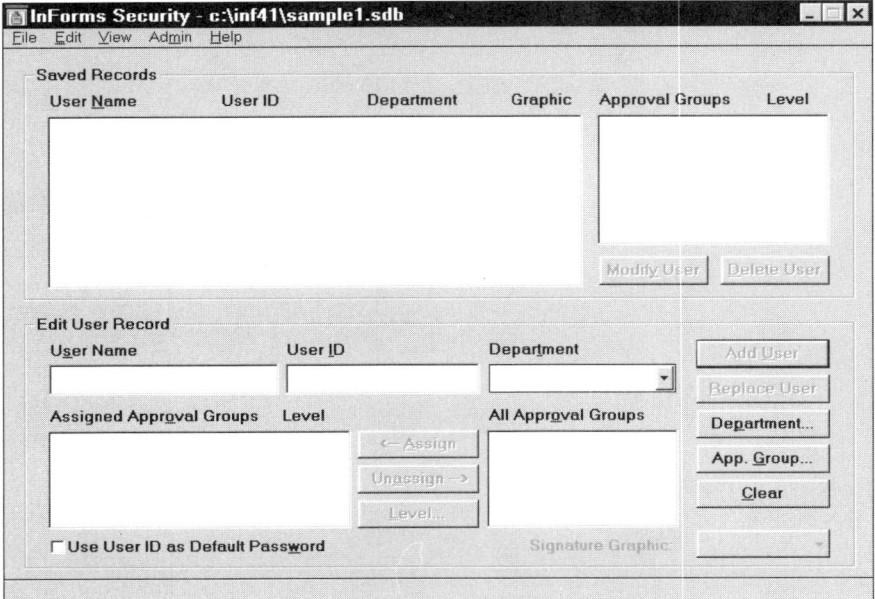

**Figure 23-27**
Departments Dialog Box.

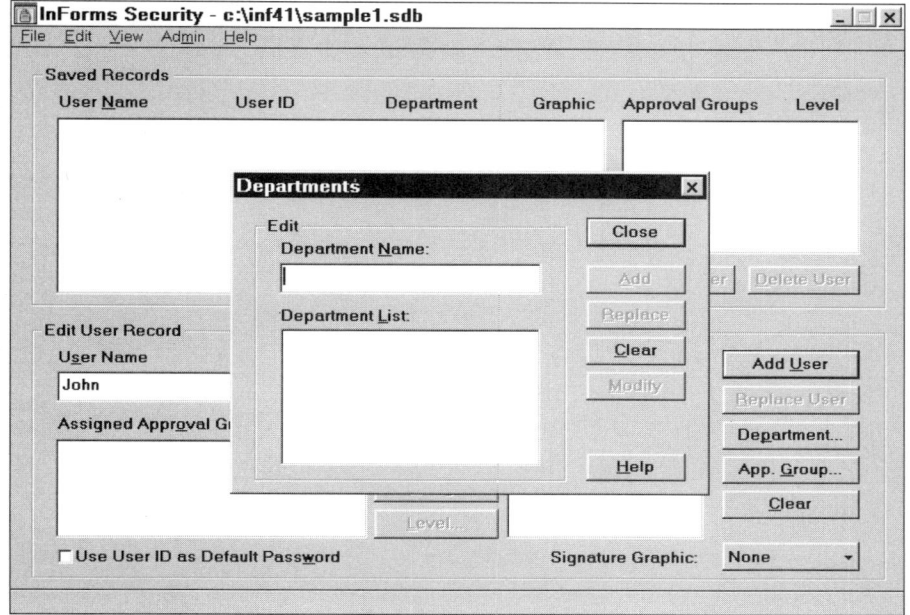

11. Click the Add Group button. You'll see the Approval Groups dialog box shown in Fig. 23-28.

12. Type *Managers* in the *Approval Group Name* field, and then click Add. InForms Security will add the new group to the list of groups stored in the database.

13. Click Close to close the Approval Groups dialog. You should see Managers in the *All Approval Groups* list near the bottom of the window.

14. Highlight the *Managers* group, and then click Assign to assign user John to this group. Note that InForms automatically assigns user John a security level of 1—you can change this setting by clicking the Level button. Your entry should look like the one shown in Fig. 23-29.

15. Click Add User to add user John to the list of people who can sign forms. You'll see an InForms Security dialog.

16. Type a password for user John. Make sure you use something other than your administrator password. InForms Security will ask you to verify the password for user John, then add John to the list of people who can sign forms. You now have everything needed to add security to the sample form we created in the previous subsection.

**Figure 23-28**
Approval Groups Dialog Box.

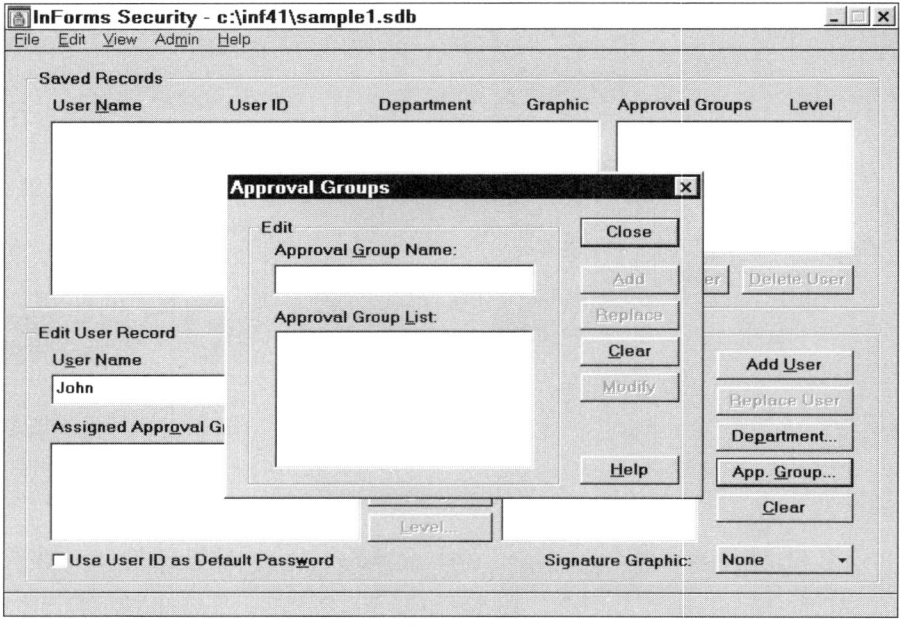

**Figure 23-29**
Assigning User John to Managers Group.

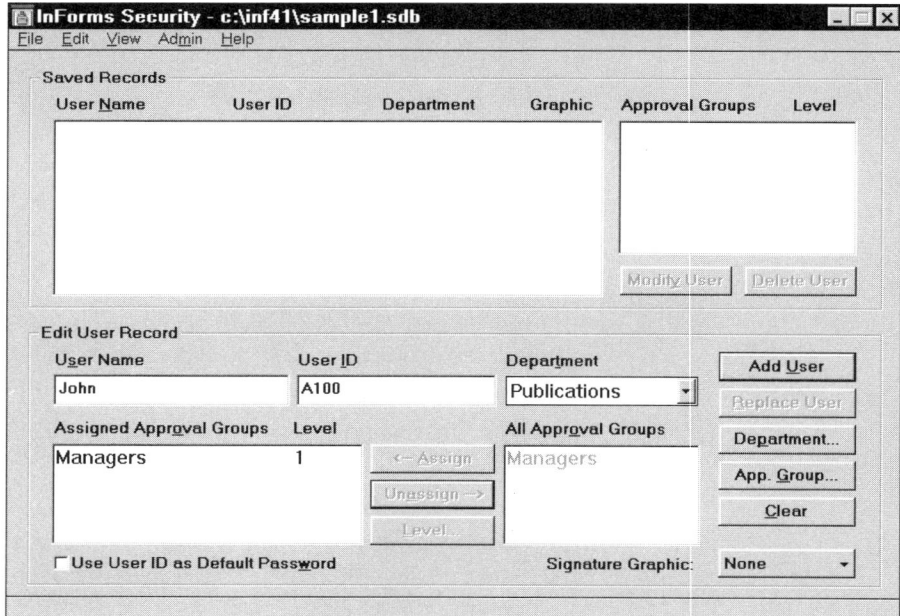

# InForms 4.x Administration and Form Design

17. Close the InForms Security utility. Open the InForms Designer utility, and then open our sample form from the previous subsection of this chapter. (You can substitute your own form if you so desire.)

18. Add a *Signature* field next to the Age field that we created previously. The example placed the field 3 in from the left side of the form and 1 in from the top. The field is 1 in long by .5 in high (which corrects the problem noted in the previous subsection of this chapter).

19. Right-click the Signature field and choose *Object Definition* from the context menu. You'll see the Entry Field Definition dialog box shown in Fig. 23-30. The first thing we need to do is change the data type of this field so that it can accept signatures.

20. Choose *Signature* in the *Data Type* field of the Entry Field Definition dialog. Note that InForms provides two methods for you to select which fields get protected by the Signature field. You can either check the *Protect Entire Form* checkbox, or choose individual fields in the *All Objects* list box (placing them in the Protected Objects list gives them the required protection).

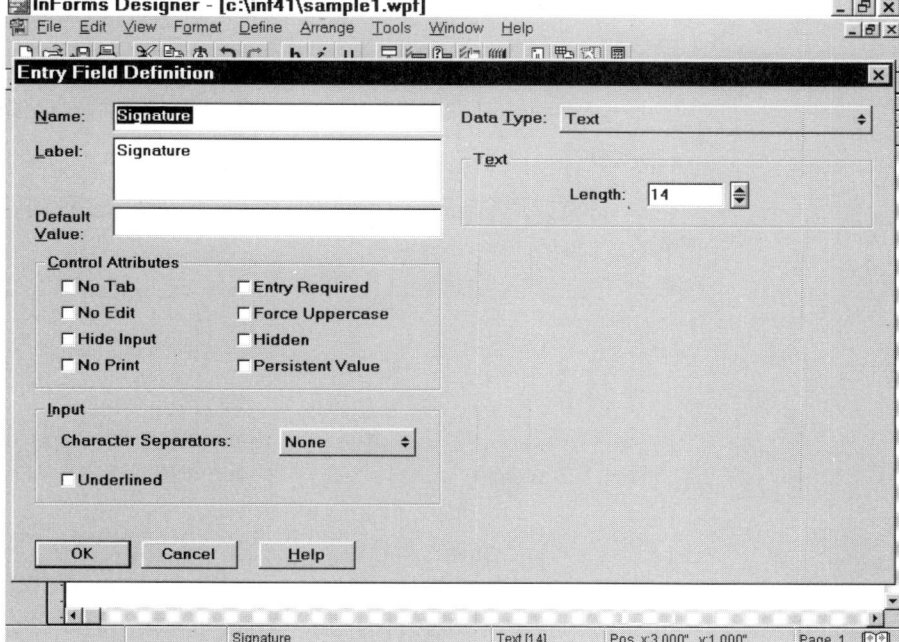

**Figure 23-30**
Entry Field Definition Dialog Box.

21. Check the Protect Entire Form checkbox. Now we need to assign some approval groups to the Signature field so that InForms knows who can sign the form.
22. Click Assign Approval Groups. You'll see the Assign Approval Groups dialog box shown in Fig. 23-31. Note that there aren't any groups available—we need to tell InForms which security database to use.
23. Click on Retrieve. You'll see an Open Database File dialog box.
24. Double-click on SAMPLE1.SDB. Now the All Approval Groups list in the Assign Approval Groups dialog contains the Managers group we created previously.
25. Highlight *Managers,* then click on Assign. Click on OK to make the assignment permanent. We've just created a Signature field for protecting the form. Note that InForms Designer places <Assigned> next to the Assign Approval Groups button in the Entry Field Definition dialog.
26. Close the Entry Field Definition dialog by clicking OK. Save the form, and then exit InForms Designer.
27. Open the *SAMPLE1* form in InForms Filler.

**Figure 23-31**
Assign Approval Groups Dialog Box.

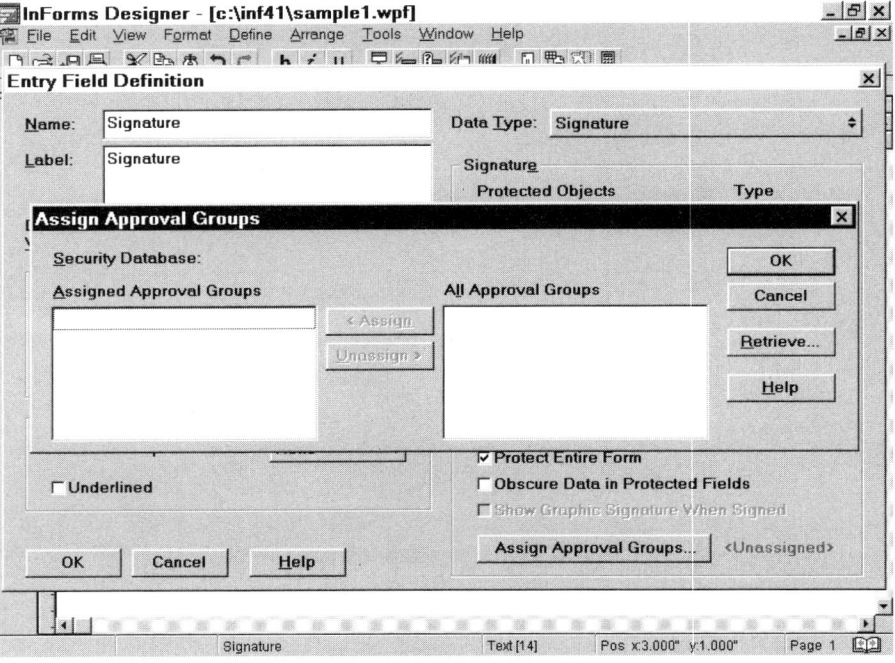

**Figure 23-32**
Register User ID Dialog Box.

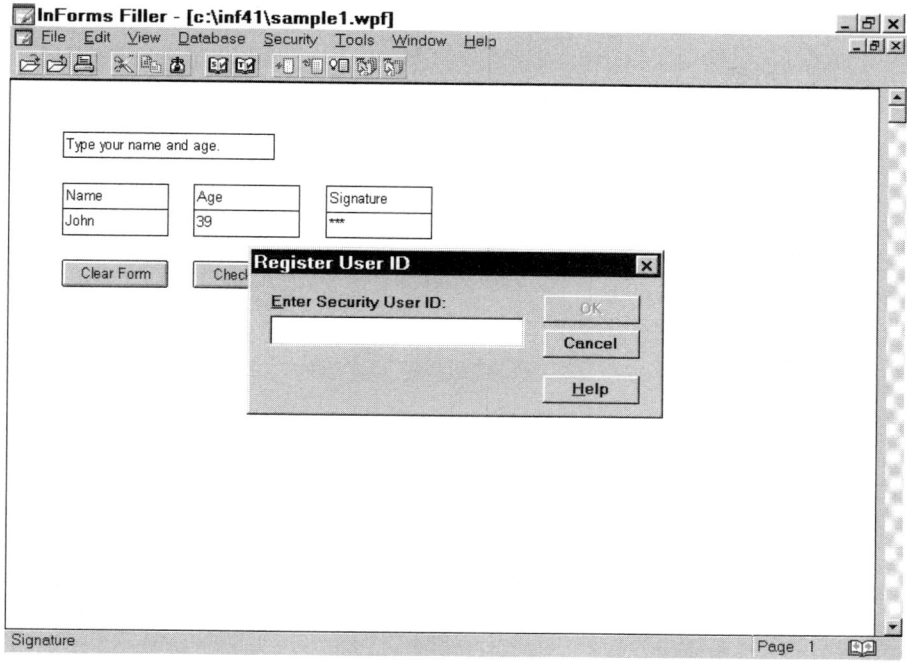

28. Type your name and age in the appropriate fields. Type your password in the Signature field, and then press Enter. You'll see the Register User ID dialog box shown in Fig. 23-32.
29. Type *A100* and press Enter. InForms will sign John to the Signature field.
30. Try changing the contents of either the Name or Age fields. InForms refuses to let you change any of the information once the form is signed.
31. Close InForms Filler.

## Study Questions

1. InForms requires _____ of memory and _____ of hard disk space for installation.
   a. 4 MB, 8 MB
   b. 8 MB, 12 MB

c. 8 MB, 16 MB

d. 4 MB, 24 MB

*d.* You must have a minimum of 4 MB of RAM to run InForms, though Novell recommends more for optimal performance. You'll also need a minimum of 24 MB of hard disk space. Obviously, you'll also need enough space to store forms, so 24 MB is a guideline for the application alone.

2. There are _____ levels of security that you can assign to an InForms form.

   a. 10
   b. 25
   c. 64
   d. 99

   *d.* You can assign any level between 1 and 99 to a particular user. Level 1 is the lowest level of security, while 99 is the highest.

3. InForms supports which of the following field types?

   a. Text
   b. Memo
   c. Integer
   d. Real
   e. Custom Data Format

   *a, b, and e.* InForms supports all three of these field types, along with numeric, date/time, autoincrement, and signature.

4. The _____ function allows the user to edit the contents of a field.

   a. @EDIT
   b. @ALLOWEDIT
   c. #EDIT
   d. #ALLOWEDIT

   *b.* You'd use the @ALLOWEDIT function to allow a user to edit a field. The @ALLOWEDIT function also needs the name of the field you want to allow the user to edit. Use the @NOEDIT function if you want to stop a user from editing a field.

5. A drop-down list box doesn't support all of the data types that a field does.

   a. True
   b. False

# InForms 4.x Administration and Form Design

    *a.* The drop-down list box only supports the text, numeric, date/time, and custom data format data types.

6. InForms allows you to rotate text in one of _____ directions.
   a. 2.
   b. 3.
   c. 4.
   d. You can't rotate the text.

    *c.* InForms allows you to rotate the text so that it aligns with the top, right, left, or bottom of the text box. This means that you can display text upside down if you want to. The right and left options are convenient ways to display longer text in little vertical space.

7. Files in the object library use this extension:
   a. SDB
   b. WPF
   c. WPG
   d. OLB

    *d.* The object library holds objects that you've created in a project, then placed there so that you can use the same object in other projects. Using an object more than once lends consistency to your forms and reduces the amount of time required to create them. One library (OLB file) can contain more than one object.

8. InForms supports which of the following database types?
   a. ODBC
   b. NetWare Directory Services
   c. Clipper
   d. Lotus Notes
   e. All of the above

    *e.* InForms supports all of these database types directly. It also includes support for Borland Database Engine (BDE), ASCII, Secondary Merge, BTrieve, DataPerfect, and FoxPro.

9. InForms Filler allows you to change the contents of _____ fields, but not _____ fields after you sign a form.
   a. Nonsecure, secure
   b. Protected, unprotected
   c. Unprotected, protected
   d. Text, signature

*c.* You can still change the contents of an unprotected field after the form is signed, InForms Filler won't allow you to change the contents of the protected fields.

10. The _____ file starts the InForms Filler utility.
    a. FFWIN41.EXE
    b. FFWIN.EXE
    c. FDWIN41.EXE
    d. FDWIN.EXE

    *b.* Use the FFWIN.EXE program to start the InForms Filler. The main InForms program file is FFWIN41.EXE—it gets started by FFWIN.EXE.

11. The acronym *IDAPI* stands for:
    a. Internet Data Access Programming Interface
    b. Intelligent Database Application Programming Interface
    c. Internet Database Application Processing Interconnect
    d. Integrated Database Application Programming Interface

    *d.* The Integrated Database Application Programming Interface is Borland's form of ODBC. You'll use it when you use the Borland Database Engine (BDE) to access dBASE and Paradox database files.

12. InForms supports forms with both a portrait and a landscape orientation.
    a. True
    b. False

    *a.* You can create forms with a portrait or a landscape orientation. The Format | Form Layout command changes the layout of the current form. If you want to change the layout of all future forms, use the Edit | Preferences command.

13. A database is composed of:
    a. Fields
    b. Records
    c. Tables
    d. Indexes
    e. None of the above

    *a, b, c, and d.* The information in a database is stored in *tables*. You view the information the tables contain in sorted order by creating an *index*—the index is ordered, the table is not. *Records* contain one complete occurrence of information in a table. For example, one customer's information in a name and address table would be a record. *Fields* are individual values within the record. For example, the customer's first name would be in one field, while the last name would be in another.

14. You need to use the _____ field type to associate a form with a security database.
    a. Security
    b. Custom Data Format
    c. Signature
    d. Text

    *c.* InForms uses a special signature field to associate a form with a security database. Of course, you must assign specific groups from the database to the field before it becomes active.

15. Which key do you need to use to place a tab character in a text object?
    a. Ctrl-Tab
    b. Alt-Tab
    c. Shift-Tab
    d. Tab

    *a.* Use the Ctrl-Tab key combination to place a tab character in a text object associated with a form object or text box.

16. The @SENDMAIL function will allow you to send mail to another person using which of the following constants?
    a. #MAIL
    b. #ROUTED
    c. #TASK
    d. #BROADCAST
    e. All of the above

    *b and d.* Use the *#ROUTED* constant if you want to send the message to a group sequentially. This option is only supported by GroupWise 4.x and WordPerfect Office 4.x and above. The *#BROADCAST* constant allows you to send the message to everyone at once. You'd normally use it with other kinds of mail systems, like Microsoft Mail.

17. InForms supports which of the following mail systems?
    a. GroupWise
    b. WordPerfect Office 4.x
    c. Microsoft Mail 3.0 or above
    d. MAPI-compliant mail systems.
    e. All of the above

    *e.* InForms supports all of these mail systems. You can also use it with WordPerfect Mail for Windows 3.x, Lotus cc:Mail 1.1 or later, Windows for Workgroups, and VIM-compliant mail systems.

18. A user with Read Only access to a database can:
    a. Modify records
    b. View records
    c. Perform queries
    d. Delete records

    *b and c.* A user with Read Only access can view the database and organize the information it contains into a more usable format, but can't change the information the database contains in any way. The user would also require Write access to actually change the database contents.

19. The acronym *QBE* stands for:
    a. Quick Bitmap Extraction
    b. Query Before Extinction
    c. Quiet Binary Exchange
    d. Query by Example

    *d.* Query By Example (QBE) is a method used to make it easier to create database queries. Normally, the QBE engine provides a graphic interface for the user. The user's selections are translated into SQL statements, which, in turn, extract information from the database.

20. If you want to find a database record that contains nothing (a blank or other nonexistent value) in a particular field, you would search for a _____ value.
    a. NULL.
    b. NIL.
    c. Wild Card.
    d. It can't be done.

# InForms 4.x Administration and Form Design

    *a.* Searching for a NULL value means that you want to find a record that contains nothing in a particular field.

21. You use the _____ command to remove the signature from a form so that you can modify its contents.
    
    **a.** Security | Unsign Signature Field
    
    **b.** Security | Sign Signature Field
    
    **c.** Security | Register User ID
    
    **d.** Security | Authenticate

    *a.* The Security | Unsign Signature Field command allows you to remove the signature from a form so that you can modify its contents. InForms will ask you to enter your password again so that it can verify that you're actually allowed to remove the signature.

22. The Windows registry loses some of the settings for your InForms setup. What do you do?
    
    **a.** Panic and call Novell support immediately.
    
    **b.** Reinstall InForms from scratch.
    
    **c.** Copy the registry from another Windows workstation.
    
    **d.** Use the INCFG41.REG and FFWIN41.REG to add the missing entries back in.

    *d.* Even though you may eventually have to reinstall InForms from scratch, you should try using the two REG (registry) files provided with InForms first. All you need to do under Windows 95 is double-click the files; under Windows 3.1 you have to import the REG files using the Registry Editor utility supplied with Windows.

23. When adding a signature to a form, you must type your name, and then InForms Filler will ask you for your password.
    
    **a.** True
    
    **b.** False

    *b.* InForms Filler requires you to type your password in the signature field to begin the signing process. It'll then ask you for your user ID. Your name will appear in the signature field once it's signed.

24. The acronym *BDE* stands for:
    
    **a.** Bad Data Entry
    
    **b.** Borland Database Entry

    **c.** Borland Database Engine

    **d.** Bitmapped Data Entry

*c.* The Borland Database Engine (BDE) allows you to access the data created by Borland products more readily than using other techniques, such as ODBC.

**25.** Downloading forms to a printer:
    **a.** Saves time because InForms doesn't have to send the form to the printer every time
    **b.** Can result in a big mess when the form gets overwritten by other data
    **c.** Is the method that InForms normally uses to print
    **d.** Allows InForms to print in the background

*a.* InForms allows you to download forms to the HP LaserJet III, HP LaserJet 4, and the IBM 4039. (You should be able to download forms to the HP LaserJet 5 as well, even though the documentation at the time of this writing didn't include it.) Using downloaded forms can also reduce network bandwidth requirements.

**26.** The acronym *ODMA* stands for:
    **a.** Open Database Management API
    **b.** Open Document Management API
    **c.** Open Database Management Architecture
    **d.** Open Document Management Architecture

*b.* The Open Document Management API (ODMA) allows you to use other document management systems that you installed in place of directory dialog boxes.

**27.** The QuickList feature allows you to:
    **a.** Define a list of the directories you use most often.
    **b.** Print all of your forms using a single command.
    **c.** Create a list of the files you use most often.
    **d.** Display the users who have accessed a particular form.

*a and c.* The QuickList feature appears on most of the File Open–type dialogs within InForms. You can use it to create a list of files or directories that you use most often so that you don't have to search for them on the hard drive.

# InForms 4.x Administration and Form Design

28. The InForms term for an NDS attribute is:
    a. Record
    b. Field
    c. Table
    d. Database

    *b.* When you access the NDS database, all the attributes associated with various objects are *fields* in InForms terminology.

29. When you launch InForms from the DOS command line using FDWIN, the _____ command line switch allows you to run it using a specific language.
    a. /la
    b. /csla
    c. /ni
    d. /l

    *d.* The /l command line switch followed by the two-letter language identifier. For example, using /l-AF would tell InForms that you want to use the product in the Afrikaans language.

30. Action buttons don't normally appear in printed output; however, you can force them to print by unchecking the No Print option in the _____ dialog.
    a. Appearance of Selected Object
    b. Action Button Definition
    c. Set Object Position and Size
    d. Formula Worksheet

    *b.* The Action Button Definition dialog allows you to change what might seem like an appearance attribute.

31. You can remove the label from a field control by selecting _____ in the _____ field of the _____ dialog.
    a. None, Label Position, Entry Field Definition
    b. No Label, Control Attributes, Entry Field Definition
    c. None, Label Position, Appearance of Selected Object
    d. No Label, Control Attributes, Appearance of Selected Object

    *c.* Most of the display attributes for a control will appear in the Appearance of Selected Object dialog. This includes such attributes as the placement of labels within the control.

32. The only InForms object not affected by the Fill Color or Line Color tools is the _____ object.
   a. Table
   b. Field
   c. Figure
   d. Action Button

   *c.* Since the Figure object is derived from an outside source, it isn't affected by the two color tools that InForms provides. If you want to change the color of a figure, you'll need to change it using an external graphics program.

33. InForms will allow you to override NDS security and access any of the objects you need.
   a. True
   b. False

   *b.* You must have access to the NDS objects and attributes that you wish to access from within InForms.

34. You would use the _____ link type if you wanted the information in one form to automatically appear in another form.
   a. Form to Database
   b. Multi Record Table to Database
   c. Form to Form
   d. Print

   *c.* The Form to Form link type allows you to automatically move information from one form to another, saving the user some data-entry time while making the forms more readable. The Form to Database link type is used when you want to use a form to view, modify, delete, or add records to a database.

35. The acronym *SDB* stands for:
   a. Single Database
   b. Security Data Bounds
   c. Standard Data Binding
   d. Security Database

   *d.* A security database or SDB file is where InForms stores the passwords, groups, departments, and users needed to secure a form.

# InForms 4.x Administration and Form Design

36. Informs allows you to link to NDS containers and objects, but you can't create _____ entries from within InForms.
    a. Schema
    b. Table
    c. Object
    d. NDS

    *a.* You can't create NDS schema entries from within InForms.

37. Microsoft Mail launches InForms Filler from the patch associated with the _____ extension.
    a. DO
    b. WPF
    c. ML
    d. DAT

    *c.* Microsoft Mail uses the ML extension for mail communications. Other mail systems, like Word Perfect Office, can use both ML and DO extensions.

38. InForms doesn't provide any statistical formulas for you to use; that's why you'll need to create your own when trying to determine statistical information like standard deviation.
    a. True
    b. False

    *b.* InForms provides several statistical functions, including average, count, standard deviation, sum, and variance.

39. InForms supports which of the following graphics formats?
    a. BMP
    b. GCM
    c. GIF
    d. PCX
    e. All of the above

    *a, b, and d.* InForms doesn't support the GIF format, which is used extensively on the Internet. It does, however, support a wide array of other graphics forms, including BMP, CGM, DHP, DXF, EPS, GEM, HPGL, IMG, MSP, PCX, PIC, PNTG, PPIC, TIFF, WMF, and WPG.

**40.** InForms security relies on _____.
   a. Users
   b. Departments
   c. Groups
   d. Objects

   *c.* Users are assigned to one or more groups and are given a security level within each group. When you assign an approval group to a signature field, any user in that group can sign the form.

# Fun Test

1. InForms doesn't provide any statistical formulas for you to use; that's why you'll need to create your own when trying to determine statistical information like standard deviation.
   a. True
   b. False

2. A database is composed of:
   a. Fields
   b. Records
   c. Tables
   d. Indexes
   e. None of the above

3. The acronym *BDE* stands for:
   a. Bad Data Entry
   b. Borland Database Entry
   c. Borland Database Engine
   d. Bitmapped Data Entry

4. A drop-down list box doesn't support all of the data types that a field does.
   a. True
   b. False

5. The Windows registry loses some of the settings for your InForms setup. What do you do?
   a. Panic and call Novell support immediately.
   b. Reinstall InForms from scratch.

c. Copy the registry from another Windows workstation.

d. Use the INCFG41.REG and FFWIN41.REG to add the missing entries back in.

6. InForms supports which of the following database types?
   a. ODBC
   b. NetWare Directory Services
   c. Clipper
   d. Lotus Notes
   e. All of the above

7. Informs allows you to link to NDS containers and objects, but you can't create _____ entries from within InForms.
   a. Schema
   b. Table
   c. Object
   d. NDS

8. The acronym *QBE* stands for:
   a. Quick Bitmap Extraction
   b. Query before Extinction
   c. Quiet Binary Exchange
   d. Query by Example

9. InForms supports which of the following graphics formats?
   a. BMP
   b. GCM
   c. GIF
   d. PCX
   e. All of the above

10. The _____ function allows the user to edit the contents of a field.
    a. @EDIT
    b. @ALLOWEDIT
    c. #EDIT
    d. #ALLOWEDIT

11. InForms security relies on _____.
    a. Users
    b. Departments
    c. Groups
    d. Objects

12. When you launch InForms from the DOS command line using FDWIN, the _____ command line switch allows you to run it using a specific language.
    a. /la
    b. /csla
    c. /ni
    d. /l

13. InForms supports forms with both a portrait and a landscape orientation.
    a. True
    b. False

14. InForms requires _____ of memory and _____ of hard disk space for installation.
    a. 4 MB, 8 MB
    b. 8 MB, 12 MB
    c. 8 MB, 16 MB
    d. 4 MB, 24 MB

15. When adding a signature to a form, you must type your name, and then InForms Filler will ask you for your password.
    a. True
    b. False

16. InForms supports which of the following field types?
    a. Text
    b. Memo
    c. Integer
    d. Real
    e. Custom Data Format

17. InForms will allow you to override NDS security and access any of the objects you need.
    a. True
    b. False

18. InForms allows you to rotate text in one of _____ directions.
    a. 2.
    b. 3.
    c. 4.
    d. You can't rotate the text.

19. If you want to find a database record that contains nothing (a blank or other nonexistent value) in a particular field, you would search for a _____ value.
    a. NULL.
    b. NIL.
    c. Wild Card.
    d. It can't be done.
20. The QuickList feature allows you to:
    a. Define a list of the directories you use most often.
    b. Print all of your forms using a single command.
    c. Create a list of the files you most often.
    d. Display the users who have accessed a particular form.
21. The _____ file starts the InForms Filler utility.
    a. FFWIN41.EXE
    b. FFWIN.EXE
    c. FDWIN41.EXE
    d. FDWIN.EXE
22. Action buttons don't normally appear in printed output; however, you can force them to print by unchecking the No Print option in the _____ dialog.
    a. Appearance of Selected Object
    b. Action Button Definition
    c. Set Object Position and Size
    d. Formula Worksheet
23. InForms supports which of the following mail systems?
    a. GroupWise
    b. WordPerfect Office 4.x
    c. Microsoft Mail 3.0 or above
    d. MAPI-compliant mail systems
    e. All of the above
24. Microsoft Mail launches InForms Filler from the patch associated with the _____ extension.
    a. DO
    b. WPF
    c. ML
    d. DAT

**25.** Which key do you need to use to place a tab character in a text object?
  **a.** Ctrl-Tab
  **b.** Alt-Tab
  **c.** Shift-Tab
  **d.** Tab

**26.** Downloading forms to a printer:
  **a.** Saves time because InForms doesn't have to send the form to the printer every time
  **b.** Can result in a big mess when the form gets overwritten by other data
  **c.** Is the method that InForms normally uses to print
  **d.** Allows InForms to print in the background

**27.** The @SENDMAIL function will allow you to send mail to another person using which of the following constants?
  **a.** #MAIL
  **b.** #ROUTED
  **c.** #TASK
  **d.** #BROADCAST
  **e.** All of the above

**28.** A user with Read Only access to a database can:
  **a.** Modify records
  **b.** View records
  **c.** Perform queries
  **d.** Delete records

**29.** The acronym *SDB* stands for:
  **a.** Single Database
  **b.** Security Data Bounds
  **c.** Standard Data Binding
  **d.** Security Database

**30.** You need to use the _____ field type to associate a form with a security database.
  **a.** Security
  **b.** Custom Data Format

# InForms 4.x Administration and Form Design 799

   c. Signature
   d. Text

31. You can remove the label from a field control by selecting _____ in the _____ field of the _____ dialog.
    a. None, Label Position, Entry Field Definition
    b. No Label, Control Attributes, Entry Field Definition
    c. None, Label Position, Appearance of Selected Object
    d. No Label, Control Attributes, Appearance of Selected Object

32. You use the _____ command to remove the signature from a form so that you can modify its contents.
    a. Security | Unsign Signature Field
    b. Security | Sign Signature Field
    c. Security | Register User ID
    d. Security | Authenticate

33. There are _____ levels of security that you can assign to an InForms form.
    a. 10
    b. 25
    c. 64
    d. 99

34. The only InForms object not affected by the Fill Color or Line Color tools is the _____ object.
    a. Table
    b. Field
    c. Figure
    d. Action Button

35. InForms Filler allows you to change the contents of _____ fields, but not _____ fields after you sign a form.
    a. Nonsecure, secure
    b. Protected, unprotected
    c. Unprotected, protected
    d. Text, signature

36. The acronym *ODMA* stands for:
    a. Open Database Management API
    b. Open Document Management API

c. Open Database Management Architecture

d. Open Document Management Architecture

37. You would use the _____ link type if you wanted the information in one form to automatically appear in another form.
    a. Form to Database
    b. Multi Record Table to Database
    c. Form to Form
    d. Print

38. The acronym *IDAPI* stands for:
    a. Internet Data Access Programming Interface
    b. Intelligent Database Application Programming Interface
    c. Internet Database Application Processing Interconnect
    d. Integrated Database Application Programming Interface

39. The InForms term for an NDS attribute is:
    a. Record
    b. Field
    c. Table
    d. Database

40. Files in the object library use this extension:
    a. SDB
    b. WPF
    c. WPG
    d. OLB

## Brain Teaser

Now that you have a better idea of the kinds of InForms administration- and form design-related questions you might see on your exam, it's time for a little fun. The cryptogram in Fig. 23-33 gives you some tips that you can use when designing forms. As you saw in our case study, creating a new form isn't all that hard. However, getting the user to actually fill the form out correctly and enjoy using it enough to not try other methods for getting information into your database can be a real chore. Fortunately, there are some simple ways to make this chore a little fun for you as well. You'll find the solution for this brain teaser in App. C, "Brain Teaser Answers."

# InForms 4.x Administration and Form Design

EBDZNFZFN M WXOP EXBDF'V RMSB VX KB M EZWWZYITV VMDG. OBPBPKBO VX IDB YXTXO VX KOZNRVBF VRB WXOP MFE PMGB ZV MVVOMYVZSB. XW YXIODB, VXX PIYR YXTXO YMF KB CIDV MD KME MD FXFB MV MTT. EXF'V KB MWOMZE VX MEE ARZVB DUMYB MD FBBEBE VX PMGB VRB WXOP BMDL VX OBME. MFXVRBO AML VX PMGB VRB WXOP BMDL VX OBME ZD VX DBUMOMVB EMVM ZVBPD ZFVX DUBYZWZY NOXIUD IDZFN TZFBD MFE XVRBO EOMAZFN VXXTD. WZFMTTL, IDZFN MF BMDL VX OBME WXFV ZD M PIDV, PMGB DIOB LXI IDB XFB VRMV'D TMONB BFXINR WXO BSBOLXFB VX DBB.

| A | | N | |
|---|---|---|---|
| B | | O | |
| C | | P | |
| D | | Q | |
| E | | R | |
| F | | S | |
| G | | T | |
| H | | U | |
| I | | V | |
| J | | W | |
| K | | X | |
| L | | Y | |
| M | | Z | |

**Figure 23-33**
InForms Forms Design Cryptogram.

**Figure 23-34**
InForms Administration Cryptogram.

$_|>/{&+ > !~_< {= ~&)} [>_/ ~! /?| %~(, /|=/{&+ {/ {= /?| ~/?|_ [>_/. <>;| =#_| }~# $~<[)|/|)} /|=/ |\|_} !~_< }~# $_|>/| #={&+ /?| {&!~_<= !())|_ #/(){/}. ~&$| /?| !~_< {=/|=/|:, <>;| =#_| }~# >:: /?| >[[_~[_{>/| =|$#_{/}.

| | | | |
|---|---|---|---|
| ! | | { | |
| @ | | } | |
| # | | [ | |
| $ | | ] | |
| % | | < | |
| ^ | | > | |
| & | | \| | |
| * | | \ | |
| ( | | / | |
| ( | | ? | |
| _ | | – | |
| + | | : | |
| = | | ; | |

If you're feeling especially knowledgeable, you can try your hand at the much more difficult cryptogram shown in Fig. 23-34. This is an InForms administration–related cryptogram that will help you remember some important tasks when using InForms in a real-world environment. Just in case the idea of working with a symbol-oriented cryptogram is a bit intimidating for you, here's a tip: All spaces really are spaces and all periods are periods. Apostrophes are also what they appear to be. Every other symbol replaces a letter.

**InForms 4.x Administration and Form Design**

## Disk Time

Don't forget to spend some time working with the disk that accompanies this book. It provides valuable and fun-to-use teaching aids that help prepare you for the exam. See "Disk Time" in the preface of this book for details about what the disk contains. Make sure you focus on the NetWare 4.x and Acronym questions if you're running out of time when playing Red Zone.

# APPENDIX A

## LIST OF ACRONYMS

| | |
|---|---|
| AARP | AppleTalk Address Resolution Protocol |
| ABM | Asynchronous Balanced Mode |
| AC | Access Control |
| ACK | Acknowledgment |
| ACS | Asynchronous Communications Server |
| ACSE | Association Control Service Element |
| ADCCP | Advanced Data Communication Control Procedures |
| ADMD | Administration Management Domain |
| ADSP | AppleTalk Datastream Protocol |
| AFI | AppleTalk Filing Interface |
| AFP | AppleTalk Filing Protocol |
| ALO | At Least Once |
| AM | Amplitude Modulation |
| AMD | Advanced Micro Devices |
| AMI | Alternate Mark Inversions |
| AMT | Address Mapping Table |
| ANSI | American National Standards Institute |
| ANTC | Advanced Networking Test Center |
| APPC | Advanced Program-to-Program Communications |
| APPN | Advanced Peer-to-Peer Networking |
| ARM | Asynchronous Response Mode |
| ARP | Address Resolution Protocol |
| ARPANET | Advanced Research Projects Agency Network |
| AS | Application System (AS/400) |
| ASCII | American Standard Code for Information Interchange |
| ASE | Applied Service Elements |
| ASK | Amplitude Shift Keying |
| ASN.1 | Abstract Syntax Notation One |

| | | |
|---|---|---|
| ASP | AppleTalk Session Protocol |
| AT&T | American Telephone and Telegraph |
| ATA | Arcnet Trade Association |
| ATM | Automatic Teller Machine |
| ATM | Asynchronous Transfer Mode |
| ATP | AppleTalk Transaction Protocol |
| AUI | Auxiliary Unit Interface |
| BB&N | Bolt, Beranek & Newman |
| BCC | Block Check Character |
| BCS | Block Check Sequence |
| BER | Basic Encoding Rules |
| BOC | Bell Operating Company |
| bps | Bits Per Second |
| BSC | Binary Synchronous Communications |
| BSD | Berkeley Software Distribution |
| CAD | Computer-Aided Design |
| CAM | Channel Access Method |
| CAM | Computer-Aided Manufacturing |
| CATV | Community Access Television |
| CBT | Computer-Based Training |
| CCITT | Consultative Committees for International Telephone and Telegraph |
| CD | Carrier Detection |
| CD | Change Directory |
| CD | Compact Disc |
| CICS | Customer Information Control System |
| CLNP | Connectionless Network Protocol |
| CLNS | Connectionless Network Services |
| CMIP | Common Management Information Protocol |
| CMIS | Common Management Information Service |
| CMOS | Complementary Metal Oxide Semiconductor |
| CMOT | CMIP Over TCP/IP |
| CMS | Conversational Monitor System |

# List of Acronyms

| | |
|---|---|
| CNA | Certified Novell Administrator |
| CNE | Certified Novell Engineer |
| CNI | Certified Novell Instructor |
| CO | Central Office |
| CONS | Connection-Oriented Network Services |
| COS | Corporation for Open Systems |
| CPS | Characters Per Second |
| CPU | Central Processing Unit |
| CR | Carriage Return |
| CRC | Cyclic Redundancy Code |
| CRT | Cathode Ray Tube |
| CSMA/CD | Carrier Sense Multiple Access/Collision Detection |
| CSU | Channel Service Unit |
| CTS | Clear to Send |
| CUA | Common User Access |
| DAP | Data Access Protocol |
| DAS | Dynamically Assigned Sockets |
| DAT | Digital Audio Tape |
| dB | Decibel |
| DCE | Data Communications Equipment |
| DDCMP | Digital Data Communications Message Protocol |
| DDE | Dynamic Data Exchange |
| DDN | Defense Department Network |
| DDP | Datagram Delivery Protocol |
| DES | Data Encryption Standard |
| DF | Don't Fragment |
| DHA | Destination Hardware Address |
| DIB | Directory Information Base |
| DIB | Device-Independent Bitmap |
| DID | Destination Identification |
| DIS | Draft International Standards |
| DMA | Direct Memory Access |
| DNA | Digital Network Architecture |

| | |
|---|---|
| DoD | Department of Defense |
| DOS | Disk Operating System |
| DP | Draft Proposal |
| DQDB | Distributed Queue Dual Bus |
| DS | Directory Services |
| DSA | Destination Software Address |
| DSAP | Destination Service Access Point |
| DSR | Data Set Ready |
| DSU | Data Service Unit |
| DTE | Data Termination Equipment |
| DTR | Data Transmit Ready |
| DUA | Directory User Agent |
| EA | Extended Attribute |
| EBCDIC | Extended Binary Coded Decimal Interchange Code |
| ECC | Error Checking and Correcting |
| ECNE | Enterprise Certified Novell Engineer |
| ED | End Delimiter |
| EIA | Electronic Industries Association |
| EISA | Extended Industry Standard Architecture |
| ELAP | EtherTalk Link Access Protocol |
| EMA | Enterprise Management Architecture |
| EMI | Electromagnetic Interface |
| EMM | Expanded Memory Manager |
| EMS | Expanded Memory Specification |
| ENQ | Enquiry |
| EOT | End of Transmission |
| ES | End System |
| ET | Electro Test |
| FAT | File Allocation Table Disk Format |
| FBE | Free Buffer Enquiry |
| FCC | Federal Communications Commission |
| FCS | Frame Check Sequence |
| FDDI | Fiber Distribution Data Interface |

# List of Acronyms

| | | |
|---|---|---|
| FDM | Frequency Division Multiplexing |
| FDX | Full Duplex Transmission |
| FEP | Front End Processor |
| FIN | Finish Flag |
| FM | Frequency Modulation |
| FRMR | Frame Reject |
| FS | Frame Status |
| FTAM | File Transfer, Access, and Management |
| FTP | File Transfer Protocol |
| GDS | General Data Stream |
| GHz | Gigahertz |
| GOSIP | Government Open Systems Interconnection Profile |
| GUI | Graphical User Interface |
| HDLC | High-Level Data Link Control |
| HDX | Half-Duplex Transmission |
| HP | Hewlett Packard |
| HPFS | High-Performance File System |
| Hz | Hertz |
| I/O | Input/Output of data |
| IAB | Internet Activities Board |
| IBM | International Business Machines |
| IC | Integrated Circuit |
| ICMP | Internet Control Message Protocol |
| IDE | Integrated Drive Electronics |
| IDG | Interdialog Gap |
| IDP | Internet Datagram Protocol |
| IEEE | Institute of Electronic and Electrical Engineers |
| IFG | Interframe Gap |
| IHL | Internet Header Length |
| ILD | Injection Laser Diode |
| IMS | Information Management System |
| INTAP | Interoperability Technology Association for Information Processing |

| | |
|---|---|
| IP | Internet Protocol |
| IPL | Initial Program Load |
| IPX | Internet Packet Exchange |
| IR | Internet Router |
| IRM | Inherited Rights Mask |
| IRQ | Interrupt Request |
| IS | Intermediate System |
| IS | International Standard |
| ISDN | Integrated Services Digital Network |
| ISN | Initial Sequence Number |
| ISO | International Standards Organization |
| ISODE | ISO Development Environment |
| ITI | Industrial Technology Institute |
| ITT | Invitation to Transmit |
| IWU | Intermediate Working Unit |
| KHz | Kilohertz |
| LAN | Local Area Network |
| LAP | Link Access Protocol |
| LAPB | Link Access Protocol—Balanced |
| LAPD | Link Access Protocol—Digital |
| LAT | Local Area Transport |
| LATA | Local Access and Transport Areas |
| LDM | Limited Distance Modem |
| LED | Light-Emitting Diode |
| LLAP | Local Talk Link Access Protocol |
| LLC | Local Link Control |
| LSL | Link Support Layer |
| LU | Logical Unit |
| MAC | Media Access Control |
| MAN | Metropolitan Area Network |
| MAP | Manufacturing Automation Protocol |
| MAU | Mainframe Addressable Unit |
| Mbps | Megabits per second |

# List of Acronyms

| | |
|---|---|
| MBps | Megabytes per second |
| MCNE | Master Certified Novell Engineer |
| MF | More Fragments |
| MFM | Modified Frequency Modulation |
| MHS | Message Handling Service |
| MHz | Megahertz |
| MIB | Management Information Base |
| MIS | Management Information System |
| MOP | Maintenance Operation Protocol |
| MOTIS | Message Oriented Text Interchange System |
| MS-DOS | Microsoft Disk Operating System |
| MSAU | Multistation Access Unit |
| MSG | Message |
| MTA | Message Transfer Agent |
| MTS | Message Transfer System |
| MUX | Multiplexer |
| MVS | Multiple Virtual System |
| NAEC | Novell Authorized Test Center |
| NAK | Negative Acknowledgment |
| NAU | Network Addressable Unit |
| NAUN | Nearest Active Upstream Neighbor |
| NBP | Name Binding Protocol |
| NBS | National Bureau of Standards |
| NCP | NetWare Core Protocol |
| NCP | Network Control Program |
| NCR | National Cash Register |
| NDS | NetWare Directory Services |
| NetBIOS | Network Basic Input/Output System |
| NFS | Network File System |
| NIC | Network Information Center |
| NIC | Network Interface Card |
| NID | Next Identifier |
| NIST | National Institute of Standards and Technology |

| | |
|---|---|
| NLM | NetWare Loadable Module |
| NOS | Network Operating System |
| NRM | Normal Response Mode |
| NRZ | Non-Return to Zero |
| NRZ-I | Non-Return to Zero—Inverted |
| NRZ-L | Non-Return to Zero—Level |
| *NSE* | *NetWare Support Encyclopedia* |
| NSF | National Science Foundation |
| NTFS | Windows NT File System |
| NVE | Network Visible Entry |
| NVTS | Network Virtual Terminal Service |
| ODI | Open Data Link Interface |
| OJT | On the Job Training |
| OLE | Object Linking and Embedding |
| ONC | Open Network Computing |
| OS | Operating System |
| OS/2 | Operating System/2 |
| OSI | Open System Interconnection |
| P/F | Poll/Final Bit |
| PAC | Data Packet |
| PAD | Packet Assembler/Disassembler |
| PAP | Printer Access Protocol |
| PARC | Palo Alto Research Center |
| PC | Personal Computer |
| PCSA | Personal Computer System Architecture (DEC) |
| PDN | Public Data Network |
| PDU | Protocol Data Unit |
| PEP | Packet Exchange Protocol |
| PLP | Packet Level Protocol |
| PLU | Primary Logical Unit |
| POP | Point of Presence |
| POTS | Plain Old Telephone Service |
| PRMD | Private Management Domains |

# List of Acronyms

| | |
|---|---|
| PSH | Push Flag |
| PSK | Phase Shift Keying |
| PSTN | Public Switched Telephone Network |
| PTT | Postal Telephone and Telegraph |
| PU | Physical Unit |
| PUC | Public Utilities Company |
| RAID | Redundant Array of Inexpensive Disks |
| RAM | Random Access Memory |
| RBHC | Regional Bell Holding Company |
| RD | Receive Data |
| REJ | Reject |
| RFC | Request For Comment |
| RIP | Routing Information Protocol |
| RJE | Remote Job Entry |
| RNR | Receiver Not Ready |
| ROM | Read Only Memory |
| ROSE | Remote Operation Service Element |
| RPC | Remote Procedure Call |
| RPL | Remote Procedure Load |
| RR | Receiver Ready |
| RS-# | Recommended Standard |
| RST | Reset Flag |
| RTMP | Routing Table Maintenance Protocol |
| RTS | Request to Send |
| RTSE | Reliable Transfer Service Element |
| RZ | Return to Zero |
| SAA | Systems Application Architecture |
| SAP | Service Access Point |
| SAP | Service Advertising Protocol |
| SAS | Statistically Assigned Sockets |
| SCS | SNA Character String |
| SCSI | Small Computer System Interface |
| SD | Start Delimiter |

| | |
|---|---|
| SDLC | Synchronous Data Link Control |
| SFD | Start of Frame Delimiter |
| SID | Source Identifier |
| SIP | Service Identification Packet |
| SLU | Secondary Logical Unit |
| SMC | Standard Microsystems Corporation |
| SMDS | Switch Multimegabit Data Service |
| SMT | Station Management |
| SMTP | Simple Mail Transfer Protocol |
| SNA | Systems Network Architecture |
| SNADS | Systems Network Architecture Distributed Services |
| SNAP | Sub Network Access Protocol |
| SNMP | Simple Network Management Protocol |
| SOH | Start of Header |
| SONET | Synchronous Optical Network |
| SPP | Sequenced Packet Protocol |
| SPX | Sequenced Packet Exchange |
| SPX | Sequential Packet Exchange |
| SQE | Signal Quality Error |
| SQL | Structured Query Language |
| SRAM | Static Random Access Memory |
| SRI | Stanford Research Institute |
| SSAP | Source Service Access Point |
| SSCP | System Services Control Point |
| STP | Shielded Twisted Pair |
| SYN | Synchronize Flag |
| TCP | Transmission Control Protocol |
| TCP/IP | Transmission Control Protocol/Internet Protocol |
| TD | Transmit Data |
| TDM | Time Division Multiplexing |
| TFTP | Trivial File Transfer Protocol |
| TLAP | Token Ring Link Access Protocol |
| TLI | Transport Layer Interface |

# List of Acronyms

| | |
|---|---|
| TOS | Type of Service |
| TP | Twisted Pair |
| TP[#] | Transport Protocol-Class # |
| TPDU | Transport Protocol Data Unit |
| TSO | Time Sharing Option |
| TSR | Terminate and Stay Resident Program |
| TTL | Time to Live |
| TTS | Transaction Tracking System |
| TTY | Teletype |
| TV | Television |
| TWX | Teletypewriter Exchange Service |
| UA | User Account |
| UDP | User Datagram Protocol |
| UHF | Ultrahigh Frequency |
| UI | Unnumbered Information |
| ULP | Upper Layer Protocol |
| UNA | Universal NetWare Architecture |
| UPS | Uninterruptible Power Supply |
| URG | Urgent Flag |
| UTP | Unshielded Twisted Pair |
| VAP | Value Added Process |
| VAX | Virtual Access Extended |
| VHF | Very High Frequency |
| VLM | Virtual Loadable Module |
| VM | Virtual Machine |
| VMS | Virtual Memory System |
| VSE | Virtual Storage Extended |
| VT | Virtual Terminal |
| VTAM | Virtual Terminal Access Method |
| WAN | Wide Area Network |
| WD | Working Document |
| WNIM | Wide Area Network Interface Board |
| WORM | Write Once, Read Many (Drive) |

| | | |
|---|---|---|
| XDR | External Data Representation |
| XMM | Extended Memory Manager |
| XMS | Extended Memory Specification |
| XNS | Xerox Network System |
| XO | Exactly Once |
| ZIP | Zone Information Protocol |
| ZIT | Zone Information Table |

# APPENDIX B

FUN TEST QUESTION ANSWERS

## Chapter 9

1. *c*
2. *a* and *d*
3. *c*
4. *a*
5. *b*
6. *a*
7. *c*
8. *b, c,* and *d*
9. *a, b,* and *c*
10. *b* and *d*
11. *c*
12. *d*
13. *b*
14. *b*
15. *d*
16. *a, b,* and *d*
17. *b*
18. *d*
19. *c*
20. *b*
21. *c*
22. *b*
23. *a, c*
24. *b*
25. *a* and *c*
26. *d*
27. *b*
28. *b*
29. *d*
30. *c*
31. *a*
32. *a* and *c*
33. *b*
34. *d*
35. *c*
36. *a*
37. *a, b, c,* and *d*
38. *a* and *b*
39. *c*
40. *e*

## Chapter 10

1. *c*
2. *d*
3. *e*
4. *b*
5. *a*
6. *a*
7. *d*
8. *c*
9. *d*
10. *a*
11. *a*
12. *a*
13. *b*
14. *a*
15. *a, b,* and *c*
16. *c*
17. *d*
18. *d*
19. *b*
20. *b*
21. *a*

22. *b*  27. *a*  32. *c*
23. *a*  28. *b*  33. *b*
24. *b*  29. *b*  34. *e*
25. *e*  30. *a*
26. *c*  31. *c*

# Chapter 11

1. *d*   13. *b*  25. *a*
2. *a*   14. *d*  26. *a*
3. *b*   15. *a*  27. *a*
4. *a*   16. *c*  28. *a*
5. *b*   17. *c*  29. *d*
6. *d*   18. *b*  30. *a*
7. *a*   19. *a*  31. *d*
8. *b*   20. *d*  32. *b*
9. *a*   21. *c*  33. *c*
10. *d*  22. *d*  34. *c*
11. *c*  23. *d*  35. *c*
12. *c*  24. *a*

# Chapter 12

1. *a*, *b*, *c*, and *d*       9. *b* and *c*              17. *c*
2. *a*, *b*, *c*, *d*, and *e*  10. *b*                     18. *a*
3. *b*                          11. *b* and *d*             19. *d*
4. *c*                          12. *a*                     20. *c*
5. *a*                          13. *d*                     21. *b*
6. *d*                          14. *a*, *b*, *c*, *d*, and *e*  22. *c*
7. *a* and *b*                  15. *a*                     23. *a*, *b*, and *c*
8. *d*                          16. *b*                     24. *b*

**Fun Test Question Answers**

25. *b*  
26. *a*  
27. *d*  
28. *a, c,* and *d*  
29. *d*  
30. *c*  

31. *b*  
32. *c*  
33. *d*  
34. *a*  
35. *b*  
36. *a*  

37. *c*  
38. *d*  
39. *b*  
40. *c*  

# Chapter 13

1. *d*  
2. *a*  
3. *c*  
4. *a*  
5. *a*  
6. *b*  
7. *c*  
8. *b*  
9. *b*  
10. *b*  
11. *c*  
12. *b*  

13. *d*  
14. *d*  
15. *f*  
16. *d*  
17. *a*  
18. *a*  
19. *b*  
20. *d*  
21. *a*  
22. *b*  
23. *c*  
24. *c*  

25. *a*  
26. *d*  
27. *e*  
28. *d*  
29. *a*  
30. *d*  
31. *b*  
32. *c*  
33. *c*  
34. *a*  
35. *b*  
36. *b*  

# Chapter 14

1. *a*  
2. *d*  
3. *b*  
4. *b*  
5. *d*  
6. *d*  
7. *a*  

8. *b*  
9. *b*  
10. *d*  
11. *d*  
12. *c*  
13. *b*  
14. *d*  

15. *a*  
16. *b*  
17. *a*  
18. *d*  
19. *b*  
20. *c*  
21. *c*

22. c
23. b
24. d
25. a
26. d
27. a
28. b
29. d
30. d
31. b
32. a
33. d
34. e
35. b
36. c
37. c
38. a
39. c
40. e

# Chapter 15

1. b
2. d
3. d
4. a
5. b
6. b
7. c
8. a
9. a
10. c
11. b
12. d
13. c
14. d
15. c
16. d
17. b
18. b
19. d
20. c
21. a
22. a
23. f
24. d
25. a
26. a
27. b
28. a
29. b
30. d
31. b
32. a
33. b
34. d
35. b

# Chapter 16

1. d
2. a
3. c
4. a
5. d
6. a
7. d
8. c
9. b
10. a
11. b
12. d
13. d
14. b
15. b
16. b
17. d
18. d
19. b
20. b
21. b

**Fun Test Question Answers**

| | | |
|---|---|---|
| 22. *c* | 27. *a* | 32. *b* |
| 23. *d* | 28. *b* | 33. *b* |
| 24. *a* | 29. *a* | 34. *b* |
| 25. *c* | 30. *d* | 35. *d* |
| 26. *d* | 31. *b* | |

# Chapter 17

| | | |
|---|---|---|
| 1. *a* | 15. *b* | 29. *b* |
| 2. *a*, *b*, *c*, and *d* | 16. *d* | 30. *d* |
| 3. *b* | 17. *a* | 31. *a* |
| 4. *e* | 18. *a*, *b*, *c*, *d*, and *e* | 32. *d* |
| 5. *b* | 19. *c* | 33. *b* and *c* |
| 6. *c* | 20. *a* and *d* | 34. *b* |
| 7. *d* | 21. *b* | 35. *d* |
| 8. *a* | 22. *c* | 36. *c* |
| 9. *b* and *c* | 23. *c* | 37. *c* |
| 10. *c* | 24. *a* | 38. *b* |
| 11. *b* and *d* | 25. *d* | 39. *c* |
| 12. *a* | 26. *b* | 40. *b* |
| 13. *a* | 27. *a* and *c* | |
| 14. *b*, *c*, and *e* | 28. *c* | |

# Chapter 18

| | | |
|---|---|---|
| 1. *b* | 8. *a*, *b*, *c*, *d*, and *e* | 15. *c* |
| 2. *a* | 9. *a* | 16. *a*, *b*, *c*, and *d* |
| 3. *c* | 10. *b* | 17. *d* |
| 4. *d* | 11. *a* | 18. *b* |
| 5. *a*, *b*, and *d* | 12. *b* and *c* | 19. *c* |
| 6. *d* | 13. *a* | 20. *a* |
| 7. *c* | 14. *d* | 21. *c* |

22. *d*
23. *a* and *c*
24. *b* and *d*
25. *d*
26. *d*
27. *b*
28. *a*
29. *d*
30. *c*
31. *a*, *b*, and *d*
32. *b*
33. *b*
34. *c*
35. *b*, *c*, and *d*
36. *a*
37. *c*
38. *b*
39. *a*
40. *d*

# Chapter 19

1. *a* and *d*
2. *a*, *b*, *c*, and *d*
3. *a*
4. *d*
5. *c*
6. *b*
7. *a*
8. *c*
9. *b*, *c*, and *d*
10. *d*
11. *c*
12. *a*
13. *a*, *b*, *c*, and *e*
14. *b*
15. *b* and *c*
16. *a*
17. *d*
18. *c*
19. *a*, *b*, *c*, and *d*
20. *b*
21. *c* and *d*
22. *a*
23. *a* and *c*
24. *b*
25. *d*
26. *a*
27. *a* and *c*
28. *b*
29. *b*
30. *a*
31. *d*
32. *a*
33. *b*
34. *c*
35. *a*
36. *d*
37. *c*
38. *d*
39. *a*
40. *c*

# Chapter 20

1. *b*
2. *b*, *c*, and *d*
3. *a*
4. *e*
5. *c* and *d*
6. *c*
7. *a*, *b*, and *c*
8. *c*
9. *a*
10. *a*, *b*, and *d*
11. *c*
12. *c*
13. *d*
14. *b*
15. *a*, *b*, *c*, and *d*

**Fun Test Question Answers**

| | | |
|---|---|---|
| 16. *b* and *d* | 25. *a* | 34. *a* |
| 17. *a* | 26. *d* | 35. *c* |
| 18. *b* | 27. *a*, *b*, and *c* | 36. *a* |
| 19. *a* | 28. *d* | 37. *b* |
| 20. *e* | 29. *b* | 38. *c* |
| 21. *b* and *d* | 30. *a* | 39. *c* |
| 22. *c* | 31. *d* | 40. *c* |
| 23. *c* | 32. *b* | |
| 24. *b* | 33. *a* and *d* | |

## Chapter 21

| | | |
|---|---|---|
| 1. *a* | 14. *b* | 27. *d* |
| 2. *b* | 15. *b* | 28. *c* |
| 3. *a* | 16. *d* | 29. *d* |
| 4. *a* | 17. *a* | 30. *d* |
| 5. *b* | 18. *a* | 31. *d* |
| 6. *a* | 19. *b* | 32. *b* |
| 7. *d* | 20. *d* | 33. *d* |
| 8. *c* | 21. *b* | 34. *b* |
| 9. *b* | 22. *c* | 35. *a* |
| 10. *d* | 23. *b* | 36. *a* |
| 11. *d* | 24. *b* | 37. *a* |
| 12. *c* | 25. *c* | 38. *b* |
| 13. *a* | 26. *a* | 39. *b* |

## Chapter 22

| | | |
|---|---|---|
| 1. *d* | 5. *c* | 9. *d* |
| 2. *b* | 6. *b*, *d*, and *e* | 10. *b* |
| 3. *b* | 7. *a* | 11. *a* and *c* |
| 4. *a* and *d* | 8. *e* | 12. *a* |

13. *b* and *c*
14. *e*
15. *d*
16. *c*
17. *a*
18. *a*
19. *c*
20. *b*
21. *b*
22. *d*
23. *c*
24. *d*
25. *a*
26. *d*
27. *c*
28. *d*
29. *a*
30. *b, c,* and *d*
31. *a*
32. *a, b,* and *d*
33. *d*
34. *a*
35. *b*
36. *d*
37. *b*
38. *a* and *d*
39. *b*
40. *a*

# Chapter 23

1. *b*
2. *a, b, c,* and *d*
3. *c*
4. *a*
5. *d*
6. *e*
7. *a*
8. *d*
9. *a, b,* and *d*
10. *b*
11. *c*
12. *d*
13. *a*
14. *d*
15. *b*
16. *a, b,* and *e*
17. *b*
18. *c*
19. *a*
20. *a* and *c*
21. *b*
22. *b*
23. *e*
24. *c*
25. *a*
26. *a*
27. *b* and *d*
28. *b* and *c*
29. *d*
30. *c*
31. *c*
32. *a*
33. *d*
34. *c*
35. *c*
36. *b*
37. *c*
38. *d*
39. *b*
40. *d*

# APPENDIX C

## BRAIN TEASER ANSWERS

This appendix contains all of the answers for the various brain teaser puzzles in this book. The puzzles are presented in order by chapter. In most cases you'll see only the answer, not the puzzle itself.

## Chapter 9

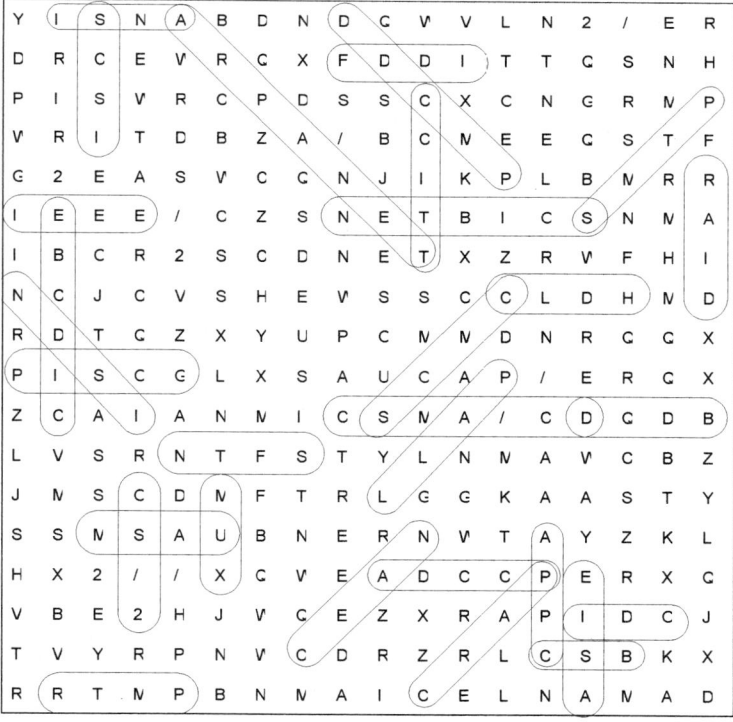

# Appendix C

## Chapter 10

|   |   |   |   |   |   |   |   |   |   |   |   |   |   |   |   |
|---|---|---|---|---|---|---|---|---|---|---|---|---|---|---|---|
| ¹E | ²L | E | ³V | E | N |   | ⁴P | ⁵C | O | N | ⁶S | ⁷O | L | ⁸E |   |
| ⁹S | E |   | L |   |   |   | ¹⁰R | O |   |   | ¹¹C | R |   | ¹²R | ¹³A | ¹⁴I | ¹⁵D |
| ¹⁶C | A | R | M |   | ¹⁷E | ¹⁸L |   | ¹⁹I | D |   | ²⁰R | E |   | ²¹A | D | S | P |
| ²²A | N |   |   | ²³C | O | N | N | E | ²⁴C | ²⁵T | I | O | ²⁶N | S |   | P |   |
| P |   | ²⁷D |   | ²⁸C | D |   | T |   | ²⁹M | A | P |   | ³⁰E | E |   |   | ³¹S |
| ³²E | ³³X | A | ³⁴M |   | E |   | ³⁵I | ³⁶S | O |   | ³⁷T | ³⁸A | T |   | ³⁹W | ⁴⁰H | Y |
|   | ⁴¹D | T | E |   |   | ⁴²N | I | S | ⁴³T |   | ⁴⁴D | W | ⁴⁵I |   | ⁴⁶I | S |
| ⁴⁷S | R | A | M |   | ⁴⁸S | I | G | N |   | ⁴⁹C | O | M | I | C | ⁵⁰S |   | C |
| E |   |   | ⁵¹B | A | Y |   | ⁵²G | ⁵³A | P |   | ⁵⁴I | R |   | ⁵⁵A | ⁵⁶L | O |
| ⁵⁷C | ⁵⁸O | ⁵⁹R | E |   | ⁶⁰S | ⁶¹K | ⁶²I | L | L |   | ⁶³O | N | E |   | ⁶⁴V | A | N |
| ⁶⁵U | S | E | R | S |   | ⁶⁶N | O | E | L |   | ⁶⁷R | I |   | ⁶⁸Y | E | S |
| ⁶⁹R | I | M |   |   | ⁷⁰G | O |   |   | ⁷¹O | X |   | ⁷²S | ⁷³N | A |   | ⁷⁴T | D |
| I |   |   | ⁷⁵S | ⁷⁶H | O | W | S |   | C |   | ⁷⁷S | T | O | W | E | D |
| ⁷⁸T | R | ⁷⁹I | V | I | A | L |   | ⁸⁰R | A |   | ⁸¹R | U | N |   | ⁸²R | ⁸³N |
| Y |   | ⁸⁴M | E | D | L | E | Y |   | ⁸⁵T | ⁸⁶I | ⁸⁷T | A | N |   | ⁸⁸E | I | A |
|   | ⁸⁹B | B | L |   | ⁹⁰S | D |   | ⁹¹T | I | N | C | T |   | ⁹²W | A | V | E |
| ⁹³P | I | E | T | ⁹⁴Y |   | ⁹⁵G | ⁹⁶R | I | O | T |   | ⁹⁷O | R | A | T | E |
| ⁹⁸I | N | D | E | N | T | E | D |   | ⁹⁹N | O |   | ¹⁰⁰R | E | D |

## Chapter 11

Proper file server tuning always begins with knowledge of the file server itself in the form of statistics, then moves on to development of a tuning strategy. Always begin the tuning process by looking at file server memory management. Once you've tuned a file server's memory, you can move on to methods of managing that memory most efficiently.

Every file server transmits both SAP (Service Advertisement Protocol) and RIP (Routing Information Protocol) information every minute. The router tracking screen displays both sets of information.

# Brain Teaser Answers

## Chapter 12

Starting the NetWare file server installation is easy. Type the drive letter of the CD-ROM followed by a colon (for example, *E:*) and press Enter. Type *CD \NETWARE.312\ENGLISH* (or the language you are using) and press Enter. Type *INSTALL* and press Enter.

The NetWare Migration utility allows you to convert a version two server into a version three server. You can also use the utility to upgrade a version three server to the current version of the software.

## Chapter 13

# Chapter 14

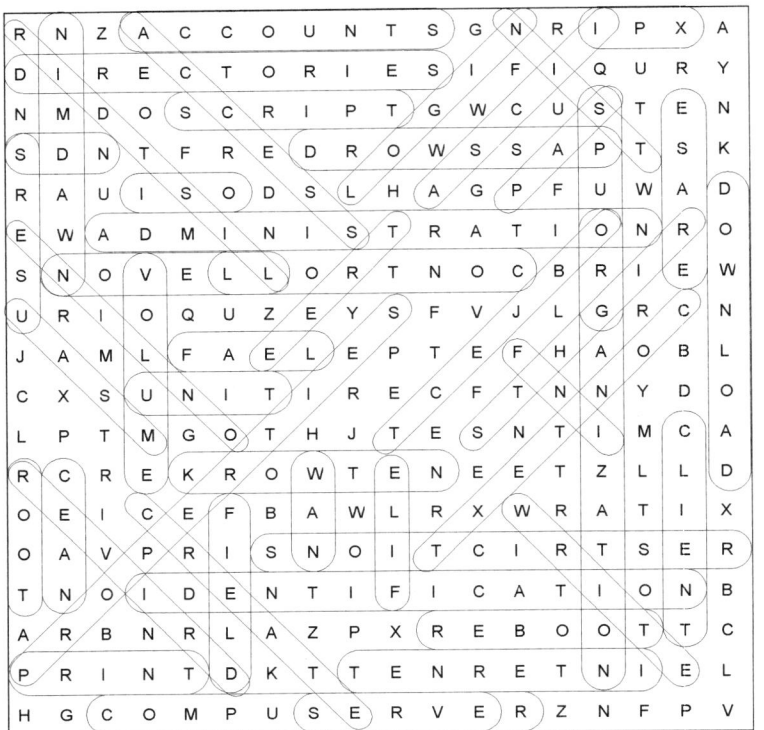

**Brain Teaser Answers**

## Chapter 15

|   |   |   |   |   |   |   |   |   |   |   |   |   |   |   |   |   |   |
|---|---|---|---|---|---|---|---|---|---|---|---|---|---|---|---|---|---|
| ¹C | ²O | ³N | ⁴S | ⁵O | ⁶L | E | ■ | ⁷D | ⁸S | ⁹R | ¹⁰E | P | ¹¹A | I | ¹²R | ■ | ¹³N |
| ¹⁴O | B | J | E | C | T | ■ | ¹⁵F | A | C | T | S | ■ | M | ■ | ¹⁶E | ¹⁷I | A |
| ¹⁸N | I | O | R | T | ■ | ¹⁹I | N | T | R | E | P | ²⁰I | D | ■ | ²¹N | L | M |
| T | ■ | ²²R | V | ■ | ²³O | N | ■ | ²⁴A | I | ■ | ²⁵I | D | ■ | ²⁶M | A | K | E |
| ²⁷E | ²⁸L | D | E | ²⁹R | ■ | ³⁰S | U | B | P | ³¹R | O | G | ³²R | A | M | ■ | S |
| ³³X | I | ■ | ³⁴R | O | ³⁵O | T | ■ | ³⁶A | T | O | N | ■ | ³⁷C | N | E | ³⁸S | ■ |
| ³⁹T | O | ⁴⁰S | ■ | ⁴¹E | X | A | ⁴²M | S | ■ | ⁴³B | A | ⁴⁴C | A | U | ■ | ⁴⁵E | ⁴⁶A |
| ■ | ⁴⁷N | O | ⁴⁸S | ■ | ⁴⁹L | E | E | K | ■ | ⁵⁰G | A | ■ | ⁵¹A | ⁵²N | T | C | ■ |
| ⁵³A | ■ | ⁵⁴F | I | ⁵⁵N | ⁵⁶A | L | ■ | ⁵⁷F | E | P | ■ | ⁵⁸L | O | P | E | ■ |   |
| ⁵⁹B | ⁶⁰U | T | T | O | N | ■ | ⁶¹S | ⁶²C | ⁶³S | I | ■ | ⁶⁴T | ⁶⁵I | ■ | ⁶⁶V | A | ■ |
| ⁶⁷P | E | W | E | E | S | ■ | ⁶⁸O | R | A | L | ■ | ⁶⁹U | N | ⁷⁰R | E | S | ⁷¹T |
| ■ | ⁷²L | A | ■ | ⁷³S | I | ⁷⁴G | H | T | S | E | E | R | ■ | ⁷⁵A | L | S | O |
| ⁷⁶B | E | R | ■ | I | ■ | A | ■ | ⁷⁷S | R | ■ | ⁷⁸E | ⁷⁹T | ■ | L | ■ | ■ | A |
| R | ■ | ⁸⁰E | ⁸¹R | S | ⁸²A | T | ⁸³Z | ■ | Y | ■ | ⁸⁴G | ■ | ⁸⁵A | ⁸⁶M | ■ | ⁸⁷I | S |
| ⁸⁸O | ⁸⁹D | ■ | I | ■ | ⁹⁰N | E | R | ⁹¹D | ■ | ⁹²O | U | ⁹³T | B | U | ⁹⁴R | S | T |
| ⁹⁴W | I | N | G | ⁹⁵B | O | W | ■ | ⁹⁶A | E | R | I | A | L | ■ | ⁹⁷A | L | ■ |
| ⁹⁸S | A | P | H | E | N | A | ■ | S | ■ | D | ■ | ⁹⁹P | E | ¹⁰⁰S | T | E | ¹⁰¹R |
| ¹⁰²E | L | I | T | E | ■ | ¹⁰³Y | A | H | O | O | ■ | ¹⁰⁴E | S | P | ■ | ¹⁰⁵T | O |

## Chapter 16

Always remember that a 32-bit operating system requires a 32-bit network client for optimum performance. Use Novell's Client 32 client when working with Windows 95 for best performance.

File compression can be enabled only when setting up a new volume and completely disabled only by removing the volume. The INSTALL.NLM will create and setup a new volume on the file server.

## Chapter 17

Security is a major problem on many networks, but you can control it by controlling data access. Remember that users must have access to their post office directory to access their mail and the working copy of the client software. They don't need access to the domain directory because the administrator software and a copy of the client software are stored there.

Fixing GroupWise problems can be very time-consuming if you don't follow the right procedure. The Rebuild Database option allows you to both correct physical problems and update the database information. Use the Recover Database option if you only need to correct physical problems in the database.

# Chapter 18

```
G A T E W A Y A D Y D A T A B A S E
R X S N E T W O R K Y T I L I T U V
O A Z Y Q I E O P N D I A R O U T E
U N I X N U T T P R O T O C O L A R
P S 2 D F C C Y I I N D I R E C T N
W I O A E L H V T L Y L S E K G S O
I W B R S I E R P I T F R V D M 2 I
S Z I X C E H J O Y T T U R Q B D T
E D N X P N X C N N B M A E S L E A
H R E M O T E L G R O U P S O O L R
E G A S S E M T L T Y U E H T C I T
T T 2 R T U V I W F P C S O W K V S
R C D D O S D S I A O E O E C E E I
O E E X F D K T F R R B B V R D R N
R J C R F N R Z P H E E N T M L Y I
R B Q F I E L D T R R Z D E P P A M
E O U L C D R E S U L T N I A M O D
C O N N E C T I O N S 2 T Y U M K A
```

# Brain Teaser Answers

## Chapter 19

GroupWise provides many features that you may not notice at first, like user-defined entries. You get 10 user-defined entries. GroupWise lets you put any kind of information needed here. For example, you could use a user-defined entry to specify the user's actual network location. Make absolutely certain, though, that you use the entries carefully by selecting data that will apply to most—if not all—of your users.

Damaged data is always a problem for any application, even GroupWise. You should back up all the USER*XXX*.DB and MSG*XX*.DB files at least once a week. Backing them up more often than that will certainly reduce the level of loss if some type of error occurs.

## Chapter 20

LAN maintenance is an essential part of every CNE's job. Just about the fastest way to destroy your LAN is to allow environmental factors like poor air circulation (heat), people with inadvertent access to cables or other components, moisture, and dust to get in the way. Records are essential to any LAN maintenance plan. Using the correct troubleshooting strategy always reduces maintenance time and increases the chances that you'll find the problem the first time around.

Knowing your hardware's enemies is the first step in eliminating them. Furnaces and microwaves both act as sources of RFI (radio frequency interference). Light switches and radar produce EMI (electromagnetic interference). Both sources of radiation can cause hardware problems, but in different ways. Make sure you know about both.

# Chapter 21

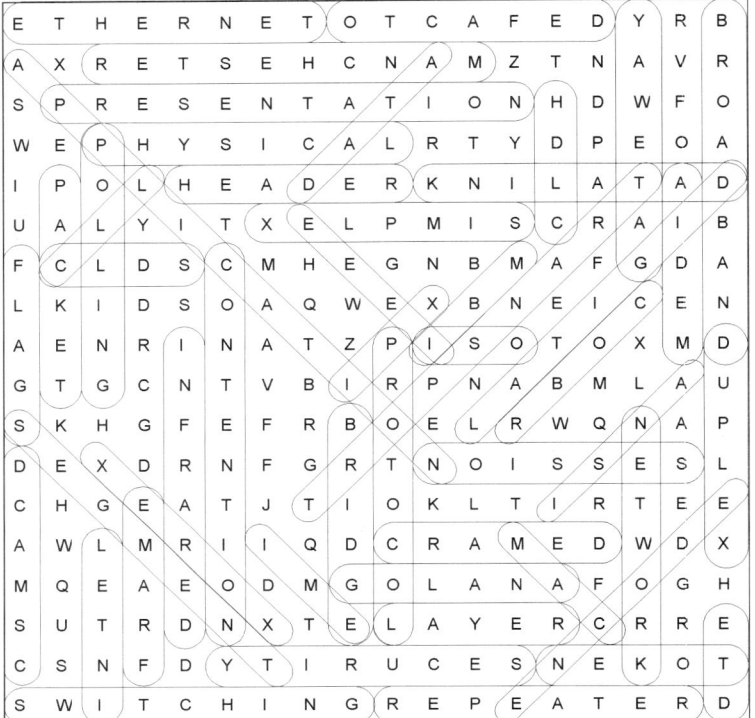

# Brain Teaser Answers

## Chapter 22

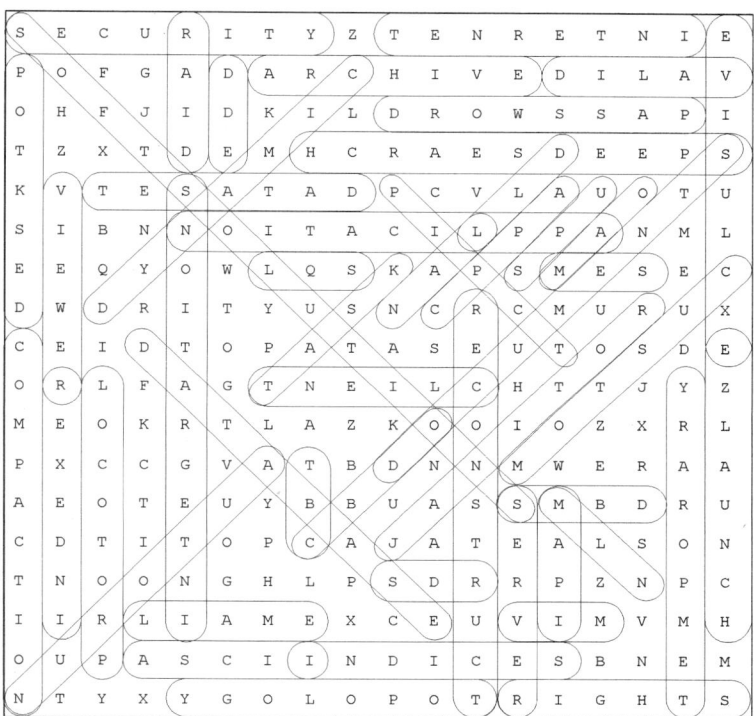

## Chapter 23

Designing a form doesn't have to be a difficult task. Remember to use color to brighten the form and make it attractive. Of course, too much color can be just as bad as none at all. Don't be afraid to add white space as needed to make the form easy to read. Another way to make the form easy to read is to separate data items into specific groups using lines and other drawing tools. Finally, using an easy-to-read font is a must—make sure you use one that's large enough for everyone to see.

Creating a form is only part of the job; testing it is the other part. Make sure you completely test every form you create using the InForms Filler utility. Once the form is tested, make sure you add the appropriate security.

# APPENDIX D

## IMPORTANT PHONE NUMBERS

*Novell Main Offices:* 1-800-453-1267.

*Novell Education Department FAX:* 1-801-429-2500.

*Novell FaxBack:* 1-800-233-3382 or 1-801-429-5363.

*Sylvan Prometric Testing Registration:* 1-800-RED-EXAM.

*Novell Technical Support:* 1-800-NETWARE.

*Novell Users International (NUI):* 1-800-873-3976 or 1-214-419-7882.

*Novell Education:* 1-800-233-EDUC or 1-801-429-5508.

*Novell After Market Products:* 1-800-346-7177 or 1-801-429-7000.

*Novell Education Materials Order:* 1-800-346-6855.

*Novell Education Area Manager, Western United States:* 1-408-747-4339.

*Novell Education Area Manager, West Central United States:* 1-214-387-7900.

*Novell Education Area Manager, East Central United States:* 1-708-228-7676.

*Novell Education Area Manager, Northeastern United States:* 1-215-647-0664.

*Novell Education Area Manager, Southeastern United States:* 1-404-698-8350.

*Novell Education Area Manager, Canada:* 1-416-940-2670.

*CompuServe Registration:* See your startup kit for instructions.

# APPENDIX E

## SOURCES OF ADDITIONAL INFORMATION

*Computer Technology Review*
924 Westwood Boulevard
Suite 650
Los Angeles, CA 90024-2910
1-310-208-1335

*Data Communications*
1221 Avenue of the Americas
New York, NY 10020
1-800-525-5003

*Data Based Advisor*
Data Based Solutions, Inc.
4010 Morena Boulevard
Suite 200
San Diego, CA 92117
1-619-483-6400
1-619-483-9851 fax

*Hands-On Guide To Network Management*
Tab-McGraw Hill
Blue Ridge Summit, PA 17294-0850
1-800-233-1128
ISBN 0-8306-4440-7

*LAN Computing*
Professional Press, Inc.
101 Witmer Road
Horsham, PA 19044
1-215-957-4269

*LAN Technology*
P.O. Box 52315
Boulder, CO 80321-2315
1-800-456-1654

*LAN Times*
Publication Office
1900 O'Farrell Street
Suite 200
San Mateo, CA 94403
1-800-525-5003

*NetWare Application Notes*
Novell
122 E. 1700 S.
Provo, UT 84606
1-800-377-4136
1-303-297-2725

*NetWare Buyers Guide*
Novell
122 E. 1700 S.
Provo, UT 84606-6194
1-800-873-2831

*NetWare Solutions*
DB Media Publications, Inc.
10711 Burnet Road
Suite 305
Austin, TX 78758
1-512-873-7761
1-512-873-7782 fax

*Network Computing*
CMP Publications
600 Community Dr.
Manhasset, NY 11030
1-516-562-5071

*Network News*
CNE Professional Association
Mail Stop E-31-1
122 E. 1700 S.
Provo, UT 84606-6194
1-800-926-3776

*Network World*
161 Worcester Road
Framingham, MA 01701-9172
1-508-820-7444

# Sources of Additional Information

*PC Magazine*
Ziff-Davis Publishing Co.
One Park Avenue
New York, NY 10016
1-212-503-5255

*PC Novice*
Reed Corporation
120 West Harvest Drive
P.O. Box 85380
Lincoln, NE 68501
1-800-544-1264

*Systems Integration*
Cahners Publishing Associates/
Reed Publishing (USA), Inc.
275 Washington Street
Newton, MA 02158
1-617-964-3030
1-617-558-4506 fax

# APPENDIX F

## COURSE DESCRIPTIONS

## DOS for NetWare Users

The DOS for NetWare Users course is a self-paced workbook-based tutorial that you can use to learn about the Novell way of looking at DOS. Most people who've used DOS on a fairly consistent basis won't need this course since they'll probably have the required knowledge from using DOS on a day-to-day basis. This course is for those who have no prior DOS experience. Anyone who intends to learn about networking using NetWare should learn about DOS before attempting any of the other courses in this book. Even though this course is no longer required for CNE certification under the new plan, you can still use it as part of the old certification program. CNAs will also benefit from the material in this course. Topics of this course include:

- Introduction to DOS
- DOS Command Execution
- Disk Drive Operations
- File Maintenance
- Directory Maintenance
- Batch Files
- Configuration of DOS Systems

This course is a workbook-only tutorial. There are no instructor-led courses associated with it. You'll need to order the workbook, part number 883-001304-003. There are no prerequisites for this course. Once you complete this workbook, order the Microcomputer Concepts for NetWare Users course described in the following section. It'll help you study for the second part of the exam associated with this course.

Course length: Approximately 6 hours

Course number: 1100

Test number: 50-15

Number of Credits: 2

# Microcomputer Concepts for NetWare Users

The Microcomputer Concepts for NetWare Users course is a self-paced workbook-based tutorial that you can use to learn about the Novell way of looking at your hardware. Even though the course emphasizes DOS, you can still use it as part of your study for the UNIX exam. Most people who have worked with the hardware installed in their machine won't need this course since they will have the required knowledge from installing and configuring hardware in the past. This course is for those who have no prior hardware-related experience. Anyone who intends to learn about networking using NetWare should learn about their machine before attempting any of the other courses in this book. Even though this course is no longer required for CNE certification under the new plan, you can still use it as part of the old certification program. CNAs will also benefit from the material in this course. Topics of this course include:

- Introduction to Microcomputer Hardware
- Introduction to Microprocessors
- Data Bus
- Memory
- Disks and Disk Drives
- Video Displays
- Serial and Parallel Ports
- Computer System Configurations

This course is a workbook-only tutorial. There are no instructor-led courses associated with it. You'll need to order the workbook, part number 883-001305-002. There are no prerequisites for this course. Once you complete this workbook, order the Microcomputer Concepts for NetWare Users course described in the following section. It'll help you study for the second part of the exam associated with this course.

Course length: Approximately 6 hours

Course number: 1101

Test number: 50-15, 50-107, or 50-207

Number of credits: 2

## UNIX OS Fundamentals for NetWare Users

The UNIX OS Fundamentals for NetWare Users course will help you understand the command line interface for the UNIX operating system. It includes material about system access, the hierarchical file system, file management, process management, and system security. This course is for the person who is a system administrator, backup system administrator, or a beginner who wants to learn more about the workings of UNIX. Topics of this class include:

- History of the UNIX Operating System
- Accessing a UNIX Operating System
- File Systems
- Performing Common UNIX Operating System Tasks
- Structure of the Operating System
- Editing Files
- Working in the Shell
- Maintaining UNIX Operating System Security
- Managing User Processes

This course includes instructor-led lectures and hands-on exercises. It concentrates on Novell's version of the UNIX operating system, UnixWare. The hands-on exercises follow the same steps and procedures used in setting up and maintaining UNIX for real companies.

The prerequisites for this class require the student to have a basic working knowledge of the hardware (see the Microcomputer Concepts for NetWare Users course description). A basic understanding of the NetWare network operating system (any version) is also helpful, but not required.

Course length: 2 days

Course number: 220

Test number: 50-107 or 50-207

Number of credits: 2

## NetWare 2.2 System Manager

The NetWare 2.2 System Manager course teaches you the fundamentals of managing and maintaining a Novell v2.2 network. This course is for the person who is a system administrator, backup system administrator, or a beginner who wants to learn more about the workings of NetWare. Topics of this course include:

- NetWare Hardware and Software Basics
- NetWare Directory Structures
- Drive Mappings
- NetWare Security
- NetWare Console and Command Line Utilities
- NetWare Menu Utilities
- Basic Printing
- Creating and Using Login Scripts
- Creating Novell Menus
- Loading Applications

This course includes instructor-led lectures and hands-on exercises. The hands-on exercises follow the same steps and procedures used in setting up and maintaining networks for real companies.

The prerequisites for this class require the student to have a basic working knowledge of DOS and to know the concepts of what a LAN is. The student's understanding of DOS must include directory hierarchy and how to create directories and ASCII files, copy files, delete files, and change directories.

Course length: 3 days

Course number: 501

Test number: 50-20

Number of credits: 3

## NetWare 2.2 Advanced System Manager

The NetWare 2.2 Advanced System Manager course covers the advanced management features of Novell NetWare version 2.2. The target student

## Course Descriptions

for this course is the person who manages an existing NetWare 2.2 network or is a consultant needing advanced information about the NetWare 2.2 operating system. Topics of this course include:

- NetWare 2.2 Installation Overview
- NetWare Accounting
- Advanced Printing
- Advanced Menu Utilities
- Performance Management
- Troubleshooting Network Problems
- Memory Management

This course includes instructor-led lectures and structured hands-on lab exercises. The lectures and lab exercises will enhance the student's understanding of the tasks and duties performed daily by system administrators and consultants working in the field of networking.

Prerequisites for this class include a working knowledge of DOS and NetWare. In addition, you must attend the 2.2 System Manager course before attending this course. The pace of the course is quite fast, making prior knowledge of NetWare a necessity.

Course length: 2 days

Course number: 502

Test number: 50-44

Number of credits: 2

## NetWare 3.x System Manager

The NetWare 3.x System Manager course centers on the basic tasks and duties of the administrator who is using the Novell NetWare 3.x operating system. Intended students of this course include network managers and networking consultants. This course will teach you the basics of using, managing, and maintaining a network running 3.x NetWare. Topics covered in the course include:

- NetWare 3.x Basics
- Setting up Directory Structures
- Working with NetWare Drive Mappings
- Understanding and Implementing NetWare Security

- Menu Utilities for Administrators
- File Server Administration Utilities
- Network Printing
- Customizing Users Access and Use to the Network
- Managing Network Applications
- Using Novell's Backup Utility

This course includes instructor-led lectures and hands-on exercises. The hands-on exercises follow the same steps and procedures used in setting up and maintaining networks for real companies.

The prerequisites for this class include a basic working knowledge of DOS and an understanding of basic LAN concepts. The student's understanding of DOS must include the directory hierarchy and how to create and manage directories, create ASCII files, copy files, and delete files.

Course length: 3 days

Course number: 505

Test number: 50-91

Number of credits: 3

## NetWare 3.x Advanced System Manager

The Novell NetWare 3.x Advanced System Manager course is an extension of the 3.x System Manager course. The lectures and lab exercises will enhance the student's understanding of the tasks and duties performed daily by system administrators and consultants working in the field of networking. Intended students of this course include system administrators and consultants. The advanced features include printing and the art of fine-tuning the network. Other topics covered in the course include:

- Advanced Command Line and Menu Utilities
- Concepts and Procedures of Performance Management
- Advanced Setup and Troubleshooting of Network Printing
- NetWare's Remote Management Utilities
- Concepts and Procedures of Open Protocol Support
- NetWare's Prevention and Maintenance Utilities

This course includes instructor-led lectures and structured hands-on lab exercises. The lectures and lab exercises will enhance the actual tasks and duties performed by system administrators and consultants working in the field of networking.

Prerequisites for this class include a working knowledge of DOS and NetWare. In addition, you must attend the 3.x System Manager course before attending this course. The pace of the course is quite fast, making prior knowledge of NetWare a necessity.

Course length: 2 days

Course number: 515

Test number: 50-82

Number of credits: 2

## NetWare 3.x Installation and Configuration Workshop

The NetWare 3.x Installation and Configuration Workshop teaches the student how to plan and install the NetWare 3.x operating system and client workstations. This course is for the person who has prior NetWare experience and whose duties include managing or maintaining the network. This includes system managers and consultants. Combining this course with the NetWare 3.x Administration and NetWare 3.x Advanced Administration courses provides a complete understanding of NetWare 3.x. Topics of this course include:

- Installing the NetWare 3.11 Server
- Upgrading a NetWare 3.11 Server to NetWare 3.12
- Installing a NetWare 3.12 Server
- Installing the Client-DOS Requester
- Configuring the NetWare 3.x Server
- Managing the NetWare 3.x Server
- Strategies for Working in the NetWare 3.x Environment
- Performing NetWare Case Studies

This course includes instructor-led lectures and hands-on exercises. It concentrates on hands-on exercises using case studies that simulate typical network setups. The hands-on exercises follow the same steps and procedures used in setting up and maintaining NetWare 3.x for real companies.

The prerequisites for this class require the student to have a basic working knowledge of the NetWare 3.x operating system. You must complete the NetWare 3.x Administration (course 508) and NetWare 3.x Advanced Administration (course 518) courses or have equivalent experience before taking this class.

Course length: 2 days

Course number: 802

Test number: 50-132 or 50-232

Number of credits: 2

## NetWare 4.x Administration

The NetWare 4.x Administration course teaches you the fundamental knowledge and skills to manage and administer a Novell NetWare 4.x network. This course is for the person who currently manages or plans to manage a network running NetWare 4.x or is a consultant planning to support the operating system. Topics of this course include:

- Introduction of NetWare 4.x
- Connecting to and Using NetWare 4.x Resources
- The NetWare Directory Services (NDS)
- NetWare 4.x File System
- File System Security
- Directory Services Security
- NetWare 4.x File Server Management
- Introduction to Printing
- Setting up the Users Network Environment

This course includes instructor-led lectures and hands-on exercises. The hands-on exercises follow the same steps and procedures used in setting up and maintaining networks for real companies.

The prerequisites for this class include a basic working knowledge of DOS and an understanding of basic LAN concepts. The student's understanding of DOS must include the directory hierarchy and how to create and manage directories, create ASCII files, copy files, and delete files. The student should also have a working understanding of Windows 3.0 or above.

>   Course length: 4 days
>   Course number: 520
>   Test number: 50-122
>   Number of credits: 3

## NetWare 4.x Advanced Administration

The NetWare 4.x Advanced Administration course continues where the 4.x Administration course stops. This course is for the manager or consultant who is working with a complex network installation. The course will teach you about planning, implementing, fine-tuning, and overseeing a complex network using NetWare 4.x. Topics of this course include:

- Introduction to Complex Novell Networks
- Planning and Managing the NetWare Directory Services (NDS)
- Advanced Security Features
- Resource Auditing Features
- Advanced Printing
- Managing Client and Network Features and Services
- Fine-Tuning NetWare 4.x for Optimum Performance

This course includes instructor-led lectures and hands-on exercises. The hands-on exercises follow the same steps and procedures used in setting up and maintaining networks for real companies.

Prerequisites for this class include a working knowledge of DOS and NetWare. In addition, you must attend the 4.x Administration course before attending this course. The pace of the course is quite fast, making prior knowledge of NetWare a necessity. The student's understanding of DOS must include the directory hierarchy and how to create and manage directories, create ASCII files, copy files, and delete files. The student should also have a working understanding of Windows 3.0 or above.

Course length: 3 days

Course number: 525

Test number: 50-123

Number of credits: 2

## NetWare 3.x to 4.x Update

The NetWare 3.x to 4.x Update course identifies the new and enhanced features of the NetWare 4.x operating system over the 3.x operating system. The course is for the person who has experience working with networks, especially Novell NetWare 3.x. This includes system administrators and consultants. Combining this course with the NetWare Installation and Configuration Workshop course offers a complete overview of NetWare 4.x. Topics of this course include:

- NetWare 4.x Overview
- NetWare Directory Services (NDS) Concepts and Implementation
- NetWare 4.x Security for NDS and the File System
- Client and Utility Changes
- NetWare 4.x Print Services
- Resource Auditing Services
- Storage Management Features and Services

This course includes instructor-led lectures and hands-on exercises. The hands-on exercises follow the same steps and procedures used in setting up and maintaining networks for real companies.

The prerequisites for this class include prior NetWare experience (preferably with NetWare 3.x). Also required is a basic working knowledge of DOS and an understanding of basic LAN concepts. The student's understanding of DOS must include the directory hierarchy and how to create and manage directories, create ASCII files, copy files, and delete files. The student should also have a working understanding of Windows 3.0 or above.

Course length: 3 days

Course number: 526

Test number: 50-124

Number of credits: 2

# NetWare 4.x Installation and Configuration Workshop

The NetWare 4.x Installation and Configuration Workshop teaches the student how to plan and install the NetWare 4.x operating system and client workstations. This course is for the person who has prior NetWare experience and whose duties include managing or maintaining the network. This includes system managers and consultants. Combining this course with the NetWare 3.x to 4.x Update course provides a complete understanding of NetWare 4.x. Topics of this course include:

- Installing the 4.x Operating System
- Installing the DOS and Windows Workstation Client
- Migrating from NetWare 3.x to NetWare 4.x
- Managing the NetWare Directory Services (NDS)
- Setting up NetWare Printing Services
- Backing up and Restoring Data Using Netware Utilities
- Managing the File Server Using New Netware Utilities

This course includes some instructor-led lectures, with most of the course consisting of hands-on exercises. The hands-on exercises follow the same steps and procedures used in setting up and maintaining networks for real companies.

The prerequisites for this class include prior NetWare experience (preferably with NetWare 3.x). Also required is a basic working knowledge of DOS and an understanding of basic LAN concepts. The student's understanding of DOS must include the directory hierarchy and how to create and manage directories, create ASCII files, copy files, and delete files. The student should also have a working understanding of Windows 3.0 or above.

Course length: 2 days

Course number: 804

Test number: 50-126

Number of credits: 2

# Appendix F

# NetWare Service and Support

The NetWare Service and Support course will teach the student various hardware topics related to installing and maintaining the NetWare operating system. During this course you'll install and configure network interface cards and disk subsystems, connect cables, and install both NetWare 2.x and 3.x. Other topics that the course will cover include:

- NetWare 2.x Architecture
- NetWare 3.x Architecture
- Multiserver Networks
- Internetworks
- Network Addressing
- Network Board Configurations
- Network Cabling
- Disk Storage
- Workstation Installation
- NetWare 2.x and 3.x Installation
- NetWare Router Installation
- NetWare Upgrading Procedures
- Troubleshooting Techniques and Tools
- Novell Diagnostics Utilities
- Common Network Problems

This course is instructor-led, with the students performing many hands-on exercises. The information and exercises in this course are the same tasks that technicians perform on a daily basis.

The prerequisites for this class include a working knowledge of the Intel-based personal computer. Other beneficial prerequisites include a working knowledge of LAN and DOS basics.

Course length: 5 days

Course number: 701

Test number: 50-46

Number of credits: 5

# Networking Technologies

The Networking Technologies course provides in-depth instruction that covers the theory and protocols of networking. Discussed in this class are the seven layers of the OSI model, the applications of each layer, and how they relate to networking. The course also includes information about the communication protocols of Novell's IPX/SPX and the TCP/IP protocol used by UNIX. Other topics and technologies of this course include:

- Understanding the History of Networking
- Standards-Setting Committees
- Data Encoding Schemes
- Data Transmission Modes
- Signal Multiplexing and Signal Conversion
- Network Topologies
- Circuit, Message, and Packet Switching Techniques
- PSTN Network
- Functions of the IEEE 802.3, 802.4, and 802.5 Standards
- LocalTalk and AppleTalk Technology
- SDLC and HDLC Protocols Used by Mainframe Networks
- NetWare Protocols of IPX/SPX
- Internet Protocols of TCP, UDP, and IP
- SNA and DNA Network Architectures

This course is lecture-only, with no hands-on computer exercises. However, the manuals provide written exercises at the end of each of the 29 chapters. The course covers many subjects related to networking in just three days. In comparison to this intensive training, a college course usually covers less material in one year.

The prerequisites for this class are a basic understanding of LANs and a strong desire to learn more about the theories of networking. Since this course covers so much material, from the general to the specific, there is no other Novell course that offers much assistance.

Course length: 3 days

Course number: 200

Test number: 50-80

Number of credits: 3

# UnixWare Installation and Configuration Workshop

The UnixWare Installation and Configuration Workshop teaches the student how to plan and install the UnixWare operating system and client workstations. This course is for the person who has prior UNIX experience and whose duties include managing or maintaining the network. This includes system managers and consultants. Resellers who require a basic understanding of how to set up UnixWare can also take this course. Combining this course with the UnixWare Administration and UnixWare Advanced Administration courses provides a complete understanding of UnixWare. Topics of this course include:

- Product Overview
- Using UnixWare
- Initial System Configuration
- Using and Configuring DOS on UnixWare
- Installing Applications
- Installing UnixWare

This course includes instructor-led lectures and hands-on exercises. It concentrates on hands-on exercises using case studies that simulate typical network setups. The hands-on exercises follow the same steps and procedures used in setting up and maintaining UnixWare for real companies.

The prerequisites for this class require a basic working knowledge of the UNIX operating system. A familiarity with UnixWare in particular is helpful. You must complete the UNIX OS fundamentals for NetWare Users (course 220) course or have equivalent experience before taking this class.

Course length: 2 days

Course number: 678

Test number: 50-133 or 50-233

Number of credits: 2

# UnixWare Administration

The UnixWare Administration course teaches you the fundamental knowledge and skills required to manage and administer a Novell Unix-

Ware network. This course is for the person who currently manages or plans to manage a network running UnixWare, or is a consultant planning to support the operating system as part of their business. Topics of this course include:

- System Administration Overview
- Managing NetWare Integration
- Managing the User Base
- Configuring UNIX Networking with TCP/IP
- Configuring File Sharing with NFS
- Configuring and Managing Print Services
- Automating System Administration Tasks
- Designing and Implementing Data Archiving Strategies
- Configuring UNIX Mail

This course includes instructor-led lectures and hands-on exercises. The hands-on exercises follow the same steps and procedures used in setting up and maintaining networks for real companies.

The prerequisites for this class include a basic working knowledge of UNIX and an understanding of basic LAN concepts. The student's understanding of UNIX must include all of the topics included in the UNIX OS Fundamentals for NetWare Users (course 220) and UnixWare Installation and Configuration (course 678) courses described in this appendix. The student should also have a working knowledge of the NetWare operating system, but this isn't a requirement to begin the course.

Course length: 3 days

Course number: 680

Test number: 50-392, 50-134, or 50-234

Number of credits: 3

## UnixWare Advanced Administration

The UnixWare Advanced Administration course continues where the UnixWare Administration course stops. This course is for the manager or consultant who is working with a complex network installation. The course will teach you about planning, implementing, fine-tuning, and overseeing a complex network using UnixWare. Topics of this course include:

- Troubleshooting Techniques
- Supporting UnixWare File Systems
- Managing System Performance
- Modifying and Upgrading System Hardware
- Modifying and Troubleshooting Network Configurations
- System Crash Recovery

This course includes instructor-led lectures and hands-on exercises. The hands-on exercises follow the same steps and procedures used in setting up and maintaining networks for real companies.

Prerequisites for this class include a working knowledge of UNIX and UnixWare. In addition, you must attend the UnixWare Administration course (course 680) before attending this course. (You may also start the course by demonstrating the requisite experiential knowledge.) The pace of the course is quite fast, making prior knowledge of UnixWare a necessity. The student's understanding of UNIX must include all of the topics included in the UNIX OS Fundamentals for NetWare Users (course 220) and UnixWare Installation and Configuration (course 678) courses described in this appendix. The student should also have a working knowledge of the NetWare operating system, but this isn't a requirement to begin the course.

Course length: 3 days

Course number: 685

Test number: 50-135 or 50-235

Number of credits: 2

# GroupWise 4.x Administration

The GroupWise 4.x Administration course teaches you the fundamental knowledge and skills required to manage and administer a Novell GroupWise network. This course is for the person who currently manages or plans to manage a network running GroupWise, or is a consultant planning to support GroupWise as part of their business. Topics of this course include:

# Course Descriptions

- GroupWise Messaging System Structure
- Responsibilities of the GroupWise Administrator
- Single Post Office Administration
- Client Administration
- Multiple Post Office Administration
- Multiple Domain Systems

This course includes instructor-led lectures and hands-on exercises. The hands-on exercises follow the same steps and procedures used in setting up and maintaining networks for real companies.

The prerequisites for this class include a basic working knowledge of DOS, microcomputer concepts, and Windows 3.x, and an understanding of basic LAN concepts. The student's understanding of DOS and microcomputer concepts must include all of the topics included in the DOS for NetWare Users (course 1100) and Microcomputer Concepts for NetWare Users (course 1101) courses described in this appendix. Successful completion of the Netware 3.x Administration (course 508) or NetWare 4.x Administration (course 520) courses or equivalent knowledge are also required. The student should also have a working knowledge of the GroupWise user tools, but this isn't a requirement to begin the course.

Course length: 3 days

Course number: 325

Test number: 50-395, 50-154, or 50-254

Number of credits: 3

## GroupWise 4.x Advanced Administration

The GroupWise 4.x Advanced Administration course continues where the GroupWise 4.x Administration course stops. This course is for the manager or consultant who is working with a complex network installation. The course will teach you about planning, implementing, fine-tuning, and overseeing a complex network using GroupWise. Topics of this course include:

- GroupWise User Administration
- GroupWise Windows Client Administration

- External GroupWise Domains
- Merging and Releasing Domains
- Domain Database Administration through Async Gateway Links
- GroupWise Administration with NetWare Utilities
- GroupWise Bindery and Novell Directory Services (NDS) Synchronization NLMs

This course includes instructor-led lectures and hands-on exercises. The hands-on exercises follow the same steps and procedures used in setting up and maintaining networks for real companies.

Prerequisites for this class include a working knowledge of DOS, microcomputer hardware, and NetWare 3.x or 4.x Administration. In addition, you must attend the GroupWise Administration course (course 325) before attending this course. (You may also start the course by demonstrating the requisite experiential knowledge.) The pace of the course is quite fast, making prior knowledge of GroupWise a necessity. The student's understanding of DOS and microcomputer concepts must include all of the topics included in the DOS for NetWare Users (course 1100) and Microcomputer Concepts for NetWare Users (course 1101) courses described in this appendix.

Course length: 3 days

Course number: 328

Test number: 50-604

Number of credits: 2

# GroupWise 4.x Asynchronous Gateways and Remote Client Support

The GroupWise 4.x Asynchronous Gateways and Remote Client Support course teaches you how to add and configure an asynchronous gateway to an existing GroupWise installation. It also shows how to provide support for a remote client. This course is for the manager or consultant working with a complex network installation. The course will teach you about planning, implementing, fine-tuning, and overseeing a complex network using UnixWare. Topics of this course include:

**Course Descriptions**

- GroupWise Asynchronous Gateway Overview
- DOS and OS/2 Asynchronous Gateways
- Microsoft Windows Remote Client
- Monitoring and Troubleshooting Asynchronous Gateways and Remote Clients

This course includes instructor-led lectures and hands-on exercises. The hands-on exercises follow the same steps and procedures used in setting up and maintaining networks for real companies.

Prerequisites for this class include having a working knowledge of DOS, Windows, microcomputer hardware, and NetWare 3.x or 4.x Administration. In addition, you must attend the GroupWise Administration course (course 325) before attending this course. (You may also start the course by demonstrating the requisite experiential knowledge.) An overall knowledge of OS/2 is also good, but is not required to complete the course. The pace of the course is quite fast, making prior knowledge of GroupWise a necessity. The student's understanding of DOS and microcomputer concepts must include all of the topics included in the DOS for NetWare Users (course 1100) and Microcomputer Concepts for NetWare Users (course 1101) courses described in this appendix.

Course length: 2 days

Course number: 326

Test number: 50-155 or 50-255

Number of credits: 1

## GroupWise 5.x Administration

The GroupWise 5.x Administration course teaches you the fundamental knowledge and skills required to manage and administer a Novell GroupWise network. This course is for the person who currently manages or plans to manage a network running GroupWise, or is a consultant planning to support GroupWise as part of their business. Topics of this course include:

- System Fundamentals and Architecture
- Installation and Configuration
- Configuring Single Post Office Messaging
- Creating a Multiple Post Office System

- Creating, Deleting, and Renaming Users
- System Backup
- Configuring Preferences
- Setting Up and Maintaining a GroupWise Library
- Security

This course includes instructor-led lectures and hands-on exercises. The hands-on exercises follow the same steps and procedures used in setting up and maintaining networks for real companies.

The prerequisites for this class include a basic working knowledge of DOS, microcomputer concepts, and Windows 3.x/95, and an understanding of basic LAN concepts. The student's understanding of DOS and microcomputer concepts must include all of the topics included in the DOS for NetWare Users (course 1100) and Microcomputer Concepts for NetWare Users (course 1101) courses described in this appendix. Successful completion of the NetWare 4.x Administration (course 520) courses or equivalent knowledge are also required. The student should also have a working knowledge of the GroupWise user tools and NDS, but this isn't a requirement to begin the course.

Course length: 3 days

Course number: 350

Test number: CNE 50-618 or CNI 50-818 (The CNE examination counts toward CNA certification.)

Number of credits: 3

# GroupWise 5.x Advanced Administration

The GroupWise 5.x Advanced Administration course continues where the GroupWise 5.x Administration course stops. This course is for the manager or consultant who is working with a complex network installation. The course will teach you about planning, implementing, fine-tuning, and overseeing a complex network using GroupWise. Topics of this course include:

- The Link Configuration Utility
- Customized Addressing

# Course Descriptions

- Database Synchronization
- Back Up MTAs
- Transfer Pull Services
- Multiple Library Configurations
- Internal and External Foreign Domains
- Migrating from GroupWise 4.x to GroupWise 5.x
- Troubleshooting GroupWise Problems
- Designing a GroupWise 5.x System

This course includes instructor-led lectures and hands-on exercises. The hands-on exercises follow the same steps and procedures used in setting up and maintaining networks for real companies.

Prerequisites for this class include a working knowledge of DOS, microcomputer hardware, and NetWare 4.x Administration. In addition, you must attend the GroupWise Administration (course 350) and NetWare Design and Implementation (course 532) courses before attending this course. (You may also start the course by demonstrating the requisite experiential knowledge.) The pace of the course is quite fast, making prior knowledge of GroupWise a necessity. The student's understanding of DOS and microcomputer concepts must include all of the topics included in the DOS for NetWare Users (course 1100) and Microcomputer Concepts for NetWare Users (course 1101) courses described in this appendix.

Course length: 2 days

Course number: 352

Test number: CNE 50-619 or CNI 50-819

Number of credits: 2

## NetWare TCP/IP Transport

This course will teach you how to install and configure NetWare TCP/IP software on a NetWare 4.x server. It's designed to meet the needs of NCIPs, though CNEs and CNIs are certainly welcome to attend. Essentially, this course is designed to help any network administrator or consultant move from an in-house network to the much wider range of possibilities offered by the Internet. Once you get the TCP/IP software installed, you'll learn how to use basic Internet applications like Telnet and FTP. Troubleshooting techniques are also part of the course. The course materials include an appendix for NetWare 3.x users, along with the NetWare 3.x TCP/IP product documentation. Topics of this course include:

- TCP/IP Installation on a NetWare 4.x Server
- Troubleshooting Procedures
- Server Monitoring
- Loading the TCP/IP NLM
- Routing IPX Packets over an IP Intranet

This course includes instructor-led lectures and hands-on exercises. The hands-on exercises follow the same steps and procedures used in setting up and maintaining Intranets for real companies.

Prerequisites for this class include a working knowledge of DOS, microcomputer hardware, and either NetWare 3.x or NetWare 4.x Administration. (You may also start the course by demonstrating the requisite experiential knowledge.)

Course length: 2 days

Course number: 605

Test number: 50-145 or 50-245

Number of credits: 2

## Understanding and Applying Internet Concepts

This course will help you get a start learning about the Internet and how it can help your business. It's designed to meet the needs of NCIP candidates, though any network administrator or consultant who plans to work on the Internet will benefit. Some types of sales and technical support personnel could also benefit from this course, though they would need some level of computer training before starting the course. The emphasis of this course is on working on the Internet itself—which means you'll spend only a modicum of time talking about networking. Topics of this course include:

- Description of Internet Components
- Locating and Accessing Information on the Internet Using a Browser

## Course Descriptions

- Identifying Internet Applications That Can Help Businesses
- Description of Internet Marketing and Information Gathering Strategies
- Defining an Implementation Strategy for Web Services
- Identifying the Various Standards Required for Internet Access
- Determining an Organization's Internet Access Configuration Requirements
- Selecting a Single E-mail System for Both Internet and Intranet Use
- Internet Security

This course includes instructor-led lectures and hands-on exercises. Most of the exercises will involve working with the Internet. The hands-on exercises follow the same steps and procedures used in setting up and maintaining Intranets for real companies.

Prerequisites for this class include a working knowledge of Microsoft Windows. The student also has to know how to use basic computer hardware like the mouse, but is not required to know the inner workings of the computer. (You may also start the course by demonstrating the requisite experiential knowledge.)

Course length: 1 day

Course number: 652

Test number: N/A

Number of credits: 0

# Web Authoring and Publishing

This course will teach you how to design and publish basic documents on the Internet using HTML. Even though the intended participants are NCIP candidates, anyone needing to create a Web site will benefit from this course. Participants could include network administrators or Webmaster candidates. The course concentrates on basic HTML formatting like creating tables, links, and forms. You'll learn about newer technologies like scripting (JavaScript). Topics of this course include:

- Creating a Basic HTML Document
- Organizing Web Documents
- Creating HTML Links (Other Computers, File Download, and Mail)

- Using Advanced HTML Features Including Tables and Images
- Creating Forms to Capture and Transfer Data

This course includes instructor-led lectures and hands-on exercises. Most of the exercises involve working with the Internet. You should also be prepared to learn some programming techniques. The hands-on exercises follow the same steps and procedures used in setting up and maintaining intranets for real companies.

Prerequisites for this class include a working knowledge of DOS, microcomputer hardware, and the Understanding and Applying Internet Concepts course (course 652). (You may also start the course by demonstrating the requisite experiential knowledge.) Some level of programming or macro scripting knowledge is a plus, but not actually required.

Course length: 2 days

Course number: 654

Test number: 50-700 or 50-750

Number of credits: 2

## Advanced Web Authoring

This course takes up where the Web Authoring and Publishing course (654) leaves off. It's designed to enhance the knowledge of potential Webmasters so that they can provide content-rich pages for a company intranet or for general use on the Internet. Most of the emphasis of this course is on server-side content, rather than the client-side content found in the previous course. Topics of this course include:

- Using SSI Commands in a Web Site
- Creating and Using PERL CGI Scripts in a Web Site
- Creating and Using JavaScripts in a Web Site
- Adding Java Applets to a Web Site

This course includes instructor-led lectures and hands-on exercises. Most of the exercises involve working with the Internet from the server rather than the client side. You should also be prepared to learn some programming techniques. In fact, the vast majority of the course is programmer-oriented. The hands-on exercises follow the same steps and procedures used in setting up and maintaining Internet and intranet servers for real companies.

Prerequisites for this class include a working knowledge of DOS, microcomputer hardware, and the Web Authoring and Publishing course (course 654). (You may also start the course by demonstrating the requisite experiential knowledge.) A good knowledge of programming techniques is a plus, though not absolutely required to pass the course.

Course length: 2 days

Course number: 655

Test number: 50-705 or 50-755

Number of credits: 2

## Web Server Management

This is one of the few NetWare-specific courses for the NCIP. It shows the student how to configure a NetWare 4.x server for Internet access. The student will also learn how to publish content using the NetWare Web Server, which includes learning how to install and configure the NetWare Web Server. In addition, the student will learn how to make the NetWare Web Server work with NDS. As previously stated, this course is specifically designed for NCIP candidates, though any potential Webmaster could learn how to better manage a Web site through this course (assuming that you're using NetWare for your Web server operating system). Topics of this course include:

- Internet Services Provided by NetWare Web Server
- Comparing Internet and Intranet Solutions (mainly content-related)
- Creating an Internet Connection
- Creating an Intranet
- Installing and Configuring the NetWare Web Server
- Using NDS with NetWare Web Server

This course includes instructor-led lectures and hands-on exercises. The hands-on exercises follow the same steps and procedures used in setting up and maintaining both Internets and intranets for real companies. Most of the information in this course is Novell-specific and deals with NetWare Web Server.

Prerequisites for this class include a working knowledge of DOS, microcomputer hardware, and the NetWare TCP/IP Transport course (course 605). The course attendee must also have a good knowledge of Internetworking technology and services. (You may also start the course by demonstrating the requisite experiential knowledge.) A good understanding of NetWare 4.x administration is a plus, but not a requirement.

Course length: 2 days

Course number: 656

Test number: 50-710 or 50-760

Number of credits: 2

## InForms 4.x Introduction for New Users

This is a beginner's course for learning to use InForms. Essentially you learn how to fill out a form with the product—just an introduction to what you'll do later. For the most part, this is a course that anyone can attend, though it's definitely geared more toward the computer novice (or at least the new InForms user). Topics of this course include:

- Filling in an InForms Form
- Signing Electronic Forms
- Managing Form Information
- Creating a Secure Environment
- Distributing Forms Using E-mail

This course includes instructor-led lectures and hands-on exercises. The hands-on exercises follow the same steps and procedures used in a company setting. There aren't any prerequisites for this course (except a desire to learn).

Course length: 2 hours

Course number: 331a

Test number: N/A

Number of credits: 0

## InForms 4.x Administration and Form Design

This course concentrates on the tasks you'll need to perform as an administrator. In other words, it assumes that you already know how to use InForms and want to know more about customizing it to meet your company's needs. The audience for this course includes both CNE and MCNE candidates, experienced network administrators, and managers who need to design forms. Topics of this course include:

- Introduction to Form Design and Tools
- Creating and Managing Forms (includes form design)
- Creating Multiplatform Forms
- Creating Form Links, Queries, and Reports
- Printing and Faxing Forms
- Understanding Ways to Minimize Data Entry Errors
- Designing a Secure Environment
- Accessing Data While Filling Forms Out
- Sending Forms to Others Using E-mail

This course includes instructor-led lectures and hands-on exercises. The hands-on exercises follow the same steps and procedures used in setting up and maintaining InForms setups for real companies.

Prerequisites for this class include a basic understanding of how to use InForms (see course 331a if you need to learn how to use the product).

Course length: 3 days

Course number: 335

Test number: 50-156 or 50-256

Number of credits: 3

## SoftSolutions 4.x Administration

This is a course designed to help CNA, CNE, and MCNE candidates, experienced network administrators, and systems integrators learn how to plan, install, troubleshoot, and maintain a SoftSolutions 4.x setup. This includes things like day-to-day maintenance procedures. The student will also learn about general document management when using SoftSolutions. Topics of this course include:

- Installing SoftSolutions
- Customizing Document Options
- Creating a Secure Environment
- Setting Up Applications
- Creating Users
- Differentiating Document Types
- Designing Screens
- Importing Documents
- Creating Reports

This course includes instructor-led lectures and hands-on exercises. The hands-on exercises follow the same steps and procedures used in setting up and maintaining a SoftSolutions setup for a real company.

Prerequisites for this class include a working knowledge of DOS, microcomputer hardware, and either NetWare 3.x or NetWare 4.x Administration. (You may also start the course by demonstrating the requisite experiential knowledge.)

Course length: 3 days

Course number: 326

Test number: 50-158 or 50-258

Number of credits: 3

## SoftSolutions 4.x Advanced Administration

This course continues where the SoftSolutions 4.x Administration course (course 345) leaves off. It's designed to meet the needs of CNE and MCNE candidates, systems administrators and integrators, and other network support personnel. Essentially, this course teaches how to manage a large SoftSolutions setup and assumes that you'll need to work with the Server Enhancement Module (SEM). You'll create multiple datasets and learn about dataset recovery procedures. Topics of this course include:

# Course Descriptions

- Maintaining SoftSolutions Utilities
- Implement a Full Text Index
- Using the Server Enhancement Module (SEM)
- Maintaining the SoftSolutions Dataset
- Repairing a Dataset

This course includes instructor-led lectures and hands-on exercises. The hands-on exercises follow the same steps and procedures used in setting up and maintaining a SoftSolutions setup for a real company.

Prerequisites for this class include a working knowledge of DOS, microcomputer hardware, and either NetWare 3.x or NetWare 4.x Administration. You must also attend the SoftSolutions 4.x Administrator course (course 345). Finally, you need to demonstrate your ability to install and maintain software on both networks and workstations. (You may also start the course by demonstrating the requisite experiential knowledge.)

Course length: 3 days

Course number: 348

Test number: 50-159 or 50-259

Number of credits: 2

# Glossary

**ACS**   See **asynchronous communications server.**

**ad-hoc solution**   A technique for solving an event or problem that requires an immediate solution. It usually refers to something that is not planned, but is implemented without consideration of any side effects. For example, an ad-hoc report solves the need to present information in a specific manner without programming that report into the application that prepares it.

**American Standard Code for Information Interchange**   See **ASCII.**

**ARCNet**   See **network type.**

**ASCII (American Standard Code for Information Interchange)**   A standard method of equating the numeric representations available in a computer to human-readable form. For example, the number 32 represents a space. There are 128 characters (7 bits) in the standard ASCII code. The extended ASCII code uses 8 bits for 256 characters. Display adapters from the same machine type usually use the same 128 uppercase characters. Printers, however, may reserve these 128 uppercase characters for nonstandard characters. For example, many Epson printers use them for the italic representation of the 128 lowercase characters.

**asynchronous communications server (ACS)**   A special network node containing one or more modems. The ACS allows users on the LAN to communicate with other LANs, BBSs, and online services. An ACS also allows off-site employees to dial into the LAN to upload and download files, use application programs, or read e-mail.

**bindery**   The set of files used to store network-specific configuration information on a NetWare network. These files contain user data, security information, and other network configuration data. You cannot start the file server without this information. Corruption of any of these files may prevent the network from starting properly, as well.

**cache buffers**   A term that refers to the smallest storage elements in a cache (an area of RAM devoted to storing commonly used pieces of information normally stored on the hard drive). Think of each buffer as a box that can store a single piece of information. The more buffers (boxes) you have, the greater the storage capacity of the cache.

**CBT** See **computer-based training.**

**CD-ROM (compact disc read-only memory)** A device used to store up to 650 MB of permanent data. You cannot use a CD-ROM in the same way as a hard or floppy disk drive since you cannot write to it. The discs look much like audio CDs, but require a special drive to interface with a computer.

**central configuration** The files required to tell an application, operating system, or application environment how to configure itself to interact with the user's workstation. This file may also contain user preferences, like screen colors or macros. Usually, these files appear on the local hard drive of each user's workstation. However, in a central configuration the files appear in one place on the file server's hard drive.

**Certified Novell Administrator (CNA)** Certified Novell Administrator (CNA) is Novell's entry-level certification. It is for the person who needs to administer the network on a day-to-day basis. Usually, these people work for one company and perform the administrator's tasks in concert with their other duties. (See Chap. 1 for more details.)

**Certified Novell Engineer (CNE)** Certified Novell Engineer (CNE) is Novell's intermediate-level certification. This certification is for people who require a higher level of expertise than a system administrator does. Many people who obtain the CNE certification are consultants, system integrators, or employees of a company that needs a person with more skills and knowledge to help maintain the overall network. (See Chap. 1 for more details.)

**Certified Novell Instructor (CNI)** Certified Novell Instructor (CNI) is Novell's advanced-level certification. This certification is for the individual who wants to teach certified NetWare courses. These courses are taught at Novell Authorized Education Centers (NAECs) and use the Novell courseware.

**channel service unit (CSU)** A device used to terminate a dataphone digital service (DDS) communications line. Terminating the line reduces noise and signal variances that could interfere with communications. A CSU is used for T-1 communications.

**character mode interface** A menu or other application selection system that uses ASCII characters to display information. The menuing system keeps the workstation's video adapter in character mode, rather than using the display adapter's graphics mode. All line drawing characters are part of the extended ASCII character set.

# Glossary

**CMOS (complimentary metal oxide semiconductor)** A shortened phrase for *CMOS memory*. It is a special form of low-power, battery-backed memory used in computer systems to store configuration information, like the number and type of floppy disk drives. It also keeps track of the system time and date.

**CNA** See **Certified Novell Administrator.**

**CNE** See **Certified Novell Engineer.**

**CNI** See **Certified Novell Instructor.**

**common user access (CUA)** A technique for creating application menus in such a way that applications that require similar functions use similar menus. For example, the *File* menu on every application will contain a *Quit* option. It also determines the order in which entries appear. For example, the File menu is always the first menu on the left side of the menu bar, while *Help* is the last menu on the right side of the menu bar.

**compact disc read-only memory (CD-ROM)** A permanent form of disk storage which relies on a single platter to store 650 MB of data (using current technology). CD-ROM drives use laser technology to read the bits of information stored on a plastic laminated disk. Data is recorded when the laser in a recording device makes pits in the aluminum- or gold-plated recording media. The pit changes the light-reflecting characteristics of the media, changing the bit's value from a 0 to a 1.

**computer-based training (CBT)** An alternative means of receiving Novell training. This method uses a combination of manuals, on-screen lessons, and simulated tests to help the candidate prepare for certification exams.

**CRC** See **cyclic redundancy code.**

**CSU** See **channel service unit.**

**CUA** See **common user access.**

**cyclic redundancy code (CRC)** A technique used to ensure the reliability of information stored on hard drives, transported across network cabling, or otherwise sent from one place to another. It uses a cyclic calculation to create a numeric check number. The computer performs the same calculation when it retrieves the data and compares it to the CRC. If the two match, there is no data error. Otherwise, either the sending machine must resend the data or the receiving computer must reconstruct it.

**DAT (digital audio tape) drive** A tape drive that uses a cassette to store data. The cassette and drive use the same technology as the audio version of the DAT drive. However, the internal circuitry of the drive formats the tape for use with a computer system. The vendor must design the interface circuitry with computer needs in mind, as well. DAT tapes allow you to store large amounts of information in a relatively small amount of space. Typical drive capacities range from 1.2 to 8 GB.

**data encoding scheme** A method for transmitting data that (1) consumes less space, (2) provides some type of error checking, or (3) makes the data unreadable to parties without the password. Products like PKZIP encode the data so that it consumes less space. A CRC provides an error-checking encoding scheme. Any product that encrypts the data fulfills the third definition.

**data-grade line** A specially constructed telephone line that uses higher-quality media and less multiplexing to reduce overall line noise and increase reliability. Data-grade lines usually use fiberoptic connections to ensure a minimum of disruption from external signal sources.

**data service unit (DSU)** A device, similar to a modem, that connects a PC or terminal to a dataphone digital service (DDS) communications line. One end of the DSU connects to the terminal through a standard serial port. The other end of the DSU connects through the CSU to the four-wire DDS line. A DSU is used for T-1 communications.

**data transmission mode** The method used to transfer data from one node to the next on a network.

**DDE** See **dynamic data exchange.**

**dial-in/dial-out connectivity** A service that allows employees to call the company network from a remote location and use the network's services. For example, if someone needed to use the company e-mail system to check their incoming mail or to create messages for other people in the company, they could use this service. This type of service also allows satellite offices to update or download information from the company database. The dial-out portion of the service allows people within the company to send faxes or to call online services using the company modem. There are a number of other uses for dial-in/dial-out connectivity.

**digital audio tape drive** See **DAT.**

**direct memory access** See **DMA.**

**dirty power** Electricity that contains impure elements, such as power spikes or noise. These impure elements may damage computer equip-

# Glossary

ment by momentarily driving the component beyond its specified limits. *Spikes* usually occur as the result of motor starts and stops. Switches and other devices that change the flow of electricity may also cause spikes. *Noise* usually comes from electric lighting, transformers, or other devices that produce radio-frequency signals.

**disk cache**  A technique that increases the apparent speed of a hard disk drive by storing some of the data in RAM. There are many methods that the disk cache software uses to determine which data remains in RAM. The caching technique determines how great a speed increase is seen from the disk cache.

**disk duplexing**  The process of running two hard disk drive subsystems in parallel. The drives are paired from one subsystem to the other and contain the same information. The drive subsystems are totally separate, which means that one drive can take over for the other in the event of any drive failure. This includes controller failures.

**disk mirroring**  The process of running two hard disk drives in parallel. The two drives share the same controller. They also contain the same information. One drive can take over for the other in the event of a drive failure. This redundant method of data storage does not provide any backup for the drive controller.

**DMA**  See **direct memory access.**

**downsizing**  The process of moving applications from a large centralized mainframe or minicomputer environment to a decentralized PC LAN environment. Downsizing may involve using the mainframe or minicomputer as a database host or storage device. All user interface, security, print, and e-mail functions reside on the local PC LAN. Many large businesses use downsizing as a means of reducing operating costs. A typical PC LAN requires fewer resources to install and maintain than a mainframe or minicomputer with similar capacity.

**Drake Testing Center**  The only company authorized by Novell to administer certification examinations. This company specializes in providing quiet and comfortable test centers that cater to a wide range of specialties, including CPA and Registered Nurse certification. The next time you fly, you will fly with a pilot tested by a Drake Testing Center. (See Chap. 1 for more details about the Drake Testing Center; App. A provides a telephone number.)

**drive mappings**  A method of assigning a drive letter to a specific volume and directory on a network drive. Drive mappings provide a quick method to access information on a network drive without worrying about the precise location of the data. Drive mappings usually range from drive G to Z (assuming that you use drive F as the first network drive).

**DSU**   See **data service unit.**

**dynamic data exchange (DDE)**   The ability to cut data found in one application and paste it into another application. For example, cutting a graphic image created by a paint program and pasting it into a word-processing application as part of a word-processing document. Once pasted, the data does not reflect changes made to it by the originating application.

**EA**   See **extended attribute file.**

**ECC**   See **error checking and correcting.**

**ECNE**   See **Enterprise Certified Novell Engineer.**

**EISA system**   A personal computer that uses the extended industry standard architecture as a bus. An EISA system provides a 32-bit data bus, contrasted with the 16-bit bus provided by an ISA machine.

**EMM**   See **expanded memory manager.**

**Emoticon**   A figure created with the symbols on a keyboard. To read an emoticon, tilt your head to the left and visualize the person's expression. Use emoticons to convey the intent behind a humorous or tongue-in-cheek comment.

**enhanced mode**   A Windows operating mode that supports the capabilities of the 80386 and above processors. This means that Windows will use any extended memory found in the workstation by using the processor's protected mode. This mode also fully supports the virtual memory capabilities of the 80386, which means that the size of the hard disk's swap file plus the amount of physical RAM determines the amount of memory available for applications. You also receive the full multitasking capabilities of the 80386 using this mode.

**Enterprise Certified Novell Engineer (ECNE)**   Enterprise Certified Novell Engineer (ECNE) is Novell's advanced intermediate-level certification. This certification is a continuation of the CNE program. A person who becomes an ECNE usually has some special requirements or interest in advanced or specialized areas of networking. For example, a consultant or a network administrator may need to connect NetWare and UNIX using TCP/IP and NFS, or need to create a wide area network using Novell's dial-in/dial-out products.

**error checking and correcting (ECC)**   This term originally referred to a self-diagnostic technique used to correct errors in RAM. The term

# Glossary

now includes the same type of diagnostics for tape, hard disk, and floppy disk drives. In all cases, the device uses some type of microcode contained in a peripheral chip to detect and correct soft errors in the data stream.

**Ethernet**   See network type.

**expanded memory manager (EMM)**   A device driver, like EMM386.EXE, that provides expanded memory services on 80386 and above machines (there are special drivers that work with 80286 and a few 8088/8086 machines). An application accesses expanded memory using a page frame or other memory mapping techniques from within the conventional or upper memory area (0 to 1024 K). The EMM usually emulates expanded memory using extended memory managed by an extended memory manager (XMM), like HIMEM.SYS. An application must change the processor's mode to protected mode to use XMS. Some products, like 386MAX.SYS and QEMM.SYS, provide both EMM and XMM services in one driver. (See the author's book *Memory Management and Multitasking Beyond 640K,* McGraw-Hill, ISBN 0-8306-3476-2, for more information on expanded and extended memory.)

**extended attribute (EA) file**   An OS/2 system file that stores the icon and other descriptive information about a particular data file or application. Extended attributes include long file names and position within the Workplace Shell. Damage to the EA file usually results in a lack of descriptive information, but no loss in application functionality.

**FAT**   See **File Allocation Table.**

**File Allocation Table (FAT) disk format**   The method of formatting a hard disk drive used by DOS and other operating systems. This technique is one of the oldest formatting methods available.

**file server**   The centralized storage area for files and applications. Special features of the NOS enable the file server to control access to these files and applications. This allows several people to share the same file or application without damage to the data. A file server usually contains larger hard drives and more memory than a standard workstation. It also provides access to one or more printers. The user-perceived capabilities of a file server depend on a combination of available hardware and NOS capabilities.

**file statistic**   Facts about one or more files on the network. These statistics can include the creation and last update dates, who created the file, who owns the file, when someone last accessed the file, who has access to it, and which user last updated it. Other statistics might include the number of file accesses, any security restrictions, or other pertinent file information.

**filter condition**   A Boolean (logical) statement that allows some part of the whole to pass. Think of a filter condition as you would any other filter. For example, a coffee filter allows the brewed coffee to pass, but retains the coffee grounds.

**graphical user interface (GUI)**   A system of icons and graphic images that replaces the character mode menu system used by many machines. The GUI can ride on top of another operating system (like DOS and UNIX) or reside as part of the operating system itself (like OS/2). Advantages of a GUI are ease of use and high-resolution graphics. Disadvantages consist of higher workstation hardware requirements and lower performance over a similar system using a character mode interface.

**graphics workstation**   A PC specifically designed for graphics-oriented work. Many workstations of this type use the UNIX operating system, although they may use OS/2 or Windows as alternatives. Tektronics and many other companies make these high-performance workstations for graphic arts or drafting work.

**GroupWare**   A special class of software designed to make interaction between the members of a workgroup easier.

**GUI**   See **graphical user interface.**

**HDLC**   See **High Level Data Link Control.**

**High Level Data Link Control (HDLC)**   A standard communication line protocol developed by the International Standards Organization (ISO). The protocol defines how two devices talk to each other. Think of the protocol as a type of language used by the two devices.

**High Performance File System (HPFS)**   The method of formatting a hard disk drive used by OS/2. While it provides significant speed advantages over other formatting techniques, only the OS/2 operating system and applications designed to work with that operating system can access a drive formatted using this technique.

**HPFS**   See **High Performance File System.**

**icon**   A symbol used to graphically represent the purpose or function of an application or file. For example, text files may appear as sheets of paper with the name of the file below the icon. Applications designed for the environment or operating system usually appear with a special icon depicting the vendor's or product's logo. Icons normally appear as part of a GUI environment or operating system like Windows or OS/2.

# Glossary

**IDE drive** A hard disk drive that uses the integrated device electronics (IDE) interface. All the components needed to use and access the drive are located on the drive itself. A cable connects the drive to a host adapter which connects the drive to the PC bus.

**inherited rights mask** The set of privileges a user obtains from directory and trustee rights settings on a NetWare network.

**Internet Packet Exchange** See **IPX.**

**IPX (Internet Packet Exchange)** NetWare's peer-to-peer communication protocol. It describes a set of rules that allows two nodes to talk to each other. Think of this as the language used on the network. If everyone speaks the same language, then all the nodes can understand each other. Messages are exchanged in the form of packets on a network. Think of a packet as one sheet of a letter. There is a letterhead saying who sent the letter, an introduction saying who the letter is for, and a message that tells the receiving party what the sending party wants to say.

**IRM** See **inherited rights mask.**

**IRQ** An acronym for *interrupt request.* A device may signal the processor that it requires servicing by sending an interrupt request to the programmable interrupt controller. (For example, the serial port does this when it has data for the processor to act on.) The controller notifies the processor that a device has requested service. The processor, in turn, interrupts its current processing activity, checks to see which device made the request, takes care of the device's needs, then resumes its previous processing task. Each device must use a different IRQ to prevent system conflicts.

**LAN** See **local area network.**

**local area network (LAN)** Two or more devices connected together using a combination of hardware and software. The devices, normally computers and peripheral equipment like printers, are called *nodes.* An NIC (network interface card) provides the hardware communication between nodes through an appropriate medium (cable or microwave transmission). There are two common LANs (also called *networks*). *Peer-to-peer* networks allow each node to connect to any other node on the network with shareable resources. This is a distributed method of files and peripheral devices. A *client-server* network uses one or more servers to share resources. This is a centralized method of sharing files and peripheral devices. A server provides resources to clients (usually workstations). The most common server is the file server, which provides file sharing resources. Other server types include print servers and communication servers.

**logic analyzer** A device that receives clock or other internal computer signals and interprets them. The resulting output is a display of the line logic. In many cases, an analysis of the logic between two components will show whether the circuitry is operating correctly. A technician may also use this data to interpret the content of the information the chips transmit between themselves.

**loopback plug** A device used to transfer signals from the output side of a computer port to the input side. A loopback plug allows the network administrator to test an entire serial or parallel port. Without a loopback plug, the administrator may only test the port internal circuitry. There are also loopback plugs for various NICs and other interface devices. (See Chap. 11 for further details on making and using loopback plugs.)

**Master Certified Novell Engineer (MCNE)** Master Certified Novell Engineer (MCNE) is Novell's advanced intermediate-level certification. This certification is a continuation of the CNE program. A person who becomes an MCNE usually has some special requirements or interest in advanced or specialized areas of networking. For example, a consultant or a network administrator may need to connect NetWare and UNIX using TCP/IP and NFS, or need to manage a group of people working in a large company networking environment. The MCNE, in comparison to the ECNE, usually possesses a better understanding of system theory and architecture.

**MCNE** See **Master Certified Novell Engineer.**

**memory footprint** The amount of memory used by an application once it loads and initializes itself. In some cases, an application requires more memory to load than to reside in memory. TSRs usually require more memory to load than to remain in memory. This is especially true when loading a TSR into high memory.

**MFM drive** An older-technology drive that uses a modified frequency modulation (MFM) storage technique. The control circuitry for this drive resides on a separate controller card which also provides an interface to the host machine.

**Microcomputer** A class of computer that uses an integrated processing and storage system. A microcomputer (or PC) normally resides on a desktop and is designed for use by a single user (although there are other applications for PCs as servers and process controllers).

# Glossary

**multiprotocol router**  A device used to connect two LANs together. The router moves signals from one LAN to the other. The difference between a standard router and a multiprotocol router is that the multiprotocol router can move signals between dissimilar LANs. For example, a multiprotocol LAN can move data between a token ring LAN and an Ethernet LAN.

**multitasking**  The ability of some processor and operating environment/system combinations to perform more than one task at a time. The applications appear to run simultaneously. For example, you could download messages from an online service, print from a word processor, and recalculate a spreadsheet at the same time. Each application receives a slice of time before the processor moves on to the next application. Since the time slices are fairly small, it appears to the user as if these actions occur simultaneously.

**multithreading**  An operating system–specific technique for breaking one or more application tasks into multiple threads of execution. Using this technique allows the operating system to devote more resources to higher priority tasks, increasing perceived system performance. The programmer must write the application to take advantage of this operating system feature when available.

**NAEC**  See **Novell Authorized Education Center.**

**NDS**  See **NetWare Directory Services.**

**NetBEUI**  A protocol used by IBM's PC Network LAN software. It allows access to the network. Most peer-to-peer network systems use NetBEUI. You will also find it used with Microsoft products, like Windows.

**NetBIOS**  See **Network Basic Input/Output System.**

**NetWare Directory Services (NDS)**  The new object-oriented configuration storage and management system used by NetWare 4.x. Every resource on the network is treated as a specific object type with properties that the administrator can set. It replaces the older bindery system used by previous versions of NetWare and offers enhanced management capabilities. NetWare 4.x can also run in bindery emulation mode.

**NetWare Loadable Module (NLM)**  An executable file that loads on a Netware 3.x/4.x file server. An NLM usually adds some capability that the entire network shares. Examples of NLMs include tape backup software, virus protection, UPS detection/management, and database servers. The NLM replaces the VAP provided in Netware 2.x. Unlike a VAP, you can load and unload an NLM while the file server is active.

*Netware Support Encyclopedia* The *Netware Support Encyclopedia* contains a complete set of Novell manuals, along with articles and other information that the certified individual requires. The professional version of the product also contains a wide variety of product patches. Most of this additional material is available on the NetWire forum of CompuServe.

**network** See **local area network (LAN).**

**network access protocol** The method a node uses to gain access to the communication path. The major protocols include CSMA/CD, token bus, and token ring.

**network administrator** The person most responsible for installing, maintaining, and upgrading the network used by a corporation. This includes managing system security and user needs, as well as equipment needs.

**Network Basic Input/Output System (NetBIOS)** This is an application programming interface (API) originally developed for IBM's PC LAN. It is a network communication protocol which resides at the session and transport layers of the OSI model for applications which use it. The NetBIOS emulation program, NETBIOS.EXE, allows applications that use the NetBIOS protocol to work with NetWare's IPX/SPX protocols. SPX replaces NetBIOS on NetWare networks.

**network cabling** The physical media used to transfer data (usually in the form of packets) across a network. There are a wide variety of copper and fiberoptic cable configurations used with networks. Each cable type has different characteristics and capabilities.

**network configuration plan** A plan that states current equipment status, network problem areas and fixes for those problems, and future upgrades. This plan can appear in either tabular or outline format and should fully answer the questions users may have about network equipment status. The plan normally includes a map, as well.

**Network File System (NFS)** A distributed file system developed by Sun Microsystems. NFS allows users of different operating systems, network architectures, protocols, or processor types to share data. More than 100 software vendors have licensed NFS from Sun Microsystems for use with their products. Novell offers NFS products to allow sharing of data from a Novell NetWare 3.x and 4.x to a UNIX host with NFS operational.

**network interface card (NIC)** The device responsible for allowing a workstation to communicate with the file server and other worksta-

# Glossary

tions. It provides the physical means for creating the connection. The card plugs into an expansion slot in the computer. A cable that attaches to the back of the card completes the communication path.

**Network Loadable Module (NLM)** An executable file that loads on a Netware 3.x/4.x file server. An NLM usually adds some capability that the entire network shares. Examples of NLMs include tape backup software, virus protection, UPS detection/management, and database servers. The NLM replaces the VAP provided in Netware 2.x. Unlike a VAP, you can load and unload an NLM while the file server is active.

**network operating system (NOS)** The operating system that runs on the file server or other centralized file/print sharing device. This operating system normally provides multiuser access capability and user accounting software, in addition to other network-specific utilities.

**network topology** The physical method used to connect the various parts of a network. The four major topologies include linear bus, star ring, star bus, and star.

**network type** A combination of network topology, access protocol, and associated hardware and software used to connect a combination of workstations and servers. There are three major network types: Ethernet (linear-bus topology and CSMA/CD access protocol), ARCNet (star-bus topology and token-bus access protocol), and Token-Ring (star-ring topology and token-ring access protocol).

**NFS** See **Network File System.**

**NIC** See **network interface card.**

**NLM** See **NetWare Loadable Module.**

**node** A single element in a network. In most cases, the term *node* refers to a single workstation connected to the network. It may also refer to a bridge, router, or file server. It does not refer to cabling or to passive or active elements that do not directly interface with the network at the logical level.

**Novell Authorized Test Centers (NAEC)** A training facility authorized by Novell to train CNA, CNE, ECNE, and CNI candidates in the latest network operating system technology. An NAEC always uses Certified Netware Instructors (CNIs) as instructors. It is the only place where you can receive training guaranteed to help you pass your Novell certification examinations.

**NTSF** See **Windows NT File System.**

**object linking and embedding (OLE)** The process of packaging a file name, application name, and any required parameters into an object, then pasting this object into the file created by another application. For example, you could place a graphic object within a word-processing document or spreadsheet. When you look at the object it appears as if you simply pasted the data from the originating application into the current application (similarly to DDE). The data provided by the object automatically changes as you change the data in the original object. Often, you can start the originating application and automatically load the required data by double-clicking on the object.

**ODI** See **Open Data-Link Interface.**

**OJT** See on-the-job training.

**OLE** See **object linking and embedding.**

**on-the-job training (OJT)** A method of training where you learn by doing the tasks you want to perform. Each mistake you make and correct helps you understand another area of the job. Often, this form of training is supplemented with advice from other people who know how to perform the work. This method works well for simple tasks. It does not work well for learning the principles of network operating systems. However, it is an important part of the posttraining learning process.

**Open Data-Link Interface (ODI)** NetWare (through IPX) uses ODI to push data in the form of packets through the IP tunnel. The IP tunnel is a software connection between two servers. Essentially, the IP tunnel looks just like a hardware connection to IPX. Its purpose is to present a standard LAN driver interface to the NetWare system. The server loads it like any other LAN driver, then binds IPX to it to instruct IPX to receive and route packets over the internetwork the tunnel is using. Workstations that load the ODI drivers can use the IP tunnel as well to communicate with a variety of NOSs, including LAN Manager and 3+Share. From the user's perspective, it appears as if they were connected to a single network.

**operating system (OS)** The software that forms the computer interface between the user and the hardware. The operating system normally provides some type of command processor along with low-level functions used by applications. The user sees these low-level services as the ability to send data to the printer or to receive information about a file on the hard drive. The operating system also schedules tasks, maintains the file system, and provides many vital security features.

**OS** See **operating system.**

# Glossary

**password protection** An operating system–enforced technique for restricting access to a network or to data. The user must enter characters, numbers, and/or special symbols in the correct sequence before the operating system will allow access.

**policies and procedures document** A set of written guidelines that the network user can refer to in case of emergency. This document also outlines the network rules and regulations. In addition, it contains the procedures for performing specific network-related tasks.

**print queue** The network version of a print spooler. It spools all print jobs for a particular printer to a network drive or to the drive of a print server. Local workstation performance is not affected by a print queue. The print queue uses file or print server CPU cycles to perform its work.

**print spooler** A special program that intercepts data going to the printer and places it in RAM or on disk. Once the application sending the data completes its work, the print spooler looks for clock cycles when the computer is not performing useful work. The print spooler sends some of the spooled data to the printer every time it sees an empty time slot. Using this technique makes it appear that the application has printed all the data when it really hasn't. The end result is that you regain control of the computer faster than if you had to wait for the printer. It also means that you use machine resources more efficiently.

**printer control sequences** A set of special control character sequences that force a printer into a specific setup. For example, one set of control characters may select a special font, while another set may change the print margins. The manual that comes with your printer will provide further details about what these control character sequences are and how to use them.

**protocol analyzer** A device used to interpret the communication packets sent between nodes on a network. Think of the protocol analyzer as a spy reading a letter addressed to someone else before they get to see it. A protocol analyzer allows consultants and network administrators to find communication errors on the network quickly.

**queue** Commonly, a programming construct used to hold data while it awaits processing. A queue uses a FIFO (first in/first out) storage technique. The first data element in is also the first data element that gets processed. Think of a queue as a line at the bank or grocery store and you'll have the right idea. There are also hardware queues which emulate the processing capability of their software counterpart.

**RAID (redundant array of inexpensive disks) system** A set of interconnected drives that in most cases resides outside the file server. There are several levels of RAID. Each level defines precisely how the data is placed on each of the drives. In all cases, all the drives in a group share responsibility for storing the data. They act in parallel both to read and to write the data. In addition, there is a special drive in most of these systems devoted to helping the network recover when one drive fails. In most cases, the user never even knows that anything has happened—the spare drive takes over for the failed drive without any noticeable degradation in network operation. RAID systems increase network reliability and throughput.

**Real Mode** A Windows operating mode which supports the capabilities of the 8088/8086 processor. This essentially limits you to loading one application within the confines of conventional memory. Windows versions after 3.0 do not support this mode. You must use these versions with workstations containing an 80286 or higher processor.

**Red Zone** The game included on the resource code disk provided with this book. Red Zone is a *Jeopardy!*-style game designed to test your NetWare knowledge. See the preface to this book for further details about the resource disk.

**RIP** See **Routing Information Protocol.**

**Router** A device used to connect two LANs. The router moves signals from one LAN to the other.

**Routing Information Protocol (RIP)** The method TCP/IP uses to communicate with other routers. It allows all the routers in the internet to exchange information about the internet configuration without human intervention.

**SAP** See **Service Advertising Protocol.**

**SCSI (small computer system interface) adapter (controller)** A computer interface card which allows you to connect up to seven devices to the computer system. The current SCSI standard is SCSI-2. Typical SCSI devices include tape drives, hard disk drives, and CD-ROM drives. SCSI devices typically provide high transfer rates (10 to 15 MB/s) and access times (device type dependent).

**SDLC** See Synchronous Data Link Control.

**Sequential Packet Exchange** See **SPX.**

**Service Advertising Protocol (SAP)** The method used by servers and gateways to advertise their service. Workstations use SAP to find the nearest server. Routers use SAP to exchange information about the

# Glossary

servers they know about. NetWare broadcasts a single SAP packet for every seven servers on the network. The packets are broadcast every 60 seconds on local segments and over high speed links.

**shell**  A command processor that allows you to directly interact with the operating system. For example, COMMAND.COM is the command processor for DOS. This also refers to menuing systems or environments which perform essentially the same task as the command processor.

**sort order**  A method of classifying and ordering a list of items. For example, you could place them in alphanumeric order. *A* would come before *B,* and so forth.

**SPX (Sequential Packet Exchange)**  The part of the NetWare shell that guarantees delivery of a message sent from one node to another. Think of SPX as the postal clerk that delivers a certified letter from one place to another. In network terms, each page of the letter is called a *packet.* SPX delivers the letter one page at a time to the intended party.

**Standard Mode**  A Windows operating mode that supports the capabilities of the 80286 processor. This means that Windows will use any extended memory found in the workstation by using the processor's protected mode. You may also load more than one application at a time (up to the limits imposed by physical RAM). This mode does not support virtual memory or page swapping. It also does not support the multitasking features of the 80386.

**static interface**  A menu that does not automatically change to reflect the current machine configuration or operating system environment.

**Synchronous Data Link Control (SDLC)**  A standard communication line protocol developed by International Business Machines (IBM). The protocol defines how two devices talk to each other. Think of the protocol as a type of language used by the two devices. This particular protocol was designed to work with Systems Network Architecture (SNA), a network architecture developed by IBM.

**TCP/IP**  See **Transmission Control Protocol/Internet Protocol.**

**Terminal Emulation Software**  A form of communications software used to connect a PC to a host. The host can take the form of a LAN, mainframe, or minicomputer. Terminal emulation software may consist of a specially designed program or be a standard off-the-shelf package, like Procomm Plus.

**terminate and stay resident (TSR) program**  An application that loads itself into memory and stays there once you execute it. The program usually returns you directly to the DOS prompt after loading. Pressing a hot-key combination activates the application, allowing you to use the application. In most cases, TSRs provide some type of utility, print spooling, or other short term function.

**token ring**  See **network type.**

**Transmission Control Protocol/Internet Protocol (TCP/IP)**  A standard communication line protocol developed by the U.S. Department of Defense. The protocol defines how two devices talk to each other. Think of the protocol as a type of language used by the two devices.

**troubleshooting procedures**  See **policies and procedures document.**

**TSR**  See **terminate and stay resident.**

**UDP**  See **User Datagram Protocol.**

**uninterruptible power source (UPS)**  Usually a combination of an inverter and a battery used to provide power to one or more electrical devices during a power outage. A UPS normally contains power-sensing circuitry and surge-suppression modules. Some UPSs provide standby power and a direct connection between the power source and the protected equipment. Other UPSs use the power source to constantly charge the battery. The protected equipment always derives its power from the inverter, effectively isolating the equipment from the power source.

**UPS**  See **uninterruptible power source.**

**upsizing**  The process of linking stand-alone PCs together into a LAN. Upsizing usually results when a business grows beyond the capacity to use a sneaker net for exchanging files. Upsizing may require the addition of a mainframe or minicomputer for storage or data manipulation purposes when using database management applications.

**User Datagram Protocol (UDP)**  Allows applications to exchange individual packets of information over a TCP/IP network. UDP uses a combination of protocol ports and IP addresses to get the message from one point of the network to another. More than one client can use the same protocol port as long as all clients using the port have a unique IP address. There are two types of protocol port: well-known and dynamically bound. The well-known port assignments use the ports numbered between 1 and 255.

# Glossary

**user questionnaire**  A set of questions designed to help users think about their needs and express them in a way that the network administrator and corporate management can understand.

**value added process (VAP)**  An executable file that loads on a Netware 2.x file server during file server initialization. An VAP usually adds some capability that the entire network shares. Examples of VAPs include tape backup software, virus protection, UPS detection and management, and database servers. You must load a VAP during file server startup. Netware 2.x does not allow you to unload the VAP while the file server is active. The NLM provided with Netware 3.x alleviates this problem.

**VAP**  See **value added process.**

**Virtual Loadable Module (VLM)**  One of several modules that comprise the NetWare DOS requester. A VLM is an executable file that provides one or more network-related functions in the form of an API (application programming interface). For example, the transport-related functions all reside within one VLM. An application requests services from NetWare by calling functions with the API. There are two types of VLM: child and multiplexor. The *child* VLM typically takes care of specific networking needs, like NDS access. A *multiplexor* VLM typically routes data from one point of the network to another by calling the appropriate child VLM.

**virtual memory**  The memory provided by an 80386 or above processor. It appears as physical RAM to both the operating system and any applications running on the system, but may or may not reside within physical memory. A special part of the operating system (known as the swapping mechanism) manages the memory which appears in physical RAM and within a swap file on disk. If the processor runs out of physical memory, the swapping mechanism removes the oldest data from physical memory in segments known as *pages* (you can view them as memory containers) and replaces it with blank pages from the swap file on disk. When the swap file runs out of blank pages the virtual memory area is full, and you must stop any unnecessary applications. If the processor requires access to data that appears on disk, the swapping mechanism removes the oldest data from physical memory and places it in the swap file, then moves the requested data from the swap file to physical memory.

**VLM**  See **Virtual Loadable Module.**

**WAN** See **wide area network**.

**wide area network (WAN)** A network that extends beyond the constraints of a single server and relies on methods other than physical connections to create the required network links. Such networks could use microwave or telephone connections to create links between two separate buildings. Some companies also rely on the Internet to create the required connections. In essence, a network must consist of two servers with no physical (wired) connection to be considered a WAN.

**Windows NT File System (NTFS)** The method of formatting a hard disk drive used by Windows NT. While it provides significant speed advantages over other formatting techniques, only the Windows NT operating system and applications designed to work with that operating system can access a drive formatted using this technique.

**workstation** The terminal provided to the user. It provides access to application programs, hardware devices, and the network. A workstation usually resides at the user's desk, but it can appear in a centralized location as well. For example, some companies provide one or more advanced technology stations in centralized locations. These workstations serve occasional graphics or engineering needs.

**WORM (write once, read many) drive** A device that uses CD-ROM technology coupled with a multiple power level laser to allow the user to write to the drive one time. Once you write to the drive, you may read the data imprinted on it multiple times. Some drives allow you to correct errors by overwriting the area of the mistake and writing the corrected data to a new area of the disk. (Of course, this assumes there is additional room on the drive for the corrected data.) The main reason for using a WORM drive is to archive data. For example, a law office could use a WORM drive to store old cases. Like the CD-ROM drive, most WORM drives limit you to 650 MB of data storage. Some use a proprietary encoding technique to allow you to store up to 1 GB of data.

**XMS manager** See **expanded memory manager**.

# INDEX

## A

Acronyms (list), 805–816
Adaptive testing technique, 131n, 135–136
AD.EXE, 540, 543, 632
Ad-hoc solutions, 871
Admin utility, 538, 633, 635
Administration Server, 581
Advanced Web Authoring (course description), 864–865
Advancement, planning for, 154–183
    company-based strategy, creating, 155–157
    interviews, 180–182
    new position, creating, 162–168
    pay raises, 171–173, 181–182
    promotions, 158–162
    and recognition of new status, 157–158, 168–171
    résumés, 173–180
    title changes, 168–171
Advertisements, using, 215–217
Allocated short-term memory pool, 321, 353
@ALLOWEDIT function, 784
Answers:
    to brain teasers, 825–833
    to sample tests, 817–824
APPEND command, 254
Apple Macintosh, 250, 255, 318
Application layer, 705
*Application Notes (see NetWare Application Notes)*
APPS directory, 269–270
ARCnet, 672, 676
ASC (*see* Asynchronous communications server)
ASCII (American Standard Code for Information Interchange), 871
*AskSam*, 191
Async gateway, 546
Asynchronous communications server (ASC), 871
Asynchronous Transfer Mode (ATM), 671, 700

/ATS Message Server, 577
Audiotapes, training from, 103–104
Auditcon, 391, 469
Auditing option (NDS), 386
AUTOEXEC.BAT, 243–245, 248, 254, 351
AUTOEXEC.NCF, 316, 353, 506
Autotuning, 669

## B

Backups, system, 7, 674
Baud rate, bit rate vs., 252
BDE (Borland Database Engine), 790
BIF Edit utility, 546
BIF files, 542
Bindery, 291, 871
BINDFIX utility, 313–315
BIOS, 242, 257
Block Suballocation option (NDS), 383, 473
Books:
    for continuing education, 196–198
    training from, 102–103
Borland Database Engine (BDE), 790
Bounded transmission media, 704
Brain teasers, answers to, 825–833
Bridges, 704
Brochures, 215, 218
Burst mode, 675
Business cards, 217–218
Busy Search feature (GroupWise), 540

## C

Cables:
    Level 3 UTP, 672
    Type 2 Token Ring, 670
Cache buffers, 871
Cache Movable memory, 321

Calendar view (GroupWise), 537, 544, 547
Calling Novell, 141–142, 150–151
    telephone numbers (list), 835
Career advancement (*see* Advancement, planning for)
CASTOFF command, 287
CBT (*see* Computer-based training)
CD-ROMs, 872
Central configuration, 872
Central processing unit (CPU), 249
Certificate, checking, 151
Certification:
    classes of, 3
    financing of (*see* Financing sources)
    as industry trend, 58–59
    and Novell support, 59–61
    recognition for, 56, 157–158, 168–171
    requirements for, 114–117
    setting goals for, 54–55
    and skills acquisition, 57–58
    time required to gain, 74–76
    (*See also specific certifications*)
Certified Novell Administrator (CNA) certification, 3–11, 171
    checklist for, 33–34
    deciding to pursue, 4, 5
    GroupWise route, 4, 8–9
    InForms route, 4, 10–11
    NetWare 3.x route, 4, 6–7
    NetWare 4.x route, 4, 7–8
    paperwork log for, 143
    path to, 62–64
    significance of, 3
    SoftSolutions route, 4–5, 9–10
Certified Novell Administrators (CNAs), 58, 163, 872
    continuing education for, 76
Certified Novell Engineer (CNE) certification, 12–19, 171
    checklist for, 34–37
    Classic, 13
    deciding to pursue, 5, 12

891

Certified Novell Engineer (CNE) certification (*Cont.*):
  electives with, 14, 15
  exam categories for, 13–14
  GroupWise route, 14, 19, 20
  maintaining, 15–16
  Master (*see* Master CNE [MCNE] certification)
  NetWare 3.x route, 14, 16–17
  NetWare 4.x route, 14, 17–19
  paperwork log for, 143
  path to, 64–66
  prerequisite knowledge for, 12
  significance of, 12
  time limits with, 14–15
Certified Novell Engineers (CNEs), 58, 163, 872
  continuing education for, 76
Certified Novell Instructor (CNI) certification, 25–31
  checklist for, 34, 43–46
  continuing education requirements, 209–210
  Instructor Performance Evaluation (IPE) for, 30–31
  paperwork log for, 146
  paperwork requirements for, 149–150
  path to, 28, 68–73
  prerequisite courses for, 30
  prerequisite knowledge for, 26–27
  significance of, 25–26
  specializations within, 27, 29–30
Certified Novell Instructors (CNIs), 872
  continuing education for, 76
  contract vs. NEAP-employed, 26
  Novell support for, 60–61
Channel service units (CSUs), 872
Character mode interface, 872
CheckIt Pro, 670
Checklists, certification, 31–46
  for CNA certification, 33–34
  for CNE certification, 34–37
  for CNI certification, 34, 43–46
  for MCNE certification, 34, 38–41
  for NCIP certification, 34, 42–43
Classes (*see* Novell courses)
Classic CNE, 13
Client 32, 424–430
Clients:
  assessing needs of, 222–224, 226
  charging, 227–229
  informing, 225–227
  installing and administering GroupWise, 9
Clipping services, 188
CMOS memory, 873

CNA certification (*see* Certified Novell Administrator certification)
CNAs (*see* Certified Novell Administrators)
CNE certification (*see* Certified Novell Engineer certification)
CNEs (*see* Certified Novell Engineers)
CNI certification (*see* Certified Novell Instructor certification)
CNIs (*see* Certified Novell Instructors)
Coach (GroupWise), 539
Common user access (CUA), 873
Company, advancement within your, 155–173
  new position, creation of, 162–168
  new status, recognition of, 157–158
  pay increases, 171–173
  promotions, 158–162
  strategy for, 155–157
  title changes, 168–171
Company-sponsored financial support, obtaining, 87–91
CompuServe, 198–205, 652–658
Computer-based training (CBT), 104, 873
*Computer Library Plus*, 191–192
Conferences, NetWire, 206
CONFIG command, 318
CONFIG.SYS, 243–248, 250, 289
Consulting, 214–233
  advertisements, using, 215–217
  brochures, using, 218
  business cards, using, 217–218
  charging for, 227–229
  and choice of services, 221–225
  and informing clients, 225–227
  and Internet advertising, 219–220
  Novell ID badge, using, 220–221
  Novell logo, using, 215, 217–218
  opportunities in, 214
  price lists, using, 218
  and professionalism, 229–232
Container Object option (NDS), 383
Container objects, 432
Context option (NDS), 382
Continuing education, 75–76, 186–207
  books, using, 196–198
  electronic media, using, 207
  and filtering information, 187–188
  magazines, using, 192–194
  Novell CompuServe forums, using, 198–205

Continuing education (*Cont.*):
  online services, using, 198–207
  organizing information for, 190–192
  sources of information for, 188–190
  trade papers, using, 195–196
Continuing education requirements, 207–210
  CNE certification, 15–16
  CNI certification, 209–210
  MCNE certification, 208–209
  NCIP certification, 209
Contract CNIs, 26
Control|Suspend utility, 584
Core exams:
  CNE certification, 13–14
  MCNE certification, 21
COUNTRY.SYS, 252
Courses (*see* Novell courses)
Cover letters, 174, 175
CPU (*see* Central processing unit)
CRC (*see* Cyclic redundancy code)
Credits, required vs. elective, 2–3
CSI file, rebuilding, 583
CSLOCAL directory, 583
CSTEMP directory, 584
CSUs (*see* Channel service units)
CUA (*see* Common user access)
Customizing desktops, 6
CX command, 384, 433, 500
Cyclic redundancy code (CRC), 873

# D

%D parameter, 741
/D switch, 584
Databases:
  components of, 786–787
  correcting errors in, 729–732
  linking forms to, 11
  maintenance of, 623–626
DATA directory, 270–271
Data encoding schemes, 874
Data-grade lines, 874
Data Link layer (OSI model), 700
Data Migration option (NDS), 383
Data service units (DSUs), 874
Data Terminal Equipment (DTE), 703
Data transmission mode, 874
DAT drives, 874
DDE (*see* Dynamic data exchange)
Dedicated Indexers, 738, 743
Default script, 350
Demarc, 706

# Index

Desktop, 6–7
Diagnostic logging level (GroupWise message server), 582
Dial-in/dial-out connectivity, 874
Directory Cache Buffers, 320
Directory structure, setting up:
  NetWare 3.x Administration, 269–271
  NetWare 4.x Administration, 410–411
Dirty Cache Buffers, 322
Dirty power, 874–875
Disk Allocation blocks, 320
Disk cache, 875
Disk duplexing, 676, 875
Disk mirroring, 875
Disks:
  floppy, 253
  hard, 254, 257
Display adapters, 251
DMA address, 344
Document Desktop, installation of, 726, 728–729
DOMAIN.NLM, 504
Domains:
  adding new, 614–619
  creating links between, 9, 565–570
  GroupWise 4.x Advanced System Administration, 614–623
  GroupWise System Administration, 524–527
  merging, 619–623
  primary, 539, 565
DOS for NetWare Users (course description), 841
DOS Micro Hardware exam, 14, 236–265
  brain teaser, 264, 265
  case study, 237–248
  companion CD-ROM, using, 264
  inventory, workstation, 238–241
  optimization, workstation, 243–248
  sample test, 258–264
  setup, workstation, 241–243
  study questions, 249–258
DOS Requester option (NDS), 385
Downsizing, 875
Drake Testing Center, 875
Drive mappings, 875–876
DSREPAIR utility, 452, 462–463, 503
DSUs (*see* Data service units)
DTE (Data Terminal Equipment), 703
Dynamic data exchange (DDE), 876
Dynamic forms, creating, 11
DynaText viewer, 191, 345, 366, 386–389

## E

EA file (*see* Extended attribute file)
ECC (*see* Error checking and correcting)
ECNE certification, 3
ECNEs (*see* Enterprise Certified Novell Engineers)
Education-based résumés, 178–180
EISA system, 876
Electives:
  CNE certification, 14, 15
  credits for, 2–3
  GroupWise certification, 16
Electro Text, 366, 374
  (*See also* DynaText viewer)
EMM (*see* Expanded memory manager)
EMM386, 244
Emoticons, 876
Enhanced mode, 876
Enterprise Certified Novell Engineers (ECNEs), 876
Environment (network), 278–281
Environment (for studying), 118, 121–124
Error checking and correcting (ECC), 876–877
ESD rules, 677
Ethernet, 499, 676, 699–701
Exams:
  and adaptive testing technique, 135–136
  failing, 110–111, 136–138
  hints for taking, 131–133
  list of, 47–50
  registering for, 130–131
  and standard testing technique, 134–135
  studying for (*see* Studying)
  taking, 110
  training for (*see* Training)
  (*See also specific exams*)
Expanded memory manager (EMM), 877
Experienced-based résumés, 176–177, 179
Extended attribute (EA) file, 877

## F

Failing the exam, 110–111, 136–138
FaxBack, 207
FDDI (Fiber Distributed Data Interface), 668
FFWIN.EXE, 786

Fiber Distributed Data Interface (FDDI), 668
Fields, 787
File Allocation Table (FAT) disk format, 877
File cache buffer, 353
File Compression option (NDS), 383
File servers, 877
  memory management, 306–310
  software installation, 333–340
  startup procedures, 304–306
File statistics, 877–878
File System Security option (NDS), 383
Filter condition, 878
Financing sources, 84–95
  company-sponsored support, 87–91
  grants, 95
  minority job-training programs, 95
  personal savings, 94–95
  scholarships, 92–93
  student loans, 91–92
  veterans' benefits, 93–94
FLAG use, 384
Floppy disks, 253
*Folio Views*, 191
FORMAT command, 249–250
Forms:
  creating, 11
  designing, 766–772
  testing, 773–775
Full-duplex transmission, 702
Full text indexer, 10

## G

Gateways, 544, 703
Goals, setting:
  for certification, 54–55
  for promotions, 160–162
  for studying, 118–119, 124–126
Grants, obtaining, 95
Graphical user interface (GUI), 878
Graphic workstations, 878
Groups, creating:
  NetWare 3.x Administration, 271–278
  NetWare 4.x Administration, 411–414
Groups, defining, 414–422
Group view (GroupWise), 537
GroupWare, 878
GroupWise:
  CNA certification, 4, 8–9
  CNE certification, 14, 19, 20
  elective courses, 16

GroupWise 4.x Administration (course description), 856–857
GroupWise 4.x Advanced Administration (course description), 857–858
GroupWise 4.x Advanced System Administration exam, 598–647
  brain teaser, 644–647
  case study, 600–626
  companion CD-ROM, using, 647
  database maintenance, performing, 623–626
  domains, adding new, 614–619
  domains, merging, 619–623
  post offices, adding new, 609–614
  sample test, 638–644
  study questions, 627–637
  user setups, changing, 602–609
  users, adding new, 601–602
GroupWise 4.x Asynchronous Gateway and Remote Client Support exam, 558–596
  brain teaser, 594–595
  case study, 560–575
  checking installation, 570–575
  companion CD-ROM, using, 596
  course description, 858–859
  links between domains, creating, 565–570
  message server configuration, 563–565
  message server installation, 561–563
  sample test, 587–594
  study questions, 575–587
GroupWise 5.x Administration (course description), 859–860
GroupWise 5.x Advanced Administration (course description), 860–861
GroupWise Remote, 544
GroupWise System Administration exam, 518–556
  brain teaser, 553–556
  case study, 520–536
  companion CD-ROM, using, 556
  domain, creating, 524–527
  post office, creating, 527–529
  sample test, 547–553
  study questions, 537–547
  testing of system, 535–536
  users, creating/enabling, 529–532
  Windows workstation, installation on, 520–524
  workstation, setting up, 532–535
GUI (*see* Graphical user interface)

## H

*Hands-On Guide to Networking, The* (John Mueller and Robert Williams), 196–197
Hands-on training, 96–98
Hard disks, 254, 257
Hardware experience, evaluating your, 221, 222
High Level Data Link Control (HDLC), 878
High Performance File System (HPFS), 878
HOSTID.DB, 541
HPFS (*see* High Performance File System)
Hypertext markup language (HTML), 22

## I

IC chip, 702
Icons, 878
ID badges, Novell, 220–221
IDAPI (*see* Integrated Database Application Programming Interface)
IDE drives, 879
IEEE 802.4 standard, 669
IEEE 802.5 token passing networks, 701
IEEE 802.7 advisory group, 701
IEEE 802.8 advisory group, 701
IEEE 802.9 advisory group, 701
IEEE 802.10 advisory group, 701
In Box, 538
Index compaction, 733–734, 736
Indexer, full text, 10
Indexes, 786–787
Information sources, 188–190
  additional information, 837–839
  books, 196–198
  electronic media, 207
  magazines, 192–194
  Novell CompuServe forums, 198–205
  online services, 198–207
  trade papers, 195–196
InForms, 4, 10–11
InForms Filler, 786
InForms 4.x Administration and Form Design exam, 756–803
  brain teaser, 800–802
  case study, 757–783
  companion CD-ROM, using, 803
  course description, 867
  designing forms, 766–772

InForms 4.x Administration and Form Design exam (*Cont.*):
  first time configuration, 763–766
  installation, 758–763
  sample test, 794–800
  security, assigning, 775–783
  study questions, 783–794
  testing forms, 773–775
InForms 4.x Introduction for New Users (course description), 866
Inherited Rights Filter (IRF) option (NDS), 383, 391, 468
Inherited Rights Mask (IRM), 292, 353–354, 879
INSTALL.BAT, 348, 501
INSTALL.NLM, 504
Instructor-led training, 98–100
Instructor Performance Evaluation (IPE), 30–31, 72–73, 149–150
Integrated Database Application Programming Interface (IDAPI), 786
Internationalization option (NDS), 386
Internet:
  advertising on, 219–220
  and consulting opportunities, 214
  (*See also* Novell Certified Internet Professional [NCIP] certification)
Internet (DOD) model packet, 691–697
Interoperability area (CNI certification), 27, 29–30
Interviews, 180–182
Inventorying workstations (DOS Micro Hardware exam), 238–241
IPE (*see* Instructor Performance Evaluation)
IPX protocol, 286, 879
IRF (*see* Inherited Rights Filter option)
IRM (*see* Inherited Rights Mask)
IRQ, 344, 879

## J

Janitor utility, 738
Jumpers, 668

## L

LANs (*see* Local area networks)
*LAN Times,* 193–194

# Index

Leaf Object option (NDS), 383, 394–395, 432–433
Links, creating, between domains, 9, 565–570
Local area networks (LANs), 187–188, 214, 699–700, 879–880
    preventing damage to, 666
    security for, 666
Logic analyzers, 880
LOGIN.EXE, 287
Login scripts (NDS), 383–384
Logo, Novell, 60, 215, 217–218
Logon script, 350–352
Logs:
    paperwork, 142–146
    phone, 146–148
Long filename support, adding, 464–466
Loopback plugs, 880

## M

Macintosh (*see* Apple Macintosh)
Macros, creating, 11
Magazines, 192–194
Maintaining certification (*see* Continuing education; Continuing education requirements)
Maintenance:
    NetWare 3.x Advanced Administration, 313–315
    of printer services, 7
    of software, 8
    volume, 322
Manuals, reading, 115–116
MAP command, 290, 384
Marketing your skills, 154, 215–221
    (*See also* Advancement, planning for)
Master Certified Novell Engineers (MCNEs), 163, 880
Master CNE (MCNE) certification, 19–24, 170–171
    checklist for, 34, 38–41
    continuing education requirements, 208–209
    electives, 22–24
    paperwork log for, 144
    path to, 67–68
    prerequisites for, 21
    responsibilities associated with, 21
    target exams, 21
Maximum Physical Receive Packet Size, 503

McAfee Associates, 658
MCNE certification (*see* Master CNE certification)
MCNEs (*see* Master Certified Novell Engineers)
MEM command, 244, 246–249
MEMMAKER utility, 243
Memory:
    adding more, 352
    CMOS, 873
    UMB, 247–248
    virtual, 889
Memory footprints, 880
Memory management:
    file server, 306–310
    and performance tuning, 311–313
*Memory Management and Multitasking Beyond 640K* (Lenny Bailes and John Mueller), 243*n*
Memory Protection option (NDS), 386
MenuItem command, 254–255
Message server (GroupWise):
    checking, 570–575
    configuration, 563–565
    corrupted messages in, 580
    installation, 561–563
    logging levels of, 582
    snapshots taken by, 580
MFC utility, 577
MFM drives, 673, 880
Microcomputer Concepts for NetWare Users (course description), 842
Microcomputers, 880
Micro House Technical Library (MTL), 676–677
Microsoft Developer Network, 192
Microsoft Mail, 793
*Microsoft Systems Journal*, 192
MIGRATE utility, 504
Minority job-training programs, 95
MLID (*see* Multiple Link Interface Driver)
MODE command, 255
MONITOR.NLM, 671
MONITOR option (NDS), 384
MSD command, 246
MTL (Micro House Technical Library), 676–677
Multiple Link Interface Driver (MLID), 286
Multiplexing, 707
Multiprotocol routers, 881
Multitasking, 881
Multithreading, 881

## N

NAECs (*see* Novell Authorized Education Centers)
Name space modules, 319
National Electrical Manufacturers Association (NEMA), 669
NCIP certification (*see* Novell Certified Internet Professional certification)
NCIPs (*see* Novell Certified Internet Professionals)
NDIR command, 384, 435
NDS (*see* NetWare Directory Services)
/NE switch, 630
NEAPs (*see* Novell Education Academic Partners)
NEMA (*see* National Electrical Manufacturers Association)
NetAdmin utility, 395
NetBEUI, 881
NET.CFG, 392
NETFIX.COM, 586
NetShield, 659
NETUSER option (NDS), 385
NetWare 2.2 Advanced System Manager (course description), 844–845
NetWare 2.2 System Manager (course description), 844
NetWare 3.x Administration exam, 268–300
    brain teaser, 297–299
    case study, 269–285
    companion CD-ROM, using, 300
    directory structure, setting up, 269–271
    groups, creating, 271–278
    network environment, setting up, 278–281
    printing of servers/queues, 281–283
    sample test, 292–297
    study questions, 285–292
    testing, prepowerup, 283–285
    users, creating, 271–278
NetWare 3.x Advanced Administration exam, 302–330
    brain teaser, 328–330
    case study, 303–315
    companion CD-ROM, using, 329–330
    file server memory management, 306–310
    file server startup procedures, 304–306
    maintenance procedures, 313–315

NetWare 3.x Advanced Administration exam (*Cont.*):
  performance tuning, 311–313
  sample test, 323–328
  study questions, 315–323
NetWare 3.x Advanced System Manager (course description), 846–847
NetWare 3.x Installation and Configuration Workshop exam, 332–362
  brain teaser, 360–362
  case study, 333–343
  companion CD-ROM, using, 362
  course description, 847–848
  file server software installation, 333–340
  sample test, 354–360
  study questions, 343–354
  workstation software installation, 340–343
NetWare 3.x operating system:
  CNA certification, 4, 6–7
  CNE certification, 14, 16–17
NetWare 3.x System Manager (course description), 845–846
NetWare 3.x to 4.x Update exam, 364–405
  brain teaser, 404–405
  case study, 365–389
  companion CD-ROM, using, 405
  course description, 850–851
  DynaText viewer, using, 386–389
  Electro Text online documentation, 366, 374
  NetWare 4.x terms and concepts, 367–382
  practice session, 380, 382
  sample test, 398–403
  study questions, 389–397
NetWare 4.x Administration exam, 408–447
  brain teaser, 445–447
  case study, 409–430
  companion CD-ROM, using, 447
  course description, 848–849
  directory structure, setting up, 410–411
  groups, creating, 411–414
  groups, defining, 414–422
  organizational units, creating, 411–414
  sample test, 439–445
  study questions, 430–439
  testing of setup, 422–424
  users, creating, 411–414
  users, defining, 414–422
  Windows 95 client, setting up, 424–430

NetWare 4.x Advanced Administration exam, 450–483
  brain teaser, 480, 482–483
  case study, 451–466
  companion CD-ROM, using, 480–481
  course description, 849–850
  DSREPAIR utility, 462–463
  long filename support, adding, 464–466
  print queue setup, 453–454
  print server setup, 455
  printer setup, 455–459
  printing software installation, 459–462
  sample test, 474–480
  study questions, 466–474
  VREPAIR utility, 463–464
NetWare 4.x Installation and Configuration Workshop exam, 486–515
  brain teaser, 513–515
  case study, 487–498
  companion CD-ROM, using, 514
  course description, 851
  sample test, 507–513
  study questions, 498–507
  workstation ODI/VLM software, installing, 496–498
NetWare 4.x operating system:
  CNA certification, 4, 7–8
  CNE certification, 14, 17–19
NetWare 4.x terms and concepts, 367–382
NetWare Administrator, 396, 433, 436
*NetWare Application Notes,* 60, 194, 207
*NetWare Buyer's Guide,* 197–198, 207
NetWare Directory Services (NDS), 7–8, 374–375, 394, 431, 434, 437, 466–467, 881
  Auditing option, 386
  Block Suballocation option, 383
  Container Object option, 383
  Context option, 382
  CX use, 384
  Data Migration option, 383
  File Compression option, 383
  File System Security option, 383
  FLAG use, 384
  Inherited Rights Filter option, 383, 391, 468
  Internationalization option, 386
  Leaf Object option, 383, 394–395
  login scripts, 383–384
  MAP use, 384
  Memory Protection option, 386

NetWare Directory Services (NDS) (*Cont.*):
  MONITOR option, 384
  NDIR use, 384
  NETUSER option, 385
  NetWare DOS Requester option, 385
  NLIST use, 384
  Novell Menu utility, 384
  NPRINTER option, 385–386
  Object option, 375
  Object Rights option, 379–380, 390
  Open Data-Link Interface option, 385
  Partitions option, 377
  PCONSOLE option, 385
  printing, 385
  Property option, 377
  Property Rights option, 382, 390, 467
  Property Value option, 377
  PSERVER option, 385
  replicas, 377, 379
  SBACKUP option, 385
  SEND use, 384
  SERVMAN option, 384
  Storage Management Services option, 383
  Virtual Loadable Module option, 385
NetWare Loadable Module (NLM), 315, 397, 438, 881
NetWare Migration utility, 352
NetWare Service and Support exam, 650–687
  brain teaser, 684–687
  case study, 651–665
  companion CD-ROM, using, 687
  CompuServe, 652–658
  course description, 852
  *NetWare Support Encyclopedia,* 662–665
  sample test, 677–684
  study questions, 665–677
  virus protection, 658–662
*NetWare Support Encyclopedia Professional Edition (NSEPro),* 60, 207, 662–665, 667, 882
NetWare TCP/IP Transport (course description), 861–862
NetWire, 61, 206–207
Network access:
  automating, 7
  protocol, 882
Network administrators, 162–163, 882
Network Basic Input/Output System (NetBIOS), 882

# Index

Network cabling, 882
Network configuration plans, 882
Network File System (NFS), 882
Network installations, company plans for, 156–157
Network interface card (NIC), 242–243, 251, 343, 344, 882–883
Network layer, 698
Network operating system (NOS), 883
Network topology, 883
Network type, 883
Networking area (CNI certification), 27, 29
Networking Technologies exam, 690–715
  brain teaser, 714, 715
  case study, 691–697
  companion CD-ROM, using, 714
  course description, 853
  Internet (DOD) model packet, 691–697
  sample test, 707–713
  study questions, 698–707
NETX.VLM, 392, 471
New positions, creating, 162–168
NFS (*see* Network File System)
NIC (*see* Network interface card)
NLIST command, 384, 435
NLM (*see* NetWare Loadable Module)
Nodes, 883
Noise, minimizing, 672
Normal logging level (GroupWise message server), 582
NOS (*see* Network operating system)
Notes, taking, 112–114
Novell:
  calling, 141–142, 150–151
  support from, 59–61
  telephone numbers (list), 835
  Web sites, 652
Novell Authorized Education Centers (NAECs), 25–26, 31–32, 98–101, 883
  government payments to, 94
Novell Certified Internet Professional (NCIP) certification, 22, 24–25
  checklist for, 34, 42–43
  continuing education requirements, 209
  paperwork log for, 145
  path to, 68, 69
Novell Certified Internet Professionals (NCIPs), 58–59, 163
Novell CompuServe forums, 198–205

Novell courses, 111–112
  attending, 115
  descriptions of, 841–869
  list of, 47–50
Novell Education Academic Partners (NEAPs), 26, 31–32, 98–101
Novell ID badges, 220–221
Novell knowledge, 115
Novell Menu utility, 384
Novell NetWare, 3
/NOVMAP switch, 738
NPRINTER option (NDS), 385–386
*NSEPro* (*see* NetWare Support Encyclopedia Professional Edition)
NTFS (*see* Windows NT File System)
NWADMIN utility, 504

## O

Object linking and embedding (OLE), 542, 884
Object rights (NDS), 375, 379–380, 390
ODBC (*see* Open Database Connectivity)
ODI (*see* Open Data-Link Interface)
ODI/VLM software installation, 496–498
ODMA (*see* Open Document Management API)
OFCHECK utility, 543
Off logging level (GroupWise message server), 582
OFUNIX40 directory, 546
OFWIN40 directory, 546
OJT (*see* On-the-job training)
OLE (*see* Object linking and embedding)
Online services, 198–207
  NetWire, 206–207
  Novell CompuServe forums, 198–205, 652–658
  Web sites, 198
On-the-job training (OJT), 57, 78, 96–98, 116–117, 884
Open Database Connectivity (ODBC), 740
Open Data-Link Interface (ODI), 317, 385, 884
Open Document Management API (ODMA), 790
Operating systems (OSs), 243, 884
Optimizing workstations (DOS Micro Hardware exam), 243–248

Organization, company, 159–160
Organizational units, creating, 411–414
OS/2, 348, 349, 471–472
OSI model, 666, 670, 674, 692, 700–704, 706
OSs (*see* Operating systems)
Out Box, 538
Outline approach to notetaking, 113

## P

Packet, Internet (DOD) model, 691–697
Paperwork, 140–152
  and calling Novell, 141–142, 150–151
  certificate, 151
  for CNI certification, 149–150
  filling out, 148–150
  initiating, 140–141
  log of, 142–146
  telephone log, 146–148
Parallel ports, 256
Partitions option (NDS), 377
PARTMGR utility, 504
Password protection, 885
Passwords, 349
PATCHMAN.NLM utility, 673
PATH, 253
Pay raises, negotiating, 171–173, 181–182
PCONSOLE utility, 323, 385
Performance, network:
  monitoring, 8
  tuning, 311–313
Permanent memory pool, 353
Personal view (GroupWise), 537
Phone logs, 146–148
Physical layer, 703
Plug-and-play, 238, 242
Policies and procedures documents, 885
Polling access scheme, 698
Port address, 344
Ports:
  parallel, 256
  serial, 249, 256
Post offices:
  adding, 609–614
  creating, 9, 527–529
  and directory access, 537
Practical knowledge, gaining, 115
Preparing for exams (*see* Studying; Training)
Presentation layer, 701
Price lists, 218

Primary domains, 539, 565
Print queue, 885
Print spooler, 885
Printer control sequences, 885
Printer services, maintaining, 7
Printing:
    NDS option, 385
    NetWare 3.x Administration exam, 281–283
    objects, creating, 455–459
    queue setup, 453–454
    server setup, 455
    software installation, 459–462
Product updates, on NetWire, 206
Professional advancement (see Advancement, planning for)
Professional recognition, certification and, 56
Professionalism, maintaining, 229–232
PROG directory, 735
Promotions, 158–162
Property option (NDS), 377
Property Rights option (NDS), 382, 390, 467
Property Value option (NDS), 377
Protocol analyzers, 674, 885
Proxy rights, to GroupWise mailboxes, 538
PSERVER option (NDS), 385

## Q

QBE (see Query By Example)
Queries, creating, 11
Query By Example (QBE), 788
Queue, 885

## R

Radio frequency interference (RFI), 669
RAID (redundant array of inexpensive disks) system, 886
RAM, 253, 320–321
RDS (see Remote Document Server)
Real Mode, 886
Rebuild Database option, 545
Recognition of new status:
    problems with, 157–158
    through title changes, 168–171
RECONSSW.EXE, 736
Records, 787
RECOVER.DDB, 631
Red Zone, 886

Referrals, 216
Registering for the exams, 130–131
Remote Document Server (RDS), 743, 744
Replicas (NDS), 377, 379
Reports, creating, 11
Required credits, 2–3
Résumés, 173–180
    cover letters for, 174, 175
    education-based, 178–180
    experience-based, 176–177, 179
RFI (see Radio frequency interference)
RIP (see Routing Information Protocol)
RMSETUP program, 542
ROM, 256
Routers, 673, 706, 886
Routing Information Protocol (RIP), 886

## S

Sample tests, answers to, 817–824
SAP (see Service Advertising Protocol)
SBACKUP option (NDS), 385, 502
Scholarships, obtaining, 92–93
SCSI (small computer system interface) adapter/controller, 886
SDLC frame, 699
Secondary domains, 539, 565
Security:
    GroupWise, 627
    implementing company-wide strategy for, 8
    InForms 4.x Administration and Form Design exam, 773–775
    for LANs, 666
SEM (see Server Enhancement Module)
Semi-Permanent memory pool, 321
@SENDMAIL function, 787
SEND use, 384
Serial ports, 249, 256
Server Always option (GroupWise message server), 585
Server Enhancement Module (SEM), 737
SERVER.EXE, 315, 505
Server Never option (GroupWise message server), 585
Service Advertising Protocol (SAP), 886–887
SERVMAN option (NDS), 384, 473, 503
Session layer, 704

SETUP program, 542
SETUPWIN command, 540
Setup, workstation, 241–243
Shells, 887
SHIFT command, 352
614 error, 739
Skills:
    certification and acquisition of, 57–58
    ranking your, 80–83
SMS (see Storage Management Services option)
SoftSolutions, 4–5, 9–10
SoftSolutions 4.x Administration exam, 718–754
    brain teaser, 752–753
    case study, 720–734
    companion CD-ROM, using, 754
    course description, 867–868
    database errors, correcting, 729–732
    index compaction, 733–734
    installation, Document Desktop, 726, 728–729
    installation, SoftSolutions, 720–727
    sample test, 745–752
    study questions, 734–745
SoftSolutions 4.x Advanced Administration (course description), 868–869
SOFTSOLW, 735
Software:
    evaluating your experience with, 221, 223
    file server installation, 333–340
    routine maintenance of, 8
    setup of, 238, 242
    workstation installation, 340–343
SOFTWIN, 735
Sort order, 887
SPX (Sequential Packet Exchange), 887
SQL (see Structured query language)
SRAM, 251
SSBack program, 744
SSPause program, 744
ST506 interface, 256
Standard Mode, 887
Standard testing technique, 134–135
Standards, 705
STARTNET.BAT, 286
STARTUP.NCF, 353, 503, 506
Static interface, 887
Storage Management Services (SMS) option (NDS), 383, 470
Streams interface, 318

# Index

Structured query language (SQL), 4, 741
Student loans, 91–92
Studying, 117–130
   and developing good habits, 126–129
   distractions from, 123–124
   environment for, 121–124
   focus areas for, 117–119
   goal-setting strategies for, 118–119, 124–126
   hints for, 129–130
   and notetaking, 112–114
   and Novell courses, 111–112
   time for, 119–121
   (*See also* Training)
SUBST command, 254
Support, Novell, 59–61
Surveys, customer, 222–224, 226
Sylvan Prometric testing center, 32
Synchronous Data Link Control (SDLC), 887
SYS.COM, 256
SYSCON utility:
   creating users/groups with, 271–278
   setting up network environment with, 278–281
SYSM Screen Access Group, 739
Sysops, 206
System backups, 7, 674
System script, 350

## T

Tables, 786
Target exams:
   CNE certification, 14
   MCNE certification, 21
TB, 257
TCP/IP (*see* Transmission Control Protocol/Internet Protocol)
TDR (*see* Time domain reflectometer)
Technical writing skills, evaluating your, 221, 225
Telephone numbers, Novell, 835
Terminal Emulation Software, 887
Terminate and stay resident (TSR) programs, 887–888
Testing (system):
   forms (InForms 4.x Administration and Form Design exam), 773–775
   setup (NetWare 4.x Administration), 422–424
   system (GroupWise System Administration exam), 535–536

Testing techniques, 134–136
Tests (*see* Exams)
Textual information, organizing, 191
Time domain reflectometer (TDR), 667
Time for studying, setting aside, 118–121
Time indicator, test, 131
Title changes, professional recognition through, 168–171
Token Ring, 700
Trade papers, 195–196
Training, 78–107
   from audio- and videotapes, 103–104
   from books, 102–103
   company-sponsored, 87–91
   computer-based, 104
   determining level of, 79–84
   financing of, 84–95
   getting the most from, 104–107
   hands-on, 96–98
   instructor-led, 98–100
   need for, 78–79
   on-the-job, 78, 96–98, 116–117
   scholarships for, 92–93
   self-study, 100–101
   student loans for, 91–92
   time spent on, 74
   (*See also* Studying)
Training experience, evaluating your, 221, 224
Transmission Control Protocol/Internet Protocol (TCP/IP), 888
Transport layer, 706–707
TREE command, 252
Troubleshooting, 9
TSR programs (*see* Terminate and stay resident programs)
TYPE command, 256

## U

UDP (*see* User Datagram Protocol)
UMB memory, 247–248
Understanding and Applying Internet Concepts (course description), 862–863
Uninterruptible power source (UPS), 888
UNIX OS Fundamentals for NetWare Users (course description), 843
UnixWare Administration (course description), 854–855

UnixWare Advanced Administration (course description), 855–856
UnixWare Installation and Configuration Workshop (course description), 854
UPS (*see* Uninterruptible power source)
Upsizing, 888
Use App Thresholds option (GroupWise message server), 585
Use Server Thresholds option (GroupWise message server), 585
User Datagram Protocol (UDP), 888
User questionnaires, 889
User script, 350
User setup, changing (GroupWise 4.x Advanced System Administration), 602–609
USERID.FIL, 630
Users, adding:
   GroupWise, 9, 601–602
   SoftSolutions, 10
Users, creating:
   GroupWise System Administration, 529–532
   NetWare 3.x Administration, 271–278
   NetWare 4.x Administration, 411–414
Users, defining (NetWare 4.x Administration), 414–422

## V

Value added process (VAP), 889
VAP (*see* Value added process)
VDM (*see* Virtual DOS Machine)
Verbose logging level (GroupWise message server), 582
Veterans' benefits, obtaining, 93–94
VGA display adapter, 253, 255
Videotapes, training from, 103–104
Virtual DOS Machine (VDM), 578
Virtual Loadable Module (VLM), 286, 346, 347, 385, 501, 889
Virtual memory, 889
Virus protection, 658–662, 672, 675
VirusScan, 659
VLM (*see* Virtual Loadable Module)
Volt-ohm meters, 671
Volume maintenance, 322
VREPAIR utility, 314–315, 452, 463–464
VShield, 659

## W

Waiting for test results, 141–142
WANs (*see* Wide area networks)
Web Authoring and Publishing (course description), 863–864
Web Server Management (course description), 865–866
Web sites, 219–220
Wide area networks (WANs), 890
WinCIM, 675
Windows 95, 244, 424–430
Windows NT 4, 244
Windows NT File System (NTFS), 890
WINFILE.INI, 635
Word-of-mouth advertising, 216
Workstations, 890
  graphic, 878
  GroupWise installation on Windows workstation, 520–524
  GroupWise setup, 532–535
  inventorying, 238–241
  setup of, 241–243
  software installation, 340–343
WORM drives, 890
WPCMAPI.INI, 635
WPDOMAIN.CSI, 630
WPINFF directory, 546
WSUPDATE utility, 472

## X

X.25 gateway, 546

## Z

/ZAR switch, 583

# ABOUT THE AUTHORS

**JOHN PAUL MUELLER** and **ROBERT A. WILLIAMS** are Certified NetWare Engineers and the authors of several other successful certification guides for McGraw-Hill.

## SOFTWARE AND INFORMATION LICENSE

...nd information on this diskette (collectively referred to as the "Product") are the property of The ...Companies, Inc. ("McGraw-Hill") and are protected by both United States copyright law and inter-...right treaty provision. You must treat this Product just like a book, except that you may copy it into a com... to be used and you may make archival copies of the Products for the sole purpose of backing up our software and protecting your investment from loss.

By saying "just like a book," McGraw-Hill means, for example, that the Product may be used by any number of people and may be freely moved from one computer location to another, so long as there is no possibility of the Product (or any part of the Product) being used at one location or on one computer while it is being used at another. Just as a book cannot be read by two different people in two different places at the same time, neither can the Product be used by two different people in two different places at the same time (unless, of course, McGraw-Hill's rights are being violated).

McGraw-Hill reserves the right to alter or modify the contents of the Product at any time.

This agreement is effective until terminated. The Agreement will terminate automatically without notice if you fail to comply with any provisions of this Agreement. In the event of termination by reason of your breach, you will destroy or erase all copies of the Product installed on any computer system or made for backup purposes and shall expunge the Product from your data storage facilities.

### LIMITED WARRANTY

McGraw-Hill warrants the physical diskette(s) enclosed herein to be free of defects in materials and workmanship for a period of sixty days from the purchase date. If McGraw-Hill receives written notification within the warranty period of defects in materials or workmanship, and such notification is determined by McGraw-Hill to be correct, McGraw-Hill will replace the defective diskette(s). Send request to:

Customer Service
McGraw-Hill
Gahanna Industrial Park
860 Taylor Station Road
Blacklick, OH 43004-9615

The entire and exclusive liability and remedy for breach of this Limited Warranty shall be limited to replacement of defective diskette(s) and shall not include or extend to any claim for or right to cover any other damages, including but not limited to, loss of profit, data, or use of the software, or special, incidental, or consequential damages or other similar claims, even if McGraw-Hill has been specifically advised as to the possibility of such damages. In no event will McGraw-Hill's liability for any damages to you or any other person ever exceed the lower of suggested list price or actual price paid for the license to use the Product, regardless of any form of the claim.

**THE McGRAW-HILL COMPANIES, INC. SPECIFICALLY DISCLAIMS ALL OTHER WARRANTIES, EXPRESS OR IMPLIED, INCLUDING BUT NOT LIMITED TO, ANY IMPLIED WARRANTY OF MERCHANTABILITY OR FITNESS FOR A PARTICULAR PURPOSE.** Specifically, McGraw-Hill makes no representation or warranty that the Product is fit for any particular purpose and any implied warranty of merchantability is limited to the sixty day duration of the Limited Warranty covering the physical diskette(s) only (and not the software or in-formation) and is otherwise expressly and specifically disclaimed.

This Limited Warranty gives you specific legal rights; you may have others which may vary from state to state. Some states do not allow the exclusion of incidental or consequential damages, or the limitation on how long an implied warranty lasts, so some of the above may not apply to you.

This Agreement constitutes the entire agreement between the parties relating to use of the Product. The terms of any purchase order shall have no effect on the terms of this Agreement. Failure of McGraw-Hill to insist at any time on strict compliance with this Agreement shall not constitute a waiver of any rights under this Agreement. This Agreement shall be construed and governed in accordance with the laws of New York. If any provision of this Agreement is held to be contrary to law, that provision will be enforced to the maximum extent permissible and the remaining provisions will remain in force and effect.